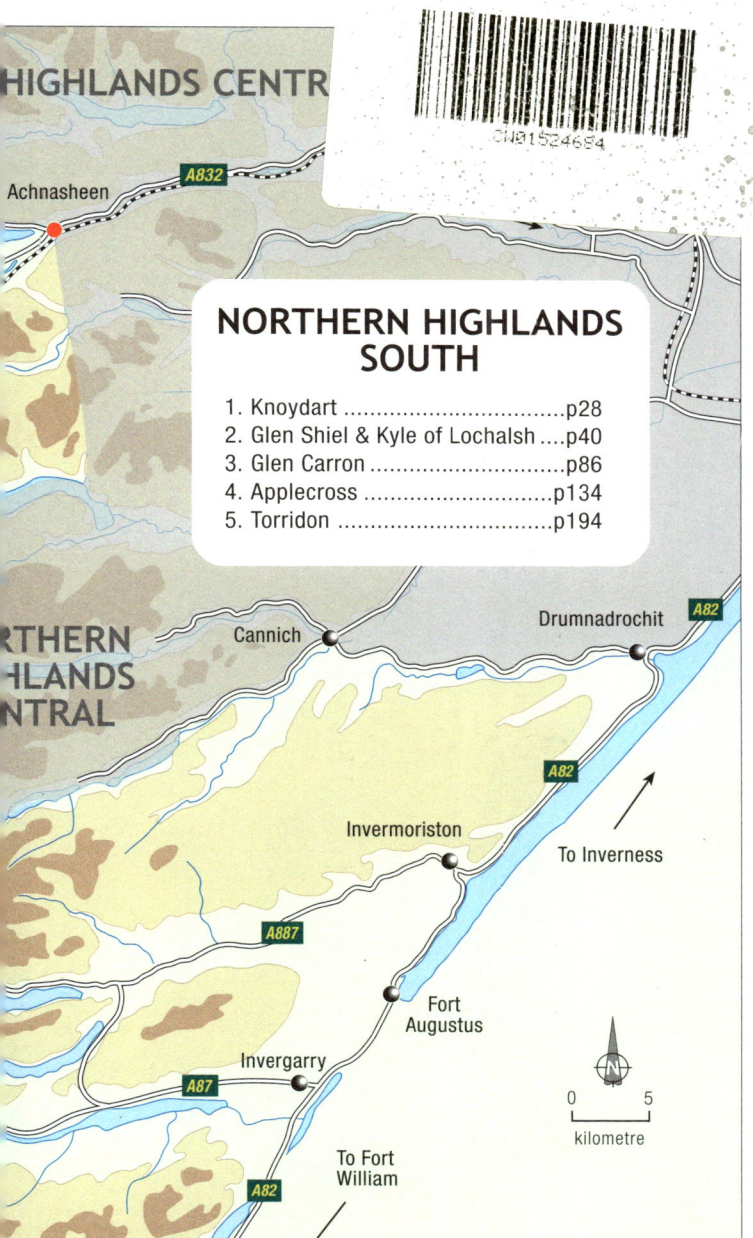

NORTHERN HIGHLANDS SOUTH

1. Knoydart p28
2. Glen Shiel & Kyle of Lochalsh p40
3. Glen Carron p86
4. Applecross p134
5. Torridon p194

NORTHERN HIGHLANDS SOUTH

Rock and Ice Climbs

including

Knoydart, Glen Shiel, Glen Carron, Applecross and Torridon

Andy Nisbet
Noel Williams

Series Editor: Brian Davison

SCOTTISH MOUNTAINEERING CLUB
CLIMBERS' GUIDE

Published in Great Britain by The Scottish Mountaineering Trust, 2007

© The Scottish Mountaineering Club

All rights reserved. No part of this publication may be reproduced, stored in or introduced into a retrieval system, or transmitted, in any form or by any means (electronic, mechanical, photocopying, recording or otherwise), without the prior written permission of the publisher.

ISBN 978-0-907521-97-6

A catalogue record for this book is available from the British Library

Front Cover: Silver Tear, V,5, Coire na Poite, Beinn Bhàn, Applecross
(photo Jon Jones)

Route descriptions of climbs in this guide, together with their grades and any references to in situ or natural protection are made in good faith, based on past or first ascent descriptions, checked and substantiated where possible by the authors.
However, climbs lose holds and are altered by rockfall, rock becomes dirty and loose and in situ protection deteriorates. Even minor alterations can have a dramatic effect on a climb's grade or seriousness. Therefore, it is essential that climbers judge the condition of any route for themselves, before they start climbing. The authors, editors, friends and assistants involved in the publication of this guide, the Scottish Mountaineering Club, the Scottish Mountaineering Trust and Scottish Mountaineering Trust (Publications) Ltd, can therefore accept no liability whatever for damage to property, nor for personal injury or death, arising directly or indirectly from the use of this publication.

This guidebook is compiled from the most recent information and experience provided by members of the Scottish Mountaineering Club and other contributors. The book is published by the Scottish Mountaineering Trust, which is a charitable trust.
Revenue from the sale of books published by the Trust is used for the continuation of its publishing programme and for charitable purposes associated with Scottish mountains and mountaineering.

Design concept: Curious Oranj, Glasgow
Production: Scottish Mountaineering Trust (Publications) Ltd
Typesetting: Ken Crocket
Diagram and map graphics: Andy Nisbet, Tom Prentice
Colour separations: Core Image Ltd, East Kilbride
Printed & bound by Elkar, Bilbao

Distributed by Cordee, 3a DeMonfort Street, Leicester. LE1 7HD
(t) 0116 254 3579, (f) 0116 247 1176, (e) sales@cordee.co.uk

For details of other SMC guidebooks see inside rear endpaper

Contents

List of Diagrams & Maps 6

Introduction & Acknowledgements 8

Geology by Andy Smith 9

History 10

Environment, Safety & Technical Notes 22

Amenities 27

Knoydart 28
Gleouraich 29
Barrisdale 29
Meall nan Eun 30
An Caisteal 32
Stob a' Chearcaill 33
Ladhar Bheinn 35

Glen Shiel & Kyle of Lochalsh 40
Meall na Teanga 41
Cluanie Dam Slabs 41
South Glen Shiel 42
Druim Shionnach – West Face 42
Creag Coire an t-Slugain 46
Aonach air Chrith 49
Sgùrr an Lochain 54
Sgùrr a' Bhac Chaolais 55
The Saddle – Forcan Ridge 57
The Saddle – Coire Uaine 58
Beinn Sgritheall 59
North Glen Shiel 59
Creag Lundie Slabs 59
Sgùrr nan Conbhairean 60
Sàil Chaorainn 62
A' Chralaig 62
Mullach Fraoch-Choire 62
Ciste Dubh 62
Sgùrr an Fhuarail 64
Sgùrr a' Bhealaich Dheirg 64
Five Sisters of Kintail 65
Sgùrr nan Saighead 65
Sgùrr Fhuaran 67
Sgùrr na Carnach 67
Sgùrr nan Spainteach 67
Beinn Fhada 69
Sgùrr a' Choire Ghairbh 69
Coire an Sgairne 70

4 CONTENTS

Dornie, Kyle of Lochalsh and Plockton	72
Biod an Fhithich	72
Cragaig	75
White Dyke	76
Duncraig – Creag an Duisilg	79
Glen Carron	**86**
Lurg Mhòr	87
Maoile Lunndaidh	88
Sgùrr Choinnich	89
Moruisg	90
Sgùrr nan Ceannaichean	92
Sgùrr na Feartaig	92
Fuar Tholl	96
Lower South-East Nose	97
North-East Flanks	100
South-East Cliff	101
Mainreachan Buttress	110
Coire Lair Approach Crags	117
Sonny Wall	117
Whispering Buttress	118
Sgòrr Ruadh	118
Raeburn's Buttress	122
North Face	125
Upper Buttress	129
Maol Chean-dearg	129
An Ruadh-stac	130
Meall nan Ceapairean	130
Glas Bheinn	131
North Strome Cliffs	133
Bad a' Chreamha	133
Reraig Coastal Cliff	133
Applecross	**134**
Kishorn Boulders	135
Meall Gorm	136
Sgùrr a' Chaorachain	143
A' Chìoch	143
North Buttresses	150
Summit Buttress	155
South Face	156
Upper Cliff	162
Hairpin Buttress	163
Beinn Bhàn	165
Coire Each	166
Coire na Feola	166
Coire na Poite	171
A' Phoit	177
Coire nan Fhamair	179
Coire Toll a' Bhein	184
Coire Gorm Mòr	187
Applecross Crags	189
Ardheslaig	189

Loch na Creige Crag	191
Camusteel Sea-Cliffs	191

Torridon 194
Beinn Damh Area 195
Kinlochdamph Crag – Creag na Saobhaidhe	195
Ben Shieldaig	198
Creag Dhubh an t-Sall	199
Creag na Speireag	200
Beinn Damh	202
Creag an Fhithich	207

Torridon Sandstone Crags 208
Annat Bouldering	208
Creag na Botaigeann	209
Seana Mheallan	210
Seana Mheallan West	219
Path Crag	226
Celtic Boulders	228
Creag nan Leumnach	230
Creag nan Uaimh	233
Hairpin Crag	234

Inveralligin to Diabaig 236
Inveralligin Sea-Cliffs	237
Creag Alligin	240
Discovery Rock	241
Big Bill's Crag	242
Beginner's Slabs	242
Diabaig	243
Diabaig Peninsula Crags	259
Rolling Wall	261
Loch a' Bhealaich Crag	265
White House Crag	265

Beinn Alligin 266
Coire nan Laogh	267
Tom na Gruagaich	267
Eag Dubh	268
Horns of Alligin	269
Sgùrr Mhòr	270

Beinn Dearg 272
Choire Mhòir	271
Coire Beag	272

Liathach 272
Stùc a' Choire Dhuibh Bhig, North	274
Coire Dubh Beag	275
Coire Dubh Mòr	279
Coire na Caime	286
Meall Dearg	297
Sgorr a' Chadail	300
Pyramid Buttress	302
Coire Liath Mhòr	304
Stùc a' Choire Dhuibh Bhig, South	305

DIAGRAMS & MAPS

Beinn Eighe	306
Coire Mhic Fhearchair	306
Far East Wall	309
Eastern Ramparts	319
Triple Buttresses	330
Sàil Mhòr	355
Coire Ruadh-staca	358
Pineapple Cliff	358
Spidean Coire nan Clach	363
Sgùrr Ban	363
Sgùrr nan Fhir Duibhe	363
First Ascents	366
Index	390
SMC Publications List	Inside Rear Endpaper

Diagrams & Maps

Knoydart	Map	28
Meall nan Eun		31
Stob a' Chearcaill		34
Ladhar Beinn – Coire Dhorrcail		36
Glen Shiel & Kyle of Lochalsh	Map	40
Glen Shiel	Map	45
Druim Shionnach – West Face		46
Creag Coire an t-Slugain		46
Aonach air Chrith		49
Sgùrr an Lochain		54
Beinn Fhada – Sgùrr a' Choire Ghairbh		69
Biod an Fhithich		72
Glen Carron	Map	86
Sgùrr na Feartaig		95
Fuar Tholl & Sgòrr Ruadh	Map	97
Fuar Tholl – Lower S-E Nose & N-E Cliff		98
Fuar Tholl – South-East Cliff, Summer		103
Fuar Tholl – South-East Cliff, Winter		106
Fuar Tholl – Mainreachan Buttress, N-E Face		111
Fuar Tholl – Mainreachan Buttress		115
Sgòrr Ruadh		119
Sgòrr Ruadh – Central Couloir		121
Sgòrr Ruadh – Raeburn's Buttress		123
Sgòrr Ruadh – North Face		126
Applecross	Map	134
Meall Gorm – Upper Cliff		137
Sgùrr a' Chaorachain – A' Chìoch Upper		144

DIAGRAMS & MAPS   7

Sgùrr a' Chaorachain – North Buttresses		151
Sgùrr a' Chaorachain – Summit Buttress		155
Sgùrr a' Chaorachain – South Face		157
Applecross Hills	Map	164
Beinn Bhàn – Coire na Feola		169
Beinn Bhàn – Coire na Poite		172
Beinn Bhàn – Coire na Poite Back Wall		176
Beinn Bhàn – Coire nan Fhamair		178
Beinn Bhàn – Coire Toll a' Bhein Left		185
Beinn Bhàn – Coire Toll a' Bhein Right		186
Ardheslaig		188
Loch na Creige Crag		191
Torridon	Map	194
Kinlochdamph Crag		197
Creag na Speireag – Left		201
Creag na Speireag – Right		202
Beinn Damh – Creagan Dubh Toll nam Biast		205
Seana Mheallan – Right		211
Seana Mheallan – Centre		215
Seana Mheallan – Left		217
Seana Mheallan West		221
Seana Mheallan West – Bedrock Buttress		225
Path Crag		227
Creag nan Leumnach		232
Hairpin Crag		235
Inveralligin to Diabaig	Map	237
Diabaig Overview		244
Diabaig – Little Big Wall & The Pillar		248
Diabaig – Main Cliff		251
Rolling Wall		260
Beinn Alligin	Map	267
Liathach	Map	273
Liathach – Coire Dubh Beag, Left		275
Liathach – Coire Dubh Beag, Right		276
Liathach – Coire Dubh Mòr		278
Liathach – Coire na Caime		287
Liathach – Coire na Caime, Am Fasarinen		288
Liathach – Coire na Caime, Bell's Buttress		294
Liathach – Coire na Caime, Northern Pinnacles		296
Liathach – Meall Dearg, Left		297
Liathach – Meall Dearg, Right		298
Liathach – Sgòrr a' Chadail		301
Liathach – South Side, Pyramid Buttress		303
Beinn Eighe	Map	307
Beinn Eighe – Far East Wall		310
Beinn Eighe – Eastern Ramparts		320
Beinn Eighe – Triple Buttresses, Winter		332
Beinn Eighe – Triple Buttresses, Summer		336
Beinn Eighe – Fuselarge		353
Beinn Eighe – Sàil Mhòr		356
Beinn Eighe – Pineapple Cliff		359

8 INTRODUCTION

Introduction & Acknowledgements

This is the third and southernmost of the SMC's three volumes to the Northern Highlands. It covers the area from Torridon south to Applecross, Glen Carron, Glen Shiel and Knoydart.

Magnificent Torridon is the highlight of this volume, offering some of Scotland's best climbing of all types, from the mountain rock and modern winter mixed routes of Beinn Eighe, to the gullies and icefalls of Liathach and the superb coastal rock climbing of Diabaig's perfect gneiss. Close by is Applecross with the winter cliffs of Beinn Bhàn, the huge Coire na Poite and the awesomely steep Coire an Fhamair. In summer Applecross has the roadside cliff with Sword of Gideon and the accessible classic of Cioch Nose.

Glen Carron is better known for winter, Fuar Tholl, Mainreachachan Buttress and Sgòrr Ruadh each having a fine selection of ice and mixed, and even some summer rock for the sandstone enthusiast. The area also has one of Scotland's best icefall venues in Sgùrr na Feartaig when the weather is cold enough. These are all just over an hour from Inverness on mostly new fast roads.

Glen Shiel is a new venue with relatively accessible routes on several vegetated schist cliffs, each linked to nearby Munros and sharp ridges for a satisfying mountaineering day. And for total contrast, the remote wilderness of Knoydart, no new roads, just peace and contentment on its quietly explored schist cliffs.

As with the rest of the Northern Highlands, there had been considerable activity since the 1993 guide. The greatest development has been on the many new sandstone crags in Torridon, several gneiss crags around Diabaig and extensive winter climbing all over the area, particularly in Glen Shiel where a handful of climbs have turned into several major cliffs. Global warming is threatening, particularly on the coastal Beinn Bhàn, but there is still the opportunity to use the new quick access to Kinlochewe and Lochcarron for winter climbing.

On a fine day, the Northern Highlands remain a uniquely beautiful and relatively unspoiled climbing location. Whether the climbs are near the road or in the mountains the views are great from them all. The west coast scenery is slightly balanced by the west coast climate, although with much less rainfall than the Fort William and Glen Coe area further south.

Andy Nisbet
Spring 2007

Thanks go to previous authors of Northern Highlands, in particular Geoff Cohen, Rab Anderson and Andy Cunningham.

Also to those who made major contributions and comments; Martin Moran, Colin Moody, Anthony (Ginger) Cain, Dave McGimpsey, Neil Hinchcliff, John Lyall, Mark Robson and John Watson.

And no guide is functional without the editing team of Brian Davison for text and Grahame Nicoll for photographs. And no guide even exists without the design and production management of Tom Prentice.

GEOLOGY 9

Geology

Much of the special character of the climbing in the North-West Highlands is associated with its unique variety of rocks. The four main types of rock are very different from elsewhere in Scotland.

Lewisian Gneiss: The rock at the bottom of the pile is Lewisian Gneiss, a coarse crystalline metamorphic rock. It is one of the oldest rocks in Europe, and can be regarded as the foundation on which the later rocks have been built. At least two major episodes of metamorphism can be recognised in the group, dated at 2800 and 1700 million years ago. It occurs extensively but tends to be confined to the lower ground. However it is generally very rough sound rock, and where it does form crags, the climbing is superb, such as at Diabaig.

Torridonian Sandstone: Resting on the Lewisian Gneiss is a very old, well stratified sedimentary rock called Torridonian Sandstone. This distinctive dark red rock forms much of the high ground and is more or less flat-lying. Its total thickness has been estimated at more than seven kilometres. Torridonian Sandstone is around 1000 to 800 million years old – much too old to contain readily recognisable fossils. The original Torridonian sediments were deposited by rivers draining from a mountainous region which lay further north-west. The conspicuous pebbles present in some beds have been linked with rocks now found in south-east Greenland. Despite its great age, Torridonian Sandstone has survived more or less unchanged since it first formed and so must have remained outwith any mountain building areas. There are not as many long mountain routes on Torridonian Sandstone as might be imagined from the amount of exposed rock. This is because frequent terraces break the bigger mountain faces. These terraces are less noticeable in winter when the direct lines of gullies and icefalls cut through them, Beinn Bhàn and Liathach being the best known.

Cambrian Quartzite: Lying on top of the Torridonian Sandstone is another contrasting sedimentary sequence. It consists largely of Cambrian Quartzite, a pure quartz sandstone which forms a distinctive capping on many Torridonian peaks, including Beinn Eighe. It is badly shattered in places, as on the east end of Beinn Eighe, but sound in Coire Mhic Fhearchair where it provides first rate climbing. One part is known as Pipe Rock because of the conspicuous vertical markings it contains – the burrows of organisms that once lived in the sea-floor sediments. These make fine rough handholds compared to the smooth vertical faces. The Cambrian Quartzite dips towards the south-east and cuts across the Torridonian strata; this is why Beinn Alligin has no sandstone, Liathach to its east has only a quartzite topping but Beinn Eighe has extensive quartzite. The quartzite was therefore deposited much later than the Torridonian Sandstone, after that rock had been tilted and eroded. The quartzite is about 550 million years old.

Moine Schists: The collision of two tectonic plates to the south-east caused a major mountain building episode that formed the massive Caledonian Mountain chain. The sediments in the ocean between the plates were squeezed and heated during the collision, producing the metamorphic Moine Schists. An extraordinary structure called the Moine Thrust Zone developed as the metamorphic rocks were pushed up and over the block of rocks to the north-west. This stable block comprised the three main rock types described above – Lewisian Gneiss, Torridonian Sandstone and Cambrian Quartzite. A great pile of schists was eventually transported several tens of kilometres north-westwards, coming to rest on top of the younger Cambrian Quartzite. The Moine Schists make up most of the Highlands to the east and south of the Moine Thrust. They are sometimes rather vegetated but can then provide winter climbing opportunities, on the cliffs of Glen Shiel and Knoydart for example.

The final moulding of all these various rocks was brought about largely by the action of the huge ice sheets and glaciers which built up and melted down many times during the ice ages of the last two million years. The last main ice maximum occurred 17,000 years ago. In the North-West Highlands glaciers flowed both east and west, carving out the characteristic U shaped valleys, corries and aretes, depositing moraines and sculpting the 'scarred and silent' landscapes in which we climb today.

History

Visits to the southern section of the Northern Highlands were sporadic until the 1970s. Since then, improved roads have brought increasing numbers of climbers north. Much of the exploration of Glen Carron and Applecross happened in the 1970s while there was an avalanche of new routes in Torridon in the 1980s. In the last 15 years, only a few very hard rock routes have shown the top level of rising standards, as much of the energy has gone into development of the many sandstone and gneiss outcrops in this area. The enthusiasm for accessible rock has been as noticeable here as anywhere. In winter, many of the ice lines were climbed in the 1980s, but mixed climbing has taken off to produce winter routes on most features. This has been helped by easier winter travel due to better roads and less snow in the valleys; the smaller amount of snow has been offset by the acceptance of poorer conditions on mixed routes.

Knoydart

The rather undistinguished rock climbs in Knoydart were climbed by various teams mainly in the late 1960s and early 1970s. The much better winter climbs have a longer history, beginning with a notable ascent by Harold Raeburn and partners during the famous SMC yachting meet at Easter 1897. Bad weather had driven the party back from Loch Scavaig on Skye. Sixty five years then elapsed before a visit by another outstanding climber, Tom Patey, accounted for two more major lines, Gaberlunzie and Viking Gully.

Ewing and Sproul added Para Handy Gully in 1971, but it was not until the late 1970s that development began in earnest. A visit by two Aberdonian teams in 1978, Andy Nisbet and Paul Tipton, and Dougie Dinwoodie and Adair McIvor, produced the first routes on Spider Buttress; Face Route and West Pillar. The sight of their footprints spurred Con Higgins into action. From his base in Fort William he began a quiet campaign to realise the true potential of Coire Dhorrcail. His first contribution, Tir na Og, was a major plum. It takes a compelling line directly up the centre of Spider Buttress. It is the hardest route in Knoydart and arguably one of the finest in the North-West Highlands. Three more routes fell to Higgins in 1978, his American partner being the inspiration for the naming of Thunderchicken and Transatlantic Bong. The following year Higgins closed his campaign with another direct line on Spider Buttress, East Rib.

Several new climbs were added by a variety of teams in the 1980s. Heriot-Watt students are believed to have ascended a number of lines in the right-hand corner of Coire Dhorrcail but these have not been reported. It was not until 1986 that Bottleneck Gully, which Patey had described in 1962 as "well deserving a visit", was finally climbed by Jeffrey and Williams. Although most of the obvious lines have now been climbed further developments have been hampered in recent years by poor winter conditions.

Glen Shiel

In the early days Glen Shiel was largely ignored for bigger cliffs elsewhere; a few summer routes were climbed on Beinn Fhada and the occasional route elsewhere. But Glen Shiel climbing is really about winter and four routes on the Five Sisters in 1957 was a long wait for the start. Little happened until Edinburgh University students started climbing from their hut in Glen Lichd in the 1980s. Most of the easier gullies above the glen were then climbed.

The big winter development started in 1993. With a nervous George Wallace on a climbing course, Martin Moran suggested that Andy Nisbet went to Aonach air Chrith where there might be easier gullies. Andy went up the wrong valley in the mist, expecting great embarrassment as he realised. But then the mist cleared and they were faced by Creag Coire an t-Slugain, with Pioneer Gully (II on the day) asking to be climbed. The other two main cliffs on the south side of the glen were visited the next winter. How there had been no previous visits when all are visible from the road is extraordinary, especially as there are now nearly 40 routes. The

West Face of Druim Shionnach was passed on the return from Creag Coire an t-Slugain and its deep central gully was noted and climbed the following February by Nisbet and Sarah Kekus (IV,4). Although short, the climbing was steep and unexpectedly helpful, always a rewarding combination and indicative of the cliff. The following month Martin Moran visited Aonach air Chrith and climbed his planned central line of Mica Schist Special (III). Conditions were generally good in 1994, so Nisbet was able a few days later to climb the easiest gully with a large novice party (hence the name, My Mother says No). The party included Rona, Tom Patey's daughter on her first new route.

The good winters of 1994 to 1996 allowed a rapid development of these cliffs, often by Nisbet with clients of Martin Moran climbing courses, similar to the development of Glen Carron and Applecross in 1969 to 1970 on Hamish MacInnes courses, also based in Lochcarron. Many of the more obscure Glen Shiel cliffs were also explored, including The Saddle (the excellent Big Gully has rarely been in condition since), Sgùrr a' Bhac Cholais and Ciste Duibh. During milder spells which have unfortunately become more common, the reliable Sgùrr a' Bhealaich Dearg and the very high Sgùrr nan Conbhairean were also explored. The latter, which is visible from a long way east in Glen Moriston, had first been approached from that direction (Ceannacroc) by Dave Broadhead to climb the so-named Couloir (II). Al Powell and friends made a five hour wade while approaching over the top through deep powder to climb two harder routes in 1995 but in the mild start to 1996, Andy Nisbet climbed two easier gullies on wet ice when there was virtually no snow anywhere else in the Northern Highlands. This has established its role as a saviour after big thaws (The Resurrection in the Fannaichs is similar).

The imposing face of Duncraig was first explored in 1971 by staff from Loch Eil Outward Bound and friends, with several routes recorded, although details were lost in the moratorium for many years, much to the irritation of Norrie Muir; most have been reclimbed recently. Ginger Cain, an artist with a studio in Plockton, climbed here with friends later in the 1970s. In the 1980s Jim Kerr climbed a couple of routes on the crag while doing rope access work on the unstable slopes above the roads on this peninsula, but did not record details. The upper crag is luxuriantly vegetated and its base so well defended by near vertical woodland that further exploration was deterred until 1996 when Martin Moran adopted the place. He climbed many routes, initially by his preferred on-sight approach but some exciting moments soon persuaded him that pre-cleaning the rock of variable quality would leave a much better route. The routes are very steep with positive holds, but the primitive appearance has limited its popularity.

The very accessible lower crag became an evening venue for local climbers, but being fiercely steep and poorly protected, a few bolts were placed in 1989 by Neil Smith; these were later replaced by modern bolts. This might have been controversial at the time but was kept very quiet; it is the type of crag happily accepted nowadays for sport climbing. Only a few outsiders like Duncan McCallum climbed there; the first bolts were quite high but a clip-stick lived at the crag. Locals have always bouldered on the overhanging cliff base, which usually stays dry. Somewhat dismissed in the 1993 guide, this is the first time the descriptions have been published (also for the upper crag) and it will be interesting to see how many visitors climb here.

Glen Carron

As early as 1895 the crags of Fuar Tholl, An Ruadh Stac and Glas Bheinn were graphically described by Lionel Hinxman, a founding father of the SMC. Coming up from Achnashellach towards Coire Lair he remarked: "Over the lower part of the glen frown the great precipices of Fuar Tholl, of which those that hem in the corrie of that ilk are 'absolutely perpendicular'. AP too appear to be the sides of the great buttress of terraced sandstone that hangs imminent over the little tarn of Coire Mainreachan... That these cliffs are also absolutely inaccessible I would not venture to affirm".

A decade later a dash by Raeburn in foul April weather allowed him to snatch his eponymous Buttress on Sgòrr Ruadh. Leaving Aviemore at 8.30am with

12 | HISTORY

E.B.Robertson he arrived in Achnashellach four hours later in dense mist, a howling sleet laden gale and 8-10 inches of slush'. Two days later, though the gale 'blew with undiminished violence' the weather was colder and the snow better. They found the climbing on the buttress 'not very easy, but icy snow usually adhering to grassy walls gave good hitches and handholds could also be cut as required'. It sounds like a typical Raeburn tour de force.

Apart from a single climb on Fuar Tholl in the 1930s, nothing of real note seems to have been achieved until 1969 when the potential of the steep sandstone cliffs of Fuar Tholl was realised by the teams of Martin Boysen and Dave Alcock and Hamish MacInnes and Ian Clough. An earlier prowl by Jimmy Marshall in 1952, and a later climb by Peter Macdonald had avoided the forbidding challenge of Mainreachan. The 1969 exploration started with Investigator, a tentative venture up the short upper right wall, and continued with several routes of some stature up the highest section of the wall; several easier climbs on the south-east cliff of Fuar Tholl were also completed, although the highest section of this was left unattended. Neither cliff has many natural lines and the steep sandstone is often loose, vegetated and greasy into the bargain. However the MacInnes guide of 1971 referred to the 'wonderful Coire Mainreachan', and the 1973 SMC Climbers' Guide described it as 'celebrated'. George Shields and Russell Sharp had indeed added another climb in 1972, and Boysen returned in 1974, but after this the cliffs lapsed into obscurity once more. Several parties reported disappointment with the quality – the climbs are certainly not in the modern idiom – but given dry conditions on the north facing cliff, the climbs are sustained and unusually exposed; sandstone may yet come back into fashion.

Meanwhile the late 1970s saw the start of an appreciation of the winter potential, with a difficult ascent of Fuar Folly by Rob Archbold and Dave Nicholls, sadly deflected from the true line by the onset of darkness. It remained for Phil Butler and Mick Fowler to take up the magnificent challenge of the steep ice in the centre of the south-east cliff (Tholl Gate, VI,6), although Alan Rouse and Tut Braithwaite had been to the cliff a month earlier in a thaw to find the ice was absent, so the line was clearly known. A couple of years later Fowler was back with Chris Watts for the obvious line of The Fuhrer (VII,6), which seems still to be unrepeated. Martin Moran had just moved into the area and started by rope soloing Cold Sweat (VI,6), an unclimbed chimney sounding attractive but taking two days and judging by the abseil gear near the start, again may have repelled all suitors. In 1987 the Fowler/Watts team Pipped Moran at the Post (V,5), having driven up from London and slept in the car, thereby being established on the route when Moran appeared from his house five miles away and not seeing the urgency. But Moran soon made his mark on the cliff with the thinner ice of Evasion Grooves (VI,6), with Simon Jenkins, and The Ayatollah (VII,7), with Ian Dring.

Sgòrr Ruadh also had to wait until the late 1960s before the first new winter climbs were made, with Bill Brooker's ascent of the north side of Raeburn's Buttress (IV,4). A spate of ascents of the more obvious gullies by Hamish MacInnes and Allen Fyffe followed. A couple of slightly harder gullies were added by Nisbet in the 1970s before Moran began to explore the North Face, adding Fox's Face (IV,4) and First Blood (V,6) with Jenkins and Superdirect (IV,6) with Paul Potter. But the best climb of all is hidden on the approach from Glen Carron, although well seen from distant Torridon. The line of Tango in the Night (VI,6) had been spotted by Steve Aisthorpe and John Lyall. Lyall regrets deciding the snow was too deep and soft, since Aisthorpe lined up Nick Forwood and Paul Yardley for an all night session on the very steep route. The second ascent waited 15 years. Allen Fyffe and Iain Peter arrived at the route amazed to find another party starting it. They were unaware that a report on the Internet the day before had claimed it as one of the best routes in Scotland to be unrepeated.

In 1995 Nisbet spent five hours trail breaking to the furthest route on Sgòrr Ruadh with Dave Bradshaw and Julie Colverd, then climbed it in 45 minutes (Riotous Ridge, II), followed by four hours returning to the car. Riotous fun? But this began a thorough exploration of an extensive cliff with lots of mostly turfy mixed routes added over the next six years. The thin ice of Tophet Gully (IV,5) was

HISTORY 13

seen as just complete after a soloing trip two days previously and The Sandstone Virgin (V,6) was the companion and much more sensible fault to Tango in the Night. Perhaps ignored on the previous assumption that it was Tango, this was Jonathan Preston's first winter route on sandstone.

In the meantime, Fuar Tholl's South-East Cliff had a large unclimbed central section between the ice lines. Moran was attracted by a hanging corner which he and Nisbet attempted in very snowy conditions. Slow going on the semi-frozen lower pitch forced an indirect line. The cliff below the corner was blank and vertical, so an easier ramp on the left was taken, leading to an overhanging corner and a point of aid before Moran made a bold entry into the corner (Sandstorm, VII,8). Nisbet couldn't help thinking that it looked easier further left, so having climbed there in the summer with Gill Nisbet, he returned in 1995 with John Lyall to climb close to the crest (Fuar Folly Direct, VI,8). This was the intended line of Archbold and Nicholls, but a very smooth but cracked corner yielded to some strenuous torquing, a technique which hadn't been refined in the seventies. Between these two mixed ascents was the icy winter of 1994, when the fine ice line left of Tholl Gate formed, but still left Dave Heselden and Simon Richardson some difficult mixed climbing to reach the ice (Il Duce, VII,7). The exploration now moved over to Mainreachan Buttress, but Ben Wilkinson and Robin Thomas thought they had climbed a new route in March 2005. Puzzled by the indirect line, it turned out they had straightened out Sandstorm and freed the aid point by bold and blind hooking on the right. Nisbet had contemplated this line but chose 'the devil he could see'.

Winter climbing on the more remote and formidable Mainreachan Buttress has only been occasional. The only winter route before 1989 was a venture into ground unprecedented in those days, when Hamish MacInnes tried Sleuth in 1970, a route he had climbed the previous summer with Ian Clough. Roping in the instructors of his courses, top climbers of the day Allen Fyffe and Kenny Spence, the route was considered the hardest in Scotland at the time, harder than Astronomy on Ben Nevis which the same team climbed the following winter. Not surprisingly, little happened until Martin Moran began contemplating an equally futuristic line, a winter ascent of Snoopy. An attempt with Nisbet in 1988 was followed by another attempt with Jenkins where they found a hidden ledge leading left out of Snoopy's big corner, only to fail high up on a smooth wall in the dark. The successful ascent in 1989 required some crucial ice forming on this wall. Nisbet long dreaded the verglassed slabs but memories fade and the possibility that Snoopy might go was re-awakened.

Years of passing by the cliff and watching the ice formations (more often, lack of them) made him realise that the route could potentially ice up. But there was no great enthusiasm until Chris Cartwright and Simon Richardson climbed Enigma (VII,7). On the path up towards the cliff they saw a flashing light ahead. Thinking it was a distress signal they continued up the path beyond the cliff only to discover it was a distant lighthouse. Undeterred but now rather late, difficult route finding delayed them further and they abseiled off. Showing the sort of determination required for hard winter routes, they returned next day for a successful ascent. Now Nisbet was thinking he might have rivals for Snoopy, so some urgency returned. After the exceptionally wet and mild February in 1998, the weather turned cold and ice formed very quickly. The required amount of ice was seen during the week with a climbing course and fingers were crossed that the weather would hold until the weekend. Chris Dale was available and the weather due to last until the Saturday afternoon. It lasted until the evening, when the road to Lochcarron was blocked, climbing clients didn't arrive and Chris Dale was spared an early start the next day.

In 1999 Nisbet had soloed Sleuth to check pitch grades and remove the dreaded Scottish VS dagger symbol from the new guide. It attracted him to repeating the winter route, which seemed a natural winter line. With the start for Sleuth being close to the recent winter Enigma, it seemed a shame that there was not a more independent start, so Dave McGimpsey and he started up an obvious but steep fault-line to join and finish up the original route. Their 11 hour ascent showed how impressive the original ascent had been. Two years later Guy Robertson, Pete Benson and Jason Currie made a fast and impressive ascent of a more direct line (Supersleuth, VII,8), although they didn't realise till afterwards that their start was the same as the recent one.

Despite all these long hard routes the Lower Nose and North-East Flanks have seen a steady stream of easier routes mostly by Martin Moran and Andy Nisbet with course members. But more unusual was an ice climbing venue which remained untouched until 1996. Although Martin Moran had heard rumours of a fine icefall on Sgùrr na Feartaig, it was Martin Welch who saw it in nick during a very cold spell. With a cold but working weekend due, he negotiated with Martin Moran to have the Sunday off in return for the information but a promise to leave the big icefall. The real beneficiary was Andy Nisbet, who was a partner on both days. Moran and Nisbet rushed up four fine routes on the Saturday while Martin Welch climbed an easier line with his clients but the best was left as promised for the Sunday when they were joined by John Lyall for The Stonker (a four pitch IV,5). Despite the thought that it was worked out, Donny Williamson and friends found a fine icefall after wetter weather formed another line (The Topper, V,5). This is one of Scotland's best icefall venues, but conditions have never been as good in recent warmer years.

Applecross

In July 1891 Hinxman visited Beinn Bhàn and described it in the Journal as having 'every attribute of hell except its warmth'. He went on to paint a marvellous picture of Coire na Poite. 'Some little way above the loch (Coire na Poite) a rock terrace .... forms the lip of the inner corrie, on whose ice worn floor lie two little Alpine tarns of green water, crystal clear. Immediately behind the highest of these rises the mountain wall, – 1,200 feet of purple sandstone – broken here and there by narrow green ledges and seamed with dark rifts, out of which pour streams of stony debris. The talus slopes are carpeted with a luxuriant growth of parsley-fern, to which succeeds a zone of delicate-fronded oak-fern; while the lower ledges, dark with dripping moisture, are lit by the bright blossoms of the globe-flower and the sea-green fleshy leaves of the rose-root.' In spite of a violent thunderstorm and the absence of companions, Hinxman managed to climb the Upper Connecting Ridge of A' Chìoch. On the summit plateau, at the head of Coire nan Fhamair, he came upon two shepherds from Applecross who 'had little of the English and were much surprised'! The fastnesses of the Karakoram are today less remote than these hills were barely a century ago.

In 1908 the redoubtable Glover and Ling visited A' Chìoch of Sgùrr a' Chaorachain having heard that 'an eminent mountaineer ..... is forming a collection of cabinet-stucke in the form of prominences in North Britain styled A' Chìoch'. One suspects Collie, who had climbed the Applecross Chìoch by a devious route two years earlier. Upon arrival Glover and Ling 'circled round it like wrestlers looking for a grip' then 'went up a succession of short chimneys which a few moments before we had waltzed up in thought .....The chimneys were lined with steep grass and loose and rounded rock'. Clearly impressed by the airiness of the situations, Glover later dreamed of the future : 'When aeroplanes become commonplace, say in three years' time, I hope to possess a 6 Sparrow-power Vol-au-Vent, or a 60 Eagle-power Soarer ... and I intend to circle around some of these towers to assure myself how really easy these cliffs would be to climb straight up.'

Nearly half a century was to elapse before these dreams were realised. It was Tom Patey and his Aberdonian comrades who first demonstrated the true climbing potential when in 1952-3 they explored the north buttresses of Sgùrr a' Chaorachain and Meall Gorm. The first visit in late March was under wet snow, having failed to winter climb elsewhere. But further exploration had to wait seven years until Patey returned with Bonington to discover that the impressive nose of A' Chìoch could be climbed with surprising ease. The following year Patey reported the fine Sword of Gideon on the roadside south face of Sgùrr a' Chaorachain and also explored Beinn Bhàn via the Upper Connecting Ridge of A' Phoit.

HISTORY 15

Strangely, another eight years were to pass before he began to exploit the obvious winter possibilities; whether this was due to the unfounded belief that the low altitude and westerly position made for infrequent good conditions or simply because he had so many other plums to pick, it is difficult now to say. At any rate the first major winter route on Beinn Bhàn, March Hare's Gully, fell in 1969 and was soon followed by exploration by leaders of Hamish MacInnes's winter courses, in particular Kenny Spence's fine ascents of Blaeberry Corner (V,6) on Meall Gorm and Wall of the Early Morning Light (now IV,5 on front points). The latter, the first route to breach the great back wall of Coire na Poite, was not rivalled until Norrie Muir and Arthur Paul's ascent of the Silver Tear icefall in 1977 (V,5 and harder than the Nevis classics).

Three years later Brian Sprunt and Andy Nisbet's success on Der Reisenwand, publicised with pictures of horrifying steepness in *Cold Climbs*, began a trend of increasing popularity of the area in winter. After a first attempt on Der Reisenwand, which Andy Nisbet had spotted in 1978 and thought looked about Grade III, Nisbet and Brian Sprunt failed high up in powder conditions. Having both climbed the North Face of the Eiger the summer before, a Nordwand approach with a team of four and bivouac gear was taken (hence the name). Although conditions were much better and a bivouac was probably unnecessary, the team were slowed down by the heavy sacks and the other two abseiled off. Having been only just short of easier ground (but unaware), the route was finished quickly the next day; several subsequent ascents have managed comfortably in a day.

The early 1980s saw Dougie Dinwoodie contribute a number of interesting new climbs in Coire na Feola and Coire na Poite but undoubtedly the most spectacular climbs were Mick Fowler's ascents of Gully of the Gods and Great Overhanging Gully in Coire nan Fhamair. These lines had of course been known to Scottish enthusiasts for years, but it took Fowler's flair, skill and weather eye to seize them. The later 1980s saw a series of good winter climbs on the north buttresses of Sgùrr a' Chaorachain, and most recently, a phenomenal 'girdle' of Beinn Bhàn by Martin Moran.

The rock climbing in Applecross developed rather spasmodically after Patey's initial impetus; his routes Cioch Nose and Sword of Gideon still receive more ascents than all the others put together. There was a flurry of climbs in the late '60s and early '70s when many of the routes on Sgùrr a' Chaorachain, which has the only good rock climbing of the three hills, were climbed (including George Shields' mysterious Big Daddy, only repeated 27 years later). There were two groups, instructors from the local outdoor centre in Applecross led by Terry Doe and outsiders mostly from the SMC. Most routes on the South Face had two 'first ascents', although the Applecross group climbed less on A' Chìoch. But they did develop many of the low level crags in Applecross, particularly the Camusteel seacliffs and Terry Doe on Ardheslaig; their belay stakes are a useful legacy. Later Paul Potter worked at the centre and discovered the Loch na Creige Crag and the cliff at Sand.

In the last ten years, despite the maritime Applecross suffering from more westerly weather, extensive development of the cliffs in winter has occurred. This has been mostly mixed climbing, for which the vegetated Applecross cliffs are ideal, since most of the icefalls had already been climbed. Most of the action has either been on Meall Gorm, suddenly much more accessible since the road is now ploughed, or on the several corries of Beinn Bhàn. Many of the easier gullies and buttresses on Meall Gorm have been climbed but the two best quality climbs, Cobalt Buttress and Blue Pillar, have seen many ascents although both are much harder than the modest grades originally given by Ian Clough and Tom Patey respectively. The front face of Cobalt Buttress gets the sun but saw two steep routes by Graeme Ettle and John Lyall in gloomy December 1993, Rattlesnake (V,7) and Blue in the Face (VI,7).

There have also been many ascents of Beinn Bhàn's classics, from the A' Chìoch ridge (II), to March Hare's Gully (IV,4) and the magnificent Silver Tear (V,5). And a few repeats of Coire an Fhamair's top routes in good style, Der Reisenwand in a day (VII,6), the amazing Gully of the Gods (VI,6) and Great Overhanging Gully climbed free (VI,6). But there is five kilometres of vegetated cliff to keep the explorers happy, most of it pretty steep too and offering some high quality routes when frozen. Pride of place goes to the fantastic Coire an Fhamair which has continued to offer routes of astonishing quality on ground thought to be impossible until someone bold enough has tried. If Gully of the Gods wasn't enough, the last decade has breached the awesome overhanging fault of Genesis and the towering walls of The Godfather. Genesis has long been admired as tiers of roofs with a few dangling icicles, but like Gully of the Gods, it needed close examination to realise that it was based on a huge deep chimney-fault. Roger Webb was close to trying the line in 2000 when Andy Cave and Dave Heselden succeeded in breaching the overhangs (VII,7).

Martin Moran had been eyeing up a big corner in the huge buttress which forms the vertical profile in the famous pictures of the cliff. When he contacted Paul Tattersall for a climbing partner on a route either on Liathach or Applecross and Paul innocently chose Applecross because he hadn't been there before, a remarkable ascent was about to happen. George Shields had tried to climb the face in summer in the '70s but had failed despite some epic pitches. A traverse line crosses the buttress, used as an early ploy to reach Gully of the Gods in 1979. Even this is gripping with the exposure underneath but yet this lower wall wasn't the crux, although some tricky route finding slowed the team down. When they reached the corner, it was dark and Martin's torch failed. Swopping torches with Paul, he led a hard pitch to the upper corner which was even steeper than expected. Paul can remember prussicking the pitch on slings in the dark on an icy rope, somehow managing to swing across to unclip his rope from a peg runner and swing back out into space. When he reached the belay below a smooth corner leading to a one metre roof and even harder beyond, he declined.

Martin says, "I met a gently impending five metre corner-crack. After failed attempts to outflank it on the left I arranged protection and went for the 'do or die' routine in a flurry of crossed axes, blind torques and other techniques. Having just got my axes planted in tufts near the top my feet came off. Not being strong enough to do a straight pull-over into a mantelshelf I hooked my heel up into a rock crevice above my head and squirmed my way out of a potential 12 metre fall." By now the halogen bulb had finished off the torch with an unknown pitch to go, but Paul remembered a normal bulb in his sack. Managing to change by the light of a mobile phone, there was just enough dim light to struggle up to an instant change from vertical ground to a horizontal plateau. It was daylight when they reached the car! The challenge is there for a repeat, and judging by the speed standards are rising, it may not be long! Certainly interest is being shown in Genesis, but in 2004, James Edwards was distracted from it by a couple of lines up the walls to its left, Revelations (VI,6) and Biblical Knowledge (VI,5).

There have been 35 new routes on Beinn Bhàn in the last ten years. In Coire na Feola, there have been a series of fine routes on Suspense Buttress, finishing with the exciting direct line of Skinflint, climbed by a team of four (VI,6). The best route in Coire na Poite was Realisation (VI,6), on the steep buttress between March Hare's and Mad Hatter's Gullies. Malcolm Bass and Simon Yearsley were inspired by the superb photo in Cold Climbs and yet again the mountain offered sustained climbing and mostly good protection on a wall with 'cool situations'. Graeme Ettle spotted the Frontal East Face of A' Phoit on a visit in 1996 with Andy Nisbet and soon returned with different partners for four steep routes. The fifth corrie, Coire Toll a' Bhein, may have first been visited by Mike Geddes in 1982 but nothing was recorded until Simon Fenwick and Phil Thornhill climbed Threatening Behaviour (V,6) and Phil soloed the good looking easier gully of Breach of the Peace (II). The names suggest that one of the team had just had a brush with the law. A mellowing Andy Nisbet has recently managed to walk past Beinn Bhàn's steeper walls for a few visits. And the very furthest corrie, the isolated gully of Flying Penguins was only known by local climbers Martin Welch and from his nickname, a mid-air Paul Potter (V,6).

HISTORY 17

Torridon Crags

The history of crag climbing in Torridon is typically recent although no doubt the rocks had been touched before the first routes at Diabaig in 1975 (although not recorded until 1981). While the willingness of Ed Grindley and Allan Austin to record routes on mere outcrops was new (Diabaig is now considered to have some of the best climbing in the country), the names of Routes One, Two and Three were more traditional. Once the cat was released, it didn't take long for further visitors, Colin Moody in 1982 with Boab's Corner, then Murray Hamilton in 1983 with The Pillar and Andy Nisbet in 1984 with Rick Allen (Dire Wall) and Richard McHardy (Northumberland Wall). Murray didn't say much about the now celebrated Pillar but in fact it was very lichenous at the time. When Dire Wall was climbed, the team chose it over The Pillar (whose ascent was unknown) because it was cleaner. Even it needed substantial cleaning and Nisbet still fell off when a hold broke. Later the crag became a happy hunting ground for Kev Howett, Dave Cuthbertson and others, who produced a host of fine and difficult routes, most notably Howett's Wall of Flame and Local Hero. In recent years it has become increasingly popular and with Route Two and The Pillar recognised as among the best routes in Scotland, they see ascents on most dry days in the summer.

The sandstone crags which catch your eye as you drive down Glen Torridon, must have caught eyes for years. But no routes were recorded before 1990. Rab Anderson had been eyeing up Seana Mheallan, but in 1989 had been distracted by competition for the routes at Ardmair. A walk up with Chris Anderson on a snowless New Year 1990 had indicated the potential. The crag was developed over five consecutive weekends during a particularly good May and June 1990 – 'Sales of wire brushes and tape increased in Edinburgh.' The mornings were cold and the crag is sunniest in the evening, so they made an early morning run up from Edinburgh, pitched the tent in the woods and walked up to the crag. Climbing continued till 10pm some Saturdays. Rab remembers a noisy cuckoo at the camping place and standing in the pitch dark throwing stones into the trees, hence the route name Shoot the Cuckoo (HVS 5a). Kev Howett was also camping there and whilst Rab was being quizzed about the location of his secret crag, which was visible as they spoke, he was aware that if he lifted his eyes over Kev's shoulder, he might perhaps give the game away! Later he conceded and Howett repeated the best route, The Torridonian (E3 6a). When the routes appeared in the 1993 guide, the most discussed item was the near impossible approach time of 20 minutes (now doubled), but the routes were soon recognised as being high quality.

Around a dozen sandstone crags have been developed since the 1993 guide, with Colin Moody the keenest activist. Around 1990, Colin spent time walking round the crags looking for possibilities on rock while his mates were winter climbing. Hairpin Crag had already been observed from the road to Diabaig and when route descriptions for Seana Mheallan were delayed until the 1993 guide was published, he paid it a visit. It later turned out that Martin Moran had soloed Walsh's groove in the said footwear, but Colin climbed several other routes, many with Ian Taylor and including the fine line of Bundle of Apathy (E4 6a). The sunny Creag nan Leumnach was explored early in 1994, the first two routes being in February and March. He returned in May with Steve Kennedy to the upper tier, then with Ian Taylor for some harder routes on the lower tier; the two also developed Creag nan Uaimh. In the summer he moved to Seana Mheallan West. This crag has slowly been developed over the years, with Nisbet actively involved, and now has more routes than any other in Torridon. To add to a busy 1994, Steve Kennedy climbed several routes on Creag an Fhithich, another crag with rumours of past climbing. Whether being visible from the bar makes this more or less likely is unsure. But Colin was not finished.

In 1995 he climbed on Creag na Botaigean and in 1996 on Creag na Speireag. After this he directed most of his attention to the sea-cliffs on Skye, most notably at Neist, but still found time for Path Crag on Liathach in 2005. Others have joined the popularity of outcrops but the keenest has been Martin Moran who with various partners, has climbed all 14 routes at Kinlochdamph Crag between 1999 and 2005. Most spectacular is the very overhanging Command and Conquer (E3 6a).

Several gneiss crags around the Diabaig area were climbed between 1998 and 2000, many by teams including Jamie Fisher. The steep crack of The Applecross Jam (E3 5c) had an abseil sling above and was rumoured to have been climbed by Gabriel Regan in the 1970s. But the best crag faced away from Diabaig and was named Rolling Wall after its waves of smooth rock; Brave New World (E2 5c) is the best route there.

Torridon, Liathach

Little of any significance was climbed on Liathach before the 1970s – Bell's Buttress had fallen in 1947 and other odd rock climbs like Reflection Wall and Dru were recorded in the 1950s. The obvious straightforward snow gullies were also climbed, like the Trinity gullies in Coire na Caime. It is possible that these and some similar routes recorded later had earlier unclaimed ascents. The most significant event of the 1970s was the ascent of Poachers Fall (V,5) by Richard McHardy and Andy Nisbet, an excellent ice route 'stolen' from Clive Rowland. Conditions were thin and none of the regular icefalls had formed, also Nisbet was not as enthusiastic as McHardy, so the chance was missed to take up the potential of Liathach.

The early 1980s saw exploration of the north side of Alligin by Steve Chadwick, but climbers were fairly slow to take up the potential of Liathach. Mild winters were part of the reason that the next route was Headless Gully (V,5) by Steve Kennedy and Andy Nisbet in 1984, climbed during a big thaw. The thaw had produced a big gap behind the steepest pitch; this made for straightforward chimneying whereas future ascents had to climb the front and upgraded the climb. At the end of that winter, Phil Butler and Mick Fowler climbed Umbrella Fall, another climb which can be Grade IV when a favourable shape (not that ice umbrellas sound favourable) but now has been upgraded.

But it was in 1986 and 1987 that a real avalanche of new ice routes was recorded no less than 23 on Liathach alone in these two winters. On the 23rd of February 1986, steep ice was climbed in three different corries, Salmon Leap (VI,6) by Cunningham and Nisbet, Dru Couloir (V,6) by Rab Anderson and Murray Hamilton in Coire na Caime and Pyramid Left Icefall (V,5) by Ken Hopper and Clive Rowland on Terminal Buttress. Partly this reflected the excellent ice conditions in these years, but at least as important was the enthusiasm of Andy Cunningham, Andy Nisbet and others. Martin Moran produced four new routes on Tom na Gruagaich of Beinn Alligin as well as two difficult ice routes on Toll a' Meitheach of Liathach.

After another spell of leaner winters, 29 more routes were climbed between 1994 and 1996. Most notable was Fubarbundy (VIII,7), the roofed corner right of Poachers. Mick Fowler and Chris Watts had tried this obvious line in the 1980s, reaching the roof but finding no cracks leading out under it. But in 1994, the ice formed down the right rib of the corner and Chris Cartwright and Dave Heselden took the chance of climbing Scotland's hardest ice route. Unable to gain the thin ice from below, Heselden tensioned from the right and made an awesome unprotected lead up the glazed rib. In 1996 Nisbet saw the ice formed much thicker up the rib but it thawed before the weekend; subsequently it has formed only to the lip of the roof rather than down the rib. But some day? In recent times many mixed routes have been climbed, but Liathach is the home of ice. Conditions were good in early March 1999; the complete icicle of Fowler's Conditions were good in early March 1999; the complete icicle of Fowler's Test Department formed and may have seen as many as 20 ascents in 10 days. The last few years have been milder but often wet and ice has formed quickly during cold spells. A sustained cold winter is in everyone's dreams.

Beinn Eighe

Hinxman again is the first to appear in the story, with a fine photograph of the triple buttresses of Beinn Eighe and an article on the rock possibilities in the very first issue of the SMC Journal (1891). A few years later he returned and made the first ascent of the Northern Pinnacles of Liathach in the company of Douglas, Rennie and W.Macdonald, the head keeper of the estate, whose protestations ("no man in the world could go up there") appear not to have hindered the party. The rock was exceedingly loose, but they felt sure that its "unstable condition would lessen with each ascent," and the route proved popular. In April 1900 it received its first winter ascent by two separate parties, led by Naismith and Raeburn. "A hitch was found, one of those rare hitches whose occurrence maketh glad the heart, as the occurrence of hitches does not always do."

The first recorded climb on Beinn Eighe was Lawson, Ling and Glover's climb on Sàil Mhòr at Easter 1899, although Collie had previously attempted Central Buttress. Writing to Douglas in 1898 he revealed "I think I have discovered the finest rock climb in the British Isles – on the precipices of Ben Eighe". After cutting steps up West Central Gully for about 800 feet he had traversed left onto Central Buttress but been stopped by a "perpendicular and overhanging cliff" at least 200 feet high.

The next day he had descended the right-hand side of Central Buttress by a complicated route to reach the cairn he had left. In 1907 came the first ascent of the East Buttress of Coire Mhic Fhearchair by Gibbs, Backhouse and Mounsey. They inspected the bottom pitch of East Central Gully but decided against it and instead went diagonally left up to Broad Terrace. "A direct ascent ... was out of the question for the holds were all the wrong way." After an excursion into East Central Gully on snow they regained the buttress by a "delightful" chimney and thereafter found "nowhere extreme difficulty, or need for great exertion. .... No better rock had been our fortune in all Scotland."

A strong SMC party attempted the West Buttress in March 1910, but were stopped by "a stretch of AP rock" and finished up Far West Gully. The first ascent of this buttress had to wait until Bower and Meldrum's visit in 1919 – they declared that for the crux sandstone slab "rubbers or stocking feet are probably essential", while they felt that the final quartzite tower "would probably succumb to a frontal attack". This was followed three years later by Pigott's Route on Central Buttress, by a raiding English party later to be more famous for their deeds in Wales. J.F.Hamilton, another climber more famous for his deeds elsewhere, added his route on Central Buttress in 1936, but nothing more of note was climbed until the 1950s.

Post-war exploration started with a fruitful June visit by Len Lovat and Tom Weir in 1954, then around 1960 Tom Patey made a few characteristic forays, producing Gnome Wall, The Gash and the adventurous Upper Girdle. An Edinburgh University Mountaineering Club meet in 1961 found Robin Smith the first to take the challenge of the Eastern Ramparts. His description of Boggle remains a classic admonition for guidebook writers. The steep quartzite was subsequently left alone for a decade apart from a fine day's climbing by Jim Brumfitt and Bill Sproul in 1966 when Kami-kaze (VS 4c) and Samurai (HVS 5a) were climbed, and another single day visit by Allan Austin.

A new era for the steep quartzite may be said to have begun with the ascent of the delightful Groovin' High (E1 5b) in 1973 by John Ingram, Greg Strange and Rob Archbold. This was instantly recognised as a classic and remains one of the most satisfying climbs in the country. The Aberdonians continued their campaign with intermittent visits, one of the most significant being a weekend in 1980 when The Reaper (E2 5c) and Pale Diedre (E2 5c) fell to Brian Sprunt and Greg Strange. The Reaper had long been recognised as a challenge and its ascent on sight was a very bold achievement; on steep ground a long way above runners a tiring Brian Sprunt had to hook his chin on a ledge to shake out. A visit the previous week had been unsuccessful when Brian forgot his rock boots. Other useful additions in this period came from Richard McHardy on the sandstone of the West Buttress and Arthur Paul and Norrie Muir on Twilight Zone.

In the later 1980s Andy Nisbet began a typically long and thorough development of the cliffs. With a variety of partners, a host of new climbs both summer and winter were produced. Worthy of particular mention are Ling Dynasty

(E5 6b), taking a spectacular roof towards the right of the Far East Wall – a phenomenal on-sight lead by Graeme Livingston; and the magnificent Angel Face (E2 5c) and Seeds of Destruction (E3 5c), which take the improbable challenge of the beautiful smooth grey wall left of The Reaper. Nisbet's best memory is of four days of cloudless weather camping under the Far East Wall with Steve Blagbrough at mid-summer, with the cliffs bone dry and the valley shrouded in cloud. Twenty hours of daylight meant for tired arms. Paul Thorburn and Gary Latter became aware of an unclimbed overhanging wall left of Ling Dynasty after Nisbet devised a spoof ascent called Pinocchio with a big nose as the crux; they had the last laugh when they climbed Fascist Groove Thang at E7 6c.

Very little was recorded in winter before 1978; East Central Gully was well known but not who climbed it first. Central Buttress was climbed by Kenny Spence and course students over two days, a notable achievement in the early 1970s but there was no record of East or West Buttresses. A renewed interest in mixed climbing after the front pointing bonanza of the early 70s saw first Alex McIntyre and Al Rouse make a one day ascent of Central Buttress in 1978, finding it so hard that the previous ascent was barely believed. But repeats of routes like Sleuth on Mainreachan Buttress (1970) have proved that Spence was well up to that standard. A rush for West Buttress (IV,4) the following year saw Nisbet and Bob MacGregor just pip Murray Hamilton and Hamish MacInnes. But surprisingly interest waned, although Nisbet found that the east wall of Central Buttress was surprisingly amenable when he climbed it with Pete Barrass in 1981 (V,4).

In the cold winter of 1986 the very hard winter Direttissima on the West Buttress (VII,8) was forced by Rab Anderson and Rob Milne; this was only repeated in 2005. In 1987 Mick Fowler and Mike Morrison seized the opportunity to climb the ferocious ice of West Central Gully. This was a well known problem but several previous attempts, by the likes of Paul Nunn and friends in 1969 and Andy Nisbet/Phil Thornhill in 1984 had failed to even see a possibility. Late season ice was the answer, as the snow is slow to thaw in that deep cleft, although the second ascent in February 2002 found ice formed in today's warmer climate.

Realising the feasibility of very steep climbing in the corrie, Andy Cunningham and Nisbet climbed the chimney-line of Kami-Kaze (VI,7) in 1988. Seeing ice formed in the huge fault to the left, they returned a week later for the high quality but unrepeated Vishnu (VII,6), nearly as improbable but not as fierce as West Central Gully. Throughout the '90s and enthused with the scope for torquing in the well cracked quartzite, Nisbet returned with many partners to climb the more obvious faults and crack-lines. The practice of approaching over the top and leaving rucksacks should have included head torches in the ascent of Glow Worm (V,6) with Sammy Dring. One pitch up with an hour of daylight left and no moon meant a finish by feel in total darkness. In fine weather in 1991, Brian Davison and Nisbet climbed Eastern Promise (VI,7) and two days later the even steeper Mistral (VII,7), the first route on West Central Wall and an indication that this wall was even more amenable than the others. Also interesting is that they were avalanched on the approach down Fuselage Gully despite several days of still and dry weather. Nisbet was fascinated by the snow profile and an air gap between layers formed by sublimation, while Davison, already psyched up for the overhanging crux of Mistral, wasn't the slightest interested and told Nisbet so! They returned the following year for the very icy Shang-High (VII,7), then Nisbet and Sean Roberts proved how snowy the West Central Wall can be even in late season with Maelstrom (VII,7).

The Triple Buttresses have seen many ascents but the harder routes are just starting to see repeats. The one route which has become almost popular and saw its fifth ascent in 2005, is Blood Sweat and Frozen Tears (VIII,8). This fairly direct and initially vegetated line up the West Central Wall was climbed in 1993 by Moran and Nisbet, and holds snow better than some of the other plumb vertical lines which are undoubtedly possible by someone strong. After this there was a lull in first ascents, partly due to a succession of failures in bad weather by Nisbet and different partners on The Sting but this was finally achieved on a fine day in 1997 with Martin Moran (VII,7). This was the start of another wave, which included a dark January finish in 1997 on Samurai (VII,7) with Jonathan Preston in 1997 and plenty of daylight in an unusually snowy April in 1998 on Gashtrognome (VI,7) with Robin McAllister. The defined HVS fault-lines were completed by Blair Fyffe and Es Tresidder on Fairytale Groove (VII,7) in 2001 and Davison, Dave McGimpsey and Nisbet on Rampart Wall (VII,8) in 2002. The E1s have hardly been touched yet!

Sàil Mhòr and Other Cliffs

The first recorded route on Beinn Eighe was Lawson, Ling and Glover's Route on Sàil Mhòr in 1899 (II). This has recently become popular and recognised as a fine mountaineering route. Since the other two main gullies were also climbed early on, this was perhaps an attempt on the central gully. But this has a fearsome finish and wasn't climbed until 2000 (Jenga, VI,7). The name is from a previous attempt in 1996 when Brian Davison displaced a crucial block from a loose pile and brought down a substantial rockfall, resulting in a helicopter lift out of the corrie. On the ride out, Nisbet spotted Spring Gully (Meall Dearg) in good condition and climbed it two days later, but the pilot declined to check out any more cliffs. Two good mixed routes were climbed on the walls of the huge gully the following winter, Overkill (V,7) by Dave McGimpsey and Nisbet and the typically intimidating The Darkness Beckons (VII,7) by Moran and Chris Dale (the name also suggests a typically late finish).

Other cliffs on Beinn Eighe have also been developed. The writing of a new Torridon Climbers' Guide by the Turnbulls in 1973 had sparked exploration of the quartzite cliffs of Coire Rudha-Staca. Four routes, including Thin Man's Ridge (Hard Severe) and the attractively named Independent Pineapple (Severe), were climbed in 1971 and 1972. Andy Nisbet's liking of the cliff started in 1976 when he and top young American climber Spaff Ackerly succeeded in finding dry rock in late October. A repeat of Thin Man's Ridge was not quite the difficulty of Foops (Spaff had just made the second ascent of this huge roof crack in the "Gunks"), nor was Autumn Rib (Hard Severe 4b). The following year an Aberdeen University Lairig Club team climbed Pineapple Chimney (VS 4c) on the opposite side of the Pineapple pinnacle. The winter story started when two routes were climbed in the '80s. But winter activity really started when Nisbet began using it as a softer option to Coire Mhic Fhearchair, usually in bad weather or conditions. Perhaps this is why both Graeme Ettle and Brian Davison have been avalanched on different days near the crag, Nisbet escaping until he later slid 100 metres and stopped with his feet dangling over the cliff edge. But recent ascents have been less eventful and fifteen winter routes of the typical steep quartzite style have now been climbed, Thin Man's Ridge (V,7) and Pineapple Chimney (VI,7) being two of the best and climbed on the same day by different teams.

Environment

Access
Part 1 of the Land Reform (Scotland) Act 2003 gives everyone the right to be on most land and inland water for recreation, education and for going from place to place, providing they act responsibly. This includes climbing, hillwalking, cycling and wild camping. These access rights and responsibilities are explained in the Scottish Outdoor Access Code. The key elements are:

- Take personal responsibility for your own actions and act safely.
- Respect people's privacy and peace of mind.
- Help land managers and others to work safely and effectively.
- Care for the environment and take your litter home.
- Keep your dog under proper control.
- Take extra care if you're organising an event or running a business.

If you're managing the outdoors:
- Respect access rights;
- Act reasonably when asking people to avoid land management operations;
- Work with your local authority and other bodies to help integrate access and land management;
- Respect rights of way and customary access.

Find out more by visiting <www.outdooraccess-scotland.com> or phoning your local Scottish Natural Heritage office.

Stalking, Shooting & Lambing
The stag stalking season is from 1st July to 20th October, although few estates start at the beginning of the season. Hinds continue to be culled until 15th February.

There is no stalking anywhere on Sundays, although requests to avoid disturbing deer on the hills may still be made, and there is no stalking on land owned by the National Trust for Scotland. This applies to most of Torridon.

The Hillphones scheme <www.hillphones.info>, run by Scottish Natural Heritage (SNH) and the Mountaineering Council for Scotland (MCofS, see below), provides daily stalking information on recorded telephone messages. In this guide, only South Glen Shiel is covered by Hillphones (01599 511425).

The grouse shooting season is from 12th August until 10th December, although the end of the season is less used. It is also important to avoid disturbance to sheep, especially from dogs and particularly during the lambing season between March and May.

Bird Life
When climbing, don't cause direct disturbance to nesting birds, particularly the rarer species, which are often found on crags (eg, Golden Eagle, White Tailed (Sea) Eagle, Peregrine Falcon, Razorbill, Guillemot, Puffin, Fulmar, Kittiwake, Cormorant, Shag, Buzzard, Kestrel, Raven). Often this is between 1st February and the end of July. Intentional disturbance of nesting birds is a criminal offence and if convicted, you face a fine of up to £5000 and confiscation of climbing equipment.

It is the individual's responsibility to find out from the MCofS (see below) about voluntary restrictions at any particular location and to obtain advice as to whether their presence might disturb any nesting birds.

Footpath Erosion & Bicycles
Part of the revenue from the sale of this and other Scottish Mountaineering Club books is granted by the Scottish Mountaineering Trust as financial assistance towards the repair and maintenance of hill paths in Scotland. However, it is our responsibility to minimise our erosive effect, for the enjoyment of future climbers.

Bicycles can cause severe erosion when used 'off road' on footpaths and open hillsides and should only be used on vehicular or forest tracks.

SAFETY NOTES

Vegetation
When cleaning routes in summer take care what you remove, some of the flora may be rare. Many crags are designated Sites of Special Scientific Interest (SSSI). This does not ban climbing, but may mean there are restrictions on activity. When winter climbing, minimise damage to underlying vegetation by only climbing routes when fully frozen. Crag and Winter Climbing Codes are available from the MCofS (see below).

Camping, Litter & Pollution
Responsible wild camping is permitted under the new access legislation, although 'No Camping' signs can still be found in the hills. If camping, do not cause pollution, and bury human waste carefully out of sight and far away from any habitation or water supply. Avoid burying rubbish as this may also pollute the environment.

Cairns
The proliferation of navigation cairns detracts from the feeling of wildness, and may be confusing rather than helpful as regards route-finding. The indiscriminate building of cairns on the hills should be discouraged.

Car Use
Do not drive along private roads without permission – the use of bicycles is covered by access legislation (see opposite) – and when parking, avoid blocking access to private roads and land or causing any hazard to other road users.

General Privacy
Respect for personal privacy near people's homes is nothing less than good manners.

Bothies
The Mountain Bothies Association has about 100 buildings on various estates throughout Scotland which it maintains as bothies. The MBA owns none of these buildings, they belong to estates which generously allow their use as open bothies. Bothies are there for use by small groups (less than six) for a few days. If you wish to stay longer permission should be sought from the owners. The increased number of hill users have put a greater strain on the bothies and their surrounding environment. It is therefore more important than ever that the simple voluntary bothy code be adhered to. This and more information can be found on the MBA website <www.mountainbothies.org.uk>:

- If you carry it in, then carry it out and have respect for the bothy, its owners and its users;
- Leave the bothy clean and dry, guard against fire and don't cause vandalism or graffiti;
- Bury human waste carefully out of sight far away from the bothy and the water supply and avoid burying rubbish.

Mountaineering Council of Scotland
The MCofS is the representative body for climbers and walkers in Scotland. One of its primary concerns is the continued free access to the hills and crags. Information about bird restrictions, stalking and general access issues can be obtained from the MCofS. Should you encounter problems regarding access you should contact the MCofS, whose current address is: The Old Granary, West Mill Street, Perth PH1 5QP, tel (01738 638 227), fax (01738 442 095), email <info@mountaineering-scotland.org.uk>, website <www.mountaineering-scotland.org.uk>.

Safety

Participation
"Climbing and mountaineering are activities with a danger of personal injury or death. Participants in these activities should be aware of and accept these risks and be responsible for their own actions and involvement."
UIAA participation statement.

TECHNICAL NOTES

Liabilities
You are responsible for your own actions and should not hold landowners liable for an accident, even if it happens while climbing over a fence or dyke. The same is true of bolted sport climbs, or routes with any protection in place. It is up to the individual climber to assess the reliability of bolts, pegs, slings or old nuts, which over time, may have become corroded and therefore fail.

Mountain Rescue
Contact the police, either by phone (999) or in person. Give concise information about the location and injuries of the victim and any assistance available at the accident site. It is often better to stay with the victim, but in a party of two, one may have to leave to summon help. Leave the casualty warm and comfortable in a sheltered, well marked place.

Equipment and Planning
Good navigation skills, equipment, clothing and planning can all reduce the risk of accident. Mobile phones and GPS can help in communications and locating your position, but mobiles do not work in many places in the North of Scotland and both rely on batteries and electronics which can fail or be damaged. Consequently, they can never be a substitute for good navigation, first aid or general mountain skills.

Rock Climbing
Two-thirds of accidents are the result of a lengthy fall, either due to holds breaking or rockfall. About one-third are the result of planning errors – being too ambitious (trying a route that's too hard) or simply failing to judge how long a route will take and becoming benighted.

Snow and Ice Climbing
These accidents are twice as likely as for rock climbing, but the fatality rate is almost half! – Perhaps the landing is softer? A substantial number are related to navigation errors, getting down from routes. Benightment and numerous other incidents are often the result of poor planning. The greatest number of accidents is caused by falls while climbing, which reflects the lack of protection and the more serious nature of snow and ice climbing!

Avalanches
Climbers venturing on to the hills in winter should be familiar with the principles of snow structure and avalanche prediction. Deposition of wind blown snow causes the largest risk, especially as snow is frequently blown around Scottish hills. Slopes between 30 and 60 degrees with fresh snow, whether freshly fallen or simply blown, should be considered suspect. The greater the amount of fresh snow, the higher the risk. Avoiding these slopes may be simple, such as choosing a buttress rather than a gully, or finding a section of cliff blown clear, but remember that some buttress routes involve steep snow at their base or more seriously, just below the cliff top. In this guide the winter cliffs are all near the coast. A wetter climate than inland can produce very heavy snowfall and high avalanche risk. But the warmer climate means that the snow tends to stabilise quicker and the absence of large plateaus reduces the collection of windslab. But on balance, the risk of avalanche should be taken as seriously in this area as any.

On meeting snow of dubious stability, climbers should dig a snow pit and examine the snow profile, looking especially for different layers of snow with different degrees of bonding. Slab avalanches are caused when a surface layer of snow is insufficiently attached to layers below and often when a climber triggers the slide. If a witness to an avalanche it is vital to start a search immediately, given it is safe to do so. Victims will often be alive at first, but their chances of survival lessen rapidly if buried. Unless severely injured, some 80% may live if found immediately, but only 10% after a three hour delay. Mark the burial sight if known, listen for any sound, look for any visual clue, search until help arrives if possible. Again, a working knowledge of first aid may save a life, as many victims may have stopped breathing.

A Chance in a Million? by Bob Barton and Blyth Wright, published by the SMC, is the classic work on Scottish avalanches (see Books, below). Avalanche predictions

TECHNICAL NOTES 25

for the major winter climbing areas are produced by the Scottish Avalanche Information Service (01463 713191), or <www.sais.gov uk>.

However, the climbing areas in this guide are not covered by SAIS reports and climbers should be more independent and make their own assessment.

Maps

Symbols are used on SMC maps to indicate different categories of summit. Tops are not marked on the maps in this guide: Munro – black triangle; Corbett – black circle; Graham – black diamond; Other – crossed circle.

Place names and map references have in general been taken from the Ordnance Survey 1:50,000 Landranger maps. The following Ordnance Survey 1:50,000 Landranger (**OSL**) and 1:25,000 Explorer (**OSE**) maps and 1:25,000 Harvey (**H**) maps cover this area.

OSL	OSE	H	Area
33	413-4		Knoydart
33-4	413-4	Kintail & Glen Shiel	Glen Shiel to Lochalsh
25	429		Glen Carron
24	428		Applecross
19, 24-5	433	Torridon	Torridon

Books

The following SMC and SMT publications, *The Munros, The Corbetts, North-West Highlands, Scottish Hill and Mountain Names, Scottish Hill Tracks, Highland Scrambles North, Hostile Habitats – Scotland's Mountain Environment,* and *A Chance in a Million? – Scottish Avalanches* are useful for hill walking routes and general mountain interest in this area. For more information and to order SMC and SMT publications, visit the SMC website <www.smc.org.uk>. See also the publications list at the end of this guide.

Technical

Summer Grades

The grading system ranges from Easy, Moderate, Difficult, Very Difficult, Severe, Hard Severe, Very Severe (VS), Hard Very Severe (HVS) to Extremely Severe. The Extremely Severe grade has been subdivided into E1, E2, E3, E4, E5, E6 and E7 and so on.

Technical grades are given for routes of VS and above where known, also sometimes for Severe and Hard Severe. The normal range for technical grades expected on routes of the given overall grade are as follows; Severe - 4a, 4b; Hard Severe - 4a, 4b, 4c; VS – 4b, 4c, 5a; HVS – 4c, 5a, 5b; E1 – 5a, 5b, 5c; E2 – 5b, 5c, 6a; E3 – 5c, 6a; E4 – 5c, 6a, 6b; E5 – 6a, 6b. Routes with a technical grade at the lower end of the range will be sustained or poorly protected, while those with grades at the upper end, are likely to have a shorter and generally well protected crux. Grading information is in some cases scanty or even lacking, particularly in some of the older or more obscure routes. A † symbol indicates that the overall grade is perhaps correct but there is no recent information for pitch grades. Where there is even less information, harder routes have been graded Scottish VS, which can encompass a range of difficulty from VS to E2. French grades have been given for a very few bolted climbs. Grades for bouldering are in a state of flux, with various systems current. The UK technical system is used for problems of 4c and below. The V and Font systems for anything harder. As an approximation, V0 is 5a, V0+ is 5b, V1 is 5c and V2 is 6a.

Winter Grades

Climbs have been graded using the two-tier system. The technical grades, which are shown by the Arabic numbers, apply to the hardest move or crux sequence of a route, while the Roman numeral gives an indication of the overall difficulty of the climb. The combination of the two grades makes the system work in a similar way to how the E grades and the numerical grades are used in summer.

In this way a V,4 is normally a serious ice route and V,5 would be a classic ice route with adequate protection. V,6 would be a classic mixed route and V,7

TECHNICAL NOTES

would indicate a technically difficult but well protected mixed route. Each route has the same overall difficulty (Grade V) but with differing degrees of seriousness and technical difficulty. Both parts of the grading system are open-ended.

Grade I – Uncomplicated, average-angled snow climbs normally having no pitches. They may, however, have cornice difficulties or long run-outs.

Grade II – Gullies which contain either individual or minor pitches, or high-angled snow with difficult cornice exits. The easiest buttresses under winter conditions.

Grade III – Gullies which contain ice in quantity. There will normally be at least one substantial pitch and possibly several lesser ones. Sustained buttress climbs, but only technical in short sections.

Grade IV – Steeper and more technical with vertical sections found on ice climbs. Mixed routes will require a good repertoire of techniques.

Grade V – Climbs which are difficult, sustained and serious. If on ice, long sustained ice pitches are to be expected; mixed routes will require a degree of rock climbing ability and the use of axe torquing and hooking and similar winter techniques.

Grade VI – Thin and tenuous ice routes or those with long vertical sections. Mixed routes will include all that has gone before but more of it.

Grade VII – Usually mixed routes which are very sustained or technically extreme. Also sustained routes on thin or vertical ice.

Grade VIII – Very hard and sustained mixed routes.

A few routes have been graded Scottish IV or Scottish V, from the older I to V system, where Scottish IV can be harder than new IV but short and Scottish V could be anything new V or above.

Pegs and Bolts

Scotland has a tradition of climbs with leader placed protection. Pegs are nowadays considered unacceptable in summer rock first ascents due to improved equipment and the option of move rehearsal as an alternative to hammered protection. Some established climbs depend on peg runners to keep their grade; these are acceptable. Bolts are also considered unacceptable on mountain cliffs. However, bolt protected sport climbs are accepted on low lying cliffs which are not adventurous in nature, do not have a history of established traditional routes and have been agreed to be better suited to sport climbing by the local climbing community. Retrobolting of traditional routes is considered unacceptable without agreement from the first ascentionist and the local climbing community.

Left and Right

The terms generally refer to a climber facing the cliff. This always applies for route descriptions and usually for descents, which are often planned before the downhill movement starts. But for a few complex descents from mountain cliffs, the direction is facing downhill (but then the direction is specified). Routes are described from left to right and this should be assumed, unless the cliff is always approached from the right, when right to left is used and indicated in the text.

Pitch Lengths

Pitch lengths are often rounded to the nearest 5m, although pitches below 20m are sometimes rounded to the nearest 2m. The descriptions assume the use of 50m ropes.

Diagrams

If a route has been numbered, this indicates that there is a diagram depicting the cliff, which will be found close to the relevant text. The numbers of the climbs in the text correspond to the numbers on the diagrams.

Recommended Routes

A star quality system has been used. No star routes may be good although nothing special, or eliminate in line, or information may be lacking. Only a few are worthless or unpleasant.

* Good climbing, but the route may lack line, situation or balance.
** A good route but lacking one or more of the features that make it a climb of quality.
*** An outstanding route of the highest quality, combining superb climbing with line, character and situation.
**** The best climbs of their class in Scotland.

In winter, quality will vary with conditions so stars, like grades, are applied for the conditions when the route is commonly climbed. In the best conditions the routes may justify more stars.

First Ascensionists

The year of the first ascent is given in the text. The full date and first ascensionists are listed by area in chronological order at the back of the guide. If climbed originally using aid or rest points, this is listed, usually with the first free ascent. Details of variations are usually given under the parent route. An ascent in winter conditions is indicated by a W at the start of an entry and a summer route by S. Winter ascents are listed separately from their corresponding summer route.

Amenities

Knoydart: Kinloch Hourn — self contained flat, B&B and tea rooms; Barrisdale — bothy, self catering accommodation (flat & house), camping <www.barisdale.com> NOTE the spelling); Inverie (NG 767 000) — pub, restaurant, post office, shop with restricted hours, assorted accommodation <www.knoydart-foundation.com>.
Glen Shiel to Kyle of Lochalsh: Cluanie Inn (NH 077 118); Shiel Bridge has shop, petrol, hotel; Inverinate has petrol. All facilities at Kyle of Lochalsh and Dornie.
Glen Carron: All facilities at Lochcarron.
Applecross: Petrol, shop, hotel with excellent bar meals <www.applecross.info>
Torridon: Kinlochewe — shop, cafe, petrol, hotel (bar meals), small climbing shop (Moru, at the village hall just on the Torridon road). Torridon village — shop and post office. Diabaig — scenery and B&B. Annat — bar with meals, petrol. Shieldaig — Hotel with excellent bar meals.
Camping: Shiel Bridge (NG 939 186), Dornie (NG 876 268), Loch Carron (NG 906 401), Applecross (NG 711 433), Torridon village (NG 905 558).
SYHA Hostels: Ratagan (NG 920 199), (0870 004 1147), Torridon (NG 904 559), (0870 004 1154).
Independent Hostels: Tigh Iseabail (near Killilan — Glen Elchaig, 01599 588205), Gerry's Achnasheallach Hostel (Craig — Glen Carron, 01520 766232), Kinlochewe Hotel bunkhouse (01445 760253).
Climbing Hut: SMC Ling Hut, Torridon, (NG 958 562, near the start of the Coire Mhic Fhearchair path).

Weather Forecasts

Weather forecasts are important as west coast weather is very changeable, but it is hard to get one with sufficient local accuracy. This is the north-west, so south-east is the best wind direction, even if caused by low pressure over England and plenty of rain in the rest of the country. The coasts often have better weather than the hills just inland. The forecasts below must be interpreted carefully. There is something to be said for "go anyway".
Radio Scotland: As well as the regular forecasts, there is an Outdoor Activities forecast. The time in summer 2005 was at 6.58pm, but 7.58pm on Sunday and an additional one at 6.58am on Saturday.
TV: Reporting Scotland forecast at 6.50 to 6.55pm is the best daily one (often starring "Heather the Weather").
Internet: The Internet has led to the withdrawal of good telephone forecasts. There is a wide variety of forecasts on the Internet (in 2007), including: <www.mwis.org.uk>. It is the best mountain forecast.
<www.metcheck.com> gives a huge range of information including mountain forecasts and long range forecasts.
<www.bbc.co.uk/weather> and <www.metoffice.co.uk> give fairly reliable forecasts.

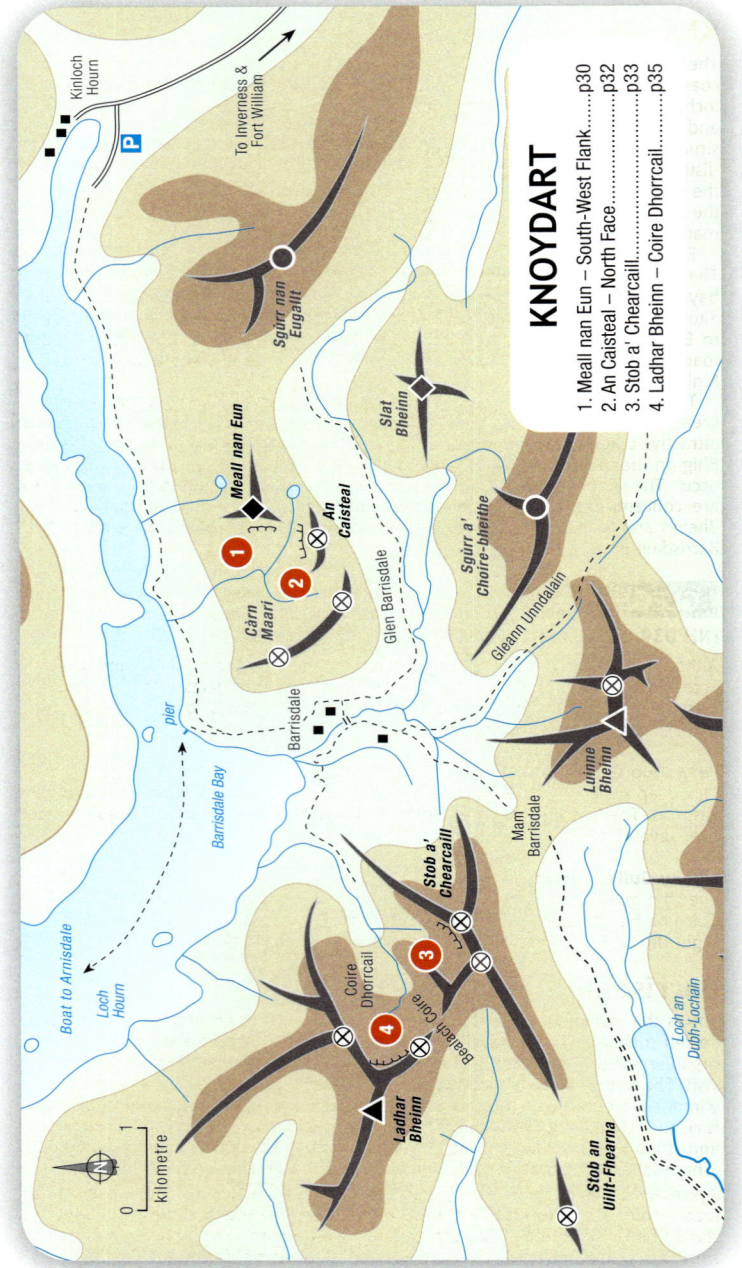

KNOYDART

The district of Knoydart is a broad mountainous peninsula, which lies on the west coast opposite the Sleat peninsula of Skye. It is bounded by two long, twisting sea lochs – Loch Hourn to the north and Loch Nevis to the south. It is an unusually wild and rugged district with a unique atmosphere. Although several fine mountains are situated here, including the magnificent Ladhar Bheinn, the special character of the district is due in no small part to its relative inaccessibility. There is no road around the coast apart from an isolated stretch on the south-west side of the peninsula by the tiny village of Inverie (the largest settlement in Knoydart). The nearest public road leads only as far as Kinloch Hourn, at the north-eastern boundary of the district.

Barrisdale Bay is a broad shallow bay situated about halfway along Loch Hourn. The best climbing in Knoydart is concentrated in two corries on either side of this bay. Consequently the most popular base for visiting climbers is at Barrisdale. The alternative is Inverie, but this makes for a much longer day. The usual approach to Barrisdale is from the A87 by a very scenic route along a 34km single track road. This runs along Glen Garry via Tomdoun, and continues past Loch Quoich to Kinloch Hourn.

There are surprisingly few rock climbing opportunities in Knoydart. Much of the area is formed from schist, which tends to encourage vegetation and rarely forms attractive crags. However, a number of routes have been recorded in Coire Chaolais Bhig on the east side of Barrisdale Bay, where better quality gneiss and pegmatite occur. The winter climbs in Knoydart are of much greater interest. The best routes are concentrated on the faces of two spectacular schistose mountains, Ladhar Bheinn and Stob a' Chearcaill, which enclose Coire Dhorrcail on the west side of Barrisdale Bay.

GLEOURAICH

(NH 039 053)   Alt 1035m

Although this Munro is not in Knoydart proper it is included here because it is also accessed by the road along Loch Quoich. Approach the routes either by crossing Fiar Bhealach (735m), the low point on the ridge between Gleouraich and Spidean Mialach, or from the north along Easter Glen Quoich.

Peekaboo Gully   200m   I/II   *(2003)*
This deep gully is situated on the right side of the north-east face leading to the east top. The true line is hidden until immediately beneath. Climb the gully direct over several steps.

Skinny Gully   100m   II   *(2003)*
The thin gully bounding the right side of the prominent buttress at the head of Coire na Fiar Bhealaich. Climb past a narrowing at one-third height and finish at a slight dip on the ridge some 200m north-west of Fiar Bhealach.

Barrisdale

This is the main centre for climbing in Knoydart. Parties visiting the area need to be self sufficient. Those travelling a long distance will need to be reasonably well organised and determined if they are to get much climbing done in a weekend visit. The protracted approach (which is possible in the dark) and the rarity of good winter conditions are sufficient to deter the masses. Long may this continue. Access is restricted in the stalking season. There are minimal rescue facilities in Knoydart, and it may be difficult to make contact with the police quickly in an emergency. (The estate manager at Barrisdale makes a daily radio check with Arnisdale.)

Approach: Barrisdale is usually accessed from Kinloch Hourn. The last section of road leading down to Kinloch Hourn itself is steep, narrow and twisty. In winter it should be borne in mind that cars can become trapped here by heavy snowfall. A small charge is made to use the car park near the group of buildings at the road head.

30 MEALL NAN EUN

Parking is not permitted on the very narrow final 400m of track where it starts to run alongside the easternmost section of Loch Hourn known as Loch Beag.

Follow a path on the south side of Lochs Beag and Hourn for 8km. This splendid walk has three sections of ascent and descent, and eventually leads to a vehicular track on the eastern shore of Barrisdale Bay. From there it is a further 2km to the stalkers' wooden cottage (NG 872 042). Quite an attractive alternative approach is to canoe along Loch Hourn to Barrisdale Bay. It is also possible to charter a boat from Arnisdale or Kinloch Hourn; see <www.arnisdaleferryservice.com> or phone (01599 522774 / 522352).

A delightful way of returning to Kinloch Hourn is to take the high level route over the hills on the north side of Glen Barrisdale and then descend from the summit of Sgùrr nan Eugallt by a stalkers' path to the ruin of Coireshubh.

The various access routes from the south are unlikely to appeal to heavily laden climbers. However, it is worth knowing that there is a regular ferry service as well as boat hire options between Mallaig and Inverie <www.knoydart-foundation.com>. A fairly good track links Inverie with Barrisdale over Mam Barrisdale – a 450m pass. Mountain bikes can be used on the track at least as far as the eastern end of Loch an Dubh-Lochain.

Accommodation: There are a number of options for staying at Barrisdale (also spelt Barisdale on the web). Next door to the stalkers' cottage there is an open bothy which can hold up to 10. The area is becoming increasingly popular with hill walkers, however, and it is unwise to rely on there being space at the bothy especially in summer. Self-catering accommodation can be booked at The Stable (sleeps 4) next to the bothy, and also at The White House (sleeps up to 12), which is situated 600m further south. The grassy ground in front of the bothy is available as a camping area. A small charge is made for both camping and use of the bothy.

Coire Chaolais Bhig

(NG 890 050)

The four tops enclosing this north facing corrie are from east to west – the west top of Meall nan Eun (666m), An Caisteal (622m), Beinn Bhuidhe (569m) and Càrn Mairi (513m). The climbs can be reached by ascending the hillside directly east of the bothy, and crossing Bealach a' Bho Chrubaich, the 461m pass between Càrn Mairi and Beinn Bhuidhe. Alternatively, the mouth of the corrie can be approached from the north by the path along Loch Hourn. The rock is generally excellent and the climbing is better than it looks.

MEALL NAN EUN - SOUTH-WEST FLANK

Alt 410m   West facing   Diagram p31   Map p28

There are several broken crags here separated by grassy gullies. Starting from the left, the first crag (NG 894 049) consists of several rock ribs culminating in a big slab. To the right of this are two buttresses set back slightly in a bay, and further right again is a rocky cone-shaped hummock, which lies near the col between Meall nan Eun and An Caisteal just to the north of a small stream.

1 Culverin   120m   Difficult   (1971)
Climbs the leftmost buttress. Start up the left-hand of the two main ribs and finish on the left side of the terminal slab.

2 Cannonade   120m   Difficult   (1971)
Climbs the leftmost buttress. Start up the right-hand of the two main ribs and finish on the right side of the terminal slab.

3 Sentinel   90m   Very Difficult *   (1971)
Climbs the left-hand of the two buttresses set back in a bay. Follow excellent rock for about 40m. Then up discontinuous ribs to slabs near the top.

MEALL NAN EUN

1. Culverin — Difficult
2. Cannonade — Difficult
3. Sentinel — Very Difficult *
4. Round House — Severe
5. Parapet — Severe
6. Bastion — Hard Severe *

32 AN CAISTEAL

4 Round House 110m Severe *(1967)*
Ascends the right-hand of the two buttresses set back in a bay. Climb the centre of a steep slab to a ledge. Traverse right to rocks on the right of a grass gully. Then go left across the gully to a grass ledge. Continue directly to another grass ledge, then more easily to the top. Low in the grade.

5 Parapet 90m Severe *(1971)*
Takes the edge facing out into the corrie on the cone shaped hummock. Easy at first, then by short vertical steps to a less steep finish.

6 Bastion 90m Hard Severe * *(1971)*
Climbs the south side of the cone shaped hummock facing the stream. Go up a crack in a steep wall, then move right to a vertical groove. Follow this to a ledge and pass an overhang above on the left. Go right to gain a left-leading gangway, followed to loose blocks and a ledge. Climb a steep mossy wall directly to slabs and a ledge above. A short wall gains the top.

AN CAISTEAL - NORTH FACE

(NG 893 046) Alt 420m North facing Map p28

The longest climbs in Coire Chaolais Bhig are found on the gloomy north face of An Caisteal, where there is a narrow central sweep of cleaner slabs, bordered by more vegetated wings. The slabs offer pleasant Etive-like climbing at Very Severe (4c) grade. The two original routes begin on opposite sides of the central slabs. A later eliminate climbs the slabs more directly.

Portcullis 215m Very Severe *(1967)*
Finds a way up the left edge of the central sweep of slabs.
1. 35m Climb a short steep crack to a rowan and continue up a groove to a ledge under overhangs. Move right and through a break in the overhang, then a groove to a grass basin. Climb the clean slab directly to a grass tuft and traverse left to a grass ledge.
2. 40m The crux pitch. Go delicately up the slab, slightly right, then left beneath an overlap to a break. Go up right to a small ledge, and move left to climb a groove to a grass ledge. Traverse right then follow a line of pock marks and quartz knobs, before moving right to gain a ledge at the foot of a prominent groove.
3. 30m Climb the groove to a small grass ledge, then a thin crack directly above a bulge. Go up grass to below the left-hand of two short grooves.
4. 25m Go up left 10m then right on a narrow grass gangway. Climb to a ledge under a prominent band of pink rock and belay beneath a recess.
5. 25m Go round right over large perched blocks to climb an overhanging niche, then up left to a grass ledge above the start. Climb a further 12m directly above by a flake and short groove to a ledge.
6 and 7. 60m Follow grassy grooves and ramps leftwards to the top.

Direct Route 180m Very Severe * *(1980)*
Takes a fairly direct line up the centre of the slabs, passing just right of the obvious wet break in the upper overlaps.

Battlement Slab 205m Very Severe *(1967)*
Start below and right of the toe of the central sweep of slabs (15m right of Portcullis), at a brown slab capped by an overhang.
1. 45m Climb easy rocks rightwards, then traverse left delicately to a ledge. Take a watercourse groove above to a large grass ledge. Continue to a large ledge below an impressive slabby scoop.
2. 25m Climb the scoop trending left for about 12m. Move up rightwards until a delicate step enables a block to be gained. Climb a smooth greasy corner above to a nose and go left to a flake.

STOB A' CHEARCAILL 33

3. 35m Take a curving crack above and pull round a block overhang onto grass. Walk up to a broken corner which trends slightly left towards the centre of a big sweep of slabs.
4. 35m Follow an impressive corner come ramp which sweeps up left to a small stance.
5. 25m Move left across the slab and go up a corner on good holds. Pull out left past overhanging grass, then go up easily passing a short wall to below a small overhang.
6. 15m Go left across short walls and belay under a steep corner.
7. 25m Ascend the corner and pass an overhang block, then follow an obvious traverse left and finish up a small ramp.

Coire Dhorrcail

The winter climbs in Coire Dhorrcail are approached by a stalkers' path which starts on the west side of Barrisdale Bay and goes round the shoulder of Creag Bheithe. The path descends slightly before it swings south-west into the mouth of the corrie, from where there is a dramatic view of the cliffs some 2km away.

STOB A' CHEARCAILL
(NG 845 029)   Alt 840m   Map p28

A prominent spur, which leads to a small top called Stob Dhorrcail, juts out from the headwall of Coire Dhorrcail and divides off a subsidiary corrie to the left (south) called Coire na Cabaig. This corrie is dominated by the spectacular north-west face of Stob a' Chearcaill. The face does not come into view until shortly after the stalkers' path peters out about halfway up Coire Dhorrcail.

NORTH-WEST FACE
Alt 550m   North-West facing   Diagram p34

This face is divided into several soaring buttresses by long straight gullies. It is some 250m high and has been likened in appearance to the Grandes Jorasses. The most prominent feature of the face is the central gully, Gaberlunzie.

Descent: Possibly the quickest way back to Barrisdale from the summit is to descend the steep southern flank of Stob a' Chearcaill and then head eastwards into Coir' a' Chearcaill.

1 North-East Ridge   100m   I   (1897)
Gain the easy north-east toe of the ridge, called Creag Bheithe, either by the stalkers' path from Barrisdale at NG 859 047, or from the north side of Coir' a' Chearcaill. At the steepening zigzag along ledges and up steep slabs. As the angle eases, continue directly to the summit.

2 North Spur   260m   II/III   (1994)
Climbs the narrow spur immediately left of the next route. Start up a short chimney just left of the toe of the spur. Move right and continue upwards keeping mainly to the crest.

3 Para Handy Gully   240m   III   (1971)
Climbs the most prominent gully on the left-hand half of the face. Slant up leftwards from the base of the cliff to reach the start. The gully is continuously steep. The entrance and exit are likely to prove the hardest parts of the climb.

4 Bottleneck Gully   290m   IV,4 *   (1986)
This long narrow gully starts a short distance left of the lowest point of the face. A 50m rope is recommended. Climb icefalls directly to reach a stance at the start of a narrow chimney. Ascend the chimney, passing a constriction with difficulty.

LADHAR BHEINN | 35

Bottleneck Gully, IV,4, North-West Face, Stob a' Chearcaill. Climber Willie Jeffrey

Surmount an awkward step and continue to a stance just above a jammed boulder. Climb a short steepening to reach a long section of easier gully. After a slightly steeper section, take a belay on the right-hand arete overlooking Gaberlunzie. Return to the gully and climb it, mainly on the right side, to the summit ridge.

5 Gaberlunzie 280m IV,4 * (1962)
This is the main central gully, Grade III with a good build-up. It starts just right of the lowest point of the face. Above a snow fan, 30m of steep climbing leads to a snow channel. This steepens to a large cave beneath a chockstone at 55m. Surmount the chockstone on the left with difficulty to reach easier ground. The walls begin to converge again 60m from the top. The last 20m of climbing up the right-hand gully wall are perhaps the hardest on the route.

6 Marguerite 220m IV,4 * (1986)
Climbs the first prominent chimney to the right of Gaberlunzie. Follow easy snow up rightwards. Then ascend mixed ground to the foot of a steep narrow chimney. Climb the chimney in two long pitches (90m). Continue up the more open gully in two further pitches (90m) to gain the summit ridge.

A gully on the north-west flank of Stob Dhorrcail has also been climbed.

LADHAR BHEINN

(NG 823 039)   Alt 1020m   Map p28

This is the highest and finest mountain in Knoydart. Coire Dhorrcail is situated on the east side of the summit, and is approached from Barrisdale as described above. The most obvious feature in the headwall of the corrie is a prominent gully with an enormous chockstone at half-height. This is Raeburn's Gully. Immediately to its right is Landlubbers Buttress. Some distance to its left is another broader and much

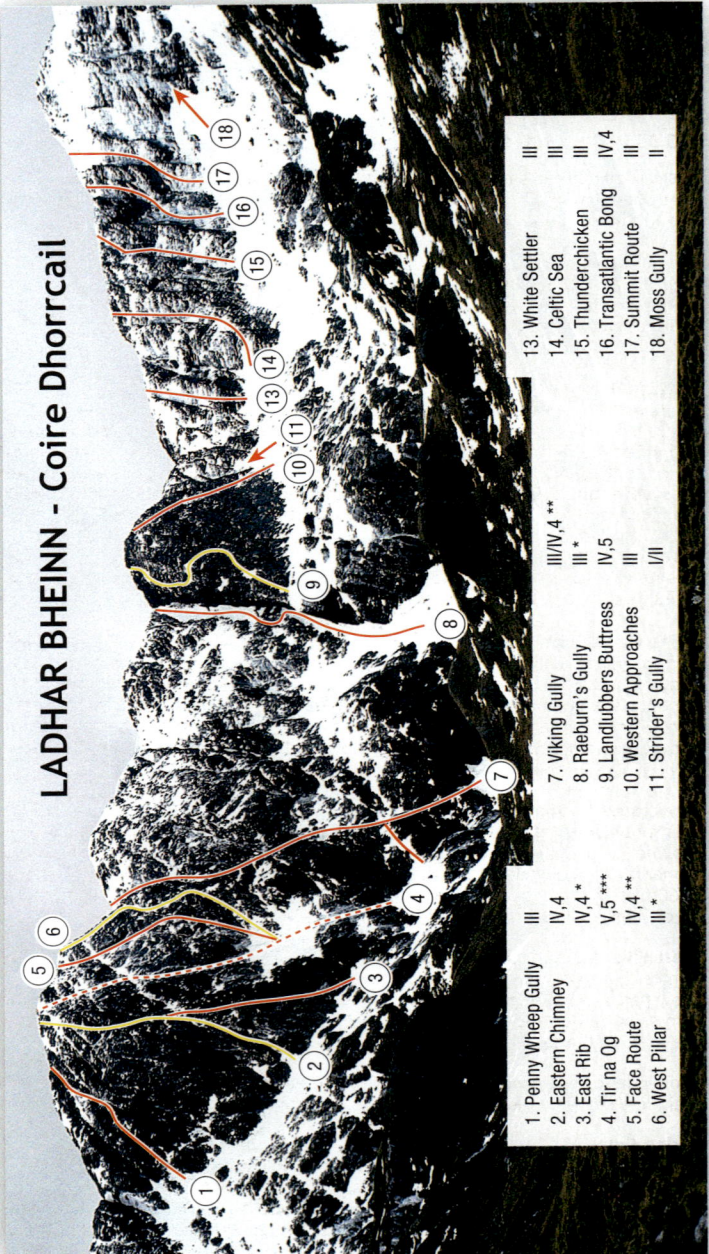

higher buttress characterised by a large snowfield at one-third height. This buttress is known as Spider Buttress because its snowfield is reminiscent of the White Spider on the Eiger. The first six routes lie on this buttress.

SPIDER BUTTRESS

(NG 835 035)   Alt 490m   North-East facing   Diagram p36

Descent: From the summit of Spider Buttress (NG 832 033, 858m) descend the ridge south-eastwards to Bealach Coire Dhorrcail from where an easy slope leads down into Coire Dhorrcail.

1 Penny Wheep Gully   180m   III *(1986)*
High up on the east flank of Spider Buttress there are three gullies. This route climbs the rightmost and largest gully. Climb a succession of short ice steps for 100m to an easy snow slope leading to a large chockstone. Turn this by ice on the right wall, and continue to a large amphitheatre. Exit out right to gain easy ground.

2 Eastern Chimney   270m   IV,4 *(1979)*
The left side of the Spider snowfield is bounded by the East Rib. This route follows a fault-line which rises from a square-cut bay, some 90m above and left of the base of the East Rib. The fault-line is extremely narrow in places, and after 120m it joins the crest of the rib. Short walls and grooves then lead in 60m to easier ground. An alternative finish is to continue along the fault-line, high above the Spider snowfield, and finish by the obvious gully used by Face Route (Route 5).

3 East Rib   360m   IV,4 * *(1979)*
This route follows the left-hand rib of the buttress. Start at the lowest rocks and maintain a central line where possible.

4 Tir na Og   350m   V,5 ***** *(1978)*
This magnificent climb takes a very direct line up the centre of Spider Buttress. Climb directly to the central snowfield (The Spider) by obvious ice grooves. Continue straight up the snowfield to the central groove system. Climb this by three pitches to finish left of the buttress summit. (After the second and crucial pitch above The Spider an easy ramp can be followed rightwards to join the final easy gully of Face Route).

5 Face Route   360m   IV,4 *** *(1978)*
This route avoids the obvious challenge taken up by Tir na Og. Gain the central snowfield either directly or more easily from the left. Aim for the top right-hand corner of the snowfield. Climb the right-hand of two grooves, turning an overhang at 60m on the right by another groove. Just short of the crest of the West Pillar take an obvious gully on the left which leads to the buttress summit.

6 West Pillar   360m   III * *(1978)*
Climbs the right-bounding rib of Spider Buttress. Gain the central snowfield by a snow patch and easy grooves to the left of the direct line. Traverse diagonally right across The Spider, and continue up a snow ramp onto the crest of the pillar. Follow the pillar to the top.

Hidden in the angle where the right-hand side of Spider Buttress abuts against the main line of crags is a long narrow gully. This gives the line of the next route.

7 Viking Gully   360m   III/IV,4 *** *(1962)*
Climb the gully directly, or in lean conditions enter it by a slanting snow rake on the left. Some ice pitches and a narrow snow trough lead to a narrow twisting channel. Continue to the recessed upper portion of the gully. A series of abrupt 15m ice pitches then follow. A long snow fan of some 90m leads to a col between two small peaks on the main ridge.

38 | LADHAR BHEINN

Face Route, IV,4, Spider Buttress, Ladhar Bheinn. Climber Paul Tipton

To the right of Viking Gully there are steep rocks, and then an unnamed broad gully (Grade II). A little further right is the very prominent gash of Raeburn's Gully.

8 Raeburn's Gully   240m   III * (1897)
This gully is quite straightforward as far as the enormous chockstone at half-height. Circumventing this huge monolith, however, can prove surprisingly difficult. It involves climbing awkward slabby rocks on the left wall, by two pitches totalling some 60m. The remainder of the gully is easy.

9 Landlubbers Buttress   240m   IV,5 (1978)
This is the obvious slabby buttress immediately right of Raeburn's Gully. Not sustained. Climb the left side of the buttress to a rock band. Head for a prominent flake on the right skyline. Pass it and go back left by a snowy groove. Continue diagonally left past the next rock band to a snow ledge. A large block pinnacle above and slightly right is a cul-de-sac, so make a descending traverse left. Cross a crucial slab to reach an easy ramp which leads back to the crest of the buttress. Scramble to top.

10 Western Approaches   180m   III (1984)
Climb the narrow and interesting gully on the right-hand flank of Landlubbers Buttress.

11 Strider's Gully   120m   I/II (1991)
This is the gully in the angle where the right-hand flank of Landlubbers Buttress meets the headwall.

SPIDER BUTTRESS 39

12 John Muir Trail 100m I/II
This takes the shortest section of the headwall by a right-trending line to a low point on the rim of the corrie.

13 White Settler 140m III (1991)
The prominent right-facing slabby corner, situated to the left of a deep twisting gully. Start just right of the line of the corner. Gain a narrow chimney which leads leftwards to a short wall at the base of the main slab. Climb the wall and follow the corner above to a final steep rock band. In good conditions it is possible to climb this direct, otherwise traverse right to find a way to the top.

14 Celtic Sea 180m III (1984)
Start at the lowest tongue of rock to the right of Landlubbers Buttress. Gain a right-facing corner, either from the right by steep icy rock, or from the left by an easier snow ledge. Climb the corner with a steeper section part way up. Finish at a step on the ridge.

15 Thunderchicken 210m III (1978)
This climb follows a corner situated about 50m right of Celtic Sea and just to the left of two prominent stepped corners.

16 Transatlantic Bong 210m IV,4 (1978)
Climbs the left-hand of two prominent stepped corners at the top right of the corrie.

17 Summit Route 290m III (1978)
Climbs the right-hand stepped corner. Ascend snow then ice to belay left of an icefall. Traverse right, then climb to belay in a groove. Continue in grooves until a traverse right can be made to belay above the icefall. Climb the snowfield and summit buttress direct to top.

A number of lines have been climbed (mainly at Grade II or III) on the more broken slabby rocks to the right of Summit Route.

18 Moss Gully 150m II
The black rift in the most westerly recess of Coire Dhorrcail, which leads to a col on the ridge linking Ladhar Bheinn with Stob a' Choice Odhair. It cannot be seen properly until well up in the corrie near the foot of the previous routes. (It was originally climbed and appropriately named in summer conditions at Difficult – 1939.)

Loch Nevis

SOURLIES BOTHY CRAG

South-West facing

A solitary rock climb lies on the opposite side of Knoydart near the eastern end of Loch Nevis. A few hundred metres east of Sourlies bothy (NM 868 950) there is a large slab and wall situated below and right of an obvious pillar with a horizontal roof. The crag is prominent when approaching from the east, but is not visible from the bothy.

A Good Day Spoilt 40m E3 5c (1996)
The lower slab is very smooth; the climb starts 5m further left and thrashes rightwards up jungle. From the top tree, move right in a wide diagonal crack, then up to a thinner break and move left in this for 3m. Climb a flake-crack to a cleaned jug in the next break. Go left again and ascend another excellent flake-crack past a good spike. Finish up a blunt arete to trees and an abseil descent.

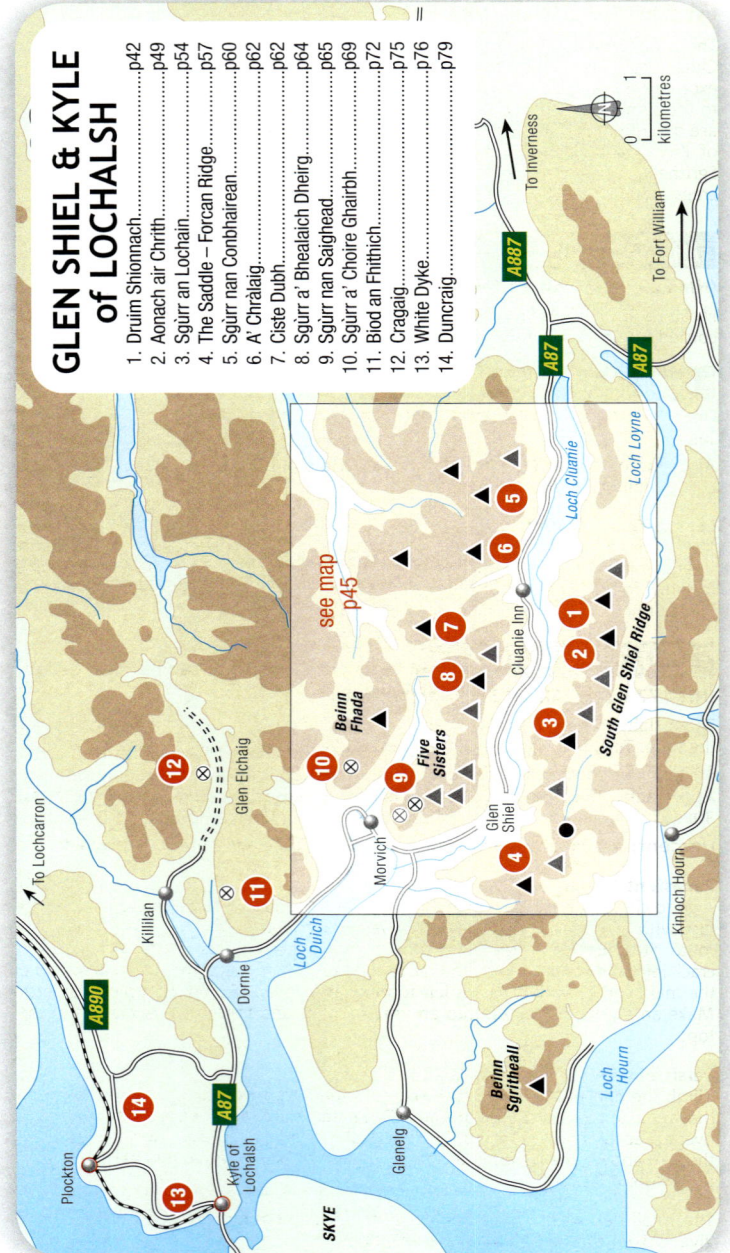

GLEN SHIEL & KYLE of LOCHALSH

1. Druim Shionnach.................p42
2. Aonach air Chrith................p49
3. Sgùrr an Lochain..................p54
4. The Saddle – Forcan Ridge......p57
5. Sgùrr nan Conbhairean..........p60
6. A' Chràlaig..........................p62
7. Ciste Dubh..........................p62
8. Sgùrr a' Bhealaich Dheirg......p64
9. Sgùrr nan Saighead.............p65
10. Sgùrr a' Choire Ghairbh.......p69
11. Biod an Fhithich.................p72
12. Cragaig.............................p75
13. White Dyke.......................p76
14. Duncraig...........................p79

GLEN SHIEL & KYLE OF LOCHALSH

The mountains of Glen Shiel lie on either side of the A87 road between Loch Cluanie to the east and Loch Duich to the west. In general the mountains provide excellent hill walking and some good winter climbs, but they provide less interest to the summer climber in search of clean rock. The mountains south of Glen Shiel are described first, followed by the north side of the glen, including the Five Sisters of Kintail and Beinn Fhada. The Loch Lochy hills to the south-east and Beinn Sgritheall to the west are included in this section, which finishes with rock climbing crags around Dornie, Kyle of Lochalsh and Plockton to the north-west.

MEALL NA TEANGA

(NN 220 924) Alt 917m

Meall na Teanga and Sròn a' Choire Ghairbh (NN 223 945, 935m) are two deeply corried Munros on the west side of Loch Lochy.

COIRE LOCHAIN

One climb has been recorded in this corrie, south of the summit of Meall na Teanga.

Approach: Park at Clunes and walk or cycle along a forestry track above Loch Lochy until below the corrie.

Central Gully   120m   III   *(1986)*
The north-east facing crag in the upper corrie is split by an obvious gully. Climb steepening snow, with a little ice, to where the gully closes in (40m). A good long ice pitch follows with two steep sections before the gully eases and fans out (40m). The exit line will be dependent on the cornice (40m).

CLUANIE DAM SLABS

(NH 177 094)   Alt 330m   North-West facing

These slabs can be clearly seen across the loch from the road at the north end of the dam. They are bigger than they look and offer a good climb on rough granite, although dry conditions are required.

Approach: Cross the dam and follow a faint path west to the foot of the slabs, 30mins.

Descent: A 50m abseil from a tree, or go up a little and descend either side.

Persistent Reward   50m   VS 5a *   *(1996)*
A good climb, but a little mossy. From the path the slabs present a steep north-east face with two obvious crack-lines. Above and right of this face is a long corner, the route. Start just left of the foot of this corner, which is black at the base. Climb a crack left of the black corner and move right to a ledge (peg, possible belay). Climb the main corner until it curves left forming an overlap (Friend 2.5 up on the left). Make an awkward step up into an upper corner and follow this and slabs to the top.

Persistent Arete   60m   HVS 4c   *(1988)*
Climb the right-hand of two crack-lines on the North-East face to a poor belay on the arete left of Persistent Reward. Climb the slab above directly to reach the overlap at the crack with the Friend 2.5 placement. Climb this crack to finish up the slab above. The right-hand crack-line has also been used as an alternative start to Persistent Reward.

The small slab with a huge boulder at its foot and about 50m east of the above gives a 10m climb of about Very Difficult.

42 | DRUIM SHIONNACH

South Glen Shiel

The South Glen Shiel Ridge links Creag a' Mhaim (947m, NH 088 077) on the east and Creag nan Damh (918m, NG 983 112) on the west. It includes seven Munros and is a classic hill walking expedition.

The fine looking Coire an t-Slugain lies on the north side of the ridge between Druim Shionnach and Aonach air Chrith, towards the east end of the main ridge. The corrie has two main crags, the West Face of Druim Shionnach in the south-east corner of the corrie and Creag Coire an t-Slugain, facing the road from the back of the corrie.

Beyond the seven Munros, the ridge continues past a Corbett, Sgùrr a' Bhac Chaolais to another Munro, Sgùrr na Sgine to finish on the complex mountain of The Saddle.

DRUIM SHIONNACH
(NH 074 085)   Alt 987m

WEST FACE

(NH 069 084)   Alt 860m   West facing   Maps p40, 45   Diagram p43

This accessible crag is clearly seen from the road further down Glen Shiel but hidden on the approach. The routes are short but exciting as the helpful strata allows steep climbing. Largely for winter, it offers turfy mixed climbing which varies unexpectedly between poorly protected slabs and the most helpful cracked ground.

Approach: Start just east of the Cluanie Inn and cross the loch by the old road. Take a stalking path on the right to reach the north ridge of Druim Shionnach. Follow the ridge, then move right along unusual small ridges before making a descending traverse in to the base of the cliff, 2hrs.

Descent: Descend easily northwards from cliff or summit (10mins away) to gain the north ridge of Druim Shionnach and reverse the approach.

The dominant feature of the crag is the large central and aptly named Cave Gully while the Silver Slab is the second buttress left. Routes are described right to left.

1 Hurting II 70m III *(2005)*
A ramp leads diagonally right from near the base of Cave Gully across much of the right section of the cliff. Below the top of the ramp, where it nearly reaches the plateau, is a wide gully which descends into a wide capped chimney. Start right of the capped chimney and climb a groove which gives good climbing but exits too soon (30m) into the easy wide gully.

2 Poems 90m III *(2006)*
An ice line which crosses the diagonal ramp. Start at a small bay 25m right of an icy groove which feeds from the base of the main ramp. Climb into the bay, out left on ice which forms left of a left-facing corner and up to the ramp. Follow the ramp up to an obvious chimney beyond steep walls. Climb this to the top.

3 Bowling Alley 90m VII,6 ** *(2006)*
The fault of Bow Peep, a shallow left-facing corner in its central section, is an obvious feature. This climbs the face to its right. Start about 10m right of Cave Gully.
1. 50m Climb the icy groove to the base of the main ramp. Step left and climb more steeply to the base of a chimney which leads diagonally right (this is the chimney on pitch 2 of Cross-Bow).
2. 40m Move left and pull through a steep but helpful wall to the base of a turfy fault which leads slightly leftwards up the wall above. Climb the fault with increasing exposure and decreasing protection (three knifeblades used initially and

DRUIM SHIONNACH - West Face

1. Hurting II
2. Poems III
3. Bowling Alley VII,6 **
4. Bow Peep V,6 **
5. Cross-Bow IV,5 *
6. Cave Gully IV,4 **
7. Boxer's Buttress IV,4 *
8. Capped Gully II
9. Silver Corner V,5 **
10. Silver Edge IV,5 *
11. Silver Slab VI,7 **
12. Deceptive Chimney III *
13. Eurhythmics V,5

GLEN SHIEL & KYLE OF LOCHALSH

John Lyall

two hooks higher up), moving at the very top into a parallel fault on its right. Finish up a 10m slope.

4 Bow Peep   90m   V,6 ** *(1995)*
On the face right of the obvious central gully (Cave Gully) is a left-slanting, slightly bow shaped fault finishing up a wide chimney. The fault was climbed throughout, the first pitch being the hardest.

5 Cross-Bow   110m   IV,5 * *(1995)*
A left to right slanting line crossing Bow Peep. Start at the foot of Cave Gully.
1. 50m Climb straight up on vegetated ledges until an easy traverse right crosses Bow Peep to belay.
2. 30m Continue right and up a chimney to a ledge below a steep corner.
3. 30m Avoid the corner to the right and regain the fault which is followed to the top.

6 Cave Gully   110m   IV,4 ** *(1994)*
The prominent central gully, containing a cave. The route is the right corner of the gully, bypassing the cave by a narrow chimney with a steep entry (50m). Straightforward snow to finish.

7 Boxer's Buttress   100m   IV,4 * *(1995)*
The snub nosed buttress left of Cave Gully. Two pitches of interesting and sustained mixed climbing up the right side of the buttress, starting from the same bay as Cave Gully but 5m left.
1. 30m Go up left into a shallow weakness and climb it to a huge detached block.
2. 30m Go up left then back right to surmount steep steps and bulges.
3. 40m Easy mixed ground then snow to the top.

8 Capped Gully   110m   II *(1994)*
A shallow gully next left which tapers to an awkward chimney slot near the top.

Mid-way between Capped Gully and another cave to the left is a silvery slab high up and forming the next buttress, Silver Slab. At the cliff base are two chimneys.

9 Silver Corner   100m   V,5 ** *(1995)*
A serious first pitch, then a steep but well protected second. Climb the right-hand of the two short chimneys at the base of the buttress. Trend slightly right to flakes below a big right-facing corner (40m). Climb the corner (20m), and continue more easily to the top.

10 Silver Edge   90m   IV,5 * *(1995)*
A slightly easier route on the Silver Slab, but high in its grade. Start as for Silver Corner up the right-hand chimney to a ledge, then trend left up an apparent line of weakness to finish up a wide and obvious easy trough left of the upper Silver Slab.

11 Silver Slab   100m   Hard Severe 4b * *(1938)*
A short but pleasant climb in dry weather. Start left of the left chimney to the ledge. Trend right crossing Silver Edge to climb a short difficult crack through a bulge leading to the easier upper slab.
Winter: **100m   VI,7 ** *(1996)*
A winter ascent close to the summer line. The route started in the left-hand chimney but pulled out steeply on to its right rib before moving back left to its top and joining Silver Edge. This was followed up left to its belay (35m). The line is now a fault central to the slab but on the right of the belay. It has a prominent small flake low down and leads up to a crack through a steep smooth girdling wall. Gain the fault by following Silver Edge for a few metres, then traversing right (thin). Climb the fault and the crack (nut for aid) and continue up on flaky ground until a ledge leads out left (45m). Easy to the top (20m).

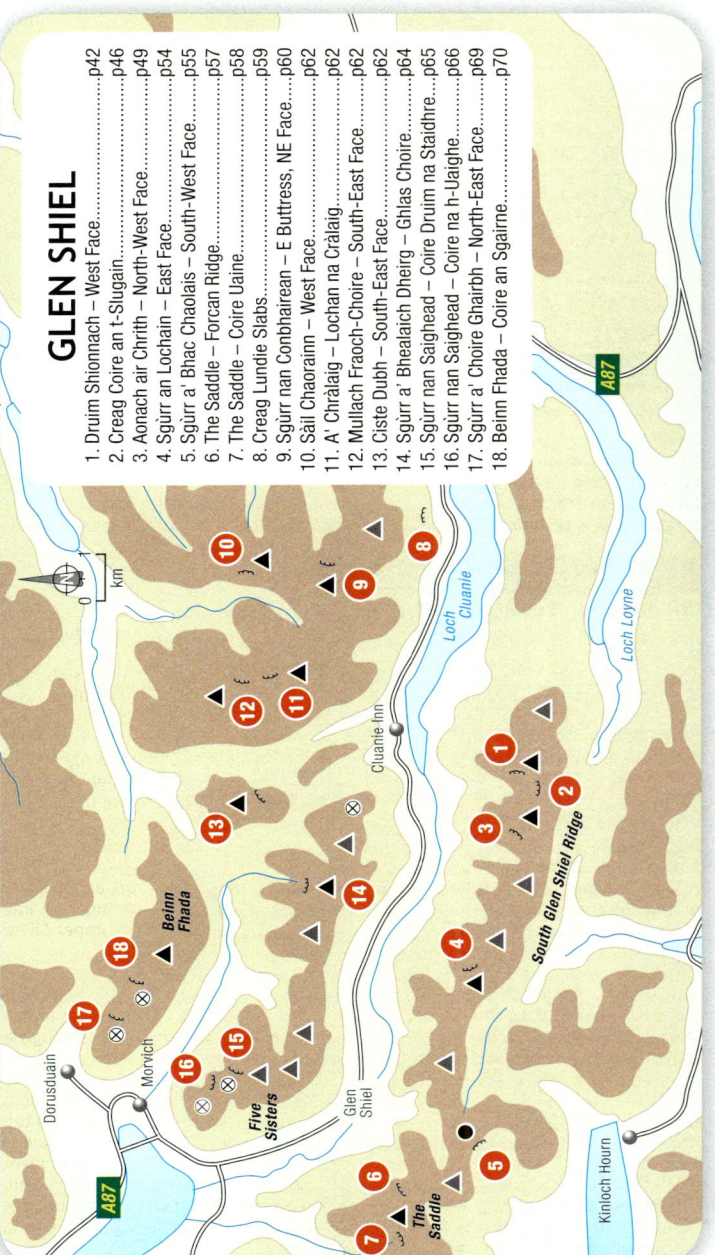

DRUIM SHIONNACH

12 Deceptive Chimney   70m   III * *(1995)*
A line of weakness left of Silver Slab buttress and just left of the left cave. Start left of a lower cave in the fault leading to the main cave. Climb turfy ground up and then right to a narrow chimney hidden on the approach from below. This leads left to easier ground.

13 Eurhythmics   70m   V,5 *(2006)*
Climbs a rib left of the two caves and Deceptive Chimney. Start below a groove with a prominent sod of turf. This is some 10m right of a right-facing corner-chimney. Climb the steep groove and continue above to reach a ramp leading up left. Follow this to below a step (25m). Continue up the ramp to below steep walls. Break back right up a small ramp (under powder, a right break right may be easier) and step right into a groove. Continue until a move right up a big flake leads to easier ground, perhaps common to Deceptive Chimney. Follow this left (35m). Finish easily (10m).

MID-WAY BUTTRESS

(NH 066 084)   Alt 850m   North-West facing

About midway between the two main crags in the corrie is a smaller crag with two gully lines. The left-hand gully, with a chockstone at mid-height, is **Mid-way Gully** 100m II (1996), with a through route. The buttress left of the gully, starting centrally and trending right to near the gully, then following grooves parallel to the gully, is **Mid-way Buttress** 100m III (2005).

CREAG COIRE AN T-SLUGAIN

(NH 060 082)   Alt 850m   North facing   Diagram p48

Offers largely turfy mixed climbing but collects more snow than Druim Shionnach West Face and later in the season, after thaws and freezes, can hold ice. The snow collection also means a potential avalanche risk, particularly from a snow bowl high up and just left of the crag.

Approach: Park opposite the Allt Coire an t-Slugain; a ruin on its right bank identifies the stream. Cross the main river, wide but shallow so often one can splash across with dry feet, and follow the left bank of the Allt until the angle eases. Go up left and climb the obvious gully in the lower crag band, the first half of Double Gully (easy Grade I); continue up steep snow to the crag base, 2hr.

Descent: Several choices.
1. By Double Gully (Grade I if the cornice allows).
2. Head towards Druim Shionnach, traverse above its West Face and descend easily northwards to gain the north ridge of Druim Shionnach. Return to the Allt Coire an t-Slugain; it is easy to return too soon down steep slopes.
3. Given enough snow, an entertaining descent is to head west towards Aonach air Chrith and descend a narrow valley parallel and west of the approach valley , the two valleys joining part way down. This is easy and unusual if the stream in this gorge is snow covered.
4. To make a mountaineering day out, head west to Aonach air Chrith and descend its North Ridge. Continue to the furthest point of the ridge and descend right on steep grass to rejoin the approach.

1 Far Left Gully   100m   I *(1996)*
The leftmost gully on the crag, left of and touched by Left Ridge. A difficult corniced exit.

2 Left Ridge   130m   II *(1995)*
The blunt ridge bounding the left edge of the crag. Start at the lowest rocks, which are about 15m right of the base of the crest. Climb up right to a barrier wall (which

CREAG COIRE AN T-SLUGAIN 47

could be climbed direct in better conditions, but much harder). Traverse left to the crest (25m). Climb the crest into a shallow gully on the left. Go up this to regain the crest, followed to the top.

3 Tipperary   140m   III * *(1995)*
Start about 30m right of the left-bounding ridge of the buttress (Left Ridge) where a ramp leads up left towards the ridge. Climb the ramp to a depression ahead of slabby ground before the ridge (35m). Go up the depression until forced by steep ground to go right, initially traversing, then rising, to reach a flake on a small ridge (35m). Pull over a bulge and move right again to climb the fault on the right (40m). Continue up to finish by the crest of the ridge.

4 Hong Kong   140m   IV,5 ** *(2004/2005)*
Start right of Tipperary. Gain and climb a fine chimney set in a prominent left-slanting slab-corner. Move left to blocks (45m). Continue left up slabby corners to join the normal route at its flake on a small ridge. Pull over the bulge but go straight up a groove to an overhung recess (30m). Pass the recess by the rib on the right, then go up left under a steep wall until it is crossed more easily (30m). Follow grooves until the crest of the ridge is joined.

5 Ploughshare Groove   130m   V,5 *(1997)*
Start at the base of Rowaling and climb the first groove (left-facing corner come chimney) on the left (25m). Continue left to reach and climb a steep turfy groove (45m). Move right to a wide slot; climb this, then more easily to the top (60m).

6 Rowaling   135m   V,6 ** *(1997)*
Climbs the most prominent groove towards the left side of the crag, a regular ice forming line. A serious first pitch, which would be much easier with thick ice, followed by a technical second. The groove is right of a slab with a wide crack set against a prominent vertical wall. Climb the groove to a ledge on the right (45m). Return to the groove, pull over a bulge and climb the next wall by a turfy pull-up on the left. The final section of groove may be possible with more ice. Instead, a short overhanging chimney on the right led to an easier turfy fault, climbed to easier ground (45m). Easier turfy climbing to the top (45m).

7 Rose Garden   120m   IV,4 ** *(1997)*
Climbs an ice line between the deeper grooves of Rowaling and The Furrow. Climbed on continuous ice; perhaps a grade harder if mixed. Start 5m right of Rowaling and climb direct to a barrier wall, taken at its top left corner. Move right on to a big inset and usually iced slab above The Furrow and obvious from below (45m). From the top of the slab a short iced rib led into a long groove, the source of the ice. The angle slowly eased (40m, 35m).

8 The Furrow   120m   IV,6 * *(1994/1997)*
Another potential ice holding line on the cliff, just left of centre. A shallow trough with a overhung recess, almost a cave, at half-height and immediately left of a blunt ridge with many flakes. Climb directly up and into the recess and out of its back left corner, followed by an immediate traverse right across its lip to rejoin the line to finish. An easier (the original) version is to go right on to the ridge from below the recess and climb it until a ramp leads left to regain the trough immediately above the recess (Grade III overall).

9 The Ridge Direct   130m   III * *(1997)*
A fairly continuous line of shallow grooves on the crest of the blunt ridge in the centre of the crag. Start just right of The Furrow and climb a shallow groove trending right to below the more defined section of crest. Climb the flaky crest, then climb the ramp for 10m, common with the original line of The Furrow, after its easy traverse. Break off the ramp through a slot, otherwise being forced into The Furrow, then move right to a well defined groove in the crest which leads to an easier finish.

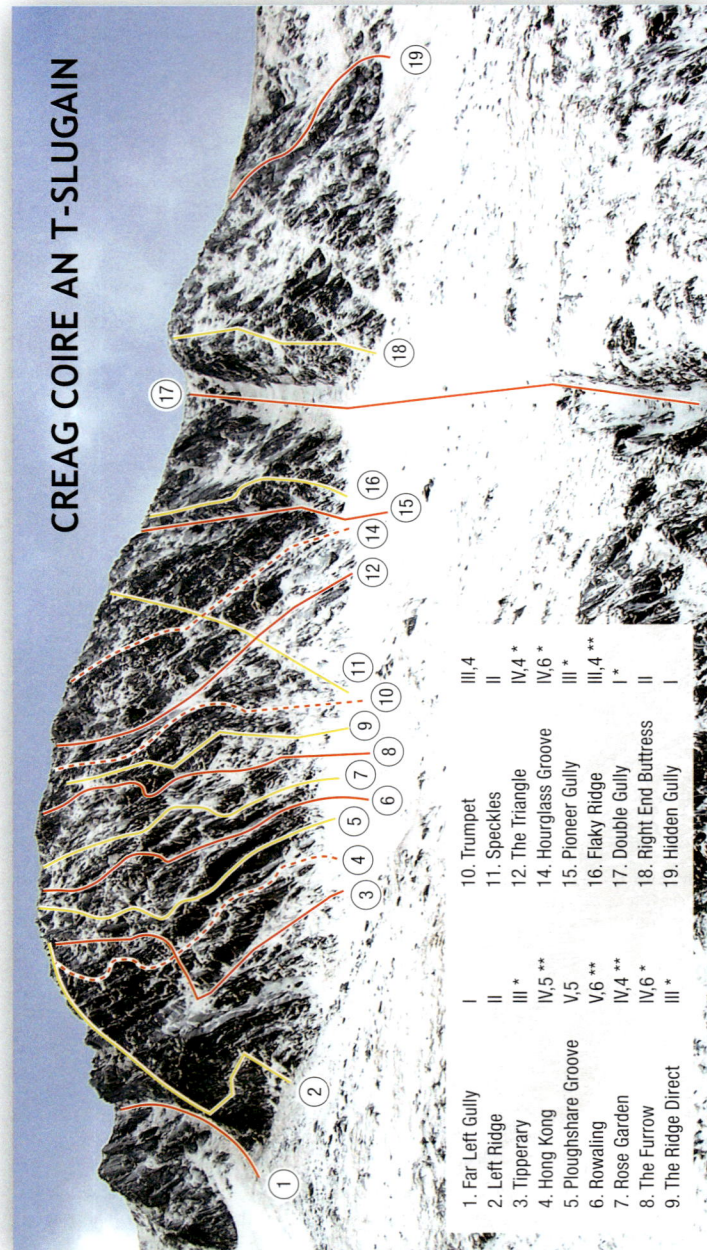

CREAG COIRE AN T-SLUGAIN

1. Far Left Gully — I
2. Left Ridge — II
3. Tipperary — III *
4. Hong Kong — IV,5 **
5. Ploughshare Groove — V,5
6. Rowaling — V,6 **
7. Rose Garden — IV,4 **
8. The Furrow — IV,6 *
9. The Ridge Direct — III *
10. Trumpet — III,4
11. Speckles — II
12. The Triangle — IV,4 *
14. Hourglass Groove — IV,6 *
15. Pioneer Gully — III *
16. Flaky Ridge — III,4 **
17. Double Gully — I *
18. Right End Buttress — II
19. Hidden Gully — I

Andy Nisbet

CREAG COIRE AN T-SLUGAIN 49

10 Trumpet 140m III,4 *(2004)*
Start below the ridge and take a groove which leads to the right side of the ridge (50m). Continue into the left corner of the triangle (see below), then leave the triangle by a line of turf and flakes which leads slightly left into the well defined groove in the crest of the ridge (40m). Finish up this (50m).

11 Speckles 120m II *(1995)*
A right-slanting line of weakness left of Pioneer Gully, which shows up as speckled snow patches. Start just left of The Triangle, cross it rightwards and continue up the line to the top.

12 The Triangle 120m IV,4 * *(1995)*
Climbs through a big triangular niche/snow patch at half-height and right of centre on the cliff. Take a left-slanting line into the triangle, out its top (crux) and straight up to the cornice.

13 Hypotenuse 120m III *(2004)*
A line of grooves parallel and right of the bigger grooves of The Triangle. Start just right of The Triangle and climb a parallel groove (may not be distinct with a good build-up). Exit right through a slot in a right-bounding wall into the main groove system. Follow this to the top, finishing close to The Triangle.

14 Hourglass Groove 120m IV,6 * *(2003)*
A narrowing groove system on the vague crest between Hypotenuse and Pioneer Gully. Start just left of Pioneer Gully and climb an icefall into the turfy groove system. Climb this to where it narrows into twin shallow grooves and go up these, keeping left above to reach an easier finishing pitch.

15 Pioneer Gully 110m III * *(1993)*
The narrow gully parallel to and 10m left of Double Gully. Low in the grade; II in good conditions.

16 Flaky Ridge 110m III,4 ** *(1995)*
The unusual arete of stacked flakes between Pioneer Gully and Double Gully. Start up a groove in its base, then follow the crest as directly as possible. Take many slings for runners and belays.

17 Double Gully 300m I *
The lower gully and its continuation up the right end of the cliff. Steep at the top, often with a big cornice. Holds snow well in lean conditions.

18 Right End Buttress 130m II *(1996)*
The crest immediately right of Double Gully. Undistinguished, but an option if the gully is full of soft snow or heavily corniced.

19 Hidden Gully 120m I *(1997)*
On the right side of Right End Buttress and well hidden is this deep, narrow but easy gully. Normally an easier descent than Double Gully, not having the steep finish.

AONACH AIR CHRITH

(NH 051 083) Alt 1021m Maps p40, 45

NORTH-WEST FACE

(NH 047 083) Alt 780m North-West facing Diagram p50

A big slabby cliff, the routes follow good lines, but are slightly broken by long easy sections. A winter climbing venue; the grooves can be icy or mixed.

AONACH AIR CHRITH

1. Boa Constrictor — IV,4 *
2. Mummy Knows Best — II *
3. My Mother Says No — II
4. Mica Schist Special — III *
5. Thin Groove Alley — IV,4 **
6. Get into the Groove — IV,6
7. Deep Freeze — V,4 *
8. The Deerstalker — IV,4

Andy Nisbet

NORTH-WEST FACE 51

Boa Constrictor, IV,4, North-West Face, Aonach Air Chrith. Climber Gill Nisbet

Approach: A rough vehicle track starts at NH 053 114, opposite a forestry track. Follow this up the west side of the Allt Coire nan Eirecheanach, 2hrs.

Descent: The north ridge of Aonach air Chrith is the best, an enjoyable but tricky 'scramble' (Grade I). The cliff base can be regained from the west, cornices permitting.

The cliff is composed of a steep slabby tower high on the left containing one route and an extensive slabby right-hand section. The two sections are separated by twin parallel gullies.

1 Boa Constrictor   270m   IV,4 * (1996)
Takes a constricting line up the tower at the top left of the crag. Start at the base of the left buttress, left of the twin gullies. Climb a shallow gully which splits the lower buttress and leads to a central snowfield. Follow this to its top and a belay below the big left-facing corner on the left of the crest of the tower (120m). Start up the corner until forced left by a big bulge. Climb a line of cracks parallel about 5m left of the corner to a flake (40m). Continue up the crack-line until one can go easily back into the corner. Go up this into a wide slot, an apparent cul-de-sac. An unexpected chimney splits the steep wall on the right and involves wriggling behind a chockstone leading to the crest (40m). The crest is unhelpful, so traverse a ledge rightwards with an awkward step down and climb the first sensible option, a thin crack filled with turf and leading to a big spike (40m). Easy to the top.
Summer: **Severe** (1995)
The rib on the left has been climbed in summer followed by a traverse right to the unexpected chimney and a finish up Boa Constrictor. Vegetated.

AONACH AIR CHRITH

Thin Groove Alley, IV,4, North-West Face, Aonach Air Chrith. Climber Calum Milne

2 Mummy Knows Best 180m II * (1995)
The narrower and left-hand of the twin gullies contains a short but awkward chockstone which becomes a short ice pitch in good conditions. Where exit from the top is blocked by a steep chimney and capstone, move right up a groove in the right-hand rib to reach its crest. Return left and climb a block filled groove to the top.
Variation: **Direct Finish III,4** (1997)
Requires icy conditions. Climb the chimney to a cave belay below the capstone. Pass the capstone by ice on its left side.

3 My Mother Says No 150m II (1994)
The right-hand of the twin gullies is easier with a big build-up, when a chimney pitch low down can largely bank out. There is always a small pitch high up.

4 Mica Schist Special 180m III * (1994)
Takes shallow grooves left of the crest forming the left edge of the slabby face. Start immediately right of My Mother Says No.
1 and 2. 60m Climb a turfy groove, then trend right to a deeper and steeper groove.
3 and 4. 60m Climb the steeper groove, then at an obvious block go easily rightwards across the crest.
5 and 6. 60m Take thin grooves in the slabs just right of the crest to gain easy ground 50m below the summit ridge.

NORTH-WEST FACE

The slabby and larger right section of this face has three main groove systems right of the crest which is right of Mica Schist Special (which also follows a big groove on pitch 2). Each starts from a triangular bay and the rightmost is the deepest.

5 Thin Groove Alley   250m   IV,4 **   (1996)
Takes a series of corners parallel to the right of Mica Schist Special and forms the left-hand of the three main groove systems. Start at the left toe of the slab face just right of a brown rock scar and 20m right of Mica Schist Special.
1. 50m Climb the open groove with the difficulty depending on the amount of ice but always poorly protected (crux). When lean it is necessary to escape left after 25m on to a ledge. Go up left again and back right to a belay above the top of the groove.
2. 30m Climb easily up and right into a big open book corner. Belay out right at a spike.
3. 30m Climb the corner to a steep exit.
4. 40m Follow the continuation groove to belays at a terrace below the final slab wall of Mica Schist Special.
5. 50m The continuation groove is the logical line but is Mica Schist Special. The big groove on the right is Get into the Groove. Between these two and 5m right of the belay is a shallow groove, the best independent line. Climb the groove to easier ground.
6. 50m Easy to the top.

6 Get into the Groove   250m   IV,6   (1996)
The middle groove system, about 25m left of the big right-hand one.
1. 35m Climb the groove to below a 3m step into a clean-cut groove (were there ice here, the route could reduce to III). Move out right to a flake.
2. 25m Get stood on the flake and step left awkwardly on to turf next to the groove. Continue up beside the groove to easier ground.
3. etc. 190m Continue in the same line, ignoring the bigger groove on the right (Deep Freeze).
Variation: **Rib Start   50m   III,4**   (1996)
Starting up the rib on the right gives a better start when lean and reduces the whole route to III. Start up the bigger groove on the right (Deep Freeze) but soon move left along the lower of two traverse lines to below a shallow chimney-slot (15m). Climb the left side of the slot (15m). Move right and up a turfy slot to join the original route.

7 (Dreaming of the) Deep Freeze   250m   V,4 *   (1996)
Climb the big right-hand groove. The start requires some consolidated snow or ice, for which it is graded, but on the first ascent was slushy and very poorly protected.

8 The Deerstalker   250m   IV,4   (1996)
This climbs the rib to the right of the big right-hand groove (Deep Freeze), then moves into it. From about 10m up the big groove (depending on build-up), traverse right to gain a steep line of turf which leads to a ledge below a smooth groove (50m). Unless the smooth groove is iced, climb an easier groove on the right (50m). Easier ground now leads back left over the rib into the top part of Deep Freeze, which is followed to the top.

Coire na Eirechanach

(NH 043 086)   Alt 570m   North facing
Airy Icefall   120m   IV,4   (1996)
Low down on the headwall of the corrie is a slabby buttress with a prominent icefall. This route climbs the thickest ice, which forms from a slabby gully, down a wall, then down the centre of the main slab and finally over a short steep wall at the base. The first pitch is the crux with a strenuous start (technical 4), then unprotected up the slab (40m, technical 3). The route is excellent in cold conditions with little or no snow but the slab soon snows over and the whole route can disappear.

54 | SGÙRR AN LOCHAIN

Airy Corner 85m II *(1996)*
The corner at the right side of the slab gave two long pitches on thinner ice. Soon banks out under snow.

SGÙRR AN LOCHAIN

(NH 005 104)   Alt 1004m   Maps p40, 45

EAST FACE

(NH 007 105)   Alt 800m   North-East facing   Diagram p55

An impressive triangular face but, apart from the central gully, the lines are disappointing.

Approach: Start from a lay-by at NH 034 119 on the A87. Go up a shallow valley east of a wood and curve right up the hillside above to a shoulder, Maoile an t-Searraich, followed by a descending traverse westwards to below the face, 2hrs to 2hrs 30mins.

Descent: Perhaps via Sgùrr an Doire Leathain and its north-east ridge; the day can then include two Munros and the route.

1 Right Gully   200m   I
The shallow gully bounding the right side of the cliff. A possible descent. In ascent, a harder left branch is worthwhile.

2 Flying Gully   200m   I * *(1990)*
The gully in the centre of the face. Could be described as a scooped ramp. High in its grade, often steep low down and at the cornice.
Variation: **Left Finish   70m   II *** *(1990)*
A steeper gully leads left from just above half-height, sometimes to a big cornice, but there is a left branch of the left finish which is often uncorniced.

**3 The Beast and The Beast   50m   VIII, 8 ** ** *(2007)*
Takes cracks in the steep walls left of Flying Gully. A full set of cams from 3 to 6, with doubles in the larger sizes, are useful for protection. Start 5m right of a monolithic corner-crack.
1. 18m Climb the crack which is unremittingly hard and strenuous. Belay on a terrace below a second tier.
2. 32m Climb a steep hard crack and easier groove line near the left edge of a tower to belay as for the last stance on Once Bitten, which is then followed to the top of the cliff.

4 Once Bitten, Twice Shy   130m   VI,6 *(2007)*
Takes a harder right-hand line up the buttress left of Flying Gully, with some thin climbing on pitch 2. Start on the left wall of Flying Gully, about 10m down from its narrows.
1. 40m Climb a chimney which leads up left to the top of a big pinnacle. Step on to easier ground and head up right over a step to below a steep wall (belay as for The Beast and The Beast).
2. 40m Move left to below a slabbier left face and climb the first corner. Step left into another corner and climb this to a steep pull on to turf. Continue more easily to join Direct Evasion and a big ramp leading up right.
3. 50m Continue up to an arete on the right and make exposed moves just right of the crest to reach easy ground.

5 Direct Evasion   150m   IV,5 * *(1996)*
Climbs the buttress between Flying Gully and a wide easy gully. Start 20m left of the Flying Gully and climb slabs to a narrow well defined gully (15m). Continue up through a steepening of the gully. Cross a wide ledge and up to a narrow cave.

SGÙRR AN LOCHAIN

1. Right Gully — I
1a. Left Branch — I
2. Flying Gully — I *
2a. Left Finish — II *
4. Once Bitten, Twice Shy — VI,6
5. Direct Evasion — IV,5 *
6. Lochain Buttress — II

Climb out on the right wall and continue up steep ledges above to a wide belay ledge. Climb up via a wide notch directly above to an easing snow slope and the top (or better by pitch 3 of Once Bitten, Twice Shy). Variations on the left but using the same belays produce a slightly easier route.

6 Lochain Buttress   200m   II   (1994)
Left of the main face is a wide easy gully. The route climbs the buttress on its left. Start at the toe of the buttress and climb rightwards to a large block near the gully (50m). Cut up and left on to the buttress via a snow groove. Follow the buttress crest, generally on its left side, with one short rock wall at half-height.

7 Enchanted Falls   150m   III   (1996)
The stream cascading from the north-east corrie of Sgùrr an Lochain passes through an enchanting ravine (to join the Allt a' Choire Reith). For much of its length it is enclosed by slabby walls and is inescapable. Needs a good freeze.

SGÙRR A' BHAC CHAOLAIS
(NG 958 110)   Alt 885m   Map p45

SOUTH-WEST FACE
(NG 957 107)   Alt 660m   South-West facing

This hill lies west of Creag nan Damh, the westernmost Munro on the ridge. Two good but short routes with a lovely outlook over Knoydart. Seriously affected by sun (effect depends on season).

Approach: Follow the stalking path up Allt Mhalagain, then leave it to gain the col between Sgùrr na Sgine and Chaolais. From the east end of the col, descend about 100m to a shelf and follow it until under the crag, 2hr.

Descent: Via the summit and Bealach Duibh Leac is satisfying and as quick as any.

The crag has a deep-cut gully with a well defined buttress on its right and a scrappy one on its left.

56 THE SADDLE

Climbers on the Forcan Ridge, I/II, The Saddle (photo Jim Teesdale)

Snowdrop 100m IV,4 * (1994)
The deep gully. The highlight is an ice pillar falling from the lip of a cave (and near subterranean belay). Poorly protected; ice screws perhaps useful.

Mayfly 60m VS (1985)
Climbs the buttress right of the gully starting near the right-hand side of the frontal face. Probably 4c.
1. 20m Climb a cracked slab and right-trending groove, then gain the edge above by a rising traverse left on a slab. The crest leads to a ledge.
2. 15m The corner above leads to a roof with a strenuous exit right. Short walls and ledges lead up and left onto the slabby crest.
3. 25m Ascend the gangway leftwards to climb an obvious crack. An easier crack and rib leads to the top.
Winter: **100m V,7** (1995)
A line based on the summer route but staying just right of the crest throughout. The "rising traverse left on a slab" is quit to climb direct up a pillar of wedged blocks into the corner of pitch 2, pulling out right at its top (40m). Gain a right-slanting turfy ramp and follow it to increasingly easy ground.

FORCAN RIDGE 57

THE SADDLE

(NG 935 131)   Alt 1010m   Maps p40, 45

The shapely mass of The Saddle is west of the main South Glen Shiel Ridge directly across the A87 road from the Five Sisters of Kintail. The best ascent of the mountain is undoubtedly by the east ridge of Sgùrr nan Forcan; the Forcan Ridge.

Approach: Park at NG 968 144. Walk via an obvious stalkers' path leaving the road at NG 968 143.

Forcan Ridge   Moderate **

The ridge is an excellent scramble in summer especially if one sticks to the crest. The crux is a short steep descent from Sgùrr nan Forcan on good flaky holds, but one can pass this on either side, easier but muddy.

Winter: **I or II ***

A classic Alpine style ridge. Climb close to the crest (Grade II) or take minor variations just below it if wished (Grade I). The steep descent can be abseiled or climbed down on either side. The route is usually climbed with one axe, as there are excellent handholds on the steep sections.

THE SADDLE

FORCAN RIDGE SOUTH SIDE

Alt 700-850m   South-South-East-facing

The south side of the Forcan Ridge presents a face with three main slabby buttresses, although the topmost, situated below Sgùrr na Forcan, consists of several ridges close together.

Millennium Chimney   130m   III,5 *   (2001)
A prominent chimney in the centre of the first and lowest buttress on the south-east side of the Forcan Ridge, doglegging left below a roof and often with ice on the slab below the roof. Climb the chimney and its cogleg left to traverse left to a ledge (30m). Continue up the chimney-groove and over an overhang at the top (20m). Finish more easily (45m, 35m).

My Learned Friend   100m   III   (1995)
Climbs the shallow continuous groove left of Millennium Chimney. Low in the grade if there is a good build-up of ice.

Cioch Buttress   120m   IV,5   (1994)
The isolated buttress is the central of the three main cliff sections. A distinctive tower seen from below becomes a Cioch (Skye) shaped block seen from the side. The described line is initially a ramp just right of the crest (with an unreasonably hard start) leading to a 2m block on the crest. Follow the crest until forced to traverse steeply left on flakes to a flake-crack leading back to the crest, which was followed more easily to finish. Difficult in summer.

Higher up the corrie there is a more complex buttress which leads to the upper part of the Forcan Ridge. The rightmost ridge of the buttress provides the following route.

Easter Buttress   100m   Severe 4a   (1961)
Stick to the crest and the standard is Severe. The climb finishes a few metres from a horizontal knife-edge just below the summit.
Winter: **100m   IV,5 ***   (1996)
Good technical crack pitches but one can walk off after pitch 1. Start on the left side of the toe at a large block. A short awkward corner and subsequent ramp leads up to the crest, followed via a smooth slab to below a prominent crack on the right of the crest (35m). Climb the crack to a platform just left of the crest (25m). An overhanging step ahead is passed on the left, then the final step taken by a turfy groove on the right (40m).

Biped Buttress   120m   II   (1994)
Left of Easter Buttress is a more broken ridge with two toes forming a bay and providing this route. Climb to the top of the bay and up the groove above. Below a steepening, move out on to the left leg. Up this and the main crest to the Forcan Ridge.

COIRE UAINE

(NG 930 130)   Alt 650m   North facing   Map p45

A couple of climbs have been recorded in Coire Uaine (north-west of the main summit of The Saddle).

Approach: Park at NG 938 187 and walk along the stalking path up Coire Undalain, then leave it to walk up Coire Uaine.

Big Gully   200m   Very Difficult   (1926)
At the left or north-east end of the cliffs is a "grand gully". It includes "Chockstones, a sentry box, short stretches of vegetable climbing, and a final wriggle under a rock

arch. Well worth a visit by a moderately strong party."
**Winter: III ** *(1994)*
A fine route, which needs cold conditions. Much steep snow and containing four ice pitches, the third being by far the longest (25m) and steep, though eased by being formed in a narrow chimney.

Little Gully   300m   I *(1994)*
To the left of Big Gully is a grass covered face which runs into a narrow gully near the top. The route starts up snow covered slopes and icy rocks to finish up the gully.

BEINN SGRITHEALL
(NG 836 127)   Alt 974m

A Munro overlooking Loch Hourn, well south of Glen Shiel but approached by a drive from it. The north side of the north top offers a couple of climbs to date, but the face is somewhat broken. Looking up from Loch Bealach na h' Oidhche (NG 831 138), a big gully splits the north face **Sgritheall Gully** (Grade II), with several short steps. To the left is a shallower gully, and left again is North Buttress. It has three rock steps separated by grassy ledges and has been climbed in both winter and summer (Difficult or Grade III). Beinn a' Chapuill, to the north-west of Beinn Sgritheall, has a steep North-West Face which has been climbed at Grade II, but lacks defined lines.

North Glen Shiel

An area covering the hills north of Loch Cluanie, the Five Sisters and 'the Brothers' north of Glen Shiel itself and finally Beinn Fhada which is beyond another valley to the north.

CREAG LUNDIE SLABS
(NH 152 108)   Alt 450m   South facing   Map p45

Creag Lundie is a small hill (508m) which lies 8km east of the Cluanie Inn, above Loch Cluanie. Just below the summit are some slabby granite crags, best seen when approaching from the Cluanie Inn and from a large parking area on the shore side at NH 145 103. The rock is just steeper than friction angle and fairly clean. Protection is very limited and the slabs have been used for scary evening soloing by locals for years until recent documentation. Leaders will be close to soloing but a rope is useful for seconds or top-ropers, although belays are hard to find.

Approach: By a ridge which runs up the hill from the south-west, followed by a short traverse right. There is a long lay-by directly under the ridge on the landward side but the large parking area is only 5mins further away, 30mins.

Descent: Traverse right across the top of the slabs and down grass.

At the west end is a steeper discontinuous wall with a prominent tree at mid-height. Right of here are three slabs of about 50 degrees, the rightmost being 20m high and characterised by a series of flared vertical channels while the others are 10 to 15m. More routes will have been done but only the longest have been recorded.

The Lost Knuckle   40m   VS 5a *(1996)*
On the steeper left wall. Right of the tree is a large heather patch. Right of the heather is a white slab with a short V-chimney and crack running up its left side. Above the slab is a deep right-slanting flake-crack. Start at a small buttress directly below the white slab. Climb a short overhanging crack (boulder problem) on to a small slab. Go up this and left along a heather terrace to the V-chimney. Go up the chimney and crack to a good ledge. Climb the deep right-slanting crack to heather.

Problem Arete   15m   4c
The well defined arete at the right end of the first slab, with a stiff start.

The rest of the routes are on the larger right-hand slab.

Small Gutter   20m   Very Difficult
The leftmost of three channel features.

Crackpot   20m   4a/b
The cracks 2m right of Small Gutter are of unknown grade but look good.

Broken Cracks   20m   Very Difficult
A further 3m right is this smaller channel, with better gear.

Low Diagonal   25m   4b *
Start at the base of the Big Gutter and traverse rising leftwards. Pleasant enough and mostly easy.

Big Gutter   20m   Very Difficult
This channel is 2m right again, the most striking feature of the cliff, but proves to be less noble from close up.

**Bald Slab   20m   5b ** **
Start 4m right of Big Gutter at the last crack. Climb this to its end (possible runner) and continue up the bald slab on red knobbles (unprotected).

Wee Baldy   20m   5a *
Start a further 2m right and climb a parallel line finishing slightly rightwards.

SGÙRR NAN CONBHAIREAN

(NH 130 138)   Alt 1109m   Maps p40, 45

The eastern flanks of Sgùrr nan Conbhairean and its neighbours are clearly but distantly seen from the A87, driving west through Glen Moriston. The cliffs are high and hold snow well, so may be good when lower crags in Glen Shiel have thawed out. They are also not quite as wet and misty as further down the glen.

Approach: Park at NH 126 105, walk along the main road for 200m, then follow a stalking path up Coire Lair until it ends. Continue up the corrie, although it is better underfoot away from the Allt, to approach Glas Bhealach. For the East Buttress, descend north-east to reach the foot of the buttress. For the North-East Face, pass just north of Glas Bhealach to reach the summit of Sgùrr nan Conbhairean. Walk north-west, then north, before descending eastwards (probable cornice) under the face, 2hrs 30mins to 3hrs.

EAST BUTTRESS

(NH 135 139)   Alt 800m   East facing

The East Buttress consists of two ridges separated by a prominent gully.

East Ridge   300m to walking terrain   II *   *(1996)*
Climbs a shallow gully in the left-hand ridge. This ridge continues on as the main ridge to the summit. Start from the same snow bay as Ceannacroc Couloir but take the shallow gully on the left (initial icefall/chockstone avoided on the right). Follow the gully, ignoring a left branch which gives an easier but less satisfying option, passing another chockstone on the right, to increasingly easy ground. The final snow crest to the summit cairn is easy but in some ways the highlight.

Ceannacroc Couloir   300m   II **   *(1992)*
Climbs the deep and narrow gully. From the top of the gully trend left to gain the

crest of the left ridge which leads to the fine snow arete and summit finish.

NORTH-EAST FACE

(NH 132 140)   Alt 850-1000m   North facing

The North-East Face is the north facing side of the right ridge mentioned above. It angles up the wall of the corrie to meet the north ridge of Sgùrr nan Conbhairean. A grassy slope traverses the face and produces a discontinuity (and escape) to the following two routes, whose main feature are icefalls below the slope.

Misty Byway   200m   IV,4 * *(1995)*
Climb the obvious icefall at the left-hand side (lower end) of the face (50m). Continue up the groove above (50m). Traverse diagonally right on snow to the foot of a gully, followed to the ridge (70m, 30m).

Fog Monster   200m   V,5 *(1995)*
Take the line 20m right of Misty Byway turning the ice column on the right (possible direct in more clement conditions) 50m. Step across the wall into the right-hand groove and follow this (50m). Traverse right on snow as for Misty Byway (70m). Climb the obvious steep chimney in the buttress left of Misty Byway (40m).

Crystal Couloir   120m   II * *(1996)*
An easy slope slants up left from the cliff base above the lower section of the previous two routes. This route is a right-slanting gully right of the upper section of Misty Byway. Climbed in cold but thin conditions, it provided a lot of ice, but might have much steep snow normally.

Sunny Side Up   100m   IV,4 *(1995)*
Climbs an icefall in the centre of the wall above the left-slanting slope and right of Crystal Couloir.
1. 45m Climb the icefall and groove above to below a steep wall.
2. 50m Step right and climb a recess in the wall. Head up to belay just below the ridge.

At the top right corner of the face are two prominent icefalls which form in shallow gullies. At their best during snowless conditions because they soon bank up and become easier, or even disappear. Being very high they can resist a big thaw.

Corn in Egypt   150m   III *(1996)*
The left icefall gave two long ice pitches, the first easier, the second steeper. A shorter third on frozen turf, then snow or easy turf to the top.

Liquid Gully   100m   II *(1996)*
The right icefall. Easy angled ice, then a short steep section lead to an ice runnel. Follow turf to finish out right on the north ridge.

LOCHAN UAINE BUTTRESS

(NH 132 145)   Alt 840m   North-East facing

Approach: By descending the north ridge of Conbhairean to the second flattening, which is the joining point of an easy ridge which is the upper continuation of the buttress. The cornice is likely to be at its smallest here, so descend and turn right (back towards Conbhairean) to curve back under the buttress. It is clearly seen in profile from the North-East face of Conbhairean but most of it, including the steep section containing the following routes, faces away (north-east).

Anne Frank's Chimney   90m   IV,4 *(1996)*
About 10m from the left end of the steep section of face is a fault with sections of

chimney high up. An initial steep step, then turf (45m). Chimney under a small chockstone (a distinctive feature seen from the route base, but small) and continue into a left-slanting steep upper fault (45m).

The Green Man 90m III *(1998)*
Climbs the face right of Anne Frank's Chimney, starting about 5m to its right. Climb turf to a block, then traverse right to reach a line leading diagonally right to end at a steep headwall (40m). Traverse back left to enter and climb a steep groove, gradually easing.

WEST CRAG

(NH 124 136) Alt 900m North-West facing

A rather broken crag on the north side of the west ridge of Sgùrr nan Conbhairean.

Approach: Start as for the other crags on the mountain but continue to Gorm Lochan and go up a gully to the col between it and Drochaid an Tuill Easaich. Go west for 30m and descend a gully on the north side. The only significant buttress is on the east of the descent gully.

Category Five 100m II *(2002)*
Climb a system of grooves just right of the crest of the buttress.

SÀIL CHAORAINN

(NH 133 154) Alt 1002m Map p45

WEST FACE

(NH 133 158) Alt 900m West facing

The crag is on the west side of the north top (1001m) and is clearly seen when walking north from the south and higher top (1002m). It is also disappointingly small.

Distant Groove 70m III *(2000)*
The route takes a central groove, trending right to a rockfall scar, up its left edge before moving left to a steep finish. The left edge of the crag has also been climbed (scrappy Grade II).

A' CHRÀLAIG

(NH 094 148) Alt 1120m Maps p40, 45

LOCHAN NA CRÀLAIG

(NH 094 156) Alt 850m East facing

The crag lies above the lochan. Left of centre is a right-slanting easy gully with a short step low down and used for descent. This gully is Grade II in lean conditions so it is then better to descend further north, outflanking all the cliff. Right of this is a sharp ridge with a distinctive S-shaped wide crack in a smooth wall at its base. Next is a bay with various grooves leading out of its top. Right again is an easier angled buttress which curves up left. The grooves start low angled, then steepen up so the route lengths varies greatly with the build-up.

Spiked 80m III,4 * *(2002)*
The ridge with the S shaped crack, but bypassing the initial steep wall on the right. Start on the left side of the bay, immediately beyond the steep wall. Climb up left on steep turf to reach the crest left of a pinnacle (30m). Pass the pinnacle on the far side, then continue up short steep walls near the crest to a final horizontal arete (30m). Finish easily along this (20m).

CISTE DHUBH

Kraken 60m VI,6 *(2002)*
The biggest groove, which leads to the end of the horizontal arete. Start at the top left corner of the bay. Go up left and back right to join the groove, thereby missing an overhanging step. Climb the groove, step right into its continuation, go over a strenuous bulge and continue steeply to the top.

Curly Gully 100m III * *(2001)*
The gully leading out of the top right corner of the bay, finishing by the gully continuation on the left.

Curled Buttress 120m III,4 *(2001)*
The easier angled curving buttress. Start by a steep chimney just left of its base. This leads to an easier upper section.

MULLACH FRAOCH-CHOIRE
(NH 095 171) Alt 1102m Map p45

SOUTH-EAST FACE
(NH 096 168) Alt 900m East facing

Frayed at the Edges 150m II *(1996)*
The scrambling section on the south ridge of the mountain has three buttresses on its east side. This takes the rightmost (northmost) buttress, with a tower and col towards the top. It finished immediately north of the trickiest section of ridge. Spoilt by an easy gully on the left leading to the col. The leftmost of the three buttresses has also been climbed, starting by a short gully between two toes but petering out on to open slopes near the top.

CISTE DHUBH
(NH 062 166) Alt 979m Maps p40, 45

SOUTH-EAST FACE
(NH 063 166) Alt 860m South-East facing

The face is clearly seen but distant from the A87 road. The rock is steep slabby schist, fortunately well turfed but unhelpful away from the fault-lines. These offer good although disappointingly short climbs. The face is susceptible to sun.

Approach: Park 400m west of where the An Caorann Mòr track meets the A87. Follow the track and subsequent path to the col before Glen Affric, then follow the stream directly to the cliff, 2 to 2hrs 30mins. The routes finish 5mins from the summit of the mountain.

Descent: The quickest descent is reversing the approach.

The deep Coffin Gully (Grade I) splits the cliff into two halves. The left half is fairly broken, but has been climbed by the gully near its right side, moving right on to the ridge overlooking Coffin Gully (Grade II). The right half provides the following routes.

Coffin Gully 100m I
The deep central gully, short and steep.

Kissed Ye Quick 70m II *(1995)*
The left edge of the face, almost overlooking Coffin Gully, has a prominent turfy groove, though not well seen from below. Near the top it splits into parallel turf grooves; this follows the left groove.

The Mantelshelf 70m V,6 *(1996)*
Climb the crest on the right of Coffin Gully (and right of Kissed Ye Quick). Short but

sustained. Start at it the base of the crest and move out right to a turfy line, followed to a flake (30m). Return left to reach a turfy ledge. Axe traverse the ledge left to a key foothold (crucial warthog runner in the ledge) and mantelshelf. Belay on huge flakes above (20m). Take the line of flakes diagonally right to finish (20m).

Rest in Peace   80m   IV,6 * (1996)
The front face is split roughly into three by two parallel faults, almost shallow gullies. Between them is a short but prominent right-facing corner, not a route. This route climbs the left-hand parallel fault. Start 10m right of the fault.
1. 25m Gain a left-slanting ramp which leads into the fault. Climb this until close to an overhang and belay out right.
2. 25m Climb through the overhang (excellent runners) and up another hard step.
3. 30m Continue up the fault passing through a short chimney to finish past a big spike on the right.

The Undertaker   70m   III,4 (1995)
The route climbs the right-hand fault, initially easy, then a deep groove, and finishing by the right of two options, with a long step left as the final move (crux; a less direct right finish would be easier).

SGÙRR AN FHUARAIL

(NH 055 125)   Alt 400m

One for the Road   130m   II (1996)
The right-hand frozen stream coming out of Coire na Cadha, bypassing a vertical section (not frozen).

SGÙRR A' BHEALAICH DHEIRG

(NH 033 143)   Alt 1031m   Maps p40, 45

This hill forms part of the easterly continuation of the Five Sisters ridge. It has a fine summit about 50m north of the main ridge.

GHLAS CHOIRE

(NH 036 147)   Alt 750m   North facing

The following climbs have been recorded in Ghlas Choire, the corrie to the north of the mountain. The cliff is composed of V shaped gullies rising from the top of a large bay with a prominent pinnacle in its centre. The gullies hold snow well even after a big thaw.

Approach: Park near NH 038 119. Go through a gap in the forest on to Meall a' Charra. Traverse east of pt.806 (or go over it) to reach the col at NH 039 139. Traverse the west side of Coire nan Eun to gain the north-east ridge of Sgùrr a' Bhealaich Dheirg at about NH 042 151. Descend east from here, which should be north of any cliffs, into the Ghlas Choire and traverse back south to reach its lochan. The cliffs are directly above. It may take as long to reach the cliffs as to do a route and return to the car!

Solution Gully   200m   II ** (1997)
The left gully of the V shape starting from the top of the bay. Two steeper pitches, then two easier leading to the crest of the north-east ridge which makes a fine easy finish to the summit cairn.

Beinn Gunn's Buttress   150m   III (1997)
The buttress between the two gullies. Start just inside Solution Gully and climb a steepening groove followed by a right-sloping ramp to the crest (50m). Follow the crest in two long pitches to reach scrambling up the north-east ridge.

SGÙRR NAN SAIGHEAD | 65

Resolution Gully   150m   III *(1986)*
The right gully of the V shape. The rock on the gully wall is very poor; ice screws recommended for protection. A steeper final icefall was avoided by an exit right on to a broken buttress which leads easily to the summit ridge.
Variation: **Direct Finish: 50m   IV,3 *** *(1999)*
Climb the final steep icefall and easy finishing gully.

Resolve   50m   IV,5 *(2004)*
A steep icefall 50m right of the prominent pinnacle flows over two vertical rock walls interspersed by a sloping ledge with a large block belay. Ice screw protection. An easy traverse off left and down a ramp reaches the base of Resolution Gully.

Five Sisters of Kintail

Situated on the north side of the road, the Five Sisters (Sgùrr na Moraich, Sgùrr nan Saighead, Sgùrr Fhuaran, Sgùrr na Carnach and Sgùrr na Ciste Duibhe) provide little climbing interest in summer. But the north side of the ridge formed by these peaks and Sgùrr nan Spainteach, provides some good easier winter routes. Virtually all the older climbs have been recorded by Edinburgh University Mountaineering Club with their convenient base at Glenlicht House.

Approach: Take the minor road to Morvich and leave the car at the start of the landrover track up Gleann Lichd (NG 967 210). Walk (or cycle) along the track, then climb straight up into the corries.

SGÙRR NAN SAIGHEAD
(NG 975 178)   Alt 929m   Maps p40, 45
There are two corries of interest to the climber.

COIRE DRUIM NA STAIDHRE

(NG 975 176)   Alt 720m   East facing
The corrie to the east of the summit is Coire Druim na Staidhre. It comprises several slabby buttresses separated by gullies which provide lower grade winter routes among impressive scenery.

Descent: There is no easy descent into the corrie. A possible descent is to go to the summit of Sgùrr nan Saighead and descend into Coire na h-Uaighe. The quickest descent is Dog-Leg Gully, the first obvious gully seen when heading north-west down the ridge from the summit.

The most obvious feature when approaching the corrie is a huge rake slanting up from right to left to end at a sharp crest overlooking Forked Gully, the deep gully in the centre of the face. All routes in the corrie are winter routes with the exception of **California** (80m Severe 1956) which climbs "an obvious S-shaped crack at the apex of the left-hand of two large scree cones".

Twisting Gully   120m   II *(1986)*
This is the leftmost gully on the face, well left of Forked Gully. It contains three short pitches separated by easy snow. Grade III in lean conditions. It fits the description for California but looks horrible in summer.

Forked Gully   140m   II * *(1957)*
The deep gully in the centre of the main face has been climbed by both forks. Its left fork gives a steep climb to finish with a short ice pitch and a spectacular exit onto the summit ridge. The right fork is Grade I.

Saighead Slot   180m   I * *(1984)*
From the start of Forked Gully take the narrow steeper gully, almost a ramp, to the

right of the right fork. The route is obvious and finishes at The Slot, a deep fissure, exiting onto the summit ridge.

Edge of Reason   210m   IV,4 ** (1986)
This scenic route climbs the sharp right arete of Forked Gully and Saighead Slot by mossy grooves. Keep to the crest for the best climbing, pass the top of the ramp and finish up easier grooves just left of the crest.

Hidden Gully   150m   II * (1984)
Climb the prominent left-slanting rake to the second snow bay on the right and proceed up a well defined gully on the right, with chockstones of varying difficulty. A large intractable chockstone presents itself. Crawl through a tiny hole on the right into a large cave and up a vertical shaft to a good belay. Easier ground leads to the summit.

Easy Gully   150m   I
To the right of the rake the face becomes less steep. This gully starts well right of the foot of the rake.

COIRE NA H-UAIGHE

(NG 972 180)   Alt 780m   North-East facing
The corrie to the north of the summit of Sgùrr nan Saighead. It provides the most westerly climbing on the Five Sisters ridge and like the other areas it is far more suited to winter climbing.

Descent: Dog-Leg Gully is the best descent from the summit buttresses. A wide open gully between the main crag and Babylon Buttress is the best descent from these.

High on the left of the corrie are some buttresses which end on the ridge right of the summit. A shallow gully left of these leads direct to the summit (Grade I).

Dog-Leg Gully   150m   I
A well defined gully with no pitches, turning right to end on the ridge.

Canine Buttress   150m   IV,4 * (2004)
The most prominent buttress, which lies between Dog-Leg Gully and another shorter gully with a steep finish (Grade I/II) to its right. The start is poorly protected. Start just right of its base and take the rightmost of three possible turfy lines slanting left to a short steep wall (30m). Climb the wall to a bay, then make a descending traverse left to pull through a shorter wall (20m). Climb a groove to the crest and follow it to a barrier wall (40m). Go up a turfy fault on the right to regain the crest and follow it more easily to the top (60m).

At the back of the corrie, well right of the summit and where the main ridge is roughly horizontal, is a compact crag of four ridges split by three shallow gully lines.

Left-Hand Gully   120m   III (1987)
Climb the left-hand gully system, with a short steep pitch near the top.

Flying Ridge   120m   IV,4 ** (2004)
The second ridge from the left, but situated somewhat centrally, features twin crests at its base, the right-hand crest being a prominent rock arete. Start up a well defined V-groove between the crests and from its top, gain the right crest. Move steeply up left (crux) and up a shallow groove to an easier section. The crest becomes a well defined arete. Climb this for a few metres, then move right into a long groove. Climb the groove to finish up the crest. The route has been climbed in summer but is very vegetated (Difficult 1987).

COIRE NA H-UAIGHE

Grovel Gully   120m   II   *(1986)*
Climb the central gully-groove system, starting just right of the lower rock arete.

Hanging Garden   120m   II   *(2004)*
The rightmost ridge, and just left of a wide open gully (easy descent). Climb shallow grooves in the lower crest, then easier ground to where the crest steepens (easy escape right here). Move right on to the gully wall, then left up two short steep walls to regain the crest. After a small descent, go up left to finish just left of the crest.
Just right of this section and the wide open gully, is a high broken pinnacled buttress leading to a top on the ridge (NG 969 182).

Babylon Buttress   220m   Very Difficult   *(1985)*
This route climbs the pinnacled buttress; start at the toe of the buttress. Climb into a cave then out left and up to a broad grassy ledge. The first pinnacle is climbed by a groove slanting left in two pitches then up right on grass to a pinnacle. The steep arete beyond is turned by a gully on the right. The second pinnacle is turned on the left and climbed from behind. Climb final slabs over detached blocks followed by a traverse right to finish just below the summit.
Winter: **III,5 ***   *(1995)*
Approximately follows the summer route. There is one very hard move off the third belay, and the final slabs can be climbed direct by twin torque cracks (again hard but only 5m before easy ground) or outflanked to the right by an easier groove.

Much further right, the east curving gully near the entrance to the corrie has been climbed and named after a well known local landmark often visible at the local hostelry; **Brenda's Cleavage** (100m I 1985). The obvious deep gully between Babylon Buttress and Brenda's Cleavage which twists and narrows near the top is **Little Gully** (100m I 1987).

SGÙRR FHUARAN
(NG 978 167)   Alt 1068m

The north face of Sgùrr Fhuaran has a steep dark crag immediately below the summit. An obvious gully splits this crag from top to bottom with a triple fork in its upper reaches. This is **Trident Gully** and has been climbed at 220m II/III (1957). From the summit of Sgùrr Fhuaran a ridge runs east towards Glenlicht House. The small top on this ridge is called A' Charraig (NG 988 165). The big gully on the north flank of this ridge has been climbed in disappointingly banked-out conditions **A' Charraig Gully** (180m I/II 1986).

SGÙRR NA CARNACH
(NG 977 159)   Alt 1002m

The east face of Sgùrr na Carnach is very steep and broken and has one prominent gully, **Dog's Leg Gully** (180m II 1957). It starts near the foot of the face and forks halfway up, the left fork finishing within a few metres of the summit.

SGÙRR NAN SPAINTEACH
(NG 992 150)   Alt 990m

Although not technically one of the Five Sisters, this peak forms the eastern end of the ridge. **Window Gully** (180m III 1985) is the gully splitting the north face of Sgùrr nan Spainteach. A frozen ramp leads into the groove which is followed via two chockstones to the window on the summit ridge (visible from the base of the climb). Right of Window Gully is **Solo Gully** (120m II 1957). This is the obvious line on the left side of the corrie north of the ridge between Sgùrr nan Spainteach and Sgùrr na Ciste Duibhe. It finishes 200m east of the summit of Sgùrr nan Spainteach.

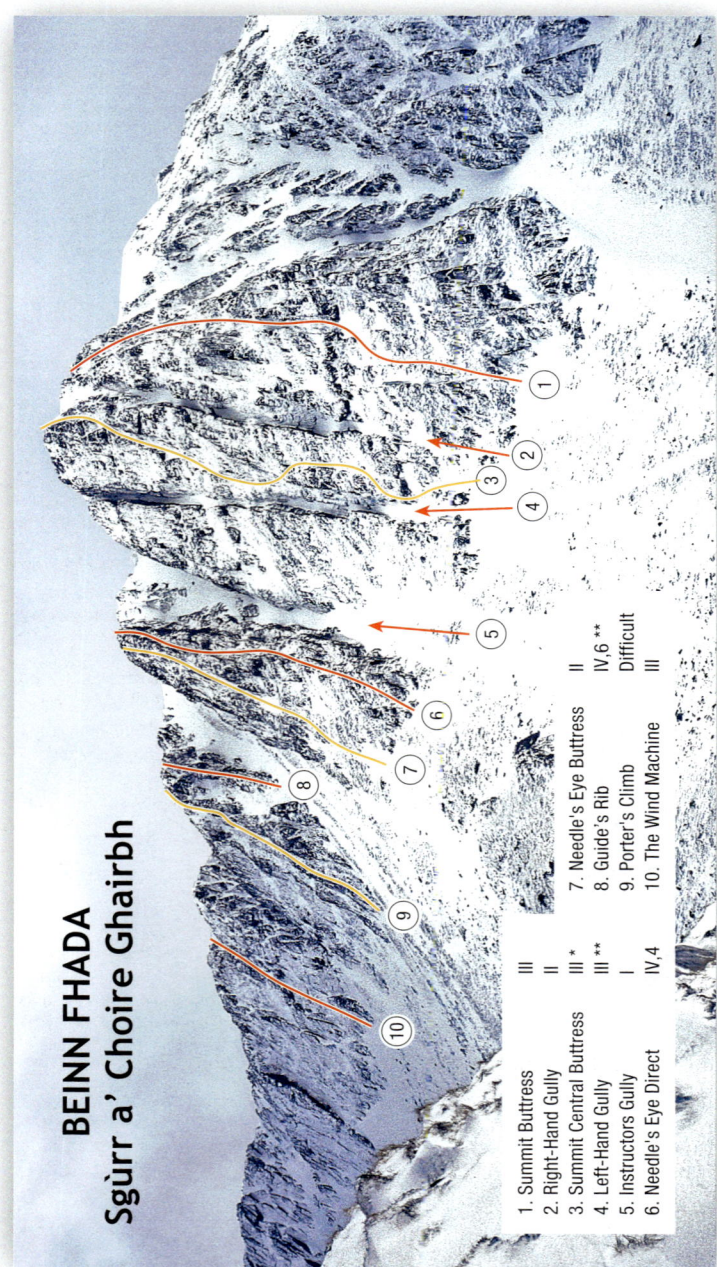

SHIEL BRIDGE CRAGS

Many routes up to 30m on good rock have been climbed on the hillside above Shiel Bridge.

BEINN FHADA
(NH 018 192)   Alt 1032m

This hulk of a mountain is relatively uninteresting if approached from Gleann Lichd, but its west ridge provides an interesting means of ascent and the corries on the north side of the mountain are impressive. Most of the climbing on Beinn Fhada is concentrated on the east face of Sgùrr a' Choire Ghairbh (NG 994 207) where a series of slabby buttresses overlook the Choire Chaoil. Coire an Sgairne, the east of the two corries is smaller and a little disappointing.

SGÙRR A' CHOIRE GHAIRBH - NORTH-EAST FACE
(NG 995 205)   Alt 650-700m   East facing   Maps p40, 45   Diagram p68

Approach: Drive up past Lienassie near Morvich to a car park just before Dorusduain House (NG 980 223). There are discouraging signs but it is a public road. Walk up the continuing track for a short way until a small path branches off rightwards through a kissing gate and crosses the river to gain the main stalker's track leading to the Bealach an Sgairne. This excellent path is followed to the junction of two burns about 1km before the Bealach an Sgairne. From this point the summit buttress of Sgùrr a' Choire Ghairbh is clearly visible and is the nearest buttress on the right-hand side as you look up.

Descent: Northwards along the Sgùrr a' Choire Ghairbh ridge and steeply down to the path.

Under the summit of Sgùrr a' Choire Ghairbh there is a broad buttress split into three parts by two narrow gullies. The following routes have been climbed here.

1 Summit Buttress   200m   III   *(1984)*
Start to the right of the right-hand gully and climb slabs to a prominent bulge at about mid-height. Continue directly to the top. The route has also been climbed in summer by traversing left across the right-hand gully at the mid-height bulge (Difficult). A disappointing climb in both summer and winter.

2 Right-Hand Gully   160m   II   *(1951)*
The right-hand of the two gullies.

3 Summit Central Buttress   200m   III *   *(2001)*
Climbs the buttress between the two gullies. There was good quality snow on the only ascent. Start in Left-Hand Gully below where it narrows and traverse on to the centre of the buttress. Climb the buttress until it narrows and traverse left (just below a short left-facing corner) into a large right-trending fault. Follow this, easy at first, then over a step. Continue up the line which eventually becomes a shelf overlooking Right-Hand Gully. A hard slabby step gains the top of the buttress (but it is easier to gain the top of Right-Hand Gully).

4 Left-Hand Gully   150m   III **   *(1983)*
The narrow gully immediately left of Summit Buttress. It contains numerous short steps which can bank out reducing the climb to Grade II.

5 Instructors Gully   140m   I   *(1991)*
To the left of Summit Buttress is a broad snow gully enclosed by steep walls. There are no pitches even in lean conditions.

BEINN FHADA

6 Needle's Eye Buttress Direct   150m   IV,4   (2000)
The left wall of Instructors Gully forms the edge of Needle's Eye Buttress, so called after a square projection halfway up the buttress which is pierced by a hole. The crest of the buttress provides a poor climb of Difficult standard (1949). The winter line follows the crest of the buttress up slabby rock, threading the needle halfway up the buttress.

7 Needle's Eye Buttress   150m   II   (1994)
This easier winter route climbs a central turfy trough left of the crest.

To the left of Needle's Eye Buttress is another broad grassy gully with a broad buttress to its left. The right-hand edge of this buttress is formed, in its upper half, by a steep narrow rib. This provides Guide's Rib.

8 Guide's Rib   100m   IV,6 **   (1996)
Basically following the crest, this gives an exciting outing. The steepest section is ascended on the right; the next section is taken on the left and the final horizontal crest is particularly airy. Very Difficult in summer (1955).

9 Porter's Climb (and Continuation)   160m   Difficult   (1955)
To the left of Guide's Rib and starting at the lowest point of the same buttress is this route. At its top and 20m to the right is Continuation Climb (30m).

10 The Wind Machine   140m   III   (1994)
The next buttress left has three rectangular ribs separated by gullies. This is the right-hand gully, well defined in its upper half.

At the back of the corrie are two large slabby buttresses, separate from the main mass and facing north-west.

11 Tropical Buttress   140m   II *   (1983)
This climbs the right-hand buttress. Start at a small bay below the middle of the buttress and follow an obvious right-trending depression to the top.

The larger left buttress contains the following summer and winter routes.

12 The Needle   110m   Severe   (1952)
The route goes up the north edge of the buttress. Starting from the lowest point, climb the groove to the edge of the slab. Traverse right to a rib of porphyry (spike belay); the direct ascent of this slab is severe. Climb the rib in several pitches (60m). Traverse up to the right for 10m to a large vibrating flake and climb the wall above to the top of a pinnacle (20m). Cross a narrow gap and scramble to the main ridge.

13 Fisherman's Blues   180m   IV,4 *   (1992)
Start a short distance up the gully between the two buttresses at the first obvious ramp-line. Climb leftwards up the ramp over some steep steps to reach the crest of the buttress. Continue up the crest by a series of grooves to reach a large detached block on the right. A further series of grooves and steps lead to easier ground.

COIRE AN SGAIRNE

(NH 003 203)   Alt 750m   East facing   Map p45

Approach: Approach as for the other corrie but stay on the path which branches into Coire an Sgairne.

Descent: Northwards down the ridge between the two corries.

The first buttress encountered is twin tiered and provides the following route.

SGÙRR A' CHOIRE GHAIRBH

GLEN SHIEL & KYLE OF LOCHALSH

Guide's Rib, IV,6, Sgùrr a' Choire Ghairbh, Beinn Fhada. Climber Graeme Ettle

The Kintail Blanket   185m   VS *(1989)*
Start at the toe of the buttress a few metres right of a large embedded boulder at a pink rock intrusion.
1. 50m 4c   Climb an easy slab then the obvious broken groove above to a prominent square-cut overhang at 40m. Turn the overhang on the right to belay on a grass ledge at the foot of a hanging groove.

BEINN FHADA

2. 45m 4b Climb the groove above and cross the terrace to belay at a 2m overhanging wall.
3. and 4. 90m 4c Climb past the right side of the overhanging wall and up by short grooves and walls to finish up a short hard corner. Take belays as required.

The Funnel   180m   I * (1994)
The gully left of The Kintail Blanket is well hidden until either directly below or from beyond. Slant in from the left and finish up a square-cut slot.

Left of the twin tiered buttress is a long section with three right-slanting ramps, before reaching the most impressive feature of all; a great black vertical wall which faces down the corrie.

Tramlines   140m   IV,6 (2000)
This climbs the crest left of the great wall. Start up a groove system left of the crest until flaky ground leads out to the crest above its first steep section. Pull over a bulge and climb twin cracks in the second corner left of the crest. The finishing crest is easy. Grade II apart from one short pitch. The route has been climbed in summer (Severe 1996), including both the steep sections on the crest, but is rather vegetated.

Left of this crest is an easy gully, then a broad buttress and followed by a narrow buttress with a snow gully either side.

Fatties Gully   150m   I (2006)
The gully on the left side of the narrow buttress. It has a short overhanging rock wall forming its right side and steepens at the finish.

Lightning Gully   150m   I (2006)
About 100m left is this well defined gully with a kink left near the start.

At the back left of the corrie, at NH 007 197, is a prominent ridge with a steep left wall dropping into a snow gully.

Atta Buttress   120m   II * (2006)
A pleasant and scenic route, suitable en route to the summit, but otherwise a long way to walk. Start just inside the snow gully and climb steeply up and right to the crest. Descend slightly on the other side and pull through a wall at the first possible place. Head left towards the crest past a short difficult step. The crest itself has many spikes and is much easier.

Dornie, Kyle of Lochalsh & Plockton

Most of the country between Glen Croe at Morvich and Loch Long (mouth at Dornie) has numerous small bluffs and crags. The largest crag in the area is Biod an Fhithich, near Dornie. There are also crags up Glen Elchaig, White Dyke crag near Kyle and the steep, intriguing and fairly extensive Duncraig near Plockton.

BIOD AN FHITHICH

(NG 915 274)   Alt 200m   North-West facing   Map p40   Diagram p74

The cliff offers quite an extensive area of rock with surprisingly good holds for schist. The rock is reasonably clean considering its aspect but runners are spaced.

Approach: The approach to this crag is along the path north of the River Glennan with a steep climb up heather to the foot of the buttress, about 45mins.

Descent: Start down the ridge at the west end of the crag (Ankle Ridge) but soon move into heathery grooves on the gully side of the ridge (or stay longer on the ridge, nicer but harder). When nearly at the base of the gully, move right on to the

BIOD AN FHITHICH 73

terrace which is formed at the top of the rake. Descend the rake to the cliff base.

Features of Biod an Fhithich are the overhanging scoop forming the base of the left half of the cliff, and bands of heather above the scoop, the much cleaner slabby right half, and the easy angled ridge which bounds it on the right. Immediately to the right of this ridge is a narrow grassy gully, and beyond it a smaller vegetatious crag. A grassy rake rises to the right below the crag and gives access to the foot of the steep wall below the slabs. The rake ends at a terrace at the base of the ridge and beside the base of the gully.

1 Ginger's Gully   Severe (1974)
This takes the vegetated gully come corner-line bounding the main face on its left. It contained an eagle's nest during the first ascent.

2 Bionic   30m   E3 *** (2000)
A spectacular and sustained route up an overhanging stepped corner at the left end of the main face. Much steeper than it looks. Initially quite bold but well protected in the corner. Two rest points were used high in the corner, which was seconded free (E4 free?).
1. 10m 4c The initial corner is black and vegetated so climb the rib on its left to a good ledge.
2. 20m 6a Move out left and climb the wall left of the corner before moving back into the corner. Make a hard move up over an overhang, then pull up left to jugs. Return to the corner and climb it to a block. Abseil from a 2m sling round the block (in-situ, but may blow off); reaching easy ground on the left would be about 4c but involve much gardening.

3 Biodiversity   110m   HVS * (1998)
Cleaner left-hand variations to Biodirect but with some unprotected 4c. Start at a small groove which forms the first reasonable break in the overhanging lower section of cliff as one moves right up the rake.
1. 50m 4c Climb up to the heather at the base of the groove. Step up left and make a short traverse along the lip of the overhang until better holds (but no runners) lead up left to a ledge. Climb fairly directly up a vague rib (a similar one further right is the original route) to a small grass ledge.
2. 25m 4c Go directly up over a small bulge to the recess below the corner.
3. 35m 4c Step left and climb the rib left of the corner to finish up the final tower direct.

4 Biodirect   110m   VS * (1974)
A direct line on fairly clean rock with positive holds but not many runners. The line is open to variation in the middle (i.e. follow your nose). Start as for Biosynthesis at the first reasonable break in the overhanging lower section of cliff as one moves right up the rake.
1. 45m 4c Climb up into the heather filled groove and step right near its top. Climb up, then slightly left and straight up to a small grass ledge.
2. 30m 4a Go up into a slight corner which trends slightly left to a recess below a corner which is the only distinct feature in the upper half of the cliff.
3. 35m 4c Go diagonally right across a slab below the corner (the corner is Hump) and step delicately into a shallow groove parallel with it. Go up this for a short way, then trend slightly left to a heather terrace below a final tower on the left. Go up the final tower on its right side to the top.

5 Hump   120m   Hard Severe ** (1971)
Start immediately at the right end of the overhang at the cliff base, just past the last step scrambling up. Fine clean rock but with very few runners and requiring some route finding. The 50m pitch can be split.
1. 25m Climb straight up to a grass ledge.
2. 50m 4a Take a line trending slightly left to reach the recess; belay common to Biodirect.

3. 25m 4a Climb the corner above over the first overhang, passing the second overhang by going left then back right and finishing awkwardly on to a heather terrace below the final tower.
4. 20m Finish easily left of the tower.

6 Wrong Turn 100m Very Difficult (1971)
On the right-hand side of the slabs. Start about 6m right of Hump. Climb to a big heather patch, then continue very slightly rightwards up a clean tongue of slab to a platform near the right-bounding ridge above a heathery recess. A short chimney leads to easier climbing.

The following two routes are on a subsidiary buttress below the right side of the main face and formed below the terrace. The buttress has a left-facing corner on its crest.

7 Intro One 60m VS 4b (1974)
Climb the corner, then move out on to an undercut slab on its left and up its outside edge to finish up two slabs separated by heather.

8 Intro Two 60m Severe (1974)
Climb the rib right of the corner and continue up the two slabs keeping right of Intro One.

9 Ankle Ridge 120m Difficult (1971)
The right-bounding ridge of the main crag just left of the obvious gully. There is considerable scope for variation but lots of heather.

CRAGAIG

Map p40
This group of crags lie on an unnamed hill in Glen Elchaig. They are a long walk and are more accessible with a bike.

Approach: Park at the end of the public road at NG 940 303. Cycle on a tarmac estate road to NG 970 280, then the continuing unsurfaced track to the crags, 7km.

An impressive wedge shaped buttress dominates the approach but is both formidable and vegetated when seen close up (NG 990 273, Alt 220m). Much nearer the track is the steep Arabian Wall. Above it but less obvious is The Cioch. High on the hill and somewhat in profile are The Tongues.

ARABIAN WALL

(NG 990 271) Alt 90m South facing (Main Wall) & West facing (Sidewall)
The crag forms an overhanging main wall of very clean schist facing the road and at right-angles, a sidewall which decreases in size as it runs up the hillside

Fritillary 25m E3 6a ** (1998)
A series of cracks in the centre of the main wall. There is a tree in the last crack, 1m below the cliff-top. Start below this, just left of a black streak. Climb a thin crack to a break (Friend 4), then continue up slightly left to gain and climb a better crack. Finish up the prominent crack past the tree.

Elchaig Arete 18m HVS 5a * (1998)
The left end of the main wall forms a sharp arete with the sidewall. Climb this on the left (sidewall) side. Near the top move further away from the arete. Sticking to the arete would probably be E2.

The sidewall wall has a long overhang; the crack at the left (top) end is 8m Severe.

CRAGAIG

THE CÌOCH

(NG 991 272)   Alt 180m   South-West facing

This is above and right of Arabian Wall, obvious from its top.

Pine Processionary   25m   Severe * *(1998)*
At the left side of the crag is a vague crack-line which is shaped like an inverted S.

Drinking with the Priest   25m   E1 5b *(1998)*
Right of Pine Processionary is a big roof at 5m and above its right end is a detached looking flake come block. Gain the flake and climb its left side to an easy top section.

THE TONGUES

The rock here is gneiss. The routes usually involve padding with very little protection and have always been soloed. Other lines are possible and like the following, are reputed to have been climbed by locals.

Middle Tongue

(NG 994 273)   Alt 320m   South facing

This is broken into lower and upper slabs.

St. Andrew's Slab   30m   Very Difficult *
A lower left slab has a cross low down formed by a vein and a crack. Climb straight up through this.

Shining   50m   Hard Severe *
Above St. Andrew's Slab is a shining slab with a crack running up left. The base of the slab forms a wall. Climb cracks to gain the slab at a moss streak. Step left and follow the crack up left.

Boomerang   30m   Difficult
A lower right slab, right of St. Andrew's slab, is the correct shape. Starting by trending right, the route bends left.

Right Tongue

Blanco   100m   Moderate
Follow the slab slightly leftwards to the top, past a grass ledge at one-third height.

WHITE DYKE

(NG 758 287)   Alt 40m   South-West facing   Map p40

A small but interesting quartzite crag, very accessible from Kyle of Lochalsh and used by locals for many years, generally for bouldering, but the routes can also be led. A bouldering mat is recommended. The following routes were climbed mainly in 1983 and others may exist.

Approach: Drive north from Kyle of Lochalsh on the Plockton road for about 2km to the first open section without houses. The new bridge is visible behind and left (to the south-west). Here is a small roadside crag overlooking a wooded valley (containing the An Garbh Allt, hidden in vegetation) and the main crag is clearly visible above it. Park on the old road, of which a short section remains inland (and by the time you see the crag, you've probably just missed its entrance). Cross the old bridge and find a small path leading up to the centre of the crag at a section with an overhanging base.

WHITE DYKE   77

Descent: At either end.

The path arrives at an overhanging section quite near the left end of the crag. There are three routes left of here, then the left descent route. Left of here the crag peters out. The first climb starts from the descent route.

Terminal Groove   6m   HVS 4c
A clean slabby groove is an obvious feature (Sunset Slab). Climb the wall left of the groove until possible to move right to the base of a short slim groove which is climbed to the top. Not technically hard, but a bad landing.

Sunset Slab   8m   Severe 4a
Climb the clean slabby groove starting from boulders.

Slab Climb   9m   Very Difficult *
Immediately to the right is a large slab. Start on the left and take a diagonal line rightwards. Poorly protected.

Next is the overhanging section of the crag, where the path arrives. It is severely undercut at the base and provides a number of steep hard routes. The traverse of this section, keeping very close to the ground, is 5c in either direction. The following two routes are usually climbed as boulder problems, descending from the ledge. The top-out looks overgrown.

Yankee Groove   10m   5c
Start beneath the large overhang at the left end of the overhanging section, beneath a sloping clean-cut ledge. A gymnastic move over the overhang leads to the ledge. Step right and climb an easier black lichenous groove.
Variation: Gain access to the ledge from the left (5a).

Clare   10m   5c
Spectacular, technically hard and strenuous but somewhat artificial. Start 1m left of the groove through the overhanging section. Climb straight up to reach a good sidepull, then a good hold at 5m. Hand traverse left along a distinct break, then move up (junction with Yankee Groove) and right to a heathery ledge to finish up.

Walkers Climb   10m   VS 5a *
The fairly obvious groove in the overhanging section, with some loose blocks marking the start. Climb past the blocks, then move right for a short way until it is possible to swing back left (well protected crux) and continue up the still awkward groove.

The impressive overhanging section now becomes vertical and goes round a slight corner opposite as pile of boulders. Directly above these is an obvious ledge at about 6m.

Defying Destiny   10m   E1 5b **
Start below and slightly right of the obvious ledge. Climb diagonally leftwards (bold crux) to the ledge. Step right and pull over an overhang on good holds (also tricky).

Anthrax   9m   VS 4c
Start 2m right of Defying Destiny and climb straight up. Reported as nice, but looks hard and unprotected.

Crack Climb   9m   Severe 4b
At the right-hand end of the steep section is this obvious crack twisting rightwards. The crux is at the start (needs big gear). Frequently started up a small corner and slab to the right (easier).

Shilling Corner   12m   Hard Severe 4b ***
An obvious left-leaning corner gives an excellent well protected climb. Climb the corner, then the left rib to pass the final overhang (crux).

Easy Slab   Difficult
An obvious slab round the corner on the right.

Mary Greaser Crack   12m   VS 5a *
The very steep wall overlooking Easy Slab seems not to have been attempted. This takes the left-leaning crack forming the right edge of the impressive wall. Start at an arrow and climb the crack direct.

Heart of Darkness   6m   E1 5c
Three metres right of Mary Greaser Crack is a very imposing short wall, slightly undercut at its base. Climb the wall with difficulty to an obvious pocket. Use this to make a wild finish. Strenuous and sustained, possibly unprotected. **Maurice's Variation** escapes right after 3m (HVS 5b).

Groove and Prow Climb   12m   VS
Start just right of Heart of Darkness.
1. 6m 4c Climb diagonally right to a block, step left into a faint groove and go up to a ledge.
2. 6m 4b Go down right and step off a boulder on to the steep buttress and climb it first on the left, then on the right.

Continuing rightwards underneath the crag, one comes to an imposing and often wet chimney-crack (Severe). Immediately right of this the crag becomes very steep again and undercut at the base with trees close. The left arete of this overhanging section has a very faint short groove (5b).

Separate Reality   8m   HVS 5b
Start just right of the left-hand arete and climb the discontinuous crack and wall, stepping right to finish at a useful bush. A tree now interferes with the route. There are good problems and traverses in this area if you can avoid the tree.

Overhanging Crack   8m   VS 5a
Start 2m right of Separate Reality and climb the crack direct.

Sorrow   8m   5b
Round the corner on the right, the crag forms an impressive slabby wall. This route climbs the left end of the wall. Start below a little ledge at 3m and directly beneath a projecting nose of rock at 6m. Gain the ledge, then step left and up (crux, unprotected).

Maurice's Slab   9m   HVS 5a *
Start 3m right of Sorrow. Climb up the centre of the slab (crux) to a ledge and continue straight up the crack above. An excellent climb but the hard climbing is unprotected.

Corner Climb   9m   Severe 4a
The big corner right of Maurice's Slab is protectable.

Narrow Buttress   9m   5b
Climb the very narrow buttress between Corner Climb and Flake Climb, without using either crack.

Flake Climb   9m   Very Difficult
The obvious flake-crack 1m right of Corner Climb is protectable.

DUNCRAIG - CREAG AN DUISILG 79

Capitalist Pig   6m   5b
Climb the wall direct immediately right of Flake Climb.

Overhanging Groove   8m   Severe 4a
The obvious groove right of Capitalist Pig; climb it and exit right. The right arete of Overhanging Groove can be climbed at 5a. The next corner right provides an interesting jamming exercise and the next buttress right is also good (both Severe 4a). The crag now decreases to 5m high and shortly one comes to the right-hand descent route by a small tree.

DUNCRAIG - CREAG AN DUISILG

(NG 836 336)   Alt 200m   North-North-West facing   Map p40
Duncraig (named on the 1:50000 map as Creag an Duilisg) is situated across the bay from Plockton. Its upper crag is terrain adventure, steep and exciting, in places loose and vegetated, but also with fine features and solid rock. The stars are subjective, as there have been few visitors, but there is some good climbing. There is also a lower roadside crag which offers an alternative with a mixture of old sport climbs and one pitch traditional.

Approach: Duncraig can be reached by a minor road leading west from the A890, Kyle of Lochalsh to Lochcarron road, through Achmore towards Plockton.

The easiest approach to the upper crag when the bracken is short (spring) is from Fearnaig Cottage to the east (NG 846 336), where there is parking space for two or three vehicles. By climbing the brackened slopes diagonally right up and over an obvious knoll, a broad terrace is gained which runs below the crags for 600m to a deep gully. The left end of the upper crag can also be reached directly from the west side of the lower crag from a marked parking place, by trending left up a small stream line until the knoll is visible on the left and the crag above. This is rough but preferable in summer (as against spring) when the bracken on the Fearnaig Cottage approach is deep. The cliff base rises gently along this traverse and maintain this line, even when the cliff temporarily disappears into steep heathery ground. It is easy at one point to be conned into descending and end up traversing under a lower tier of cliff. But if this happens (or you are unsure), keep traversing until a step and easy slope leads up right to directly under the main crag, 30mins. The lower crag is very close to the marked parking place, 30 seconds.

Descent: Generally by abseil from the many birch and rowan trees at the top of the routes. See the Main Crag for details of its descent.

Just beyond the knoll, a vile and grossly overhanging section of crag is passed, the Left Wing. This peters out into a broken and slimy tier of crag, but 300m further along the terrace a more compact and continuous section of cliff is reached, first a black streaked section of wall, the Black Walls, then an impressive slim wall with a square-cut overhang and ivy at its base, the Animal Farm Wall. Beyond is a shorter overhanging section with a big terrace at one-third height, then a fine white lichened wall, the 007 Wall, a tree filled bay and a large verdantly vegetated ramp which gives access to a much higher section of cliff some 100m high. Right of this ramp is another steep 35m wall, the Brigadier's Redoubt, then a diagonal stone shoot. The terrace can be followed for another 150m to a big gully, beyond which it peters out. The Western Cliff is beyond the end of the terrace but approached from below.

Despite the prevailing vegetation, the quality of some routes is considerable, and the situation and beauty of the crag are exceptional. The rock is a horizontally bedded schist, but with a variable amount of metamorphosis from shale, so that in places it is solid with plenty of flat holds but in others is loose and particularly prone to horizontally stacked flakes. The crag doesn't get any sunshine until mid-afternoon even in mid-summer, and takes a few days to dry out after a really wet spell. The main crag does not take much drainage, but any wetness makes the rock very slippery. Once dry the rock will not be affected by light rain or showers

DUNCRAIG - CREAG AN DUISILG

because of its steepness and horizontal stratum. The midge rating is extreme! All of the new routes required gardening, but only the hardest were gardened on abseil.

LEFT WING

Bungle in the Jungle   50m   E2 5b   (1996)
At the left end of this section, just left of a big bay festooned with trees, is a bulging grey wall. Gain the ledge below the wall, move slimily right to the left edge of the big bay, then climb up left on to the wall and up to a sloping break. Go right along the break for 5m and up a flake-crack on to a long narrow ledge (possible belay here). From 3m along the ledge climb a bulge on big pockets then move right and finish into the trees. Abseil off. Can only improve with traffic!

THE BLACK WALLS

Crocodile Shoes   40m   E2 5b ***   (1996)
At the right hand end of this section, just right of the area of black rock, is a steeper tower with a ledge at one-quarter height. Climb on to the ledge, then up the face of the tower, moving right through bulges to a finishing slab (tree belay).

ANIMAL FARM WALL

This lies 8m right of Crocodile Shoes and is easily identified by the block overhang at one third height with ivy beneath it. The wall is steep and imposing and bounded on the left by a tree filled corner-line.

My Sex Romp with Llama Sid   40m   E5 6a/b ***   (1996)
Climb the left-bounding corner for 8m to a holly, then follow the seams and thin cracks directly up the wall of black rock on the right (sustained, Friend 0.5 useful). Finish up right to trees or, better, go slightly left through final bulges of sooty rock.

Seals Guaranteed or your Money Back   40m   E2 5c ***   (1996)
Start at a tree just left of the square-cut roof. Pull up into the bay beneath the roof, then make thin moves left and up alongside the overhang and a delicate crux step on to a hold on the lip. Follow a good break up right, go up the side of a flake then back left and finish up a massive flake in the final wall. A good route, probably at the top end of its grade.

Hamish Quick-Death   30m   E4 5c ***   (1996)
Right of the Animal Farm Wall there is a shorter wall with a terrace at 8m. In the centre of this is an obvious bulging crack. Climb this to a gripping finish; prior arrangement of a rope loop from the top is recommended to avoid an exit on vertical heather.

Between Animal Farm Wall and The 007 Wall is a line of three consecutive corners stepping left and with oak trees on each of the two steps. This is the line of Lonesome Traveller, which then continues to the top of the cliff.

Lonesome Traveller   85m   HVS ***   (1971)
A well protected route with some strenuous moves.
1. 40m 4c Climb the arete just left of the initial corner to the first oak, up the second corner to the second oak, then the third corner to heather. Go left and back right to a wooded terrace and belay at a 1m flake lying against the upper wall.
2. 30m 5b Starting from the left end of the flake (about 10m left of the second pitch of The Three Legged Race), climb a flake-crack leading to a ledge at 10m. Continue up the groove above to a prominent capping brown roof. Climb over this and up a short crack before swinging left to a small ledge. Go up and slightly right

to belay.
3. 15m 4c Trend rightwards to tree belays and an abseil descent.

007 WALL

The next obvious feature is a fine white wall with an overhang split by a groove at its top. The two routes are cross diagonals, described as such for consistency of grade, finishing on the wooded terrace just left of the main section of crag.

Jim Kerr Knew my Father   35m   E2 5b ** *(1980s/1996)*
Start up the corner on the left (the first of the three consecutive corners mentioned above), then break out steeply up cracks in the wall. Traverse right at two-thirds height and pull through the roof into the obvious groove to finish (JK may have done this in the 1980s).

James Bond is Alive and Well and Living in Plockton   35m   E4 6a * *(1996)*
Start towards the right-hand side of the wall at a blunt rib. Go up the rib trending left (runners out right), then utilise hidden slots to climb the bulging wall above (just left of a roof), mantelshelfing on to a small ledge to easier ground. Move left, crossing Jim Kerr Knew my Father, and go up into a niche below a bulging roof. Swing strenuously over this and exit left to the terrace.

MAIN CRAG

The highest section of crag. The rock is generally good with square-cut holds providing steep exciting climbing but the ledges are very vegetated. This is much quicker to dry than the walls on the approach but there can be seepage from the jungle above.
  The Main Crag has two big left-slanting corners high up (Shenavall and Easy Rider) with smaller direct corners either side (Cypress Avenue on the left and Can of Worms on the right). The best view of the Main Crag is from a little further along the cliff base (or further below).

Descent From all routes finishing at the top of the Main Crag, the easiest descent is to abseil off trees down the left-hand side (looking up) to the wooded terrace, and then down the Animal Farm Wall to the base of the cliff. Go to the biggest rowan tree near the top end of a cliff-top fence. Scramble easily down right, then left (looking down) to more rowan trees directly below. Make a 25m abseil from the biggest of these (sling and krab in-situ) to the 'wooded terrace'. Walk left to a tree near its end (sling) and a 35m abseil.
  Right of the 007 Wall is a small black mossy bay with a tree 1m up the rock and below the leftmost corner in the upper section of the crag. The left arete of the bay holds the start of the following route.

The Three Legged Race   80m   HVS * *(1971)*
Climbs the hanging arete which is formed between the 007 Wall and the small bay (which is Cypress Avenue). A scary start (which can be avoided by starting 5m to the right and traversing left to the top of the groove) leads to exposed climbing on good holds. Start at a small groove on the crest (scratched arrow at head height).
1. 35m 5a Climb the groove (crux), then trend left as soon as possible to the arete and up cracks and blocks to the wooded terrace.
2. 45m 4c Climb up zigzag ramps, initially vegetated, to a prominent roof above. Traverse out left and return right above the roof to climb a corner on the right, passing over a small overhang to a heather ledge. Finish up the wall above to reach a terrace and tree belay (abseil descent).

Cypress Avenue Direct   80m   E1 ** *(1971/1996)*
Starts at the small bay and tree, finishing up the leftmost corner in the upper crag. The original pitch 1 climbed a big vegetated corner up left to the wooded terrace,

82 | DUNCRAIG - CREAG AN DUISILG

then went back right to a lichened wall. This version climbs a shallow curving groove with small stepped overhangs in the lower headwall as a direct pitch 1 to gain the upper corner direct.

1. 40m 5a From the top of the bay, ascend the curving groove to a ledge, then up a delicate lichenous wall to gain a ledge at the foot of the main groove.

2. 20m 5a Climb the corner groove to a wide crack and belay behind a detached monolith.

3. 20m 4c Go left and up a steep wall and corner, finishing on good holds. Belays are 20m further at the top of the crag.

To the right of Cypress Avenue is a steep ramp of luscious vegetation.

Chanter   110m   Scottish VS   (1971)

Chanter crosses Shenavall from the left to gain a short but obvious overhanging chimney corner in the hairy rib between the big corners of Shenavall and Easy Rider, then aids up the final overhanging tier. Unrepeated. Start up a corner at the base of the vegetated ramp.

1. 40m Go up behind a large flake and out right steeply to a ledge followed by a short wall and groove. Climb through the grass above to a good stance.

2. 25m Climb the groove line to the right of the belay to a tree; continue right and over another overhang to a tree. Go up and right over blocks to the foot of the corner on Shenavall.

3. 25m A short way up the corner, hand traverse right to the foot of an overhanging corner-chimney, climbed to a large block.

4. 20m   Directly above is an overhanging corner (4PA). Escape left under overhangs and up blocks.

Shenavall   80m   HVS *   (1971)

Takes the left-hand big corner, the one with the most prominent cracks and leading to the detached monolith common with Cypress Avenue. Unfortunately, this line can only be accessed by scrambling up the ramp and, due to the fragile and possibly precious vegetation here, the start is not recommended. Since Chanter starts from the bottom of the ramp it offers an environmentally more friendly start to Shenavall. Otherwise, start up the vegetated ramp for about 25m, then climb up blocks to the left to belay by a large flake.

1. 20m 4c Go up a crack above the flake to a recess below an overhang. Go strenuously up the wall above to a large block strewn ledge.

2. 20m 5b Climb the impressive corner-crack to the ledge with the monolith.

3. 40m 4c Go up and right to climb a corner below a triangular overhang (20m). Belay in a further 20m.

Easy Rider   55m   HVS   (1971)

Climbs the right-hand big corner, almost a ramp. Start at the top of the ramp beneath the overhangs at the top of the crag. This is best accessed by climbing It Ne'er Rains but it Pours (see below), and traversing across the top of the ramp (rather than climbing the ramp).

1. 25m 5a Traverse left to the bottom of a steep left-slanting corner-crack and climb it.

2. 10m 5a Climb the short hairy wall to the left (strenuous).

3. 20m 4c Go up and left to join the last pitch of Shenavall.

The impressively overhanging headwall of the Main Crag has a right diagonal break sandwiched between roofs which is best gained by climbing a route on the Brigadier's Redoubt and the first pitch of Easy Rider.

The Hanging Traverse of Babylon   40m   E4 6a *   (1996)

From the finely poised stance at the top of the corner climb the 'hairy' wall on the left and pull out on to the ledge, as for Easy Rider.Go straight up the brown wall above to gain a break, which leads rightwards into a corner directly above the belay. Move out along the top of a hanging flake, then swing across the impending wall and follow the fault for 5m to a break in the final overhangs. Pull through this to the top. An impressive pitch.

Can of Worms   50m   E1 *   *(1971)*
An unusually exposed route for its grade. Based on the rightmost corner, starting from the top of the vegetated ramp 5m right of Easy Rider but diverging rightwards. Reach the start as for Easy Rider.
1. 20m 5a Climb a corner and traverse left to a ledge in the main corner-line. Go up the steep corner until below a roof. Go out left to a hanging slab which is climbed to an airy grass ledge.
2. 30m 5b Continue up the corner, initially awkward, then the slab on its right to rejoin the corner. Move out right on to its arete to avoid the last bulge and gain ledges above. Climb walls on the left to the top.

THE BRIGADIER'S REDOUBT

This is the wall to the right of the vegetated ramp which terminates in a diagonal stone shoot. The routes here are worthwhile in themselves, but are equally useful for getting to the top section of the Main Crag.

Brigadier Braggart's Little Secret   35m   E3 5c   *(1996)*
Takes the central line. Pull through a flake overhang at the right-hand end of the wall, then traverse left until below a hanging groove. Go up this to a roof (peg runner), and then launch out left with conviction to gain a ledge. Step left, then go straight up with continuous interest to finish at a tree belay.

The Queen's Garden Party   30m   E2 5b   *(1996)*
Start as for Brigadier Braggart. Pull through the roof, then go up the arete on the right edge of the wall to gain big sloping ledges out right. Finish up the corner above and go left at the top to tree belays.

It Ne'er Rains but it Pours   35m   VS 4c *   *(1996)*
A good approach or warm up for the upper Main Crag. Originally climbed during a deluge. Start 10m up the diagonal stone shoot and step out left onto the face. Go up a short corner to roofs, then traverse left to sloping ledges and finish up the corner above, as for The Queen's Garden Party.

Trundle   60m   VS   *(1971)*
A disappointing route with easier vegetated ground always to the left. To the right of the Main Crag and Brigadier's Redoubt is a diagonal stone shoot, which gives access to the upper section of cliff containing Trundle. The shoot has loose blocks but the underlying rock is water washed and clean. It is reasonable for ascent (when dry) but unpleasant for the descent. Ascend the shoot for about 60m to start at the bottom right corner of a large square block slab on the left-bounding wall of the shoot.
1. 25m 4c Traverse left for 10m along grassy ledges to the groove bounding the left edge of the slab. Climb the groove for 3m, then step right and climb the left edge of the slab to overhangs on the left (or climb the groove, easier but vegetated).
2. 35m 4c Go left through a break in the overhangs and immediately return right to weave a line through steep blocky ground generally trending right to the top.

A new section of cliff begins 60m further right of the shoot at an impressive overhanging arete. The routes here are single pitch and lack the convenience of tree belays at their tops, but give a variety of grades on quick drying rock. Two routes from 1971, Very Difficult and Severe, may have been on this section of cliff but can not been identified.

84 | DUNCRAIG - CREAG AN DUISILG

Roseroot Ramp   40m   Severe 4a   *(1997)*
The obvious left-slanting ramp in the centre of the crag. Climb the centre, enjoying the clean shield of rock in the middle. Exit left on thick heather to birch belays. Abseil from large rowans 15m left of the top.

Plockton Plonkers   40m   Severe 4a   *(1997)*
Start 15m right of Roseroot Ramp at the right end of the sector. Climb a clean curving crack into a corner system. Exit left and climb a short corner to the top. Peg belay and abseil point in-situ 5m higher.

Miracle of the May Midge   30m   E1 5b   *(1997)*
A clean wall with cracked blocks at its foot lies 8m left of Plockton Plonkers. Climb up to the right of the blocks and go delicately up the wall to a ledge. Take the centre of the impending wall of brown rock above, following a vague crack-line, to finish at a higher terrace (the peg abseil of Plockton Plonkers is 10m higher).

WESTERN CLIFF

Five hundred metres west of the Main Crag, well beyond the prominent gully which cuts the centre of the crags, is a prow of beetling green overhangs. Some 80m high, well coated by the sea lichen or dulse which gives these crags their name, and defended by vertiginous vegetation this crag looks as impressive as it is repulsive.

Approach: This sector is best approached from a good lay-by at NG 832 335 from which a 20mins struggle through birch woods leads to the base.

Descent: Best to the west of the crag via a stony gully and steep heather slopes. Peregrine falcons were seen preparing to nest here, so the crag is best avoided during the May to August nesting season. The following route climbs directly up the prow. Stars are unknown.

King Prawn Deathwish   115m   E3 5c   *(1997)*
A route of unusual character and considerable excitement, a real Plockton special! Start just left of the prow at a blunt rib with a tree at 6m.
1. 20m 4c Climb the rib past two trees to a long vegetated ledge.
2. 25m 5a Go 3m up a wide crack on the right, then move awkwardly left and up to a cleaned ramp. Follow this for 15m up under roofs, where it peters out at a vegetated break. Pull round right and go straight up a wall to a tiny ledge directly below a groove cutting the main roofs of the prow (peg belay in-situ).
3. 20m 5c The route now bears its teeth. Climb the groove above the stance through bulges for 15m. Committing moves right gain a ledge with precarious stacked blocks. Climb through the bulging wall above to a fine stance beneath the capping roof (peg and Friend belay).
4. 15m 5b Hand traverse left 3m and pull on to a ramp. Go back right and swing across the lip of the roofs on good holds to ledges. Belay 4m right on another ledge with a view.
5. 35m 4c Go slightly left, then up heathery grooves and flake-cracks to the top.

No Stars No Moon No Nothing   150m   E4   *(1998)*
Features the fine hanging corner at the right-hand side of the crag. More direct variations look possible, particularly a more direct finish up a fine groove line starting at the base of the grassy ramp. Start at a flake-crack at the lowest point in the buttress.
1. 20m 5b Climb the flake-crack to a ledge (peg runner). Step left and go up a steep wall to below a roof.
2. 25m 5a Traverse right under the roof passing a peg runner, step down and then go diagonally right up a fault to the base of the corner. Traverse 6m left to a ledge with a two peg belay.
3. 35m 6a Step back into the corner and go up this passing a peg to a small niche

(peg). The overlap above is the crux. Exit up the left wall to a grassy alcove.
4. 45m 4c Step up left to gain a grassy ramp. Go up this to a short vertical crack down and left of a large flake.
5. 25m 5a Go up the flake (Friend 4) to its end. Hand traverse left and mantelshelf on to a ledge. Continue to the left arete and go up this (peg) to grassy bays.

LOWER CRAG

(NG 838 338)   Alt 30m   North facing

The lower and roadside crag. Hang Over and Levitation have no bolt runners.

Hang Over   20m   E2 5b *(1989)*
At the left end of the crag is a cave, with a fire place. Down to the right is a flat wall with an arete at its right end. Follow the arete to an overhang which is turned on the right.

Long Reach   20m   E2 5b *(1989)*
The prominent slab to the right of Hang Over. Start in the corner. Move right, passing a bolt, to reach the right end of the overhang. Step left and pull through the overhang passing a further bolt. Continue up to a bulge, then traverse left.

Gordon's Route   25m   E3 6a *(1989)*
Climb directly up the wall to the right of Long Reach. Pull through the overhang and climb cracks trending right. The top bulge is turned first right then left to reach a tiny corner.

Pine Martin   25m   F7a/b *(1989)*
Right of centre of the crag are large overhangs. Two bolt lines take direct lines through the overhangs. This is the left line. The upper overhang is the crux.

Wild at Heart   25m   F7a/b *(1989)*
The right-hand line of bolts taking the overhangs directly, the upper one being the crux. Joins Pine Martin for the last 5m.

Levitation   60m   E3 5c *(1989)*
A rising traverse from left to right. Start at and follow the prominent rising crack come fault to the right of Long Reach. Two pitches; the second has a 6m section providing a strenuous but protected crux. Finish at the top right-hand corner of the crag, after passing Wild at Heart.

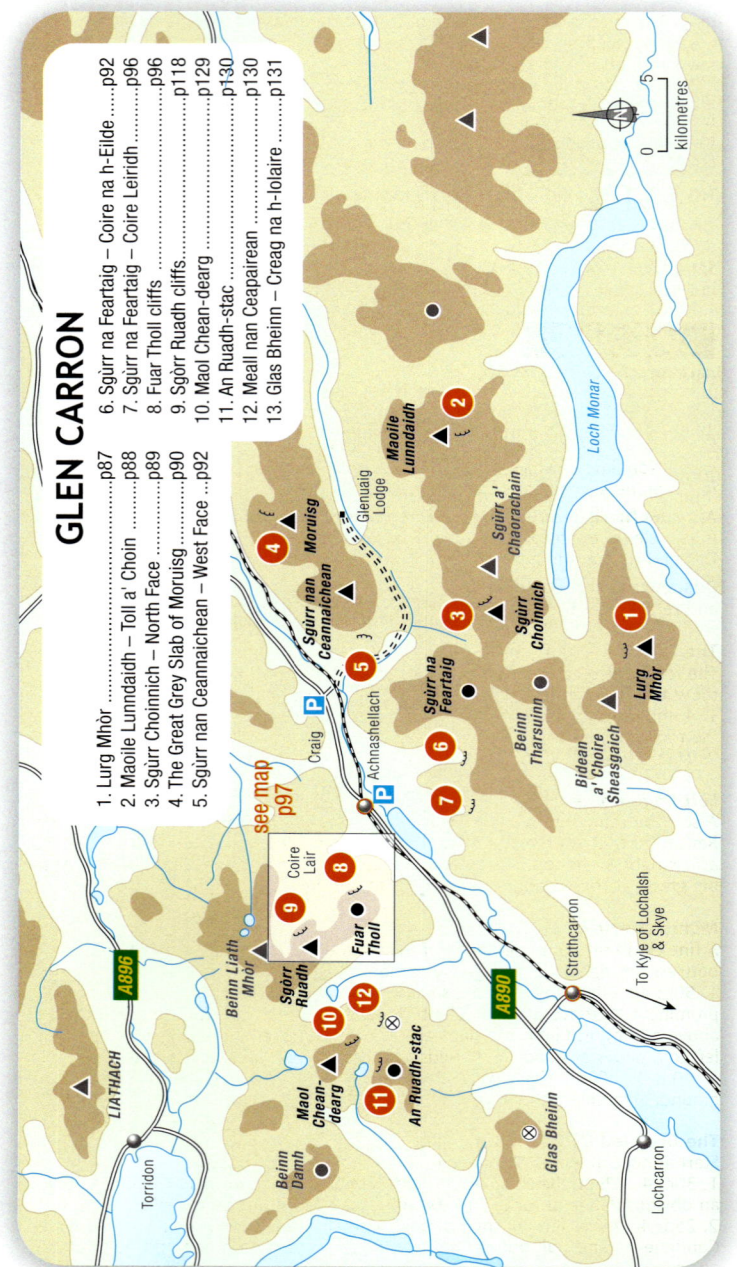

GLEN CARRON

This is the next valley system south of Torridon and a major geological fault, with older Torridonian sandstone and Cambrian quartzite to the north and largely Moine rocks to the south. The valley stretches from the sea loch, Loch Carron up towards the major junction of roads at Achnasheen. Much less popular than the famous cliffs of Torridon, there are still some big steep cliffs on its north side and some hidden gems to the south.

The cliffs described in this section are normally approached from Glen Carron. First are five cliffs to the south, a mixture of summer and winter routes and on different rock types. Next the big sandstone cliffs of the very craggy Fuar Tholl and Sgòrr Ruadh further up Coire Lair. And finally some smaller cliffs on the north side but nearer the coast.

LURG MHÒR

(NH 062 405)   Alt 790m   North facing   Map p86

The mountains surrounding the head of Loch Monar are remote and have seen little climbing development. But a large crag of excellent rough and clean quartzite lies high on the flank of Lurg Mhòr, above Loch Monar. The climbing has an expedition flavour which may involve an isolated camp; there are excellent pitches for camping at the head of Loch Monar.

Approach: There are a number of options. The most feasible one for a day visit is to cycle up the track south-east from Craig, then walk to the Bealach Bhearnais. Descend to near the head of Loch Monar, then go up to the base of the crag.

Descent: To the west of the crag. But the aesthetic (and fit) may climb with sacks and return over Bidean a' Choire Sheasgaich and Beinn Tharsuinn.

The Far Side   60m   Severe *(1993)*
The route lies on a clean area of slabs some 200m east of, and slightly lower than, the start of Munroist's Reward. Start at the lowest point of the slabs.
1. 45m Climb directly up aiming for a notch to the left of the steep upper wall at the top. Belay below this wall.
2. 15m Climb the wall by any of a choice of unappetising lines to the top.

Left Edge Route   90m   Severe 4a *(1993)*
A scrappy route, not as good as it looks from below. Start just left of Munroist's Reward and climb the big inset slab with thin cracks to its top left corner. Pull across right to the top of a short arete. Climb a narrow rib close on the left of the big grassy corner to a more broken finish out right.

**Munroist's Reward   90m   VS ** *(1988)*
A fine climb taking the left edge of the main slabs. Start at the lowest point of the buttress 5m right of a long grassy corner.
1. 50m 4c Climb the slab with a small steepening, then move right to the foot of a prominent V-groove at 10m. Climb the wall to the right (crux) to reach the slab above and right. Climb the slabs and two further overlaps above, moving slightly left to a pedestal stance on the edge of the buttress. An excellent pitch.
2. 40m 4b Climb the groove above, then the exposed wall to its left to easier ground. Scramble to the top.

The Dreaded Lurgi   125m   VS * *(1995)*
Start about 5m left of Monar Magic at a distinctively red slab.
1. 30m 4c Climb the slab, which slants left, and cross two small overlaps to below an obvious flange of rock which protrudes out from the main overlap.
2. 25m 4c Move left and pull through a small overlap until level with the flange. Continue up and pull out right above the flange. Go up a slab and pull out right again.

MAOILE LUNNDAIDH

3. 30m 4b Move left and climb a clean raised slab.
4. 40m Easier slabs, blocks and vegetation leads to the top.

**Monar Magic   140m   VS ** *(1988)*
This excellent climb takes a direct line up the centre of the slabs. Start just left of a fault which slants from left to right (most easily seen from below) near the middle of the crag. There is a shallow inverted U shaped overlap just to the right of the start at the foot of the crag.
1. 45m 4b Climb straight up slabs, then thin cracks to the right of a grassy corner to a slight steepening at 30m. Move up then diagonally left to a tiny ledge in a short open corner. A poorly protected pitch.
2. 20m 4c Climb straight up to an obvious V-niche in the main overlap. Climb this on good holds, then the slab above to belay in a small overhung niche.
3. 45m 4c Move up and right into a corner in the next overlap. Swing out onto the right arete then climb directly up the slabs.
4. 30m 4a Pleasant slabs above lead to the top.

MAOILE LUNNDAIDH
(NH 135 458)   Alt 1007m   Map p86

This flat topped mountain has the big corrie of Toll a' Choin to its south.

TOLL A' CHOIN
(NH 135 449)   Alt 800m   North-East facing

The left wall of the corrie is steep and vegetated, with an impressive steep buttress of overlapping smooth slabs.

FB Gully   100m   IV,4 *(2003)*
The fine narrow gully defining the left side of the steep buttress. It provided around 80m of continuous water ice in perfect conditions.

**Hellfire and Brimstone   110m   VII,7 ** *(2003)*
The steep buttress has two obvious gully lines at its left end. This route starts at the base of the right-hand gully and trends up slightly right before tackling the bulging headwall direct. It provides unlikely and often strenuous climbing on good hooks, torques and turf.
1. 45m From the base of the gully, traverse right into a steep groove and climb this to gain easier ground (similar start to Spiral Search). Continue in the same line then pull on to an obvious right-slanting hanging ramp. Belay at its right end below a very steep groove with a crack in its right wall.
2. 15m Climb the groove to its apex, then make hard moves out right into another groove that leads to a commodious belay in a recess.
3. 50m Exit the recess via a flared chimney on the left then continue up an overhanging groove to below a roof. Pull leftwards through the roof and continue up more or less directly with diminishing difficulty to the top.

Spiral Search   120m   IV,5 * *(2000)*
A diagonal line of weakness across the steep buttress. Start at the bottom left corner of the buttress and trend right, generally with awkward moves up and easy moves right. On the first ascent there was some ice and the crux, gaining a slab above a short wall to reach an easy ramp on pitch 2 probably requires some.

The Shiner   80m   III,4 *(2003)*
This takes the wider and less steep icy scoop defining the right side of the Spiral Search buttress. A fine if short climb on more or less continuous water ice.

Mica Ridge   100m   II *(2000)*
It follows the left-hand of two definite ridges (the right being shorter) well to the

SGÙRR CHOINNICH

Munroist's Reward, VS, Lurg Mhòr

right of the steep wall and at the top end of the cliff. It has a slabby crest and vegetated grooves just to its right. The summer route stays more on the crest (Difficult 1954) while the winter route is more often in the grooves. The first summer ascent had a snow comb and a big cornice to lend atmosphere.

SGÙRR CHOINNICH

(NH 076 446)   Alt 999m   Map p86

A shapely, more accessible mountain.

NORTH FACE

(NH 076 446)   Alt 800m   North facing

The crag is often in condition. The rock is a variety of rather demoralised schist that lends itself to form tottering crannies and rather unreliable protection. All this is irrelevant if properly frozen and the turf is excellent. There are five right-slanting gully-lines on the face.

Occluded Ridge   150m   II   *(2003)*
Start up and right of the long toe at the left-hand end of the main face. From the back of the bay, climb turf up and left into the left-hand of the twin gullies above. Climb two tricky steps then continue up easier ground, moving into the right-hand gully below the top.

**Stirling Moss   250m   III **   *(2003)*
This takes the discontinuous hanging ramp directly below the summit (leftmost gully). A fine line with much variety. Start 40m left of the easier angled curved ramp-line that is the most obvious line on the cliff. The discontinuous ramp is

bottomed by mixed ground and ice with a straight snow section which is prominent from below.
1. 50m Climb up to and past the snow section to a little cave.
2. 55m Step left on to thin ice that leads to tricky rock and turf steps which lead to the hidden ramp above (possible belay). Continue up snow to a shelf on the right.
3. 50m Climb pleasant snow and ice steps up the ramp to a tiny cave below a steep iced corner.
4. 45m Climb the fine corner either by ice or turf and continue straight up the ramp to below the steep headwall up on the right.
5. 50m Step right, then move back left and climb past a rockfall scar with some difficulty. Continue straight up steep walls and little ledges to finally traverse left to below a jutting block. Climb past this and up snow to the summit cairn. A complex pitch with some dubious rock.

**Chemical Alley   140m   IV,4 ** *(2003)*
The second from the right of the five gully-lines. It has a steep middle pitch.

The buttress between Chemical Alley and The Bow, starting just up and right of the base at a steep left-slanting groove is 100m II (2003).

The Bow   100m   II * *(2003)*
Climb the long right-facing corner at the right-hand end of the main face. It offered an excellent 50m pitch of continuous ice on this occasion.

Downhill Racer   150m   II * *(2003)*
This is a Y shaped and rightmost gully. On this occasion it was descended on perfect neve coated with a thin layer of water ice and was quite steep and had a little ice pitch near the narrows at its base. The gully also has a left-hand exit which looks a similar grade.

MORUISG

(NH 101 499)   Alt 928m

This extensive but rounded mountain offers some climbing.

COIRE NAM MANG - THE GREAT GREY SLAB OF MORUISG

(NH 103 508)   Alt 750m   East facing   Map p86

A large low angled grey schistose slab lies above Loch Cnoc na Mointeich. The slab is remarkably smooth and undulating, offering some unusual friction climbing. A remarkable property about the rock is the friction which is relatively unaffected in the wet owing to a lack of lichen. It is perfectly possible to ascend the easier routes in the rain with little change in grade. The rock is very clean but protection is almost entirely lacking. A light rack including small Friends and small Rocks and one rope will suffice. The routes are not sustained and, taken in the right spirit, the complete set can be climbed in an exhilarating day. Due to its low angle it receives the sun until mid-afternoon and dries quickly.

Approach: The slab is well seen when driving from Achnasheen along the A890. Park at a turn off close to the east end of Loch Sgamhain (NH 107 533). Go under the railway at the first stream to the south-east and follow the west bank of the stream until a rising traverse above the loch leads to the slab, 1hr 30mins.

Descent: Down smooth (slippery) grass at the north end of the slab.

The slab is 120m high on the easier angled right to about 90m on the left near a grassy corner. Above this corner lie further corners and inset slabs, diminishing in height leftwards. The routes are open to variation; choose the smoothest line you

GREAT GREY SLAB OF MORUISG 91

dare. Routes are described right to left.

Disposable Slab   100m   Moderate   (1996)
Climbs a smaller slab right of a dirty groove which defines the right edge of the main slab, starting above broken rocks. Follow the best line just left of the edge.

Close to the Edge   120m   Difficult *   (1996)
Follows the right edge of the main slab, left of the dirty groove which cuts up the slab left of Disposable Slab. A pleasant excursion with some easy friction, but almost no protection. Start 10m left of a large flake above the broken rocks and climb a slab rightwards to gain the edge overlooking the groove. Follow the edge all the way to a terrace. Move left to a clean slab between two corners. Climb this and its narrower continuation to the top.
Variation: **Very Difficult**
From the terrace, move further left to the arete left of the left corner and either follow this, or easier, up a crack to step back right to the edge at a dirty chimney-crack (good flake belays). Step right to finish up the narrower slab between the corners.

Rock Surfer   95m   VS *   (1999)
Moving about 30m diagonally left up the rake below the main slab, there is a horizontal ledge at the base of the slab and below a right-rising overlap with an A shaped notch cut out. Start here.
1. 45m 4c Climb up to the notch on friction (crux) and through it to continue up the slab to a terrace and belay by Close to the Edge.
2. 50m 4b Climb the initially easy slab left of that route to the steeper top section. Climb straight up to the shallow corner right of the more obvious double overlapped corner of The President's Men and finish up this on better holds.

Slapstick   95m   HVS *   (2002)
A direct line up the blankest slab available. Start from the ledge at the base of the right-rising overlap.
1. 45m 4c Climb up, then go diagonally right above the overlap along a line of quartz before going straight up the smooth slab left of Rock Surfer to the terrace. A very direct line can be climbed if dry, using a runner to the right.
2. 50m 4c Climb the easy slab as for Rock Surfer, but then continue direct up the blank slab right of the corner and between two grassy cracks.

The President's Men   90m   VS *   (1996)
Above the left end of the horizontal ledge is a higher ledge below some overlaps. Start from the left end of this higher ledge. Perhaps the best route here.
1. 50m 4c Climb to and up a slab with quartz dimples set between two overlaps. The climbing soon gets easier above the top overlap. Continue straight up to the terrace, then up the slab above to below a double overlapped right-trending corner.
3. 40m 4b Climb to the corner, then follow it up and right to finish through an overlap and better holds to the top.

Brittle Times   90m   HVS   (1999)
This route takes the slab to the right of the big grassy corner and left of The President's Men. Slight variations would make it a grade harder. Start from the left end of the higher ledge.
1. 20m 4c Climb a shallow corner between two smooth slabs, then move on to the right slab and go straight up to the terrace.
2. 45m 4a Climb the slab right of the big corner and just left of an overlapped edge to an easing and Friend belay in a slot above.
3. 25m 4c Climb the steeper slab mid-way between the big corner and the top pitch of The Presidents Men.

SGÙRR NA FEARTAIG

COIRE TOLL NAM BIAN

Low down at the east entrance of the corrie is a prominent buttress split by a gully (NH 090 501). **Short and Silly** (90m II/III 1978) the only climb recorded here done in several short pitches.

NORTH-WEST SLOPE

Moruisg Icefall   40m   V,6 * *(1995)*

The icefall is situated in a slot gully in the north-west facing slope of Moruisg at NH 095 505. The top section of the icefall can be seen from the road.

1. 15m   Climb steep ice to gain a cave stance on the left of the main fall (peg in situ).

2. 25m   Move right and slightly down from the stance to climb a vague scoop in the steep ice wall. Peg in situ on the right at the top.

On the second ascent, when water was flowing down the original line, a line about 6m right was taken and the climb done in one pitch. Same grade but perhaps less sustained. The iced corner some 10m further right has been climbed at Grade IV,4.

SGÙRR NAN CEANNAICHEAN

(NH 087 481)   Alt 915m   Map p86

A hill walking companion to Moruisg, but with an impressive face looking down Glen Carron.

WEST FACE

(NH 077 480)   Alt 350m   West facing

This prominent face has two big gullies, easily seen from down the valley.

White Heather Club   350m   IV,4 or 6   *(2001)*

Take the rambling buttress left of North Gully, aiming for the obvious open corner high on the face. A reasonable challenge with a thick snow cover and a good low freeze. Starting from the foot of North Gully the buttress on the left was gained on steep heather with awkward moves up a slanting groove. Climb the buttress for two pitches to easy ground. Zigzag up to the open book corner. Climb this in a big 50m pitch, exiting either to the right (technical 4) or more sportingly by a direct finish up an ice filled groove (technical 6). Easy scrambling leads to the top.

North Gully   420m   III,4   *(1987)*

Several interesting pitches lead to a huge chockstone, which has a remarkable through route. The exit window frames a superb panorama stretching from Liathach round to the Applecross peaks. The upper part of the gully is straight forward. Moderate in summer.

South Gully   400m   I

A big easy gully, the right-hand of the two on the face, sometimes with an ice pitch near the top.

SGÙRR NA FEARTAIG

(NH 054 454)   Alt 862m   Map p86

This Corbett on the south side of Glen Carron is well seen from across the glen from the better known climbing venue of Fuar Tholl and has recently become recognised as a fine waterfall ice climbing venue in cold weather. The reclusive Coire na h-Eilde is the jewel, although the more visible Coire Leiridh has a couple of routes.

The Stonker, IV,5, Sgùrr na Feartaig. Climber Martin Welch

COIRE NA H-EILDE

(NH 030 454)   Alt 450-550m   North facing   Map p86   Diagram p95

The head of the corrie has several waterfalls, even marked as such on the 1:50000 map. Very cold weather is required for a full freeze but it then offers a superb ice climbing venue.

Approach: There are two options with little difference in time (about 1hr 30mins). The first involves wading the river while the second requires a bike.
1. Approach by the stalkers' path up the east side of Coire Leiridh from Lair. The bridge at NH 011 482 no longer exists. The crossing is wide and shallow when the river is low (dry in Yeti gaiters) but impossible in spate.

94 SGÙRR NA FEARTAIG

2. Start from Craig and cycle upstream and downstream to the Allt Coire a' Bhainidh which is then followed via a stalkers' path into the corrie. The path starts as a narrow vehicle track which should be left at a wooden post when it heads away from the Allt (only 5mins extra if this turn is missed). The path is not in as good condition as the Coire Leiridh path but saves the descent into the corrie.

Descent: The Coire Leiridh path is easily found above the cliff. For a return to the cliff base and the Allt Coire a' Bhainidh path, there are two options.
1. Scramble down and abseil from a tree near the east end of the icefalls (just west of The Ice Channel).
2. Go to just east of the icefalls and walk steeply down, either just east of Wee Nipper or the next open gully to the east.

The biggest feature of the face is the main watercourse set in a gully (The Stonker). A wide steeper icefall to the left is more obvious, however, from the approach col and briefly visible from the A890 just east of Craig. Either side of the wide fall are thinner falls and leftmost of the set is an ice filled gully. Routes are described right to left.

1 The Wee Nipper   170m   II *(1996)*
In the centre of the broken ground right of the main falls is a less steep ice gully. Its crux is a steep pitch towards the top.

2 The Stonker   180m   IV,5 *** *(1996)*
The tremendous icefall that forms in the main stream bed right of the more visible icefalls. It drops into a small gorge so its full height is not immediately obvious. It gives four long ice pitches, continuous water ice between 50 and 70 degrees, finishing through some huge ice umbrellas (crux). The first pitch in the gorge may be reluctant to form, particularly after wetter weather, but one can traverse in.

3 The Topper   210m   V,5 ** *(1997)*
The icefall which forms on the left wall of The Stonker recess, gained by climbing the first pitch of The Stonker. Steeper and more sustained than The Stonker, with the fourth of five pitches the crux. The amount of ice is variable according to the amount of drainage during freezing (very little ice in Feb 1996, but a lot in 1997). Ice screw belays used throughout.

4 High Flier   110m   IV,4 ** *(1996)*
The thinner fall right of the wide fall (The Fast Lane). A low angled initial pitch may bank out (25m). The fall then steepened to below a crest (20m). This was climbed direct (technical 5), but the second ascent took its left side, less steep but more sustained (35m). Then an easier section, followed by a steep finish out left. Initially soloed, but ice screw belays used throughout on the second ascent.

5 The Fast Lane   90m   IV,4 ** *(1996)*
Very sustained but never vertical up a vague groove towards the right side of the wide fall. Ice screw runners will have to be placed on steep ground.

6 The Big Dipper   90m   V,5 * *(1996)*
Two consecutive pillars on the left side of the wide fall lead to a relatively easier middle section and a capping bulge (led in a 60m pitch). Easy angled to finish.

7 Aerial Runway   70m   III *(1996)*
Start at the same place as The Big Dipper but take a big left-slanting ramp below Damoclean icicles, passing behind the largest (40m). The ice peters out into stepped mixed ground, climbed up and out right.

8 Wee Dribble   70m   IV,5 *(1997)*
Start a few metres to the right of Running on Empty. Climb via a series of icicles draining down a vague groove to blocky ledges to the left of a huge recess (30m).

SGÙRR NA FEARTAIG
Coire na h-Eilde

2. The Stonker — IV,5 ***
3. The Topper — V,5 **
4. High Flier — IV,4 **
5. The Fast Lane — IV,4 **
6. The Big Dipper — V,5 *
7. Aerial Runway — III
8. Wee Dribble — IV,5
9. Running on Empty — III,4 *

FUAR THOLL

Climb over the blocks and short corners to easy ground, with one further short step to the top (40m).

9 Running on Empty   90m   III,4 * (1996)
The left-hand thinner fall has an impressively steep section low down which was passed by 70 degree ice on the left and a short bulge to gain a long easier angled finish.

10 The Ice Channel   80m   III * (1996)
This forms in a left-curving gully as the leftmost main ice line. A steep entry leads to a long runnel of ice.

About 200m left of the icefalls is a left-slanting deep gully with a big step. Left of here is a long face descending to a big north pointing spur.

11 In the Pink   150m   II (1996)
A shallow gully in the middle of the long face between the deep gully and the spur. The route lies at NH 035 453.

Immediately right of the spur are two easy scree gullies, then a buttress with another easy vegetated gully cutting back on to it. The following route starts close on the right of the latter easy gully and about 50m left of the previous route.

12 Willy Wonka   200m   III (1996)
Start up the narrow well defined gully, then follow its right-trending fork up steepening ice steps to a wide icefall. Take this direct to an easier left-trending gully, then through mixed ground to the top.

COIRE LEIRIDH

(NH 022 454)   Alt 500m   North facing   Map p86
The Gully that Time Forgot   150m   II * (1994)
The narrow central gully at the head of the corrie. A similar but shorter narrow gully further left is Grade I when full, Grade II when lean.

Whites of Their Ice   85m   IV,5 ** (1996)
A fine route but somewhat reluctant to form. At the right end of the cliff is an icefall featuring a prominent icicle. The route takes a zigzag line up ice ramps passing the icicle on the left and stepping on to its top (exposed crux) before moving up to a good thread belay on the left (40m). An easier second pitch followed an ice groove (45m).

FUAR THOLL

(NG 975 489)   Alt 907m   Maps p86, 97
This fine mountain on the north side of Glen Carron has two major cliffs, an extensive band of more broken crag, and particularly good scope for winter climbing. The major cliffs are the South-East Cliff, which overlooks a small corrie just south-east of the summit, and Mainreachan Buttress, which rises from a north facing corrie and abuts the north-west ridge. The South-East Cliff, visible from the road at Achnashellach, should not be confused with a lower band of small crags which line the south-east face of the mountain. Further up this band, as seen from the Achnashellach approach, is a clean nose which falls from the south-east ridge of the mountain. The band continues round to the north-east side of the mountain, facing the grand Coire Lair, where there are more broken crags and gullies, suitable for lower grade winter climbing.

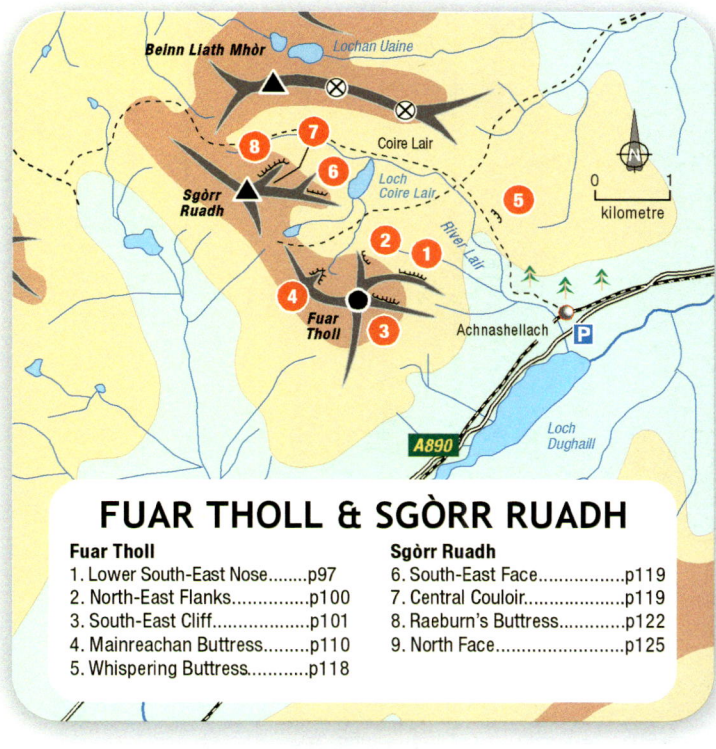

FUAR THOLL & SGÒRR RUADH

Fuar Tholl
1. Lower South-East Nose........p97
2. North-East Flanks..............p100
3. South-East Cliff...................p101
4. Mainreachan Buttress.........p110
5. Whispering Buttress............p118

Sgòrr Ruadh
6. South-East Face.................p119
7. Central Couloir....................p119
8. Raeburn's Buttress.............p122
9. North Face..........................p125

LOWER SOUTH-EAST NOSE

(NG 984 491)   Alt 500m   North-East facing   Map p97   Diagram p98

These cliffs give a good selection of routes for short days or wild weather. The climbs come into condition after a low snowfall and a couple of days of hard frost. The nose itself provides a pleasant rock climb. The cliff has no crag symbol on the 1:50000 map, but only the 50m contours are marked.

Approach: Start as for the South-East Cliff (see below) until below the fence at 200m altitude. Traverse right to a hint of a path in deep heather. Fight your way up the side valley which passes close under the Nose. 1hr 30mins under snow, 1hr in summer.

Descent: Either go over the crest heading south and down to join the South-East Cliff approach and descent beside its stream, or to return to the cliff base, descend the wide gully at the west end of the cliff (summer or winter).

Initially (the lower end) the cliff is in two tiers with several left-slanting chimney-lines at the right end of the lower tier, but the routes are higher up where the tiers merge into one. The Nose itself is roughly where the cliff turns from north-east to north facing but only becomes obvious when close underneath where it shows up as a clean blunt rib in a triangular buttress with an obvious diagonal fault in steep ground to its right. Left of the Nose are two chimneys and just left again a left-slanting grooved fault.

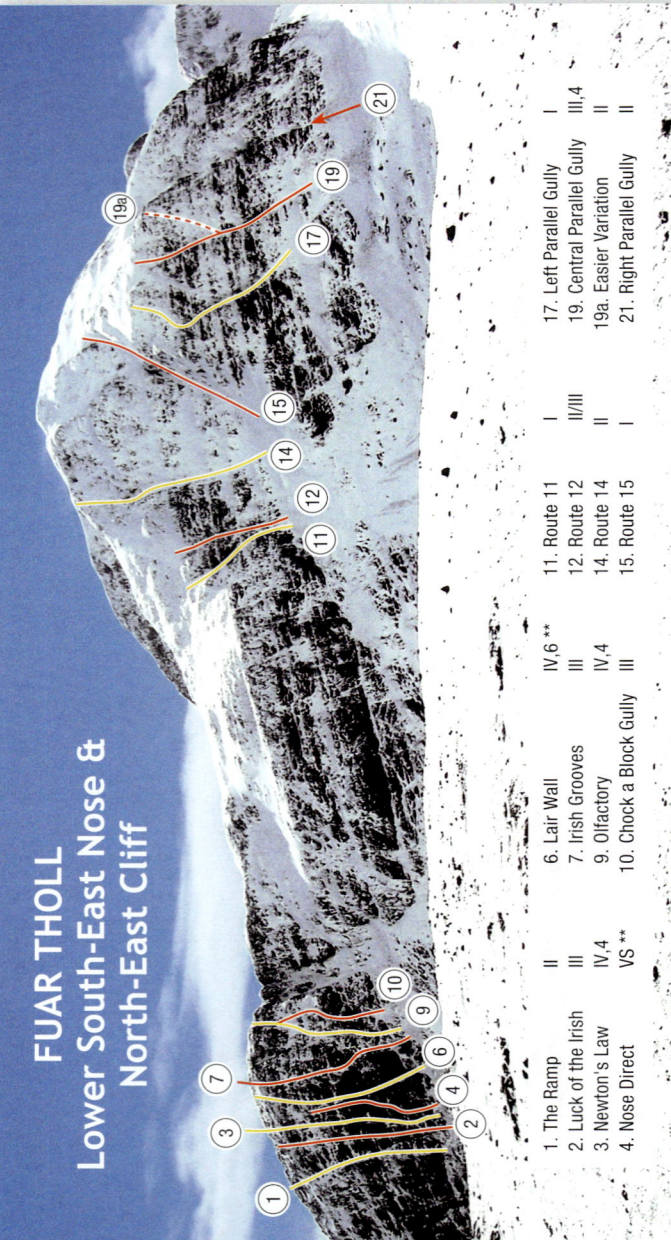

FUAR THOLL
Lower South-East Nose & North-East Cliff

1. The Ramp	II	6. Lair Wall	IV,6 **	11. Route 11	I
2. Luck of the Irish	III	7. Irish Grooves	III	12. Route 12	II/III
3. Newton's Law	IV,4	9. Olfactory	IV,4	14. Route 14	II
4. Nose Direct	VS **	10. Chock a Block Gully	III	15. Route 15	I

17. Left Parallel Gully — I
19. Central Parallel Gully — III,4
19a. Easier Variation — II
21. Right Parallel Gully — II

Andy Nisbet

LOWER SOUTH-EAST NOSE

1 The Ramp 150m II *(1998)*
The left-slanting turfy grooved fault, climbed for three pitches. Either finish up the groove or traverse right for an extra pitch.

2 Luck of the Irish 175m III *(1992)*
This takes the left-hand chimney 10m right of The Ramp and about 7m left of Newton's Law.
1. 45m Climb icy ground trending slightly left, then a steeper iced chimney to a small ledge.
2. 35m Steep moves lead into the main groove line. Follow this to a small terrace.
3. 25m Continue up the groove to a steep exit, then belay on the terrace above.
4. and 5. 70m Climb a little chimney, then surmount easier steps and grooves to reach the top.

3 Newton's Law 170m IV,4 *(1992)*
This is the more obvious right-hand chimney-groove line just left of The Nose.
1. 40m A wandering line on icy ground leads to a ledge and stance where the rock steepens.
2. 30m Climb turfy iced grooves direct to the base of an obvious hanging chimney.
3. 20m Climb the chimney, then exit right to a recess.
4. 45m Follow the continuing fault-line to easy ground.
5. 35m Climb the easy final steps.

4 Nose Direct 140m VS ** *(1961)*
A sustained route of largely clean rock, but dry weather is recommended. The line is open to variation but the following is suggested. Start left of the crest of the nose.
1. 30m 4b Take a right-trending line up clean slabs and a steeper section to below another clean slab.
2. 25m 4b Go out right on to the nose in an exposed position and climb this to ledges.
3. 15m 4b Climb the crest on good holds to a good ledge.
4. 15m 4c Climb a steep wall right of a flake system (old rope thread in the flake) to join and finish up the flake.
5. 25m 4b Go up blocky ground to below overhangs. Traverse right, climb a corner and return left to the crest (direct looks possible, perhaps 4c). Climb the crest to easier angled ground.
6. 40m 4b A short slabby section followed by a rib on the left keeps to clean rock as long as possible.

5 A Right Cheek 130m VS * *(1999)*
A route up the steeper ground right of the Nose, crossing the fault of Lair Wall. Start below a lighter coloured rib which forms the right side of a bay with a rowan tree.
1. 45m 4c Climb the rib to the first stance of Lair Wall.
2. 45m 4c Move right and climb near a crack-line which goes to the right end of a roof system. Move out right in a spectacular position and up to a terrace.
3. 40m Move left and climb a rib of booming flakes to scrambling (also an alternative finish to Nose Direct).

6 Lair Wall 145m IV,6 ** *(1992)*
This route climbs the left-slanting fault which lies immediately right of The Nose.
1. 40m Climb the fault to a good stance below steeper ground.
2. 45m Continuously interesting climbing in the same line leads to a large terrace.
3. and 4. 60m Easy ground leads to the top.

7 Irish Grooves 140m III *(1998)*
A left-slanting line of turfy grooves. Start 10m left of and lower than Olfactory. Climb a well defined V-groove, move right to avoid its steep continuation and return left to the main line (50m). Continue in two long pitches to the top.

100 FUAR THOLL

8 Welsh Grooves 150m III,4 * (2005)
Start just left of Olfactory.
1. 35m Climb mixed ground to a steep wall. Traverse left and join Irish Grooves until it goes left. Go right instead. Starting up Irish Grooves is easier.
2. 25m Go rightwards up a ramp system until below a big groove hidden from the start.
3. 30m Climb a steep step to gain the groove. Follow the groove, then the rib on the left before moving back right above the groove.
4. 60m Easier ground with short steep steps leads to the top.

9 Olfactory 150m IV,4 (1986)
Right of the Nose Direct are two narrow gullies. The left gully gives a good climb in four pitches, of which the second is a steep narrow chimney followed by steep ice on the left, and the fourth is another short steep chimney.

10 Chock a Block Gully 150m III (1990)
The right-hand gully, including a deep chimney with a chockstone.

Right of Chock a Block Gully is a deeply recessed easy gully, a possible descent.

NORTH-EAST CLIFF

(NG 978 494) Alt 550m North-East facing Map p97 Diagram p98

The buttresses are rather broken but there are some pleasant easier gullies, particularly when combined with a visit to the summit.

Approach: The normal approach is as for Sgòrr Ruadh up the Coire Lair stalking path but turning left up a branch towards Bealach Mòr and Mainreachan Buttress. This passes quite close to the cliff base. An alternative is to start as for the Lower Nose but continue on below it to the cliff, shorter but rougher, only recommended when the river Lair is high. 1hr 30mins to 2hrs.

Descent: The routes finish high on the mountain either near the top of the south-east ridge, which could be descended, or on the north spur, from where it is easiest to visit the summit and descend as for the South-East Cliff.

To the right of the Lower Nose a line of broken cliffs seamed by gullies stretches for over a kilometre around the north-east flank of the mountain. Beyond the recessed gully right of the Nose lies a craggy spur traversed by a shorter band of cliff, then an obvious shallow corrie. At the top left of the corrie are two narrow gullies, close together and diverging (almost a V shape). The left is Grade I (Route 11); the right is Grade II or III (Route 12), according to the build-up on one steep pitch near its base. At the top of the corrie is a fine gully leading up to a small col on the upper south-east ridge of the mountain (Route 14 300m II). The buttress on its left is Grade II/III (Route 13). Leading up right from the corrie is another Grade I (Route 15), only well defined for a short narrow section and leading to slopes north-east of the summit. On the face to the right of the corrie are three parallel gullies split by narrow spurs leading to the same slopes, just before the face turns to the north and bends back into Mainreachan corrie.

16 The Pile 200m II (1971)
The rib on the left of the Left Parallel Gully. A line has also been taken further left.

17 Left Parallel Gully 200m I (1990)
As named.

18 Spare Rib 210m III,4 (2000)
The crest of the rib between the left and central parallel gullies, the crest being near the central gully. Start left of the crest and slant up right to join it. Follow the crest or close to it with one short technical but well cracked section to the final tier.

SOUTH-EAST CLIFF 101

This is easiest on the left but a fine twin cracked chimney-groove just right of the crest gives a good finish. Moderate in summer (2003).

19 Central Parallel Gully   200m   III,4   *(1994)*
The highlight is a two tiered upper icefall, which does not form readily. One can escape out right below it, when the route becomes Grade II.

20 Solicitor's Rib   200m   III   *(1995)*
Climbs the buttress between the central and right-hand of the three parallel gullies in the right-hand section of the face just before it turns to the north and bends back into Mainreachan corrie. One interesting mixed pitch up the broad lower tier, then pleasant scrambling up the rib above.

21 Right Parallel Gully   200m   II   *(1994)*
As named.

SOUTH-EAST CLIFF

(NG 978 488)   Alt 750m   North-East facing   Map p97   Diagrams p103, p107

This is a typical Torridonian sandstone cliff, steep and hostile, providing tremendous winter climbing. Its steep icefalls have recently gained a good reputation, but there is also hard mixed climbing which is icy in good conditions and two good easier climbs. The cliff is lower than the Liathach corries, so the season is shorter and more susceptible to thaw. It faces the road so conditions can be assessed (weather permitting) from the car, but mid-season is most likely. The corrie is sheltered from winds south-westerly through to northerly and this can provide a venue when other cliffs are wind exposed. The disadvantage is that the corrie collects snow and is prone to big unstable cornices and windslab avalanches. The summer climbing is typically Torridonian too, slow to dry, a bit vegetated and out of fashion, but the climbs are adventurous and on good rock.

Approach: The face is best approached from the south-east via the small plateau named Sgùrr a' Mhuilinn on the 1:50,000 map. Obtaining this point from Achnashellach Station is problematical, as the River Lair is difficult and possibly dangerous to ford and the only bridge over the river carries the railway, along which there is no legal right of access. Once over the river climb the hillside to a doorway in a fence (NG 994 483) at about 200m altitude. Continue up steep rough slopes to the plateau at 420m. Reach the burn issuing from the corrie and climb its right side past a small lochan to gain the corrie, about 2hrs.

Descent: The summer descent is obvious although very rough so the following applies to winter.
1. In bad weather or complete snow cover (when the cornices cannot be seen), head away from the cliff southwards to the flat area near Càrn Eididh, descend a gully eastwards and traverse back to the plateau at altitude 420m (or continue from Càrn Eididh to Balnacra).
2. The more direct alternative is to descend south-eastwards along the top of the cliff (cornices). When the ground begins to steepen (after about 200m), turn right (west) and soon reach a snowy trough which leads south-east again. The slope is convex and briefly 50 degrees. Follow snow as long as possible, because the ground here is very rough, and trend left to the plateau at altitude 420m.
3. To return to the corrie, Access Gully is rarely used, as the cornice has to be abseiled. The usual choice is to descend the ridge on the north side of the corrie until it is possible to go down the short 'Right-Hand Gully', Grade I, to the floor of the corrie.

The left side of the corrie is the main face and the climbs are described from bottom left to right. The big corner of Fuhrer is to the left while the icefall of Tholl Gate in the centre is often the most obvious feature. At the top of the corrie there are two snowy gullies, the cul-de-sac of Cold Hole is the left one and Access Gully

FUAR THOLL

the right one, with Right End Buttress between them. Below the main cliff and on the left side of the approach valley is a lower cliff.

Lower Cliff

The left side of the lower cliff has a band of steep compact rock towards its top. This is broken by a groove which forms a weakness for the following route. Right of the steep ground is a prominent gully, Butcher's Dog. Right again is a turfy buttress (Grade II), then two shorter gullies (Grade II) and further right, an icefall (Grade II) leading to a diagonal ramp which forms the lower left end of the main cliff.

Placa 80m Hard Severe 4b *(2005)*
Climbs pleasant but artificial slabby ground to reach a rib left of the groove which breaks the upper overhangs. Start at a tongue of rock about 30m right of a flat topped pedestal at the base and near the left end of the cliff. Trend up rightwards on steepening slabs towards the groove. Climb the rib left of the groove (a move into the groove and back out may help) to a ledge. Finish up a continuation rib.

Butcher's Dog 80m II *(1994)*
The route is situated approximately 200m below and left of the diagonal ramp which forms the lower left end of the South-East Face. It takes the obvious gully for 60m to a shallow terrace, then up a steeper gully for 20m to the top.

Main Cliff

1 Blue Finger 150m Severe *(1969)*
Start 30m from the left end of the main cliff, below a break before the rock gets much smoother and steeper. This is left of a corner with a smooth rectangular left face.
1. 40m 4a Climb up easily, follow a short groove and hand traverse up to a higher ledge. Move back up right and follow a groove to belay in a corner.
2. 15m Climb a crack to an overhanging block on the left, then move left and follow a groove to a terrace.
3. 95m Continue easily to the top.
Winter: **V,6** * *(1993)*
Follow the summer line except the third tier which was climbed by a steep spike filled chimney and the last tier which was climbed by working left, then finishing straight up.

2 Cold Sweat 130m VS * *(1969)*
This is the line of a definite black chimney right of the harder section of wall and facing the much bigger corner of Fuhrer.
1. 35m Climb up to the chimney making a few excursions to the right.
2. 15m 5a Climb up right past an old peg and on to the wall. Move back left into the chimney above the overhang and so to a ledge. This is more pleasant than struggling up the chimney, which may be slimy.
3. 80m Continue up easier chimneys to the top.
Winter: **VI,6** *(1986)*
A back roped solo ascent was made over two days, the rope being left in place and the high point regained by jumaring. There was sustained mixed climbing in the lower section, the crux chimney being verglassed and very strenuous.

3 Boat Tundra 150m Severe *(1969)*
Start near the centre of the wall between the obvious black chimney (Cold Sweat) and the line of the big corner of Fuhrer, which starts halfway up the cliff.
1. 45m Climb up for 7m, traverse left for 6m, then climb up and right to a small grassy bay. Continue up then diagonally right to the base of the big corner.
2. 45m The corner is vegetated and unattractive; the cliff is more broken here and

FUAR THOLL
South-East Cliff

1. Blue Finger	Severe	
2. Cold Sweat	VS	*
3. Boat Tundra	Severe	
5. Fuar Feast	HVS	
6. Fuar Folly Direct	VI,8	**
7. Sandstorm	VII,8	***
9. Original Route	Severe	*
9a. The Fuar	Severe	
15. Via Wellington	HVS	*

GLEN CARRON

Tholl Gate, VI,6, South-East Cliff, Fuar Tholl. Climber Roger Wild

variations are possible. Climb up and left, passing a pleasant smooth slab at about 25m, to belay on a terrace by a large pinnacle.
3. 60m   There is a clean headwall above a short black corner left of the big vegetated corner which gives a good finish to the climb. From the pinnacle belay continue up broken ground to the headwall and climb it using a fine layback crack to start.

**4 Fuhrer   190m   VII,6 ** *(1986)*
This fine route takes the big corner up the left-hand side of the cliff. It was climbed in very icy conditions (perhaps at a lower grade) and may be unrepeated. An earlier route, Fuar Folly, escaped left from the corner under threat of darkness, possibly via Boat Tundra. Start at the obvious mixed line trending right to the foot of the hanging corner.
1. 45m   Start in a short corner and trend up right to belay just below the start of the big corner. This is likely to be up Cold Sweat for 5m, then trending right to join Boat Tundra. The line further right as marked in the 1993 guide would definitely need ice.
2. 35m   Gain the corner and follow it over ice bulges to a good flake on the right.

Take to ice streaks on the slabs on the left and belay 8m below and left of the overhang which caps the groove.
3. 25m Just left of the stance thin ice leads through a steep wall to below an ice-choked chimney.
4. 25m The ice chimney gives access to the left end of a ledge which is followed 15m rightwards to a right-trending break in the wall above.
5. 60m Take the break in the wall above and further tricky ground to the top.

5 Fuar Feast   190m   HVS *(1993)*
Climbs the crest of the buttress right of Fuhrer. Start right of a line below the big corner of Fuhrer, at a big low angled ramp which leads up right.
1 and 2. 55m 4c Climb the ramp for a few metres, then move left on to the lower buttress right of The Fuhrer, zig-zagging to find the easiest line of clean rock and belay on the main horizontal ledge.
3. 35m 5a Leave the ledge just right of the crest, climb slightly leftwards and finish up the right of two short prominent V-grooves (obvious from the corrie floor) to the ledge above.
4 and 5. 100m Trend right up easier ground to finish up Sandstorm.

6 Fuar Folly Direct   190m   VI,8 *** *(1995)*
This was the original intention of Fuar Folly, climbing direct up 'the great rock bastion' right of Fuhrer. The original Fuar Folly traversed into The Fuhrer along the ledge, tried this, then escaped left when darkness arrived. This route criss-crosses Fuar Feast to take the natural winter line. Start right of Fuhrer.
1. 30m Climb the big low angled ramp to the start of a snow shelf.
2. 40m Go up, then take a second right-trending ramp, until a short steep crack gains the ledge which is followed left to the crest just before the ledge curves round into Fuhrer.
3. 20m Climb a left-slanting ramp (groove) to a short overhanging corner. Climb this and pull left on to a smooth rock terrace with a big block at its right end.
4. 10m Fuar Feast crosses here and goes up a short overhanging groove on the left. Instead, pull up right on spikes to the base of a shallow right-facing corner with a perfect crack. Climb this (excellent protection) to a precarious finish on to the ledge above.
5. 45m A long pitch straight up leads to the right-slanting break of Fuhrer.
6. 45m Finish by this.

7 Sandstorm   180m   VII,8 *** *(1993)*
This route climbs the steep and compact rock right of the crest of 'the great rock bastion' to provide a demanding climb. Start 30m right of the initial ramp of Fuar Folly Direct.
1. 50m Follow a vague left-trending ramp, then go up right to an easement before moving back left to join Fuar Folly Direct. Follow its "second right-trending ramp" to the ledge. There is a short blank wall below a higher ledge, above which is a turfy ramp leading into a steep cracked corner. Avoid the wall by a dog-leg to the right to reach good belays right of the ramp and corner.
2. 30m Climb the ramp to a ledge, then go direct up the very steep corner (1PA) and swing left to moss ledges. Further strenuous moves lead up and right to a small stance just left of a big bottomless groove.
3. 45m Swing up to the exit of the groove, then go direct up the walls to a stance in the right-facing corner where the cliff steepens.
4. 30m Go up right on flakes, then move back left to the crest of the buttress and a hard exit to easier ground.
5. 25m Short steps lead to the top.
Variation: **VIII,7**   *(2005)*
The line of the second ascent. Instead of climbing the second right-trending ramp and dog-leg on pitch 1, a direct line was taken to the belay. Pitch 2 was climbed free, perhaps passing the 'very steep corner' on the right and entering the 'big bottomless groove' lower down. Different belays were used.

2. Cold Sweat — VI,6
4. Fuhrer — VII,6 **
6. Fuar Folly Direct — VI,8 **
7. Sandstorm — VII,8 ***
8. Il Duce — VII,7 **

FUAR THOLL
South-East Cliff

10. Tholl Gate — VI,6 ****
11. The Ayatollah — VII,7 ***
12. Evasion Grooves — VI,6 **
14. Pipped at the Post — V,5 **
16. Cold Hole — VI,5 ***
18. Right End Buttress — III,4 *

Simon Richardson

108 | FUAR THOLL

8 Il Duce   200m   VII,7 **   *(1994)*
Three parallel ice lines form down the central section of the cliff. This varied ice and mixed line takes the thin left streak to the left of Tholl Gate. Start mid-way between this and Sandstorm below a short steep wall topped by a narrow ice ramp.
1. 25m Climb the wall and make a difficult exit on to the ramp which leads to a crescent shaped snowfield. Belay below the wall above. Missing out this pitch and starting up Tholl Gate would reduce the grade to VI (in good conditions).
2. 15m Cracks lead to a tongue of ice after 10m. Climb this to the terrace at the top of the first tier.
3. 50m An intimidating pitch, but considerably easier than it looks. Move up and right to gain a narrow icy groove. Climb this for 10m, then traverse up and left past a precarious pointed block along a vague ramp to a ledge. Continue up and right on good ice to a stance on the left.
4. 50m Climb the hanging icicle fringe on the right and continue directly to a stance.
5 and 6. 60m Continue up the vague depression above, keeping left of Tholl Gate to the top.

9 Original Route   220m   Severe *   *(1933)*
An indirect adventure with some good rock in the lower part and some loose rock in the upper part. The drier the better! Start below and right of an obvious, large 'semi-lunar' green shelf right of centre on the cliff. This is just left of the watercourse which is the first pitch of Tholl Gate.
1. 25m Climb to the right end of the shelf, then traverse left along it.
2. 45m From the left end of the shelf, make a hard move up, then trend right to a long ledge. Follow this right under the crux of Tholl Gate until under the smooth corner of Ayatollah.
3. 40m Traverse round the nose on the right to climb a steep groove.
4. 40m Climb to a large ledge.
5. and 6. 70m Climb two successive chimneys to rotten rock, then continue easily to the top.
Variation: **The Fuar   180m   Severe**   *(1969)*
A more direct start, although the rest appears similar.

10 Tholl Gate   170m   VI,6 ****   *(1984)*
This takes the magnificent icy line in the centre of the cliff, 50m right of Fuhrer. Start slightly right of the line in a shallow bay.
1. 40m Climb a shallow icy groove (or mixed climbing trending left then right) to a ledge line. Traverse left for 10m to belay below the ice streak.
2. 35m The difficulty will depend on how far the icefall extends down an overhanging wall to the ledge below. Moving out right below the thick ice will probably be easiest. Once gained, follow the ice to a good ledge.
3. 50m The steep and fine icy corners on the right lead to a good ledge.
4. 45m Move left and continue straight up by corners and a final gully.

11 The Ayatollah   190m   VII,7 ***   *(1989)*
Takes an uncompromising line right of Tholl Gate, following an obvious steep slab corner in the second tier, and then a series of icy grooves directly above. The key to the route is reaching the ice on the slab (pitch 2). Start, as for Tholl Gate, at a shallow bay beneath the highest part of the cliff.
1. 50m Climb as for Tholl Gate, tricky icy grooves to a snow terrace, then a right traverse to a spike beneath the slab corner.
2. 30m Make some radical moves up the smooth corner until usable ice can be gained on the slab on the left. The second ascent climbed an ice smear which can form between the corner and Tholl Gate's icefall. Follow the ice smears to a narrow terrace, traverse right under an icicle, then up a rocky groove for 4m to belay at a cracked block.
3. 35m Bridge across left to gain the icicle, then climb up directly. If no icicle is present it can be mixed climbed. A short groove, an easier snow bay and a further

SOUTH-EAST CLIFF 109

iced groove lead to belays at a wedged block below a steeper icefall.
4. 45m Climb the icefall, then go left and back right in easier angled mixed grooves to gain a terrace below the final rock wall.
5. 30m Traverse 5m left, then go up steep snow and a runnel to the cornice.

12 Evasion Grooves   210m   VI,6 ** *(1988)*
This is a mixed alternative to Tholl Gate, up the big buttress to its right. It is more frequently in climbable condition than its neighbours. The line is similar to the summer Original Route apart from a more direct start. An excellent climb. Start, as for The Ayatollah and Tholl Gate, at a shallow bay below the highest part of the cliff.
1. 50m Climb tricky ice grooves, as for Tholl Gate, to a snowy terrace, and go right along this to the spike beneath the smooth corner of The Ayatollah.
2. 40m Traverse right for 4m to a very steep groove (Original Route). Climb this direct to a hard exit, then continue to giant spikes.
3. 40m Go right on to a big easy snow ramp. Follow this for 25m to a left-sloping break in the tier above. Struggle up this to reach another terrace directly beneath a fine ramp.
4. 40m Climb the ramp to belay in an overhung corner.
5. 40m Traverse left for 15m, then trend left up snowfields and rocky grooves to a possibly large cornice.

A prominent gully, the Cold Hole, separates the right and higher side of the cliff from an easier buttress. The gully ends in a cul-de-sac. The first three routes climb the right side of the main cliff, starting just inside the gully.

13 Mixed Post   100m   IV,5 * *(1993)*
In good conditions an icefall forms partly connected to Pipped at the Post but offering a slightly easier separate line. Without ice, a mixed route with a short hard section on pitch 1 (V,6). Start immediately left of Pipped at the Post. Gain a shallow chimney from the right. Climb it and the continuation fault slanting leftwards to the top.

14 Pipped at the Post   100m   V,5 ** *(1987)*
About 30m down the gully from the cul-de-sac of Cold Hole is a continuous ice streak on the left wall. Often the best line of ice is the steep first pitch of this route, then moving left to finish up Mixed Post.
1. 40m Climb the ice to a thinly covered wall at 15m (crux) and continue to a big spike belay on the right.
2. 30m Continue in the same line to belay below an overhanging wall.
3. 30m If there is sufficient ice, climb the wall; otherwise traverse delicately right to easier ice or mixed ground leading to the cornice. Finish directly on mixed ground.

15 Via Wellington   100m   HVS * *(1994)*
Climbs the slabby wall right of Pipped at the Post. Start just above the step in the Cold Hole introductory gully.
1. 45m 5a Climb the wall just right of Pipped at the Post (wet streaks) to the big spike belay.
2. 35m 5a Move 3m right and climb a thin crack to a ledge, then another wall to a ledge.
3. 20m Finish straight up, keeping to rock.

16 Cold Hole   50m   VI,5 *** *(1987)*
The gully is easy up to the cul-de-sac which forms a very steep 45m step. This climb takes the ice sheet forming the left corner of the step. Though short it is highly recommended and often in condition even when the other routes are too thin. This is a big and tiring pitch, but never vertical, and the crux is at the top. Finish either on steepening snow or traverse left and climb a long pitch on lower angled ice (Grade III).

FUAR THOLL

17 Tubular Bells   40m   VII,7   *(1991)*
Takes the obvious icicle ridden corner just right of Cold Hole. Short but noteworthy; certainly not sensible!
1. 25m   Battle up through overhanging Damoclean icicles to a belay in a cave beneath the final overhangs.
2. 15m   Break left through the icicle fringe, round the overhang and gain easy slopes leading to the cornice.

18 Right End Buttress   180m   III,4 *   *(1976)*
The separate buttress at the top right of the cliff, between the Cold Hole cul-de-sac and Access Gully, can provide a fine icy climb or an easier option in bad conditions (if safe from avalanches). The belays are good but hard to find. Start at the bottom left corner and gain the centre. Climb a steep pitch, usually mixed, then a slabby pitch, quite thin, to the left side of a big snow terrace. Regain the centre and climb rightwards, often on ice, then move back left to the upper snowfield. The buttress has also been climbed in summer (Very Difficult).
Variation: **IV,4**
Climb the steep wall above the big snow terrace at its left side, going up cracks to a ledge on the left, then straight up to the upper snowfield.

19 Access Gully   130m   II
The obvious gully to the right of Right End Buttress has a steep exit, often dangerously corniced. A steeper right fork gives an alternative finish of 50m.

20 Right-Hand Gully   50m   I
The right-hand gully in the corrie gives an easy uncorniced exit to the right ridge of the corrie, which then provides a pleasant "scramble" to the summit. The face between here and Access Gully gives a steeper and longer route to the ridge (Grade II).

NORTH-WEST FACE

(NG 974 489)   Alt 820m   North-West facing

Summit Rib   150m   II   *(2005)*
The central and most prominent of several ribs which lead up the north-west face of Fuar Tholl from Mainreachan corrie. It ends just south of the summit. It can also be approached by a slightly descending traverse from the col between the summit and the central top (895m, top of Mainreachan Buttress). Keeping as close to the crest as possible gives the most interesting climbing but the difficulties are very escapable.

MAINREACHAN BUTTRESS

(NG 973 489)   Alt 700m   North-East to North-West facing   Map p97
Diagrams p111, 115

This cliff has never regained popularity after a period of enthusiastic exploration in 1969/70. It is, however, one of Scotland's great cliffs and provides an adventurous day out. Many of the holds and runners are cracked or wedged blocks although the underlying rock is solid and fairly clean; consequently the climbs are worrying. The cliff is slow to dry and particularly prone to seepage. Sandstone enthusiasts will like the cliff; others may hate it. The winter routes are fantastic but all hard. The buttress presents a steep north face with a scree slope below it rising sharply from left to right. Several gangways slant up leftwards from the scree marking the starts of the routes. This upper right side of the buttress is an awesome place, particularly in winter, occasionally forming some ice between the overhangs!

Approach: Follow the very scenic stalker's path from Achnashellach to a height of 360m in Coire Lair where a second path branches left, crossing the River Lair (difficult in spate) and climbing up to the Bealach Mhòr between Fuar Tholl and

FUAR THOLL
Mainreachan Buttress, North-East Face

1. Hanging Imminent   IV,6
2. Nebula   VI,6 **
3. Mainline Connection   VI,6 **

Sgòrr Ruadh. Just below the bealach branch off left to reach the base of the buttress, 2hrs (summer) to 2hrs 30mins (winter). There is running water about 10mins below the crag (also potential camp sites). Alternatively, less scenic but perhaps slightly quicker, particularly useful if rucksacks are to be left at the top, start from Balnacra in Glen Carron (NG 983 463), climb to the summit of Fuar Tholl and descend either the west or east flank of the buttress to its base (depending on the intended route).

Descent: Descent back to the cliff base is easier on the west (left looking down), but both sides are possible.

At the left end of the north-east facet of the buttress are two obvious steep corner-lines and a third smaller one on their left.

1 Hanging Imminent   160m   IV,6   *(2001)*
Climbs the smaller corner left of the two main corner-lines. Climb a steep icy crack (crux, easier with more ice) and follow the ramp corner to the terrace. Continue to the left end of the upper tier and climb up right by a groove and ledges to the top.

2 Nebula   195m   VI,6 *   *(1994)*
The left-hand corner-line is an ice trap, not often in prime condition, but a natural winter route. Start below the left-hand of twin grooves.
1. 35m Steep mixed climbing (crux) leads into the groove. Climb ice to a ledge and belay on the left.

112 FUAR THOLL

Chris Cartwright on Enigma, VII,7, Mainreachan Buttress, Fuar Tholl, prior to the first winter ascent

2. 40m Continue up the icy groove to the terrace.
3. 25m Move up the terrace to the foot of the ice groove cutting through the upper tier.
4. 45m Climb the groove, which continues in the same line as the lower groove.
5. 50m Continue up easy snow and mixed ground to the top.
This offers a rather dirty Severe in summer (1971).

3 Mainline Connection   200m   VI,6 ** *(1989)*
This climbs the right-hand corner-line. Start below the right-hand groove, 15m right of Nebula.
1. 50m Climb the corner over several steps to a good ledge.
2. 45m Ascend the fault directly above the belay and just left of the corner, then continue in the corner to the terrace.
3. 15m Traverse left and belay below the first obvious groove (Nebula is further left).
4. 45m Move up left and traverse right into the groove, which is climbed to smaller twin grooves, the right-hand of which leads to easy ground.
The route approximates to the line of **Nimrod** (Hard Severe 1968).

4 Enigma   200m   Hard Severe *(1952)*
A rather scrappy and vegetated route. The upper half of this description may prove difficult to find; recent ascents have followed their nose. Start at the left end of the lowest terrace on the north-east face. Go up the left edge on easy rock to a mossy stance (10m). Climb the crack on the right to a ledge (20m). Traverse left into steep grooves and up to a large grass platform. Go up right for 20m to a moss patch, then up left to a big ledge. Climb a groove for 10m, then a crack to the top of a large flake. Traverse right and climb a steep wall on good holds to a ledge (15m). Traverse left and climb a rib for 10m and scramble to below a steeper rib. Climb this on small holds for 20m, then trend left and climb short pitches and easier rock for 60m to the top.
Winter: **230m   VII,7 ***   *(1997)*
A sustained mixed route up the front face of the buttress. The route is loosely based on the summer route of Enigma, and lies between the winter routes of Sleuth and

MAINREACHAN BUTTRESS 113

Mainline Connection. Above the Great Terrace, the natural winter line of Sleuth was followed. Start just left of the first tier and below a short gully (about 5m right of Mainline Connection).
1. 20m Climb the gully to a terrace.
2. 15m Continue up the prominent V-groove to a ledge.
3. 20m Move up and right along a narrow slabby ramp to below a steep wall (junction with Sleuth, which traverses left to reach this point and then goes back right along a horizontal ledge). Move left below a big square flake and continue up and left to a niche overlooking the corner of Mainline Connection.
4. 15m Climb the groove just left of the niche to a bay.
5. 15m Mainline Connection takes the corner up and left. Instead, traverse horizontally right for 3m below an overlap, and move up to a small ledge. Climb the short groove above to flat ledge.
6. 20m Climb the bulging groove just right of the left edge to reach the Great Terrace which girdles the cliff at two-thirds height. Move up to belay below a steep pillar.
7. 45m Traverse right along a dwindling ledge for 25m, then go up on mixed ground to reach a right to left diagonal line of weakness where the angle eases.
8. 30m Climb up diagonally left for 15m until about 10m below a big nose with a protruding flake. Traverse horizontally left along a ledge for 10m, then move up to the left edge of the buttress.
9. 50m Straightforward mixed ground leads to the top.

5 Sleuth   240m   VS (1969)
A pleasant start below the Great Terrace, but not as good above it. Nearly worth a star in dry conditions. Start at the right-hand end of the lowest terrace on the north-east face. Climb cracked blocks and the continuation line until it is possible to traverse right round the corner to easier rock leading up left to a ledge and belay (30m, 4c). A more direct line up an obvious corner left of this line has also been climbed (HVS 5a). Continue up leftwards to a broad terrace, the First Terrace. Above is a smooth barrier wall. Continue rising leftwards, then go up a small corner to a higher ledge in the middle of the wall. Return right along this, despite heading for improbable ground, and include two short descents to reach a groove; go up this using a spike (4b), then slightly right to near the edge and back left to belay. Go straight up a small wall to the Great Terrace, then up to its right end under huge jammed blocks. Climb the main crack through these (surprisingly solid, 4b) to reach a left to right line of weakness with loose rock which leads to a nose with a protruding flake. Go up under the nose, then traverse right under it (4b) to reach easier ground leading to the top.

6 Sleuth, Original Winter Route   240m   VII,7   *** (1969)
A long hard route, probably the hardest in Scotland at the time, although the crux section is relatively short. Start close to Enigma, just left of the first tier and below a short gully (about 5m right of Mainline Connection). Climb the gully to the First Terrace, then traverse right to join Sleuth. Follow its summer route left then right to pass the barrier wall and up the crux groove to ultimately reach the Great Terrace. Go up left and back right along the dwindling ledge, now having joined Enigma (pitches 7-9). The summer route reaches this point more directly up the jammed blocks. Climb up diagonally left until about 10m below a big nose with a protruding flake (the summer route goes up to the nose and traverses right under it). Traverse horizontally left along a ledge to reach a turfy groove which leads to the top.
Variation: **Sleuth Start   60m   VII,7** (2000)
A recommended start near the summer route which keeps the route nearly separate from winter Enigma below the Great Terrace and, although slightly harder than the Original Route crux, is in keeping with it. Start right of Sleuth summer and about 25m up from the toe of the cliff at a short ramp which slants up leftwards into a steep groove of vertical flakes. Climb the ramp and groove to a ledge (20m). A line of weakness now slants up left to join the summer route and continues to the First Terrace, joining the Original Winter Route (40m).

GLEN CARRON

114 FUAR THOLL

7 Supersleuth 240m VII,8 *** (2002)
Takes the Sleuth Start, then a very direct line up the rest.
1 and 2. 60m Start just up from the right end of the lowest terrace and climb the Sleuth Start to the First Terrace.
3. 40m Above is a smooth barrier wall. Climb the very prominent thin torquing crack to a hard move below a steepening (crux). Step horizontally left and up into grooves which trend back right over an overhang to a good stance common to Sleuth, Original Winter Route.
4. 20m Step left into a short steep groove and climb this to easier ground which leads to the Great Terrace.
5. 40m Ten metres above is another steeper barrier wall, the only break in which is a groove just right of centre. Climb into and then up this with difficulty then with more ease to a ledge.
6 and 7. 80m Trend up rightwards (junction with Sleuth summer), then back left to the top.

8 Sherlock 200m HVS * (1969)
A sustained route, worthwhile but with moves on hollow blocks. Start at the obvious left-trending gangway below and parallel to that of Snoopy. The gangway starts above a small overhung bay.
1. 45m 4c Climb the gangway for 25m to a small ledge (original belay, but awkward without pegs). Climb cracked blocks trending right to a good ledge. Combining these pitches causes rope drag, so an intermediate belay may be better.
2. 15m 5a From a huge block on the ledge, go left under roofs into a groove. Go up the groove and on to a ledge out left.
3. 20m 5a Step back into the groove and climb it to a bulge. Move left round the corner to a grass ledge. Trend right across the wall above (poorly protected) to a block on a ledge.
4. 30m 4b Climb a groove trending left then back right.
5. and 6. 90m Follow the vague crest on loose rock to the top.

9 Moriarty 180m E4 (1999)
A line just right of Sherlock, but forced to share two belays and a short section with that route. An independent line up this section of cliff would be 'well hard'. Start at a small rib right of the bay at the base of Sherlock.
1. 30m 5a Climb the rib, then go diagonally left across a steep wall above the bay to enter and climb a chimney-corner which leads to the right end of the ledge of Sherlock.
2. 15m 6b Climb the groove above the right end of the ledge to roofs. Swing out left on to the arete and traverse delicately left to the belay of Sherlock.
3. 15m 5b This pitch is a direct version of Sherlock's pitch 4. Start up the groove of Sherlock but continue over a bulge and the groove above.
4. 40m 5a Traverse right, then go up to a ramp. Follow this a short way, then climb straight up grooves.
5. 50m 4b Take a right-trending line up a depression (parallel to Sherlock).
6. 30m Finish straight up.

10 Reach for the Sky 200m VII,6 *** (1989)
This route follows the ramp of Snoopy before breaking out left on very steep mixed ground to gain finishing grooves. Although nowhere desperate, it is a sustained and intimidating climb with some spectacular exposure. Start as for Snoopy at the gangway leading left into the bottom of the ramp.
1. 35m Follow the gangway to a bay beneath the ramp.
2. 30m Climb the corner of the ramp, generally on tufts and verglas (poorly protected), to a terrace on the left.
3. 40m Continue up the ramp corner to the corner-chimney at its top. Climb this and exit left up to loose wedged blocks beneath a sheer corner. A narrow ledge leads left out of this impasse to a well poised belay on the front of the buttress.
4. 30m Climb mixed ground trending left to an overhang. Mantelshelf over this

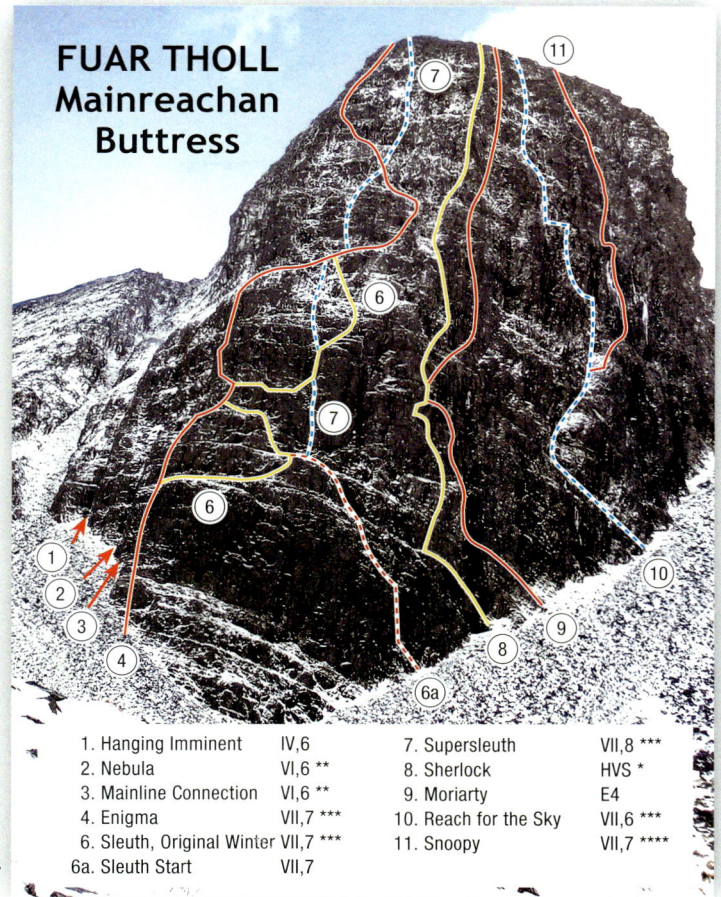

FUAR THOLL Mainreachan Buttress

1. Hanging Imminent	IV,6	7. Supersleuth	VII,8 ***
2. Nebula	VI,6 **	8. Sherlock	HVS *
3. Mainline Connection	VI,6 **	9. Moriarty	E4
4. Enigma	VII,7 ***	10. Reach for the Sky	VII,6 ***
6. Sleuth, Original Winter	VII,7 ***	11. Snoopy	VII,7 ****
6a. Sleuth Start	VII,7		

then make a long left traverse, gaining a turfy ramp beneath iced grooves (exposed and unprotected), belay up and left at a huge cracked block.
5. 30m Step right and climb an ice column to gain easier angled grooves which are followed first left then back right and left again.
6. 35m Go up and right to regain the groove line which is followed through two further tiers to a sudden ending.

1 Snoopy   190m   HVS * *(1969)*
Start at the obvious gangway near the middle of the face, well up the sidewall from the lowest rocks. A good route when dry, but this takes several days.
1. 35m Go left up the gangway.
2. 45m Climb back right up a slabby ramp to its top right corner, a ledge below steep walls (ignoring the chimney-corner of Reach for the Sky on the left).
3. 15m 4c Traverse right to below a shallow brown and usually wet groove and climb on the right of this to a ledge.
4. 40m 5a Trend right to below a steep mossy groove; traverse hard right on steep

FUAR THOLL

rock to gain another groove (belay on the right if required); follow the groove, moving left at the top to reach a large grass ledge.
5. 60m 4c Traverse left round an edge to a chimney with a large pinnacle forming its left side. Climb this and the groove above to the top.

Winter: **180m VII,7 ****** *(1998)*

Very spectacular, with bold pitches on thin ice leading to a strenuous but well protected section through roofs. The more ice, the easier it would become. It would seem to finish left of summer Snoopy. The 'brown groove' is not visible from the ramp so ice conditions are difficult to assess until arrival (but the summer route on the right may be possible).

1 and 2. 35m, 30m Follow the ramps of Snoopy for two pitches (as does Reach for the Sky).
3. 15m Continue a short way up the ramp-corner, then traverse right along a foot ledge to climb the right side of the ramp to its top. Move right to belay.
4. 25m Climb steep rock trending right to gain the iced 'brown groove' and follow it, probably on increasingly thick ice to a ledge below a prominent ice column.
5. 15m Climb the ice column into a recess. Make unlikely moves round the arete on the left to easier ground leading back right above the recess.
6. 30m Climb the chimney above and continue to a terrace.
7. 30m Move right and finish easily up grooves.

12 Private Eye 150m Scottish VS *(1974)*

This route climbs the buttress in the centre, through the obvious black cave at half-height. The most obvious gangway in the centre of the face marks the start of Snoopy; this climb starts at the next gangway above. The route looks very hard and is reported as such.

1. 45m Climb the gangway with some awkward moves.
2. 30m Continue slightly right to belay in the back of the cave.
3. 30m Exit over the roof of the cave past a thread runner to a belay above (difficult and wet).
4. 45m Continue up cracks and steep loose walls to the top.

13 All the Way 120m E1 * *(1972)*

Some fine climbing on clean rock, but also very serious (perhaps E2 5a). The climb starts from a shelf below the gangway of Investigator and takes a fairly direct line to the big nose of Investigator at the top of the cliff.

1. 40m Go left up the shelf to near its end where a corner come ramp leads back up right.
2. 20m 5a Start on the left to make tricky moves up right to reach the base of the corner which leads to the gangway of Investigator. Go left on this until just past its narrowing.
3. 45m 5a The peg runner on the next pitch is now visible above and slightly left. Climb up on to a large block and continue up until a step left gains the bulge below the peg. Clip the peg, move left through the bulge and go up to a recess. Move right below a nose then up and left on to a slab. Continue up to finish, as for Investigator, by pulling on to the overhanging nose on the right.

14 Investigator 120m Hard Severe * *(1969)*

A spectacular route, but the quality of the climbing doesn't match the position. Start at an obvious narrow slab gangway near the top right-hand end of the cliff (lower down than a big low angled slab and gangway which is level with the col on the right).

1. 40m Climb the gangway easily.
2. 25m 4b Continue up the gangway past a narrowing and another awkward mossy section to reach a nose on the skyline.
3. 25m 4a Go left around the nose and climb up a broken groove, then traverse right to belay.
4. 30m 4a Climb up and right to gain an overhanging nose, pull up the overhang and continue to the top.

COIRE LAIR APPROACH CRAGS   117

Society of Whispers, E2 5b/c, Sonny Wall, Coire Lair. Climber Carlos Las Heras

Winter: **VI,7** ** (1991)
Follow the summer line, as spectacular an outing.

WEST TOP - NORTH FACE

(NG 969 491)   Alt 750m   North facing

Western Pinnacle   90m   III (2005)
This buttress is much shorter and somewhat broken but offers some easier lines. Its base angles rightwards up the hillside, then levels off below some steeper and blocky ground as its aspect changes more to north-west. This is high on the right, in profile from the point where the Mainreachan approach leaves the path. Start just left of the steep ground and climb a groove which leads into a ramp below the steep ground. Continuing up the ramp would probably be Grade II. Make a short traverse right and climb a prominent short chimney to gain a squat pinnacle. Move up and left to reach easy ground.

COIRE LAIR APPROACH CRAGS

The following crags are near the Coire Lair path, on the approach to Sgòrr Ruadh.

SONNY WALL

(NG 995 490)   Alt 170m   South-East facing

The wall can be clearly seen above the tree plantation from where the Coire Lair path leaves the vehicle track. The wall is 100m from the path when it turns north-west away from the deer fence. The lines climb the main wall left of a heather filled corner.

Transoceanic Chicken   15m   HVS 5a * (2005)
Climb the shallow cracked groove system on the left side of the wall.

118 SGÒRR RUADH

Sonny Jack 15m HVS 4c *(2005)*
Start 3m left of the corner and climb stepped ground up to a small overhang on the right. Pull through this into a shallow groove on the left and climb to the top.

WHISPERING BUTTRESS

(NG 993 499) Alt 370m South-West facing Map p97

The prominent buttress on the right of the path. The routes lie on the large central section. A Dog Named Corrie takes the broken groove up the biggest section of the buttress from the lowest point.

The Custodian 35m E1 5a * *(2005)*
Start at the bottom of a left-slanting ramp to the right of a grassy gully on a terrace 5m from the bottom of the buttress. Climb the ramp and then the crack up the wall above. Step right with difficulty into a small niche. Either climb this direct, or for the faint hearted, dogleg right for 3m and then back to climb the wall above to the top. Good climbing. Gear is poor and sparse.

A Dog named Corrie 35m Severe 4a *(2005)*
Belay on the terrace below a broken groove. Start 3m left of the groove and traverse in to the groove after 3m. Climb this to the top.

Society of Whispers 40m E2 5b/c * *(2005)*
This climbs the most prominent corner-groove of a series of cracked grooves that start 8m right of the above route. Climb the groove and wall above with difficulty to easier ground at 20m. Continue to the top.

SGÒRR RUADH

(NG 959 505) Alt 960m Maps p86, 97

Sgòrr Ruadh, the highest peak of the Coulin Forest, presents an impressive north-east and north face to the walker ascending Coire Lair from Achnashellach. The rock is sandstone throughout and rather broken, so the summer climbs are somewhat indeterminate. In winter the gullies and faces provide good climbs in a fine situation.

Approach: The best approach is on the good path from Achnashellach station to upper Coire Lair. There is a good parking place on the A890 near the sign to Achnasheallach Station. Walk up to the station and continue on the track which crosses the railway. Turn left at a junction (this is obvious) and through felled ground until a fence and kissing gate can be seen close on the left (small sign). Behind the fence is the stalking path which is followed into Coire Lair, 2hrs 30mins. A notice says that the Achnasheallach Estate stalks from 15 Sep to 20 Oct and to contact 01520 766266 for information. The alternative approaches from Torridon are considerably longer but also very scenic. Either follow the track from Annat to the Bealach na Lice and then via Bealach Bàn to upper Coire Lair; or, starting from the Ling Hut (NG 958 562) take the path climbing southwards. It disappears after a few kilometres but later on the Bealach Bàn track is joined.

Descent: The normal descent is down Central Couloir although North Gully is an alternative for those who have left rucksacks below the North Face. A pleasant and only slightly longer alternative is to descend south-east, crossing the stream below Loch a' Bhealaich Mhòir and join the stalking path which leads back to the Coire Lair path. Another option is to bag the Munro (about 15mins away).

The climbs are described as for the Achnashellach approach. Seen from Loch Coire Lair, the furthest skyline ridge marks Raeburn's Buttress, with the North Face behind it. Coming left from this is a broken face overlooking the broad Central Couloir, and then, in front of the Couloir and partially hiding it, the long line of Academy Ridge with an easy section in the middle and a steep upper part. Left of

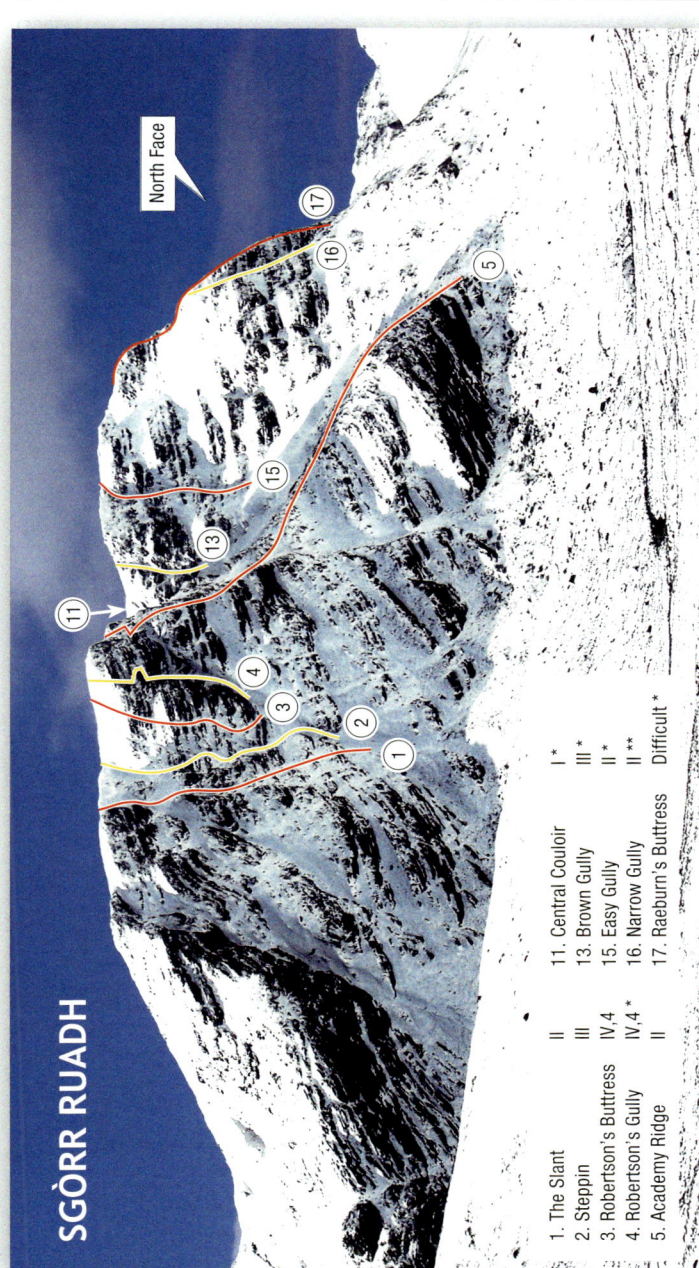

SGÒRR RUADH

1. The Slant	II	11. Central Couloir	I *
2. Steppin	III	13. Brown Gully	III *
3. Robertson's Buttress	IV,4	15. Easy Gully	II *
4. Robertson's Gully	IV,4 *	16. Narrow Gully	II **
5. Academy Ridge	II	17. Raeburn's Buttress	Difficult *

GLEN CARRON

SGÒRR RUADH

this is another large broken area, the South-East Face, with a number of rakes running up from left to right terminating in gullies. Robertson's Gully defines the left boundary of Academy Ridge and the next buttress left is Robertson's Buttress. From a diagonal snow ramp going up rightwards to Robertson's Gully, two lines may be seen climbing directly up and passing left of Robertson's Buttress.

SOUTH-EAST FACE

(NG 969 505)   Alt 650m   East facing   Map p97   Diagram p119

1 The Slant   350m   II   *(1969)*
The left-hand line rising from the ramp. An easy climb with several possible variations.

2 Steppin   250m   III   *(1969)*
The right-hand line rising from the ramp is an obvious corner. Follow this for two pitches then move right and go up a small steep step. Continue up easier ground to the top.

3 Robertson's Buttress   200m   IV,4   *(1994)*
This takes a central line on the face of the buttress right of Steppin. Start at the toe of the buttress and climb by snowfields, short rock steps, a shallow icy gully and a steep groove in the final rocks to reach easy ground.

4 Robertson's Gully   180m   IV,4 *   *(1976)*
A long snow approach climbing diagonally right leads to this steep gully on the left of Academy Ridge. There is a deep cave just over halfway up. Climb the gully by a series of chockstone filled chimneys to the cave (this section can largely bank out). Traverse right and re-enter the gully by the higher of two traverse lines above the cave.

5 Academy Ridge   350m   Very Difficult   *(1948)*
The lower part of the ridge is scrambling. Above there is a discontinuity in the crest, which re-appears on the left. Rejoin it as soon as possible and climb the steep upper section with a fine 25m pitch.
Winter: **II**
A long mountaineering route, mostly easy. Follow the summer line, except that the steep upper pitch is avoided on the right, probably involving a short descent into the upper section of Post Box Gully, regaining the ridge above the steep section.
Variation: **Direct Finish   25m   IV,5**   *(1994)*
Climbed direct, the steep upper section gives a sustained pitch. Gain grooves just to the right of the arete by a 3m traverse, then follow the grooves to a loose spike. Gain the arete by awkward steps, and follow the arete more easily to the top.

CENTRAL COULOIR

(NG 966 506)   Alt 700m   North or South-East facing   Map p97   Diagram p121

6 Post Box Gully   180m   II ***   *(1969)*
This is a narrow well-defined gully, recognisable by a huge chockstone near its foot and situated low down in the left wall of the Central Couloir, where the couloir is wide and open. Climb up to the chockstone and continue beneath it to emerge from a slot. Continue direct over small pitches to the top of Academy Ridge. Ice is not required, the route is climbable in most conditions.

7 Gravesend   200m   IV,4   *(1998)*
At the base of the steep section of the Central Couloir left wall is a prominent left-slanting gully, almost a ramp under a smooth steep wall. Climb the gully to a cave (50m). Exit the cave by ice on the left and cross a big terrace (50m). Enter a big scoop in the upper buttress and finish up a chimney from its top right corner. Perhaps Grade III with the first pitch well frozen.

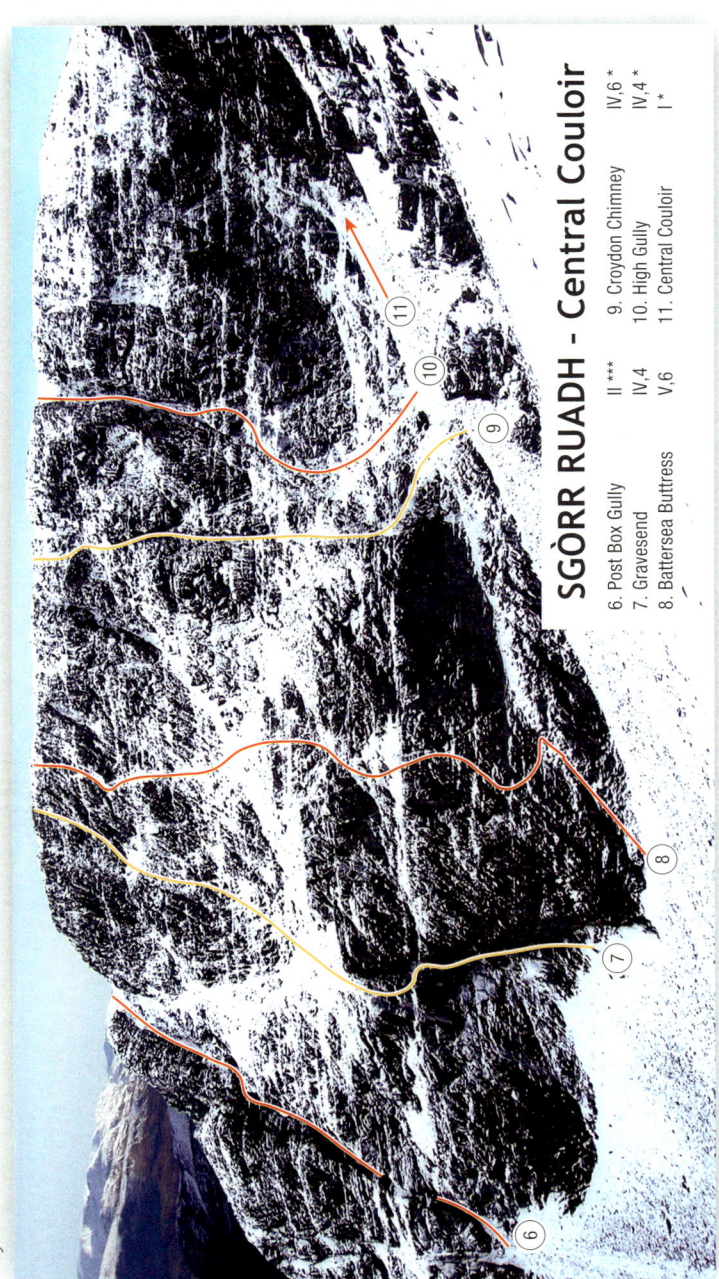

SGÒRR RUADH - Central Couloir

6. Post Box Gully — II ***
7. Gravesend — IV,4
8. Battersea Buttress — V,6
9. Croydon Chimney — IV,6 *
10. High Gully — IV,4 *
11. Central Couloir — I *

GLEN CARRON

SGÒRR RUADH

8 Battersea Buttress   250m   V,6   *(1996)*
Climbs the buttress right of Gravesend and where the cliff base turns sharply upwards into the narrow section of the Couloir. Start about 30m right of Gravesend where an easy turfy ramp leads up right.
1. 30m Climb the ramp.
2. 30m Work out left by a devious line on steep ground, always keeping right of a slabby left-facing corner, to reach easier angled terrain.
3. 50m Climb up right to a big terrace.
4. 50m There is a Grade I escape rightwards up a gully here. Instead, cross the gully leftwards and go up a turfy line on the buttress above.
5. 25m Continue to the crest on the left and climb it steeply.
6. 25m To the top.

9 Croydon Chimney   180m   IV,6 *   *(1969)*
Just left of High Gully is a left-slanting chimney-line. It can be very icy but this is not essential. Climb this direct with a hard slot (crux, mixed) at mid-height and a sustained upper groove. Escape left to easy ground below the final capstone.

10 High Gully   120m   IV,4 *   *(1976)*
High on the left wall of the Central Couloir, just below and opposite Brown Gully, a large two-tiered icefall can form below a deep narrow gully. Climb the icefalls trending right and enter the gully from the right. Grade III in its best condition.
Variation: **V,6**   *(1988)*
The route has been climbed without ice, starting further right (SMCJ 1994).

11 Central Couloir   300m   I *
The huge shallow gully with climbs leading out either side. Only just steep enough to be given Grade I and therefore a popular route to the summit of Sgòrr Ruadh.

12 Ruayahua   110m   V,6   *(2001)*
This route climbs the broken buttress high up on the right of Central Couloir and left of Brown Gully via the front face of the prominent tower. Start at the bottom left side of the buttress below a turfy groove just left of the first tower.
1. 25m Climb the turfy groove trending right to a chimney; climb this to the top of the first tower.
2. 25m Traverse left along the ledge on to the front face of the second tower. Climb a black groove and traverse hard left until established in the steep cracks in the middle of the face. Climb these (crux) and continue in the same line to the top of the tower.
3 etc. 60m Climb the broken buttress above to the top.

13 Brown Gully   100m   III *   *(1969)*
This is the narrow gully on the right of and starting high up Central Couloir. Climb up right past a bend in the gully and go up an ice pitch. Climb straight up the gully to where it narrows and steepens. Follow a groove on the right and return to the gully as soon as possible. Continue easily to the top.

14 Parallel Lines   100m   III   *(1994)*
Shortly after the start of Brown Gully is a right branch. This is easy until an awkward overhung 3m wall. Easy snow grooves to finish.

15 Easy Gully   180m   II *   *(1969)*
Halfway along the right wall of Central Couloir is an obvious long gully starting just right of an isolated pinnacle. It may have several short ice pitches.

RAEBURN'S BUTTRESS

(NG 966 509) Alt 630m North-East to North facing Map p97 Diagram p123

The ridge forming the right side of the Central Couloir formation, clearly seen in

SGÒRR RUADH
Raeburn's Buttress

16. Narrow Gully	II **
17. Raeburn's Buttress Direct	V,6 *
18. The Jigsaw	III **
19. Tritium Chimney	V,7 **
20. Brooker's Route	IV,4 *
21. Raeburn's Superdirect	IV,6 **

profile from the Coire Lair approach. Although it appears on the approach to have a well defined crest, in fact its upper part is much better defined than the lower, which has a broad frontal zone consisting of steep, slabby walls separated by discontinuous terraces. This lower face has two chimney lines, a narrow one in the centre and a big obvious one (more of a gully) forming its right side. The crest arrives at a shoulder followed by the upper section, which is easier-angled but a well-defined crest. Routes on the north face of the buttress finish at differing heights on the upper crest. Route lengths, apart from Raeburn's Buttress and its Direct, are given to the crest which is Grade II for its upper section. It is also possible to escape from the shoulder by descending diagonally left into the Central Couloir, finishing by the base of Easy Gully.

**16 Raeburn's Buttress via Narrow Gully   350m   II ** *(1904/1978)*
Start up the prominent narrow gully bounding Raeburn's Buttress on the left. The 1904 ascent gained the buttress after its first two pitches. The 1978 ascent climbed the gully throughout. Continue up the crest, with a couple of tricky sections but mostly easy, to the top.

17 Raeburn's Buttress (Direct)   350m   Difficult *
This climb follows the skyline silhouetted on the approach from Coire Lair. The first two short pitches are on fine sound rock and quick to dry; thereafter the climb becomes a Moderate scramble with much heather and loose rock. It is however a good, natural mountaineering route. Start immediately right of Narrow Gully, at the base of its right wall. Climb the crest on good holds to a terrace (20m). Move right and climb the short steep tier above by a left-slanting ramp-corner to a boulder covered terrace and easier ground (20m). Keep as near to the crest as seems sensible to reach the shoulder. The easier upper section follows.

124 SGÒRR RUADH

Winter: **130m to shoulder   V,6 ***   (1999)
A fine line following the summer route, but a rather hard start compared to the upper section. The steep first pitch has several thin moves but is well protected by blade pegs. After the ramp-corner, follow grooves close on the right of the crest to reach easy ground leading to the shoulder.
Variation: **Severe**
The line described in the 1993 guide, much less pleasant, mostly Very Difficult but with a move of at least Severe. Start about 25m down and right from the base of Narrow Gully, on a terrace below the front face and about 10m left of a narrow ramp leading diagonally rightwards up the face, the first big feature right of the crest. Climb on to a big square block, move right, up a tricky wall and back left to follow a left-slanting flaky-line to the terrace after pitch 1 above. Walk left to regain the normal route.
Winter: **160m (to shoulder)   V,6**   (1998)
Not quite as hard as the more direct route above, this route omits the first pitch of the summer variation (which would be very hard in winter). The line is separate line from the direct route, only the last pitch coinciding. Start at the foot of the right wall of Narrow Gully, at the same place as the direct route.
1. 20m   Traverse horizontally right along a narrow ledge to join the summer variation.
2. 30m   Find the left-slanting flaky-line leading to a bigger ledge.
3. 20m   Traverse right and climb two short steep walls to a big terrace.
4. 45m   Climb easier ground just right of the crest.
5. 45m   Climb the crest to the shoulder etc.

18   The Jigsaw   200m   III **   (1998)
Provides a more difficult mixed start to Raeburn's Buttress, but not sustained. Start only a little right but much lower than Narrow Gully where a ramp leads rightwards up the face. Climb the ramp to its top (60m), traverse right along a ledge (50m) and reach a fault-line leading diagonally back left to the crest (70m). A short pitch on the crest leads to the upper section (20m).

19   Tritium Chimney   140m   V,7 **   (1997/2006)
Based on the narrow chimney line right of Raeburn's Buttress Direct and which cuts directly through The Jigsaw. The chimney, which is hidden from below, feeds ice into a groove which is rarely in condition. A mixed line near the groove is the current start. Start up the groove but immediately move right. Climb steep ground about 3m right of the groove before stepping into it. Climb the groove to a bay (20m). Vertical ice leads into the chimney but a mixed line just left gains a ledge. Crawl right to the chimney and follow it to the top of the ramp on The Jigsaw and below the upper chimney (20m). Two steep steps in the upper chimney (crux – 30m) and the easier continuation of the line (40m) lead to the crest and the short pitch as above to the top of the steep section of the buttress (20m).
Variation: **Original Start**
Climb the blocky rib on the left of the groove, leading into the top of the Jigsaw ramp, followed rightwards back to the upper chimney-line.

20   Brooker's Route   300m   IV,4 *   (1967)
Called Raeburn's Buttress Direct in the last guide, but renamed because it is not a direct version of the original route. It starts well to the right and takes a completely separate line to reach the upper crest. It crosses the big chimney of the Superdirect (name retained). Start at a bay below and right of the big shelf and just right of Tritium Chimney. Take a turfy line leading rightwards to the brink of the big Superdirect chimney. Climb the wall on the left of the chimney to a ledge and continue to another terrace. Here a steep wall rises for 30m forming an incipient tower close to the chimney. Follow a groove leftwards passing an icy section by ledges on the vertical right wall. From a narrow terrace make a sensational traverse right for 15m over large detached blocks beneath an overhang to gain a recess in the Superdirect chimney. Cross the chimney, moving right to reach easy ground, then follow the upper crest to the top.

NORTH FACE | 125

**21 Raeburn's Superdirect   190m   IV,6 **   *(1989)*
This big chimney line is an obvious feature just before the buttress curves round to form the North Face.
1. 45m Climb a short ice pitch, then a right-slanting iced groove passing a chockstone to a terrace.
2. 45m Go up the groove above to a steeper iced exit.
3. 40m Climb over short walls into an overhung cul-de-sac which is surmounted by tricky mixed climbing up the left wall, then bridging across to reach ice leading to easier ground. Belay on the right.
4. 40m Climb a chimney and a short step. Belay on the left.
5. 20m A final awkward step leads to easy ground and the upper crest of Raeburn's Buttress.

NORTH FACE

(NG 963 508)   Alt 750m   North-North-West facing   Map p97   Diagram p126

Raeburn's Buttress gradually bends round to form the 250m north face. This is bounded on the right by a deep scree or snow gully with an impressive vertical left wall (North Gully). The most obvious feature is the gully of the Superdirect which somewhat arbitrarily forms its left side. The route lengths apply to reaching the upper crest of Raeburn's Buttress. The best finish is to follow the crest to the top (Grade II at first) although there is an easier option to traverse left and finish up a shallow gully.

22 Spanner in the Works   230m   V,6   *(1996)*
Climbs the buttress right of the Superdirect, between it and and Tophet Gully. Start mid-way between the two at a 5m icefall at the base of V shaped diverging faults; this is 8m left of a tree. Climb the icefall to a ledge, then traverse left into the left fault, almost a shallow chimney. Follow this to a bulging section which forces a 6m traverse left to a large flake against the wall. Climb steep cracks above the flake to a terrace (45m, could be split). The fault continues left to join the Superdirect, so traverse easily right and up to the right-hand of parallel grooves (35m). Climb the right-hand groove to a notch on the skyline and easier ground (70m). Follow the easy features to the upper crest of Raeburn's Buttress.

23 Sticky Fingers   240m   V,5   *(2006)*
This is the vague crest left of the obvious fault of Tophet Gully, requiring a devious route to avoid steep blank walls. Start as for Tophet Gully.
1. 10m Move up and left on turf to find a belay.
2. 25m Traverse left along a ledge with a gap to easier ground leading up left.
3. 25m Gain the top of a platform on the left and climb the first break beyond smooth walls.
4. 25m Climb a left-slanting steep crack with chockstones to a ledge. Move left and back right to a higher ledge.
5. 50m Traverse the ledge right to easy ground and go up to a platform below smooth walls.
6. 25m Starting on the left, climb some thin steps rightwards to easier ground.
7. and 8. 80m Climb the vague crest to the upper crest of Raeburn's Buttress.

**24 Tophet Gully   200m   IV,5 *   *(1995)*
The obvious left slanting fault in the centre of the North Face. It leads to the top of the steep lower section of Raeburn's Buttress. Access to the fault appears to be blocked by a big overhang. Attention is attracted by extensive smears of ice, but a thinly iced slab tucked in to the fault on the right is the key. A second barrier wall can be climbed on ice at its left side leading to an easier upper gully and in turn to the upper crest of Raeburn's Buttress.

**25 Fox's Face   260m   IV,4 **   *(1987)*
A good mixed route up the highest part of the north face, finishing near the top of

GLEN CARRON

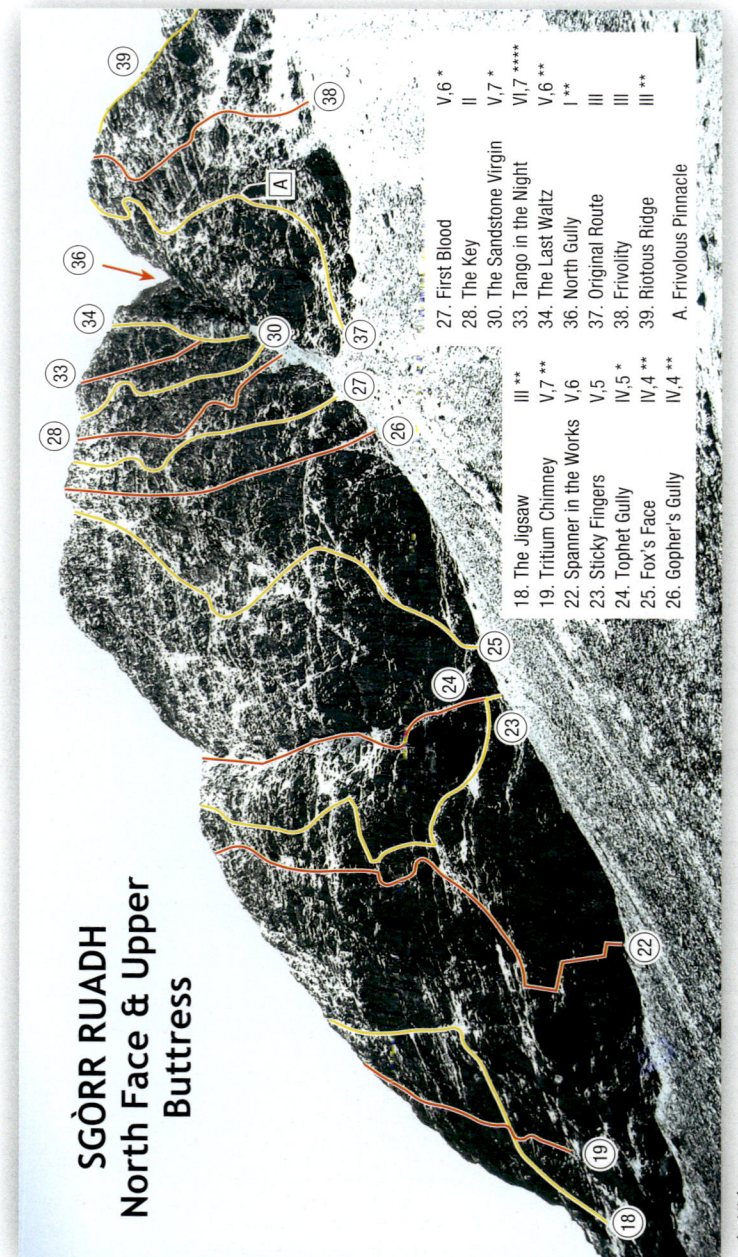

SGÒRR RUADH
North Face & Upper Buttress

18. The Jigsaw	III **
19. Tritium Chimney	V,7 **
22. Spanner in the Works	V,6
23. Sticky Fingers	V,5
24. Tophet Gully	IV,5 *
25. Fox's Face	IV,4 **
26. Gopher's Gully	IV,4 **
27. First Blood	V,6 *
28. The Key	II
30. The Sandstone Virgin	V,7 *
33. Tango in the Night	VI,7 ****
34. The Last Waltz	V,6 **
36. North Route	I **
37. Original Route	III
38. Frivolity	III
39. Riotous Ridge	III **
A. Frivolous Pinnacle	

Andy Nisbet

the Raeburn's Buttress. The lower part is the crux, originally graded III. Start 10m right of the obvious left-slanting fault-line of Tophet Gully. Take a right-slanting crack-line through the very steep lower tier (40m). Make a rightward deviation, then move back left into the big central depression of the face (40m). Go left at the top of the depression, then weave back right and take the final wall direct by grooves.

26 Gopher's Gully   200m   IV,4 ** *(1996)*
Takes a shallow gully starting below First Blood and just outside North Gully. It has the very obvious feature of a large chockstone on the first pitch underneath which one must chimney. The second pitch continues up the gully, also steep and leads to an easy broad rib and the upper crest of Raeburn's Buttress.

27 First Blood   185m   V,6 * *(1988)*
Start just inside the right-bounding North Gully, about 50m above Fox's Face. A shallow bay leads to a steep corner with a prominent crack in its left wall.
1. 20m Climb the bay to belay beneath the crack.
2. 25m Follow the crack direct, finishing over a roof to a good block belay, a fine hard pitch.
3. 45m Go up grooves, moving slightly left then traversing back right under roofs and up easily to belay beneath a left-slanting groove.
4. and 5. 95m Now climb the groove (awkward to start) to gain easy ground which is followed to the top of the buttress.

28 The Key   170m   II *(1995)*
Start about 50m up North Gully, where an easy ramp leads out left. Follow the ramp to the first crest after which it continues as a traverse line. Traverse initially, then make a difficult move on to a higher ramp leading to the main crest. Follow this easily to the top.

29 Highland Scottische   150m   IV,5 * *(1995)*
This climbs intimidatingly steep but helpful ground. Start about 15m above the ramp of The Key. Climb the vague scoop in the wall trending slightly left towards the top, to finish up the easy crest, joining The Key.

30 The Sandstone Virgin   130m   V,7 * *(1996)*
On the gully wall higher than the left-leading ramp of The Key is a shallow gully which clearly steepens.
1. 35m Climb up into the gully and follow it with a deviation to the left to avoid a short wall, to the steep section.
2. 25m Climb the steep section, imposing but very helpful (and crucial that many blocks are frozen in place).
3. 45m Continue and reach easier ground over a big chockstone with a very hard exit (technical crux) on to scree. This would be a lot easier with a little ice.
4. 25m Finish easily up a groove and the final 10m of Raeburn's Buttress.

31 Ruadh Awakening   120m   VI,6 * *(1988)*
This climb is a direct winter version of Splintery Edge. Start in the middle of the buttress below Splintery Edge, where a system of grooves can be seen running up the face.
1. 40m Move left along a ledge for about 5m, then climb up and right to a good ledge. Step right and continue up to a flake. Move up and right then up to a wide crack which is ascended to a ledge. Traverse left then up to a belay on blocks.
2. 20m Move right off the blocks to regain the groove line. Climb this briefly then its right edge. Climb the bulge above and from a small recess below a steeper bulge traverse right to a ledge near the edge of the buttress.
3. 30m Continue up the groove line above. On the first ascent poor ice just short of the top necessitated a short deviation left then up the crest.
4. 30m Climb the final buttress by the right-hand of two grooves.

Gopher's Gully, IV,4, North Face, Sgòrr Ruadh. Climber Martin Moran

32 Splintery Edge 100m Very Difficult (1961)
Follow the scree-filled North Gully for about 100m to a concealed left branch which ends in a formidable cul-de-sac. Climb the crumbly bed of the branch gully for 15m, then follow a shelf leftwards over loose blocks to the edge. Now climb straight up for 75m on improving rock to the top.
Winter: III,4 (2001)
By the summer route. The top part obviously coincides with Ruadh Awakening.

33 Tango in the Night 100m VI,7 **** (1989)
One of the best short routes in Scotland, taking a superb line up the huge imposing depression lying halfway up North Gully on the left. Start as for Splintery Edge but soon diverge right into the main corner. Follow this, soon becoming a very steep succession of chimneys, which can be climbed in several short pitches. Despite the steepness, there are excellent cracks and many flakes (essential that it is well frozen). Almost at the top, the line is blocked by a final overhang. Move up right on blocks and finish on the left (the first ascent made a sensational but harder traverse right to finish).

34 The Last Waltz 110m V,6 ** (1996)
This takes the unexpected easing in angle between Tango in the Night and steep walls higher up the gully. Start as for Tango but at the start of its difficulties, traverse right along a narrow grass ledge above a steep wall to a spike (30m). Take a line of cracks slanting slightly right and leading to a right-facing slabby corner with a fine crack. A belay was taken in a niche above the corner (45m). Make a strenuous pull out of the niche, then follow a right-trending line via a groove to an easier finish (35m).

MAOL CHEAN-DEARG   129

35 Pit Bull Polka   65m   VI,7   *(2001)*
Short but brutal! A steep line on the left wall of upper North Gully, above its concealed left branch. The line takes a shallow groove on a slight crest between two big overhangs. Start about 40m above the left branch and below the upper overhang. Take a line leading diagonally left, including an awkward move left round a bulge to the base of the groove. Climb the groove (crux) until flakes and blocks lead left to a good ledge (35m). Climb a ramp with a wide crack up left to a slight crest. Finish up a turfy groove and snow (30m).

36 North Gully   200m   I *
The deep gully bounding the right side of the main face is scenically impressive because of its imposing left wall. Initially easy, it steepens and narrows in the upper half.

UPPER BUTTRESS

(NG 961 506)   Alt 750m   North facing   Diagram p126

Upper Buttress is on the right of the deep scree-filled North Gully. **The Frivolous Pinnacle** (Difficult), the pinnacle on the right of Original Route and near the base of North Gully, is very obvious on an approach along the base of the North Face, but not from directly below. It can be reached from the foot of North Gully by ledges and a short chimney.

37 Upper Buttress, Original Route   150m   Very Difficult   *(1955)*
Start at the left edge of the buttress. Climb a 3m corner near the overhangs on the left edge and traverse 12m right to cracks on the face between these overhangs and the prominent Frivolous Pinnacle. Climb more or less straight up the buttress, with slight traverses as necessary. The main difficulties end about half-way up where a through route is made behind a boulder jammed in the right-hand crack. Scrambling leads to the top.
Winter: **III**   *(1972)*
The original description (SMCJ 1977) sounds more like Fox's Face, but the 1973 guide also notes a winter route leading from the back of The Frivolous Pinnacle straight up the buttress. Presumably this route moves leftwards to join Original Route on the crest after about 50m.

38 Frivolity   150m   III   *(2006)*
Start in the centre of the face, about 20m right of the Frivolous Pinnacle. Climb straight up steep turf for about 50m to reach and follow a gully leading left. Shortly before reaching the crest, break back right and finish direct.

39 Riotous Ridge   140m   III *   *(1995)*
The right bounding ridge of Upper Buttress. Missing the lower crest by a depression on the left and passing the upper crest on the right makes it Grade II.

MAOL CHEAN-DEARG

(NG 924 498)   Alt 933m   Map p86

Meal Chean-dearg and An Ruadh-stac can be approached on excellent paths either from Coulags, about 7km south-west of Achnashellach, or from Annat at the head of Loch Torridon. There is a line of quartzite crags on the east side of the south-east ridge of Maol Chean-dearg leading towards Meall nan Ceapairean. The two biggest buttresses are at NG 931 492 and are clearly visible from the east. The left-hand buttress gives a pleasant climb, **Ketchil Buttress** (120m Difficult 1969). In winter conditions, Grade III, starting just right of the crest by a groove which leads up left to a few tricky moves on the crest (2001). The right-hand buttress has also been climbed, **Ketchup Buttress** (Moderate). A long groove on its right flank gives a 100m II (2001).

130 AN RUADH-STAC

There is also some climbing on the steep north face of Maol Chean-dearg, overlooking Loch an Eoin. **Hidden Gully** (300m II 1968) lies at the left-hand side of the face, running from low down right up to the summit. Two climbs lie on a conspicuous light coloured quartzite cliff about 150m above the loch, below a darker band of crags (NG 923 505). The cliff has a horizontal ledge at one-third height and two big left-slanting ramps near the top. **No Birds** (100m Very Difficult 1971) starts below the right-hand ramp, just under some very light coloured rock. It climbs up to the ramp in two pitches and follows it to the top. **But Midges** (110m Severe 1971) starts below the left-hand ramp. It reaches the horizontal ledge via a steep groove and then climbs right to a short vertical step, left into a steep recess and right to reach the ramp.

AN RUADH-STAC

(NG 922 481)   Alt 890m   Map p86

The north face of this peak has two tiers of blocky quartzite giving climbs of up to 180m.

North Face   180m   Very Difficult   *(1960)*
Climb a prominent slabby rib just left of an obvious white scar on the lower tier. Above is a curving damp chimney. Go 30m left and climb diagonally left for 45m to a big recess. Continue directly to the top.
Winter: **300m   III**   *(1993)*
Climb the lower tier close to the summer line, then follow the terrace rightwards to the large depression in the upper tier and climb this to the summit.

Foxtrot   180m   Severe   *(1967)*
This route lies to the right of North Face. There is a large black cave on the bottom terrace with an ill-defined buttress of ribs and grooves on its left. Climb the buttress up to the large depression on the right of the upper tier. Follow the left edge of the depression to scrambling.

Quartzice   160m   V,5   *(1994)*
A winter ascent close to Foxtrot. Towards the right end of the lower tier, directly below the depression in the upper tier is a prominent icefall. Start in a snow bay just left of a big cave, about 20m right of the line of the icefall.
1. 45m   Climb a vegetated groove, trending slightly left to a ledge.
2. 20m   Continue in the same line and move left to the base of the icefall.
3. 45m   Climb the icefall and belay on the terrace above.
4. 50m   Follow the left edge of the depression via grooves to scrambling.

EAST FACE

(NG 925 482)   Alt 600m   East facing

On the east face of the mountain is a recessed slabby area which forms twin icefalls. These look good under cold snowless conditions but disappointing as soon as there is any snow, when they bank out considerably.

Left Icefall   90m   II   *(1996)*
The left icefall.

Right Icefall   90m   II   *(1983)*
The right icefall.

MEALL NAN CEAPAIREAN

(NG 938 486)   Alt 677m   Map p86

A small hill whose face is seen on the approach up Maol Chean-dearg from the south-east.

GLAS BHEINN 131

NORTH FACE

(NG 939 487)   Alt 500m   North facing

A very turfy face, steeper than it looks, but disappointing as the natural lines are diagonal and do not lead to the top. It is, however, a useful accessible option when deep soft snow prevents a visit to the higher or more remote cliffs. The Coulags bothy makes a useful stopping point.

Approach: The obvious route via the staking paths, 1hr 30mins.

Descent: On a broad ridge leading south-eastwards until an easy slope leads straight down to the bothy.

Stressful Buttress   180m   IV,5   (1998)
A fairly direct line, unfortunately escapable on to easier options. The steep central section of the face forms a nose between a big bowl on the left and steep broken ground on the right. A ramp leads up right from the bowl to the crest of the nose at about half height. The nose is also cut horizontally and near its base by parallel ledges close together. Climb a short gully to reach the left end of the upper ledge. Find a way through the steep turfy ground above to reach the ramp and follow it until just short of the crest. A fairly direct line keeping left of the crest was taken, involving some short difficult walls, to finish at the top of the crest.

Restful Buttress   200m   II   (1996)
Reach the left end of the upper ledge as for Stressful Buttress but traverse the ledge rightwards round the crest to where it curves up at its right end, then take a left-trending line to finish near the crest of the nose.

GLAS BHEINN

(NG 901 436)   Alt 711m   Map p86

CREAG NA H-IOLAIRE

(NG 899 445)   Alt 480m   North facing

This impressive, though unfortunately rather dirty, crag of gneiss directly overlooks the Bealach a' Glas-chnoic. It has a remote feel and the views are very fine. The climbs are described from right to left.

Approach: Park on the A896 2km north-east of Lochcarron near the track leading to Tullich (no easy parking place). Walk past Tullich on a signposted route and up beside the river on a deteriorating track. Where the track becomes merely tyre tracks in the heather, head away from the river to pick up the path. It barely exists at first and is never good, but lies close to where it is marked on the map, although it seems a long way up from the stream (much easier in descent), 1hr 30mins to 2hrs.

Right-Hand Gully   150m   III   (1999)
The gully bounding the right end of the crag.

Slab and Groove   150m   Severe   (1984)
At the right (higher and further away) side of the crag is a slabby corner just left of a gully. Climb this for 90m (Moderate) to a grassy terrace. The slabby corner continues to the top of the cliff. To its left is a deep groove, entrance to which is barred by a wall with overhangs. Follow the slabby corner for about 5m until above the first overhang then traverse left across the wall and climb through the second overhang to reach the groove. Follow the groove to the top.

Slab Boys   150m   IV,4   (2000)
As for Slab and Groove, except climb the slab all the way on a strip of ice.

132 GLAS BHEINN

The wall of the main crag left of Slab and Groove has a large flake. A route has been climbed, but not properly recorded, which takes walls up to the flake on the left, then goes right and up the flake.

Black House   175m   HVS   (1972)
Start below the centre of the crag.
1. 30m From a pinnacle go right up a crack.
2. 35m Go left round a rib and up a wide scoop.
3. 40m Climb directly, sometimes grassily, to a stance below overhangs and a small white slab.
4. 25m Climb the slab on the left, traverse right, and exit steeply on the right to a ledge at the left end of a terrace.
5. 45m Finish directly up steep walls.

Clean Compromise   170m   E1 *   (1984)
Start at the centre of the crag below a groove with an overhang at 10m.
1. 40m 4c Climb the groove to below the overhang, then go right and up easily for 10m. Climb a steep shallow groove on good holds to a small stance.
2. 40m 4c Move right along a ledge, climb up slabs, a steep wall and then a rib to a slanting grass terrace.
3. 25m 4b Go up the terrace to the white slab of Black House. Climb this on the left and continue up to a ledge below a steep wall. (A more direct variation is possible on this pitch.)
4. 35m 5b Climb a steep wall to gain a short groove on the right. Climb this and the overhang above on the right (strenuous). Continue up short walls and grassy ledges.
5. 30m Continue to the top.

Adul Suh   165m   HVS   (1974)
Start about 30m left of Black House. (This start would seem to be common with Clean Compromise).
1. 35m Climb a large groove with an overhang and luminous green moss above. Escape right below the overhang.
2. and 3. 65m Continue directly to below the steep grooves on the nose of the crag (taken by Clean Compromise), just left of the white slab on Black House.
4. and 5. 65m Go left and finish by shallow chimneys.

Left-hand Route   120m   VS   (1984)
This lies on the left-hand section of the crag.
1. 25m Climb a chimney past a flake to a large terrace.
2. and 3. 95m Go up a steep wall for 10m and trend left above an overhang onto black slabs. Climb black walls to the top.

Greenhorn Gully   190m   IV,4 **   (1996)
A big north facing gully bounding the left side of the main face and round the corner from the rock routes. A fine route when iced but this is rare due to the crag's low altitude. Easy angled ice terraces led to an obvious large ledge on the right (40m). The gully now steepened for two long pitches, with a short vertical crux low down, before narrowing and trending left. Finish by broken and turfy ground out right.

Frozen Pipes   90m   III   (1995)
Start up a curving gully seen on the approach from Tullich (New Kelso Couloir). Go easily along a terrace to the right until an obvious pinnacle or huge flake is reached (route length from here). The right end of the terrace overlooks Greenhorn Gully. Go up the icefall left of the pinnacle, then easier up a gully to the top.

New Kelso Couloir   180m   II   (1995)
The curving gully, via its right fork (the left fork is hidden on the approach).

NORTH STROME CLIFFS

SGÙRR A' GHARAIDH

(NG 890 446)   Alt 450m   North-East facing
A subsidiary peak to the west.

The Beast's Lair   200m   IV,5 * *(1999)*
From the Bealach a' Glas-chnoic, walk just south of west for 1km until a deep chimney come gully appears on the left. This is the route, a narrow chimney providing the crux.

NORTH STROME CLIFFS

Two crags on the north side of Loch Carron have a lovely view to Plockton, Skye and Applecross.

BAD A' CHREAMHA

(NG 849 362)   Alt 280m   West facing
A nose of quick drying juggy schist provides a good evening venue, hopefully in the sun. There are two buttresses of clean rock with a few heather ledges.

Approach: Start from Leacmashie, about 1km west of North Strome, on the road from Lochcarron to Ardaneaskan. There is a good parking place at the start of the footpath to Reraig (NG 851 356). Follow the path to the top end of a forestry road. Go 140m down the road to where the path leaves on the right (cairn). Go up the path to a col and the crag (right buttress) appears high on the right just before the col is reached. Leave the path just beyond the col and find a way up to the crag, 20mins.

Descent: Easily down the south side.

Floating Rib   60m   Moderate * *(1983)*
The right-hand and smaller buttress, following the left side of the crest.

Spare Rib   70m   Severe * *(1983)*
The main buttress lies about 60m left of Floating Rib. Start about 6m from the left edge of a steep lower section at a groove.
1. 25m Go up steeply past a small holly and another small tree in the V-groove above. Go left and up to a terrace, then a little way right to a clean wall.
2. 25m Find a way up the middle of the wall, probably bearing slightly left.
3. 20m Move left and easily up the crest to the top.

RERAIG COASTAL CLIFF

(NG 826 363)   Non-tidal   South facing
A steep 15m crag of bedded gneiss, reached by a 30mins shoreline walk from Reraig Cottage (9km west of Lochcarron).

The Schtroumpf   15m   E3 6a *(2001)*
A fierce corner-line at the left end of the crag.

Twinkle Toes   18m   HVS 5b *(2001)*
Climbs the big ramp from the left side of the crag with a short tricky section where it narrows.

Roaming the Gloaming   16m   Severe 4a *(2001)*
A parallel ramp-line below and right of Twinkle Toes, finishing up a steep corner.

GLEN CARRON

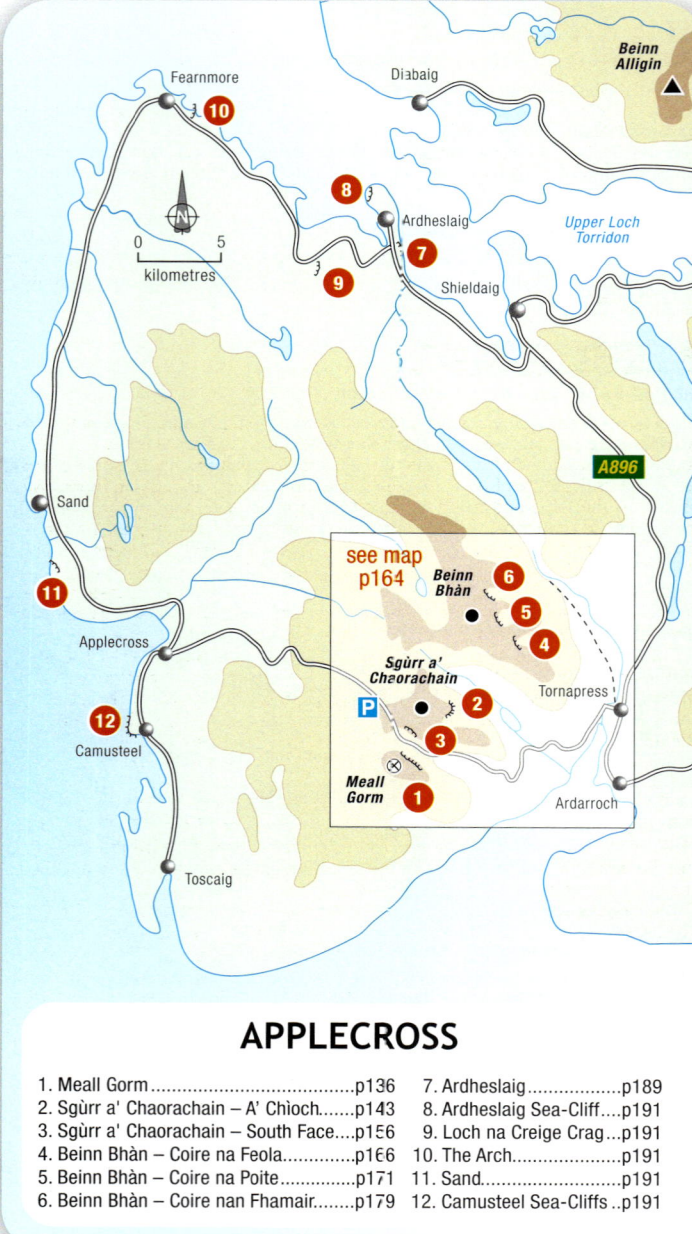

APPLECROSS

1. Meall Gorm.....................p136
2. Sgùrr a' Chaorachain – A' Chìoch.......p143
3. Sgùrr a' Chaorachain – South Face....p156
4. Beinn Bhàn – Coire na Feola..............p166
5. Beinn Bhàn – Coire na Poite...............p171
6. Beinn Bhàn – Coire nan Fhamair........p179
7. Ardheslaig..................p189
8. Ardheslaig Sea-Cliff....p191
9. Loch na Creige Crag...p191
10. The Arch....................p191
11. Sand..........................p191
12. Camusteel Sea-Cliffs ..p191

APPLECROSS

The Applecross peninsula has a group of three fine mountains, Meall Gorm to the west, the central Sgùrr a' Chaorachain and the larger Beinn Bhàn to the east. Britain's highest road outside the Cairngorms crosses a pass between Meall Gorm and Sgùrr a' Chaorachain and provides extraordinary access to Meall Gorm's winter routes and the fine rock climbing on Sgùrr a' Chaorachain. Its Cioch Nose is one of the great classics while its South Face offers roadside multi-pitch routes. Beinn Bhàn is a magnificent winter cliff, arguably Scotland's best were it further from the coast and less affected by global warming. Coire nan Fhamair is a truly awesome steep face while Coire na Poite's huge icefall of Silver Tear is the biggest steep icefall in Scotland. The Kishorn Boulders are described first, being on the south side of the peninsula, whereas the other crags on the north or west side are described after the mountains.

KISHORN BOULDERS

Map p164

Also known as the Applecross Boulders, but given a more specific name since there is much scope on the Applecross peninsula and more action has been promised soon. On the approach from Tornapress towards the Bealach na Bà, some of these large but isolated boulders are seen on a ridge across the Russel Burn. Most obvious is the large and heather topped Kishorn Stone on the skyline; this is the main point of reference. The Kishorn Stone is also seen from the parking place, a small layby for one car (two might just fit) at NG 8116 4082. This is on the uphill side of the road whereas the ridge and boulders are below. There were 25 routes on these boulders in early 2006. The rock is typical Torridonian sandstone, clean and featured. The landings are good and there are plenty of new lines still to be climbed. As an approximation, V0 is 5a or less, V1 is 5c and V2 is 6a.

The **Kishorn Stone** with nine routes is 250m down the ridge at NG 8136 4060, next to an old path. Its delightful north face has many some introductory wall lines, with the north-west arete (V1) providing a suitable exercise in balance. The underclin problem just to the left also provides a moment of essential control (V1). The south face is steeper and blanker with the obvious hanging groove, which seems frustratingly just out of reach, going at V8 (font 7b). The east face has two good easy cracks (V0, V0) and the west face a fine north-west layback crack (V0). There is also a good dyno problem on the south-west arete, (V2ish from a standing start).

Brains Boulder with four routes is 50m south, right of the ridge crest at NG 8137 4055. Its west face has a good travelling crack started from the arete (V1) and the east face groove provides a technical bridging exercise (V2), with a choice of exiting left or right.

The large **Ledge Boulder** is 80m down the ridge crest from Kishorn Stone at NG 8142 4051. It has a heavily ledged south face, which is problematic in that it is slightly green and highball and crevassed enough to be terrifying. The wee boulder below it has a more amenable juggy traverse on a roof (V2).

The **Swamp Boulders** with four routes on the East Boulder are 200m further downhill. The west wall has two good cracks (both V1), its east wall has a propped roof problem, and the south wall has two obvious projects, the slopey bulging roof and the technical wall just left of this.

Visible on the drive up and from the Kishorn Stone (north at the same altitude) but not from the parking spot although only 200m east and quite near the road, is the **Russell Boulder** with five routes (NG 8133 4092). It has a highball slabby west face (V0 at either end), a double-cornered north face (V1 at either end) and a steep and powerful line on the east face, V10 (font 7c+). The north-east arete is a good blunt power problem on diminishing slopers from a sit-down start (V8).

MEALL GORM

MEALL GORM

(NG 779 409)   Alt 710m   Maps p134, 164   Diagram p137

The northern side of Meall Gorm presents a broken line of cliffs overlooking the Allt a' Chumhaing, the valley leading up to the Bealach na Bà. Scotland's most accessible winter cliff! It may not be as impressive as others in the area but 15mins from the road makes it an important option. The Bealach na Bà road is now often ploughed and even when not open over the pass, one can often get as far as the climbs. Meall Gorm is near the sea and the most important factor for good conditions is that the turf be frozen (which happens more quickly on the steeper pitches than on the terraces which are often insulated by snow). The climbs near the top end of the cliff are much more likely to be frozen. The cliffs are too terraced and vegetated to provide rock climbing of the high quality of the Chaorachain face opposite but in dry weather there are some fair climbs.

Approach: *Upper Routes*: Park opposite and slightly below the climbs just beyond the roadside South Face of Sgùrr a' Chaorachain (Sword of Gideon cliff). Walk across and up to the routes.
  Lower Routes: There is a car park, really an extended lay-by, opposite the lower cliff.

Descent: *Upper Routes*: Descend to the first hairpin (sometimes via the summit trig point), having walked beyond the top end of the cliffs. The broad snow gully above Cobalt and Wedge Buttresses is also useful, particularly from that area.
  Lower Routes: There are some Grade I gullies in the centre of the cliff, the choice depending on where the car is parked (see below and make a plan before leaving the car).
  Lowest Routes: The slope south of the three big gullies and beyond the cliffs, close to another shallow gully.

1 Bypass Buttress   350m   II   *(1998)*
A scrappy but scenic route. Climb the central of the three lowest gullies to its blocking cave, traverse out right for 60m along a ledge to the buttress crest, then climb a steep pitch on the crest to an easy finish up the buttress.

2 Global Warming   300m   III   *(1995)*
Climbs the right-hand of three big gullies at the bottom end of the cliff, just left of the buttress with the Spiral Terrace. The right branch was taken, the left being easy. The three chockstone section was avoided by a groove on the right.

The first major feature when travelling up the Allt a' Chumhaing is the large eastern buttress which has a prominent terrace at half-height. When seen on the approach up the road, the terrace is crossed at right angles by a long, well defined gully which starts near the base of the uppermost of the three big lower gullies. A shallow gully line ascends from a scree cone to the right-hand end of the terrace, and then divides into three branches. This forms the start of the Spiral Terrace and Trident Gully climbs.

3 Shamrock Gully   300m   III   *(1999)*
The well defined gully which starts near the base of Global Warming but angles rightwards up the large buttress. Climb the gully for two pitches, then make an easy traverse right to reach the base of the long well defined section. Below the Spiral Terrace there is a short vertical pitch avoided using the rib on the right, otherwise the gully is followed.

4 Spiral Terrace   600m   II   *(1986)*
Ascend the shallow gully for 100m to the right end of the terrace. Follow the terrace leftwards for 300m to a defined gully (Shamrock Gully). Cross the gully and continue diagonally left for 100m to a large flat ledge in front of a short, steep wall. From the right end of the ledge ascend to a shallow gully slanting up right for 100m to the plateau.

MEALL GORM - Upper Cliff

16. Gormless Grooves	III	22. The Smooth Creep	VS	28. Wedge Buttress	III,4
17. Gorm Gully	II **	23. The Blue Lamppost	HVS	29. Boulder Problem Buttress	III
18. Blaeberry Corner	V,6 *	24. Rattlesnake	V,7 **	29a. Right Version	III
19. Blue Pillar	V,6 **	25. Blue Velvet	V,6 **	30. The Six-track Mono Blues	II
20. Lobster Gully	IV,5 **	26. Cobalt Buttress	IV,5 ***		
21. Blue in the Face	VI,7	27. Turquoise Gully	III **	d. descent	

APPLECROSS

Variation: **Direct Finish** 100m III,4 (1998)
Finish up the buttress right of the "defined gully", the crux being a short vertical wall low down.

5 Blue Moon 200m III,4 * (1991)
This route follows the crest of the buttress left of Trident Gully left branch. Start on a terrace left of the gully and climb a steep wall trending right towards the gully, then a harder one to the left. If well frozen and a sustained climb sought, the best line is now to traverse left to a gully come groove on the left. Otherwise, follow an easier turfy line nearer the gully. Finish by a short flaky wall.

6 Trident Gully, Left Branch 350m II * (1986)
Climb the shallow gully to the terrace (100m). One can also traverse in to this point from the right. Continue up the gully, keeping left where it forks, to the plateau (250m).

7 Trident Gully, Central Branch 350m III (1999)
From the fork, climb the central branch, which contains several short steps and one 15m barrier near the top, climbed by a chimney.

8 Trident Gully, Right Branch 380m III (1982)
Ascend to the terrace (100m). Continue up the gully to where it forks below twin chimneys (50m). Climb the left chimney to regain the gully (40m). Climb easily to a large roof (100m). Traverse left to a narrow gully, exiting right to gain the plateau (90m).
Variation: **Direct Finish** III (1999)
Move right from the large roof and a cave along a shelf, then up a corner to easier ground.

9 The Vegetable Sheep 270m IV,4 * (1995)
An obvious gully just right of the Trident Gullies. A chimney pitch at half-height and subsequent boulder choke are passed on the buttress on the left. Climbed and graded for semi-frozen.

Moving right (west) from Vegetable Sheep there is a well defined buttress, then a left-slanting gully with several indefinite branches to its right.

10 Wee Beastie 210m II (1986)
Climb the left-slanting gully.

To the right of Wee Beastie is a stepped buttress, then a V shaped gully system, the left branch being deeper and left-slanting, Grade II but would bank out to Grade I with only a little solid snow. The right branch is shallow, scree filled and is the best descent to the road from routes below this gully. Next is a scrappy buttress, then a shallow gully. At this point there is a steep step in the valley floor, the big feature which divides the cliff into upper and lower halves. Immediately above the step is a big rounded buttress split by two deep gullies, the left-hand only defined high up. To the right lies a wide gully, **Easy Gully**.

11 Way Out 210m II (1980)
This route is the least obvious and furthest left on the big rounded buttress, left of the two more obvious gullies. It is shallow and trends continuously left, taking in icy grooves and turfy walls to finish on the left skyline of the ridge.

12 Chockstone Gully 100m II
The left-hand gully, well defined high up and containing an obvious chockstone (which could bank out). Gain the deep section of the gully by a number of possibilities (not included in length), then climb it past two short pitches, the second being the chockstone, sporting if lean.

MEALL GORM 139

13 Crescent Gully 200m II
The right-hand gully, starting near Easy Gully and slanting left into the buttress before curving right to the summit of the buttress. Reach its start by a terrace leading left from Easy Gully. Two low angled ice pitches lead to a fork. Take the right branch, giving turfy grooves to the top.

14 Stonner Falls 95m IV,4 *(1980)*
This climb lies on the buttress right of Easy Gully, and follows a right-trending gully topped by a large cascade of ice. The ice rests on a broad terrace running the width of the buttress.
1. 40m Climb a short ice step then an easy gully to a wide terrace.
2. 30m Follow ice bulges on the left; belay below the final icefall.
3. 25m Climb the icefall on the left through bulges to a broad terrace.

15 Scampi Fries 90m IV,4 *(1994)*
Right of Stonner Falls is a fault. Climb this to a cave belay. Go up thin ice and two further steepenings (50m). Easy to the top.

Moving right, there is an area of broken ground, then the deep Gorm Gully, then a three-tiered buttress, then a broken buttress followed by the narrow Blue Pillar and the biggest buttress, Cobalt Buttress with its big steep left-hand face.

16 Gormless Grooves 130m III *(1995)*
The somewhat broken buttress to the left of Gorm Gully. Keep slightly left of centre up a series of stepped tiers following the natural grooves. The first tier is the crux.

17 Gorm Gully 150m II ** *(1970)*
This good wee route holds snow better than the other climbs on this face. Climb the deep narrow gully left of a three-tiered buttress (the third gully left of Blue Pillar) via easy snow to a final ice pitch. There is an escape left below the ice pitch.

18 Blaeberry Corner 105m Severe *(1955)*
This climbs the left side of the three-tiered buttress. It is a steep climb often on good rock, but with occasional loose blocks. Start up Gorm Gully (on the left of the buttress). After 15m traverse right over a block and up a wall to a terrace. Climb up the steep wall ahead for 25m to the top of the first tier. Climb the second tier by the vertical wall straight ahead, over some flakes, ending by a traverse right. Climb the third tier by the crest.
Winter: **75m V,6 *** *(1971)*
Start at the foot of the first tier.
1. 30m Go left up a weakness for 10m, then move right up a steep flake on to the buttress crest and the belvedere above.
2. 25m Gain the black groove on the buttress crest by delicate moves up the wall on the left and climb it direct with continuous interest; an excellent pitch.
3. 20m Move 3m right to a chimney ramp which leads to the top.

9 Blue Pillar 180m Severe * *(1953)*
A good mountaineering route up an excellent line, but some loose rock and vegetation. This is the conspicuous narrow pillar on the left of the massive Cobalt Buttress. Start at the foot and follow the crest. At mid-height a vertical step is climbed by a crack on the right with a precarious jammed flake at the top. Cracks about 10m round on the left wall is another possibility. Surmount the final tower by a deep chimney on the right.
Winter: **V,6 **** *(1958)*
Follow the summer route, except that the 'vertical' step at mid-height can either be climbed direct as for summer or by the cracks about 10m round on the left wall (the crux either way).

APPLECROSS

140 MEALL GORM

**20 Lobster Gully   200m   IV,5 ** *(1987)*
This is the prominent gully separating Blue Pillar from Cobalt Buttress. Several short steep steps lead to two fine well protected chimney pitches in the upper section. Some ice forms in the back, along with frozen vegetation, but requires cold conditions.

21 Blue in the Face   215m   VI,7 *(1993)*
This route lies on the steep left wall of Cobalt Buttress, right of Blue Pillar and Lobster Gully. Start at the foot of Lobster Gully and go up rightwards to a terrace. The first main tier is then climbed on the left by a zigzag line which reaches a belay below the smooth corner of The Smooth Creep (110m). Follow the next corner to the left up a line of a thin icefall to a ledge (25m). Step left and pull into a turfy groove which leads to a ledge and flake (25m). Traverse 10m left, past a blocky left-facing corner to climb an unlikely vegetated crack-line up the wall. Belay in a right-facing roofed corner (30m). Step down to make an exciting axe traverse left on turf. Slant up left to a wide crack, climb this and finish straight up (25m).

22 The Smooth Creep   90m   VS *(1971)*
Lies in the centre of the wall. High in the grade, partly because of some vegetation. Scramble up preliminary tiers to the foot of a smooth corner about halfway along the wall.
1. 20m 4b Start up the corner, trend right and climb a crack to below a steep wall.
2. 20m 4b Step right and climb to a stance below the left-hand of two corners.
3. 10m 4b Climb the corner to a ledge below a small overhang.
4. 35m 4c Go 5m left along a ledge and climb a steep cracked corner, then its right rib and up over two huge poised flakes to a good ledge.
5. 5m Finish by a short overhanging chimney.

23 The Blue Lamppost   90m   HVS *(1996)*
Scramble up vegetation through the easy lower tiers to the big ledge below the steep upper wall. At the right edge of the wall is slightly slabbier ground bounded on the left by the first right-facing corner which is about 20m left of Rattlesnake. Start left of the corner.
1. 10m Climb vegetation rightwards to the base of the corner.
2. 40m 5a Climb the slabs right of the corner to a long roof with a fine crack splitting its left side and the clean wall above. Climb the roof and crack, then move left past some unpleasant large jammed spikes, and further left to a large flat block sitting on a ledge.
3. 40m 5a Climb the crack above, initially off-width and awkward, until a step left is made into a shallow chimney with wedged blocks (not a bigger chimney further left). Climb the chimney back into the crack and continue until it is easier to trend right to finish close to Rattlesnake's left arete.

24 Rattlesnake   135m   Severe *(1965)*
This route follows the obvious line of corners running up the centre of Cobalt Buttress, at the right edge of the long wall.
1. 35m Scramble up to the first unavoidable tier and climb directly below the line of corners some distance left of a large black patch.
2. 35m Follow grass to the foot of the first and most impressive corner. Climb a smaller corner to the right until a right-slanting crack leads more easily to a grass ledge.
3. 35m Traverse left into the line of corners and climb to the top of the third tier.
4. 30m Climb the last set of corners directly.
Winter: **200m   V,7 ** *(1993)*
Climb close to the summer line, providing sustained and varied climbing. The first unavoidable tier was climbed by a groove line a short way right of the black patch (crux). Climb the first and most impressive corner to half-height, then take the edge on the left. Follow the corner system to the top with sustained and varied climbing.

MEALL GORM 141

Cobalt Buttress, IV,5, Meall Gorm. Climber Alastair Matthewson

25 Blue Velvet 240m V,6 ** (1996)
A direct line on the crest between Rattlesnake and Cobalt Buttress, but largely a direct start to Cobalt Buttress. Start 10m left of the lowest rocks at the right side of the crag. Above the initial turf field are three corners, the central and most obvious holding a wide crack.

1. and 2. 85m Head directly towards the central corner up steepening ground.
3. 25m Climb to a short corner and wide crack, then pull out left and continue to beneath the main central corner.
4. 15m Climb the corner and the crack in its right wall to gain a terrace and belay on the left beneath the most obvious corner in the crest.
5. 15m Climb the corner to reach a terrace.
6. 45m An obvious fault-line slants up rightwards in the crest. Follow this, then traverse right to join Cobalt Buttress for its crux move. Go rightwards to a terrace and continue to a higher terrace (as for Cobalt). Walk left up the terrace for 10m to the crest.

7. 30m Above is a wedged spike just left of the crest. Climb up and left to reach the spike, then pull carefully behind this and climb rightwards to a small terrace. Join Cobalt Buttress and follow short tricky walls and a block filled chimney leftwards.

8. 25m Climb a short difficult wall, then trend left to easier ground.

26 Cobalt Buttress   140m   Very Difficult *(1953)*

Some good climbing when dry, but also some vegetation and loose blocks. Previously graded Moderate, so perhaps low in the grade. Start about 80m up to the right from the toe of the buttress, in Turquoise Gully, just above the toe of Wedge Buttress and below a short, steep pitch in the gully bed. Follow a ledge to the left to a belay below a short corner.

1. 25m Climb the corner with difficulty and make an awkward traverse left to easier ground. Go up to the first terrace.

2. 25m Go up to a higher terrace and to its back below a steep wall.

3. 40m Climb an initial wall, then a slabby line of weakness leftwards to the crest and a barrier wall. Make the crux moves up this, then go rightwards to a terrace and continue to a higher terrace.

4. 25m Climb short walls right of the crest to a small terrace, then tricky short walls until a short overhanging block-filled chimney leads left to the crest.

5. 25m Climb a short difficult wall, then trend left to easier ground.

Winter: **IV,5 *****   *(1970)*

Short hard sections, but generally well protected, following the summer line. Pitch 4 is made better quality by walking left for 10m up the terrace and following pitch 7 of Blue Velvet past the wedged spike.

27 Turquoise Gully   200m   III **

Wedge Buttress is the triangular buttress immediately to the right of Cobalt Buttress. This is the narrow gully between the two. The first pitch is the steep crux and rarely forms good ice combined with a snow build-up, but if so, can be Grade II. Above are several short ice pitches. For a Grade II route, or if the first pitch is not formed and the rest looks good, traverse in from the right across Wedge Buttress immediately above this pitch.

28 Wedge Buttress   150m   III,4   *(2000)*

The triangular buttress with a narrow base which starts higher up than the base of Cobalt Buttress. The lowest tier has not been climbed so start from the traverse in to Turquoise Gully, immediately before entering the gully bed. Climb this tier steeply, then the next one just left of the crest, leading to an easier finish.

To the right of Wedge Buttress is a broad easy gully, then a terraced buttress divided by a narrow gully, which gives the following two routes.

29 Boulder Problem Buttress   130m   III   *(1997)*

The buttress just right of the broad easy gully has two routes which join near the top. For the Left Version, start by a turf chimney about 50m up the easy gully and continue by turfy walls generally on the left side of the crest to finish by a 2m boulder problem wall (which banks out unless lean).

Variation: **Right Version**

Start at the base of the buttress and climb easily up its right side to a short ice pitch in a barrier wall (hard without ice). Continue by a turf chimney to the same boulder problem finish.

30 The Six-track Mono Blues   210m   II   *(1978)*

Climb the narrow gully, which has two short pitches. Low in the grade; could bank up to Grade I.

The right side of the terraced buttress holds a 25m steep icefall, very near the hairpin (technical 5).

SGÙRR A' CHAORACHAIN

(NG 797 417)   Alt 792m   Maps p134, 164

A' CHÌOCH

(NG 795 426)   Alt 300m (Lower), 400m (Upper)   South-East to East facing   Diagram p144

This justly famed sandstone bastion forms the end of the east-north-east ridge of Sgùrr a' Chaorachain, known as the A' Chìoch ridge (despite another ridge of the same name on nearby Beinn Bhàn). It is composed in the main of excellent rough sandstone, beautifully clean on its upper frontal face, though more vegetated in the lower reaches and on the flanks. In addition to the classic Cioch Nose route, there are many good climbs in the Severe to HVS grades.

From the col between A' Chìoch and the start of the A' Chìoch ridge, South Gully runs down on the south side and North Gully on the north side. The buttress of A' Chìoch is divided into two tiers by Middle Ledge – an obvious heathery terrace that runs right from the bottom of South Gully, gradually narrowing to a rocky ledge as it comes onto the front of the buttress. Most of the rock climbs are on the south-east and east faces of the upper tier although there are climbs on the vegetated lower tier which can be combined with those on the upper. In general the climbing is easier than it appears, with a generous supply of holds. The excellent quality of the climbing and the superb views make this a most attractive crag.

Approach: The recommended approach is from the top in order to include the fine traverse of the A' Chìoch ridge on the return to the car. Park at the big car park on the summit of the Bealach na Bà. Walk back south-east for about 300m, then go up the locked landrover track almost to the radio mast on the summit of Sgùrr a' Chaorachain (776m). From the last bend about 50m short of the summit, cut left and after about 100m reach the north-west corner of the corrie which forms the south side of the A' Chìoch ridge. A short steep descent on bits of path gains the top of the corrie floor. Descend the corrie, passing under the steep but vegetated south flanks of the A' Chìoch ridge, until nearly at the lip of the corrie. Go up over boulders to below South Gully which comes down from A' Chìoch and reach a small path which leads along Middle Ledge to reach the start of the routes. The easiest line is hard to find but take the lower of two ledges which form Middle Ledge. Middle Ledge gradually narrows as it comes on to the front of the buttress. A short step up on to the upper of the two ledges gains the start of Cioch Nose, only a few metres along the ledge. For the Lower Tier, angle down left from the lip of the corrie to its base.

The alternative is a low route. From the bridge over the outlet of the River Kishorn follow the road to the Bealach na Bà for about 2.5km to the bridge over the Russel Burn (NG 814 413). The huge tower of A' Chìoch is well seen from here. Walk past Loch Coire nan Arr, then slant up left towards South Gully, which flanks A' Chìoch on the left. For climbs on the lower tier continue near the corrie floor.

Descent: The immediate descent from A' Chìoch is via South Gully, but this requires two short abseils. A longer scrambling route can also be found by traversing terraces rightwards from near the top of the gully. The main advantage of the approach from the Bealach na Bà is to enable parties to continue up and along the very fine east-north-east ridge of the mountain (see the description for Cioch Nose).

The first two routes follow lines up the east facing buttress left of South Gully and near the left end of Middle Ledge. They only have one good pitch but the descent is quick. Grassy ledges lead right into South Gully left fork (Anonymous Gully). Abseil down the gully or continue traversing to abseil down South Gully itself.

1 Rapid Pulse   70m   E1 * *(2002)*
1. 25m 5b Climb a left-facing corner 10m left of Impulse.
2. 45m Easy ribs and slabs lead to the descent ledges.

A' CHÌOCH   145

2 Impulse   70m   HVS   (1997)
Start directly below an obvious narrow left-facing corner near the right end of the wall.
1. 40m 5a Climb directly to the base of the corner and up it until possible to swing rightwards on to the rib using a flaky handhold on the wall. Climb up, then rejoin the corner at the opening of a crack. Move up and right to the top of a pinnacle and continue directly upwards to the left end of a grass ledge.
2. 30m Continue above trending rightwards the descent ledges.

3 Anonymous Gully   230m   III   (1980)
From the bottom of South Gully this rises directly to the end of the east-north-east ridge, some 100m above A' Cioch. On the first ascent there was an initial ice pitch, followed by a long easy section ending in a rock cul-de-sac. Owing to the paucity of ice, recourse was made to the rocks of the ridge on the right.

Upper Tier

Following Middle Ledge along from South Gully one passes successively two grassy bays. Then the ledge becomes narrower and there is a conspicuous long low roof only about 3m above it. Beyond this the ledge continues with rather more broken ground above until the steep clean rocks of the 'Nose' are reached. Here the ledge becomes very narrow and rocky but continues right round the front of the buttress. Climbs in the area just right of South Gully were made in the early days of the SMC by Collie, Ling, Glover and others. In particular, **Glover's Route** (Very Difficult, III) climbs a series of chimneys starting from the first grassy bay right of South Gully.

4 Sideburn   80m   Severe   (1968)
Start from the second grassy bay up the buttress on the right.
1. 35m Climb the rather ill-defined buttress, to the right of a corner, to reach a grassy ledge from which the corner can be reached without difficulty.
2. 45m Climb the corner. Exit left to easy ground.

**5 Parting   95m   Hard Severe **   (1970)
Start 5m left of the left end of the low roof overhanging Middle Ledge.
1. 35m 4b Climb an obvious steep right-angled corner for 30m, then traverse up and right for 5m across a grass ledge to gain the bottom of a big diedre with a slab on its left.
2. 25m 4a Climb the diedre using the slab on it left. Belay beneath overhangs.
3. 35m 4a Avoid the overhangs on the left via a steep wall, after which the angle relents and easy scrambling leads to the top.

**6 Gritstone Grooves   110m   HVS * **   (1969)
A fine line with sustained climbing, low in its grade, although the first pitch is a little slow to dry. Start at a clean corner just left of the low roof overhanging Middle Ledge.
1. 25m 5a Climb the corner and groove above to a grass ledge.
2. 20m 5a Continue up and climb a steep corner, the corner right of the bigger slab corner of Parting.
3. 20m 4b Go up the steep corner above.
4. 45m More easily to the top.

The next three climbs start from Upper Ledge, a grass ledge about 25m above Middle Ledge, which runs across from the top of the first pitches of the last two routes to the top of the first pitch of Cioch Nose. It may be reached by scrambling up vegetated ground or by climbing the first pitch of Cioch Nose, which runs up the steep and cleaner rock about 20m right of the low roof. Cioch Nose then continues from Upper Ledge by a conspicuous V-chimney, which provides a useful marker.

146 SGÙRR A' CHAORACHAIN

Cioch Nose, Severe, A' Chìoch, Sgùrr a' Chaorachain. Climber Walter Taylor

7 African Waltz 90m VS (1969)
Start from Upper Ledge 35m left of the chimney of Cioch Nose and 10m right of where Gritstone Grooves crosses the ledge.
1. 20m 4b From a small niche climb up for 15m and traverse right to a grass ledge on the left of an obvious corner.
2. 15m 4b Follow a left-trending crack through a niche to a ledge.
3. 15m 4c Go right and up the wall to another niche left of the main corner, which is climbed with difficulty.
4. 40m Continue more easily in the same line to the top.

8 Forgotten Corner 90m HVS * (1975)
A good first pitch worth a star but heathery further up. Taking a diagonal line rightwards after the first pitch to join Snothard gives the best climbing. An abseil from the junction gains the start of Snothard. Start from Upper Ledge about 10m

left of the chimney of Cioch Nose, below an obvious corner. Climb up into the corner-line and follow it through a bulge (5b) to reach a ledge (30m). Continue up the corner to easier ground.

9 Snothard 90m VS ** (1969)
Fine clean rock and low in the grade. Start at the foot of a groove 5m left of the chimney of Cioch Nose.
1. 35m 4b Climb the groove until it is possible to move left onto a slab on the lip of a conspicuous overhang. Climb the slab to a ledge and continue up a steep corner to belay.
2. 25m 4b Move left and climb a crack past three overhangs.
3. 30m Easier climbing to the top.

10 Cioch Nose 125m Severe **** (1960)
This is the classic of the area, a most enjoyable climb. Best climbed as a circuit from the Bealach na Bà (car park), therefore including the long upper ridge (see below). Some technical moves on each of the first three pitches, but very well protected, therefore low in the grade. Still enjoyable in the rain, as the friction remains good, but approximately VS to lead. Start from Middle Ledge about 20m right of the low roof where the rocks become cleaner. Here the path returns from a lower ledge to the foot of the wall.
1. 30m 4a Immediately above a step up in the path is a flake-crack. Gain and climb this wide crack (10 or 11 Hex useful) to a ledge. Move left up over a block and climb consecutive tricky corners to the Upper Ledge. Belay here, then transfer 5m right to below a short V-chimney with an undercut base.
2. 15m 4a Climb the chimney and exit on the right, continuing up right over clean easy rock to a splendid ledge and belay.
3. 35m 4a Step out right on to exposed ground, then diagonally right for 5m on excellent holds to a peg runner. Step up, then traverse left until one can go straight up to a ledge below a small overhang (or a more direct left-trending line, only slightly harder). Pass the overhang on the left and return right immediately above it to a big ledge.
4. 45m A straight up line is now possible but the normal route is to walk 10m right and belay. Climb on to a big block. Move up, then step round the arete to the right and take the natural left-trending line of grooves and flakes to the top of A' Chìoch.
Variation Pitch 1: **Hard Severe**
This slightly harder variation starts from the ledge above the flake-crack. Step right and go up a wall followed by a slim corner next to a roof. This leads more directly to the V-chimney, arriving just to its left.
Winter: **V,6**
It is unlikely ever to be in full winter condition, when it would be very hard. It is graded for "very snowy", but could one justify the crampon scratches?

The most enjoyable route is to continue to the top of the mountain instead of descending South Gully. If so, cross the neck connecting A' Chìoch to the ridge behind and scramble up vegetation and short rock steps to reach a steep wall girdling the nose of the ridge. Climb this on its left edge using alternating sides of the arete (Very Difficult) or up the centre (Severe). The ridge soon levels out and then climbs gradually, with several summits and sharp gaps, avoidable if wished by clever route finding, to the summit. A direct line on the crest of all the towers gives moves up to Severe.

11 Cioch Nose, Direct Start 50m Hard Severe ** (1968)
From the ordinary start continue walking along Middle Ledge, where it becomes narrower, underneath steep rock with overhangs, until a large dark diedre is reached.
1. 40m 4b Climb up 5m then traverse left on steep rock to gain a short vertical crack. Climb this to reach the rib on the left edge of the diedre. Follow the rib and wall above on good holds to a ledge and belay.
2. 10m Go left and up to the second stance of the normal route.

148 SGÙRR A' CHAORACHAIN

Harder variations have been made on both the ordinary and direct starts to Cioch Nose. Easier but less clean starts to Cioch Nose have been made further left.

12 Cioch Corner 125m HVS ** *(1969)*

This climb is perhaps best combined with Cioch Corner Superdirect, on the lower tier (described below). Start at the large dark diedre as for Cioch Nose Direct.

1. 35m 5a Climb directly up the diedre to the roof, step right to a ledge and go straight up to a grassy recess.
2. 40m 4c Follow the line of grooves over a bulge. Climb a pleasant slab on the right of the corner, then return to the corner-line. Climb a chimney-groove to a grassy bay.
3. 40m 4a Climb more easily, with a final steep corner.
4. 10m Scramble to the top.

The next three climbs lie on the steep area of rock between Cioch Corner and North Wall which lies about 40m further right. Numerous variations are possible as the rock is climbable almost anywhere at a sufficiently high standard. This is true also for the routes already described. It must be admitted that some of the features mentioned in the descriptions may be hard to identify; however the rock is generally so good that any route here will be found rewarding.

13 The Maxilla 130m VS *(1968)*

Start at the first break right of Cioch Corner.

1. 20m Climb the break through the overhangs, passing a small tree, to a triangular ledge below a corner capped by a large overhang.
2. 20m Traverse 5m left and climb the left edge of the corner.
3. 25m Above are four parallel grooves. Climb over a small roof into the leftmost groove and follow it and the exposed slab above to belay below a large corner.
4. 20m Climb the corner.
5. 50m Easier rocks lead to the top.

14 Mantissa 130m VS *(1975)*

Start as for The Maxilla.

1. 20m The Maxilla, pitch 1.
2. 10m Climb the crack just right of the stance and cross the rib rightwards into a large recess.
3. 35m Leave on the right and traverse right about 12m below a steep concave wall. Start up a faint rib with cracks and continue, making a move right near the top of the wall. Move left to belay.
4. 25m Trend diagonally left through overlaps to the skyline.
5. 40m Climb easily to the top.

15 Lost Wall 130m HVS *(1984)*

About 30m right of The Maxilla a narrow slab can be seen slanting up right, the start of North Wall. Another groove breaking through the overhangs starts just to the left.

1. 30m Climb the groove and the wall above to a small stance below a corner capped by an overhang.
2. 30m 5a Climb the corner passing the overhang on the left. Or, if wet, traverse left 8m at the level of the stance and climb easier rock up and back right to above the overhang. Now climb the steep wall slightly left to a break.
3. and 4. 70m Continue straight to the top.

16 North Wall 140m Hard Severe *(1952)*

Start about 30m right of The Maxilla where a narrow slab, undercut at its base, slants up to the right.

1. 15m 4b Gain the slab and climb to a ledge at its top (crux).
2. 15m Climb up and right to a terrace.

3. 40m 4a   Move right past the foot of a deep-cut rock funnel crowned by overhangs until below a prominent layback crack. Climb the crack, then the groove on its left to a ledge. Continue up the groove, or the rib on its left, to large terraces.
4. 30m 4a   The ground is more broken above. The left skyline forms a tower. Move left from the belay, start up a chimney on the right of the tower then traverse left onto its front and climb up, with a delightful airy move.
5. 40m   Continue easily to the top of A' Chìoch.
Winter: **VI,6**   (1993)
By the summer route. Well protected but sustained.

17 Lap of the Gods   150m   VS   (1969)
Well right of North Wall this route finds a way up the steep overlapping slabs on the left of the North Gully of A' Chìoch. The start is best reached by scrambling in an exposed position along the continuation of Middle Ledge, then climbing up the gully to the point where it becomes a steep, open chimney. Alternatively, go right round the lower tier and scramble up 170m of vegetated ground and broken rocks left of the lower reaches of North Gully.
1. 10m   Climb a steep grey rib just right of the chimney.
2. 20m   Traverse left across the slab to a fine airy stance on the far lip.
3. 15m   Go straight up the 5m wall above to a good ledge. A steep groove above is barred by overhangs, so traverse left to flakes below an overhanging nose.
4. 15m   Pass just left of the nose to a shallow corner which leads to easier ground. (It is now possible to traverse left onto North Wall, or right into the upper part of North Gully.)
5. 45m   Scramble up 20m to the prominent rib above. Climb it to the base of the steep final wall.
6. 10m   Go slightly right up a black slabby wall to a ledge.
7. 45m   Continue steeply leftwards past a poised pinnacle into a groove leading strenuously through a break left of the overhangs. Step back right and climb straight up to the top of A' Chìoch.

Lower Tier

Cioch Corner Superdirect   160m   HVS *   (1970)
The climb takes the obvious line of grooves which runs the full length of the lower tier below Cioch Corner. It is best combined with the latter to give an excellent, sustained climb of seven long pitches. Although there is some vegetation and loose rock on the lower tier, the climb has a lot of interest and can be recommended in dry conditions. Start at the foot of the grooves by a huge pinnacle. Climb directly up the groove line all the way in four pitches (5a, 5a, 4c, 4b) to reach Middle Ledge.
Winter: **VII,8 ***   (2003)
Five pitches of sustained technical well protected climbing. Pitches two and three are the hardest.

Cleavage   160m   HVS   (1968)
This route climbs the next corner right of the Superdirect. The corner starts about 30m above a slabby spur at the foot of the face, and has a prominent overhanging beak on its left.
1. 30m   Climb a right-slanting slab and heather to a ledge at the foot of the corner.
2. 12m 4b   Climb the corner to a small stance below a slight overhang, between the offset continuation of the corner on the right and a steep layback crack on the left.
3. 25m 4c   Climb the layback crack for 3m, pull across the left wall on to a small ledge (committing), and climb up and right to a ledge and belay above the corner.
4, 5. and 6. 90m   Trend right to a rib and climb directly up to Middle Ledge, reaching it below the start of The Maxilla.

150　SGÙRR A' CHAORACHAIN

NORTH BUTTRESSES

Map p164　Diagram p151

Beyond North Gully there is a row of five buttresses supporting the north side of the long east-north-east ridge of Sgùrr a' Chaorachain. They are numbered 1 to 5 from left to right, numbers 1 and 2 being the largest. In summer they offer somewhat grassy routes, but both buttresses and gullies give good climbs in winter.

Descent: In winter the best way off the top will often be to continue along the east-north-east ridge to the 776m top of Sgùrr a' Chaorachain. From the top it is a long walk back down via Bealach na Bà if transport has been left at Russel Bridge.

1 North Gully　160m　III *　　　　　　　　　　　　　　　　　　　　(1995)

North Gully is complex but only one line avoids big overhangs. Start by the right-hand of three gullies (ice), as for Voyager. Climb this, curving left to join the central gully. Follow this to the A' Chìoch col.

2 Voyager　350m　V,4 **　　　　　　　　　　　　　　　　　　　　(1986)

A fine corner-line on the left of No.1 Buttress. Gain the base of the corner by climbing up and left for two pitches towards North Gully and then traversing easily right. First ascent details were as follows. After a start up the corner, a deviation left and back right led to the base of an icefall. The ice was thin and the steepest section was avoided by a difficult bulge in the corner on the right. The ice led to a roof in the corner, split by a very co-operative chimney. Two pitches in the same line, the second a deceptively awkward chimney, led to the top of the buttress.

3 Jupiter　300m　Severe　　　　　　　　　　　　　　　　　　　　(1952)

This is a good summer climb up the centre of No.1 Buttress. From the lowest rocks climb indeterminate ground to the base of the first big tier (60m). Start to the right of a recessed chimney which is right of some mossy overhangs. Diverging from the chimney, go up 20m to a platform. Here a thin ledge under an overhang leads back left above the top of the main chimney. At its end a 3m chimney leads to easier ground. The middle tier of the buttress rises in front. Climb a deep 5m chimney, a 5m flake-crack and an 8m groove on the left. From here a perched spillikin can be seen on the right in an exposed situation. Balance round this then go straight up to a terrace (25m). Go a few metres right then climb another 20m with one awkward move. The buttress now falls back somewhat, but a steep 20m band circles it, barring the way. Follow a thin crack; at 3m there are some awkward jammed blocks and the crack remains hard for 6m above. After another 15m serious difficulty ends. Climb easy rock for 60m, then a narrow arete sweeping up for 60m gives a good finish.

Winter:　**440m　V,5 **　　　　　　　　　　　　　　　　　　　　(1991)

Frozen turf is unusual but close to essential. Start from the toe of the buttress about 50m right of Voyager.
1. 40m　Climb a turfy groove.
2. 40m　Climb a steep chimney.
3. 50m　Go up to the base of the largest tier.
4. 45m　Take a heavily vegetated trough left of the crest.
5. 45m　Go diagonally right passing a tree to a ledge. Climb a vertical wall with a good crack, passing a roof on its right.
6. 60m　Go up to the next tier and a corner on the left.
7. 50m　Climb the wall left of the corner on big flakes, then take a slabby wall on the right up to the next tier.
8. 50m　Climb the central corner, then a right-slanting line of flakes to easier ground.
9. 60m　Blocky ground leads to the top of the buttress.

4 White Dwarf　300m　III *　　　　　　　　　　　　　　　　　　　　(1984)

Towards the right side of No.1 Buttress is a narrow gully ending at a steep band of

SGÙRR A' CHAORACHAIN
North Buttresses

A' Chioch

1. North Gully	III *	
2. Voyager	V,4 **	
3. Jupiter	V,5 **	
4. White Dwarf	III *	
5. No.1 Gully	III	
6. Sinister	III	
8. No.2 Gully	III	
9. No.3 Gully	I	
10. Totem	IV,5	
12. No.4 Gully	Scottish IV	
13. Turret Buttress	IV,5	
14. No.5 Gully	I or II	
15. High Domain	IV,6	
16. The Gully in 3D	II	

APPLECROSS

rock (not to be confused with a slabby corner further right, ending at the same height in a big overhang). Climb the gully with some deviations on the right, and when stopped by the steep band of rock crawl right along a ledge past a tree to a V-groove. Climb the groove until it is possible to step awkwardly onto some jammed blocks on the right wall. Trend slightly right for 70m until past the steep part of the buttress. Return easily left to the crest and follow it over short walls and blocks to the top.

5 No.1 Gully (Lang Tam's Gully)   180m   III
The gully on the right of No.1 Buttress. Climb to an obvious cave, which is turned on the right by an icy curtain. Near the top take the right fork to gain the ridge. Probably graded for ideal conditions; a recent ascent thought Grade IV despite a less direct line.

6 Sinister   150m   III   (1984)
Climb the left edge of No.2 Buttress to a small rock tower facing No.1 Buttress. Climb with difficulty for 10m above this, then continue more easily to the top. This route has been climbed in summer at Very Difficult, but is not recommended.

7 Dexter   150m   Difficult   (1953)
Scramble up the right side of No.2 Buttress for 90m to a partly detached tower. Pass the tower by a dark chimney on the right. Step off a flake to a ledge and go round a corner to the right to a large platform. Climb a slab with small holds (20m) and continue easily to the top.
Winter: **IV,4**   (1991)
Follow the summer line, except avoid the dark chimney by the wall on its right, which leads to a short icefall at the right side of the slab.

8 No.2 Gully (London Welsh Gully)   150m   III
This is the gully between No.2 Buttress and No.3 Buttress. No details are available but it has some steep ice pitches which rarely form.
No.3 Buttress is shorter than the others and no climbs have been recorded.

9 No.3 Gully   120m   I
Short and eas with a good build-up. It has a short but impossible cave pitch in lean conditions.

10 Totem   135m   Very Difficult   (1952)
A curious rock pillar, seen on the skyline near the top of No.4 Buttress, gives this climb its name. Start on the right flank of the buttress below an obvious 5m chimney. Climb the chimney and make an awkward exit to a grassy depression which leads to a terrace. Follow the terrace to the left side of the buttress then return right as soon as possible to the crest. Surmount a small rocky nose to reach a steep tower above. On the left climb a deep chimney to ledges. Ascend a short pitch over huge blocks to a ledge below the final rampart. Finish by a steep chimney on the right.
Winter: **150m   IV,5**   (1993)
This is a winter version of the summer climb, taking a series of steep blocky grooves just left of the crest and finishing past the right side of the Totem pinnacle. Easier options further left were avoided.

11 Tomahawk   170m   IV,6   (1996)
Climbs the right side of Totem Buttress. Start mid-way between the 5m chimney of Totem and No.4 Gully. Climb a shallow gully line until easy ground leads to a deep wide chimney. Move left below the chimney to climb a steep left-facing corner with a wide crack and helpful chockstones. Follow the continuation fault to the top.

12 No.4 Gully   150m   Scottish IV   (1977)
Between No.4 and No.5 Buttresses is a narrow gully. After an initial ice pitch a

NORTH BUTTRESSES

huge cave is reached at 60m. Climb the steep pillar on the right to easy slopes. Continue to where the gully forks. Take the left fork leading to two short awkward pitches and a final snow slope. Seems to be unrepeated and may have been climbed in unusually good conditions.

13 Turret Buttress   200m   Severe   *(1952)*
This is No.5 Buttress, which is right at the back of the corrie, facing Beinn Bhàn. Seen from below it appears to culminate in a pinnacle 50m below the top, but this is just a promontory linked by a narrow ridge to the upper cliff. Start on the left, at the foot of No 4 Gully. Climb mixed rock and grass to the first tier (30m). Climb this about 8m from the edge of the gully at a short steep corner. Follow easier rocks to the second tier, which is climbed up the left edge by a short slab. The third and steepest tier is gained and the only line of weakness is in the centre. Surmount a steep, narrow slab by a layback crack on the right (10m). Another 60m of interesting climbing leads to the narrow arete behind the promontory. On the first ascent the final 45m of the upper cliff looked wet and unpleasant and was avoided by a gully on the left.
Winter: **IV,5**   *(1986)*
Follow the summer line approximately. On this ascent the first tier was the crux. The final upper cliff was avoided on the left, but not in the gully.

14 No.5 Gully   200m   I or II
The gully has two major branches separating at half-height, the junction being easily reached. The left branch has a pitch, usually Grade II but can bank out to Grade I. The right branch has no pitches in summer, usually straightforward in winter but under heavy snow can steepen to a cornice (when it would be worth Grade II).

15 High Domain   110m   IV,6   *(1997)*
A big groove line running straight up the buttress between the forks of No.5 Gully, which can be descended for access to this route. The first pitch leads to a terrace, then the upper groove gives superb climbing with the crux near the top, a disproportionately hard move compared to the rest.

FAR NORTH BUTTRESSES

North of the North Buttresses are two large more broken buttresses separated by a descent depression marked on the map as a break in the cliffs at NG 788 430 (just south-east of a small lochan).

16 The Gully in 3D   400m   II   *(1995)*
The left buttress has a well defined gully and shallower left branch on its right side (i.e. next to the descent, directions looking up). Climb the gully, with one awkward pitch, past the fork to a big chockstone (which might ice in good conditions, steep) 170m. Traverse left on to the far side of the buttress between the branches, regain the crest and follow many short grooves and terraces to the top.

High up on the north side of the descent depression (left of Chocks Away) is a steep wall at NG 787 432 with two routes.

Independence Day   50m   Hard Severe   *(1996)*
Climbs an arete at the left-hand side of the wall.
1. 20m Climb the obvious chimney which is left of the foot of the arete to gain the arete after 5m. Follow the left side of the arete and move right to gain large holds and a steep move to a belay ledge.
2. 25m 4b Climb a steep crack for 5m and move out right on to a broad sloping shelf. Make an awkward exposed move right round a corner, then climb up and across a broken gully to gain a large ledge finishing left.

154 SGÙRR A' CHAORACHAIN

Chopper Chimney   50m   VS 4c   (1993)
1. 25m   Climb a steepening corner for 15m, then traverse out left on to the buttress.
2. 25m   Go left and up into a narrowing chimney.

Chocks Away   150m   II   (1996)
On the south side of the right-hand (northern) buttress, facing the descent depression, is this gully. All easy bar 15m of chockstone chimney, passing behind the first chock and outside the second.

Very Y-Gully   220m   III   (1996)
The obvious gully on the east (facing Coire nan Arr) side of the same buttress. It splits into right and left gully finishes below a steep wall at the top. The very lowest shallow section of gully was not climbed; a traverse from the left led to the deeper section. The two steepest steps were bypassed on the left, otherwise the gully was followed, finishing by the easier right branch.

Far North Gully   300m   I   (2006)
On the north side of the northern buttress is this hidden gully. Starting at NG 789 435, some 200m north of Very Y-Gully, is a long shallow gully leading up into steep ground. If not snow-filled, this can be avoided by traversing in from the right. The gully then takes a sharp left turn and takes a line parallel to the cliff and leading to the top.

SUMMIT BUTTRESS

(NG 787 422)   Alt 650m   East facing   Map p164   Diagram p155

This is the large and impressively steep wall at the head of the corrie between the south-east and east-north-east spurs of the mountain. It takes some drainage and requires dry weather for rock climbing. A cold spell is required in winter, but also not too dry.

Approach: The approach for A' Chìoch passes under the buttress. From the Bealach na Bà car park, go up the landrover track. From the last bend about 50m short of the radio mast on the summit of Sgùrr a' Chaorachain, cut left and after about 100m reach the north-west corner of the corrie, from where the crag is obvious and gained by a short steep descent on bits of path.

The cliff is split into three sections by two prominent steep gullies which fill with ice during a cold spell.

1 Excitable Boy   100m   V,5 *   (1986)
This is prominent icefall which forms in the left-hand gully, distinctive because a shallow gully carries on down the slope below. The ice is steep and somewhat slow to form.
1. 20m   From the terrace at the foot of the cliff climb steepening snow to a good block belay.
2. 40m   Climb very steep ice to a small snow bay.
3. 40m   Leave the bay by a short chimney on the left and trend right over short snow steps to the top.
Variation: **Triple Echo Finish**   (1995)
For pitch 3, take an ice streak on the right wall (steep at first) to the cornice.

2 Big Daddy   100m   E3 **   (1972)
Climbs a right-trending line of hanging slabs on the left side of the central section which is between the two gullies. Dry conditions are required. The hardest of George Shields' routes; a mind boggling sandstone experience. Start about 30m right of the gully of Excitable Boy, at a break in the bottom overhangs where a shallow groove leads up to overhangs and a continuation corner above.

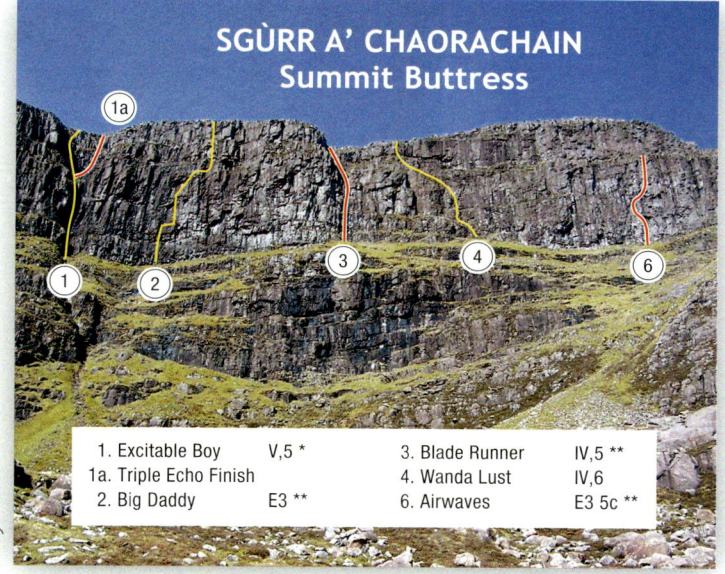

SGÙRR A' CHAORACHAIN
Summit Buttress

1. Excitable Boy V,5 *	3. Blade Runner IV,5 **
1a. Triple Echo Finish	4. Wanda Lust IV,6
2. Big Daddy E3 **	6. Airwaves E3 5c **

Andy Nisbet

1. 25m 5c Climb the initial groove, then through the overhangs and up the corner above until it is possible to break out left and move up to a grass ledge. Two or three peg runners would nicely replace a multitude of poor nuts and Friends.
2. 30m 5a Return down to the corner, then traverse right until a line leads straight up to the right end of a roof. Climb past the roof, then make a rising traverse right under a bigger roof system to a small ledge.
3. 45m 5a Go up right to a blaeberry ledge on the skyline and step right into a big corner. Climb this to a terrace which runs across the whole cliff, then two more corners above to the summit plateau.

3 Blade Runner   105m   IV,5 **
(1986)
The right-hand icefall forms more often than Excitable Boy. The chimney is mixed so only pitch 1 requires ice and the route has seen several ascents.
1. 30m Climb steep ice to belay below a chimney.
2. and 3. 75m Climb the right-slanting chimney (crux) to easier ground, which leads via one short step to the top.

4 Wanda Lust   80m   IV,6
(1997)
A mixed line slanting left up the buttress, starting 50m right of Blade Runner. A short easy pitch leads to a terrace. Gain a ledge leading left to a short chimney come crack. Climb it and move right on another ledge until the diagonal fault is followed back left to a terrace (this section can be climbed more direct at V,6). The final steep wall is climbed by a tricky move to gain an icy recess.

5 Synergy   80m   HVS
(1989)
Follows "a big corner", but the precise location is unsure (below is the original description, but the start was related to a cairn, long gone). The most likely possibility is a corner 20m left of Airwaves.
1. 25m 4c Climb the vegetated corner using the right wall for entry before a hollow flake gives access to a good belay ledge.

SGÙRR A' CHAORACHAIN

2. 25m 5a Follow the steep corner above to a bulge, which provides the crux, then take an excursion to the right to a wide terrace.
3. 30m 5a On the left an obvious crack-line leads to a final overhang which is climbed on the right by exciting moves. Care is required with the last few moves. Belay well back.

**6 Airwaves   50m   E3 5c ** *(1997)*
An exciting route; the middle section is space-walking. The route is two-thirds along the right-hand section of cliff i.e. near the approach path. Immediately below the cliff is a narrow terrace. Walk along this past two pillars to a point where there is a rocky spur on the slope underneath. Above the far end of the spur is the widest section of terrace with a cubic block lying on it. The wall above is beetling with overhangs but the key feature is a big roof with a downward-pointing lip about 10m up. Start at a black right-facing corner which leads up to the left end of the roof. Climb the corner, move left and up a shallow groove to a break below overhangs. Go diagonally right by sensational moves round overhangs to a hidden grass ledge. Finish up the final corner passing a roof.

A' CHÌOCH RIDGE - SOUTH FACE

Yodel   200m   IV,5 *(1995)*
Most of this face is broken, with easy gullies leading down from cols on the ridge, most of which have been descended. At the top end, however, next to the descent slope from near the radio mast, is a well defined steep straight gully. Pitches 3 and 4 involve steep ice.

SOUTH FACE

(NG 788 413)   Alt 400m   South facing   Diagram p157

This is the crag that rises steeply on the right of the road to Bealach na Bà at a point opposite the waterfalls in the floor of the corrie. It offers very pleasant, clean sandstone climbing, near the road, and is often warm and dry. The crag consists of six buttresses numbered from left to right. No.1 is the best, having a broad 40m wall of excellent clean rock in its middle section (Patey's Wall). This is the most obvious area of clean rock halfway up the nearest buttress to the car park. No.2 is more broken, hidden behind No.1 from the car park and is separated from No.3 by a square-cut, mossy gully. Nos.3 and 4 are narrow pillars separated by a narrow gully with caves. These are close together and left of the skyline buttress, which is No.5, a much larger buttress coming down almost to the road. No.6 is a broken buttress beyond a broad gully to the right of No.5.

Approach: There is a small incut parking place below the top end of the crag with room for about three cars. The buttresses are visible from here, 5 to 10mins.

Descent: From No.1 Buttress, go right (north, towards the Bealach na Ba) down a big grassy ramp (small path) until directly above the car park. From Nos.2 to 5, which finish higher, descend another grassy ramp north until the No.1 Buttress ramp and small path can be seen below. Descend to it and follow as before.

No.1 Buttress - Patey's Wall

The lower 45m of No.1 Buttress gives delightful, easy climbing up to a ledge at the base of the steep middle section, the clean reddish wall of Patey's Wall. Alternatively, walk onto the ledge from the left. The climbs are described from here (except Sword of Gideon). The easiest way to climb several routes is to make a 35m abseil from the top of their difficulties back to the ledge and retrieve the abseil point after the last route. Finish by an easy pitch to the descent terrace (as described for Sword of Gideon).

SOUTH FACE 157

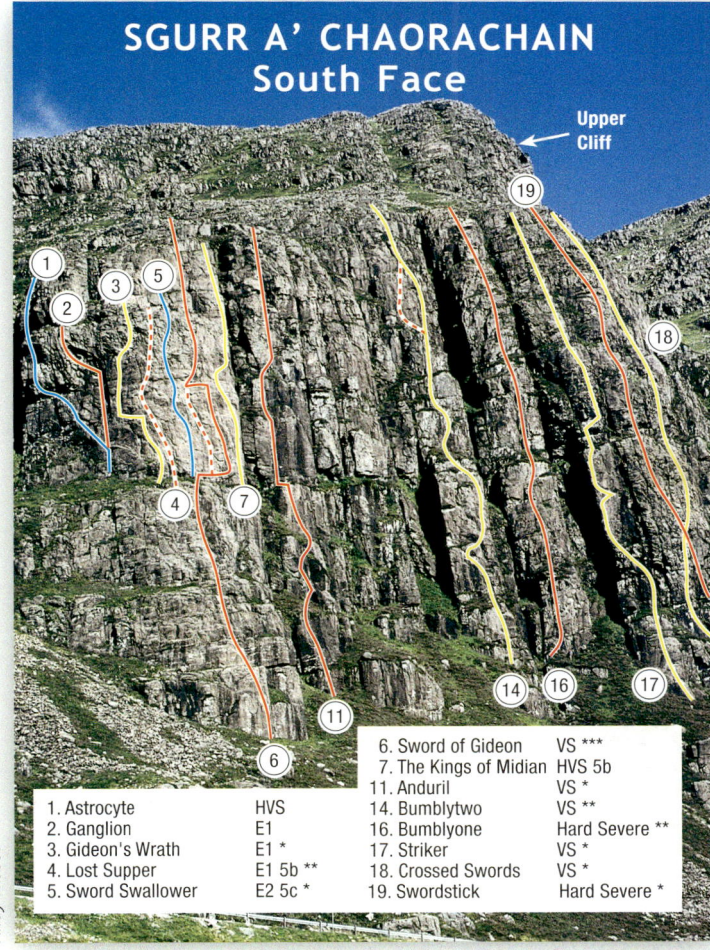

SGURR A' CHAORACHAIN South Face

Upper Cliff

1. Astrocyte	HVS
2. Ganglion	E1
3. Gideon's Wrath	E1 *
4. Lost Supper	E1 5b **
5. Sword Swallower	E2 5c *
6. Sword of Gideon	VS ***
7. The Kings of Midian	HVS 5b
11. Anduril	VS *
14. Bumblytwo	VS **
16. Bumblyone	Hard Severe **
17. Striker	VS *
18. Crossed Swords	VS *
19. Swordstick	Hard Severe *

Andy Nisbet

1 Astrocyte   40m   HVS *(1997)*
Climbs the bulging buttress at the left end of the wall and left of the groove of Ganglion. Start as for Ganglion.
1. 25m 4b Start up the groove as for Ganglion but soon move left and climb a left-slanting ramp to the halfway ledge. Traverse left to blocks where the ledge turns the corner towards the left-bounding gully.
2. 15m 5b Pull through the roof at a wedged block (just left of a central groove). Finish trending left under overhangs.

2 Ganglion   35m   E1 *(1971)*
To the left of the clean wall is an obvious groove leading to a large black recess below an overhanging section. The route used to be graded E1 – hence the abseil tat in the recess.

SGÙRR A' CHAORACHAIN

Sword of Gideon, VS, South Face Sgùrr a' Chaorachain

1. 20m 4b Climb the groove and crack to belay in a recess below overhangs.
2. 15m 5a Traverse the halfway ledge left for 4m and make scary moves up to a large flake under the capping roof. Finish round the left end of the roof.
Variation: **Original Route**
The original route climbed the groove direct; a little dirty and looks no easier.

3 Gideon's Wrath   40m   E1 *   (1971)
Start towards the left end of the main ledge, where the reddish wall takes a gentle curve and forms a slight crest (3m right of a white patch under a small roof). Here is a shallow left-slanting groove 5m up the wall. Good climbing, low in the grade. The first pitch is not well protected but perhaps only 5a.
1. 15m 5b Gain a higher ledge, then climb up into the groove. Go up the short groove, then traverse 4m left and move up to below an overhang.
2. 25m 5b Climb the overhang above and follow a line trending right to reach a short wide crack. Continue up and right to finish just right of the biggest bulge.
Variation: **Direct Finish   5a or 5b**   (1973)
Instead of the 4m traverse on pitch 1, go up a thin crack to a triangular niche, then trend right to join Lost Supper at the small roof and peg. Finish up this direct (5b) or on the right (5a) – see Lost Supper.

4 Lost Supper   35m   E1 5b **   (1973)
A fine direct line on good rock, if a little lacking in protection. The peg is now very rusty and E2 has been suggested. Immediately right of Gideon's Wrath is a patchwork of short cracks in a grey piece of rock 5m up. Climb up through these and continue up to a small roof with an old peg and tat. Either pull through the roof to easing ground (5b), or from immediately under the roof, traverse right for 3m to a tiny ramp forming a break. Climb this to the easier ground. The traverse version reduces the overall grade to E1 5a, technically easier but still with an exposed feel.

SOUTH FACE 159

5 Sword Swallower   35m   E2 5c * *(1993)*
A direct line up the centre of the wall, featuring thin moves near the start; the crucial runner is hard to find. Start 2m left of Sword of Gideon Direct Start and climb easily to the right end of a ledge 3m up. Go up cracks (crux) until moves left lead to a small pod. Go up this, then straight up to pass close on the left of Sword of Gideon belay (possible use). Trend left up the wall to join Lost Supper up the tiny ramp in a smooth wall and climb it to easier ground. A finish independent of Lost Supper but very close on its right has also been climbed (5b).

6 Sword of Gideon   100m   VS *** *(1961)*
This is the original route of the crag, immaculate rock, good protection, very enjoyable and low in the grade. Start at the lowest point of the buttress.
1. 45m Easy climbing on perfect rock leads to the terrace above the lower tier.
2. 15m 4c Starting from near the right end of the terrace, climb a shallow corner bending slightly left (the Kings of Midian groove -see below- is easier but not as good, would reduce the grade to 4b), then traverse left for 4m to beneath prominent cracks.
3. 20m 4b Climb the two short cracks to easier ground and pick a line to a ledge.
4. 20m Pick a line to the descent terrace.
Variation: **Direct Start   12m   E1 5b ****
Gain the thin groove with difficulty (although the tall may think HVS 5a) and climb it directly to the prominent cracks in the upper part of Sword of Gideon.

7 The Kings of Midian   35m   HVS 5b *(1993)*
Climbs the right edge of the steep section of wall. Easier pitches could be climbed below and above. Start just right of Sword of Gideon at the wall's right arete. Climb a parallel line to Gideon (which has been used as an easier start to Gideon, as on the first ascent), then traverse right across a wall with twin cracks to gain a big ledge. An easier finish goes straight up the scooped wall above.

8 Orcrist   60m   E2 * *(2005)*
A crack in the right sidewall of the buttress gives sustained but well protected climbing.
1. 15m 5a Climb the chimney-line which forms the right side of Patey's Wall (Skullsplitter) to where a crack-line leaves the chimney.
2. 15m 5c Climb the crack-line to a bulge where it ends. Move right through the bulge to another crack-line and climb this to the arete.
3. 30m 4a Finish up the arete.

9 North Circular   65m   E1 5b *(1973)*
This is a girdle traverse of No.1 Buttress from left to right. A full description is given in the SMC Journal for 1976.

10 Skullsplitter   130m   V,6 *(1999)*
Climbs the chimney line between No.1 and No.2 Buttresses.

No.2 Buttress

A broad buttress split into four vague pillars by the corner-crack of Anduril and two narrow chimneys further right.

11 Anduril   100m   VS * *(1970)*
This route follows a line of cracks towards the left side of No.2 Buttress. Start just right of the gully separating buttresses 1 and 2 (Skullsplitter). The first three short pitches are avoidable by traversing in below Patey's Wall.
1. 15m 4a Climb the left edge of clean slabs to a grass ledge.
2. 20m 5a The wall on the right has a thin groove going slightly left. Climb this awkwardly then continue up a short rock step and grass to the next clean wall.
3. 10m 4c Climb the left edge of the clean wall to a good hold and continue easily to the Terrace.

4. 20m 4c Climb the crack in the wall above to a small terrace, then continue to a larger terrace.
5. 35m 4b Move right to a bay below a clean overhanging crack in a corner. Climb this direct, then continue up a conspicuous deep corner to easier climbing and the top.
Variation:
5a. 35m 4b The pillar above the crack of pitch 4 and left of the overhanging corner-crack is pleasant and slightly easier.

12 Swordthrust   100m   Scottish VS   *(1971)*
The line is uncertain. The following is assumed but it may have climbed the top of Anduril, which is much better climbing, and its ascent was not known at the time. Start at a square-cut corner near the right edge of the buttress.
1. 30m Climb the corner and break out left on to the Terrace.
2. and 3. 70m Traverse left along the Terrace and climb the left-hand of the dividing chimneys. Continue up the prominent but vegetated crack-line above.

13 The Smoke   80m   Severe 4a   *(1970)*
The right-hand of the dividing chimneys between Nos. 2 and 3 Buttresses. Gain the start either by traversing the ledge under Patey's Wall and continuing the traverse on to No.2 Buttress or by climbing the first pitch of Anduril, passing the harder second by heather on the left and climbing the third by easier rock on the right. Traverse rightwards beyond Swordthrust until a deep narrow chimney is reached. Climb the chimney and the continuing fault to the top. Rather vegetated but not unpleasant.

14 Bumblytwo   140m   VS **   *(1970)*
Some fine climbing but with poorly protected sections. Start at the foot of No.3 Buttress.
1. 25m Climb two walls to a spike on the left.
2. 25m 4b Make a delicate step up on to a sloping ledge, then traverse right to climb delicate and unprotected ground to a ledge.
3. 25m Continue straight up and avoid a steep wall by going left up a ramp to a ledge.
4. 25m 4a Step up and traverse right to slabby ground. Go up this to a crack, climb this, then go back left to the centre of the face and up left to a large block.
5. 45m 4a or 4b The next pitch is up a steep wall which is avoidable on the left. Either step across a gap and climb a groove (4a) or for a better but harder finish, go further up and left, trend right across smooth pink rock to finish straight up (4b, unprotected, possibly HVS). Finish more easily.

15 Park Lane   120m   Severe   *(1971)*
The prominent deep cleft between Nos.3 and 4 Buttresses.
Winter: **Bee Gully   120m   IV,5**   *(1987)*
The highlight is the last pitch, a fine narrow ice smeared chimney.

16 Bumblyone   130m   Hard Severe **   *(1970)*
Start at the left corner of No.4 Buttress.
1. 45m 4a Go right up a ramp to an obvious flake-crack. Better but 4b is to start off a block on the right and climb a steep wall to the flake-crack. Climb the crack to a terrace, then up the easier crest to a tree.
2. 30m 4a Climb a corner to a ledge, then a clean wall (or as two pitches, both 4a).
3. 55m Easier up the crest.

No.5 Buttress

17 Striker   140m   VS *   *(1970)*
Climbs the clean left edge of No.5 Buttress. Some lovely rock, but with occasional blemishes. Requires dry conditions although the hard sections dry faster. Start at

the lowest point of a small rib at the left edge of the buttress and lower down than most starts.

1. 20m 4a Climb the rib moving left into a zigzag crack. Belay above on the grass terrace below a black overhang, usually wet.
2. 20m 4c Ascend dry rock moving right to a large loose block below a wet chimney. Traverse out left to pass the overhang left of the chimney and up to below a clean rib, an attractive feature seen from the start.
3. 30m 4b Climb the rib until forced by a smoother section to the edge of the wet groove on the right. Return left immediately and continue up the rib. The direct line is possible at 4c or 5a, but bold.
4. 20m 4b Turn an overhang on the left, returning right on hollow jugs across its lip to reach easing ground.
5. 50m Climb the pleasant clean rib (easy) to the top.

The line of the wet groove may have been climbed (described in the last guide as Trundler) although the original Trundler was the same as Swordstick.

18 Crossed Swords   120m   VS *   (1997)
This takes a direct line in the crest of No.5 Buttress, crossing Swordstick. Start 5m left of the more obvious groove of Swordstick.

1. 35m 4c Climb a rib and small V-groove, then trend slightly right, crossing Swordstick, to follow the crest to a tiny but prominent roof. Pass it immediately on the right up a small groove to reach a big terrace.
2. 30m 4c Climb directly through the overhangs above, taking a line right of centre (other lines possible). Climb easier rock above, taking a direct line.
3. 55m Pleasant easier rock to the top.

19 Swordstick   120m   Hard Severe *   (1968)
This takes a slightly less direct line on the crest of No.5 Buttress, using a deep groove blocked by a roof and with a lower wet continuation. This is left of a big overhanging prow in the steep section of the buttress and about 10m left of the recess of Recess Rib. Start by scrambling easily across to the base of the steep section.

1. 35m 4b Climb the right wall of the deep groove for 6m to a ledge. Step left and climb the left wall, passing the overhang. Trend slightly left, then up to a big terrace and below overhangs.
2. 30m Climb the chimney on the left of the overhangs (or the easier but dirtier one on the right), then pleasant easier rock.
3. and 4. 55m Easy climbing leads to the top.

20 Recess Rib   125m   Hard Severe   (1969)
A pleasant route, good rock but some vegetation, on the extensive area of rock right of the crest of No.5 Buttress. Directly above a passing place on the road (the second down from the parking place) and to the left of a big square-cut and often wet corner with a smooth and black streaked left wall forming a big recess is another slightly less obvious recess with a vertical left wall and some 10m right of the groove of Swordstick. Above the recess are two parallel V-grooves and another corner above on the skyline (as seen from the lay-by). The line follows a thin crack in the right wall of the recess, then the right-hand groove and the corner. Start by climbing easy slabs up to a ledge below the recess.

1. 40m 4b Climb up, then traverse right to a large square ledge on a promontory. Climb up the thin crack in the right-hand rib of the recess. Go up to and climb the right-hand V-groove and continue to a terrace.
2. 35m 4a Climb up to a square chimney, climb this and belay below a long corner.
3. 50m 4a Climb the corner and scramble to the top.

21 Vine Street   175m   HVS *   (1971)
Climbs the arete between the two recesses followed by the aretes right of the

SGÙRR A' CHAORACHAIN

square chimney and the long upper corner of Recess Rib. Good pitches, although the line is very artificial with Recess Rib so close. Start from the second lay-by down from the parking place (the belayer need not leave the car!).
1. 20m 4b Climb the slabby wall nearest the lay-by (easiest on the left edge).
2. 30m Climb pleasant slabs trending right to stacked flaky overhangs below the square ledge of Recess Route.
3. 30m 4c Climb through the right side of the stacked overhangs and up to the square ledge. Climb a wall and groove just right of the rib of Recess Route, then step left to belay below its V-groove and the prominent right arete.
4. 20m 5b Climb the prominent arete to below Recess Rib's square chimney.
5. 25m 5a Climb the bulging arete just right of the square chimney (very artificial), then a slabby corner-crack until it is possible to step right on to a slabby nose and make thin moves up to a ledge.
6. 50m 4c Starting from a huge rocking block on the right, climb short aretes right of the final corner of Recess Rib.

22 Yer Dirt Box   135m   VS   (1973)
A mucky start leads to an improvement. Climbs the rib right of the larger and wetter recess. Start right of Recess Route, close to Vine Street, either by scrambling across No.5 Buttress or by starting up the first two pitches of Vine Street.
1. 35m Go right across potentially wet ground to the rib right of the wet recess.
2. 45m 4b Climb the arete and continue to a steep barrier wall right of the final big corner of Recess Rib.
3. 45m 4c Climb the centre of the wall, starting up a small left-facing corner, then trending right and back left until above the initial corner, to finish straight up.
4. 10m An easier wall to finish.

Right of the big wet recess is a left-facing diedre, then a big vegetated V-groove forming on its right side a prominent rib, almost appearing as a separate buttress. **Sausage Machine** (Severe 1974) climbs the rib. The ribs right side forms a vertical wall with a thin zigzag crack.

23 Roadhog's Wall   20m   E3 5c   (1996)
Climbs the zigzag crack, which can be seen from the road below. Well worth the 150m approach scramble. Enter the crack from the right and climb it direct to the top. Sustained and well protected.

24 Broken Buttress   90m   Severe   (1970)
This route lies on No.6 Buttress. Much variation is possible. Start at the right foot of the buttress. Climb the right edge on easy rocks for 30m and scramble up the next tier to the foot of a steep wall. From a good belay below the wall climb the slab above to the overhang and turn it on the right. Continue on good holds to the top.

UPPER CLIFF - CONTINUATION BUTTRESS

(NG 790 414)   Alt 550m   South-East facing

This cliff is above and right of the six buttresses forming the South Face. It presents a steep face above a gully which runs down to the road below the lay-by for Sword of Gideon. The cliff is clearly seen in the distance when driving up from Loch Kishorn, just after a right-hand bend at NG 808 405. It can be reached after climbing a route on the main cliff or independently.

Approach: Go straight up the hillside from the car park, then angle rightwards up ramps and terraces until above Nos.2-5 Buttresses (this is reversing their descent). Continue up rightwards, when the profile soon becomes visible. Follow a terrace rightwards along its base, which is a short smooth vertical wall, 30mins. It is only 10mins from the top of Nos.2-5 Buttresses on the main cliff, so a route here is recommended as the approach. But it is then recommended to carry trainers as the total descent is very long in rock boots.

UPPER CLIFF - CONTINUATION

Descent: A grassy trough just left (looking up) and round the corner from the cliff. It is easily seen on the approach.

Pommel   60m   VS *   (1984)
At the left end of the cliff and above the left end of the short smooth vertical wall is a steep clean wall with a very prominent deep diedre above two corners (left of an enormous block).
1. 25m 5a Take the crack into the right-hand corner and climb it.
2. 35m 4b Climb the slab and arete on the right to easier ground.

Rig-Veda   105m   HVS **   (1984)
A climb which would improve with traffic; a fine expedition. Start at a grassy corner at the right end of the short smooth vertical wall and directly beneath the upper wall of the cliff. This is about 40m left of the gully. About halfway up the upper wall a small undercut nose can be seen with a short wide crack on its right. The line goes directly up corners and grooves to this.
1. 20m 4c Climb grassy corners to a terrace.
2. 20m 5a Continue up black cracks just left of a corner to belay on the grass terrace beneath the upper wall.
3. 40m 5a Climb cracks and a corner to reach the left side of the undercut nose. Step right, go up a right-facing corner and continue up cracks to the terrace.
4. 25m 4b Finish up the corner on the left.

Hotline   70m   HVS **   (1991)
Scramble up from just right of Rig-Veda to the ledge below the steep upper section of the wall. Start mid-way between the Rig-Veda belay and the right end of the ledge, where there is a small ledge at head height.
1. 30m 5a Climb past the ledge and up the central of three small left-facing corners to a bulging section. Go through this trending right, then straight up to a grass ledge 5m below the terrace. (Rig-Veda is just to the left).
2. 40m 4b Move right then straight up to the top.

Sanctuary   80m   E2 *   (1988)
Scramble up as for Hotline, and start at the right end of the ledge. This route climbs a series of flake-cracks up the right side of the overhanging band at 25m before breaking left.
1. 40m 5b Follow the left-slanting crack-line with a hard move to gain a good ledge. Ignore the hollow flake on the left and follow the improbable crack-line on good holds before moving boldly right through the hanging band to a rest. Traverse left to gain the easier continuation crack which is followed over several breaks to a good stance.
2. 40m Easier climbing leads to the top.

Dougie's Climb   90m   Severe   (1971)
This climbs the obvious arete at the right-hand end of the cliff. Scramble up left of the arete to the flat top of a large jammed boulder.
1. 20m Climb on to the wall and step delicately left around the corner. Continue up until it is possible to step on to a sloping ledge. Climb over broken ground to a grass ledge.
2. 30m Climb an overhanging crack containing a jammed block. Continue up a grass filled gully.
3. 30m Step right and climb a shattered arete to a 3m wall, taken by a groove on the left to reach a terrace.

HAIRPIN BUTTRESS

(NG 781 417)   Alt 550m   South facing   Map p164
The black water streaked buttress on the right of the road level with the second hairpin when travelling up the road towards the Bealach na Bà.

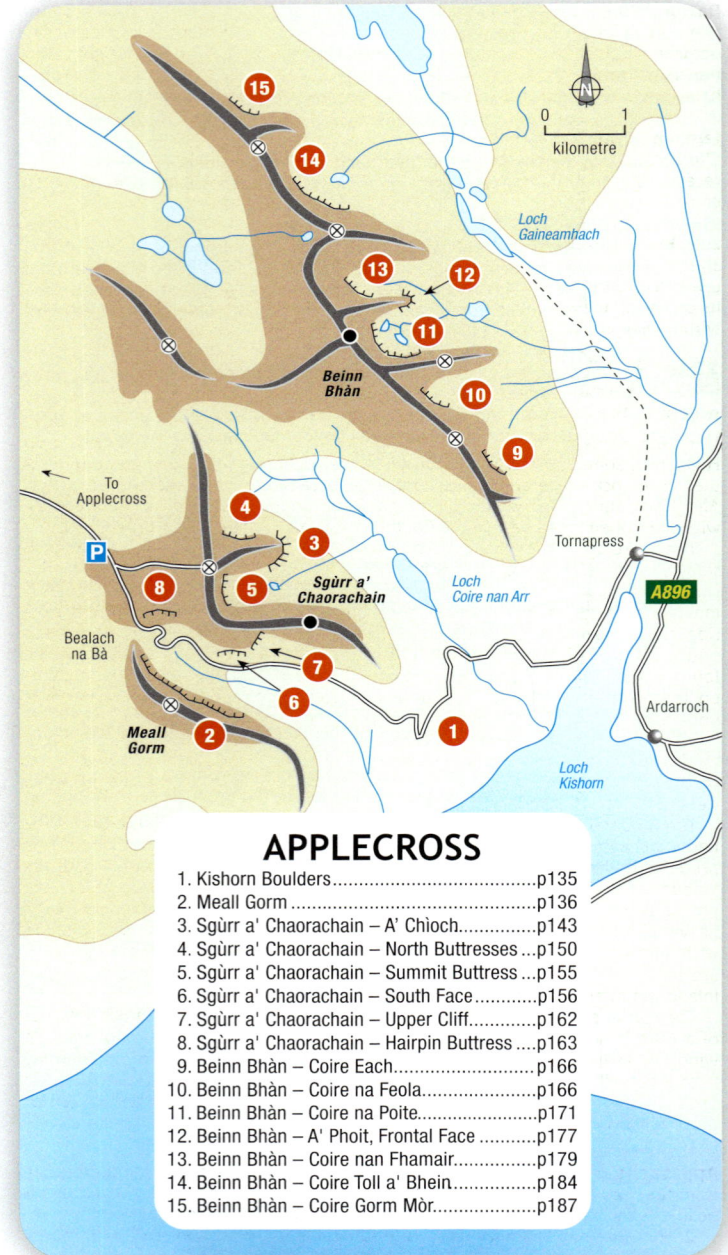

APPLECROSS

1. Kishorn Boulders p135
2. Meall Gorm p136
3. Sgùrr a' Chaorachain – A' Chìoch p143
4. Sgùrr a' Chaorachain – North Buttresses ... p150
5. Sgùrr a' Chaorachain – Summit Buttress ... p155
6. Sgùrr a' Chaorachain – South Face p156
7. Sgùrr a' Chaorachain – Upper Cliff p162
8. Sgùrr a' Chaorachain – Hairpin Buttress p163
9. Beinn Bhàn – Coire Each p166
10. Beinn Bhàn – Coire na Feola p166
11. Beinn Bhàn – Coire na Poite p171
12. Beinn Bhàn – A' Phoit, Frontal Face p177
13. Beinn Bhàn – Coire nan Fhamair p179
14. Beinn Bhàn – Coire Toll a' Bhein p184
15. Beinn Bhàn – Coire Gorm Mòr p187

Rastus 50m Severe 4a *(1974)*
The slowest line to dry, on the left. Climb black, water streaked rock until a massive detached boulder is reached in a recess. Pass the boulder on the right, then traverse leftwards to a large flat ledge (belay). Move out right on to the wall and hand-jam into a V-groove leading to a lush green ledge at the top.

Jemima 50m Severe 4a *(1975)*
Climb directly up the lower wall to arrive right of the huge detached boulder in the recess. Gain twin vertical jamming cracks on the right and climb them to easier ground.

Lulu Belle 50m Hard Severe 4b *(1975)*
Start right of Jemima and climb the wall on holds that appear to have been cemented to the face. Move left and up to the right edge of the recess. Step round its corner on the right to gain a hanging slab. Traverse 3m right and climb a groove with a wide crack to easier ground.

BEINN BHÀN

(NG 804 451)   Alt 896m   Maps p134, 164

This superb mountain offers some of the finest winter climbing in the Northern Highlands. Some summer climbs have been recorded but few are of great merit as the loose rock, vegetation and horizontal breaks are not generally attractive. Altogether, summer or winter, the magnificent mountain scenery of these corries, with their open views east to the Coulin Forest, make them well worth a visit.

There are six corries lining its north-east face. The first corrie, Coire Each is somewhat open and less impressive than its neighbours. The second and third corries, Coire na Feola and Coire na Poite, each rise from an outer corrie to a high inner corrie with a magnificent backwall. Coire na Poite is enclosed by two narrow ridges with precipitous sides whose outer ends form the great castellated buttresses of A' Chioch on the left and A' Phoit on the right. Beyond A' Phoit the fourth corrie, Coire nan Fhamair, contains on its south side one of the steepest cliffs on the Scottish mainland. There is a fifth corrie, Coire Toll a' Bhein, which is unnamed on the 1:50000 map and a smaller sixth corrie, Coire Gorm.

While there are a number of excellent gully climbs, the climbs on the buttresses tend to be open to traversing variations owing to the horizontal bedding of the sandstone. So, typical of sandstone, many of the best climbs here are gullies or icefalls.

The mountain is quite often in good winter condition, basically the colder the better, because of the low altitude of the cliff base. Conditions are not completely predictable, however, varying with the length of the cold spell coupled with the amount of drainage water; January and February are the most likely before the proximity to the sea allows damaging thaws. Applecross sometimes escapes a heavy snowfall, and it may be worth visiting when inland mountains are swamped with unconsolidated powder. On the other hand, being low and near the sea, there are inevitably times when the climbs have little snow and ice while the higher inland mountains are in good condition.

The corries can be very sheltered during strong westerly winds. But the presence of a 60m band of 50 degree snow around their rims makes them very prone to windslab avalanches. It is easy to underestimate the deposition of windslab because the cliffs are so big and the puffs of spindrift seem far away. The traverse of A' Chioch is largely safe from avalanche and can be a bad weather option; descent down Suspense Gully may then be preferred as an escape from the wind (assuming this is safe from avalanche).

Approach: 1. Coire Each, Coire na Feola and Coire na Poite are all approached from the road bridge at the head of Loch Kishorn, via a good track. The ground is heathery and takes longer than expected, especially with fresh snow.

2. For Coire nan Fhamhair and Coire Toll a' Bhein, either approach as above or,

BEINN BHÀN

if the Bealach na Bà road is open (nowadays it is often ploughed) and high level walking conditions are good, follow the stalkers' path across Coire nan Cuileag to the col between Sgùrr a' Chaorachain and Beinn Bhan, climb to the Beinn Bhàn plateau and descend into the corries from their top; Fhamair by the slope under the cliff from the north and Toll a' Bhein by the most convenient of its Grade I gullies. Note that the start of the path and the shieling at NG 763 437 are hidden from the road. The remote Coire Gorm should only be approached by this high level route when walking conditions are good.

Descent: A straightforward descent to the road bridge at the head of Loch Kishorn may be made by following the summit ridge and the south-east flank of the mountain. In white out conditions, admittedly rare on the windswept plateau, there will be a serious problem with cornices, particularly where the plateau projects out towards A' Chioch. Suspense Gully is a useful descent into Coire na Feola, also into Coire na Poite by crossing A' Chìoch ridge over its final col.

COIRE EACH

(NG 818 438)   Alt 500m   East facing   Map p164

The first corrie, nearest to the road.

Deep Gully   200m   III   *(1978)*
The deep snow gully in the centre of the corrie. There is an ice pitch at two-thirds height, which may bank out after a heavy build-up.

Skidmark Buttress   180m   III   *(1980)*
This takes the buttress left of Deep Gully. Start at the foot of a wide groove. Follow corners and ledges for two pitches to reach the top of a right-trending ramp. Climb the steep, exposed groove above (crux) to gain a wide ledge. Traverse left for 5m and continue up grooves and corners to the top. Good protection throughout.

Donkey's Doobrie   160m   IV,4   *(1980)*
This takes the line of an obvious narrow gully in the centre of the main face (right of Deep Gully).
1. 45m Climb the initial icefall direct for 20m, then avoid a 5m bulging section by a short corner on the left. Regain the gully and follow it to a belay.
2. 30m Continue to the base of an ice-choked chimney.
3. 40m Make a short traverse right followed by a short chimney and groove for 40m to regain the main gully just above the ice-choked chimney and a prominent chockstone.
4. 45m Climb easily to the top.

Hors d'Oeuvres   150m   III   *(1980)*
This takes the rightmost gully on the main face using a direct start. An easier start is possible further right.
1. 40m Climb the obvious icefall to belay under rocks on the right.
2. 45m Follow the icefall on the left through short ice bulges and grooves to a snowfield with a spike belay on the backwall.
3. 65m The main gully is now gained which leads to easy ground.

COIRE NA FEOLA

(NG 810 444)   Alt 600m   North-East facing   Maps p134, 164   Diagram p169

A corrie which has been visited much less frequently then its more famous neighbour. The amount of ice in the corrie is more variable and the same routes have been described as brilliant ice to tedious turf; stars have therefore been given conservatively. The mixed climbs are more reliable and of generally good quality but require well frozen turf. There are some interesting features on the walls of the enclosing arms of this corrie, but the best routes are probably on or near the

COIRE NA FEOLA 167

backwall. This curves round to the left into the prominent Suspense Gully, which is split into parallel runnels by a narrow ridge with an apparent tower, and may be used as a descent route. To the left of this is Suspense Buttress, which has the summer climb Rory-Pory in its lower part. The first two routes lie on the left, just at the entrance to the corrie, to the left of a large, black cave like recess.

1 Couldoran Gully   170m   III *(1986)*
Start 45m left of the recess at the foot of an obvious Y shaped gully. On the first ascent a 10m ice pitch was climbed at the start, and another small pitch at 45m. Above follow the right branch to the top.

2 Grey Hair Gully   170m   III,4 *(1986)*
Start 10m left of the black cave like recess at a steep ice filled chimney. Climb this with a hard move right at the top (15m). Follow the gully above to the top of the buttress.

3 Winklepicker   150m   IV,4 *(2001)*
On the broken ground on the left side of the corrie, before reaching Suspense Buttress, are two icefalls which are particularly prominent in cold conditions with little snow (for which they are described). This is the left icefall which flows over several tiers, the lowest being a narrow partially hidden groove and the crux being two steep walls of ice, always prominent.

4 Musselman   100m   IV,5 *(2001)*
The right icefall which flows down a shallow right-slanting gully with a steep exit which forms a wide groove of ice (with awkward ice umbrellas on the first ascent but could perhaps be Grade III,4). The lower pitches of low angled ice can bank out. The start can be reached easily from the top of Winklepicker by making a descending traverse. The next gully further in to the corrie is an easy descent (about Grade I).

5 Weakest Link   150m   III *(2004)*
This route is on a left continuation of Suspense Buttress, with its base slightly higher. The only obvious break in a steep lower tier is a groove left of centre on the buttress. Climb a groove through the lowest tier to reach the main groove. This was entered from the left over flakes and followed (45m). Continue up the groove to easier ground (40m). Continue in the same line (45m) to a finish on the left (20m).

Suspense Buttress

This is the triangular buttress at the far end of the left wall of the corrie and left of Suspense Gully, the snow gully at the back left corner of the corrie (the gully is hidden on the approach up the corrie). The steep lower rock band of the buttress is sub-divided into three subsidiary buttresses by a steep wet recess at each end, the central subsidiary buttress being much wider than the others.

6 Rory-Pory   75m   Scottish VS *(1981)*
This route takes the left rib of the left-hand subsidiary buttress, just right of a grassy chimney and minor broken rib. Start at the toe of the rib and go up to climb an obvious crack-line up slabs. Surmount the bulge at the top direct (just right of a grassy recess) and gain a terrace. Climb up the left side of the rib and move right into a groove system. Climb grooves to finish up the furthest left groove.

7 The Acid Queen   150m   V,4 * *(1984)*
The slender icefall which sometimes forms in the left recess of Suspense Buttress. It is usually accompanied by an icicle mass hanging up on the left and a twin strip of thinner ice running up just to the right. Climb the icefall in two pitches, starting up a short chimney and snow funnel. The ice at the top may be thin and this will normally be the crux. A right traverse then easier grooves lead to the top in 90m.

BEINN BHÀN

**8 Bounty Hunter   170m   IV,5 ** *(2001)*
A sustained mixed route up a central line on the buttress. The lower rock band is breached by a right-slanting line of weakness. Start on the left side of the central subsidiary buttress, down from The Acid Queen. Climb turf to gain the base of the diagonal line and walk a few metres right (10m). Go up, then traverse left to reach the diagonal line above its initial steep section. Follow it to a ledge (30m). Continue up the line and finish on the right to reach the terrace above (40m). Suspense Buttress traverses this terrace. Move right and climb a long V-groove (40m). Two short walls and a steep flaky groove just left of the crest lead to the start of the final horizontal arete (50m).

**9 Skinflint   190m   VI,6 ** *(2005)*
A spectacular line up a groove in the front face of the central subsidiary buttress. Avoid the steep but minor lowest tier and start about 15m from the left end of the next tier (this tier is also optional).
1. 10m Climb a fault with turf leading to a cracked wall. Walk left about 10m to twin cracks in a corner, the only sensible break in the right half of the next tier.
2. 25m Climb the cracks and their right-slanting continuation, passing the last crack on the right. Walk 5m right to below the main groove.
3. 15m Climb the initial overhanging section by chimneying and bridging, then go up and right to a ledge on the right of another overhanging section.
4. 30m Return to the groove and climb it to a final bulge. Move left and back right above this. A final wall is climbed by another move left and back right. Cross the terrace to an embedded flake.
5. 40m Start up a groove on the left (the harder version of Suspense Buttress goes up this and Bounty Hunter climbs a groove on the right), then walk right along a ledge (direct may be possible). Climb the buttress above to a ledge.
6. 25m Climb a groove with a steep finish.
7. 25m The final groove of Cliffhanger is on the right. Climb a steeper smaller groove to the flat top of the buttress.

10 Cliffhanger   170m   V,6 * *(2001)*
A mixed route featuring a prominent chimney-crack high on the left side of the right recess (high in the grade). Start at the back of the right recess and traverse a ledge leftwards (10m). Move up and left to climb a short cracked corner (left of a spikey rib) which gains the base of the chimney-crack. Step into the crack from the right and climb it to a ledge. Climb an exposed flake on the arete on the right to gain the terrace (50m). Traverse easily right to the left-hand of two grooves which lie above the recess. Climb the left-hand of these grooves to a ledge (30m). Continue up the groove to the crest and finish up this (40m).

11 Suspense Buttress   200m   III
Start at the base of the right recess of Suspense Buttress. Go diagonally right to reach the crest next to Suspense Gully and follow it to a terrace (50m). Make an exposed traverse left above the recess (45m). Pass the V-groove of Bounty Hunter and either climb a second groove above, including a short chimney of technical 5, or traverse a little further towards the easier grooves of Acid Queen and climb a series of short walls broken by terraces to reach the top arete of the buttress.

**12 Suspense Buttress Direct   175m   IV,5 ** *(2001)*
A much better way of doing Suspense Buttress, keeping close to the crest, which runs parallel to Suspense Gully.
1. 50m As for Suspense Buttress.
2. 40m The original route now makes an exposed traverse left above the recess. Instead, go up the crest and climb a steep tier in the front face diagonally from right to left.
3. 45m Traverse 15m left on a steep terrace until a slim groove allows the next tier to be surmounted; belay at the next break 10m higher (more direct versions will be considerably harder).

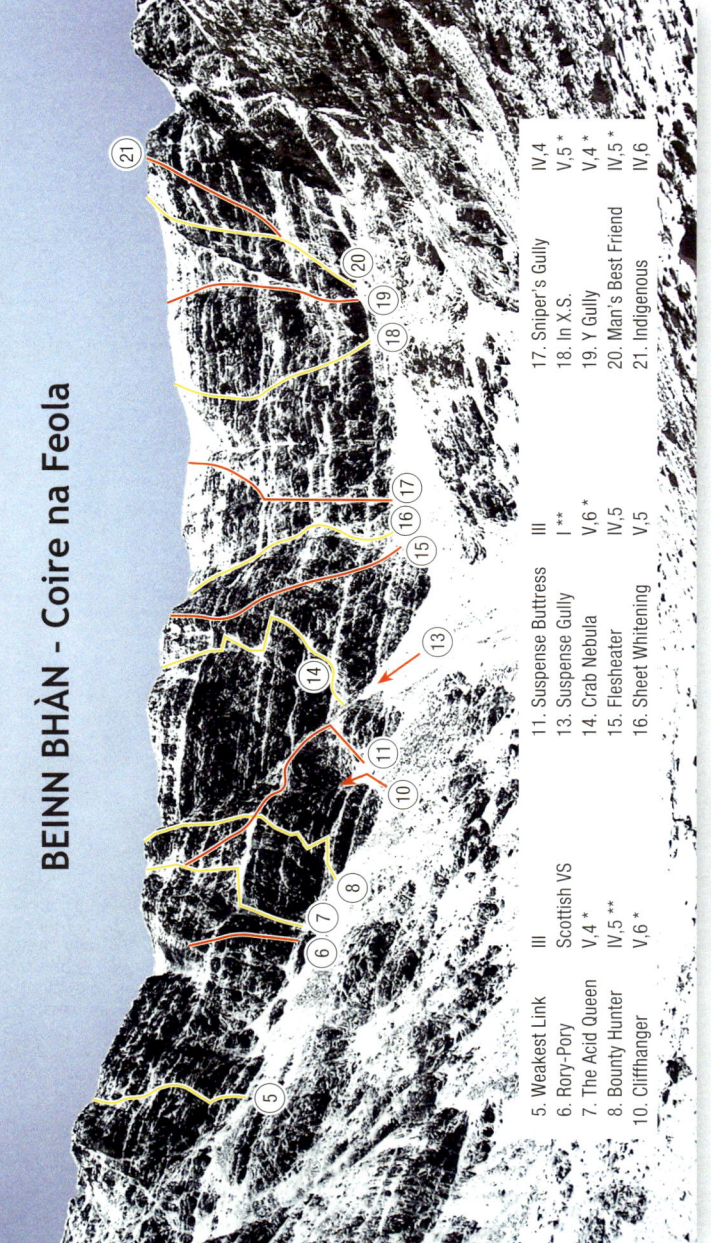

4. 45m Climb an attractive corner-line in the final tier to the top (probably the same flaky groove as for Bounty Hunter; the crest is easier but less good).

13 Suspense Gully   150m   I **

A straightforward snow climb between Suspense Buttress and the main backwall. There are two parallel lines separated by an arete; the right one is more scenic but may be corniced or threatened by avalanche whereas the left one has a tricky finish. The right branch is the more likely descent.

14 Crab Nebula   275m   V,6 *   (1980)

This takes the line of the hanging snowfield at about half-height in the huge buttress right of Suspense Gully. The two lower tiers are avoided on the left. Start by traversing right on a snow terrace from the base of the gully. Climb diagonally right up ramps and grooves for two pitches then break left up a short wall to gain the snowfield. At the top of the snowfield climb a short ice pitch to reach a higher snow patch. On the first ascent a traverse was made from here to gain a bulging icicle formation, and two rock pegs were then used for aid to reach easier ground. Finish up steep snow slopes.

15 Flesheater   220m   IV,5   (1989)

Takes a prominent diagonal fault-line in the steep cliff to the right of Suspense Gully. The line slants steeply leftwards between Sheet Whitening and the hanging snowfields of Crab Nebula. Start at the foot of the fault.
1. 20m Climb easy snow to steeper grooves, belay on the left.
2. 50m Go right into the grooves with a hard start. Follow the grooves, trending slightly right then back left to a good belay at a cracked wall.
3. 40m Climb a short chimney, then continue to a deeper chimney which is quit to a belay on the right.
4. 40m Follow grooves above directly to an entertaining exit on to a good terrace.
5. 45m Go up a shallow chimney behind the belay, then follow the rocky buttress crest in a fine position to easy ground.
6. 25m An easy arete leads to the top.

16 Sheet Whitening   245m   V,5   (1981)

This is the leftmost of the obvious runnels on the backwall of the corrie. The crux is a hard ice pitch up a steep barrier rock band at 90m. The rest of the climb is straightforward.

17 Sniper's Gully   280m   IV,4   (1986)

The shallow gully just right of Sheet Whitening. A series of icy grooves lead to an easy ramp leading out right to snow slopes.

18 In X.S.   250m   V,5 *   (1986)

This route follows a continuous ice smear starting in a small basin about 45m left of Y Gully and not visible until under that route. On the first ascent the climb gave four excellent long pitches on good quality thin ice, with a big ice filled corner as the highlight. It rarely forms as well, and the line is not obvious unless iced.

19 Y Gully   300m   V,4 *

At the right side of the backwall is a very prominent Y shaped feature. There is one big pitch but the rest is easy. The lowest band may be climbed slightly right of the steepest ice. After crossing some easier ground climb a long steep ice pitch in the 'stem' of the Y. Higher up either the left or the right branches of the Y may be taken, both giving pleasant climbing to the top.

20 Man's Best Friend   220m   IV,5 *   (1994)

Climbs the big corner-line to the right of Y Gully. Start from the bottom of Y Gully trending right to the foot of the corner (as for Indigenous). Climb the right-facing corner as directly as ice and turf allows, with a superb through route on the way. The final wall is easier than it looks from below.

21 Indigenous   170m   IV,6   *(1993)*
This is the obvious right-rising diagonal line which starts from the bottom of Y Gully. Start up an easy chimney, then follow mixed ground to the foot of the ramp. (Man's Best Friend goes straight up from here.) Climb the ramp, which on this ascent gave one turfy and one iced pitch, with an evil chockstone slit to finish. Easy steps then lead to the top of the A' Chìoch ridge.

An easy gully, just Grade I, leads from the corrie to the final col on the A' Chìoch ridge (and at a similar standard from the col down into Coire na Poite). The gully leading to the central col on the A' Chìoch ridge is easy Grade II with one tricky step which would bank out with more snow.

COIRE NA POITE

(NG 808 451)   Alt 650m   North to East facing   Maps p134, 164
Diagrams p172, 176
Surely one of the most dramatic of Highland corries.

1 A' Chìoch Traverse   II *   *(1968)*
This is the best mountaineering route on Beinn Bhàn, and also a good choice for those who wish to venture out on a wild westerly day. Climb easily up and along A' Chìoch, then with more difficulty down to the col; an easy line exists but requires good route finding. The crux is the ridge from this col to the summit plateau, which has some tricky little walls. One in particular (after 50m) is losing its turf but there is an easier option further right. A direct line up the last of three long pitches is harder; the normal route deviates left after an initial chimney to reach easy ground. The route ends with an easy crest to the plateau.
Variation: **II ****
Start by North Gully (route 3). It finishes on the ridge before the start of its difficulties (therefore misses nothing!).

2 Consolation Buttress   130m   IV,5   *(1996)*
Climbs the buttress left of North Gully, taking a line of weakness which forms intermittent chimneys and corners about 30m left of the gully. Perhaps Grade III in good conditions and taking an easier finishing pitch on the left.

3 North Gully of A' Chìoch   140m   II *   *(1969)*
This is the prominent chockstone gully on the left side of the Coire na Poite face of A' Chìoch. It finishes halfway up the A' Chìoch spur and therefore makes an excellent combination with The Traverse, including all the difficulties of the latter. Start easily, then climb a couple of steeper pitches near the top. Still good and the same grade, although more technical, in cold lean conditions.

4 North Buttress of A' Chìoch   150m   Severe   *(1950)*
This is the large, stepped buttress above the lower lochan on the left and bounding the right side of North Gully. Start near the foot of North Gully. Trend right over walls and terraces to the top of A' Chìoch.
Winter: **375m   IV,4 ***   *(1996)*
The crest right of North Gully, close to the summer route initially. Start just inside North Gully on the right wall. Traverse easily round to the front, then climb the crest through four tiers to below the clearly steepest tier (100m). Climb the steep tier by a turfy corner just left of a small tree on a ledge (25m). Traverse away right until it is possible to breach the next tier by a short steep wall (100m). Return left diagonally through the next tier and continue trending left until an easy chimney on the crest leads to A' Chìoch. Finishing rightwards after the traverse and the short wall would probably be no harder.

5 Dormouse Chimney   85m   IV,5 *   *(1980)*
Towards the right side of the north face of A' Chìoch and above vertical ice smeared

BEINN BHÀN
Coire na Poite

1. Traverse of A' Chioch — II ***
2. Consolation Buttress — IV,5
3. North Gully — II ***
4. North Buttress — IV,4 *
5. Dormouse Chimney — IV,5 *
9. March Hare's Gully — IV,4 ***
10. The Adventures of Toad — IV,4 *
12. Harlequin Rib — IV,4
13. Mad Hatter's Gully — V,5 **
15. Silver Tear — V,5 ****
16. The Cooler — VI,6 ***
17. Wall of the Early Morning Light — IV,5 ***
17a. Moonshine — IV,5
18. Meanderthal — V,5 *
20. Upper Ridge of A' Phoit — V,6 *
21. White Bhan Man — V,5
22. Gingerbread — V,6
23. Bhantasia — VI,6
24. Beinn Bhan Grooves — IV,5 *

Coire nan Fhamair

Dave Broadhead

tiers is a prominent ice filled chimney which forms its ice readily during cold weather. It provides two long pitches with steep and varied climbing on continuous ice. The start is reached by traversing in from the right along a good ledge from the upper corrie. Above the chimney go easily right up a snow ramp to the crest. If descending A' Chioch ridge is the intention, a left-trending line through easy tiers can be taken.

Teapot Buttress is the buttress high up and right of the North Face of A' Chioch, the gullies on either side of which lead up to the two cols towards the end of the A' Chioch ridge.

6 Teapot   100m   III   (1994)
There is a prominent corner near the left side of Teapot Buttress. Scramble up to a cave on the left just below the foot of the corner.
1. 50m Climb the corner with a short steep ice pitch to a tiny roof.
2. 50m Traverse right and follow a shallow snow trough to an obvious rock spike and the summit.

7 Gryphon   130m   V,7   (2005)
Climbs the front face of the buttress. Start 5m right of the small cave.
1. 30m Go up a turfy groove, traverse left and then climb a short hard groove above (crux) to a terrace below a slabby wall.
2. 40m Climb a right-trending groove, then move out right to a spike. Go up short steps, then traverse back left before climbing up and back right to easier ground leading to a short tower.
3. 30m Climb a ramp on the right side of the tower to gain its top.
4. 30m An escape left to easy ground is possible, but continue up the ridge above via short turfy steps.

8 Alice's Buttress   320m   IV,4   (1978)
At the left side of the upper corrie are two very fine gullies. This climb takes the buttress left of the left-hand of the two gullies (March Hare's Gully). Start to the left of the toe of the buttress. Climb diagonally right up a snow ramp to a point overlooking the gully (35m). Trend diagonally left then climb more or less directly to beneath a rock band at about 225m. Traverse left around a nose then go up steeply to gain the crest on the right. Follow the crest to meet the A' Chioch ridge some 45m short of the plateau.

9 March Hare's Gully   300m   IV,4 ***   (1969)
The first of the major winter climbs to be done on Beinn Bhàn and a splendid route. The hard sections are short and it takes the obvious line on the left side of the upper corrie finishing at the point where the upper connecting ridge of A' Chioch meets the summit plateau. There can be several ice pitches of which the first is often the hardest, particularly if unfrozen; sometimes it can be avoided on the left. In unusually heavy snow conditions much of this climb may bank out, but the grade will still be IV,3 because rock protection is limited. It's a bad choice if there is spindrift; windslab avalanches from near the plateau funnel down the gully.

10 The Adventures of Toad   400m   IV,4 *   (1983)
This takes the big buttress between March Hare's Gully and Mad Hatter's Gully and provides interesting route finding with a 'big route' feeling. Start at the foot of March Hare's Gully. Climb its steep first ice pitch, then take a zigzag line first away right then back left and up to a terrace below a formidable rock band. A traverse right along the terrace for a full pitch leads to a more broken area in the band where the terrace rises up. Above this climb direct to the easier crest of the buttress.

11 Realisation   370m   VI,6 ***   (2004)
A sustained climb of great character with superb situations which takes a direct line

174 BEINN BHÀN

up the front of the buttress between March Hare's Gully and Mad Hatter's Gully. It probably joins the top part of The Adventures of Toad. Good protection except for the precarious slabs on pitch 3. Start at the lowest point of the buttress.

1. 60m Climb the lower toe of the buttress and continue to the first large snow terrace via a steep corner. Belay at a large rock finger at the foot of the second rock tier.
2. 40m Climb a groove 2m left of the belay for 10m, then take a groove on the left to gain a large snow ledge. Move to its left-hand end and climb a short steep corner. Continue up and slightly rightwards to the second of two parallel snow terraces.
3. 50m Move 4m left and climb an open groove. Continue trending right then up via precarious slabs to another snow terrace. Move up to the foot of the next steeper rock tier and traverse right to a flake-crack. Climb this for 3m, then move left at its top and continue up a steep groove until it is possible to step right in a superb position on to the rocky crest. Move up and right round the toe of a small buttress.
4. 55m Climb easier ground for 20m, then a wide open fault-line cutting through the next tier.
5. 55m Continue up an open groove to easier ground.
6. 55m Up easy ground to climb a large corner cutting through the next tier.
7. 55m Easy ground to finish.

12 Harlequin Rib   260m   IV,4   *(1986)*
This takes the right edge of the buttress between March Hare's Gully and Mad Hatter's Gully. From the start of Mad Hatter's Gully go diagonally left up a huge snow covered slab until below the obvious steep wall. Turn this by a groove round the left edge, then continue up to a steep band (the crux) which girdles the buttress at about mid-height. Gain a groove either directly or by a traverse from the left, then continue up until able to move right to easier ground. Several easier pitches lead to the top.
Variation: **Right-Hand Version   V,7**   *(2003)*
A line suitable for lean conditions, which are much more common than the original ascent under good snow, but using 2 pegs for aid. Start a short way up Mad Hatter's Gully.

1. Traverse a horizontal terrace leftwards to the foot of a left-facing slabby corner-groove which bounds the extreme right edge of the 'steep wall' (the original route turns its left edge).
2. Climb the corner and turfy cracks to a 'blank exit' up a smooth slab (1PA).
3. Traverse easily leftwards for 20m.
4. Climb a slabby wall by a central turfy weakness, then continue more easily to beneath the next steep band.
5. Climb this by gaining an obvious right to left ascending traverse line. Follow this to its end, then climb a short groove to a blind and rounded finish. A poor peg was use as a handhold to traverse an undercut slab; continue up the subsequent groove.
6. etc. Continue much more easily.

13 Mad Hatter's Gully   300m   V,5 **   *(1976)*
This is the large gully in the back left corner of the corrie. A huge feature with an impressively big and steep ice pitch, but the rest is easy.

To the right of Mad Hatter's Gully is the huge backwall of Coire na Poite. The climbs here are long and impressive. In the upper part of the face traverses along the obvious snow terraces allow numerous variations, though the routes will always be serious. Recent warmer winters have meant that, with the exception of Silver Tear which forms more readily, good conditions have not been common and the routes have seen few repeats.

14 The Mock Turtle   320m   V,5   *(1986)*
Climb easily up Mad Hatter's Gully for 80m to the base of an icefall beside a

March Hare's Gully, IV,4, Coire na Poite, Beinn Bhàn. Climber Derek Bearhop

right-facing corner on the right wall. Climb the icefall for 45m. Step out right for 5m then go up a snowfield to belay below a prominent icefall (45m). Climb the icefall (45m). Continue up a snowfield to belay below the last rock band (45m). Traverse left to find the easiest corner through the rock band (45m). Two long pitches of mixed climbing lead to the top.

5 Silver Tear   350m   V,5 ****   (1977)
In good conditions this gives a superb ice climb; four stars assumes the upper icefall is complete. The great icefall somewhat left of the centre of the wall is climbed directly for 120m to a terrace. Continue to a steep upper tier which ideally holds an ice pillar, but it may be necessary to pass the tier on the right. The easiest finish is up a right-slanting natural fault-line (Wall of the Early Morning Light). A mixed line near the top icefall has also been climbed.

BEINN BHÀN – Coire na Poite Back Wall

13. Mad Hatter's Gully V,5 **
15. Silver Tear V,5 ****
16. The Cooler VI,6 ***
17. Wall of the Early Morning Light IV,5 ***

16 The Cooler   150m   VI,6 *** *(1983)*
This steep ice offers a direct start to Wall of the Early Morning Light or a steeper right-hand start to Silver Tear. Start at the right side of the Silver Tear icefall (well left of Wall of the Early Morning Light). Climb steep ice to a snow terrace, then even steeper ice to reach a terrace. Either traverse right to reach the right-slanting runnel taken by Wall of the Early Morning Light or a traverse left gains Silver Tear. The first ascent traversed right below the 'even steeper ice'.

17 Wall of the Early Morning Light   400m   IV,5 *** *(1971)*
A bigger area of less steep ice usually forms in the centre of the backwall, to the right of Silver Tear and starting slightly lower. Climb this by a number of possible lines, the easiest involving a right-slanting ice runnel, to reach a barrier wall of very steep ice. The right end of this is an icy chimney which although steep, is the easiest way through this crux section. Make a long traverse left into a natural fault-line of chimneys and grooves which lead up slightly right through the upper bands of the face.

Variation: **Moonshine   300m   IV,5** *(1978/2003)*
This mixed variation on Wall of the Early Morning Light is good when ice conditions are not. Climb the central icefalls as for that route, but where it traverses left, make a long traverse right to bypass a big rock band. Trend back diagonally left by a series of traverses and short rock steps finishing by an easy left-slanting hidden chimney to finish just right of Wall of the Early Morning Light. The original line traversed immediately back left to join the right-slanting runnel of Wall of the Early Morning Light.

18 Meanderthal   400m   V,5 * *(1979)*
A line of ice through the barrier wall right of the previous route, but rarely in condition (perhaps unrepeated). Start up the icefall well right of the centre of the backwall. Climb the icefall to a large snowfield at about 60m. Go up to the top of

the snowfield and climb steep ice up the next band to snow terraces about halfway up the wall (Moonshine arrives here too). The original route followed a line of snow terraces diagonally right to finish near the top of the Upper Connecting Ridge of A' Phoit. A left finish up Moonshine is an alternative.

19 Right Face   300m   IV,3 *(1990)*
A series of snowfields at the right side of the face gives an exposed but technically easy snow climb in good conditions. Start to the left and make a long rising traverse above an initial rock band to gain and climb the snowfields, which form in a depression left of the Upper Connecting Ridge of A' Phoit.

20 Upper Connecting Ridge of A' Phoit   180m   Severe *(1961)*
This is the ridge from the col beyond A' Phoit to the plateau. There are three tiers of sandstone leading to a more broken upper ridge. Climb the first tier centrally for 10m then climb shattered blocks on the left to a wide ledge below the third tier. From 10m left of the true nose climb a clean crack to an overhang and step right across a loose flake to reach the top of the tier quite suddenly.
Winter: **V,6** *   *(1971)*
A short hard pitch with the rest much easier. Climb a groove system with blobs of turf about 20m left of the true nose.

A' PHOIT - FRONTAL EAST FACE

(NG 810 453)   Alt 450m   East facing   Map p164   Diagram p172
This face offers some good icy mixed lines, an easy descent and not quite as big an adventure as the main corrie.

21 White Bhan Man   170m   V,5 *(1998)*
The left-hand side of the face offers a series of short corners and grooves trending leftwards near the top. Start at a large block at the left side of the face.
1. 40m   Move up a little chimney rightwards to walk along to another chimney. Above this, ascend leftwards to a steep wall.
2. 35m   Traverse left into and climb a big corner to exit right and go up the easier fault above to a big chimney.
3. 35m   Climb the chimney, then traverse up left below the very steep continuation. Keep moving left to rock ledges.
4. 40m   Step back right into the groove line on thin ice. Ascend to the next fault above, turning a roof on the left to reach the final tier.
5. 20m   Climb a thin leftwards corner into an obvious slot to finish.

22 Gingerbread   200m   VS *(1974)*
Looking towards A' Phoit from Lochan Coire na Poite one can see a line of corners starting halfway up the cleanest part of the crag. The route gains this system of corners and follows it approximately.
Winter: **170m   V,6** *(2000)*
This sustained mixed climb heads for and ascends the left-facing corner-line halfway up the cliff's most continuous section. Approximating the summer line.
1. 20m   Go easily up a leftwards fault to ledges.
2. 35m   Short walls lead up and right to a hidden corner, climbed to a big terrace and a rock rib on the right.
3. 35m   Ascend the right side of the rib to steep walls. Climb direct to the base of the corner line above.
4. 20m   Climb corners to belay on the right.
5. 20m   Go up the next corner-line.
6. 40m   Step right and climb a final corner-line to an easing.

23 Bhantasia   200m   VI,6 * *(1997)*
This route ascends the central fault-line of left-facing corners, then the steep face.
1. 50m   Follow the iced fault-line up left to a large ledge and a thread on the left.

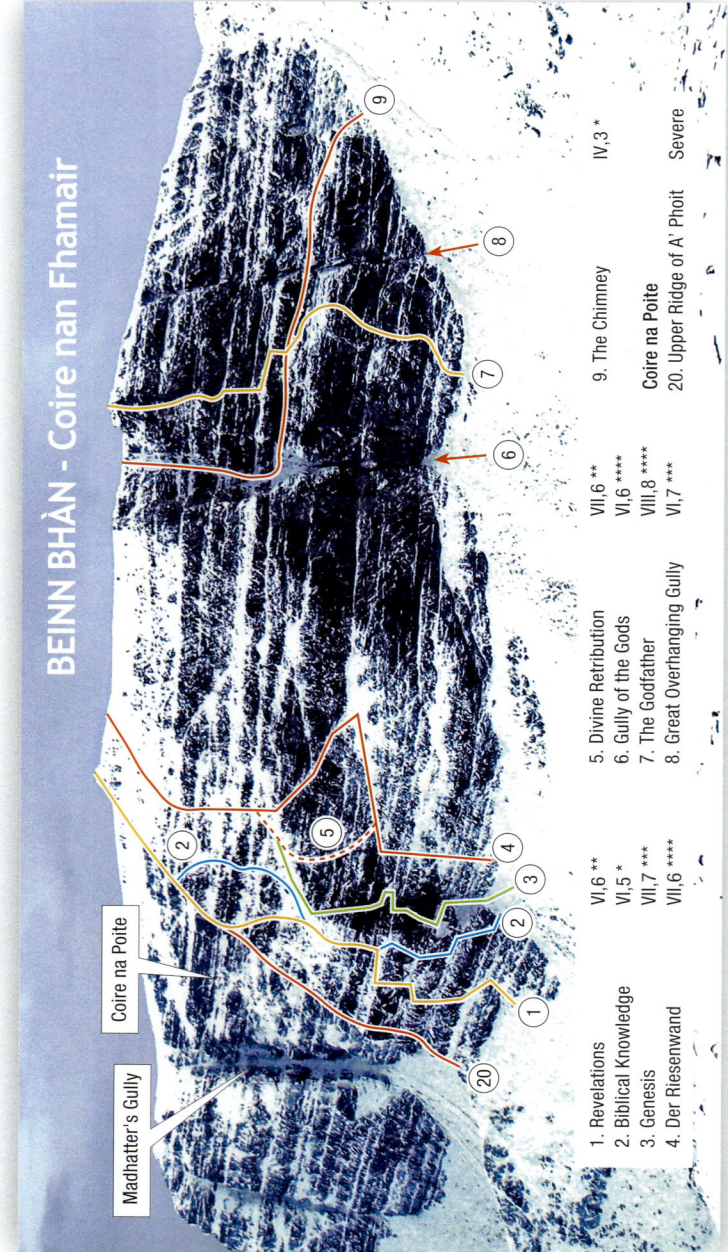

COIRE NAN FHAMAIR

2. 40m Climb an iced groove just left of the main corner to easier ground and a tree below the main left-facing corner which bounds the central slabs.
3. 25m Ascend the icy corner to an excellent thread.
4. 45m Move up and right to follow ensuing walls and cracks to a rocky rib.
5. 40m Easy ground leads to the final tier. Climb direct up good cracks.

24 Beinn Bhan Grooves   140m   IV,5 *   (1998)
At the far right-hand end of this east face, there is a large open corner system, topped by an obvious flake-crack.
1. 45m Climb an easy leftwards groove system into the base of the corner-line.
2. 25m Climb the corner-line up a wide crack.
3. 30m Continue up several icy bulges.
4. 40m Finish up the flake-crack through two tiers.

COIRE NAN FHAMAIR

(NG 803 455) Alt 600m North-East facing Maps p134, 164 Diagram p178
A huge and very steep face on the left of the corrie provides some tremendous routes. On the left of the face is a huge overhanging chimney come chasm taken by Genesis.

1 Revelations   300m   VI,6 **   (2003)
Start left of the left arete of the huge overhanging chimney come chasm below some small roofs.
1. 40m Climb up through the small roofs on thin ice to trend left to an open corner.
2. 25m Climb the corner on the left wall moving right at its top. This was tricky on the first ascent but would be easier with more ice in the corner.
3. 40m Go right along the ledge system for 7m to a short steep corner which is climbed to easier ground trending up and right to the base of a weakness above.
4. 30m Go up the right wall of the weakness to a spectacular belay on a block overlooking Genesis (or continue to make the next pitch shorter).
5. 60m Go up a short steep wall to much easier ground.
6 to 8. 105m The ground is now much easier. A hidden easy gully leads left up to the arete which is followed with a short tricky mixed section at its start to the summit.

2 Biblical Knowledge   300m   VI,5 *   (2004)
This takes the arete left of the huge overhanging chimney come chasm. Start on a ledge left of the fault-line, some 10m up from the very toe of the arete.
1. 40m Climb a corner for 20m until a zigzag right then left allows a ledge on the left to be gained (this pitch could be shortened by coming out of Genesis from higher up).
2. 40m Climb up a niche and gain a ledge on the arete via a flake. Move up the right side of a cracked slab and follow a rising left-trending ramp until below a stepped wall.
3. 40m Move up and right to a right-facing corner, then go right and up via turfy ledges until a move back left leads up to an apexed ledge right of a steep wall.
4. 60m Climb the wall on the left to reach easier ground. Go up a snow slope trending right to a large detached block, 30m right of the easier exit gully.
5. 50m Go up and right above the block to reach a left-trending break in the wall above. Climb this to reach easier ground.
6 and 7. Climb easy ground to reach the broad crest leading to the summit cornice.

3 Genesis   310m   VII,7 ***   (2000)
Climbs the stunning line formed by the overhanging chimney forming a chasm at the left side of the cliff. Sustained at a reasonable grade and with good belays, this route has an intimidating ambience. The situations are superb.
1. 30m Climb up to the base of the overhanging chimney and traverse out left along an obvious narrow turf ledge with interest to belay up and left.

BEINN BHÀN

2. 35m Climb rightwards across a steep wall on to a small ledge and then climb a short left-facing corner. Move out right to a second corner and climb its right wall on thin ice to a terrace above. Belay out left on a huge natural thread.
3. 25m Move right and climb up under a hanging icicle. Climb a steep left-facing corner on the right. At its top traverse right along turf and mantel boldly up to a huge monolithic block. Steep and exposed.
4. 45m Traverse left across the wall to reach the main line of thin ice. Follow this all the way to a giant chockstone. Climb on to the chockstone. Fantastic.
5. 25m Climb the steep groove above with interest.
6. etc. 150m Now follow easy snow to the top.

4 Der Riesenwand   400m   VII,6 ****   (1980)
This outstanding and exciting route takes the line of least resistance up the large face left of Gully of the Gods. A prominent zigzag of snow ledges marks the line in the upper part. Good conditions are advisable as a retreat from high up would be difficult. Repeats when very icy have thought it VI,5. Start towards the left of the face below a secondary corner. Climb steep ice for three pitches to a niche below a huge roof, 80m. (The second pitch climbs a short barrier wall which may be passed on the left if there is insufficient ice.) Traverse right from the niche across steep rocky ground to gain a large snow ledge, 30m. Continue traversing right for about 80m until another ledge leads back up left across the wall. Follow this for 60m passing some narrow sections and finishing with a memorable swing round a bulge in a very exposed position. The ground is now easier and a short traverse left leads to a shallow gully which gives a pleasant route to the plateau, 150m.
Variation: Direct Start   100m   VIII,8 *   (2007)
A direct and icy line which leads in two long pitches to the point where the original route traverses back left. Start in the centre of the face, below a slight recess in the initial overhanging barrier wall. Climb a short groove and pull onto a ledge, before traversing delicately left across the recess to cracked blocks. Climb up the blocks, then a short hard crack, to a swing right onto a ledge below steep thin ice. Climb the ice to an overhang and pull over directly with difficulty. Belay up on the right at the base of a groove (40m). Climb the groove to the next ledge, then move right and climb another, steeper groove to easier ground. Trend up slightly leftwards then back right to the large ledge (60m).

5 Divine Retribution   350m   VII,6 **   (1991)
A more direct route based on Der Riesenwand. Climb the first three pitches of that route to the obvious niche. Make the steep traverse rightwards until the climbing eases then cut back left up an obvious rising shelf for 20m until directly above the niche. The right-facing corner-line above develops into a groove system which is capped by a roof before easy ground. Climb the corner come groove system for 30m, chimney through the roof, then a further 150m of easier climbing to gain the top.

6 Gully of the Gods   180m   VI,6 ****   (1983)
The uniquely overhanging central gully splitting the cliff gives a tremendous climb. It is intimidating but surprisingly accommodating, providing unexpected runners and rests.
1. 25m A combination of back and foot with bridging on ice leads to an excellent ledge on the right.
2. 40m Climb the back of the gully for 5m, then back and foot out to the main ice streak and follow this into a very steep and difficult icy groove above the main overhangs. Pass the final capstone on the right.
3. 115m Climb more easily to the top.

7 The Godfather   230m   VIII,8 ****   (2002)
A mixed adventure up the face between Gully of the Gods and Great Overhanging Gully finishing up the big left-facing corner in the upper tiers. Complex and sustained climbing with the cruxes high on the route. Start mid-way across the face

COIRE NAN FHAMAIR 181

Gully of the Gods, VI,6, Coire nan Fhamhair, Beinn Bhàn. Climber Robin Beadle

right of a projecting overhang. The right-hand of two diagonal weaknesses provides the key to the lower wall.

1. 45m Climb rightwards to a terrace, move 8m right and climb a broken flaked corner to gain a narrow ledge; belay 4m back left along this.
2. 50m Go another 4m left, then make very steep moves to gain the right-slanting diagonal line which can be spotted from below the route; this leads with continuous interest to a big balcony below the girdle ledge.
3. 50m Traverse the balcony left for 30m rising slightly until a short fierce groove can be climbed to reach the girdle ledge; traverse 10m along this to belay at a

projecting block.
4. 25m Go a further 5m along the ledge to below the big corner-line then climb straight up a series of steep mantelshelves to where the corner becomes defined.
5. 15m Go right to the smooth corner, but climb a subsidiary line just left of it which is very steep but more helpful; belay up right at the base of the upper corner.
6. 25m Climb the corner past two overhanging sections (crux) to a ledge on the right.
7. 20m Go more easily up the final bulge in the corner and exit up steep snow.

8 Great Overhanging Gully   180m   VI,7 *** *(1984)*
This is the very steep line about 45m right of Gully of the Gods. Little ice is required, although it may be VI,6 if icy. Take some 4m slings for large chockstones.
1. 20m Climb turfy ground to below the overhangs.
2. 35m Climb the chimney to the overhangs; surmount these (crux unless on ice) and continue over an awkward bulge to a cave stance.
3. 35m Climb to beneath the chockstone and gain a traverse line. Continue up left to belay 5m left of the foot of a dry overhanging pitch.
4. 12m Move left and ascend to another ledge.
5. 12m Move up to reach deceptively hard turf climbing which leads back right to the gully bed.
6. 12m Surmount the overhang to belay below the final chimneys.
7. 50m Climb grooves and chimneys to the cornice finish.

9 The Chimney   270m   IV,3 * *(1979)*
The original winter line on this face takes a left traverse along the sensational snow ledges on the right of the cliff for 180m to gain the upper part of Gully of the Gods.

10 Der Rise and Shine   120m   IV,4 *(1983)*
This climbs the narrow gully splitting the largest buttress on the opposite side of the corrie from the main cliff. Start left of the foot of the buttress.
1. 45m Climb a 25m icefall at the foot of the gully. Climb small ice bulges to a belay.
2. 45m Climb a short easy chimney, then another ice pitch.
3. 30m Follow the gully to the top.

11 The Magician's Boy   150m   IV,5 *(1995)*
Immediately right of Der Rise and Shine, between it and icefalls near and just right of the crest of the buttress, is a steep turfy groove.
1. 30m Climb the groove to a stance below a steepening.
2. 30m Continue to reach a steep terrace and thread belay top right.
3. 30m Climb a corner-crack 2m left of the belay to a terrace.
4. 60m More easily to the top.

12 The Dwarf Icefall   50m   V,5 *(1986)*
The icefall just right of the crest provides two pitches of steep ice followed by an abseil off. Or trend left over easy mixed ground to join Der Rise and Shine high up.

13 Countdown to Disaster   120m   IV,4 *(2001)*
A shorter icefall which forms to the right and can be thicker than The Dwarf Icefall. Only the first pitch and a half are hard.

14 Das Rheingold   2800m   V,4 *** *(1989)*
A continuous girdle of the central triad of corries – Feola, Poite, and Fhamair – using natural ledge and terrace lines. A magnificent expedition. Careful assessment of snow conditions is required as the steep ramps are prime accumulation sites for windslab and are threatened by cornices throughout. Many crucial moves depend on turf. Start at the top of Suspense Gully above Coire na Feola where a horizontal terrace takes off across the corrie backwall.

The Godfather, VIII,8, Coire nan Fhamhair, Beinn Bhàn. Climber Paul Tattersall

Follow the ledge (generally easy apart from a few narrowings) as far as Y Gully. Climb the left branch of this for 30m, then transfer into the right branch which is followed for a further 50m until easy ground leads right onto the final crest of the A' Chìoch ridge. Continue round across the exit bay of March Hare's Gully then lose height gradually until the crest of the bounding buttress is reached. A steep rock band required a short abseil onto a broad terrace spanning the crest. Go down to the right end of the terrace, overlooking Mad Hatter's Gully. A 15m abseil and a short traverse gain the gully just below its big ice pitch. Descend a short ice groove, then down easy snow for 80m to a diagonal ramp-line on the right wall. Climb this to its top, descend the far side for 10m, then go out right to gain a large snowfield where the traverse of the Coire na Poite headwall begins.

Go diagonally right across the snowfields until a snow or ice pitch gains a higher terrace. Traverse this for 300m, then follow its slightly descending continuation to gain the Upper Ridge of A' Phoit just above its steep steps. Traverse a further 100m then go up a 20m ice pitch to gain a higher ledge line. This leads out across some spectacular ground to the upper bay of the Gully of the Gods. The terrace continues beyond but diminishes to become a fault sandwiched between the overhanging cliffs of the final headwall. The fault descends slightly, crawling alternating with some moves round bulges, until the chasm of Great Overhanging Gully is reached. Descend this for 20m, then continue along steep ramps until the cliff finally runs out onto easy snow slopes 100m below the corrie rim. The final section from the Gully of the Gods reverses the line of The Chimney.

COIRE TOLL A' BHEIN

**(NG 803 470)   Alt 600m   North to North-East facing   Map p164
Diagrams p185, 186**

This is the fifth of the Beinn Bhàn corries, and with a loch in its bowl. The cliffs are more broken than the other corries, but still steep.

Approach: The simplest approach is along the path from near Tornapress till it ends at Loch Gaineamhach. Follow the west shore of the loch, rough and deep heather, then angle up the slope into the corrie, 3hrs. The upper approach from near the Bealach na Bà, followed by descending the relevant Grade I gully, is more pleasant but requires unusual conditions of hard snow, 2hrs 30mins.

Descent: The quickest is to descend the slope under the big cliff of Coire an Fhamhair and return to the path (assuming the low approach). It is more satisfying to go to Beinn Bhàn summit and traverse the plateau.

The most impressive feature is the biggest buttress with the wide and relatively easy angled Main Gully on its right. The buttress is characterised by a ridge right of centre. This ridge has a level platform at one-third height and a small pinnacle at two-thirds height (obvious from the side but less so from below). There is also a lower tier of crag not far above the loch. Left of this Main Buttress is a narrow snow gully and left again the three ridged Breach Buttress. Right of Main Buttress is an easier angled buttress (Missing Persons), then a snow gully and right again two very steep faces split by a big right-slanting ramp broken by a vertical step.

Breach Buttress

1 Speeding Ticket   250m   II   *(2006)*
A shallow groove between the left and central ridges. The distinct crux and only real interest is a short vertical chimney high up.

2 Breach of Contract   250m   III *   *(1999)*
The central ridge, left of the well defined gully of Breach of the Peace. Follow it direct from its base. Avoiding a steep pitch at mid-height by a chimney on the left and passing the top tower on the right would reduce the grade to II.

3 Breach of the Peace   220m   III **   *(1984)*
The straight narrow gully between the central and right ridges contains two tricky steps.

4 The Weed   230m   IV,5 *   *(1999)*
Climbs directly up the rightmost ridge, right of Breach of the Peace. Start from the toe up a zigzag pitch leading to a steep band (60m). This was tackled centrally starting up a big block with jammed flakes. Two further groove pitches lead to an easier final crest and the top tower taken direct.

5 Illegal Grass   250m   IV,5   *(1988)*
A less direct route up the rightmost ridge, but with one disproportionately hard pitch. Start as for The Weed from the toe to the steep band (60m). Tackle this at its right end where it becomes more slabby and turfy but with one hard wall

BEINN BHÀN - Coire Toll a' Bhein, Left

1. Speeding Ticket	II	
2. Breach of Contract	III *	
3. Breach of the Peace	III **	
4. The Weed	IV,5 *	
5. Illegal Grass	IV,5	
6. Breach Gully	I	
7. Threatening Behaviour	V,6 **	
8. Silent Witness	III *	
10. Insufficient Evidence	V,6	
11. The Bill	II	
12. Main Gully	I	
13. Solitary Confinement	III,4	

APPLECROSS

Andy Nisbet

**BEINN BHÀN
Coire Toll a' Bhein, Right**

| 14. Missing Persons | II * | 16. Criminal Trespass | II * |
| 15. Toll a' Bhein Gully | I | 17. Policeman's Gully | I |

(crux). Easier ground leads back to the easier upper crest and the top tower passed on the right.

6 Breach Gully   250m   I
The fairly narrow snow gully between the two big buttresses.

Main Buttress

7 Threatening Behaviour   250m   V,6 **   (1984)
The face left of the pinnacled ridge has a shallow left-trending gully in its centre above some steep ground. A prominent ice column through a steep band at mid-height is the most obvious feature. Climb icy slabs for 45m, then easier ground to the steep ice pitch which may be easier if the wall on the left is iced rather than just the column. Above this, steep ice for 15m leads into the upper gully. Follow this over short ice steps to the top.

8 Silent Witness   270m   III *   (2002)
A gully which leads to the col on the pinnacled ridge provides an interesting route requiring the turf to be well frozen for the grade. Climb ice as direct as possible into the gully (similar start to Threatening Behaviour). The gully leads easily into a cave. Pass the cave by climbing the buttress to the right before making a descending traverse back into the gully just above the cave. Climb the next steep section by a groove on the left of the gully bed (crux), then continue up the gully to the col. After an awkward step, finish up the easier ridge to the plateau.

9 Indecent Exposure   290m   IV,4   (1984)
Climb the pinnacled ridge on the central buttress as direct as possible. At the top of a steep chimney traverse right across a wall to enter the upper section of the right-hand gully. Follow this to the top.

COIRE TOLL A' BHEIN

10 Insufficient Evidence 300m V,6 *(2000)*
It is unsure how this relates to Indecent Exposure so a separate description is given. Climb a shallow chimney on the face left of the crest of the pinnacled ridge to a shoulder on the ridge. Climb short chimneys up steps on the ridge crest to reach a barrier wall (old peg). Descend 10m right, then traverse a ledge leftwards for about 15m. Take a line back left up steep flaky ground (crux) to finish up a corner (which had been passed on the traverse) leading to a platform on the crest. Climb an awkward wall to the top of the pinnacle. Descend slightly along a sharp arete to the col. Climb an awkward wall, then finish more easily up the crest.

11 The Bill 200m II *(1999)*
The gully on the right of the ridge with the pinnacle, starting some way up Main Gully. A steep section in the middle can be avoided by a ramp on the left leading to an easy finish.

12 Main Gully 250m I
Right of the Main Buttress (with the pinnacle) is this broad gully. It splits at half-height, the left branch being steeper.

Between these branches is a buttress which provides the following route.

13 Solitary Confinement 130m III,4 *(1995)*
Start just inside the left branch of Main Gully and gain a shelf leading out right to the crest. Climb the crest or just right of it until blocked by a steep wall. Move right and up steep blocks (crux) to the crest again. On the right is a short icy corner leading to the upper snow slopes.

14 Missing Persons 250m II * *(1995)*
The big but much less steep buttress right of the Main Buttress. Start left of the crest up a short gully, then slant up right to a horizontal section of crest overlooking Toll a' Bhein Gully. Continue generally up the line of the crest to an easy finishing section.

15 Toll a' Bhein Gully 250m I
The big deep gully right of Missing Persons. Has a rounded exit not prone to cornicing.

16 Criminal Trespass 200m II * *(1995)*
The rightmost buttress in the corrie (next right of Missing Persons, although there is a more broken one further right) has a deep and well hidden gully cutting into its right side. One chockstone pitch (and cave belay below) and a smaller pitch higher up. The start was reached by descending Policeman's Gully from the col at NG 795 472 and traversing a terrace right (south), crossing a prominent snow ramp below a big step. It could easily be reached from the corrie floor.

17 Policeman's Gully 250m I
The last big gully on the right.

COIRE GORM MÒR

(NG 794 478) Alt 600m North-East facing Map p164

The sixth corrie has little in the way of crag, only one deep gully. The 1:50000 map only names Coire Gorm Beag; this is the bigger corrie 500m south-east.

Flying Penguin Gully 250m V,6 *(1988)*
Easy snow leads up to a big steep ice pitch, climbed via three caves (45m). Climb another step, and higher up a short chimney avoided on the right buttress before finishing up the gully.

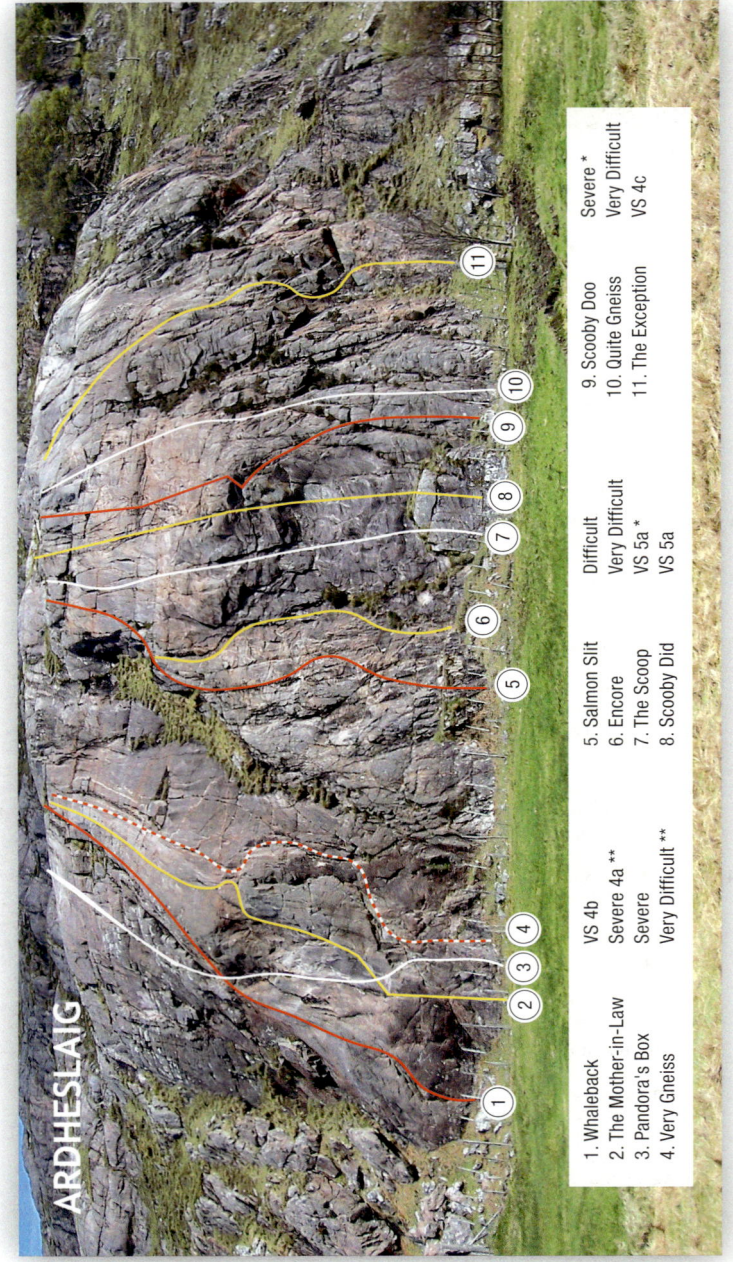

Applecross Crags

This section covers crags near the coastal (north) approach to Applecross, starting from the turn-off near Shieldaig and ending at Camusteel, beyond Applecross.

ARDHESLAIG

(NG 784 558)   Alt 30m   South-West facing   Map p134   Diagram p188

This is a clean slabby and very accessible gneiss crag with eleven 35m routes of Difficult to VS standard, generally well protected, which are ideal for a short or lower grade day. The rock is very rough and can be climbed in the rain (add about a grade). There is also some good bouldering on smaller crags nearby.

Approach: The crag is very obvious across a field from the road. Park directly opposite the crag and approach by walking west along the road, turning right (signposted Aird) and going behind the fences to the crag, 5mins.

Descent: Easy to the south-east (left looking down).

The crag is split into two halves by a big grassy fault, wide at the top but dwindling near the base and just failing to reach the ground. The fault is most obvious from the parking place.

LEFT HALF

1 Whaleback   35m   VS 4b
At the left end of the crag is a vague whaleback. Climb a tiny corner leading to a right-slanting line of downward-pointing flakes. Follow these rightwards to their end, then make thin moves left on to the blunt rib above. Follow it to the upper slabs and the top.

2 The Mother-in-Law   35m   Severe 4a *   *(1974)*
Next right is a scoop above a low bulging wall. Climb directly into the scoop, tricky but well protected, then trend right up wavy rock to the ledge of Very Gneiss. Step up into the left-hand crack and make a couple of thin moves before climbing straight up the easier upper slab.

3 Pandora's Box   35m   Severe   *(1975)*
A counter diagonal to Mother-in-Law, easier but not as good. Start 2m to its right and gain the scoop from the right. Go straight up a thin crack, then trend left under steeper ground to round the corner and gain the easier upper slab.

4 Very Gneiss   35m   Very Difficult *   *(1974)*
The best of the easier routes. Start up the slab below the right-rising overlap, then move right under the overlap to reach a vertical crack. Climb this, ignoring the first ledge on the left, to gain a second ledge (optional belay). Climb the right crack above the ledge and up the easier finishing slab.

RIGHT HALF

There are metal stake belays above this section.

5 Salmon Slit   35m   Difficult   *(1974)*
Start on a horizontal ledge 2m up and right of the base of the dividing fault. Find the easiest line up the slabby ground above to reach the right side of the turfy fault (optional belay). Keeping away from the turf, step right and climb a crack, step right again and finish over a flake.

6 Encore   35m   Very Difficult   *(1974)*
Right of Salmon Slit is a shallow corner before steeper scooped ground further

right. Climb close to a vertical line of turf to reach and follow the corner to join and finish up Salmon Slit.

7 The Scoop   35m   VS 5a * *(1974)*
The steeper ground starts with a shallow scoop leading to a bulge. Climb the left side of the scoop to a shallow left-facing corner. Climb the corner, with good but well hidden holds, to the fine but easy upper slab.

8 Scooby Did   35m   VS 5a
Climb the scoop centrally to its headwall. Pull up left on to a small scooped ledge. Step right and up cracks to the upper slab, climbed direct to the top.

9 Scooby Doo   35m   Severe * *(1974)*
Climb the rib on the right of the scoop until it steepens. Climb cracks until it is possible to step left to a ledge overlooking the scoop. Step up on to the upper slab and finish trending slightly left.

10 Quite Gneiss   35m   Very Difficult *(1974)*
Climbs the same rib as Scooby Doo but to its right, keeping just to the left of a sliver of grass. A bit scrappy.

11 The Exception   30m   VS 4c *(1974)*
A steeper route at the right end of the crag, but with slightly poorer rock. Go up an easy slab for 5m to the left corner of an overhanging wall. Step right into a short crack, up and right again to a shallow corner. Above this, step left into the continuation of the crack and follow it to trend left up the upper slab.

ARDHESLAIG SEA-CLIFF

(NG 777 575)   Partially tidal   North-West facing   Map p134

A tidal cliff of red gneiss with a fine westward outlook reached in 20mins shore walk from Ardheslaig township.

High Tide, Green Grass   20m   VS 4c *(2002)*
Climb cracks and walls just right of a bounding arete. It can be accessed at all tides.

Shaggy Crack   20m   Very Difficult *(2002)*
The obvious chimney in the crag centre reached by an entertaining 30m sea-level traverse. Not accessible at highest tides.

LOCH NA CREIGE CRAG

(NG 769 557)   Alt 110m   West facing   Map p134   Diagram p191

This compact gneiss crag in north Applecross lies one minute from the coast road. The routes have been upgraded from the last guide, but maybe the author was having a bad day.

1 Corner Route   20m   E1 5b * *(1988)*
Climb an obvious left-facing corner at the crag end nearest the road.

2 Little Plum   20m   E2 5b * *(1988)*
Very sustained, would deserve an extra star if the finish was cleaned. Start 8m right of the corner. Climb a small shallow cracked groove leading to a smooth wall.

3 Diagonal   30m   E1 5a *(1988)*
A large curving overlap dominates the right side of the crag. Follow a left-slanting break to its left end, then climb the corner on the left.

4 Slab Route   25m   HVS 5a *(1988)*
Start at the right end of the crag, just right of the bottom end of the curving

LOCH NA CREIGE CRAG

1. Corner Route — E1 5b *
2. Little Plum — E2 5b *
3. Diagonal — E1 5a
4. Slab Route — HVS 5a

overlap. A hard and poorly protected start leads to progressively easier climbing. Climb left to a flake, then up the wall above.

A' BHAINLIR

(NG 763 563)   Alt 130m   West facing

A small crag on the west side of this 192m hill. Approach from the west over a bridge. The left side of the crag has good rock but is split by a left diagonal heather rake.

Vantage Slab   25m   Severe *(2005)*
Climb the right-hand of two slight ribs which form the right side of the crag. Start over a flaky bulge.

THE ARCH

(NG 731 603)   Non-tidal   West facing   Map p134

Situated a short distance west of Fearnbeg on the crags on the east side of a large bay. The crags contain a natural arch.

Cas Chrom   12m   VS 4c *(2003)*
Left of the arch is a tree. Start just left of the tree and traverse out leftwards to gain a left-facing slabby corner. Climb the corner.

SAND

(NG 68452 47221)   Non-tidal   South-West facing   Map p134

This is an extensive area of steep compact cliff, often overhanging, just south of the Allt Tasabhaig (north of Applecross village). The two routes to date are on a slab

CAMUSTEEL SEA-CLIFFS

which is not obvious from the road but is marked by belay stakes (1988 vintage, but solid in 2005). Approach by abseil from a stake.

Mandela's Birthday 15m HVS 5a *(1988)*
Trend left above a roof to finish at the top left corner of the slab at a hollow block.

If 15m E2 5b *(1988)*
Take a direct line in the centre of the slab. A bold start with a loose flake to finish.

CAMUSTEEL SEA-CLIFFS

Map p134

The hamlet of Camusteel lies just south of Applecross village. Here are sandstone sea-cliffs which were popular in the 1970s when used by instructors and students of the local outdoor centre. Climbs were often top-roped but all or most have been led, although information is lacking. The original grades are quoted (usually technical grades only) and have not been checked; the climbs look hard for their grades. Since the climbs have seen little attention in recent years and protection is generally poor, a cautious approach is recommended, but a visit may salvage something from a showery day.

CAMUSTEEL CLIFFS

(NG 704 421) Non-tidal South-West facing

These 8-10m cliffs lie 100m south-west of the hamlet of Camusteel and have reverted to a lichenous and somewhat overgrown state. Approach along the shore from Camusteel to an obvious cave seen looking up and back. Descend by a ramp which passes under the cave. Described right to left.

Route 1 3b. A V-groove splitting an overhang just right of a crest below the cave.
Cave Roof 4c. Pull over 1m left of the cave.
Right Angle 4c. Left of the cave is a large ledge with trees. A shallow bottomless corner above the left end of the ledge.
Overhang 4a. Four metres left of Right Angle is an overhanging block. Gain this from the right and finish straight up on good holds.
Coffin Groove 5b. A bottomless groove 2m left.
Fragile Crack 4a. Near the left arete of this wall, starting round the corner and finishing on the front.
Doorjam 4b. After 10m of broken ground is a square-cut doorway. Climb its right corner but finish left under the overhang.
The Hinge 4b. The left corner to the same finish.
Easy Corner 3a. A V-groove 5m to the left.
Wall and Crack 3b. The left wall of the groove and a crack finishing left.
Bosun's Chair 3c. A left-facing corner just left of the crack.
Tippy Toes 4a. A clean bottomless wall 5m to the left.
Ape Man 5a. Left of an overhanging groove containing a tuft of grass is a steep wall with an undercut base. Pull through the overhang and climb the nose above.

TRACKING STATION CLIFFS

(NG 703 423) Non-tidal West facing

Just north of a derelict tracking station inside a small fenced area are stakes seen on the cliff top. Approach down a gully from the north. The routes are cleaner here, 10 to 14m long and described from the top of the gully wall rightwards.

Renown 5b. A line of overhanging flakes heading diagonally rightwards. Start on their right and traverse left to their base.
Eyeball 5b. Start as for Renown but continue direct to a spherical depression.

MARGARETTE CLIFFS 193

Climb diagonally left and finish as for Renown.
Centre Route 5a. Just right of the spherical depression is a "suit case handle". Climb up to the handle, then slightly right and back left.
Nautilus 5b. The wall 4m to the right.
Hard 5c. Start as for Nautilus, then go rightwards across the wall above its undercut end (formed by a cave round the corner) to exit 1m from its right end.
Darling 5c (E3). Moving round right is the cave. Climb a break between the right end of the cave and a long roof to the right (peg runner). Finish by a crack at the right corner of the cave roof.
Integrity 5c (E2). After a gymnastic start, climb the face at the right end of the long roof.
Tutae 5b. Another gymnastic start 1m right of Integrity. Traverse right for 3m, then finish diagonally right.

MARGARETTE CLIFFS

(NG 707 423)   Non-tidal   West facing

These 10 to 12m cliffs are 400m further north, just beyond a dry stone wall. There are four 5m routes on a north facing wall. **Blood** 4c is a thin crack with a peg. The three undercut cracks to the right are **Sweat** 4b, **Tears** 4a and **Mars Bar** 5a. The remaining routes are described from here northwards (right to left). After about 60m of broken cliff is a ledge of saplings at half-height, then a buttress, then a bay with saplings at half-height and a pale wall capped by a roof.

Rush Pigeon 5a (HVS). Climb up through a niche in the centre of the wall to under the roof, then finish out right.
Zig-Zag 4a. Climbs the arete beneath the left end of the roof. Start by small potholes under a small overhang. Gain a ledge on the left, then one on the right. Climb straight up and finish left.
Wall Street 4a. Ten metres to the left is the biggest roof at the top of the cliff, with a steep south facing wall below its left end. Climb the wall to a horizontal crack, traverse left and go round the left end of the roof.
Diedre 4b. A small undercut diedre which lies 6m left.
Orf 5c. The crag now becomes very undercut, ending at a south facing wall of an obvious promontory. This route is 2m right of the end of the undercut, through a large overhang split by a V-groove (1NA).
Thin Finger Crack 4b. Climb the corner between the undercut wall and the south face.
South Face 4a. Climb Thin Finger Crack for 6m, then traverse left for 3m and finish direct. A direct start is 5a.

North of the promontory the cliff becomes more broken and there is a descent. Some large blocks now lie above the high tide level. Here is a platform with ferns and a dead tree. Behind the dead tree is a line of pegs, an old aid route and a good landmark.

Pebble Climb 5b. A black north-west facing wall at the right end of the platform, right of the pegs.
The Beast 5c. Climb the overhanging wall 3m left of the line of pegs.
Overhanging Chimney 4b. To the left is a corner climbed by flakes on the right and capped by an overhanging chimney.
Letterbox 5a. The left side of the arete on the left, starting further left.
Fern Crack 5b. A thin crack 8m left of the arete, finishing by a right-facing corner on its left.
Pigeon Toes 5c. The edge of this wall is 10m north. Two pockets lie 3m right and 3m up the wall. Climb the wall using them.
Holly Wall 5c. A holly grows in a fault 10m left and well up the cliff. Climb the wall 1m right of this, starting up a line of flakes.

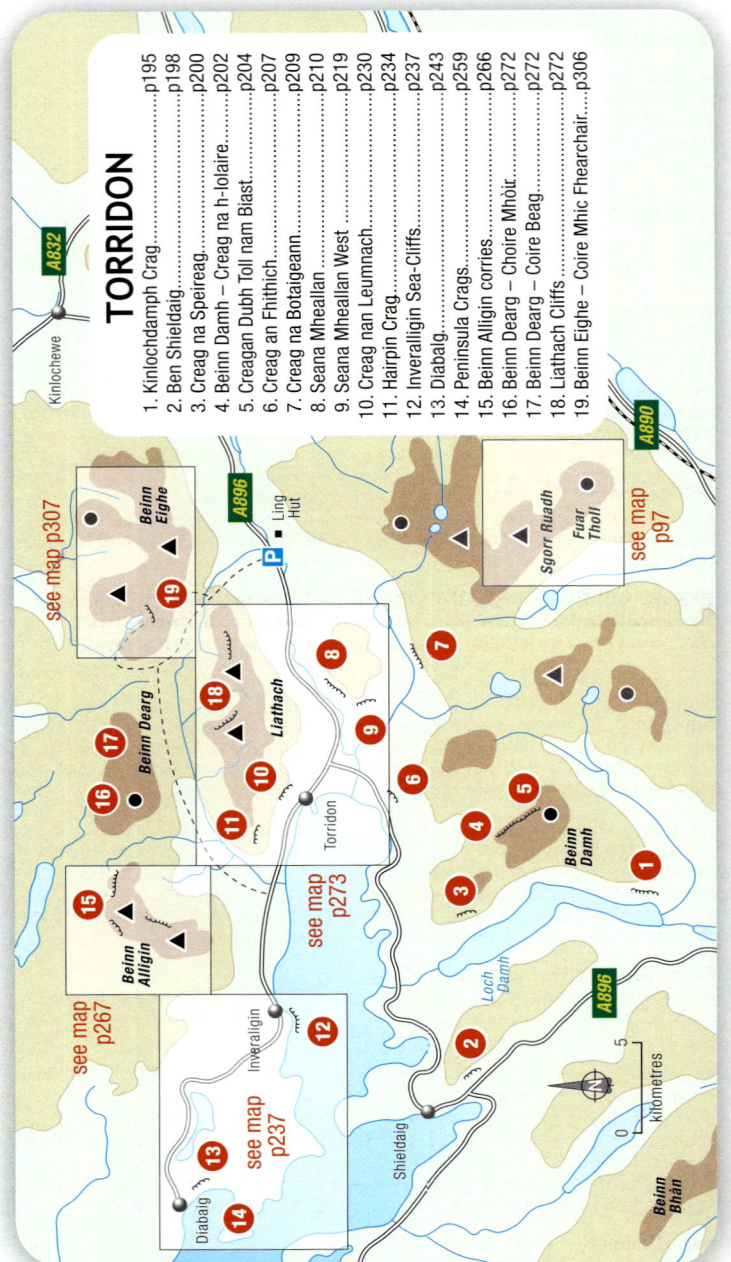

TORRIDON

1. Kinlochdamph Crag.................p195
2. Ben Shieldaig........................p198
3. Creag na Speireag..................p200
4. Beinn Damh – Creag na h-Iolaire.......p202
5. Creagan Dubh Toll nam Biast.......p204
6. Creag an Fhithich..................p207
7. Creag na Botaigeann..............p209
8. Seana Mheallan....................p210
9. Seana Mheallan West.............p219
10. Creag nan Leumnach.............p230
11. Hairpin Crag........................p234
12. Inveralligin Sea-Cliffs.............p237
13. Diabalg..............................p243
14. Peninsula Crags..................p259
15. Beinn Alligin corries..............p266
16. Beinn Dearg – Choire Mhòir....p272
17. Beinn Dearg – Coire Beag......p272
18. Liathach Cliffs....................p272
19. Beinn Eighe – Coire Mhic Fhearchair....p306

TORRIDON

Torridon is one of Scotland's most spectacular glens, with dramatic peaks and climbing to match. The main glen is formed by the two big ranges of Beinn Eighe and Liathach, before it meets Loch Torridon. Here the road splits with the south fork leading to Beinn Damh and the smaller north fork leading to the third major peak of Beinn Alligin. While the mountain routes of Coire Mhic Fhearchair used to receive all the plaudits, many crags have been developed in recent years. Diabaig, at the far end of the road along north Loch Torridon, and Seana Mheallan in the glen itself, were established in the 1993 guide, but since then some 20 less extensive crags have been discovered. These include sandstone crags around Beinn Damh and in Glen Torridon itself, as well as gneiss crags near Diabaig.

The rock layers angle slightly downhill moving inland, so the lowest layer of gneiss is seen at the coast (Diabaig), the middle layer of Torridonian sandstone dominates on the coastal mountains (Beinn Damh, Beinn Alligin and Liathach) and the more inland Beinn Eighe is largely quartzite. In winter, the compact sandstone forces water to flow out over the cliffs to produce fine icefalls, on Liathach in particular, while the more fractured quartzite of Beinn Eighe provides excellent mixed climbing on steep cracked cliffs. These two mountains rank with the best of their climbing style in Scotland.

Beinn Damh Area

Beinn Damh is a Corbett placed between Torridon and Applecross. While the mountain and its high cliffs feel close to Torridon, the crags on its west side feel closer to Applecross.

KINLOCHDAMPH CRAG - CREAG NA SAOBHAIDHE

(NG 869 477)   Alt 150m   West facing   Map p194   Diagram p197

A steep sandstone crag with impressive natural lines. A few routes are slow to dry but many are quick in the afternoon sun.

Approach: The crag is seen from the A896 Lochcarron to Shieldaig road. Park on this road and walk or cycle down the tarmac road to Ceann-loch-damh (Kinloch Damph), cross the river (no bridge) and follow the path until climbing the heathery hillside to the crag, 30 to 40mins.

The crag is separated into two halves by a large pinnacle at its base. Left of the pinnacle are several grooves. Right of it is an impressive prow high up and a smooth overhanging wall at the right end of the crag. The left end of the frontal face of the crag coincides with the end of trees at its base. Here the crag turns from west facing to north-west facing and becomes vegetated. In the arete forming this change of aspect is a slim bottomless groove, the first route from the left.

**1 Raven Seek thy Brother   30m   E2 5c **   *(1999)*
Start at the base of the cliff below the groove. Climb a short steep wall to pull on to the ledge below the groove. Climb the groove, very helpful until the last move, to gain a ledge. Finish up a difficult short wall.

2 Beauty and the Beast   30m   E2 5c *   *(1999)*
A left-rising line. Between the end groove and several big grooves to the right is a cracked overhanging wall forming the left end of the front face. Start just left of the leftmost big groove and climb a shallow chimney and slab on its left to the overhanging wall. From an obvious undercling flake, reach left over the overhang and mantel on to a big sloping ledge. Move left and gain a higher ledge. Move left again and finish up the difficult short wall as for Raven Seek thy Brother.

3 Den of Iniquity   30m   E4 6b **   *(1999)*
The leftmost of several big grooves left of the pinnacle. Start at the same point as

Beauty and the Beast but go straight up a corner to step right into the groove. Climb the groove by imaginative wide bridging over an initial overhanging section, then more easily to the top. E3 if tall and flexible.

4 Here be Dragons   25m   E1 5b *(1999)*
Climbs the next groove right, a smaller one with two chimneys. Start from the left edge of a big vegetated platform 5m up from the base of the cliff. Step left into the base of the groove (or climb direct from below) and climb a short wall to the first chimney. Climb this chimney, a wall and the second chimney to holly trees on a ledge. Fight through the hollies and up a corner to finish.

5 Ivy League   25m   E1 5b ∗∗ *(1999)*
The next groove, deep and left-facing. Start from the back of the platform. Climb a difficult left-slanting crack (originally ivy covered), making use of a flake on the right, to a ledge at the base of the groove. Continue up the main groove with one hard section near the top.

6 War of Attrition   25m   E3 6a ∗ *(2005)*
Climbs the cracked groove line 2m right of the corner with a bird's nest to the right of Ivy League. Very much harder and better than it looks. Go up to a block, swing right into the groove and climb it with sustained interest to an exit on suspect flakes. Finish up an easier flake-crack in the right side of the final arete.

7 Beasts' Lair   30m   E1 5b ∗ *(1999)*
The groove come corner behind and just left of the pinnacle. Start in the cleft behind a huge block which lies between the pinnacle and the cliff, at its outer end. Chimney up to gain a small corner and the ledge at its top. Move right into the corner and climb it to a big ledge just below the top. Move left across the back wall of the ledge to finish up a flake.

8 Cat's Claw   6m   Severe *(1999)*
Climbs the back side of the pinnacle by a stiff pull up on to the arete.

9 Needle's Edge   18m   E1 5a ∗∗ *(1999)*
Takes the smooth right-hand edge of the front face of the pinnacle; climb the lower arete to a good break then make committing moves up left on to the unprotected upper arete which eases to the top of the pinnacle.

10 Sleeping Dog Climb   45m   Very Difficult *(1999)*
Moving 15m right from the pinnacle, the last easy line before steep walls is a chimney under the left side of the prow.
1. 20m Climb the chimney.
2. 25m Traverse left where the chimney meets the overhanging upper wall, bridge across a gap and hand traverse a flake to reach a good break leading up to the top of the crag. The finish is slow to dry.
Variation: **Poshpaws Start   14m   Severe** *(2004)*
A pleasant start, also to routes in the headwall. Climb cracks on the buttress just left of the chimney, moving up and left to block belays below the headwall.

11 Tiberian Sun   40m   E2 ∗
Climbs a brief but memorable overhanging wall to gain the vice like groove in the left side of the headwall; protection is good.
1. 14m As for Poshpaws Start to Sleeping Dog Climb.
2. 26m 6a Gain the wall below the groove from the left and layback boldly into the slot. Bridge leftwards up the groove and finish up a right-facing corner.

12 Crusade Corner   50m   Severe *(1999)*
1. 25m Climb the chimney of Sleeping Dog Climb until it is possible to bridge across to a traverse shelf leading down and right to a belay under the overhanging prow.

KINLOCHDAMPH CRAG

1. Raven Seek thy Brother	E2 5c **	6. War of Attrition	E3 6a *	11. Tiberian Sun	E2 6a *
2. Beauty and the Beast	E2 5c *	7. Beasts' Lair	E1 5b *	12. Crusade Corner	Severe
3. Den of Iniquity	E4 6b **	9. Needle's Edge	E1 5a **	13. Command and Conquer	E3 ***
4. Here be Dragons	E1 5b	10. Sleeping Dog Climb	Very Difficult	14. Hasta la Bista	E2 **
5. Ivy League	E1 5b **	10a. Poshpaws Start	Severe		

TORRIDON

SHIELDAIG CRAGS

2. 25m Move right into the corner right of the prow; climb it past bushes to a deeper finishing chimney.

13 Command and Conquer 35m E3 *** *(2000)*
The stepped and overhanging arete on the right edge of the leaning upper wall gives a spectacular but largely well protected route. Start 5m right of the chimney of Sleeping Dog Climb at a corner formed by a large detached block
1. 18m 5c Climb the corner and bulging groove above, moving slightly left to gain the halfway ledge.
2. 17m 6a Move up blocks on the left, then layback right on to the prow and pull directly over the large roof to gain a break. Move 3m left to a finishing groove.

14 Hasta la Bista 50m E2 ** *(1999)*
Climbs the overhung ramp 6m right of Sleeping Dog Climb, then continues up a fine slab to a final overhang. Start under the left and lower of two roofs.
1. 22m 5c Climb right-slanting slabs under the roofs until a short overhanging crack just right of the right roof leads up to the stance under the prow on Crusade Corner.
2. 18m 4c Move 5m right to the centre of slabs and follow a vague crack-line to a stance under a jutting prow.
3. 10m 5c Go up into the recess just left of prow and make an exciting swing and mantel over the roof to a ledge then the top.
Variation: **Pitch 3 10m 5a** Climb the crack in the right side of the prow. If wet, traverse 5m to an easier finishing crack.

BEN SHIELDAIG

(NG 826 524) Alt 300m South-West facing Map p194

The following routes are on the largest and cleanest of the crags situated on the south-west slopes of Ben Shieldaig. It is situated just above the tree-line, contains some prominent overhangs and is easily seen from the road. Park about 100m south of the Applecross turn off. The best approach is by way of a clearance on the left but involves some deep heather, about 35mins. The crag is split into three sections. The left section has two large overhangs and is bounded on the right by a groove. The middle section is bounded on the right by another groove with an overhang on the right.

Gateway 35m HVS 5a * *(2004)*
This weaves a line between the two large overhangs on the left section. Scramble up steep heather to the lowest point, directly below the right end of the upper overhang. Climb a steep crack to some small trees then traverse away left directly below the upper overhang to the exposed left edge. Finish up the easier slab on the left.

Prawn Man 30m HVS 5a * *(2004)*
The prominent groove to the right of the left section. Start in a large recess below the groove, a few metres right of Gateway. Climb a short wall then a slab to a bulge at the base of the groove. Surmount the bulge (crux), continue up the groove and finish up slabs.

SHIELDAIG CRAGS
ANGIE'S BARN CRAG

(NG 822 543) Alt 35m South-East facing

A small but accessible crag located close to the east end of Shieldaig Village, slightly below the level of the road. It has a prominent square overhang in the centre, with a steep face to the right. Descents are possible on either side of the crag.

Sheep Shed Shuffle 8m Severe 4a *(2005)*
Start at the left end of the crag above a very large flat boulder. Climb a corner with some reddish rock until it is possible to shuffle across onto the wall below the small upper slab. Pull onto the slab either direct or to the right.

Unpaid Bills 10m VS 4c *(2006)*
Climb steep cracks to the left of the overhang. Pass a small tree on a ledge above the cracks before continuing easily to the top.

Threesome 10m HVS 5a *(2006)*
From the start of Unpaid Bills move right and up until underneath the overhang. Move boldly out right until it is possible to pass the overhang on the right.

Archie Gemmell 12m VS 4b *(2005)*
This route starts up a curving ramp well right of the overhang and steep face. Move up the ramp to a strangely shaped hollowed out hold. Pull into the corner below an angular block. Climb onto the right-leading ramp. Head up from this ramp onto a slab which leads to the top.

WEST CRAG

NG 813 555   Alt 5m   South facing

A photogenic crag on the west side of Shieldaig peninsula. Protection is generally good. An extra rope for belays is useful. The routes are described right to left.
Approach: Take the path that leads past the football pitch. Turn left at a cairn and follow the path over a little hill. The path soon drops down a very short scramble. Cross a little burn and go left of the path. The crag is on the right with a raised bank in front of it.

J.S. 15m VS 4c *(2006)*
A fun route with an interesting start. Start at an obvious crack on the right of the crag. Climb the crack to its end and break out right. Continue up on good holds.

Broken Flip Flop 15m VS 4b *(2006)*
Climb the crack of J.S. but break out left, fun and airy.

Midge Direct 15m Severe 4a *(2006)*
A slightly overhanging line roughly in the centre of the crag has good holds and protection.

Endless Dribble 25m E1 5a *(2006)*
A more committing route. Start as for J.S. but break left and follow an obvious crack across most of the crag. When the crack finishes go straight up to a bulge. Finish left up a small diagonal channel.

Perfect Day 20m VS 4b *(2006)*
An excellent route with a cheeky start. Start at an obvious roofed indent at the left end of the crag. Go up this and break our right at the roof to finish straight up.

CREAG DHUBH AN T-SALL

NG 862 531   Alt 210m   West facing

A small sandstone crag passed on the way to the more impressive Creag na Speireag.
Approach: Park at the start of the track to the fish farm on Loch Damh. Walk about 300m down the track, then go diagonally up the hillside to reach the crag, 40mins.

CREAG NA SPEIREAG

Descent: The north end is slightly less rough.

At the left (north) end, the crack on a side wall is a short Severe. To its right is a deep chockstoned crack (Very Difficult) which leads to a ledge. Walk right and climb the corner behind a tree to finish. The next prominent feature to the right is a big wet black corner.

Bumble   10m   Very Difficult   (2002)
Climb the arete to the right of the black corner and the wall above, trending right above a small holly.

Towards the right end of the crag is an arete with a big roof at its base.

Apis   10m   Severe   (2001)
A crack-line starting where the left end of the roof meets the ground. This leads to a finish up the right arete of a small V-groove.

Vespa   10m   Severe   (2001)
A crack-line starting 5m from the left end of the roof, passing a small tree at the halfway horizontal break.

Bombus   10m   E1 5b *   (2001)
A steep and photogenic crack-line with some strenuous moves in the wall right of the arete, then its upper continuation.

Hoverfly   15m   E1 5a *   (2002)
Two slabby right-facing corners lie 15m right of Bombus. Climb the right corner and step left on to a small ledge. Cross an overlap and finish up a wall. Small RPs useful.

CREAG NA SPEIREAG

(NG 864 527)   Alt 260m   West facing   Map p194   Diagrams p201, 202

A steep sandstone crag with surprisingly good holds and which gets the afternoon sun. A black area is slow to dry but the rest dries quickly in the sun. The black area is easily seen when driving east towards Beinn Damh on the south side of Loch Torridon but the crag is hidden on the walking approach until past Creag Dhubh an t-Sall.

Approach: As for Creag Dhubh an t-Sall but continue past its right end when the crag immediately becomes obvious, 50mins.

Descent: Walk down at the north end.

The crag is a steep smooth wall decreasing in size towards the left end, with a watercourse and black area right of centre and smaller but well defined buttresses at its right end.

1 Big Ears   30m   HVS 5a *   (2001)
At the left end of the crag, just before it starts to decrease significantly in size, is a big left-facing flake-line. Climb the flake-line (b g Friends useful) to a horizontal ledge below a capping roof. Traverse 5m left along the ledge and pull through the roof at the first obvious break.

2 One Cog Missing   30m   E2 5c **   (2001)
Start 3m right of the flake-line below cracks in the impending wall. Gain and climb the crack-line until it peters out, then traverse boldly right for 6m along a break to gain a parallel crack-line on the right. Climb this to the overhung shelf, then straight over the roof and up a crack to the top.

CREAG NA SPEIREAG Left

1. Big Ears — HVS 5a *
2. One Cog Missing — E2 5c **
3. Waggonner — E3 6a ***
4. Cuir Tigear Na Do Thanc — E3 5c **
4a. Easier Version — E1 5b
5. Telegraph Pole — E2 5b *
6. Rock Agus Roll — E1 5b **
7. Nematode — VS 4c

3 Waggonner 30m E3 6a *** (2002)
The most continuous crack-line in the middle section of crag has a hard but well protected section. A low horizontal break leads right from near the base of One Cog Missing. About 15m right is a pink streak emerging from the left end of a wide section of crack. The crack itself passes a block on its right to pass the right end of this wide section of horizontal crack. Climb the crack past the wide section and steeply above (1 rest) to make a thin move on to easier angled ground leading to the main horizontal break. Continue up the crack-line direct through two roofs, although both are easier taken on their left.

4 Cuir Tigear Na Do Thanc 30m E3 5c ** (1996)
About 5m right, just before the cliff base becomes vertical, is a crack which leads almost to a horizontal break, then another above which starts about 1m right. Go up the first crack to near its end, then step right and follow the second crack. Continue straight up, easier but with less protection finish up a left-facing corner and its arete.

Variation: **Easier Version E1 5b (overall)** (2002)
Go up the first crack to below its top, then pull out right. Traverse right (crux) to a flake-line leading back left to the top of the second crack of the direct route and finish as for that route.

5 Telegraph Pole 30m E2 5b * (1996)
At the right end of the smooth wall section of crag is a watercourse with slow drying black rock to its left. The route is a steep crack in this black area. Gain it from the left and climb it to finish up twin cracks.

6 Rock Agus Roll 30m E1 5b ** (1996)
A few metres right and quite close to the watercourse is a less obvious crack system. Climb up to gain a crack which leads to the right side of an overhang. Step right and climb a crack up leftwards. Move up right to finish up a steep crack.

7 Nematode 30m VS 4c (1996)
Climb the open corner just left of the watercourse.

8 Che Guevara 20m VS 4c * (1996)
Right of the watercourse is a protruding buttress with an undercut arete at either end. Start up the shallow chimney-corner right of it. Traverse on to the right arete and climb it. A more direct start would be harder!

CREAG NA SPEIREAG - Right

8. Che Guevara	VS 4c *	11. Pea Soup	HVS 5a
9. Gondola	VS 4b *	12. Lysfoss	E2 5b/c *
10. Someone's Crack	Severe	13. South Wall	HVS 5b

Andy Nisbet

9 Gondola   20m   VS 4b * *(1996)*
The shallow chimney-corner climbed throughout.

10 Someone's Crack   8m   Severe *(2001)*
Right of the previous route is another watercourse, then a dry wall with a hand crack.

11 Pea Soup   10m   HVS 5a *(2001)*
About 15m to the right are three thin cracks; climb the left one.

12 Lysfoss   12m   E2 5b/c * *(2001)*
The last section of cliff forms a prominent rib containing a cracked groove. Move left on a block to gain the bulge at the start of the groove. Climb the bulge and continue to the top.

13 South Wall   10m   HVS 5b *(2001)*
This route is on the south facing wall right of Lysfoss. Start near the right side of the wall. Climb up to a break, move left, then up.

BEINN DAMH

(NG 893 502)   Alt 902m   Map p194

Situated at the south-west end of the Torridon group, Beinn Damh has been less visited as a climbing venue. This is partly because of its lower altitude, partly because there is minimal rock climbing and partly because its summit is less than the magic 914m. There are three sections of cliff, Creag na h-Iolaire at its north end (nearest the road), the big face of Creagan Dubh Toll nam Biast stretching along its east side and containing most of the routes and Stùc Toll nam Biast, the ridge north-east of the highest summit. The names are taken from the 1:25000 map.

Approach: The approach for all the cliffs is a stalkers' path which starts from the road about 150m west of the bridge across the Allt Coire Roill as almost a tunnel through thick rhododendron but is well maintained through pleasant forest and out

BEINN DAMH

on to the moor. It soon forks, the right branch being the regular hillwalkers' route and also leading to Creag na h-Iolaire while the left branch crosses the Allt (no longer a bridge, possible problem in spate) and ascends gradually on the opposite side of the corrie to Creagan Dubh Toll nam Biast and further on, opposite Stùc Toll nam Biast. For these cliffs, choose a point to head directly to the chosen route, as the cliff base is very rough. In clear weather, the path is an excellent viewpoint. It is quicker for routes near Stag Gully, however, to stay on the right bank of the Allt, gradually rising to the cliff base, 1hr 30mins.

Descent: There is a choice of returning over the top of Spidean Toll nam Biast and heading north-west to the obvious col, reversing the hillwalkers' route (the easiest route and normal choice) or descending Toll nam Biast, the huge bowl between the two summits, certainly the chosen route for returning to the cliff base. The Toll is steep but easy with sufficient snow but very rough and bouldery in the more common lean state.

CREAG NA H-IOLAIRE

(NG 883 521)   Alt 400m   North-East facing   Map p194

The Professor's Lum   135m   II   *(1991)*
To the left (east) of the path leading to the first col on Beinn Damh there is a small compact buttress split by an obvious gully (near the name Creag na h-Iolaire on the maps). The gully is steep and interesting in places and contains a passage under a jammed boulder. Seldom in condition.

Aquila   110m   Severe   *(1967)*
This follows the light coloured rib bounding the crag on the left. Start at a pinnacle on the lower of two terraces that cross the crag.
1. 20m Climb a chimney and the corner above to the next terrace.
2. 35m Continue up a grassy groove to the right. Exit right halfway up and climb an open chimney and overhang to a ledge.
3. 35m Climb a corner to the right, emerging on wet slabs which converge on a corner that is climbed delicately to a large terrace.
4. 20m Finish up pleasant twin cracks.

The following route was described as 'approximately the same line as Aquila', but since the position of Aquila is in doubt, its position is also uncertain. The 'open gully' could, however, be Boundary Gully.

Aetos   200m   III   *(1984)*
This takes the left edge of the steep part of the buttress, bounded on the left by an open gully. Climb the first tier at its lowest by an easy chimney right of a steep wall. Climb the next band by a left-slanting ramp to easy ground. Continue up to two chimneys. Climb the right-hand chimney and then the arete on the left to finish up the top of the left-hand chimney. More easy ground leads to a steep corner-crack. Climb this and more easy ground to the final tier, climbed by an open chimney.

LITTLE CORRIE

(NG 881 514)   Alt 650m   North-West facing

Above the buttress containing The Professor's Lum, cradled between the two ridges at the north-west end of the mountain, there is a small corrie containing a row of buttresses split by easy gullies and chimneys. Some five of these (120m I/II 1987-1994) have been climbed. These include a broad central gully, **Neerday Gully** (Grade I). Two further chimney-gullies were climbed on the buttress right of Neerday Gully; **The Thin White Line** (Grade II) and **The Slanter** (Grade II). An unconfirmed report in 2000 claimed 'most of the buttresses have been climbed at Grade II'.

BEINN DAMH

CREAGAN DUBH TOLL NAM BIAST

(NG 890 510) Alt 500m East facing Map p194 Diagram p205

The long east face of Spidean Toll nam Biast, Beinn Damh's second summit. It offers winter routes of a mountaineering nature, very long but not sustained (the upper halves are much easier) and ending near the summit. The face has many buttresses and gullies, requiring cold conditions both for frozen turf on the buttresses and particularly for ice to form in the gullies. A large build-up of snow in the gullies is desirable but rare because its proximity to the sea limits precipitation during cold east winds.

The cliff has a long open face with several gullies bounded on its left by a steeper and more complicated buttress, Mystic Buttress. The main face and Mystic Buttress are separated at the change of aspect by Boundary Gully. It has been argued that only Mystic Buttress should be named Creagan Dubh Toll nam Biast, because of its proximity to the bowl of Toll nam Biast. In clear weather the cliff is well seen on the approach up the stalkers' path when the best locating feature is the buttress of Traveller's Trail, which leads directly to the summit of Spidean Toll nam Biast. On its left is the biggest gully, Stag Gully, with branches vaguely like antlers. With the tops in mist, the base of Stag Gully is best defined, a huge feature continuing as a parallel sided gully on the slope below the cliff base (Stalker's Gully also does so but is much less impressive). Left of Stag Gully is a shorter prominent gully, petering out into open slopes at half-height and further left is the big shallow Boundary Gully. Mystic Buttress has a left-slanting ridge (Ermine), very obvious from close up but less so from a distance when the gully on its right (Mystic Gully), also left-slanting, is a more obvious feature.

1 Stalker's Gully   400m   III   *(1995)*
The big gully bounding the summit buttress of Traveller's Trail on the right, NG 888 513. Two lower steps and a big cave at mid-height were avoided by mixed climbing on the left wall. Above, a short awkward chockstone leads to the narrow upper gully and finishing snowfield. In exceptional conditions all the steps might form ice and a direct ascent would be a fine climb.

2 Traveller's Trail   400m   III,4 *   *(1995)*
Climbs the broad buttress which leads directly to the summit of Spidean Toll nam Biast, NG 888 512. Start at its right-hand side at the foot of Stalker's Gully and climb a left-slanting line of weakness through the steep tiers of the lower buttress, gaining the easier upper crest in five pitches. This is followed for 200m finishing by a variable line through bands of crags to emerge just a few metres north of the summit.

3 Stag Gully   400m   III *   *(1979)*
The most obvious gully on the main crag. It extends as a gully on the slope below the cliff base and towards the top has several branches resembling antlers. There is a large chockstone and it may contain three ice pitches. Grade II if well built up (unusual).
Variation: **Left Fork   75m   II**   *(1994)*
Below the main pitch of Stag Gully, make a leftward rising traverse on snow to beneath a chockstone; climb this and easy snow above.

4 Erica's Ridge   450m   III   *(1998)*
The ridge left of Stag Gully. Start 60m left of Stag Gully and climb a turfy pitch (the easiest line on the lower buttress) to a terrace (45m). Traverse easily right to overlook Stag Gully (45m). Climb the crest thereafter, becoming easier after two long pitches, to finish up a chimney on the crest.

5 Fraoch Groove   450m   IV,4 *   *(2005)*
A more direct ascent of the ridge by a line of grooves overlooking the gully on the left (Calluna). Start close to Calluna and go up right to reach the grooves. Climb

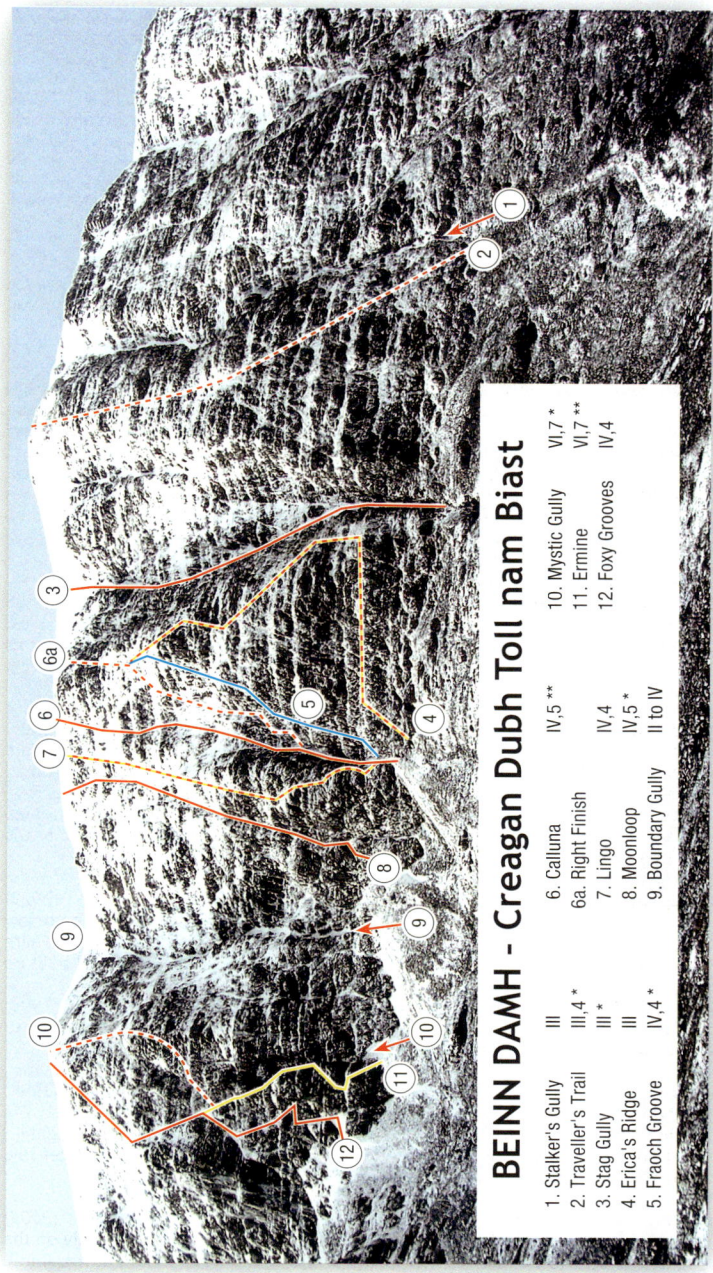

BEINN DAMH – Creagan Dubh Toll nam Biast

1. Stalker's Gully — III
2. Traveller's Trail — III,4 *
3. Stag Gully — III
4. Erica's Ridge — IV,4 *
5. Fraoch Groove — IV,4 *
6. Calluna — IV,5 **
6a. Right Finish
7. Lingo — IV,4
8. Moonloop — IV,5 *
9. Boundary Gully — II to IV
10. Mystic Gully — VI,7 *
11. Ermine — VI,7 **
12. Foxy Grooves — IV,4

Andy Nisbet

close to these for three pitches before moving right below the last steep tier to another turfy line. Finish up the easy crest and final chimney as for Erica's Ridge.

6 Calluna   450m   IV,5 **   *(2001)*
A big gully which appears to end in a steep wall halfway up the face. Its ice is hidden even when climbing the lower gully but if the first ice pitch is formed, then it should be in condition. Climb the gully, easy at first, then a 15m ice pitch leading to an overhang. A thinly iced corner just to the right was climbed to below the steep wall and the split in finishes.
Right Finish: Traverse right to an apparent line of weakness leading upwards. This was climbed, zigzagging around to find the easiest route through turfy walls and finally finishing up the last chimney on the crest of Erica's Ridge. A thinly iced corner provided the crux; the whole route might be Grade III in prime condition.
Left Finish: The direct and much better finish offering a long and steep ice pitch. Traverse left below the steep wall into a hidden icy groove and climb this to easier ground. Follow the shallower gully system to the top, with a couple of bulges passed on the left.

7 Lingo   400m   IV,4   *(2005)*
The buttress to the left of Calluna. Start just inside Calluna and traverse on to the buttress above the first wall. Go up to a steep band (15m). Climb this and the next band by corners on their right side. Go up and traverse left on to the crest (45m). Continue up the crest for two long pitches to easier ground. Finish up the crest which merges into slopes.

8 Moonloop   400m   IV,5 *   *(1995)*
Follows a shallow narrow and right-curving chimney not far left of Calluna and starting some 100m right of Boundary Gully at NG 891 508. It readily ices in cold conditions. The chimney slants easily up left for 75m before steepens and curves right over an ice bulge (25m). Climb up a sustained icefall (50m) and up the turfy wall on the left to reach open slopes and rocky steps.

9 Boundary Gully   275m   II to IV   *(1979)*
Between the main face containing Stag Gully and the steeper rockier Mystic Buttress is a long gully ending at a minor col to the left of the summit of Spidean Toll nam Biast, NG 889 508. If present the large ice pitch at its foot may vary from easy to vertical depending on snow build-up. It may be avoided by turf on the right. Above are icy steps and one good short ice pitch.

Mystic Buttress

10 Mystic Gully   370m   VI,7 *   *(1997)*
This climbs the gully on the right side of the buttress, right of a prominent ridge.
1. to 3. 100m Climb the gully over some very awkward chockstones (easier with some build-up?) leading to a big pitch.
4. 15m Gain the sharp crest of the ridge on the left by an easy traverse. This bypasses the big pitch, which would be a better choice if iced.
5. 25m Climb pitch 5 of Ermine (crux).
6. and 7. 70m Regain the gully above and climb it past a right-angle right turn to a chimney pitch.
8. 60m Climb the buttress on the right to easier ground leading after 100m to the upper slopes.

11 Ermine   370m   VI,7 **   *(2004)*
This follows the prominent ridge on Mystic Buttress, staying as near the crest as possible, but bypassing a steep second tier. Start on the right side of the ridge, below the base of Mystic Gully.
1. 30m Go up to and climb an awkward wide crack on the right side of a tier to a terrace below a steep wall. It has a clean cracked corner on its right side but instead, go to its left end.

CREAG AN FHITHICH

2. 30m Climb a grassy groove until it is possible to move right above the steep wall. Climb up steps to belay on the crest below flake-cracks.
3. 10m Climb these to an overhang, then crawl left to a small corner.
4. 30m Climb the corner and the cracked overhang above to an easy section of crest. Walk along this and climb a corner-chimney.
5. 25m Climb cracks to a rest on the right, then move up left to a steep but short wide crack. Above this, reach the easier upper crest.
6. 50m Follow the crest.
7. 60m Continue in the same line (Mystic Gully takes the gully at right angles heading right) to a crest on the skyline.
8. etc. 135m Easy turfy ground leads to the top.

12 Foxy Grooves 370m IV,4 (2006)
This is based on a groove line parallel to Ermine and situated in the steep but more broken ground between Ermine and a very steep smooth buttress. Start at a snow bay where the first terrace of Ermine reaches the hillside on the left. The groove line leaves from this bay.
1. 30m Follow the groove line to below a bulging section, which could be climbed if iced.
2. 30m Climb under the bulge, then move right on to a ledge. Follow this right, either over a pinnacle or round it, and continue to a ramp back left.
3. 20m Climb the ramp to a terrace.
4. 30m Return left to the groove and climb easily to a narrowing..
5. 30m Climb the groove up a steep V section to its end below steep walls.
6. 35m Head up right to the crest and join the upper part of Ermine.
7. 60m Go left to the skyline, as for Ermine.
8. etc 135m Easy turfy ground leads to the top.

STÙC TOLL NAM BIAST

(NG 894 506)   Alt 550m   North-West facing

Stirrup Gully   400m   III * (1991/1996)
The only route is the long gully forming the left edge of the steepest section of the face, well seen on the walk-in. In lean conditions, the lower half holds several short steep ice pitches leading to easy snow in the top half. Easier with a bigger build-up.

CREAG AN FHITHICH

(NG 892 538)   Alt 190m   North-West facing   Map p194

A low lying line of sandstone crags clearly seen from the Ben Damph Bar above the A896 Torridon road. There are two sets of crag with a shallow heather gully between them, but the main climbs are situated on an upper buttress above the left set of crags which is partially obscured by trees.

Approach: Park and start up the hill from the road bridge about 100m west of the Bar car park; follow the gully to the crag, 20mins.

The upper crags are split into two distinct sections by a grassy gully come corner. The left-hand section is slabbier and the right section is characterised by two prominent groove lines on either side of a prow.

Maculate Slab   8m   4b (1994)
The short immaculate slab up and left of the main section of crag and directly above the fence. Climb directly up the middle.

Four Trees   30m   Severe 4a (1999)
Climb the left side of the slabby left section just right of four small trees. Start at a small left-facing corner and finish up a crack beside the last tree.

Crystal Horizon   30m   Hard Severe 4b ** *(1994)*
This follows a flake-line running up the obvious slabby scoop on the left side of the left-hand section of crag. Start about 10m right of the fence line at the lowest point of the crag. Climb a short awkward corner. Pull out right and climb the flake-line to the top of the scoop. Climb up and slightly rightwards to finish just right of a small roof.

Gem Find   25m   VS 4c ** *(1995)*
Start behind the big tree closest to the base of the left section. Pull out left on to a ledge at 2m. From its left end, gain and climb a shallow groove, then continue straight up to the top.

The following routes lie on the right-hand section.

Tombstone   25m   VS 4c * *(1994)*
Climbs the prominent groove running up the left side of the prow. Start by climbing the left edge of a coffin shaped rock directly below the groove (about 5m left of the right edge of the crag). Step right into the groove and continue to a short overhanging wall. Step out right and climb around the wall into the upper groove. Climb the groove to below the prow. Swing out left to the left edge and climb directly to the top.

Fiery Cross   25m   HVS 5a * *(1994)*
Climbs the short groove running up the right side of the prow. Climb Tombstone to below the prow. Traverse right past some loose blocks to the groove which is climbed directly.

Procession   25m   Severe 4a * *(1994)*
The short roofed groove on the wall right of Fiery Cross. Climb slabby rocks at the rightmost edge of the crag to the foot of the groove. Climb the groove, roof and wall above.

Congregation   20m   Hard Severe 4b *(1995)*
The slab right of the prow section of cliff. Start at a small pine 5m up and climb as directly as possible, the difficulties soon easing.

Below the main crag is a 6m wall of impeccable rock with three routes:
Chimney Climb (Severe 4a) The obvious chimney.
Jughandle Wall (VS 4c) The best route, 3m left of the chimney.
Central Crack (Severe 4b) Right of the chimney.

Torridon Sandstone Crags

There are many sandstone crags on the steep hillsides overlooking Glen Torridon, which runs between Liathach on the north and Seana Mheallan on the south. A few unrecorded forays in the past led to the development of Seana Mheallan in 1990, just in time for the last guidebook. Since then there have been many, with Creag na Botaigeann and Seana Mheallan West to the south of the glen and several sunny crags on the slopes of Liathach to the north.

Those who like the fine natural lines of Torridonian sandstone will enjoy the climbing here. The pure features of sandstone provides top quality routes, although many crack-lines originally needed cleaning and there are occasional hollow blocks on the sunnier cliffs. Combined with the immaculate Diabaig, Torridon is a top cragging venue.

ANNAT BOULDERING

There are many short walls and free standing boulders lying above the east end of Annat. The rock is good quality sandstone and the landings are generally good.

CREAG NA BOTAIGEANN | 209

Much potential remains for new problems at all grades, although the excellent Celtic Boulders are better quality.

Approach: Park near a new house on a bend in the A896 (NG 9018 5474). All the walls and boulders are seen from here although the upper walls are hard to pick out.

ANNAT BOULDERS

Map p273

The boulders are 250m south-east from the bend, at NG 9028 5457, alt 20m. A large rectangular boulder is **Holiday Home Boulder** and has four problems on its north face, at Font 5, 5, 3, 4 left to right. Just south of it is **Metaphysics Boulder**, a church shaped boulder with a north facing gable end, Font 5+ up its left arete and 6a near the right arete.

ANNAT WALLS

(NG 902 542) Alt 160m North-East facing

Overlooking the road west of the house, at NG 9000 5457, alt 25m, is **Slipstanes Wall**. This is the upper tier of two. A tree grows out of the rock at the right end of the tier. There are three problems at Font 5, 6a, 6a.

For the upper walls, head just west of south from the back of the house to NG 9013 5449, alt 40m where the ground forms a rock slab sloping towards the sea. There are six tiers of rock above this, the first immediately above and the second hidden behind a big rowan, while the fifth tier is the most obvious. The best feature is a 3m cubic boulder which is 10m west of the fourth tier (also seen from the bend). There are two routes on the hidden third tier which has an unusual rounded formation reminiscent of gritstone (NG 9011 5445, alt 60m). These are 6b (Font 7a+) up a smooth groove with three brown streaks of rock in the centre of the wall, and a short prow forming the left edge of a chimney 5m right of the groove, 6c (Font 7c). The fourth tier (NG 9010 5444, alt 65m) has a head-height roof. Climbing the left side of the roof is 6b (Font 6b+) while pulling rightwards through the roof is 6a (Font 6a). All are sit starts.

CREAG NA BOTAIGEANN

(NG 928 533) Alt 350m North-West facing Map p194

A line of crags overlooking the Abhainn Thrail and situated behind (south of) Seana Mheallan has two fine walls. A visit can be combined with Seana Mheallan West.

Approach: Park just inside a track which leads from immediately south of the bridge across the River Torridon at NG 903 550. The track leads to a new house. Follow it and a stalkers' path along the banks of the Abhainn Thrail until steep heather leads to the crag, 1hr 30mins. When high, the river below the crag can be crossed using an unusual barrier construction. Going to Seana Mheallan West, then traversing to the river below the crag only adds 10mins, but is much rougher.

Descent: Steep heather at the west end of the crag. Also the best route for approaching the cliff top.

**Lammergeier   35m   E2 5b ** *(2000)*

In the centre of the cliff is a large steep wall. This route climbs the central groove on the wall, sustained but well protected. Start at the top of a heather bay below the centre of the wall (overlooked by birch trees on the left). Climb steep heather to reach a crack-line in the shallow groove. Climb the shallow groove to reach a block roof. Pass this on the left to finish up the deeper groove which slants slightly left.

**Tjasa   40m   E3 6a ** *(2000)*

Climbs the pink right side of the wall, facing slightly more west. The pink is perfect

water washed rock providing a superb finish, but slow to dry. Start as for Lammergeier.
1. 20m 5a Climb the heather to the crack-line. Traverse 5m right on heather and climb a corner, then go diagonally right to a ledge just short of a big grassy ledge.
2. 20m 6a Go on to the big grassy ledge and climb a tricky corner at its near (left) end. Go up slabbier ground to gain and climb an overhanging crack leading to the top.

THE BOLTING BLOCK

A huge cubic block at the right end of the cliff has three fine crack-lines in its clean smooth right-hand face, the left two being visible from a distance. The three routes have a common start, at the right end of a low roof which is at the base of the right-hand face, gained by a scramble up grass and heather (or abseil from the top).

Phantom Fencer   35m   E2 5c ** *(2000)*
This climbs the left-hand crack in a superb situation, although the crack itself is only 5a. Climb on to a ledge with trees on the right. Step left on to the lip of the roof and climb a crack (crux). Go up and slightly left to reach a bulging band. Climb through this by a crack on the right of a large block, then swing left to climb to a small tree. Traverse left to a small ledge on the arete. Climb the fine left crack to the top.

Two Bolts and Some Bailer Twine   30m   E2 5c ** *(1995)*
Originally climbed avoiding the hard initial crack on the right (then E1 5b) but better starting as for Phantom Fencer to the small tree. Climb the finger crack which runs up from the tree to the top.

Dhanakosa   30m   E5 6a ** *(1996)*
Climbs the thin crack right of Two Bolts, bold and committing. Start up the initial crack as for Phantom Fencer / Two Bolts, then climb direct to blocks. Climb the thin crack initially via pockets right of the crack to gain the overlap. Pull over the overlap and follow the continuation crack to the top.

SEANA MHEALLAN - GLAC DHORCH

(NG 925 553)   Alt 300m   West-North-West facing   Maps p194, 273
Diagrams p211, 215, 217

This excellent sandstone crag lies on the south side of Glen Torridon. It catches the afternoon and evening sun, with a superb outlook to Liathach, Beinn Eighe, and across Loch Torridon to Skye. After a showery day, the climbs may not dry until the sun appears (2pm). Those who are unfamiliar with the climbing style of Torridonian sandstone may find the grades hard.

Approach: The climbs are on the uppermost of three tiers and well seen from the road. Leave the road about 300m upstream of the two small forests on the river side of the road and where an S-bend in the river is close to the road. Cross the river at an impressive set of stepping stones at the lower bend of the S and just above some rapids. The approach is then obvious, up and then left, 40mins.

Descent: Near the top of The Torridonian is a prominent cairn. Descend rightwards (facing down) to another cairn. Make a descending traverse rightwards until the way is clearly easier below. The leftmost routes finish on this descent. For routes near the right end, an abseil descent can be made down the inset slab of A Touch Too Much, leaving a sling on a spike on a back wall (45m).

The most obvious feature seen on the approach is Crack of Ages, a prominent crack on a smooth wall which faces the approach. The climbs are described from right to left. At the right end of the main section of crag is an arete with a dark overhanging

Seams Obvious, E1 5b, Seana Mheallan

wall right of its upper section and an obvious crack in the wall right of its lower section (this is Dog-leg Crack). The first route starts beneath a short corner with a blocky overhanging right wall.

1 The Dark One   35m   E2 * (1990)
1. 15m 5b Climb the corner and its left wall to a ledge.
2. 20m 5b Walk right then climb another corner to a ledge, then take the left of two cracks to the top.

2 Edge of Enlightenment   30m   E3 5c ***   (1990)
Climb the thin crack up the left side of the arete to a ledge. Step right and climb a steep juggy wall to a slab. Move right and follow the arete to the top.

SEANA MHEALLAN | 213

3 Path of Righteousness   30m   E2 5c ** (1990)
Climb the thin crack up the centre of the slab left of the arete to a ledge. Step right and climb the steep juggy wall (as for Edge of Enlightenment) then finish up the steep corner above.

4 Elbow Room   30m   HVS 5b * (1990)
Climb the obvious corner then follow cracks to the top.

5 Dog-leg Crack   30m   E1 5a (1990)
Climb the wide crack in the wall left of the corner to the crest, then follow slabby ground and cracks left of Elbow Room.

A short distance left is a steep inset slab, the line of the abseil descent.

6 Cornered   30m   Severe (1990)
Climb the blocky corner up the right side of the slab.

7 A Touch too Much   30m   E3 5c *** (1990)
An excellent route taking the right-slanting crack-line in the right side of the steep inset slab. Move awkwardly up a thin crack to a break (bold) then take the crack to a shallow groove. Move up and climb the obvious crack to the top.

8 Seams Obvious   30m   E1 5b ** (1990)
A fine route up the crack in the centre of the slab. Gain a large elongated pocket then reach the break and a thin crack above; follow this up to a niche. Take the right branch of the crack to a ledge, then its continuation up the final wall.

9 Seems the Same   30m   HVS 5a ** (1990)
Some thin moves but well protected. At the left side of the slab climb a short crack to the break, then move right and follow a thin crack into the niche (5b without using the crack of Looks Different for initial holds). Take the left branch of the crack to a ledge and a final wall near the corner on the left (or go rightwards up the wall to finish as for Seams Obvious).

10 Looks Different   30m   HVS 5b ** (1990)
Follow Seems the Same to the break, then continue straight up until moves left (hard for the short) lead to a prominent crack which is climbed to the top.

At the left end of this recessed section of the crag is a corner leading to a roof. The next two routes start up the corner.

11 Squeeze 'Em In   30m   E1 5b (1990)
The wide crack in the corner leads to a ledge. Move up to a pocket then out right to climb a thin crack into a groove and then up the left wall to finish

12 Wide Deceiver   30m   E1 5b * (1990)
Climb the corner, then the roof and continue up the crack above.

13 In the Groove   30m   HVS 5a * (1990)
Just left is an arete. Climb a shallow groove up its right side to a heathery ledge, then take the corner and its continuation crack to the top. Low in the grade.

Around the edge to the left is a prominent crack splitting a bulge. On its left is a corner then a band of roofs. The next route takes the crack.

14 Fistfighter   30m   E4 6a ** (1990)
Start left of the thin crack which leads to the bulge. Gain a ledge, traverse briefly right and pull blindly into the crack and move up to the break. The difficult crack above leads to the top.

The Torridonian, E3 6a, Seana Mheallan. Climber Ian Taylor

15 Rock Around the Block   30m   E2 5c * (1990)
Climb Fistfighter to the ledge. Move up to the break, step right and climb left around a huge block into a short corner which leads to a swing out right. Go up to heather then climb the wall on the left of the crack.

16 Shoot the Cuckoo   30m   HVS 5a * (1990)
On the left is a corner system. Start just left of the initial short corner and climb a short crack to gain the main corner. Follow this past a recess and finish out left.

17 Hunter Killer   30m   E4 6b *** (1990)
A superb route taking the thin crack and arete just left of Shoot the Cuckoo. Climb up to stand on a small undercut shelf (Rock 1 in the right of three hairline cracks).

SEANA MHEALLAN Centre

17. Hunter Killer — E4 6b ***
18. Exterminator — E3 5c **
19. Eliminator — E3 6a *
20. The Deerstalker — VS 4c **
21. Route with a View — HVS 5a *
22. Mark of a Skyver — E2 5c **
23. View to a Hill — E1 5b *

Climb to a peg runner, then up the crack to the arete. Continue up the edge (small wires) to a small block in a break. Move right and up to the top.

**18 Exterminator 30m E3 5c ** *(1990)*
The crack and groove system up the centre of the wall.

19 Eliminator 30m E3 6a * *(1990)*
Eliminate but fine climbing up the very thin crack right of the corner. Climb easily to the break, then up the wall to the left end of a ledge. Move left to gain then climb the crack.

**20 The Deerstalker 30m VS 4c ** *(1990)*
The corner starting from a platform. There is a small rowan near the top.

21 Route with a View 30m HVS 5a * *(1990)*
Takes cracks in the buttress edge left of the corner to a blocky ledge. Finish up the cracks above, gained from the left.

**22 Mark of a Skyver 30m E2 5c ** *(1990)*
A fine route, three stars but for a slightly dirty start. About 5m left is a large flake part way up the wall. Start up a crack in a smooth wall leading to the flake. Climb the crack up its right side then take a thin crack in the wall.

23 View to a Hill 30m E1 5b * *(1990)*
The corner system on the left leads to a heather ledge (large Cams useful). Exit right to a slab then move up a crack to a niche then to the top.

**24 Crack of Ages 30m E2 5b ** *(1990)*
Climb the very prominent fine crack on the left, very sustained.

SEANA MHEALLAN

25 Sandwich 30m E3 5c *(1994)*
Climb the arete left of Crack of Ages to reach a niche. Pull left out of this to finish up the final crack of Sandpiper.

Around the ledge to the left just before the crag bends around out of sight there is a corner, one of the most prominent features of the crag. The right wall contains two crack-lines which share a common start.

**26 Sandpiper 30m E1 5b ** *(1990)*
Make a move up a crack which runs into the corner of The Torridonian, then step awkwardly up right to the thin left crack (or make a further move to a small rock scar, then step right – both are close to 5c). Move immediately across to the other crack which is climbed to the top.

**27 Sandstorm 30m E3 6a ** *(1990)*
The thin left crack provides eliminate but excellent climbing. Follow Sandpiper to the left crack, which is climbed to the top. Use a pocket on the left to start the upper wall.

**28 Thunderbird 30m E3 6a ** *(2000)*
Start as for Sandpiper. Climb the crack which trends left into the corner of The Torridonian. Go up this for a few metres and take the flying hand traverse out towards the left arete. Fortunately, the first moves provide the crux, perhaps only 5c. At the arete, step left and follow a short crack in a good position to easier ground.

29 The Torridonian 30m E3 6a ** *(1990)*
The excellent corner gives a delightful technical exercise, with the crux right at the top.

Around the edge to the left is a short overhung corner with a wall above containing three parallel cracks.

**30 Middle of the Road 30m E3 5c ** *(1990)*
Climb the steep corner to a ledge. Move right to climb the central crack.

**31 Left in the Lurch 30m E1 5b ** *(1990)*
Climb Middle of the Road to the ledge, some powerful moves for E1, then take the crack on the left to a niche. Step right and climb the wall to the top.

32 Dirty Dancing 30m E2 5c *(1999)*
On the wall left of Left in the Lurch. Start steeply via a crack in a prow and followed by a difficult entry into a shallow steep left-facing corner. Climb to the easing, move right, easier climbing to finish.

On the left is a recessed area of rock. It consists of an inset slab with a steep headwall which angles into a corner with a vertical left wall. Forgotten Corner, Rejection and Reject all finish up the twin cracks in the corner.

33 Skirting the Issue 25m VS 4c *(1999)*
Start at the foot of Forgotten Corner and climb a short steep groove and diagonal crack to a triangular vegetated niche. Continue up the corner-cracks above and exit right below the top. Finish easily.

34 Forgotten Corner 25m VS 4c *(1999)*
This is the big right-facing corner. Climb the corner, slabby at first, and continue up the steepening to step left to the obvious ledge. Finish up the twin cracks in the corner.

SEANA MHEALLAN
Left

25. Sandwich	E3 5c	
26. Sandpiper	E1 5b **	
27. Sandstorm	E3 6a **	
28. Thunderbird	E3 6a **	
29. The Torridonian	E3 6a ****	
30. Middle of the Road	E3 5c **	
31. Left in the Lurch	E1 5b **	
32. Dirty Dancing	E2 5c	
33. Skirting the Issue	VS 4c	
34. Forgotten Corner	VS 4c	
35. Rejection	HVS 5a *	
36. Reject	VS 5a	
37. Rowantree Crack	HVS 5a **	

Andy Nisbet

TORRIDON

218 SEANA MHEALLAN

Thunderbird, E3 6a, Seana Mheallan. Cl'mber Dave Cuthbertson

35 Rejection 25m HVS 5a * (1999)
The obvious jam crack in the left wall. Gain the crack from the foot of Forgotten Corner and follow it to the ledge on the left. Finish up the twin corner cracks.

The next two routes take lines on the left retaining rib of the recess.

36 Reject 30m VS 5a (1993)
Climb the crest of the rib. Follow an obvious shelf right, then finish up twin corner cracks.

**37 Rowantree Crack 30m HVS 5a ** ** (1990)
An excellent line, but one strenuous move is much harder than the rest ("Gritstone

SEANA MHEALLAN WEST 219

VS"). Climbs cracks near the crest of the arete. Start just left of the crest and climb a series of cracks, passing a small rowan and a bulging section (Friend 3.5 or 4 useful).

38 Mackintosh Slab 30m E1 5b *(1990)*
The thin crack in the slab immediately left of Rowantree Crack leads into a corner under the obvious slanting roof. Pull out right then continue up a crack and its thin continuation.

39 No Brats 30m E2 5b *(1993)*
Start left of Mackintosh Slab. Climb the slab rib left of the undercut slanting roof, traverse right above the lip and follow thin cracks to finish up the final crack of Mackintosh Slab.

The following route climbs a clean slabby wall above the descent route and with two obvious cracks (the right one peters out at the bottom and does not reach the ground).

40 Neville the Hedgehog 10m VS 5a * *(2006)*
Climb the left-hand crack to a ledge, step right and continue up a short corner to the top. Nice delicate climbing pulling on some unusually large pebbles.

SEANA MHEALLAN WEST

(NG 921 547) Alt 280m South-West facing Maps p194, 273 Diagrams p221, 225

Offers some good climbs on very clean rock with a pleasant and sunny outlook which, although shorter and more scattered than the main cliff, provide a good venue on a cold day, for those looking for lower grades or a morning ahead of the main cliff which is only 10mins away. The sector, on the western prow of the hill, can be clearly seen from near Torridon village.

Approach: Start as for Seana Mheallan but branch off right up a defined grassy trough to join a terrace descending slightly westwards from it. Reach a main aspect change from north of west to south-west, 40mins from the road, 10mins from Seana Mheallan. Maol Chean-dearg comes into sight at this point. Now the rock becomes cleaner and pinker due to the sun, but the penalty is the occasional loose block.

Descent: There are no easy descents other than abseil but each piece of crag has its own scrambling option. The corner beside the ramp of Flaky finishing down the flakes (Difficult) is one option. A line right of Clingfilm is easier but finishes on some near vertical heather. The descent from Bedrock Buttress is easy to the south.

THE PROW

The first routes are on a prow with three grooves (cairn below) which offers a preliminary change of aspect 50m before the main change.

1 Cairn Terrier 15m VS 5a * *(1999)*
The left groove has a bulge blocking access to a well defined V-section leading to the top.

2 Cairnaholics Anonymous 15m Severe 4a * *(1999)*
The middle and right grooves diverge about 5m up. This is the slabby right groove, almost a ramp.

3 Incognito 15m E1 5b ** *(1998)*
Right of the three grooves, on a small west facing wall, is a fine snaking crack-line, started direct (crux).

220 | SEANA MHEALLAN WEST

The arete which forms the main change of aspect has huge blocks forming its base and holds the following route.

4 Moaning Minnie   15m   Hard Severe 4b *(1994)*
Start left of the arete and climb a right-slanting crack to a ledge on the arete. Move left and up a short corner to finish.

5 Tarsam   12m   HVS 4c *(2006)*
Right of the arete and immediately right of the huge blocks is a rib which leads to a crack.

PINK WALLS

6 Yak   12m   VS 4b *(2006)*
The previous route is on the left wall of a bay. At the top of the bay is a right-slanting slight rib passing the left end of a roof. This gives a pleasant but escapable route.

7 Fleeced   15m   Hard Severe 4c * *(1994)*
Climb a prominent rib close to the left end of the Pink Walls to a crack in a steepening where the rib ends. Climb the crack (the only hard move) and continue up the right-slanting corner above.

Immediately right of Fleeced is a steep wall with a rightward-slanting crack-line, then a crack rising from a triangular slot and a left-facing corner just right again. Beyond the corner is a left-slanting stepped corner forming a hanging slab.

8 Skye and Kyle against Trugs   15m   HVS 5a * *(2000)*
The right-slanting crack right of Fleeced.

9 Fish and Chips   15m   E1 5b ** *(1999)*
The crack rising from the triangular slot and finishing left of a bulging nose.

10 Unmasked   20m   Hard Severe 4b ** *(1994)*
Climb the slabby corner, starting on the right up the first move of Flaky and going left round an arete (or more direct).

11 Flaky   15m   Very Difficult *(1994)*
Climbs the slabby wall of a ramp feature just right of Unmasked. Start just left of a dirty corner and climb flakes to finish up a crack on the left.

To the right of Flaky is a fine steep wall and right again, a very obvious overhung corner.

12 Outswinger   15m   E2 5c * *(2000)*
Climbs a corner with two stepped roofs on the left side of the fine steep wall. Start at the dirty corner beside Flaky (high runner) and pull up right into the start of the stepped corner. Climb this, initially bold, then follow it round the roofs and up to the top.

13 Nasal Abuse   20m   E1 5b ** *(1994)*
Climbs the right side of the fine steep wall. Start by climbing on to a ledge formed by a removed block at head height. Go diagonally right up the line of a thin crack to a ledge on the left side of an arete. Climb up from the left side of the ledge and finish up an easy corner.

14 The Age of Confusion   20m   E3 5c *** *(1998)*
The rib between Nasal Abuse and the corner (Mechanical Sheep). Start left of the rib. Move up right to a horizontal break (Camalot 4 useful). Reach above the

SEANA MHEALLAN WEST

7. Fleeced — Hard Severe 4c *
8. Skye and Kyle against Trugs — HVS 5a *
9. Fish and Chips — E1 5b **
10. Unmasked — Hard Severe 4b **
11. Flaky — Very Difficult
12. Outswinger — E2 5c *
13. Nasal Abuse — E1 5b **
14. The Age of Confusion — E3 5c ***
15. Mechanical Sheep — E2 6a ***
16. Clockwork Rat — E2 5b *
17. Skate — HVS 5a *
18. Hadrian's Wall — E1 5b **
19. Heather Said Sunshine — HVS 5a *

TORRIDON

Andy Nisbet

222 | SEANA MHEALLAN WEST

Off With Her Head, VS 4b, Quartz Slab, Seana Mheallan West. Climber Bruce Taylor

break, then right to a crack. Follow the crack, step left before the final overhang and climb the arete.

15 Mechanical Sheep   20m   E2 6a * * * (1994)
The obvious corner with an overhang at one third height and another near the top. Sustained but very well protected passing the first roof (crux). Unfortunately the rock is a little dirty.

16 Clockwork Rat   20m   E2 5b * (1999)
Strenuous but well protected. Start up the corner of Mechanical Sheep but move right to gain a crack in its right wall. Follow the crack round the right arete to a roof and rockfall scar. Go through the left side of the roof and finish up the continuation crack.

17 Skate 20m HVS 5a * (1994)
Right of the corner of Mechanical Sheep is a short rib below the roof and rockfall scar. Climb the rib then a crack passing through a break in the overhangs right of the scar to finish up a corner. Same route as The Brotherhood. Some loose rock.

18 Hadrian's Wall 20m E1 5b ** (1995)
Gain the top of a 2m pinnacle about 2m right of Skate. Climb the crack on the right, moving over an overhang to finish up a short steep wall.

19 Heather Said Sunshine 20m HVS 5a * (2002)
Right of Hadrian's Wall is a line of roofs 6m up, then a slabby corner with a high roof on its left. Start at the right end of the 6m roof. Climb a short black corner, go right over the right end of the roof and follow either a crack up leftwards or juggy ground just to its right.

20 Polythene Bag 15m Severe 4a (1994)
Start at the base of the corner and trend left to pass the left side of the high roof.

21 Better than a Slap in the Face 15m Severe (2002)
Right of Polythene Bag is a slabby wall topped by an overlap. Pass the overlap by a rib and bulge on the left.

22 Clingfilm 15m Very Difficult * (1994)
About 10m right again and just right of another grassy corner is a narrow clean buttress containing a blocky crack.

About 20m right of Clingfilm is a wall with a large prominent roof in the lower section. The two routes through the roof have boulder problem starts and easy finishes.

23 Luing Rib 12m Very Difficult (2002)
Climb the short slabby wall left of Mr Bean. Go left into the corner to avoid the overhang then back right and continue up pleasant rock right of the edge.

24 Mr Bean 12m VS 5a (1994)
Climb directly up a crack to the left end of the roof in the centre of the buttress. Pull out left and finish up slabs.

25 Sleeping Sickness 12m HVS 5a (1999)
At the right side of this wall just right of the roof are three faint crack-lines running up slightly left; follow them.

26 Right Edge 12m E1 5a (2005)
The left side of the wall's right arete (bold) and the slab above.

27 The Black Streaked 20m Very Difficult * (2005)
Some 30m right of Right Edge are some low roofs with pleasant black streaked slabs above. Climb past the right end of the right roof and up the slab above.

QUARTZ SLAB

Beyond some broken slabby rocks is a concave quartzy slab (about 90m right of Mr Bean).

28 Mind the Trench 20m Severe (2003)
The left side of the slab is separated from the right by a left-slanting corner. Start about 4m left of the corner at some white patches. Climb up past the right side of a nose at 8m, step left and continue up the slab to a grass ledge. Climb a short steep wall between the overhangs.

SEANA MHEALLAN WEST

29 Trench at Top 20m Very Difficult * *(2003)*
Start immediately right of the corner. Climb past the left end of an overlap at 6m. Continue to pass a smaller high overlap by a shallow left-facing corner to a grass ledge. A short easy wall leads to the top.

30 Lap Land 20m Severe * *(2002)*
Start 3m right of Trench at Top. Take a direct line through the overlaps to a heather ledge, then a short wall to finish.

31 Quartz Warts 20m Severe * *(2000)*
Climb a short left-facing corner and pass the right end of the overlap at 6m. Continue rightwards up a crack, slab and headwall.
Variation: After the 6m overlap, continue to pass the right end of the higher overlap to finish up two right-facing corners.

32 Off With Her Head 20m VS 4b ** *(1998)*
On the quartzy slab just left of the main part of Bedrock Buttress. At the right side of the slab is a vertical grassy crack. Start left of this. Climb straight up to a shallow right-facing corner and finish up this.

33 The Black Queen 15m Severe 4b * *(1998)*
Climb the slab just right of the grassy crack to finish up a steep juggy crack in the headwall. Good protection for the final move (crux).

BEDROCK BUTTRESS

This is a small compact buttress next right and featuring a prominent crack (Archangel).

34 Bedrock 8m Severe 4a *(1994)*
Takes the concave corner left of the prominent crack of Archangel.

35 Wriggle 10m VS 4c *(1998)*
Wriggle right on to a shelf to gain the start of Archangel. Step left and climb the arete, slabby then cracked.

36 Archangel 10m VS 5a * *(1994)*
Climb the prominent crack with an awkward steep start.

37 Porpoise Scandal 10m E1 5c *(1998)*
Right of Archangel is a short right-facing corner with a dead tree under a roof system just right again. Climb the corner, step left on to its arete, then back right to climb the crack.

38 Turned Turtle 10m E1 5c *(1998)*
The roof crack and easier continuation right of the dead tree and in the centre of the roof system.

39 Bleached Whale 10m E2 5c ** *(1998)*
A good looking line. Go up a short block, gain an overhanging hand crack and its continuation.

40 Dolphin Friendly 10m E1 5b ** *(1998)*
The big right-facing corner next right. Sustained but well protected.

41 The Knob 10m HVS 5b * *(1998)*
Right of the big corner is a short corner leading to a roof. Move left round the roof and up cracks to finish up the arete.

SEANA MHEALLAN WEST

Bedrock Buttress Area

Quartz Slab

28. Mind the Trench	Severe	
29. Trench at Top	Very Difficult *	
30. Lap Land	Severe *	
31. Quartz Warts	Severe *	
32. Off With Her Head	VS 4b **	
33. The Black Queen	Severe 4b *	
34. Bedrock	Severe 4a	
35. Wriggle	VS 4c	
36. Archangel	VS 5a *	
37. Porpoise Scandal	E1 5c	
38. Turned Turtle	E1 5c	
39. Bleached Whale	E2 5c **	
40. Dolphin Friendly	E1 5b **	
41. The Knob	HVS 5b *	

TORRIDON

Andy Nisbet

PATH CRAG

FLINTSTONE BUTTRESS

This is 150m further on and slightly higher, above a flat area.

42 Wilma 12m HVS 5a *(1998)*
The right-hand of two ramps (the left is capped by a roof) and the groove above.

43 Pebble 12m Hard Severe 4b * *(1998)*
The slabby wall to the right. Start 6m right and climb up to an alcove, then out left and up to the top.

PATH CRAG

(NG 936 573) Alt 400m South facing Map p273 Diagram p227

These sandstone crags on the south side of Liathach have fine views over to the Achnashellach hills.

Approach: From a car park at NG 935 566, follow the path on the right of the Allt an Doire Ghairbh to an easing at 370m. Cross the Allt, climb a little, then traverse west to the crags, 40mins.

Upper Tier Descent: A diagonal line east of the climbs.

LOWER TIER

Lower Leftist 15m VS 4c * *(2004)*
At the left end of the crag is a shallow gully. Climb a corner-crack right of the gully formed by the left side of a huge block. Step left and finish up an arete.

Foxglove Crack 15m VS 4c ** *(2004)*
Start just right of centre. Climb a right-slanting flake-crack and finish past a small overhang. The wall to the left is black.

UPPER TIER

Left of the clean central section of crag is a recessed area with a left-facing two stepped corner forming its right side. Right of here is a slightly curved slabby wall with a prominent right arete.

1 Pitching 22m VS 4c *(2005)*
The left-facing two-stepped corner.

2 Space Face 22m E1 5b * *(2005)*
Start up two shallow corners to reach the foot of the slabby wall. Climb up the face above past a prominent recess in its centre.

3 Spaceman 22m HVS 5a ** *(2005)*
Start up the two shallow corners to reach the foot of the slabby wall. Hand traverse right and step up to climb a right-curving crack, then the crack just left of the arete in an impressive position.

4 Path Corner 22m HVS 5a ** *(2004)*
Right of the arete are two recessed corner-cracks facing each other. The left (right-facing) is the most obvious feature on the approach. Start under the left-hand corner-crack. Move up under a big roof, go right to a ledge, then continue up and move left on to a heather ledge. Climb the left-hand corner-crack.

5 White Fingers 22m E2 5b * *(2005)*
The right corner (left-facing) is barred by a short off-width crack above a roof. Start

PATH CRAG

1. Pitching   VS 4c
2. Space Face   E1 5b *
3. Spaceman   HVS 5a **
4. Path Corner   HVS 5a **
5. White Fingers   E2 5b *
6. Path Flake   VS 4c
7. Swirl   VS 4c **

228 CELTIC BOULDERS

up a corner to the right and go up left to the off-width. Climb this with difficulty (large Cams useful) to gain and climb the corner.

6 Path Flake   22m   VS 4c *(2005)*
Next right are several huge blocks piled up to half-height on the cliff. Start on their right, climb walls and a corner, then the flake-crack above.

7 Swirl   20m   VS 4c ** *(2004)*
A swirl formation of rock lies 8m right. Climb up right through it to gain and follow a left-facing corner-crack formed by a huge block. Step left to follow an easy slab up right.

CELTIC BOULDERS

(NG 909 557)   Alt 20m   South-West or South-East facing   Map p273

This set of huge boulders lies below a small angular outcrop, situated behind the gap between two young roadside plantations. The venue is easily seen when driving down Torridon and approaching the Torridon village turn-off, although the individual boulders are not.

The crag and boulders offer some excellent bouldering and short routes up to 10m, an intriguing cave (if you can find it!) and some 'Celtic' carvings. The routes and boulder problems are on clean sandstone, quick drying and of all grades; only the larger boulders are described and many shorter problems can be climbed. The crag has several sharply overhanging south-east faces and more friendly south-west faces. The boulders are spread over a wider area and with different aspects, although many are sunny. As an approximation, V0 is 5a, V0+ is 5b, V1 is 5c and V2 is 6a.

Approach: Park at the Torridon village turn off, walk 100m towards Kinlochewe and follow a faint path on the far edge of the first wood, 5mins.

THE CRAG

As distinct from The Boulders. First seen on the approach is an undercut wall with a thin boulder touching its top; this is part of the crag. The scoop left of the undercut is **Dished Wall** 4b. Heading round to the right is a bay under an overhanging face and next to a triangular boulder with a celtic carving (Celtic Boulder – see the boulders below). A very overhanging arete is close to the boulder. Round to the left of the arete are a **Fat Crack** 4c on the left and a harder **Thin Crack** slanting right from its base.

The wall right of the overhanging arete is also overhanging below a left-rising fold which starts near the corner on the right. A hanging ramp leading left into a crack-line and a straight up line on better holds have been climbed (grades unknown). The fold itself is **Frantic** V10 (Font 7c) while a straight up line from its start is V2 (Font 6a+). The right bounding corner is VS 5a but now overgrown. A fine arete bounds a more broken section which leads on to a bay with a big tree and at its back, an overhanging leaning corner-crack with some superb holds (VS 4c). The right wall of the bay holds a narrow chimney with a chockstone (VS 4b). The wall right of this gives the next impressive route.

Trend Setter   10m   E5 6b/c *(2003)*
Start just left of a small tree. Climb a thin crack to the first break, make a desperate move to gain a good hold at the base of a thin crack above. Follow the crack up right, then straight up to finish.

Right of here are two overhanging walls separated by a small south facing wall of knobbly rock which gives two good Very Difficult routes with a common start. Beyond is a long smaller wall descending rightwards. Its right section has a thin crack, then a wider forked lightning crack above a roof (grades unknown).

Chris Anderson on the Celtic Boulders – Seana Mheallan in the background

Wave Wall

(NG 9096 5573)

Next is a very broken section followed by the fine Wave Wall, a south-east facing wall most easily reached by rising rightwards for 60m through a break in the boulders from Spaceship Boulder (see below). This 8m wall, 20m long, is clearly seen from The Ship boulder but an approach from here involves a heather cornice. The left arete is **Kate's Arete** (E1 5a). The centre of the wall gives **Muir's Masterpiece** while the right side has **Bramble Crack** (Severe 4b). The wall is traversed at mid-height by **Neils's Traverse** (5c). The right end forms a deep cleft (descent) formed by a boulder on the right, climbed by **Pegasus**, past a detached flake on the right and continuing beyond on the main cliff

Celtic Boulder

(NG 9085 5572)

The triangular boulder near the first overhanging wall on the crag is also known as 5a Wall. There is a Celtic carving on its north wall. The centre of the face trending right above the carving is **The Edge**, V0. Right of the carving is **Scott's Wall** V1. The right arete is **Launch** V1. On the east face, the right arete is V0 or 4c with a deviation on to the face at mid-height.

Further boulders are described going east from here, approached by walking below the boulder field along a vague path until they are seen. Between Celtic Boulder and Morning Wall is Tip Toe Wall. The overhung arête facing Celtic Boulder gives a fine problem V2 (SS)

230 CREAG NAN LEUMNACH

Morning Wall

(NG 9087 5571)

This is 35m east, with the best wall facing away from the approach. On the left side is a shallow corner **Zig-Zag** V1. There are three lines in the centre of the wall (all V10) while a diagonal crack at the right side is **No Skoosh** 4c.

Immediately east of Morning Wall is a cave formed by a large jammed block with a hanging arête. Either dyno for the obvious hold on the arete (V1) or, better, start from the break in the cave and pull out onto the arête at V3.

Spaceship Boulder

(NG 9090 5572)

This large low-angled slabby boulder is 25m further east and slightly hidden behind another boulder. There are three main lines of **Playtime Padding**, right, centre (right of a small overlap) and left.

The Ship

(NG 9100 5570)

This impressive boulder is 100m further east (160m from Celtic Boulder) and slightly out from the main boulder field. First seen when approaching from the west is a severely overhung face. The left arete is **Squelch** V4. The severe right arete, **Malcolm Smith's Arete** V6 with a V7 SS. Anti-clockwise, a slim groove in south face is **The Mission** V9 (Font 7b+). Next is **The Dandy Don's Arete** V3. **The Bogmen** V3 takes the face to the right. Nedi V0+ follows a short crack diagonally left from the north face. **North Face Direct** is V1, with a blunt arete to the right **Swamp Monster** V4 V5 SS. The scooped (north-west) face is **Indentation** V1.

Angel Boulder

(NG 9106 5569)

This fractured boulder is 40m further east and has many ledges on its overhanging outward face. **Trapping** V1 hand traverses the first ledge from the left and continues. **Jump** V2 takes the left and **Biscuits** V0 the centre of the ledged face. **The Nose** 4a climbs the centre of three right-slanting faults while **Layback** 4b climbs the wide crack which is the right fault. **Dyno** V0/1 is the face right of this.

Dinosaur

(NG 9109 5569)

This is 25m further east, with a small concave overhanging front face and routes round to its right on a better wall (south-east facing). The left arete (right end of the concave face) is **Dinosaur Leg** V1, immediately left is a mantle problem at V2. A central capped crack is **The Hook** 4c. To its right is a large wedged boulder at 2m. Traversing from its right to above it is the **Dino Traverse** V0.

CREAG NAN LEUMNACH

**(NG 899 569)   Alt 270m   South-South-West facing   Maps p194, 273
Diagram p232**

The crags can be seen directly above Torridon village shop at the top of an open gully filled with boulders. This is the approach (the boulders are generally solid and better than the heather/bracken), 30mins. There are two long crags; the lower is very steep; the crag directly above gives easier climbs. Like all the sandstone crags, many lines seep and take at least a couple of days to dry after heavy rain (but Warmer Cleaner Drier is quicker).

LOWER CRAG

The crag is divided into two sectors by a big right-slanting break.

Left Sector

Descent: Scramble down the big right-slanting break.

1 Global Warming 25m Severe * (1994)
There is an arete at the left end. Start left of it, step right and climb it.

2 Blind as a Frog 25m E1 5b * (1994)
The slanting corner-crack just right of Global Warming.

3 Squeezin' yer Heid 30m E4 6a * (1994)
Climbs the wall just right of Blind as a Frog. A boulder problem start gains a flake on a ledge. Climb the middle of the wall (gear), trend rightwards to stand on a pinnacle (small flexible friends). Move up and left and continue to the top. It is possible to traverse in to the top of the pinnacle but this would avoid some good climbing.

4 The Vanishing Frog 30m E5 6b ** (1996)
Climbs the streaked rounded nose in the centre of the wall right of Squeezin' yer Heid. Bold and unobvious. Start up the second groove right of a wide flake-crack to gain a break. Climb the shattered wall to the next break and using hidden holds above, make a hard move rightwards round the nose. Climb the right-hand side of the nose until a move left at the top gains a ledge.

5 Kermit's Crack 30m E3 6a * (1999)
Climbs a thin crack between Vanishing Frog and the big right-slanting break (descent). Bridge up the descent chimney to a ledge, then pull left on to the wall. Climb to a break, then pull through a steepening above. Go up the wall, then trend right and go up to finish on a heather ledge.

Right Sector

Descent: Either scramble down a chimney at the right end of the crag, or walk right for another 50m past all the rock.

6 Torridown Man 25m E2 5c *** (1994)
An excellent route, well protected. In the centre of the wall right of the slanting break is a steep crack. Climb the crack to a ledge (strenuous), step left and climb another crack (technical), move left and climb a third crack.

The next three routes are near the right end of the wall where there is a jagged crack (Warmer Cleaner Drier).

7 The White Streak 20m E1 5b (1994)
A good route but still a bit mucky. Halfway up the wall about 10m left of the jagged crack is a white streak; the route climbs the crack left of it. Move left and right to gain the crack. Either finish through a heather cornice or by a tree over to the left.

8 Cross Dressing 20m E3 5c ** (1996)
Climbs the bold wall left of Warmer, Cleaner, Drier. Five metres from the top, traverse right and finish up Warmer, Cleaner, Drier.

CREAG NAN LEUMNACH

1. Global Warming — Severe *
2. Blind as a Frog — E1 5b *
3. Squeezin' yer Heid — E4 6a *
4. The Vanishing Frog — E5 6b *
5. Kermit's Crack — E3 6a *
6. Torridown Man — E2 5c ***
7. The White Streak — E1 5b
8. Cross Dressing — E3 5c **
9. Warmer Cleaner Drier — E2 5b **
10. Block and Beak — HVS 5b **
11. Completely out to Lunge — E5 6b *
12. The Great Brush Robbery — E4 6a **
13. A Million Years B.C. — E1 5b *
14. Don't Just Sit There — VS 4b
15. Big Tree — Severe
16. Sky a Jy — VS 4c

Andy Nisbet

9 **Warmer Cleaner Drier   20m   E2 5b** ✶✶ (1994)
A fine line, quick drying. Climb the steep jagged crack at the right end of the wall, trending right then back left.

UPPER CRAG

Access from the lower tier is up the most convenient "descent" route. Descent is by walking past the crags at the east end (left looking down). The left half of the crag features a prominent leaning block on the terrace below. The right half of the crag is split by a terrace. At the right end of the terrace is a structure, possibly a burial cairn.

10 **Block and Beak   25m   HVS 5b** ✶✶ (1994)
A fine upper section, well protected; the beak is a small feature on the skyline. The cliff above the block starts with a small overhang. Start left of the overhang, move right above it (direct is harder than it looks) and follow the groove and crack-line above to finish at the beak.

11 **Completely out to Lunge   25m   E5 6b** ✶ (1999)
A bold route with a bouldery crux, which climbs the shallow scoop right of Block and Beak. Start up Block and Beak to a ledge, then go right and pull on to a small ramp. Climb the wall above until a long lunge gains a projecting hold. Just above is a good break for large Friends. Finish more easily.

12 **The Great Brush Robbery   25m   E4 6a** ✶✶ (1994)
High in the grade. Right of Block and Beak is a huge block against the cliff. Climb the chimney formed by its left side. From the top of the block, place runners on the right. Move left to flat holds and climb straight up to a ledge. Finish up the cracked wall (crucial rock 3 placement halfway up the left-hand crack).

13 **A Million Years B.C.   30m   E1 5b** ✶ (1994)
Climb the chimney as for the previous route to the top of the block; move right and climb the obvious crack in a left-facing corner, passing a wedged block which is best not touched (not a problem). Move left to finish.

14 **Don't Just Sit There   25m   VS 4b** (1994)
This route climbs the clean buttress above a terrace which divides the right end of the cliff. Climb a right-slanting crack below the buttress. Move left, then step right on to the buttress and follow the line of weakness up right.

15 **Big Tree   25m   Severe** (1994)
Start below the biggest tree on the terrace; climb a right-slanting crack to the terrace. Climb the right-slanting crack up the ramp just right of the tree.

16 **Sky a Jy   25m   VS 4c** (1994)
Start just right of the previous route. Move up to gain a flake, step right and climb cracks to the terrace. Follow the edge to the top.

CREAG NAN UAIMH

(NG 894 570)   Alt 220m   South-South-West facing   Map p273

This crag is on the hill 100m past the last house in Torridon village going west. It consists of several short ridges. The rock is slightly worrying. 25mins steep approach.

Reach the Road   15m   HVS 5a ✶ (1994)
Climbs the right-hand edge of the left-hand buttress. Climb a corner-crack, move up right on a large flake (left of the chimney with the holly trees) and finish up the wall.

234 | HAIRPIN CRAG

Caterpillar Ridge   20m   E1 5b (1994)
Further right is a prominent arete. Climb up just right of it, traverse left with the hands in the higher of two breaks, pull on to the arete and climb it.

En Route   20m   Severe (1994)
Climb the wide crack left of Holly Tree Rib and the continuation corner to the ledge; climb the ridge on the left.

Holly Tree Rib   20m   Difficult (1994)
Climb the ridge, easy despite the initial holly. At the top, either move right and descend a gully or go up leftwards on vegetation.

Kanko the Bone   20m   E2 5b * (1994)
Climbs the clean east facing wall. Start past the tree to gain and hand traverse a break left. Move up to flakes and follow a flake-crack to a thin move at the top (ignore an escape left).

HAIRPIN CRAG

(NG 880 573)   Alt 150m   South-East facing   Maps p194, 273   Diagram p235

The sandstone cliff which overlooks the hairpin bends on the road to Diabaig, shortly after leaving Loch Torridon. An impressive but slightly primitive crag. The black routes can seep for weeks but some routes dry fairly quickly, although leave a couple of days after heavy rain.

Approach: The best parking spot is 100m west of a cattle grid which is in turn 200m west of the obvious place to leave the road. Make a gently rising traverse on to a terrace well below the crag, then approach direct. 15mins. Easier in the spring before bracken grows, when a higher traverse is quicker.

Descent: There is a steep sheep track at the west end or steep heather at the east end. Abseil is quickest but there is no convenient tree.

The most obvious feature from the terrace below the crag is a roofed cracked corner just right of a change in angle from south facing at the left end to south-east facing at the right. There is another roofed corner just to its right. Two separate prominent buttresses lie to the left of the main crag. The furthest left has a V-groove on the left and a clean east facing wall on the right and has the following routes.

1 A Range Apart   10m   VS 4c (2006)
The V-groove.

2 Bluebell Crack   15m   E1 5b (2006)
Climb the crack-line up the centre of the right wall to a vegetated ledge, then the groove to the left to the top.

30 metres right is a second prominent buttress which is 50m left of the big roofed corner on the main cliff and has the following two routes.

3 Man-Eating Troll   15m   HVS 5b (2005)
A bottomless narrow V-groove and crack above.

4 Speckled Frog   15m   VS 4c (2005)
A wider and more obvious groove to its right.

5 Becalmed   30m   E2 5c * (1993)
On the main cliff and left of the roofed corner is a tree filled V-chimney. Start here. Climb the steep crack on the left to a ledge on an arete. Climb the arete to a horizontal break, move up left to a crack, then step back right and continue to the top.

HAIRPIN CRAG

3. Man-Eating Troll	HVS 5b	8. Bundle of Apathy	E4 6a **
4. Speckled Frog	VS 4c	9. Grey Matter	E2 5b
5. Becalmed	E2 5c *	10. Black and Blue	E1 5b *
6. Walsh's Groove	VS 4c *	11. Indian Winter	E3 5c *
7. The Text Book	E1 5a *	12. The Black Struggle	HVS 5a
		13. Wind Break	E3 5c *
		14. Nut the Rock	HVS 5b **
		14a. Direct Finish	E2 5c

HAIRPIN CRAG

6 Walsh's Groove   30m   VS 4c * *(1990)*
The large roofed corner formed in the top half of the cliff, particularly obvious from a distance. An exciting route with initial jungle but a fine finish. Start below a tree. Go slightly left and back right to pull into the base of the corner using the tree. Move up the corner, then step left to climb the crack on its left wall to a ledge. Finish up two short walls.

7 The Text Book   30m   E1 5a * *(1993)*
A big but less obvious right-hand corner gives a fine varied climb although the start is sometimes wet. Climb steeply up blocks to the corner, followed to its top. Traverse right to the arete (bold) and climb a jam crack directly above (strenuous).

8 Bundle of Apathy   30m   E4 6a ** *(1993)*
Right of The Text Book is an overhanging east face with a prominent crack. Climb the crack to the first of several overhangs high up, move right and climb a finger crack.

9 Grey Matter   30m   E2 5b *(1992)*
To the right and 5m up is a ledge with deciduous trees and one big pine. Gain the pine ledge. Climb the crack left of the pine until it finishes, step right and go up a short corner, then step left and finish up the wall.

10 Black and Blue   30m   E1 5b * *(1993)*
Gain the pine ledge. Go up a crack right of the pine and finish up a wide corner-crack in the black streak.

11 Indian Winter   30m   E3 5c * *(1993)*
Gain the pine ledge. Step off a block and climb the wall just right of a holly bush to reach the left end of a slight ramp. The ramp leads right to an overhang. Move left under it and climb the wall.
Variation: **Windy Wall   30m   E3 6a** *(1997)*
An alternative start. Start beneath the right side of the wall right of the holly. Move up left to a flake just right of a small oak. Go up this for 3m, then traverse left to a good flat hold. Move directly up to reach a small ledge on the normal route.

12 The Black Struggle   30m   HVS 5a *(1992)*
At the left side of the pillar is a corner-crack in a black streak. Follow it, then move right and go past a holly to finish past a large corner.

13 Wind Break   30m   E3 5c * *(1993)*
A bold route. Start at the middle of the pillar and move up left to a short corner on the arete. Climb the corner and a couple of moves up the arete (the unprotected section). Continue up the arete to finish up a crack in the upper wall.

14 Nut the Rock   30m   HVS 5b ** *(1992)*
Climb the wide crack on the right side of the pillar and step left. Climb the right arete of the pillar to finish up a crack containing a small rowan.
Variation: **Direct Finish   E2 5c** *(1997)*
Instead of stepping left, continue up the crack.

Inveralligin to Diabaig

Various crags lie near the coastal path between Inveralligin and Diabaig. The Inveralligin Sea-Cliffs, Creag Alligin, Discovery Rock and Big Bill's Crag are nearer Inveralligin and described from there while White House Crag is about halfway but described from Diabaig. Near the road end at Diabaig is the excellent Diabaig itself. Crags on the Rubha na h-Airde peninsula are described next, then heading away from Diabaig to end with White House Crag.

INVERALLIGIN to DIABAIG

1. Inveralligin Sea-Cliffs........p237
2. Creag Alligin p240
3. Discovery Rock................p241
4. Big Bill's Crag...................p242
5. Beginner's Slabs..............p242
6. Fish Farm Crags...............p243
7. Diabaig Pillar.....................p245
8. Diabaig Main Cliff...............p250
9. Twin Walls.........................p259
10. Crofter's Crag....................p259
11. Rolling Wall p261
12. Rubha na h-Airde p263
13. Loch a' Bhealaich Crag........p265
14. White House Crag...............p265

INVERALLIGIN SEA-CLIFFS

(NG 841 572) Mostly Non-tidal South-East to South facing Maps p194, 237

These small sunny crags of mostly good sandstone are of borderline size between bouldering and roped climbing. There are eight buttresses in a 200m stretch of crag.

Approach: In Inveralligin, turn right at a public phone box and park before a bridge at the end of the public road. Walk to the end of the road, follow the Wester Alligin footpath, then along the shore to the last building, a boathouse, 5mins.

The buttresses and routes are described in the order of approach, right to left.

BOATHOUSE CRAG

The biggest crag, 15 to 20m high, situated behind and beyond the boathouse.

Back Close (VS 4b). Start at the back right corner of the boathouse. Climb steeply leftwards to the right end of a big heather patch, then rightwards up slabs to finish right of a jutting block.
The Evil One (Difficult). The obvious heather filled crack behind the boathouse.
Born Again (Hard Severe). Start 2m right of a boulder which is 10m from the left end of the crag. Climb up, then slightly right to the right end of a long ledge. Climb a crack and trend right up slabs.

INVERALLIGIN SEA-CLIFFS

Wobbly (Very Difficult). Start behind the boulder. Trend right, then back left to the long ledge. Climb a left-slanting crack and easier slabs to finish over a jutting block.
Left Edge (Severe). The left arete to heather. Traverse 5m right to finish at a small jutting block (more direct is harder).

CATHKIN BUTTRESS

This is 20m to the left. Routes are 6 to 10m long.

Cathkin Capers (Difficult). The wall at the right end of the buttress.
The Joshua Tree (Moderate). A left-slanting fault-line.
Oops! I did it Again (Severe). Right of an arete above boulders is a concave section of wall. This is a fault-line on the right side of the concave section.
Analwaterjet (Difficult). Climb left out of the concave section to the top of the arete.
Justice of the Peace (Difficult). The arete and wall above.
Eejit (Difficult). A south-west facing wall left of the arete.
Gentlemen Prefer Blondes (Very Difficult). A south-east facing wall immediately to the left.
Little Mermaid (Difficult). The left arete of the front face.
Stinky Cheeky (Moderate). A crack on the right wall of the bounding gully, The Lum.
Up the Lum (Very Difficult). The deep gully forming the left side of the buttress.

ROOF BUTTRESS

The buttress left of The Lum is 15m high.

Cranium (VS 4c). Climb a lower wall until a vertical crack is reached. Traverse out right, on the overhang and finish up the convex face.

THE SKULL

The buttress close on the left is 10m high and a suitable shape.

Babes Bombshell (Very Difficult). The chimney between this and Roof Buttress. Finish up a groove on the right.
Shakey Spider (Severe). Climb the right face of the skull, up a groove to the bulge which is passed right and back left.
Post-Op (Severe). Start in the big cave below the skull. Climb a right-slanting ramp to the middle overhang. Traverse left under the overhang. Pull awkwardly to gain a crack. Climb straight up.
Becker's Bounce (Hard Severe 4b). Start as for Post-Op but continue to traverse right to join Shakey Spider.

DAYTIME BUTTRESS

A small smooth triangular buttress some 8m left.

The End of the Day (Moderate). A wall forming the left wall of the cave of The Skull.
Perfect Day (Moderate). A deep groove 3m from the right side of the buttress.
Sandpaper (Very Difficult). The triangular face.
Dinny Faw (Very Difficult). A rib at the left end of the triangular face.

SAMMY'S BUTTRESS

The next buttress close on the left is 6 to 10m high.

DEALAIN CRAG

Jose Nose (Very Difficult). Climb up a nose at the extreme right side of the buttress.
Sammy's Belt (Difficult). Start at the same point and climb up to gain a horizontal crack. Traverse left across the south face of the buttress to reach Six of the Best.
Pre-Op (Very Difficult). This full height vertical crack is on a south facing wall.
Number 7 (Hard Severe). Climb Pre-Op till about 2m from the top. Hand traverse leftwards for about 5m and finish up on to a big shelf.
Six of the Best (Moderate). Halfway along the buttress is this easy groove.
Scary Monsters (Difficult). Start from the top of a flat topped boulder. Traverse left and up to a wee knob. Traverse up and left for 3m, then straight up. Watch out for the monsters!
The Love of My Life (Severe). A shallow corner leading into a crack.
Kyle's Konundrum (Severe). At the left end of the front face of the buttress is an arete. Just right of the arete is this cracked groove.
20th Century Boy (Severe). Start just left of the arete on a north facing wall. Climb a groove, then move right on to a large shelf. Finish straight up.
Suzie's Heaven (VS 4c). Climb the groove of 20th Century Boy, then traverse left to reach a wide overhanging crack. Using an anvil stone, climb the crack. A direct start is 4c.

BOULDERS AREA

The north face of Sammy's Buttress is separated by a gully from a small amphitheatre with two parallel grooves.

Wee Gully (Difficult). The right groove.
Shuffle and Pinch (Severe). The left groove.
Left of here are two boulders and a fallen pillar. These are Severe either on the front or on the right side.

DEALAIN CRAG

About 50m left of the distinctive boulders is the start of this crag, 6 to 10m high. The crag consists of four south facing front walls, each stepped out from the one on the right by a short east facing sidewall. The last front wall is tidal. There are two routes on the sidewall right of the first front wall, both Severe but loose.

A Corner (Hard Severe). A right-facing corner on the first front wall.
The Boak (Hard Severe). A clean prominent section of wall.
Spud's Slab (Severe). A narrower pillar climbed to an overhang passed on the left or climbed direct.
Sabre Squadron (4c). Left of the narrower pillar and behind the next wall is an enclosed smooth wall with horizontal cracks. Climb its centre, hardest at the start. The right edge of the wall is **PFs Lay** (Difficult).
Jugs (Very Difficult). Within the hidden recess on the opposite wall to Sabre Squadron is an overhanging wall. Climb the obvious line on big jugs.
Slippy's Cherry (Very Difficult). A flake-corner on the right side of the second front wall.
Ken (Very Difficult). A right-rising shallow corner-crack in the centre of the second wall.
Descent Chimney (Moderate). A corner chimney which is the back corner of the third step.
Pink Panther (Hard Severe). Climbs the left side of a prominent jutting flake on the sidewall.
Jimpy (VS 4c). On the third front wall, starting 2m from its left end. Steep slab climbing on good friction holds leads to an overhang. Traverse up and right to a ledge. Follow a horizontal crack system rightwards and finish up Pink Panther.
Breezy (VS 4c). As for Jimpy but climb the overhang and continue up a steep wall.
Fruit Route (Severe). Left of the third wall is a corner with a huge jammed block.

240 CREAG ALLIGIN

Climb the right side of the block.
Isa Tamson's Bairn (Severe). Climb the left side of the block.
Blistering Barnacles (4c). The most westerly slab. Climb the obvious overhang and continue up on to a slab shelf.

CREAG ALLIGIN

(NG 805 577)   Alt 120m   West facing   Map p237

This is a 15m high 70 degree slab of gneiss with many crack-lines offering generally lower grades.

Approach: Go to the west end of the road end at Wester Alligin – Alligin Shuas (NG 825 576). About 30m beyond the tarmac is one of the starts of the path to Diabaig (probably signposted). Follow the path out of the forest to a gate. Soon after, the path deviates from its route on the map and takes a slight loop round the first peninsula. Either follow it (5mins longer) or take the marked line with only the odd cairn to guide you, and join the upper path. Follow the path until it crosses a stream at NG 806 575, then make an ascending traverse right to the crag. The crag is 100m below the obvious wall seen in apparently the right direction but the correct one is to the left, on the far side of a knoll and faces away, 1hr. A high route on the return, passing close to Loch a' Choin Duibh, makes a pleasant change (same distance). A 15m rope attached to a hidden thread behind a boulder provides a quick belay for all the routes. Combined with an easy descent to the south, all the routes can be climbed quickly.

Route 1 (Very Difficult). The left arete, gained by a left-slanting crack. Poorly protected.
Route 2 (Difficult). Slant up left on pockets, then climb a thin crack just right of the arete.
Route 3 (E1 5a). The left section has the only uncracked area of slab. Climb the 'blank' slab direct, passing grey rock at 5m and a big pocket at 10m, finishing by a thin crack.
Route 4 (Difficult). A prominent right-slanting crack come tiny ramp. A thin start, then easier.
Route 5 (Severe 4a). A straight up crack forming an X with Route 4, but with a small left deviation after their crossing point.
Route 6 (VS 5a). Very thin cracks between the more obvious Routes 5 and 7. Move left into pockets at 6m and avoid being tempted right on to the easier Route 7.
Route 7 (Severe). Twin cracks at the base, then a thin crack, finish by either of two cracks curving up to reach the cliff top at the top of Route 4.
Route 8 (Very Difficult). A deep crack 2m right of Route 7 and converging with it towards the top.
Route 9 (VS 4c). A thinner crack 1m right.
Route 10 (Difficult). A deep crack 3m right.
Route 11 (Difficult). A left diagonal crack near the right edge, joining Route 10 near the top. Two possible starts, the direct one being better.

LOWER SLABS

(NG 805 576)   Alt 90m   West facing

Best reached by descending a grassy gully from just south of the south end of the upper slabs.

Gin Crack   35m   VS 4c   *(1993)*
Start at the lowest point and climb the slab to reach a crack in the headwall which runs parallel to the right arete. Quite sustained and protection spaced for moves left and back right to gain the deeper part of the crack.

DISCOVERY ROCK | 241

Teacher's Pet, VS 4c, Discovery Rock. Climber Jonathan Preston

DISCOVERY ROCK

(NG 810 570)   Alt 90m   South facing   Map p237

A clean outcrop sited on the Rubha na h-Airde Glaise peninsula above the narrows of Loch Torridon with an interesting variety of routes, ideal for novices. The routes were climbed in 2003 or 2004. Approach by the coast path from Wester Alligin in 40mins, turning off right when the crag appears on the skyline, 500m before the tip of the peninsula. The arete in the centre of the crag is the obvious identifying feature from which routes are described.

Teacher's Pet   18m   VS 4c **
The arete gives a pleasing route.
Variation: **Teacher's Finish   6m   HVS 5b** *
Move right after the arete and climb cracks on the left edge of the headwall.

242　DISCOVERY ROCK

Susie's First   20m   Very Difficult
A direct line 5m left of the arete, starting up to a block then taking a brown wall to gain finishing slabs.

Neville's Post   18m   Severe *
Start 5m left of the arete; climb up left to a big block in a corner, then take a thin curving crack up the slab above.

Captain Haddock   15m   Hard Severe 4b *
From a recess in boulders on the left side of the crag, move out right along an undercut ramp and pull over a roof into a finishing groove.

Rack Rental   13m   E1 5c *
A short powerful climb up an overhanging crack in the prow 2m left of Captain Haddock.

The next routes start right of the arete in the centre of the crag.

After the Horse has Bolted   20m   Severe *
A crack-line in the right wall of the Teacher's Pet arete, finishing direct up the cracked wall above.

The Wanderer   20m   Difficult *
Zigzag right then left up ramps right of the arete, then step out right at the cracked wall at the top.

The Moore's Last Sigh   18m   Severe *
Climb flake-cracks in the wall just right of The Wanderer, then go up the wide chimney-crack in the headwall of the crag.

Dundee Cake   18m   HVS 5a *
Climb the lower wall 2m right of Moore's, then take a right-facing corner in the headwall.

Othello   16m   HVS 5b **
Climb the lower wall 2m right of Moore's, then a thin crack-line in the headwall 3m right of the chimney; well protected.

Long Tall Jonny   14m   VS 4c
A finger-crack in the headwall 3m right of Othello.

BIG BILL'S CRAG

(NG 811 568)   Partially Tidal   South-South-East facing   Map p237

A fierce crag, viciously undercut and dipping into the sea, well seen from A896 on the south side of the loch, which is reached by turning left from the Rubha na h-Airde Glaise path at a ruined cottage 500m before the tip of the peninsula. A ramp drops to the sea under a large black roof. A great crag for thugs with 'pump-fests' guaranteed

Who Needs Kalymnos?   16m   E4 6a **   (2004)
Start at a block on the ramp 6m down from the left end of the crag. Use knee bars and heel hooks to climb through the obvious roof crack and gain a finishing groove; well protected.

BEGINNER'S SLABS

(NG 825 586)   Alt 200m   South-East facing   Map p237

An area of clean sandstone slabs on rough rock just a short distance west of the first hairpin above Alligin Shuas. There are four slabs between 15 and 30m high; each can be climbed between Moderate and Difficult choosing a line with all the holds and Severe for padding (ie not using the holds). The routes are fun if somewhat trivial, the 90 second approach being a justification. There are few runners. On the left is **Pink Slab** (Difficult), the largest. Moving right are **Right Slab**, **Long Thin Slab** and **Short Slab**.

DIABAIG

(NG 801 596)   Maps p194, 237   Diagram p244

Diabaig is one of the finest outcrops in Scotland. The setting is exquisite, above a picturesque inlet and village at the end of the road north of Loch Torridon (through Torridon village and passing Beinn Alligin). The rock is excellent gneiss, usually rough, clean and slabby but occasionally overhanging and juggy. Protection is often excellent. The only disadvantages are the long approach drive and bad midges in the summer. The rock is quick to dry after showers but there is drainage and many routes seep for a day after heavy rain. The main cliffs are situated around the knoll called Meall Ceann na Creige.

Approach: Park just before the pier at Lower Diabaig. From here the craggy hillside is obvious, but the Main Cliff and the Domes face away from the village. Walk to the end of the road and follow the right of way path towards Inveralligin (signposted through a garden). Walk up the wooded hillside and follow the path through a gate – access to Diabaig Pillar is by descent to the right. Further up, the path reaches an open gully, at the top of which is The Red Wall. The path crosses the gully and turns south, gradually descending until the steep slabs of the Main Cliff are visible up on the left. To reach the parallel cliffs of the Condome and Charlie's Tower, continue a little further along the path and cut up left.

FISH FARM CRAGS

(NG 800 602)   Alt 100 to 140m   South to South-East facing   Map p237

A line of crag starting in the birch wood above the Marine Harvest warehouse and continuing uphill and overlooking a stream which flows down to the road end. There are other possible lines but the rock is scrappy.

Approach: Find a way into the wood behind the fish farm and go up to the crag. Approaching via the path to the main cliffs is less suitable because the stream is difficult to cross.

Grandad's Wall   18m   VS 5a   (1994)
On a black compact section of crag in the birch wood above and left of the Marine Harvest warehouse. This is below the end of the main line of crag and its top is visible from the car park. Take a start just left of centre, up left past a black streak, then step right on to a cleaner shield of steeper rock, and go direct to the top.

Copping's Crack   28m   Very Difficult   (1994)
The first clean slabby crag above the highest and rightmost trees overlooks the stream gorge and has a vague nose. The route climbs a crack just right of the nose, with a steep start on its right.

APPROACH WALLS

Diagram p244

The next routes are left of or above the path to the main cliffs and are therefore seen from the parking place.

The Mynch   30m   HVS 5b   (1990)
The obvious overhung cleft on a low crag directly overlooking the village and car

RED WALL

park and below The Red Wall. Reach the start by following the fence up left from the gate on the approach path. It ends at the cliff base about 20m from the start of the route.

Red Wall

Diagram p244

The Red Wall lies higher up the gully where the path turns south and flattens out. It is directly above the gate on the path. A fine wall with sustained bold routes but the rock is slightly worrying. Apart from the first route, protection is just adequate with small cams, Rocks and RPs. Descent is easiest on the left (other side from the gully).

An Offensive Man   20m   E1 5a (1990)
The left blunt arete starting just on its left and staying on the right side thereafter. Very poorly protected.

Animal Magic   20m   E2 5b ** (1990)
The thin crack-line just right of An Offensive Man.

Porpoise Pun   20m   E3 5c ** (1990)
The best route on this wall. Sustained. Climb the centre of the wall via a series of obvious pockets.

Batwing   20m   E3 5c (1990)
Climb the right arete of the wall with difficult initial moves up the wall then moving on to the arete.

Dental Trauma   30m   HVS 5a (1994)
A route on the crag which is about 50m left of and very slightly below The Red Wall. Approach from the base of The Red Wall or by climbing The Mynch. Takes the main central break in the crag. Climb steeply through a bulge (crux) to the base of a heather filled groove, then break out right and climb a clean slabby wall to the top (initially bold).

Continuation Route   55m   VS (1995)
A route on the upper crag which is above and left of Red Wall. The route involves some rock, some scrambling and some walking. The original line is hard to find (says A.Nisbet, but he has climbed a similar start at the same grade). 'Start to the left of Red Wall, at the foot of a large angled block below a rowan sapling. Climb past an overlap to the rowan (20m). A heather terrace leads to an obvious slab trending rightwards to a grass ledge (10m, 4b). Walk up grassy slopes to the next buttress: an obvious corner and slabby face to the right of an overhang (15m). The obvious corner on big jugs (10m). Scramble to the summit.'

DIABAIG PILLAR

(NG 799 596)   Alt 30m   West facing   Map p237   Diagrams p244, 248

Diabaig Pillar, the most prominent section of cliff visible from the village, is an impressive steep wall fairly low on the hillside which faces out to sea. The approach path to the Main Cliff initially runs up near its left side. Access to its base is by scrambling down and right through bracken. From below, a large inset slab is obvious at its top left. Between this and the pillar is a sharp arete, the line of Dire Wall.

1 Diabaig Corner   20m   E1 5b * (1991)
The corner left of The Pillar, which overlooks the village. An easy shelf leads right into the corner from just above the fence.

The Pillar, E2 5b, Diabaig Pillar. Climber Kevin Kelly

2 Diabaig, the Hard Way 35m E5 6b ** *(1993)*
A very powerful problem through the obvious roof left of The Pillar (close to 6c). Start left of Dire Wall beneath a flat topped pinnacle. Gain the top of the pinnacle via the brambly crack (or from the left). Step right and follow the open scoop to the roof. Tackle this using the obvious undercut flake and continue up a crack just right of the arete. Where the angle changes, move right to the centre of the fine slab and wander pleasantly up this. The short headwall has an obvious hanging V-notch – 'the Tail'. Arrange protection in a crack in the slab to the left and boulder up into the notch 'the Sting'.

DIABAIG PILLAR

3 Dire Wall 35m E2 *** (1984)
A fine route, but not as pure a line nor as well protected as The Pillar. Start about 3m left of The Pillar on clean rock, at a small step in the cliff base.
1. 20m 5a Go up and left to the edge of a groove which comes up from ground level (or climb the groove). Continue up to join The Pillar but soon move left to the base of the arete.
2. 15m 5b Climb the arete.
Variation: **Slab Finish**
After pitch one, continue out left across the slab. This is easier but a bit of a cop-out.

4 The Pillar 35m E2 5b **** (1983)
A superb quick drying route up the continuous wall of the pillar. Despite its intimidating smooth appearance, there are good holds and runners, and it provides a good sustained pitch at the lowest limit of its grade. Start from a bay below the wall. Climb to and up a crack in the centre of the wall (same as Dire Straights) until it is possible to make a short traverse left towards the top of a groove which comes up from ground level (or start as for Dire Wall). Gain an intermittent crack-line which trends right into the centre of the wall and climb straight up.

5 Dire Straights 35m E2 5b *** (1991)
A parallel line up the wall about 5m right of the Pillar. Not as sustained as The Pillar, but with a poorly protected section. Start as for The Pillar, but instead of moving left continue up a bulging crack, then an easy ramp, and then thin cracks in the upper wall to finish at an obvious V-notch.

The following two routes start from a ledge above and right of the start of The Pillar, reached by awkward scrambling or abseil.

6 Upper Corner 25m HVS 5a * (1975)
Climbs the corner which bounds the upper right side of The Pillar and curves over leftwards into a roof. Climb the wall below the roof, place runners in the roof, then step down and traverse left until a finish is made past the left end of the roof.

7 The Frieze 25m HVS 5b * (1993)
A ramp breaks right out of Upper Corner into very impressive but surprisingly helpful ground.

LITTLE BIG WALL

(NG 799 595) Alt 20m West facing Diagrams p244, 248

Immediately down and right from Diabaig Pillar is a shorter overhanging wall, Little Big Wall, which looks insignificant from the village because its lower half is hidden. Access is by descending right from the base of Diabaig Pillar. The best descent is by abseil.

8 An Eyeful 10m E3 5c (1987)
The left end of the Wall is a short steep wall with a vertical crack in its centre. Start 2m left of the crack. Strenuous and serious. Climb the wall to half-height passing a small spike. Traverse to the crack and climb it. Finish on the left.
Variation: **The Gritty Finish E4 6a**
Continue slightly leftwards where the normal route moves right into the crack.

9 (Once upon a Time in) The Wild West 25m E5 6a * (1994)
The highest section of cliff is bounded on the left by an obvious right-slanting corner-line. This takes the left arete of the corner. Two Friend 2s are useful. Start in the recess. A couple of layback moves lead to a comfortable ledge on the left. Move up rightwards to gain a bulge in the arete proper. From an undercut gain

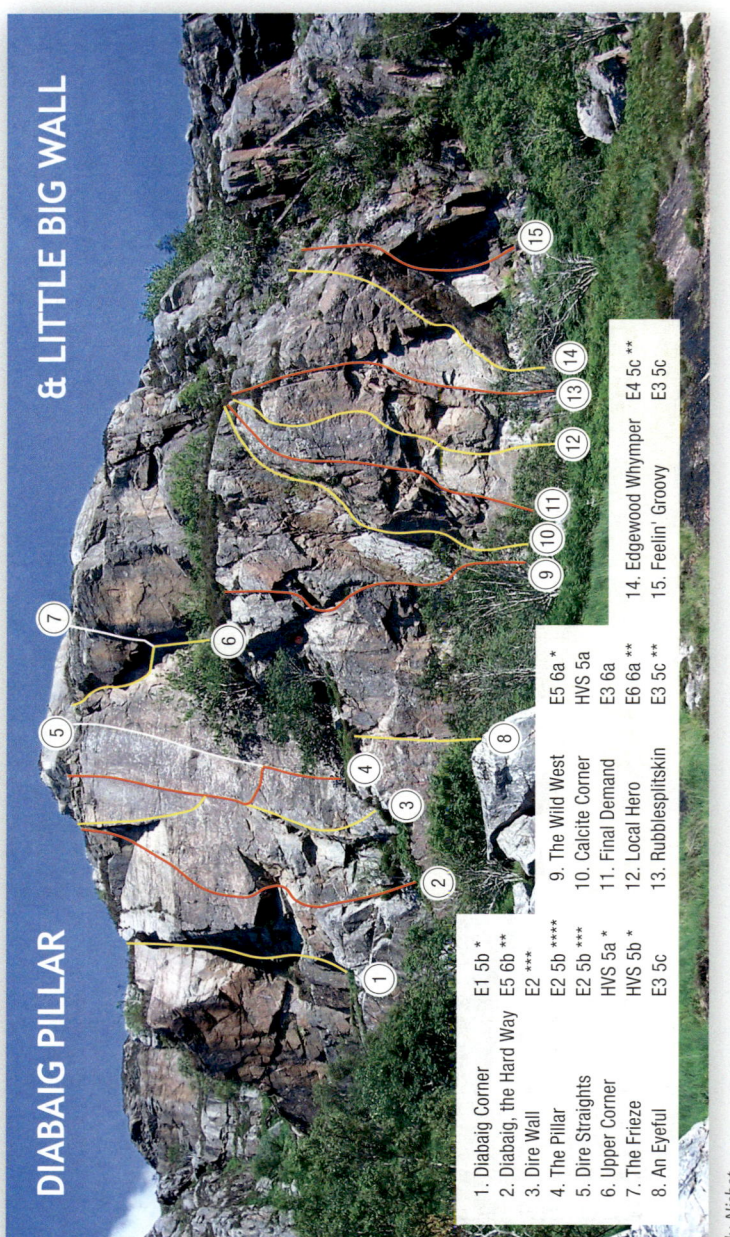

Rubblesplitskin, E3 5c, Little Big Wall, Diabaig. Climber Ian Taylor

layaways over the bulge. Continue with decreasing difficulty up the groove in the arete to a comfortable position. It is possible to escape up left to the ledge from which starts The Pillar etc. Move up slightly left, however, then step rightwards to gain the continuation groove. Go up this to the top.

10 Calcite Corner   30m   HVS 5a *(1998)*
Steep well protected climbing, taking the prominent right-trending corner at the left end of the highest section of wall. Follow the corner passing an ancient peg and stepping out right near the top to finish on the heather and tree covered terrace. The fine Upper Corner up on the left provides a worthwhile continuation.

11 Final Demand   25m   E3 6a *(1988)*
Climb the crack in the left side of the steep wall, gained direct round bulges. The crux is at the top before an easier finish near Calcite Corner.

250 DIABAIG

12 Local Hero 30m E6 6a ★★ *(1987)*
Superb, bold climbing up the highest section of the crag, to the left of a system of cracks and grooves (Rubblesplitskin). Start just to the left of the crack. Climb up to the 'block' in the centre of the wall. Turn it on the left, then go up and right to a good resting place. Using two pockets move up to the bulge with a hard move. Reach left over the lip to good holds and a runner placement. Pull over the bulge rightwards gaining a good semi-rest below the obvious red streak in the headwall. Climb up the wall trending left to pull over on to a slab. Finish up and right around a rib to a tree belay. Several RP1s are required.

13 Rubblesplitskin 25m E3 5c ★★ *(1987)*
Just left of the undercut right arete is a twin crack-line. Climb the right-hand crack (sustained and steep) to an awkward exit into an open niche. Move up to a good rest, then pull over the roof to easier ground.

14 Edgewood Whymper 25m E4 5c ★★ *(1987)*
Fingery to start, strenuous in the middle and bold and exciting at the top. Start just right of Rubblesplitskin at the undercut right arete. Pull onto the wall, then follow the edge rightwards to a groove. Go up this to pull out right onto a good ledge. Keep following the edge all the way.

15 Feelin' Groovy 25m E3 5c *(1998)*
Spectacular well protected climbing up the prominent right-slanting overhanging groove bounding the right side of the wall. Scramble up easy slabs to belay on a small ledge. Climb the groove, with hard moves to pull round onto the slab. Follow a left-trending line up the slab to a small rowan.

MAIN CLIFF

(NG 801 594) Alt 80m South facing Map p237 Diagrams p244, 251

The superb main cliff is a south-facing 70m wall of steep rough slab bounded on the right by a wet gully and split just below half-height by a less steep section with patches of vegetation. The routes generally have two pitches with belays at this halfway point. From left (downhill) to right (gully) are the following features on the lower cliff: broken blocky ground topped by a heathery ledge 20m up decreasing to 5m from the ground at its finish in the centre (Gamhnachain's Crack and Route Three cross it; Route Two touches its right end); a short left-facing corner (Northumberland Wall); a big right-facing corner which leads into a roof and sprouts a holly tree (Route One), with a thin crack 3m left of the corner (Black Streak). The upper wall has continuation crack-lines, the best defined being The Black Streak and Route Three. The routes are well protected and on near perfect rock, occasionally with a gritty surface which will disappear with popularity. Being less than vertical, good footwork is the key to success.

Descent: The best descent is to make two abseils down the line of The Black Streak (in situ threads). The alternative is intricate and often muddy scrambling. Traverse right from the cliff top and cross the gully to gain a vague ridge. Descend a shallow gully just beyond the ridge (the upper section of the gully right of Condome) until the ridge can be crossed rightwards and finished steeply next to the start of Evasion. The easiest but longest option is to walk over the top and down past Charlie's Tower.

1 Pointless Eliminates 20m E2 5c *(1999)*
Above the path on the approach to the Main Cliff (approximately 100m left of Dead Mouse Crack) is a prominent gully with a large holly immediately above the initial barring chockstone. This route climbs the centre of the slab forming the left side of the gully and is well named, with the crest immediately to the left having been climbed at Very Difficult. Descend by traversing right (looking down) or by abseil.

Brimstone, E2, Main Cliff, Diabaig. Climbers Roger Everett and Dee Gaffney

2 Dead Mouse Crack   25m   VS 5a * *(1985)*
A pink wall lies just above the path where the Main Cliff turns to face the sea. Towards its right end is an obvious crack. Climb the crack with a strenuous start. Good climbing, but hard to avoid starting with wet feet. Abseil off. Alternatively, go diagonally right on rock and heather, including a short corner, to join and finish up the last pitch of The Grunter.

3 Emerald   30m   HVS 5a * *(2005)*
This route aims for the sharp arete leading to the left end of the large roof just right of Dead Mouse Crack. Start a few metres right of Dead Mouse and climb into a slabby recess via a short steep wall (directly or easier on the right). Continue up left to a corner, then pull left on to the arete. From the top of the arete make an awkward step on to a slab. Cross the slab on the left then move back right to the edge. Finish at the abseil point at the top of Dead Mouse Crack.

4 Apprentice Bhoys 20m Severe 4a * (2003)
A pleasant but short easier route. Close to the lowest point of the Main Cliff (to the left of The Grunter) lies a short slabby corner leading to the right end of a prominent roof. Climb the corner, then pull out right by a cracked block. Continue up a short corner, then move leftwards to the buttress edge. Finish up the edge to the abseil slings at the top of Dead Mouse Crack.

5 The Grunter 70m VS * (1991)
This is a logical combination of previously climbed pitches. Start at a flake right of a heather recess at the lower left end of the wall.
1. 20m 4c Step left, then work back right and climb a crack. Continue to a belay at a birch (down and left of the holly belay of Gamhnachain's Crack).
2. 20m 4c Climb the crack and slab above to a belay at a dead tree stump.
3. 30m 4c Step right on to slabs, then trend left up cracks before finishing straight up on easing slabs.

6 Gamhnachain's Crack 75m HVS (1976)
A vegetated start leads to better climbing. Start as for Route Three.
1. 20m 4c Step left on to a slab, climb it then traverse left into a crack which leads to the heathery ledge.
2. 20m 4c Climb to the holly tree. Traverse right and climb slabs just right of heather to belay at the top right corner of a big heather patch.
3. 35m 5b Go right to a crack which takes a dog-leg to the right and continues up as a wider crack.

7 Route Three 80m E1 *** (1975)
The route follows an obvious crack-line (more distinct than Route Two) which starts from a triangular roof near the right end of the low heathery ledge. Start 8m left of Route Two.
1. 15m 4b Climb a right-facing blocky corner to belay below a prominent holly.
2. 30m 5b Step right and climb up the wall for 3m until it is possible to traverse right into a scoop below a turfy ramp. Follow this rightwards to join the crack (taken throughout by the direct start). Climb the crack-line to belay below where it steepens.
3. 35m 5a Follow the crack to the top.

8 Brimstone 75m E2 *** (1991)
An enjoyable route, with good but fiddly protection on the first pitch. Start as for Route Two.
1. 35m 5c Gain the heathery ledge but move left to a triangular roof. From the apex of the roof, pull out left into the left of two thin cracks. Move up, then return to the right and follow it to a junction with the original route. Trend over right to the Route Two belay.
2. 40m 5c Follow Route Two until possible to go left under the overlap. Where it ends follow a thin crack to the top.

9 Route Two 75m HVS **** (1975)
Highly recommended and probably the best introduction to the wall. Start below the right end of the low heathery ledge 5m up.
1. 35m 5a Climb to the right end of the ledge, then pull awkwardly up right into the start of the crack. Follow it, then go slightly right to a large grass clump below a thin crack.
2. 40m 5a Climb the crack.

10 Northumberland Wall 70m E2 *** (1984)
This follows intermittent cracks between the more continuous cracks of The Black Streak and Route Two (nearer the latter). Fine technical climbing.
1. 30m 5c Start up a short, left-facing corner, step left over its capping roof and climb slightly leftwards up a shallow groove to a thin horizontal crack. Traverse

back right to follow the intermittent cracks to belay at the abseil point.
2. 40m 5c Go up The Black Streak to the first overlap and traverse left underneath it to its end. Climb a faint crack and subsequent cracks above.

11 Wall of Flame   70m   E4 *** (1987)
Climbs a rather blank and intimidating section of wall. Possibly E5 for the short, who will struggle to find a high runner for the crux. Start just right of the initial corner of Northumberland Wall.
1. 30m 6a Go up the wall just right of the arete to a faint diagonal line running right. Follow it to its end, then pull over a bulge and a small overlap, stepping right to reach a large flat hold (just left of the crux of The Black Streak). Go direct up a blank slab to an impasse below an isolated overlap. Go diagonally left (crux) to gain the base of a thin crack and up to belay at the abseil point.
2. 40m 6a Climb the slab left of The Black Streak to gain the left end of an overlap. Climb a faint crack and subsequent cracks above (as for Northumberland Wall).

12 Afterglow   80m   E4 * (1988)
A left-trending diagonal line taking in the best rock and as many independent features as possible.
1. 35m 6a Start up The Black Streak to a hollow block at 5m. Break out left and follow a diagonal line crossing Wall of Flame and going direct over a small overlap in the centre of the wall, before moving left into Northumberland Wall at its bulge. Take a horizontal crack out left and across a quartz blotch to join Route Two and belay at its grass clump.
2. 45m 6a Go left and up a slab to a jug below a blank looking runnel. Go up this until 2m below the overlap. Pull out left round a rib to a flake. Go up to the right end of the roof split by Route Three and follow a thin crack from here to its end. Make a hard move left round a slabby rib via a thin diagonal crease to gain an easy crack and the top. Instead of the hard move left, a step right and a finish up Brimstone makes the pitch 5c.

13 The Black Streak   65m   E1 *** (1976)
An excellent route following a thin crack-line just left of the big right-facing corner. Start just left of the big corner.
1. 25m 5c Go up to and follow the thin crack (crux, overhead protection) to belay at the abseil point.
2. 40m 5b Climb the faint crack just left of the tree. It leads directly into a prominent crack which forms the right boundary of a black streak.

14 Going Home   70m   E1 (1988)
Climbs through the roof right of the big corner. Start just right of the big corner.
1. 25m 5c Go up the slab, cross the left traverse of Route One and go up to the roof. Pull over above an obvious block and go up to the belay.
2. 45m 4c Climb a series of cracks right of Route One, probably the same as Foil pitch 2.

15 Route One   70m   HVS ** (1975)
Start 5m right of the big right-facing corner.
1. 30m 5a Climb the wall until it is possible to traverse left to the holly. Step left onto the face and climb it diagonally left, then a long step left to a fault leading to a grassy ledge and block belay beside a tree.
2. 40m 5a Climb the thin crack which starts just right of the tree. Step right and back left at a hard section after about 10m. Climbing the hard section direct is maybe 5c. An easier (4c) alternative start goes up a groove to the right.

16 Foil   70m   VS * (1982)
1. 25m 5a Climb the wall right of Route One to its capping roof. Go through the roof by a right-slanting crack to a ledge.
2. 45m 4b Go up a crack beside a black streak (the left-hand of three cracks in this

Route Two, HVS, Main Cliff, Diabaig. Climber Dave McGimpsey

section of wall) until 1m short of grass, then go diagonally left to the base of a steep crack. Climb this to a ledge, then easier slabs.

17 The Dominie   65m   E1 *   (1996/1997)
A line up the right edge of the wall. Start beneath a crack on the right side of the wall, just left of the gully.
1. 30m 5a Climb the crack and over the right side of a roof to belay up on the right, beneath an orange coloured wall with three vague discontinuous cracks.
2. 35m 5b Follow the central of the three cracks. Only the middle section presents any difficulty, with the lower section about Severe and the upper crack easing back to about Difficult.

18 Big Glossy Book Route   50m   Severe   (1994)
The gully right of the main section of wall. Walk to the back of the gully, back and foot up and out to the edge of the chimney, then traverse back in. Step off a large chockstone and climb the gully wall; traverse in again and follow the easy gully.

The following routes climb the wall right of the gully and left of the scrambling descent.

19 Bogie 40m E2 5b * (1990)
Start at the base of the gully. Pull over a rounded nose on the right, then pass left of a red roof and go up cracks parallel to the gully. Pull over a small roof to reach a tree on a big ledge (invisible from below). Abseil descent or traverse right to the descent path.

20 Evasion 55m VS ** (1990)
Start about 10m down and right from the gully at the lowest point of clean rock.
1. 45m 4c Make thin and poorly protected moves up left to gain and climb a series of shallow scoops trending slightly left. Pull out right at the apex of a small roof system (after 35m, about 10m right of a prominent dead tree which is next to the gully) to a small tree. Move left above the roof to reach a crack leading up and left to a larger tree (or go up a heathery groove above the small tree). Abseil descent, traverse right to the descent path, or climb the next pitch and scramble down right.
2. 10m 4c Climb the corner above the tree, pulling over a bulge and out right on jugs to finish easily up a rib.

THE DOMES

(NG 802 593) Alt 70m South facing
Continuing along the path beyond the Main Cliff, an apparent dome of smooth rock becomes visible beside the top right end of the slope under the Main Cliff. This is the Condome. To the right of this is a recess beyond which the cliff turns again to form a long face parallel to the Main Cliff but of less continuous rock. Charlie's Tower is the bottom nose of this long cliff.

Condome

Diagram p244

Condome 30m E4 6a ** (1987)
Climbs the discontinuous crack on the left of the dome. Start just left of a large boulder at the base of the cliff. Gain and climb the obvious hanging crack, move left to ledges on the edge, then return right to climb the upper crack. It is possible to climb direct to the ledges, missing out the hanging crack, at E3 5c.

The Con-Con 30m HVS 5b ** (1987)
Climb the crack right of Condome, soon becoming right-curving twin cracks, to a ledge. Move right into a left-facing flake-corner and follow it leftwards to the top, the technical crux being the thin crack at the top (avoidable on the right). Sustained, some say E1.
Direct variation: **E2 5c ** * (1988)
From the ledge, continue direct past small right-facing overlaps.

Shunned 30m HVS 5a (1993)
Right of The Con-Con there is an awkward step in the grassy gully. Start just below this and climb slightly leftwards into a crack. Climb this line until it becomes more broken, then follow the middle of three rising traverse lines right (initially a ramp) to climb to and finish by a short right-facing corner at the cliff top.

Charlie's Dome

Diagram p244

The quickest descent from this, the second dome, is to follow a ramp which overlooks Boab's Corner down to a terrace under Terrier Trauma and finish down the short gully between this face and the Condome.

CHARLIE'S DOME 257

Condome, E4 6a, The Domes, Diabaig

Terrier Trauma   22m   E3 6a (1993)
On the steep wall to the right of the Condome slab, facing west. Take the crack-line on the right side of the wall, starting at a recess. Climb on to a slab, arrange runners with care (the route might be E4), then climb the overhanging wall very strenuously to a ledge and finish more easily up the corner above.

Charlie's Tower   60m   Hard Severe 4b (1976)
The route follows the rounded buttress right of the Condome wall, the lowest point of the next wall. Start from the top right corner of the slope next to the Condome. Climb cracks on the left edge of a small dome. Near its top, go into the centre and on up the dome. Continue via a groove and easier slabs (variation possible). Rather scrappy but still pleasant.

Variation: **Original Start   5b**
Start at a short wall which forms the lower end of the next face to the right. On this wall is a short stepped corner with an oak tree. Start about 8m to its left. Climb the wall (crux), then a clean crack above. Traverse down left to join the easier route.

Apprentices Route   50m   Severe   *(1997)*
Also starts from the top right corner of the slope right of the Condome but traverses 50m rightwards, beyond Charlie's Tower and Boab's Corner. Climb a short steep wall for 3m. Go straight up the groove above and follow a crack to easier ground.

Boab's Corner   60m   VS   **   *(1982)*
The best of the easier climbs, taking the slabby wall right of Charlie's Tower via an obvious right-slanting, stepped and capped corner for its second pitch. Start at the short corner and climb to the oak.
1. 30m 4b Step right and climb straight up cracks in the wall on the right to the base of the groove.
2. 30m 4c Up the groove (hard for the short, can be avoided on the right by the short corner of Oor Wullie, returning immediately). Finish up slabs.

Oor Wullie   60m   E1   *   *(1996/1998)*
Climb a line just right of Boab's Corner. Start 2m right of the stepped corner.
1. 30m 5c After a boulder problem start (the original start to Boab's Corner), go diagonally right up scoops overlooking a steep wall to reach a roofed recess. Leave it out of its left corner and make thin moves to heather.
2. 30m 5c Go up to a black streaked section of wall. Climb this with difficulty to reach a short corner right of Boab's crux corner. Climb this and continue up a dwindling ramp rightwards to reach easy ground.

Right of Boab's Corner, the cliff soon becomes more vegetated. After about 100m there is a clean light coloured pillar in its top half (Bromide). Down to the right is a shallow left-trending slabby scoop which leads up to an ash and holly tree below overhangs (Plunge).

Bromide   40m   HVS   *   *(1988)*
1. 10m 4c Start up a cracked wall left of the smooth undercut cliff base below the tree. Climb it on good holds to a ledge.
2. 30m 5b Climb up the overhanging nose on the right, then move right round the corner, up an overhanging groove and swing back left on to the crest above the nose. Follow the crest to the top.
Variation: **The Original Start   15m   5a**
Move up to an overhang left of the scoop of Plunge. Climb a crack through an overhang, past a loose block, to the tree belay shared with Plunge. Now move up left to join the second pitch.

Plunge   40m   HVS   *(1982)*
1. 20m 5b A boulder problem start, then the scoop to the trees.
2. 20m 5b Climb the overhang directly above (3m right of Bromide groove), then follow the buttress, finishing as for Bromide.

Up and right from Plunge is a short south-east facing slab with right-rising rounded overlaps. The routes finish on a heather ledge below the easy upper rock. The climbing is pleasant but the routes short for Diabaig.

Deputy Dawg   25m   Severe   *(2005)*
Start on the left side of the slab between heather patches. Go up to a slanting overlap, climb a crack through the overlap and continue up a rib.

Musky   20m   Very Difficult   *(2005)*
Start at the right side of the right heather patch. Go straight up to a crack near the right end of the overlap two-thirds of the way up the slab. Climb a crack and continue up the slab.

Like Pine Bark 20m Very Difficult (2005)
Climb a line about 3m right of Musky.

UPPER SLABS

Diagram p244

The Gooseberry 60m Severe (1994)
The route starts at a small bealach at the top of the gully which bounds the right wall of the Main Crag. This is the gully called Big Glossy Book Route but the bealach is about 10mins above the climbing and crossed by the long easy descent (also 5mins from the top of Plunge). Climb slabs directly to a large ledge (30m). Climb just left of a left-slanting diagonal crack on good holds, then up slabs to the top (30m). The diagonal crack can also be climbed at 5a.

Top Cat 30m VS 4b (2005)
About 100m (distance) up and right from the Deputy Dawg slab and obvious from it is a dome of clean slabs on the skyline (this may be close on the right of The Gooseberry). This route climbs the upper right-hand skyline slab. Start at a flake filled recess at its base. Climb up through the flakes into a right-slanting crack. Follow this to where it ends, move left and back right on friction to finish up a continuation crack.

Peninsula Crags

Diagram p244

There are a number of gneiss crags on or near the Rubha na h-Airde peninsula which forms the south side of Loch Diabaig. Many are west facing and like the west facing walls on Diabaig itself, offer steep juggy climbing with some exciting situations despite their smaller size. Beware of ticks!

Approach: Follow the Diabaig to Inveralligin path until just past Charlie's Dome, then leave the main path at a cairn and follow a faint path down to follow the shore until a flat area between the mainland and the peninsula is reached. A temptation to follow the shore from the start should be resisted. Here is the derelict croft of Araid, from where the approach to various crags is described. But the first crag is reached from the shore before the flat area.

TWIN WALLS

(NG 500 589) Alt 40m West facing Map p237

Approaching the peninsula, just beyond a birch woodland, is a fine wall of orange rock (well seen from the peninsula).

Hot Head 15m HVS 5a * (2001)
Climbs the left side of the smaller left-hand wall. Start beneath a steep juggy wall. Climb straight up to a prominent projecting block at two-thirds height. Pass this on the right and finish up quartz cracks.

Red Crescent 15m E1 5b * (1998)
Climbs the centre of the left-hand wall. Start up a short steep ramp to a shallow crescent corner. Above this, climb an obvious left-slanting crack leading to a pod. Go directly to the top.

CROFTER'S CRAG

(NG 794 587) Alt 40m North-West facing Map p237

Situated opposite the ruined croft of Araid is an area of steep broken crags but one clean wall has a crack. Described left to right

ROLLING WALL

4. Beside the Point	VS 4c
5. Rolling Baba	E2 6a *
6. The Ice Bulge	HVS 5a *
7. Aquamarine	E4 6a **
9. Brave New World	E2 5c ***
10. The Sea, The Sea	E2 5b **
11. Rolling Home	E2 5c **
12. The Feelies	VS 4c
13. Submission	VS 5a
14. Boatman's Call	E1 5b

Andy Nisbet

ROLLING WALL 261

Diabaig Tiger 20m E3 6a ** *(2000)*
The corner and crack-line right of Applecross Jam provides another excellent route. Finish up the left-hand slanting crack.

The Applecross Jam 20m E3 5c *** *(1998)*
A clean central wall is split by a compelling overhanging crack. Very strenuous. A brushing of the top half may be worthwhile after the winter. Descend by abseil (sling and maillon in place).

8-Ace 20m VS 5a * *(1998)*
The left arete of the clean wall follows a curving ramp. Climb the corner on its left, place a high runner and step right into the ramp. Climb to the same belay and abseil descent.

Right of Tenure 20m Hard Severe *(2000)*
The obvious corner left of 8-Ace, swinging right below the unappealing final overhanging section.

The Act 15m E1 5a *(2000)*
In the centre of a small overhanging wall left of the corner is a curving shallow corner. Climb it, go over a bulge, then trend right to the top.

Jammy Dodger 12m 4c *(1999)*
The left side of the overhanging wall is climbed largely on jugs but unprotected.

ROLLING WALL

(NG 788 588) Alt 110m South-West facing Map p237 Diagram p260

The crag, well named from its shape, is situated on the south side of the peninsula. It catches the sun for most of the day and its exposed situation may allow a breeze which will deter midges. The best climbs follow well protected crack-lines which provide steep and strenuous climbs.

Approach: From just before the derelict croft of Araid, head up diagonally leftwards up the hillside above a fenced enclosure to the base of a crag high on the left skyline. Rolling Wall is its continuation round the corner. 1hr of rough going from the car park.

Routes are described right to left. At the right end the crag diminishes to become a smooth white slab split by three diagonal lines which give good short routes.

1 Epsilon 6m Hard Severe 4b *(1998)*
The right crack.

2 Delta 8m E1 5b *(1998)*
The central crack, sustained.

3 Gamma 10m Very Difficult *(1998)*
The left line, a right-trending ramp.

The central section of cliff is the crag's showpiece, a fine formation of smooth bulges split by impressive crack-lines.

4 Beside the Point 15m VS 4c *(1998)*
The crack-line left of a vegetated ramp.

5 Rolling Baba 20m E2 6a * *(2004)*
Climbs the walls right of The Ice Bulge; dries quickly after rain. Start as for Beside the Point. Traverse a hand-crack across a steep wall to gain a ramp, then move up and left across an impending wall to good holds and gain a sloping terrace. From

ROLLING WALL

a horizontal crack, climb through the bulging wall above on orange quartz rock with a hard crux sequence.

6 The Ice Bulge 20m HVS 5a * *(1998)*
Climb an initial wall, then continue direct to an obvious quartz bulge, put your crampons on and …

**7 Aquamarine 25m E4 6a ** ** *(2000)*
The impressive right-hand crack on the wall. Start easily, then swing through the bulge strenuously from the right to gain the crack, which is sustained to easier ground.

8 The Low Girdle 30m E1 5b *(1998)*
Start beneath the crack of Aquamarine and right of Brave New World. Climb up to the start of the crack. Make thin moves left until easier climbing continues the traverse.

9 Brave New World 22m E2 5c * ** *(1998)*
An angelic climb up the impressive cracks in the centre of the Rolling Wall. Climb the initial crack until a delicate traverse leads left to above the first bulge. Return to the crack and follow it on good holds to a hard finish (crux).

**10 The Sea, The Sea 25m E2 5b ** ** *(1998)*
Another gem up cracks left again. Start 2m right of the thin starting cracks, traverse in beneath the first bulge and continue up the crack to below the final bulge through which the cracks peter out. Step up and left, then back right to finish in an exposed position up the left edge of the Rolling Wall.

**11 Rolling Home 40m E2 5c ** ** *(1998)*
Start 2m right of Feelies crack. Climb cracks up the blunt arete to a junction with The Sea, The Sea. Step delicately on to 'The Roll' and traverse beneath it, exiting up the far right crack (crux).

The following three routes have upper and lower sections separated by easier ground and therefore feel disjointed despite some nice moves. They can be climbed in one or two pitches.

12 The Feelies 30m VS 4c *(1998)*
The crack at the left end of the wall, finishing up a steep spike choked corner (or the wall just on its right, stepping back into the corner at the top – 4b).

13 Submission 30m VS 5a *(1998)*
Start left of The Feelies at an embedded spike just right of a wild rose bush. Climb a diagonal crack rightwards for 2m, then go up and right to a flake. Climb the arete left of Feelies corner.

14 Boatman's Call 30m E1 5b *(1998)*
Start at the same place as Submission but climb straight up past the right end of two overlaps. Cross Submission and The Feelies to finish up the mossy corner right of The Feelies.

ORANGE WALL

Two small buttresses lie 30m left of the Rolling Wall; each is split by cracks.

Ewar Woowar 8m Hard Severe 4b *(1998)*
Cracks up the right side of the right buttress.

Mustn't Grumble 10m VS 5a *(2000)*
Start at a Y shaped crack. Follow the left-slanting crack through a bulging slab. Step

left and finish up another cracked bulge. Well protected. This may be a variation of Ewar Woowar.

Alice's Overhang   8m   VS 5a *(1998)*
A slab and bulge up the left-hand buttress.

RUBHA NA H-AIRDE

(NG 790 591)   North facing   Map p237
On the side of the peninsula facing Diabaig, clearly seen from the pier, is a wide grassy gully narrowing near the top and leading to an apparent col between two summits. There are sections of crag on either side of the gully but the rock is not as clean as the sunnier crags on the south side of the peninsula. The direct approach is over a shoulder at NG 793 591, but some of the routes were approached by canoe from the pier. The first route is on the lower left side of the gully at NG 791 592, alt 30m. Here are overlapping slabs then heathery ground topped by a red wall above small trees.

Diabaig Diamond   55m   E1 *(2005)*
Start at the toe of the overlapping slabs.
1. 30m 5a Trend left to access a right-trending corner leading to a big block. Move back left and up cracked slabs to a tree. Scramble up a rib and into trees below the red headwall.
2. 25m 5b Climb a steep corner trending right before traversing back left to a crack finish.

The following two routes are on a buttress further up the left side of the gully (alt 80m), left of a left branch of the gully at NG 790 591. This is level with a distinctive "mottled wall" on the right side of the gully. The buttress has a steep sidewall facing the gully and an even steeper base wall facing down the gully. Above and left of this is a clean narrow rib.

Beached Boat Buttress   60m   HVS * *(1998)*
This climb starts in the gully and climbs a lower wall, then climbs the rib via a corner.
1. 20m 4c Start down and left of a thin crack. Climb the arete.
2. 40m 5a Scramble down and left for 20m. Climb the corner past a holly, then up the rounded rib.

Bitch Witch   10m   E4 6a *(2005)*
Start just left of a break in the base wall. This wet break leads up to a ramp and pitch 2 of Beached Boat Buttress. Boulder bulging rock to gain a steep crack. Use the right arete to top out.

The next route is on a clean dome low down on the right of the gully and clearly seen from the parking place.

Diabug   40m   HVS *(2000)*
1. 15m 4a Climb a lower tier via the right branch of a Y shaped crack.
2. 25m 4c Start just left of a rock platform below the right side of the upper tier. Go diagonally right below a steepening (unprotected), then move back left through it and follow a rounded crest to the top.

Shipwrecked   50m   Hard Severe 4a *(2006)*
On a left-hand slab 50m left of Diabug. Climb the cleanest strip to a grassy ledge 4m up a central crack. Traverse left to a left-hand crack and finish up this.

Above the dome with Diabug is a distinctive mottled wall of unusual but sound rock.

264 UGLY CRAG

Mottled Wall   18m   E1 5b * *(2005)*
Climb through brown rock before moving left to gain a prominent crack which lies right of centre and starts halfway up. Finish up the crack.

Above a small bay right of the dome, two slabs separated by a vegetated crack rise out of the sea. They are also clearly seen from the parking place. The left slab is **Sea Otter** (12m VS 4c 2005). The right slab is **Fish Eagle** (12m HVS 5a 2005). Both are reached by a short traverse above the sea.

The next four crags are most easily reached by following the main path from Diabaig beyond Diabaig crag and towards Inveralligin.

UGLY CRAG

(NG 800 587)   Alt 100m   West facing

The crag is visible in profile from the Diabaig car park as the left wall of the central of three small high cols on the skyline. It is seen better from the last section of road before the car park. Pretty Crag is also seen in profile right of its base. The crag is overhanging but with very juggy rock. It is most easily approached from the Inveralligin path near Loch a' Bhealaich Mhòir, otherwise very rough from just beyond the birch wood (it can also be seen from here). At the left end of the crag is a big corner with overhanging walls to its right.

Ugly Mug   55m   E2 *** *(1998)*
A rising girdle from bottom left to top right provides a wild route, steeped in exposure. Start 10m right of the big corner at a pile of blocks beneath a big block in an open corner.
1. 25m 5c   Climb up and rightwards, then pull steeply over a bulge to a ledge below a large triangular niche. Traverse strenuously rightwards on good holds to a precarious exit on to a hanging slab. Belay at its right end.
2. 30m 5c   Drop down and continue traversing rightwards on huge holds in a spectacular position to the flake on Ugly Wall (good runners). Step up and right to a good slot (Friend 2), then make a hard move rightwards to another good flake. Pull directly over the bulge above. Exit leftwards.

A Mugs Game   20m   HVS 5a *(2000)*
A straight up line through the start of Ugly Mug. Start 2m right of the pile of blocks and climb direct over a bulge, then a second bulge (common to Ugly Mug) into the triangular niche. Exit the niche leftwards along a small ramp to finish more easily.

Handsome Hog   20m   E3 5c * *(2000)*
A strenuous direct line with reasonable protection up the highest and steepest part of the wall. Start at the left side of a black wedge of rock under the lowest overhang. Pull through the overhang, then move 2m right along a handrail and pull leftwards through the next overhang. Climb up past a knob of rock to a cramped rest. Pull through the next overhang and reach into a small V-niche. Finish direct through more overhangs.

Ugly Wall   20m   E1 5b * *(1998)*
Start just right of the highest part of the crag and 5m left of an orange corner. Climb up and left on big holds to a large flake below a roof. Pull over directly and make an awkward exit leftwards. An exciting outing.

PRETTY CRAG

On the other side of a small ridge which is in front of Ugly Crag is a slab of immaculate white gneiss (facing away from Ugly Crag and slightly lower).

WHITE HOUSE CRAG 265

Pretty Scoop   8m   VS 4b (1998)
A scoop at the left end of the slab. Poorly protected.

Pretty Crack   8m   VS 4c (1998)
The left-hand crack.

Pretty Midgie   10m   E1 5b (2000)
The right-hand crack-line gives a sustained route.

LOCH A' BHEALAICH CRAG

(NG 800 584)   Alt 100m   North-West facing   Map p237

A crag above the stream just below the outflow of Loch a' Bhealaich Mhòir (there is no crag symbol on the 1:50000 map). The crag has a large overhanging wall at its top right side.

Parasol   35m   E1 5b * (2000)
This route climbs the pillar on the left side of the crag, with an overhanging downward-pointing toe. The hard sections are well protected. Climb a groove which curves up left of the toe to reach a capping roof. Swing right and traverse right to reach the crest. Climb the flat fronted crest to a tree growing out of a horizontal crack. Go right, then up on to a sloping ledge. Finish slightly leftwards to a belay 5m below the top (it is easy to the top but there is no belay).

WHITE HOUSE CRAG

(NG 802 577)   Alt 30m   South-West facing   Map p237   Diagram p244

The crag is a 50m dome of gneiss with a steep juggy band at 20m and a terrace at 35m. On the terrace is a lone tree from which an abseil is possible, omitting the much easier second pitches. The most obvious feature is a short, shallow but well defined central groove in a slabby lower section (taken by the original route Rendezvous).

Approach: Follow the Diabaig to Inveralligin path past two lochans and down to a bay with a white house. Approaching from Wester Alligin is a similar distance and time. The crag is directly behind the path, 1hr.

Bare Faced Cheek   45m   E1 5b (1998)
A steep brown slab lies to the left of the grassy groove of Rock Stripper. Climb the central plinth to a horizontal, then take the bulge above to a foothold. Continue up the central cracks in the slab, a good pitch (25m). Continue up right of a dirty corner-crack, following the best line, rather scrappy (20m).

Rock Stripper   50m   VS 4c (1998)
Start left of the short central groove and right of a grassy groove. Climb the slabby wall to a chockstone in a bulge which is climbed to a step right and up directly to twin overhangs. Surmount the lower (crux) and traverse left beneath the upper to enter a groove which is climbed up and right to the terrace (40m). Continue straight up to finish (10m). Quite bold in places.

Indecent Exposure   50m   HVS 5a * (1998)
Either start as for Rock Stripper or to the left of its grassy groove and climb blocky rock to surmount the chockstone. Continue up a steep slab with a small aspen to the overhangs on the right. Move right on huge jugs to a small triangular niche on the nose (exposed). Climb the crux wall directly above to the terrace (35m). Finish up the top tier (15m). Well positioned climbing with a short crux.

Rendezvous   50m   HVS 5a * (1993)
The original route on the crag taking a central line (and approached by canoe from

Applecross). Scramble up easy rocks to a short wall beneath the central groove. Climb a wall and thin crack to enter the groove which is climbed to overhangs. Step right and surmount the overhang, then another and continue up on holds that keep appearing to the terrace (35m). Climb the wall left of the tree and a slab to the top (15m).

The Full Monty   50m   E1 5b **   *(1998)*
A better companion to Rendezvous, more exposed and sustained. To the right of the central groove is a thin red crack. Climb the slabs directly up to it, then climb the crack to the overhang. Move right and pull over this to climb the wall to a horizontal crack. Move left, surmount the bulge and climb the exposed wall directly, making a step left near the top to the tree (35m). Climb the wall to the right of the tree and slab above to the top (15m).

Promiscuous Groove   30m   HVS 5b   *(1998)*
To the right of The Full Monty is a red wall. Start left of a juniper bush and climb the slab to the wall. This provides awkward climbing to a better wall above which leads to a blocky groove of suspect rock.

Above White House Crag is a slab.

Walking on Crystals   40m   Moderate to Very Difficult   *(1998)*
The slab is easiest on the left but more entertaining up the red crystalline gneiss to the right.

Quartz Inspector's Slab   10m   Very Difficult to Severe   *(1998)*
At the top of the slab is a 10m slab of faultless white gneiss to the left. Various lines climbed.

BEINN ALLIGIN

Maps p194, 267

Beinn Alligin, the most westerly of the three great mountains of the Torridon Forest, has fewer ice climbs than its neighbours and is less often in good winter condition. Although it has some steep sandstone faces they are rather vegetated and crossed by ledges; no summer climbs have been recorded. Despite these comparisons it is a noble mountain, well worth a visit for its winter climbs, or for the traverse of its tops.

Approach: Leave the road from Torridon to Diabaig at a large car park by the bridge over the Coire Mhic Nòbuil burn and follow the good path on the east side of the burn through beautiful Caledonian forest. The first corrie to be seen high on the left is Coire nan Laogh, which offers some sporting winter possibilities. The next corrie, Toll a' Mhadaidh Mòr, between Tom na Gruagaich and Sgùrr Mhòr is much more impressive and offers several good ice routes on the north-east face of Tom na Gruagaich. There are further winter climbs around the Eag Dubh, on the north side of the 'Horns' of Alligin and further round the mountain in Toll nam Biast.

Beinn Alligin Ridge Traverse   I **
The ridge can be traversed in either direction but anti-clockwise is easier; this goes over the Horns of Alligin first. There is a considerable path leading up towards the Horns, which involves some short and awkward, but unexposed walls. The Horns can be traversed on the crest (Grade II in very icy conditions, the hardest section being descending from the First Horn) or passed on the left (south) by a long exposed traverse. The ascent to Sgùrr Mòr is steep but only walking. On its descent, the initial bearing will appear to lead diagonally off the ridge, but thereby misses the Eag Dubh. Continue easily towards Tom na Gruagaich; on its ascent there is some easy scrambling, exposed at one point. Normally the summit of Tom na Gruagaich would be included but it can be passed on the right by traversing into a snow gully which leads up and over directly to the descent down Coire nan Laogh. This leads fairly directly to the car park.

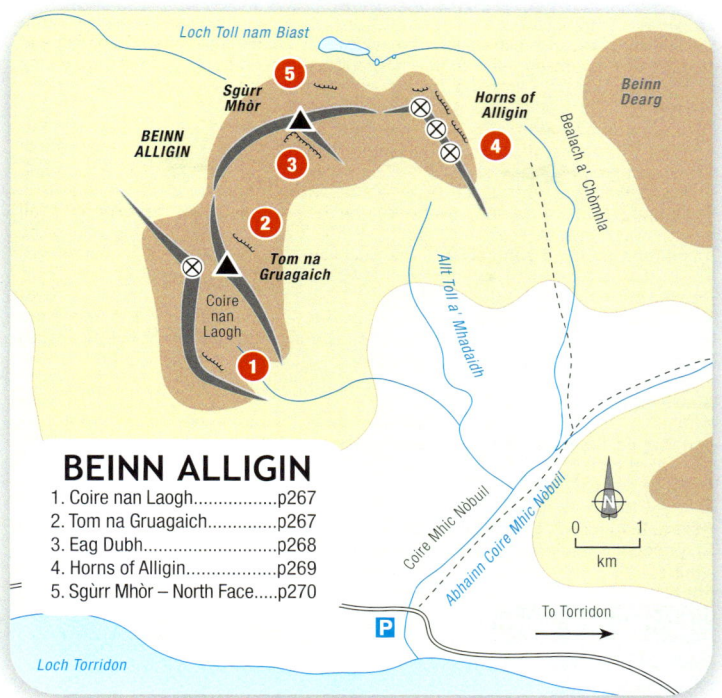

BEINN ALLIGIN

1. Coire nan Laogh.................p267
2. Tom na Gruagaich..............p267
3. Eag Dubh..........................p268
4. Horns of Alligin..................p269
5. Sgùrr Mhòr – North Face.....p270

COIRE NAN LAOGH

Map p267

Gardener's Choice   100m   III (1994)
The cliffs of Coire nan Laogh are on the left side on ascent. The corrie and cliffs take a distinct bend at about 600m, the cliffs being separated into two sections by an easy gully. The highest section of steep cliff is below the bend and is north-east facing. This route is the highest gully on this steep section of cliff, rising out left from the bottom of the easy gully.

High on the left side of Coire nan Laogh are three parallel icefalls at NG 858 596 and altitude about 750m. Each had a direct entry pitch of 35m Grade II followed by the main icefall. Descent from the right two was by abseil down the right icefall but the left icefall continued for 10m as an ice umbrella and a 100m traverse right regained the corrie base. An alternative is a Grade I continuation of the right icefall. The grades were (left to right): 45m IV,5; 35m III; 35m IV,4 (2001).

TOM NA GRUAGAICH

(NG 861 603)   Alt 600m   North-East facing   Map p267

West Coast Boomer   300m   IV,4 ** (1973)
The obvious gully on the left of the face can be recommended as a sustained and scenic route. Pass the lower crag on the right and angle up left to reach the main gully. There are numerous short pitches in the lower part and a continuous steep section in the upper part.

268 BEINN ALLIGIN

Ice Gem 150m IV,5 *(1986)*
On the left of the tier below West Coast Boomer a prominent icefall forms on right-trending ramps. Trend left into the ramp corner then climb direct to the top.

The upper face right of West Coast Boomer has four lines of weakness which can hold good snow and ice.

Crown Jewel 350m IV,5 * *(1986)*
This is the left-hand line. Climb steep iced tiers, then a 50m mixed pitch to gain an upper gully. This has many icy steps and finishes just right of the summit trig point.

The Moonstone 300m IV,5 * *(1986)*
The central line is gained by thinly iced ramps and leads to a steep finishing corner.

Koh-i-Noor 270m IV,5 * *(1986)*
A well iced stepped scoop further right. Follow the scoop, moving slightly left, then head directly up by mixed climbing in steeper grooves to the top.

Bilas 300m IV,4 *(1987)*
A thinner icefall right of Koh-i-Noor. After three pitches go left, up a further 15m and then left again to join the easy upper part of Koh-i-Noor.

Light of Bengal 270m IV,4 *(1989)*
The first icefall right of Bilas, directly in line with a large V notch on the summit ridge. Start close to Bilas and climb a succession of short steep ice pitches leading to a deep gully splitting the upper rocks. Finish up the gully in two pitches.

Shezan 255m IV,5 *(1989)*
Climbs the icefall right of the previous route which leads into an obvious narrow chimney in the upper part of the face. Climb the chimney in two pitches (crux) and finish up a short gully.

EAG DUBH

(NG 866 610) Alt 700 to 800m South-West facing Map p267
On the north side of the corrie under Sgùrr Mhòr is a very impressive vertical wall with an easy gully running up beneath it, the Eag Dubh. The other wall of the gully is a buttress forming the minor peak of Sgùrr na Tuaigh (as named on the 1:25000 map). About 3hrs approach to the top of the Eag Dubh.

Under the Hammer 110m V,6 *(1993)*
The left side of the final gully of the Eag Dubh is a buttress which is both steeper and larger than it appears. This route is based on a central corner system, with frequent deviations on to the right wall.

For the Chop 100m III,4 *(1999)*
Climbs the ramp system overlooking the Eag Dubh on the left. Start just inside the Eag Dubh, climb a short wall and traverse left round the corner to a groove which leads to a ledge with a large block (25m). Stand on the block to gain and follow the ramp proper (50m). Finish up the upper of two ramps (the lower would be easier) to the summit of Sgùrr na Tuaigh (Hatchet Peak) – 25m.

Eag Dubh 400m I or II *
The deep narrow snow gully at the top of the diagonal vertical wall is Grade I. The gully can either be gained by a long scramble up the ramp immediately below the impressive wall or more directly up a shallow gully further left. The latter requires some consolidated snow but it can have several low-angled ice pitches and is a more satisfying approach (Grade II). The gully is a windy place, susceptible to a fierce updraft.

EAG DUBH

Wall of the Outcry   105m   VI,8 ** (1996)
Climbs the steep right wall of upper Eag Dubh, aiming for a big right-facing corner which forms high up at the right side of a shield of rock, the left side being a left-facing corner and well seen from the main ridge at the top of Eag Dubh. Start on the immediate right of the entrance to the narrow upper gully between Sgùrr Mhòr and Sgùrr na Tuaigh (flake belay close against the wall and about 6m above the gully bed in summer).
1. 30m Bridge past a good spike and go awkwardly up grooves to the left. Go up to a steeper rock tier and traverse 5m left to a flake belay.
2. 25m Just right of the stance pull into a vertical corner with a large flake on its right-hand side and climb it strenuously to a terrace. Move out right on turf ledges and make thin moves back left to a bay directly beneath the big corner.
3. 35m Make hard moves off the right side of the stance to an easement, then move into the corner. Bridge up to a roof and from a spike, use tension to swing down to a ledge on the right. Make a hairy mantelshelf up right again to a thin foot ledge. Traverse this right for 6m and pull into a ramp which leads back left to a terrace.
4. 15m Traverse 6m left and climb a left-trending line of flakes to the top.

Wailing Wall   110m   VII,7 *** (1999)
A very steep fault-line to the right of Wall of the Outcry. Climbed in icy conditions, useful to solidify the mossy vegetation. The hardest moves are well protected. Start as for Wall of the Outcry.
1. 45m Climb the initial left-slanting grooves of Outcry (about 20m), but then go straight up to the ledge system of its traverse. Traverse right under some huge blocks (now under the main fault-line) and climb just on their right to belay on top.
2. 10m Step right into the fault-line and follow it to a ledge under an overhanging smooth section.
3. 35m Traverse a ledge right for 6m to a crack. Use this to gain a prominent grass ledge above and left. Pull out left on to a flake (technical crux) and continue left, hopefully on ice, into the fault-line. This ascent pulled out on to its left arete and went 5m up left for runners, returning down to the fault. Climb the fault to a ledge with no protection. Traverse 15m right, climb the short wall above and return part way left.
4. 30m Traverse easily right, climb a short wall and easy ground to the top.

Hatchet Man   80m   III * (1993)
Mid-way up the long right wall of the Eag Dubh is the only easy break, a slabby ramp which ices readily. Climb this in three pitches, entirely on ice in good conditions.

HORNS OF ALLIGIN

(NG 877 613)   Alt 500m   North-East facing   Map p267
On the north-east face of the Horns of Alligin are the following climbs, reached by continuing along the vague path towards the col between Beinn Dearg and Beinn Alligin, after the more obvious path to the ridge has been left. The first main gully, Deep South Gully, finishes between the first (lowest) and second Horn.

Deep South Gully   250m   I ****
This is the first gully seen up on the left from the path and one of the best snow gullies in Scotland through magnificent scenery, especially when used as a start to the traverse of Beinn Alligin. It curves from left to right. In lean conditions there is a big chockstone with an easy through route followed by an easy ice pitch. It is often lean nowadays but four stars assumes snow over the lower boulders.

Depth Charge   130m   VI,8 * (1996)
Climbs the headwall of the Horn which overhangs Deep South Gully. Fine situations and a tough finish. Climb Deep South to just past the narrows where the gully bends rightwards. Start at a corner ramp. Directly above, a black crack splits the final headwall; the route aims for this.

BEINN ALLIGIN

1. 55m Climb iced corners and steep mixed ground, finishing by the left of two shallow chimneys; belay at a block. The pitch can be split at 20m.
2. 40m Follow an icy gully above for 20m. Where it peters out traverse 10m right and go up a cul-de-sac to belay at the foot of the black crack.
3. 35m Climb the left-slanting V-groove immediately left of the black crack to a ledge. Continue in the same line up a second overhanging groove to the top.

Errors Cleft   250m   II *(1987)*
To the right of Deep South Gully are two obvious lines of weakness. This climb gains the left-hand line by traversing up from the right. Follow the line to the top.

Diamond Cleft   260m   IV,4 * *(1988)*
This is the right-hand line of weakness. Approach from the right to the start of the gully formed by a buttress on the right and a huge sandstone monolith on the left. Climb an initial steep section, then more easily into the cleft. The steep V-cleft of ice leads to a cave belay (45m). The climbing now eases.

Deep North Gully   250m   II ***
The gully, which finishes between the second and third Horns, requires a good build-up; otherwise an introductory pitch can be very hard.

Backfire Ridge   200m   II * *(1981)*
This takes the most northerly of the ridges which form the north-east face of the Horns. It runs left of the triangular north-west face above Toll nam Biast. Climb the ridge direct, with three short rock steps and a good finish at the top of the third Horn.

Diamond Fire   225m   IV,4 *** *(1985)*
Recommended as an adventure into the unknown, to climb a deep cleft on the north-west face above Toll nam Biast. First climbed in very lean conditions, it held good ice even when the surrounding buttresses had little snow. The steepest ice pitch was avoided on the left, but with a good build-up it may not be too difficult.
1. 35m Climb ice steps to a shelf below a corner.
2. 35m Climb the short corner on the left and go up easier ground to below a short icefall.
3. 35m Climb the icefall and go up to a deep, wide cleft.
4. 45m The icefall above is avoided. Climb the left wall, traverse left to a snow slope and climb the narrow gully above.
5. 30m Follow a snowfield to the back wall.
6. 45m Climb the final corner to the main ridge.

Backyard Gully   150m   I *(1984)*
In the corrie above Loch Toll nam Biast, two gullies rise to the col between the northern Horn and Sgùrr Mhòr. The right-hand gully is short and uninteresting. The left branch is longer and entertaining in early season but later banks out.

Backyard Buttress   110m   III *(1986)*
The short buttress immediately right of Backyard Gully.

SGÙRR MHÒR

(NG 860 602)   Alt 985m

The highest peak on Beinn Alligin.

North Face

(NG 868 615)   Alt 630m   North facing   Map p267

Curve Stone   350m   II *** *(1996)*
Left of centre on the face is a long shallow gully, initially left-trending, which ends

HORNS OF ALLIGIN

Deep North Gully, II, Horns of Alligin, Beinn Alligin

on a shoulder of the north-west ridge of Sgùrr Mhòr. An ice pitch leads into the gully. After another 150m, the line turns right and enters the icy narrows. Two pitches lead to the exit snows.

Black Opal   200m   IV,4 *(1995)*
On the right-hand side of this large north face is a buttress with a steep line of weakness clefting its centre.
1. and 2. 80m Approach by steepening snow slopes till beneath the main pitch.
3. 50m Two icy steps lead to the ice runnel. Climb this and the continuing corner groove to gain the wall below an overlap. Pull over into the upper groove, rock belay 5m up and left.
4. 30m Steep snow to the exit gully.
5. 40m Climb the gully and move right over final snows to reach the north-west ridge.

BEINN DEARG

(NG 895 607)   Alt 914m   Map p194
Carn na Feola North Ridge   500m   II *(1994)*
A fine mountaineering excursion. Approaching from Coire Dubh Mòr, skirt below the evil dripping crag at the foot of the ridge, traversing back up a series of short icy steps to gain the crest. A scramble in summer (1994), with some short tricky walls, the drier the better.

CHOIRE MHÒIR

At the top of this corrie is a triangular buttress (NG 899 607).

Red Rag 90m VII,7 *** (2000)
This climbs the extremely obvious and steep icy groove that descends from the apex of the crag.

Red Chimneys 90m VI,6 (2001)
Start from the lowest point of the crag, down and right of Red Rag at a deceptively steep chimney-crack. Climb this to a ledge and move right to an obvious chimney, followed by a higher ledge below a smooth corner. Climb the right arete of the corner to gain the base of a wicked off-width ice smear. Grovel horribly up to a welcome ledge. Climb straight up to reach a vicious narrow chimney. Either squeeze up painfully or take the outside option (bold) to finish.

COIRE BEAG

Red Dwarf 100m IV,6 * (2001)
A short but well cracked ridge at NG 907 609 and climbed in five short pitches. Start just left of the toe and go easily up right on to the crest. Climb a right-slanting ramp (steeper than it looks) leading to a terrace. Cross this and pass a steep wall by going left and back right. Climb a well cracked slabby wall on the right, then finish by two short walls with good cracks.

Liathach & Beinn Eighe

These two magnificent mountains dominate the north side of Glen Torridon and offer some of the best mountain routes in the country, in both winter and summer.

LIATHACH

Maps p194, 273

Liathach comprises a range of seven peaks forming an 8km chain running east to west on the north side of Glen Torridon, towering directly above the road. The highest point on Liathach is Spidean a' Choire Lèith at 1055m, mid-way between Stuc a' Choire Dhuibh Bhig 915m, guarding the east end of the chain, and Mullach an Rathain 1023m, at the west end above Torridon village. A broad shoulder extends west for 2km from Mullach an Rathain rising slightly to Sgòrr a' Chadail before dropping steeply, but easily, down to Coire Mhic Nòbuil and the footpath. Since most of the rock on the high cliffs of Liathach consists of broken vegetatious Torridonian sandstone terraces, usually wet streaked, only a handful of rock climbs have been recorded.

However, in winter the mountain is transformed to produce some of the best icefall climbing in Britain. The traverse of the mountain in both summer and winter gives one of the classic ridge expeditions of the mainland, with sensationally exposed views onto the surrounding prehistoric looking hills of the Torridon area.

In the past, winter climbing conditions on Liathach were renowned for being fickle. However, increased popularity has confirmed that good ice forms regularly every season at any time from January to March. A warm weather system may strip the buttresses and thin icefalls, but the ice will re-form quickly on a return to colder conditions. The most reliable climbs will be found in Coire Dubh Mòr and high up in Coire na Caime. There are also many big gullies which with good snow cover offer fine easier climbs.

Apart from Coire Liath Mhòr east of Spidean a' Choire Lèith, the south side of Liathach offers fewer climbs despite its continuous steepness and very little in the way of continuous gullies.

LIATHACH

1. Annat Bouldering....................p208
2. Seana Mheallan.......................p210
3. Seana Mheallan West...............p219
4. Path Crag................................p226
5. Celtic Boulders.........................p228
6. Creag nan Leumnach................p230
7. Creag nan Uaimh.....................p233
8. Hairpin Crag............................p234
9. Stùc a' Choire Dhuibh Bhig......p274/305
10. Coire Dubh Beag....................p275
11. Coire Dubh Mòr.....................p279
12. Am Fasarinen.........................p289
13. Upper Coire na Caime............p295
14. Meall Dearg – North Face......p297
15. Sgòrr a' Chadail.....................p300
16. Pyramid Buttress....................p302
17. Coire Liath Mhòr – Toll a' Meitheach..p304

BEINN EIGHE see map p307

TORRIDON

Liathach - North side

Approach: The climbs on the north side of Liathach are described from east to west, approaching via the Coire Dubh footpath, starting from the National Trust car park in Glen Torridon (NG 958 568). The path rises under the east buttress of Stuc a' Choire Dhuibh Bhig and round the back to give access to the three northern corries of Coire Dubh Beag, Coire Dubh Mòr and the larger spectacular Coire na Caime. Access from the footpath to each corrie, and also the descents, are described for each corrie individually. Coire na Caime can also be accessed directly over the main ridge while the north face of Meall Dearg is usually accessed from the Beinn Alligin car park.

Liathach Main Ridge Traverse   4km   II ****

A superb expedition with continually interesting walking and spectacular mountain and loch scenery. It is usually traversed from east to west. Leave the Coire Dubh path at about NG 954 582 and climb steep slopes towards Stùc a' Choire Dhuibh Bhig. On reaching a high rock band, traverse right to reach its north-east ridge. Go up a short tricky section and the bouldery ridge to the top. For convenience of transport, non-purists may start up the Allt an Doire Ghairbh path. Access Gully (Grade I) in Coire Dubh Beag is an alternative. The hardest part is the traverse of the Fasarinen Pinnacles which warrants Grade II, but all sections of the traverse involve Grade I up, down and traversing. In summer a low traverse of Am Fasarinen on the south side provides a path but this is often steeply banked in winter and more difficult than the crest, especially in bad snow conditions. Usually a mixture of traversing and the crest will be taken, the recommended route being to traverse initially (at the eastern end) round the pinnacles, but follow the crest over Am Fasarinen. The main ridge finishes at Mullach an Rathain.

STÙC A' CHOIRE DHUIBH BHIG - NORTH

(NG 942 582)   Alt 915m   Map p273

The following routes are on the East and North side of this peak. Routes on the South side are described at the end of the Liathach section.

East Buttress   Difficult   *(1899)*
Recorded for posterity. To quote: 'This is the black, broken, unwholesome-looking cliff low down on the main north-east ridge of the mountain, overlooking the Coire Dubh track'. It was originally climbed by Lawson, Ling and Glover on an SMC Easter Meet in wet and windy conditions. The first tier had some steep little pitches, the second was passed by a grassy gully on the left, and the third was climbed by steep rock and a small chimney.

Chi Squared   450m   IV,4   *(1968)*
This takes the watercourse descending the north flank of Stuc a' Choire Dhuibh Bhig, before the entrance to Coire Dubh Beag. Initially shallow, it becomes a well defined gully higher up where the left fork is hidden from below. Consistent climbing on water ice, requiring very cold weather to freeze, leads to the crux at a band of crags high up. Take the left fork to finish.

COIRE DUBH BEAG

(NG 938 583)   Alt 750m   North facing   Map p273   Diagrams p275, 276

This is the first of the northern corries, a classic bowl with an easy snow gully on its back left side and broad steep terraces sweeping round to the right. From a distance, the cascades of ice look discontinuous, but the lines become more apparent on closer inspection.

Approach: From the Coire Dubh footpath, the best approach is to follow the burn draining from the corrie, the chosen side depending on snow deposition, 2hrs 30mins.

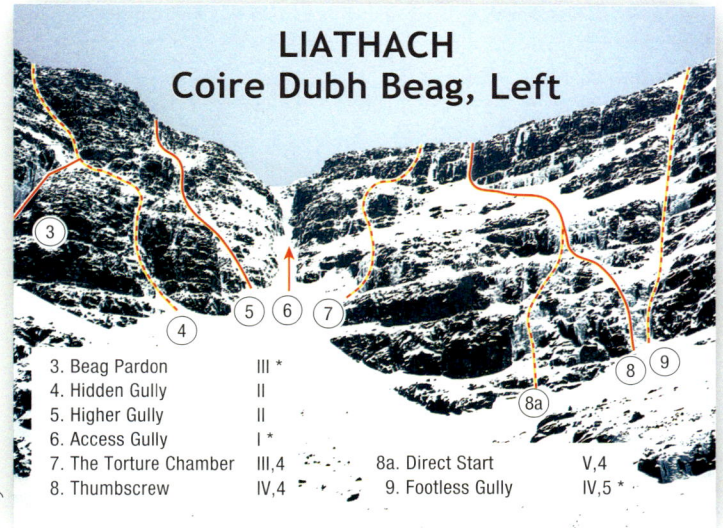

LIATHACH
Coire Dubh Beag, Left

3. Beag Pardon	III *	
4. Hidden Gully	II	
5. Higher Gully	II	
6. Access Gully	I *	
7. The Torture Chamber	III,4	8a. Direct Start V,4
8. Thumbscrew	IV,4	9. Footless Gully IV,5 *

Descent: The quickest descent is to go down Access Gully and return by the approach. Alternatively, continue along the ridge east beyond Access Gully to traverse Stùc a' Choire Dhuibh Bhig and descend off the east end of the ridge. The third option is to descend the opposite side of Access Gully (i.e. southwards) or from a point just to its west, then turn right (west) to traverse into Coire Liath Mhòr.

1 Left Gully   200m   II
A shallow gully line on the hillside left of Beag Pardon, gained by a traverse left from below it, and finishing in a snow bowl below the summit of Stùc a' Choire Dhuibh Bhig. There is another shallow gully of similar grade much further to the left.

2 The Snotter   40m   VI,6 ** (1986)
The very steep icicle that drools down the left wall at the start of Beag Pardon. Descend by abseil, or continue very easily to the summit.

3 Beag Pardon   200m   III *
At the back left corner of the corrie is the easy snow gully. Left of its base is a snow terrace leading left, then up into a narrow cleft. Climb the cleft, requiring chimneying on steep ice. From the top of its narrows, traverse right and finish up Hidden Gully, Grade I from here.

4 Hidden Gully   210m   II (1977)
This climb sneaks up left, usually on ice, from the lower reaches of Access Gully, breaking into a snow gully directly above.

5 Higher Gully   150m   II
A parallel but less distinct line to the right of Hidden Gully, sometimes icy. Start further up Access Gully.

6 Access Gully   120m   I *
The obvious snow gully tucked into the left side at the back of the corrie. It gives a

pleasant route on to the main ridge and without a cornice and not steep for the grade, may also be used as a descent.

7 The Torture Chamber   160m   III,4   *(1999)*
Between Access Gully and Thumbscrew is a large snowfield above the first sandstone tier. This route takes three short ice falls through the left side of the snowfield and just right of Access Gully. Go part way up Access Gully until below the icefall on the right. A short lower icefall on the left-hand side of the lower tier leads to the left side of the snowfield (20m), then easy ground to a rock buttress on the left side of the snowfield (70m). A second fall goes through this and leads (50m) to a third icefall directly above and going through the final rock tier (20m).

8 Thumbscrew   200m   IV,4   *(1989)*
This climb links a series of icefalls to the left of Footless Gully. Start some 8m left of the Footless chimney and take a short left-slanting groove to the foot of a very steep narrow icefall. Climb this to a large terrace and continue up and left to climb a large icefall leading to a second terrace. Mixed ground leads to an obvious deep chimney cleaving the final tier.
Variation: **Direct Start   60m   V,4**   *(1989)*
A two pitch steep icefall start straightens the line. Start about 40m left of Thumbscrew. Climb a steep right-facing icy corner up the first tier. Follow the same line in the second tier then move 5m right into Thumbscrew.

9 Footless Gully   150m   IV,5 *   *(1977)*
The obvious line on the back wall. The first 10m is the crux, an awkward narrow vertical chimney slow to fill with ice. The climb is often only Grade III after the first pitch. Although there are many terraces, the direct line feels natural.

10 Headhunter   200m   V,5 **   *(1994)*
An obvious chimney left of the aspect change taken by Headless Gully; more of a gully than Headless. From the Coire Dubh path it appears straight up whereas Headless slants right. The route starts up a steep icefall, leftmost of several (can be the crux, easier with more build-up) to gain the first terrace. A short awkward

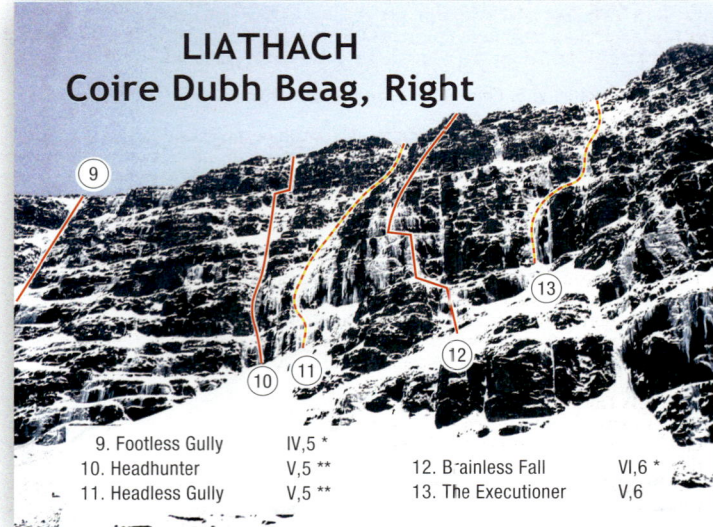

LIATHACH
Coire Dubh Beag, Right

9. Footless Gully	IV,5 *
10. Headhunter	V,5 **
11. Headless Gully	V,5 **
12. Brainless Fall	VI,6 *
13. The Executioner	V,6

Andy Nisbet

COIRE DUBH BEAG 277

The Snotter, VI,6, Coire Dubh Beag, Liathach. Climber Andy Cunningham

corner gains the bottom of the chimney, which can be led in one long pitch or split. Follow the chimney for 20m before leaving on the left to gain a good ledge. Regain the continuation chimney on the right and follow it to below a steep rock wall and icy slab on the left. Climb the slab to turn the rock wall on the left and reach a final steep ice pitch leading to easy ground.

11 Headless Gully 150m V,5 ** (1984)
The main line on the right (east facing) wall and the route most likely to form regularly. Start by the highest point of snow under the middle of the wall. Climb an initial short steep icefall to the first terrace. Move left into the main icefall which is steep for 25m (crux) before easing onto more terraced ground. Finish via an ice filled corner through the top tier onto the summit snowfield.

12 Brainless Fall 140m VI,6 * (1999)
Climbs some steep ice which occasionally forms on the wall right of Headless Gully. Climb ice leftwards to reach a ledge below the ice which forms on the wall just right of overhangs which run across from Headless (10m). Climb an icefall on the wall which is just below vertical (25m). Move 5m left and climb thicker vertical ice which soon eases (30m). Go up a short wall and easier ground to the final tier (50m). Climb the tier by a groove on the left to easy ground.

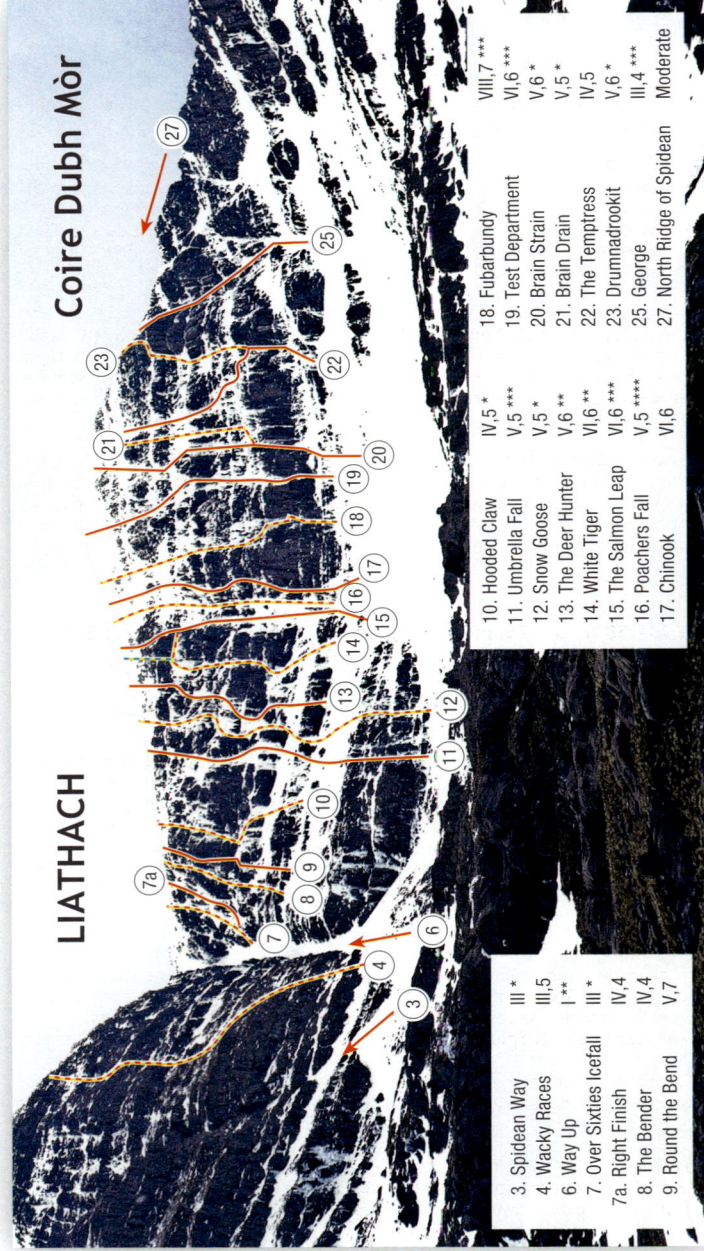

13 The Executioner 140m V,6 *(1986)*
A large snow ramp leads right from under the line of Headless Gully, to finish at an overhang at the base of a shallow gully. The Executioner gains the gully higher up, avoiding the overhang on the left. Start halfway up the ramp and follow a very steep ice filled corner, vertical to start, to a pinnacle belay on the right. The icefall continues right of the pinnacle in two steps to a big snow ledge. Move right into the main gully which leads to the top.

14 Nil Can't 250m II *(2000)*
A somewhat scrappy line up an obvious line of weakness up the face. Start up the large snow ramp passing under The Executioner and continue to its end where it becomes a shallow chimney. Go up this to a terrace, then turn straight up and climb short walls and terraces to finish on the crest at the top of the final tower of Rambler's Rib.

15 Rambler's Rib 350m II * *(1987)*
This route follows the rib bounding the left side of a narrow curving gully (Hillwalk) and bounding the west of Coire Dubh Beag itself. Start in the gully and climb out onto the rib at the earliest opportunity. Climb the rib direct, with short technical walls above big ledges, avoiding the final rock tower on the left or right. Not a safe option in avalanche conditions, as either finish is on snow slopes.

16 Hillwalk 300m II ** *(1966)*
The fine curving narrow gully immediately right of Rambler's Rib is also known as Trotters Gully. It can give several short pitches through interesting scenery, but often banks out to Grade I. It opens into a bowl after its narrow section, and it is common for windslab to build up here (there have been accidents).

COIRE DUBH MÒR

(NG 931 583) Alt 750m North facing Map p273 Diagram p278

This corrie is topped by Spidean a' Choire Lèith, the highest peak of Liathach, and provides the best concentration of ice climbs on the mountain.

Approach: Leave the Coire Dubh footpath just before the watershed and angle up to join the burn draining from the corrie itself, 2hrs 30mins.

Descents: 1. For the main face, the quickest descent is to make a rising traverse left to join and descend the east ridge of Spidean to the col between it and Stob a' Coire Liath Mhòr. From the col, Way Up can be descended northwards back into the corrie, but it is quicker to descend in the opposite direction (south) down a shallow gully (Grade I) to a flat area. Go straight on from the base of the gully to the south rim and descend another gully. Continue in the same direction down a shallow continuation to cross the stream and gain the footpath. In favourable conditions much of this can be glissaded.
2. If the summit of Liathach has been visited, either as an option or after George, one can still descend the east ridge to the col, or in very good conditions glissade from near the summit, but the least steep option is to descend the south ridge (a notorious dead end) until it becomes level, then turn left (east) and descend diagonally leftwards to gain the descent gully part way down from the col.
3. From West Gully or Spidean Way, one can either go west to the col and descend as above or go east and descend as for Coire Dubh Beag ('six and two threes').
4. From the top of George, or routes nearby, a quick descent back to the corrie is down steep slopes just west of the North Ridge of Spidean, either traversing back into the corrie at the base of George, or lower down on to the floor of the corrie.

The corrie has huge rambling buttresses on the left cut by two obvious gullies, West Gully and Spidean Way, followed by a deep snow gully, Way Up, bordering the left end of the steep back wall. Way Up leads to a col on the main ridge. The 200m back wall extends rightwards to a left-curving gash, George, before merging into

280 LIATHACH

Poachers Fall, V,5, Coire Dubh Mòr, Liathach

the North Ridge of Spidean. In the centre of the back wall, and obvious from a great distance, is the magnificent ice cascade of Poachers Fall, the line that forms most readily.

1 West Gully   300m   I * (1978)
This is the first obvious gully line in the mouth of the corrie, with a steep right wall and bounding the left side of a terraced buttress. Normally banked up, it can be very icy in lean conditions.

2 Penelope Pitstop   300m   IV,5 (2001)
The right side of the terraced buttress (the left side is easy). Climb the icefall which forms centrally in the lowest tier and up the terrace above (45m). Move left and climb a short icefall, then go 10m left and up two grooves with a left step (50m). Gain the big terrace above and traverse right to near the right edge of the buttress. Climb tricky walls on this crest, then two easier pitches up the crest leading to easy snowslopes.

3 Spidean Way   300m   III * (1977)
The next gully line, left-slanting and formed between the first terraced buttress and a larger one in the back left corner of the corrie. Often two short steep pitches followed by a longer one, but the short pitches disappear under heavy snow.

4 Wacky Races   300m   III,5 (2000)
A route up the large rambling terraced buttress forms left of the snow gully of Way Up. Start at the base of the buttress and find the easiest line on turf or ice to reach

a barrier wall at half-height. Climb this fairly centrally (crux), then finish trending right.

5 Under Thirties Icefall   140m   IV,5   (1994)
An icefall on the left wall of Way Up, starting just above where some icicles hang down and just below Over Sixties Icefall on the opposite side. Slow to form. The large terraces are less spoiling than they look, as the ice takes a direct line. The first and crux pitch was steep ice (hidden from below behind two ice columns), the second mixed (the ice line being thin), the third a less steep wide icefall and the fourth an ice filled chimney.

**6 Way Up   250m   I **
The straightforward snow gully leading to the bealach on the main ridge. The grade does not vary with build-up, nor does it form a significant cornice.

The next four routes finish on a slope which is too low angled for avalanches so can provide a safe option in poor snow conditions, particularly if approached by the initial icefall of Umbrella Fall.

7 Over Sixties Icefall   100m   III *   (1994)
A shorter and more friendly route than others in the corrie. On the right wall of Way Up about halfway up is a lower angled icefall which is excellent when formed, but poor in some years. There are often two lines, a left-hand which is low in the grade and a right-hand up steeper pillars which is nearer Grade IV. The icefall leads in three pitches of largely continuous ice to a big terrace from where a rising traverse leads left to the ridge just above the col (and descent).

8 The Bender   150m   IV,4   (1999)
Climbs the leftmost icefall on the main face, virtually on the corner where the face bends round on to the gully wall of Way Up. The difficulties are short but useful as a second route, being accessible from the col by descending Way Up and traversing from 50m below the base of Over Sixties Icefall. Start below the icefall and climb easily to an iced corner which leads to the main icefall. Climb the icefall to a ledge at its top. Move left to slabby mixed ground leading to a big terrace. Finish easily by a choice of lines.

9 Round the Bend   150m   V,7   (1999)
Climbs an iced groove right of the icefall of The Bender (which is often prominent). Start up a series of shallow iced grooves parallel and right of The Bender to reach the main iced groove. Climb the groove to where it overhangs and the ice finishes. Step left and climb a shallow, parallel but less overhanging groove to a terrace. A Friend 0 was used for aid to clear snow from the exit (almost managed free). Finish up a chimney on the right, then a shorter chimney.

10 Hooded Claw   150m   IV,5 *   (1987)
The icefall towards the left edge of the main face and the next prominent ice line left of Umbrella Fall. Start from a long traverse left along the terrace above the first tier (or climb a line on the tier a bit to the right). The fine crux pitch follows a steep iced groove to an ice 'hood', bypassed on the right via a short icicle.

11 Umbrella Fall   230m   V,5 ***   (1984)
This is the largest and most obvious icefall on the face between Way Up and Poachers Fall. The crux pitch is much harder than the rest. It can be Grade IV with ideal ice formations, when a groove may form. Either start by a steep icefall on a ramp immediately right of Way Up or climb ice directly below the upper icefall to reach the first terrace. Trend right or straight up to below the main fall. The main fall steepens to its crux pitch. Often this forms a deep groove on the right of a pillar (sometimes with a big ice umbrella) which can be eased by bridging, or even chimneying. In leaner conditions a line left of the pillar may be easier. The final optional pitch is also quite steep, or escape left.

12 Snow Goose   230m   V,5 * (1986)
The left-hand thinner icefall and just right of Umbrella Fall. The line includes a pitch up the lowest tier. The ice is continuous over six tiers; the fourth a steep iced wall of a right-facing corner and the fifth tier (crux) a weave through two overhangs by a corner on the right and an icicle above.

13 The Deer Hunter   200m   V,6 ** (1986)
The middle of the thin ice lines left of The Salmon Leap. The line is obvious at mid-height as a thick ice cased right-facing corner. The first short bulging tier may be turned on the left. Again, the last tier is bare of ice and a short right traverse leads to a strenuous chimney with a difficult exit (crux).

14 White Tiger   220m   VI,6 ** (1987)
The nearest ice line to The Salmon Leap, and slow to form, but can form very thick, and then excellent. Vertical sections, but not too long, and with good belays and ledges. The first main tier, if not formed, can be avoided by a right traverse from an icy bay left of the main line. Four steep tiers lead to a final rock barrier. Follow a delicate right traverse into the final pitch of The Salmon Leap. The obvious direct finish has also been climbed in mixed conditions at technical 7.

15 The Salmon Leap   200m   VI,6 *** (1986)
This is the left side of Poachers Fall, separated in the top half by a rock rib. It has a short vertical section when ice conditions are average, but in prime conditions this can be avoided by a groove on the right, and then it may become easier than Poachers, which can form a big ice bulge at mid-height. Good rock belays on the left wall. The line finishes naturally up a left-slanting chimney-crack, but if the ice in this has thawed, finish on the right towards Poachers.
Variation: **VI,6** (1995)
Take a parallel icefall on the left of the lower half, rejoining the main route after its end.

16 Poachers Fall   180m   V,5 **** (1978)
Take the right side of the obvious steep wide icefall draining the middle of the back wall. The top section is in a deep groove right of the separating rib and is partially hidden on the approach to the corrie. The route comes into condition quickly and the top groove can be climbed even when thin. There is a good rock belay at the right end of a ledge between the two steepest sections and about 60m from the start; but at least one ice screw belay should be expected and most of the runners are ice screws.

17 Chinook   160m   VI,6 (2000)
Climbs the ice line which sometimes forms 15m right of Poachers; a good independent route.
1. 50m Climb icy grooves passing a big pedestal on the right to a cramped stance under an overlap.
2. 40m Swing on to an ice fringe at the lip and follow the slab corner above to belay in a dry corner left of an icicle.
3. 25m Climb the steep icicle and move right to block belays.
4. 55m Move 5m back left, climb iced rock, an ice corner and a mixed chimney to easy ground.

The face right of Poachers Fall forms two obvious icefalls draining down a very steep first tier, giving the crux of the climbs.

18 Fubarbundy   200m   VIII,7 *** (1994)
The obvious hanging icefall right of Poachers; it often stops at the lip of a roof 30m left of Test Department, but can form down the arete on its right. A free ascent is possible in the right conditions, but they have yet to be caught. Start beneath the roof.

COIRE DUBH MÒR 283

Poachers Fall, V,5, Coire Dubh Mòr, Liathach. Climber Grahame Nicoll

1. 35m Climb icy grooves trending right to belay in a small corner directly below a large left-facing corner (right of the one leading to the roof).
2. 30m Climb up to the large corner, followed for 6m, then tension left on to the hanging slab. Climb this on thin ice trending left above the large roof. The slab culminates at a small overhang; belay at its left side.
3. 30m Climb the icy groove to the left of the belay and continue up the icefall.
4. 40m Continue up the icefall trending right.
5. 45m Move right to the obvious buttress, move around its prow to belay below an icy groove.
6. Climb the groove, then easy broken ground to the top.

284 | LIATHACH

Test Department, VI,6, Coire Dubh Mòr, Liathach. Climber Andy Nisbet

19 Test Department   190m   VI,6 ***   (1987)
The second icefall right of Poachers, distinctive as forming two consecutive ice columns (but normally seen as hanging icicles). After a 20m pitch to gain them, climb the ice columns and steep ice above (50m). On the first ascent the lower icicle did not reach the ground so a start was made to the right and two aid pegs were used to gain a traverse line back to the icicle. Take the left-hand of two ice lines, then more easily up to the final wall (50m). Mixed icy ground trending slightly left, following a shallow groove almost directly above the lower pitches,

leads through a small niche to easy ground.
Variation: **70m VII,7** (1999)
A mixed finish up the final wall, trending right up thin slabby ground to a vague crest.

20 Brain Strain   180m   V,6 * (1991)
This takes a series of ice streaks in line with the first pitch of Brain Drain. Start up a shallow chimney-groove 15m right of Test Department (Brain Drain) – 45m. Trend slightly right to belay beneath a vertical ice smeared corner (30m). Climb the corner and continue to the next steep band (30m), which is climbed by an ice line just left of Brain Drain, or more easily further left (60m). Finish through the final tier (15m).
Variation: **The Stem   50m   VII,6** (1994)
Provides an independent start to Brain Strain. Climb the very steep and thinly iced corner immediately to the right of the shared initial chimney of Brain Drain and Brain Strain. Unrepeated but would have been VI,6 in the good conditions when the parallel icefall of Brainstorm was climbed.

21 Brain Drain   180m   V,5 * (1987)
The next main fall to the right, most obvious at mid-height, forms a thin bulging first pitch. This is avoided on the left by a hidden icy chimney-groove (crux), followed by a traverse right to join the main line. Continually interesting and varied climbing on ice leads in three or four pitches to easier ground.
Variation: **Brainstorm   50m   VI,6** (1999)
A direct start. The thin bulging pitch provides a steep icefall some 10m right of the chimney start and 6m right of The Stem.

22 The Temptress   220m   IV,5 (1988)
The rightmost icefall on the face, much less continuous than the others. A short steep introductory pitch leads to a steep shallow left-facing ice groove. Climb the groove (crux), step left into a shorter groove and go up to small walls (50m). Traverse left, then go up to a left-slanting icefall right of Brain Drain. Finish more easily.

23 Drumnadrookit   220m   V,6 * (2002)
The intended line of The Temptress, but the upper ice pitch doesn't always form. Climb the introductory pitch and the steep groove as for The Temptress. Step right and climb a long easier groove to bulging walls left of an impressive prow which sits high on the right side of the face. Ice forms through a slot about 20m left of the prow. Climb this finishing with a short overhanging section to a terrace. Traverse the terrace rightwards until above the prow and finish up the crest formed above it.

24 Sinister Prawn   230m   V,6 (2000)
This is on a rib left of the gully of George. Start at the base of George but move out left on fairly steep ice on to the rib. Climb a series of icy turfy grooves to the impressive prow. Pass this on the right via grooves and a final awkward short wall (which could be easier or harder depending on the amount of ice). Finish direct up mixed ground.

25 George   230m   III,4 *** (1967)
The steep back wall of the corrie finishes at a deep gash, the next feature left of the north ridge of Spidean; this is the line. Almost always in condition, even when lean, and both forks give short but technical difficulties. The first half of the gully is easy, sometimes with short ice pitches, but then it steepens and narrows. Here is the fork, the more obvious chimney on the left being the harder Sinister Prong. For the normal route, climb rightwards out of the gully on steepish ice. One can now crawl under a big chockstone to a narrow exit (looks improbable). Alternatively, climb over the top on ice (slightly harder unless there is a good

build-up). Climb right to left over an awkward bulge of jammed blocks, then finish up a shallow groove on the right to the crest of the north ridge. The summit of Liathach is easily visited and recommended from here. Alternatively, descend the north ridge (on which the route finishes), keeping left of the crest until a large snow shelf leads back into the base of George.

Variation: **Sinister Prong   IV,5 *****   *(1978)*

This takes the left fork of George below the steep upper section. Move left into the chimney at one of two possible places. There are two difficult bulging sections (both well protected) leading to the same belay as the normal route. Finish up the continuation line, a shallow groove which is recommended when iced. Otherwise, move right to finish up the final groove of the normal route. Grade III,5 in good conditions.

26 Georgina   80m   III   *(1998)*

A line going out diagonally right from the base of George on to the North Ridge of Spidean.

27 North Ridge of Spidean   150m   Moderate

Stick closely to the crest overlooking George to provide some tricky steps and good exposure. It is easy to walk off right in a few paces to steep grassy slopes which are the winter descent.

COIRE NA CAIME

Diagrams p287, 288, 294, 296

Walking west along the Coire Dubh path, this is the third, the most scenic and largest of the northern corries. Its relative remoteness ensures that it is less popular than the others and it will appeal to those who wish a day with a mountaineering atmosphere and an element of exploration. There is a bigger selection of lower grade routes but it lacks the steep icefalls of Coire Dubh Mòr.

Approach: 1. Leave the Coire Dubh path near the watershed as for Coire Dubh Mòr (p279) and skirt round under the north ridge of Spidean into the corrie. The exact height of approach depends on destination but all are bouldery unless there is hard snow. This takes 2hrs 30mins in good conditions but 3hrs is more normal. This is the easiest approach but returning to the car is much longer.

2. Recommended for Bell's Buttress and the Upper Corrie, perhaps for Am Fasarinen, is an approach over the top. Park between two woods, at the east end of the western wood and close to the river (NG 914 554). A path starts 10m east at a small cairn. It is indistinct at first over small crags but soon becomes a constructed path; the intention may be to construct it all the way to the road. Cross a deer fence by a stile and follow the path up a shallow valley before moving right to join the Allt a' Tuill Bhan. Continue as if heading for Mullach nan Rathain, but leave the path and climb direct up a shallow gully which leads towards a small top formed by Bell's Buttress (NG 916 576). For Bell's Buttress, descend the gully immediately to the west (this can be corniced) and turn right. For the Trinity Gullies, descend the gully but turn left as soon as possible into the base of the Upper Corrie. Alternatively, or if approaching from Mullach nan Rathain, descend the gully from the small col just east of Mullach (NG 912 576). Both gullies are Grade I and descending the wrong one means only some easy traversing.

3. Useful for Am Fasarinen and the east end of the corrie, this option is similar to number 2 but trends right on the final slopes (further right than appearances might suggest), and reaches the ridge near the west end of Am Fasarinen. The broad Gully 7 (easy Grade I and the cornice can be passed easily on the right) lies at a col (NG 921 574), before a 5m rise to a bump. After this the ridge starts to narrow and gently drops to another col (the top of Twisting Cully) ahead of a steep rise to Am Fasarinen. If the steep rise is reached, Gully 7 is 100m back.

Descent: See each section of the corrie.

LIATHACH - Coire na Caime

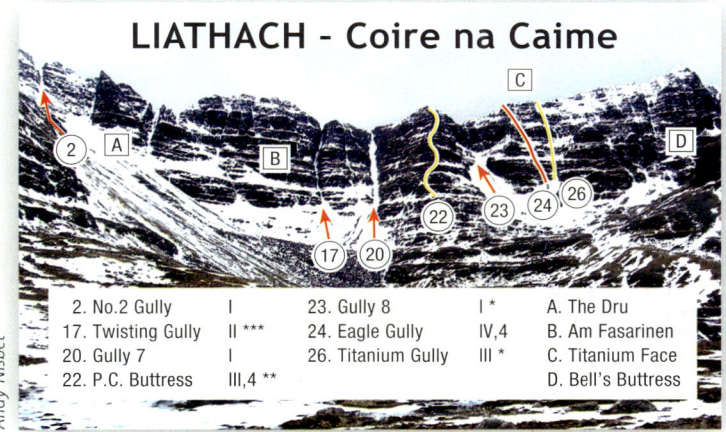

2. No.2 Gully	I	23. Gully 8	I *	A. The Dru	
17. Twisting Gully	II ***	24. Eagle Gully	IV,4	B. Am Fasarinen	
20. Gully 7	I	26. Titanium Gully	III *	C. Titanium Face	
22. P.C. Buttress	III,4 **			D. Bell's Buttress	

As the name may suggest, Coire na Caime, the 'crooked corrie' is more complicated than the typical bowl shape. Loch Coire na Caime lurks at the entrance, with Meall Dearg on the west and Spidean towering above to the east. The broad ridge of P.C. Buttress divides Coire na Caime leaving a small hanging bowl on the left enclosed by the Fasarinen Pinnacles and Am Fasarinen, and a larger three stepped corrie reaching high to the right, finishing in upper Coireag Cham overshadowed by Bell's Buttress, Mullach an Rathain and the Northern Pinnacles.

The routes are described from left to right, starting with the Fasarinen pinnacles and Am Fasarinen. The first two pinnacles have slabby faces which can hold ice and are flanked by easy gullies. The Dru is the third pinnacle, impressive from the ridge and the corrie (the triangular tower high up on the left from the loch).

The Pinnacles

(NG 926 577) Alt 800m North-West facing

Descent: This can be serious as there is no immediate descent to the south. The choice of direction may depend on the location of your transport. It may be best to traverse the ridge eastwards and go to the summit of Spidean. Descend from here as described for Coire Dubh Mòr. The last 30m below the summit can be traversed on the right to the top of Pyramid Buttress. Or go west over Am Fasarinen and descend as described for it (see p289).

1 No.1 Gully   100m   I
A straightforward snow slope running up the left side of the first pinnacle.

2 No.2 Gully   100m   I
The right-trending gully between the first and second pinnacles.

3 First Face   200m   III   *(1994)*
Climbs an obvious wide icefall in the centre of the First Pinnacle face. A start was made right of No.2 Gully up a huge sheet of ice below and right of the upper icefall and leading into No.2 Gully. A left traverse across the gully led to the upper icefall.

4 3rd Pinnacle Gully   120m   II   *(1955)*
The gully between the second and third pinnacles. After 75m, traverse left along a snow ledge into a subsidiary gully and climb this to the main ridge. The main gully, with a steep final pitch, is Grade III.

5 Dru   150m   Severe   (1959)
The third pinnacle forms a rocky tower, which, with a bit of imagination, might seem similar to the slightly bigger Chamonix mountain of the same name! From the lowest point of the pinnacle, climb into an open groove at 12m and move out left at 30m to a broad grassy ledge. Climb just left of a chimney-crack to a narrower ledge (20m). (This point can be reached by a long right traverse along the ledge from 30m up 3rd Pinnacle Gully, making it possible to climb the fine final arete at an overall grade of Very Difficult). Traverse 20m right then gain the top of a small detached needle from the right. Follow the narrow crest behind in a superb situation to easier ground and the top.

6 Dru Couloir   150m   V,6 **   (1986)
The left-slanting chimney-gully on the Dru Pinnacle. Start right of the foot of the pinnacle at a left-facing tapering corner, directly below the chimney-gully. Climb the corner to a ledge at 30m (crux). Gain the chimney-gully and follow it for 30m to a belay on the left. Continue in the same line to the bealach where the detached needle of the summer line abuts the summit ridge. Take the easiest line up the ridge to the top.

7 West Face of the Dru   140m   III,4   (1996)
As per title. Start below the steep lower tier, about 30m right of Dru Couloir, at the first easier break right of steep smooth walls. Step out right into a crack-line leading to turfy ledges. A short awkward corner on the left gains a turf terrace (25m, crux). Trend left to a shallow fault just right of the face's left bounding crest (45m). Climb the fault to the peak (20m, 50m).

Bordering the fourth pinnacle are two gullies which form a V.

8 4th Pinnacle Gully   120m   II
The left-hand gully usually has good but short ice pitches.

9 Gully 5   120m   I
A straightforward snow gully, the right-hand of the V.

10 Red Herring   140m   IV,4 *   (1995)
The buttress right of Gully 5. Start just right of the toe of the buttress, which is close to Gully 5. Climb a steep turfy groove until a narrow ledge leads left to the crest (30m). Climb a groove on the left leading to a pinnacle, its top gained by a narrow chimney. Belay just above (20m). Continue near the crest past a level section (45m). A shallow chimney on the right and the crest leads to the top (45m).

Next is the 5th pinnacle (as seen from the corrie) before the main ridge swings west over Am Fasarinen, forming the back wall of a small hanging corrie, which in turn is bounded on the right by P.C. Buttress. Between 5th Pinnacle and Am Fasarinen is an easy snow slope only defined in the top half and split by a rock rib at the top, Grade I.

Am Fasarinen

(NG 924 576)   Alt 750m   North facing   Map p273   Diagrams p287, 289
On close inspection Am Fasarinen sports five fine looking thin ice lines, the middle three being the most obvious chimney gullies directly under the summit. Of these three, the left one (Jerbil) is the deepest, the middle one (The Andes Couloir) is essentially a right-facing corner and the right one (Echo Couloir) is only defined in its upper part.

Descent: Quickest is to traverse the ridge westwards to a col where the ground opens out to a level area (top of Gully 7). Descent south-west on steepening slopes to reach the Allt a' Tuill Bhàn. Descend the path If there is a good build-up, go south-south-west from the col to a gully at NG 921 573 which runs south-west towards the Allt a' Tuill Bhàn (not just east of south, crucial!). This is a very quick descent if conditions are favourable for glissading, but take great care as there are drops below chockstones into which one could fall in lean or thawing conditions. It is unusual to be able to glissade all the way to easy ground but one can escape out right lower down.

11 Forking Gully   160m   IV,4   (1995)
This is the left-slanting gully which starts from the snow bay of Jerbil.
1. 45m Climb the left-slanting gully to the first terrace.
2. 30m Move left and climb the deep fault on the left side of the main depression.
4. 45m Above the gully forks. Climb the left fork on steep ice to reach easy ground and the next terrace. Move right to above the main fault. (With a good build-up it should be possible to climb the right fork which starts with a short step. This would probably make the climb Grade III.)
4. 40m Climb the very open turfy corner to a left-slanting fault leading to the ridge.

12 Jerbil   120m   V,5 **   (1985)
The deepest and often iciest of the gullies is steep. Start in a high snow bay shared by a left-slanting gully. Climb a steep ice pitch leading to a small snow amphitheatre in the deep gully (45m). Continue in the same line avoiding difficult obstacles on the left or right as necessary to an easy bay leading to the main ridge.

13 The Andes Couloir   180m   V,5 **   (1986)
A steep start up an ice curtain, quite slow to form, leads to a snow ledge under a steep iced corner. Pull into the corner over a strenuous bulge (where the ice may be thin) and take the superb right-facing ice corner above to an easing below the main ridge.

14 Echo Couloir   250m   III **   (1993/1994)
This, the fourth ice line is seen (in good conditions) as a wide slabby icefall forming below a big final corner. Start up the initial gully below Andes Couloir, then trend diagonally right on mixed ice and turf to reach the slabby icefall. Climb this and the very obvious upper gully.
Variation: **Direct Start   V,6**   (1993)
The original ascent started more direct but is harder and the ice forms less readily. Climb two consecutive steep icefalls leading to the right side of the slabby icefall. Either climb the slabby icefall (if formed) or a right-facing turfy corner further right to gain the upper gully.

15 Toll Dubh Chimney   250m   V,5 *   (1987)
This route follows the left-trending chimney-line on the buttress 100m left of Twisting Gully; it is the furthest right of the five obvious chimney-lines. Climb to the foot of the deep icy chimney at one-third height in two pitches. On the first ascent, the chimney was overhung at the base and was climbed by a dry crack in the right wall until the ice was regained after 25m. The next pitch culminates in a short overhang after which difficulties eased. A good route.

16 The Shining Path   160m   IV,6 *   (1993)
A big icefall forms right of Toll Dubh Chimney to the left of the edge of Twisting Gully. Start just left of the gully at a slanting groove. Climb thin awkward ice up the groove, then trend more easily left up iced steps until a short steep ice corner leads to the foot of the main ice wall. The wall is normally split by a diagonal right-slanting weakness which gives a fine 40m pitch. Climb turfy corners above to the top.

17 Twisting Gully   200m   II ***   (1955)
The deep snow gully on the right of Am Fasarinen is very scenic, with lovely ice

formations. With a good build-up, it is easy except for a short steep ice pitch at two-thirds height. But it is perhaps a better choice when lean but frozen. Short easy ice pitches lead to the main pitch where there is a window through a screen of icicles making this crux pitch less steep.

18 Bannockburn   200m   IV,5 *(1987)*
Climbs the fine obvious line of icy chimneys and grooves up the middle of the buttress right of Twisting Gully, starting near the foot of the gully and moving out right on to the crest. The steep crack in the final rock band provides the crux.

19 Bannock Gully   150m   II *(1995)*
The well defined but easy gully right of Bannockburn. One ice pitch.

20 Gully 7   180m   I
The wide open couloir left of P.C. Buttress. Easy for the grade and the cornice is always passable on the left.

21 WPC Gully   120m   II *(1997)*
The shallow gully that runs from Gully 7 up the left side of P.C. Buttress to reach its crest at the final col.

22 P.C. Buttress   250m   Very Difficult *(1939)*
This is the terraced buttress bounding the west side of the small 'Fasarinen' corrie. The lower terraces are easy, but the upper section narrows and steepens where the route climbs to the right of centre up a precipitous tower to a small summit (some loose rock). Scrambling leads to the top. The grade assumes keeping to rock; the winter line is easier.
Winter: **III,4 ****
A fine mountaineering line, with some short tricky walls but not sustained. Start from the large platform on the lower part of the buttress. Climb an easy gully and move right to the crest. Thereafter, climb close to the crest, choosing the easiest line through each tier. Avoid tempting terraces leading away left. About half-height there is a 5m pinnacle on the crest. Climb up to the neck at its back (technical crux, but the devious may find a through route) and steeply above but soon becoming easier and leading to the small summit and subsequent col.

23 Gully 8   120m   I *
This easy snow gully starts high up at the top of a huge snow slope on the west side of P.C. Buttress, and finishes through a deep narrow section, steepest at the top. A good scenic gully, but disappointingly short considering the long approach.

Titanium Face

(NG 918 576)   Alt 750m   North facing   Diagrams p287, 294

West of P.C. Buttress and Gully 8 is this broad broken face cut by numerous shallow chimney lines. These can be filled with ice or partly bank out in snowy conditions. Although escapable on to the many terraces, this is not obvious during the routes and would often only lead to another chimney of similar standard. The face ends in a large buttress of more compact rock, Bell's Buttress, situated above the entrance to upper Coire na Caime and forming a small summit on the main ridge.

Descent: Head south down steep slopes perhaps picking up the gully which descends directly from the top of Bell's Buttress (Approach 2) and in ideal conditions provides a long glissade.

24 Eagle Gully   220m   IV,4 *(1995)*
The leftmost icy line on the face. Start 30m left of Titanium Gully at an icy depression. Climb this (50m, crux), then go straight up and climb the left-slanting gully to the top.

Titanium Gully, III, Coirie na Caime, Liathach. Climber Hamish Irvine

25 Titanium Buttress   200m   III *(1999)*
Go up snow to the start of Titanium Gully. Climb the buttress to the left in 2 pitches to reach snow and climb up to where Titanium Gully goes through the next buttress. Cross to the right and trend up right on snow to a gully which is sheltered by a rock buttress to its left. Climb the gully and belay on the left before the crest above is reached. Make a traverse right on to the buttress and then up to reach the snow slopes above in 2 pitches.

26 Titanium Gully   200m   III * *(1984)*
Towards the left end of the face and starting at a snow bay just above the lowest rocks is an obvious narrow ice line running virtually the height of the face. A good line in lean icy conditions, perhaps grade IV at the start, but it can fill up with snow and all but disappear.

27 Fat Man's Folly   250m   IV,5 * *(1993)*
In the centre of the face is a squat triangular buttress ending at half-height. This climb starts up a deep gully forming the right side of this buttress and slanting left, then breaks right to follow a slanting corner.

28 The Faultfinders   250m   IV,5 *(1994)*
Follows a shallow fault-line between the more obvious lines of Fat Man's Folly and

Valentine Buttress. Start below the twin chimneys of Valentine Buttress. Slant up left on mixed ground and climb a bulging ice wall (crux, may not form often) to gain the fault. Follow this to the top (may finish as for Fat Man's Folly).

29 Valentine Buttress   250m   IV,4 **   *(1987)*
A fine chimney-line in the buttress at the right end of the face, left of the couloir bounding the left side of the Bell's Buttress (Vanadium Couloir). Start 30m left of Vanadium Couloir at the top of a snow bay and take the right-hand of two chimneys close together. Climb the chimney line for about 100m, with unusual subterranean moves, until easier climbing leads out right onto the buttress. Follow a series of grooves up the rocks above leading to the ridge.

30 Vanadium Couloir   300m   III   *(1979)*
The obvious steep open gully line immediately left of Bell's Buttress, starting from the highest point of the snow bay. Trend right from the base, then go back left into the upper runnel (or if approaching from above, traverse under Bell's Buttress into the upper runnel). This has icy steps, but can be largely banked out in good conditions, when it becomes Grade II. There are no cornice problems, as the finish is near the top of Bell's Buttress.
Variation: **Direct Start   45m   IV,4**   *(1979)*
The obvious direct start is steep and good quality when formed, but this is rare these days.

Bell's Buttress

(NG 916 577)   Alt 750m   North facing   Diagrams p287, 294

Bell's Buttress is a high area of steep compact rock streaked with shallow chimney-gully lines on the left side and cut by two deep gullies on the more continuous right side; the left one is a cul-de-sac and the right one the line of Bell's Gully. All the routes merge into an easy finish up the upper crest. A snow terrace at the base of the routes can be gained from either end.

Descent: Head south down steep slopes to pick up the gully which descends directly from the top of Bell's Buttress (approach 2) and in ideal conditions provides a long glissade.

31 The Doctor's Ear   230m   IV,6   *(1995)*
Climbs the crest at the left edge of Bell's Buttress. Start about 10m left of Bell's Buttress Left Chimney below a narrow chimney. Climb the chimney to the terrace above the steep lower tier and move slightly right to a small bay round the corner from Left Chimney's block belay (30m). Climb a vague groove above to steep ground, then traverse right and go up another groove (40m). Turfy ground leads to a steep wall (25m). Climb a chimney formed by a distinct ear of rock (10m, crux). Finish easily up the crest to the top.

32 Bell's Buttress, Left Chimney   230m   IV,5 *   *(1987)*
A fine route taking the furthest left chimney-line on Bell's Buttress. Start up the left of a pair of chimneys and step into the right-hand one at 10m. Where it overhangs, climb out right and up the gully above to a huge block belay on the left (30m). Continue up the chimney-line to snow ledges, turning two blocking overhangs on the right (30m). Follow the gully on the right through several narrowings past a rightwards ramp at 45m, and continue in the same line to finish.

33 Bell's Left Buttress   230m   IV,4   *(1996)*
The buttress between Left Chimney and Cube's Chimney. The same start was used as for Bell's Right Buttress i.e. the initial chimney of Last Orders followed by a (longer) traverse left to the buttress. A left-slanting line gained a higher terrace. A slabby corner on the left side of the buttress led to a flaky chimney and terrace above (45m). A short chimney on the right led to the easier upper section.

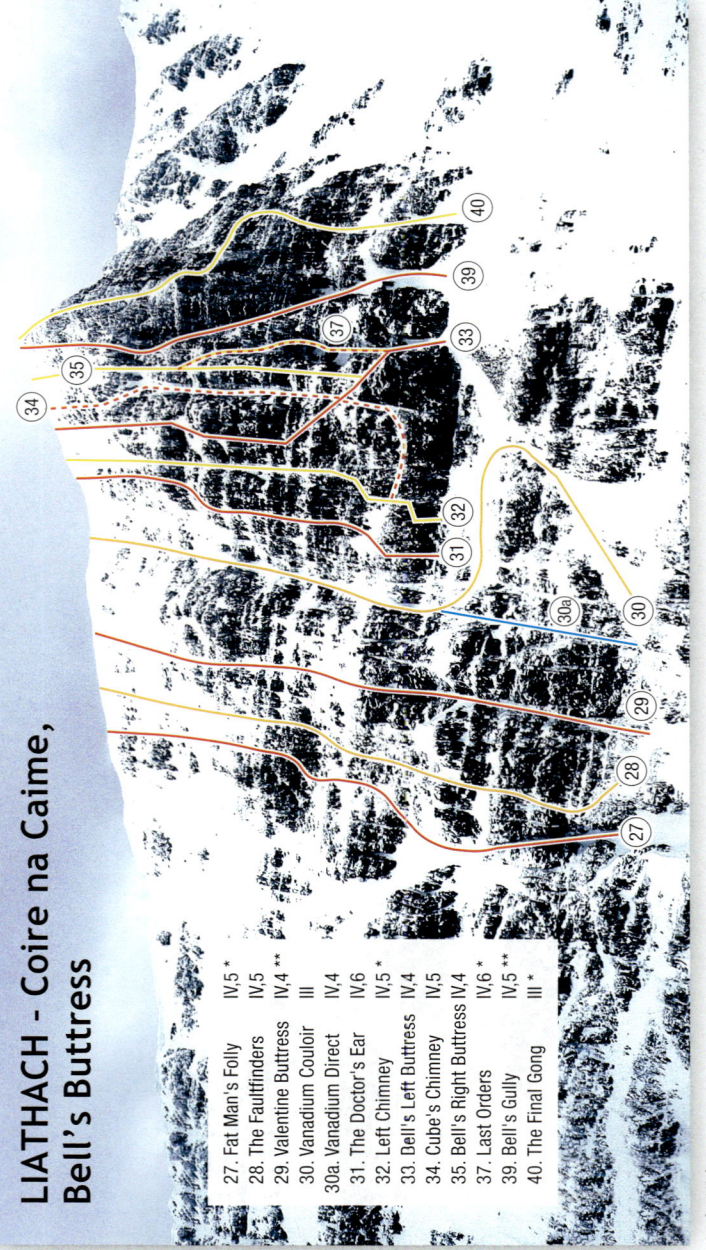

LIATHACH - Coire na Caime, Bell's Buttress

27. Fat Man's Folly IV,5 *
28. The Faultfinders IV,5
29. Valentine Buttress IV,4 **
30. Vanadium Couloir III
30a. Vanadium Direct IV,4
31. The Doctor's Ear IV,6
32. Left Chimney IV,5 *
33. Bell's Left Buttress IV,4
34. Cube's Chimney IV,5
35. Bell's Right Buttress IV,4
37. Last Orders IV,6 *
39. Bell's Gully IV,5 **
40. The Final Gong III *

Andy Nisbet

COIRE NA CAIME 295

34 Cube's Chimney   280m   IV,5 *(1994)*
The central chimney on Bell's Buttress, which fails to reach the base of the cliff, despite the attempts of an icicle to bridge the 10m gap. Start up Left Chimney, then take a traverse line right on diminishing ledges to gain the central chimney just above the icicle. Starting steeply, then easing, the ice-choked chimney gives superb climbing to the buttress top.

35 Bell's Right Buttress   230m   IV,4 *(1995)*
This climbs the buttress between Cube's Chimney and Last Orders. This seems the most likely buttress to have been climbed by the Bells. The very steep first tier was passed by starting easily up Last Orders and moving left. The crest was followed for two pitches before the route merged with Campanology for a final chimney pitch on the right of an isolated tower.

36 Bell's Buttress   150m   Severe *(1947)*
Climb "the left-hand narrow buttress in the middle of the face" in three pitches. Scrambling then leads to the top. The left buttress looks better rock, but is overhanging to start. Perhaps the start was up the right buttress (still looks hard), later transferring to the left.

37 Last Orders   230m   IV,6 * *(1993)*
This is the left-hand of two gully lines on the right side of Bell's Buttress, blocked by a huge roof.
1. 40m Climb easy snow.
2. 40m Climb two icy steepenings to below the large roof, then move right and climb the right wall via difficult moves to reach a crack above the overhang. Move back left into the main gully line and continue to a belay.
3, 4 and 5. 150m The gully gradually eases, and after 20m gives straightforward climbing to the top.

38 Campanology   230m   IV,6 *(1995)*
Climbs the buttress between Last Orders and Bell's Gully. Start above the first steep tier, passed by the easy start to Bell's Gully. Climb a fault just right of the crest, moving on to the crest higher up.

39 Bell's Gully   230m   IV,5 ** *(1986)*
The right-hand and most obvious of the two gully lines on the right side of Bell's Buttress. Follow the increasingly difficult gully over two steepenings to a cul-de-sac at 125m. A dribble of ice may flow down from the upper gully but it looks reasonable without. Move left and take the shallow gully above to easy ground.

40 The Final Gong   200m   III * *(1995)*
A good easier route up the terminal buttress right of Bell's Gully. Start up an easy chimney in the lower tier, then trend slightly right to avoid slabby ground on the left. Return left to the crest between two steep tiers, climb the second, then a right-facing corner and continuing line to easy ground.

Upper Corrie

Map p273   Diagram p287, 296

The upper corrie of Coire na Caime, Coireag Cham, feels almost alpine. It is guarded on the left by Bell's Buttress and on the right by the spectacular Northern Pinnacles of Mullach an Rathain, rising from the outrider of Meall Dearg. Mullach an Rathain itself tops the back of the corrie. Since this corrie is high and sheltered it seems to come into condition sooner and holds snow longer than elsewhere on the mountain. The wide snow slope leading up to the col just west of Bell's Buttress or the col just east of Mullach an Rathain may each be used as a short Grade I descent or ascent to the main ridge.

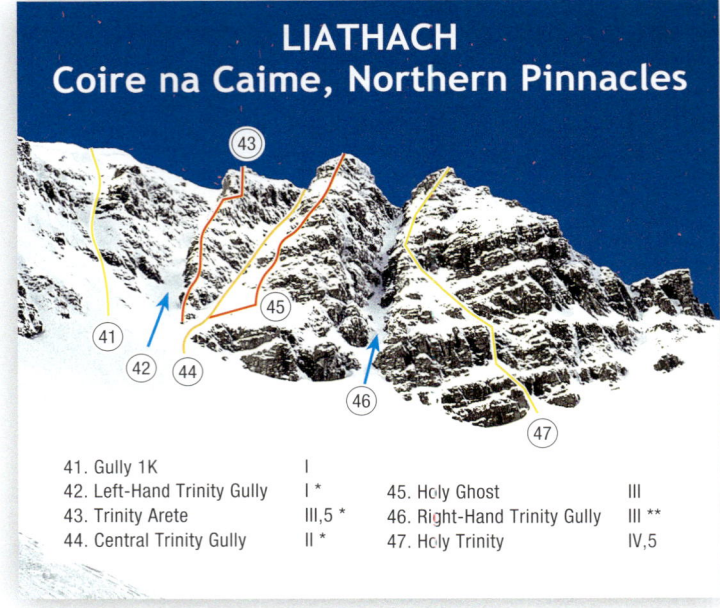

LIATHACH
Coire na Caime, Northern Pinnacles

41. Gully 1K	I
42. Left-Hand Trinity Gully	I *
43. Trinity Arete	III,5 *
44. Central Trinity Gully	II *
45. Holy Ghost	III
46. Right-Hand Trinity Gully	III **
47. Holy Trinity	IV,5

Andy Nisbet

Descent: From the top of Mullach an Rathain, descend by the normal hillwalkers' route, probably down the gully heading south from the summit to the Allt a' Tuill Bhàn.

41 Gully 1K   120m   I   *(1928)*
The shallow snow scoop, not quite a gully, leading to the main ridge immediately east of the summit of Mullach an Rathain. Start from the highest point of snow at the back of the corrie.

Northern Pinnacles

(NG 913 578)   Alt 850m   East facing   Diagram p296

These are numbered ascending from right to left, One to Five. The gullies between the top pinnacles provide good winter routes.

42 Left-Hand Trinity Gully   90m   I *   *(1928)*
The gully between the fifth pinnacle and Mullach an Rathain. Usually snow but icy in lean conditions.

43 Trinity Arete   110m   III,5 *   *(1996)*
Climbs the sharp crested buttress between Left-Hand and Central Trinity Gullies. Very helpful and well protected when necessary. Starting at the very toe, the first pitch held a barrier wall climbed by a central thin crack (crux) and higher up a steep shallow corner (40m). The easier crest (50m) led to an overhanging rock nose passed by the first groove on the right (20m).

44 Central Trinity Gully   105m   II *   *(1955)*
The gully between the fourth and fifth pinnacles normally gives two ice pitches, but can bank out to Grade I.

45 Holy Ghost   150m   III   (1996)
Climbs the buttress between Central and Right-Hand Trinity Gullies. Start on the left side of the buttress, next to the base of Central Trinity Gully. Traverse a ledge horizontally rightwards to the centre of the buttress, then go diagonally left to a barrier wall (50m). Pass this on the left and return right to a vague groove line. Follow the groove line for two pitches, then finish up the final crest over several small pinnacles.

**46 Right-Hand Trinity Gully   120m   III **   (1955)
This lies between the third and fourth pinnacles. It is usually the best and most difficult of the Trinity gullies.

47 Holy Trinity   150m   IV,5   (1990)
The obvious chimney-flake and left-slanting ramp-line up the front face of the Third Pinnacle. Start in the middle of the buttress and climb the chimney-line for 90m to the edge overlooking Right-Hand Trinity Gully. Climb the crest, turning a steepening on the left.

MEALL DEARG

(NG 916 582)   Alt 620m   North facing   Map p273   Diagrams p297, 298

Meall Dearg, the right-hand 'gatepost' to the entrance of Coire na Caime, has a steep north face. A combination of a route here followed by the Northern Pinnacles in a circuit from the Beinn Alligin car park makes a fine long mountaineering day.

Approach: While it is possible to approach from the Coire Dubh car park, a much more enjoyable circuit is provided by starting from the Beinn Alligin car park and via the Coire Mhic Nòbuil path. Cross the first bridge as for the Beinn Alligin approach but turn right very soon (cairn) and continue round the back of Liathach. Cross the Abhainn Coire Mhic Nòbuil (no bridge!) and angle up to below the cliff. The first route, however, starts just inside Coire na Caime.

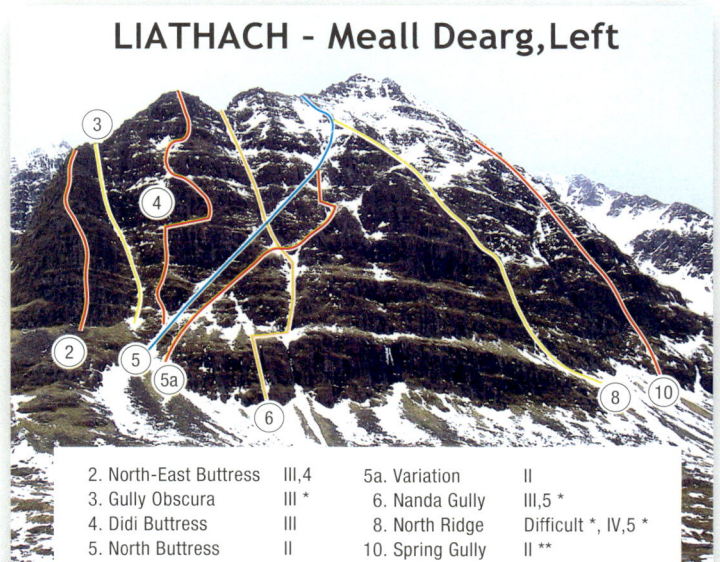

LIATHACH – Meall Dearg, Left

2. North-East Buttress	III,4	5a. Variation	II
3. Gully Obscura	III *	6. Nanda Gully	III,5 *
4. Didi Buttress	III	8. North Ridge	Difficult *, IV,5 *
5. North Buttress	II	10. Spring Gully	II **

Andy Nisbet

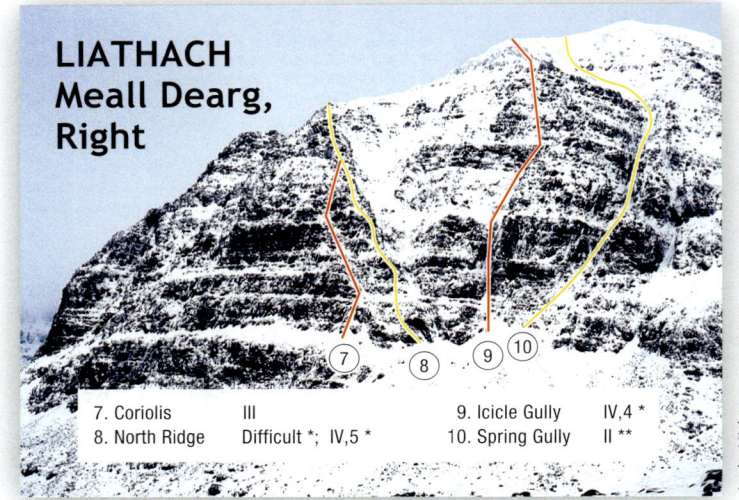

LIATHACH
Meall Dearg,
Right

7. Coriolis	III	
8. North Ridge	Difficult *; IV,5 *	
9. Icicle Gully	IV,4 *	
10. Spring Gully	II **	

Descent: It is highly recommended to continue to the top of Meall Dearg, then continue up the Northern Pinnacles to Mullach an Rathain (Grade II, Route 11). From here, descend westwards past Sgòrr a' Chadail, keeping to the crest of the ridge, easy apart from one short steep section, until heathery slopes, then a wooded stream lead to the road about 200m east of the car park.

1 Terminal Buttress 180m III * (1986)

This is the line of least resistance up the crest of the conical buttress at the base of the east ridge of Meall Dearg, at the left end of the north face. Start in a bay on the left side of the east facing buttress (just inside the corrie). Climb a snowy depression up and left until a line can be taken back right to a shoulder on the ridge (100m). Interesting climbing leads up walls, towers and terraces to the top.

2 North-East Buttress 200m III,4 (1992)

This buttress forms the left wall of Gully Obscura and provides good climbing up some steep walls on the crest. Start near the foot of the gully. Details unsure.

3 Gully Obscura 200m III * (1999)

The leftmost gully on the north face starting at the same point as the two diagonal shelves of North Buttress but going straight up to join Terminal Buttress at the shoulder on the crest leading up to Meall Dearg. The steepest pitch was climbed by the leftmost chimney close against the left wall, returning right to the main line immediately above.

4 Didi Buttress 250m III (2001)

The buttress between the two well defined gullies at this end of the face and above the start of the ramps of North Buttress. Start at the lowest point of the buttress, close to Gully Obscura. Climb a groove system to a steep band. Traverse right along a ledge to an easing in the steep band and climb shallow grooves to its top. Traverse back left to the original groove and follow it to a steep tier near the top. Move right to a crest and zigzag up to the crest of Meall Dearg.

5 North Buttress 200m Easy

Starting at the left end of the North Face below the first gully, this route follows the lower of two right-slanting diagonal shelves crossing the face to join the easy top

section of the skyline North Ridge. An easy scramble, unless you dislike grass.
Winter: **II**
The upper of the two shelves gives a better and more direct line; the lower is very easy to start but you have to gain the line of the upper at its end.

6 Nanda Gully   250m   III,5 * (2001)
A long and fairly well defined gully right of Gully Obscura and crossing the two diagonal shelves. The first pitch is usually insufficiently iced so start by climbing a turfy groove 10m to the left to reach the first shelf. Cross this, gain the gully and follow it throughout, all straightforward except for a short vertical pitch which was passed by climbing the corner on its immediate left (although the pitch itself might have been easier). The gully continues to the crest of Meall Dearg.

7 Coriolis   250m   III (2000)
The face to the right holds a left-slanting ridge with several rocky tiers (North Ridge). Gain and climb a turfy groove left of the ridge. Where this peters out, climb steep turf direct to the final tier of the ridge. Climb this on the crest, then continue up the easier upper crest to reach the east ridge of Meall Dearg.

8 North Ridge   250m   Difficult *
The best rock climb to the top of Meall Dearg, although with some loose rock and vegetation. Slippery in the wet. Start in the middle of the north face, just left of a small left-slanting watercourse which widens with height, and climb a narrow left-slanting blunt ridge through several tiers. The third tier is the best, steep but juggy. Previously called North Flank.
Winter: **IV,5 *** (2000)
A pleasant route keeping to the crest as closely as possible. Easily escapable but the line feels natural. The third tier is the crux, with some thin moves.

9 Icicle Gully   280m   IV,4 * (1996)
The shallow watercourse forming a gully right of North Ridge and two other gullies to its right form a diverging set of three; this route is the central one. It is well defined to half-height, where it bends right and peters out on to mixed ground. The third pitch is the crux by far, involving 15m of 75 degree ice, so perhaps low in the grade.

10 Spring Gully   300m   II ** (1996)
The right-hand of the set of three, initially shallow then deepening, contains several short ice pitches. The gully combines well with the Northern Pinnacles in a circuit from the Beinn Alligin (Coire Mhic Nobuil) car park and makes a three star outing when the gully is in good condition.

11 The Northern Pinnacles   200m   Moderate * (1894)
The rock is somewhat shattered and muddy but nevertheless an enjoyable ridge. The line is the same as in winter (see below). Not recommended as a descent to Meall Dearg from Mullach an Rathain; it is quicker to head east and descend the second scree gully into Coire na Caime, traverse under the Trident gullies and climb to the col at the base of the Pinnacles. Return up the Pinnacles.
Winter: **II **** (1900)
Short and sharp, the Northern Pinnacles guard the north ridge of Mullach an Rathain. Combined with a west to east traverse of Liathach's main ridge, this gives one of Scotland's finest winter round trips. With this in mind, approach via the Coire Dubh Mòr path from the National Trust car park to the base of Meall Dearg (2 to 3hrs), with ascent via the northern corries. An ascent of Meall Dearg by North Buttress (or even Terminal Buttress) seems appropriate, but Meall Dearg can be bypassed by entering upper Coire na Caime (Coireag Cham), from where a short Grade I leads to the col between Meall Dearg and the first pinnacle. The shortest approach from the west (Beinn Alligin car park and via the Coire Mhic Nòbuil path) is up the north-west flank of Meall Dearg leading into a narrow gully, a short but rather steep Grade I, and so to the col before the first pinnacle.

There are five pinnacles in all; the first two are small and can be passed on the right (appearing to be one), the third has the longest ascent including a tricky chimney just left of the crest, and the fourth is perhaps the crux (either by flakes on the left or a chimney on the right). The fifth is passed on the right; a tempting direct line on the left has a boulder problem finish, Grade III.

GLAS TOLL BOTHAIN

(NG 911578)   Alt 850m   North-East facing

A corrie immediately to the north and below the summit of Mullach an Rathain.

Pearl Ridge   150m   II/III   *(2004)*
A prominent ridge is present on the right of the corrie. The route follows this ridge until it merges into the final summit slopes of Mullach an Rathain. Difficulties can often be avoided on the right to give consistent Grade II climbing but the ridge becomes better defined in the upper half.

COIREAG DHEARG

(NG 906 578)   Alt 730m   North facing

This corrie may bank out after heavy snow.

Boxing Day Romp   100m   II   *(2004)*
Two easy gullies split the left side of the back wall of the corrie This route follows the right rib of the right gully. It is straightforward but with a steep finish if taken direct.

Liathach - South side

In comparison to the northern corries, the south side of Liathach offers fewer climbs despite its continuous steepness. The Glen Torridon glacier has scraped and plucked the south side relatively smooth, leaving only one small hanging corrie, Coire Liath Mhòr east of Spidean a' Choire Lèith, and very little in the form of continuous gullies. The rock tends to be terraced and vegetatious. In winter, the sun will quickly affect the icefalls that regularly form, particularly later in the season. The climbs are described from west to east.

SGÒRR A' CHADAIL

(NG 887 578)   Alt 630m   South-West to South facing   Map p273
Diagram p301

The crag is at the very west end of Liathach, overlooking Loch Torridon and offers the only good rock climbing high on the mountain. At 60m the crag is not as big as would appear from below and perhaps too much effort for those who don't appreciate the sunny and spectacular outlook over Loch Torridon (although as good as the sandstone crags nearer the road).

Approach: Start just above the hairpins on the Beinn Alligin road and flog up steep grass and heather to the crag. A gentler approach is from the Beinn Alligin car park followed by a traverse under the crag.

Descent: Reverse the approach.

1 Trench Foot   40m   E1 5b   *(1993)*
Towards its left side, the crag has a wide square-cut slot with a sharp right arete. About 10m to the right is a deep left-facing V-groove which leads into a crack-line. The route climbs the deep V-groove and its right arete, then the continuing crack-line.

2 Reflections of my Mind   50m   E2 ***   *(1993)*

LIATHACH
Sgòrr a' Chadail

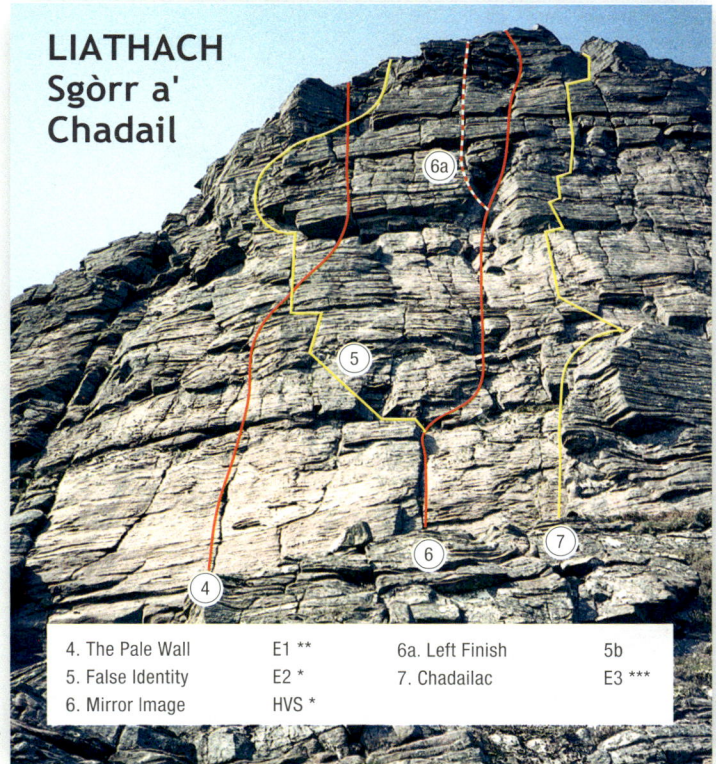

4. The Pale Wall	E1 **	6a. Left Finish	5b
5. False Identity	E2 *	7. Chadailac	E3 ***
6. Mirror Image	HVS *		

Climbs a blunt cracked nose a further 12m right where the crag changes aspect from south-west to south. Start just right of the crest.
1. 25m 5c Climb an overhanging groove (crux). Traverse awkwardly left into the base of a left-facing corner on the left side of the crest. Climb the corner to a ledge. A very sustained pitch with excellent protection.
2. 25m 5a Continue up the corner-line to easier ground.

Continuing right is a steep section with blocky overhangs and discontinuous corners. After about 50m the crag changes aspect again to a south-east facing cleaner wall with a light coloured square wall low down. This pale wall is the most distinctive feature from the road and above it is a 10m long blocky roof. Near its left edge is a line of flakes which continues on to near the top.

3 Reflection Wall   60m   Very Difficult * (1952)
The line of flakes forming the left edge of the pale section of wall.

4 The Pale Wall   60m   E1 ** (1993)
Takes a crack-line through the centre of the pale wall right of Reflection Wall.
1. 30m 5b Climb the crack (second from the left) and its continuation to below a crack in the blocky roof.
2. 30m 5b Climb the roof-crack and up into a recess. Go up the crack at its back (the right arete looks equally possible) and on up to easy ground.

302 LIATHACH

5 False Identity 60m E2 * *(2005)*
This route starts in a shallow right-facing corner-crack defining the right edge of the pale wall. It takes a rising diagonal line leftwards to cross The Pale Wall before climbing a left-facing overhanging groove marking the left edge of the blocky roof.
1. 35m 5c Climb the initial corner to a break, then pull across leftwards and up into a small recess. Pull up and left out of the recess and step delicately leftwards to another crack (crux). Follow cracks up and left, crossing The Pale Wall, to the overhanging groove. Climb the groove up into The Pale Wall recess above.
2. 25m 4b Finish out of the recess as for The Pale Wall.

6 Mirror Image 60m HVS * *(1993)*
This route starts as for False Identity but continues straight up following crack systems into an overhung groove with two exit cracks.
1. 40m 5a Follow the crack system into the overhung groove. Take the right-hand exit and on up cracks to a big ledge. The left-hand exit crack is 5b.
2. 20m Finish up blocky walls.

7 Chadailac 65m E3 * *(2005)*
To the right of the Mirror Image exit cracks on the upper wall are two more cracks. This route aims for the left-hand of these cracks and is reached by an unlikely direct line linking a series of short cracks and horizontal breaks. Start right of False Identity/Mirror Image in an easy left-facing corner.
1. 40m 5c Climb easily up the left-facing corner for 10m and step rightwards onto the wall above below two stepped overlaps. Pull back left between the overlaps aiming for two side by side cracks. Climb these then rightwards into a break. Pull through onto the next wall and another break. Find the perfect two finger pocket in the next thin crack and use this to reach the next break (crux) and continue to below the steep final crack. Commit to this excellent finale to a great pitch.
2. 25m 4c Climb a big final groove.

PYRAMID BUTTRESS

(NG 932 577) Alt 800m South-East facing Map p273 Diagram p303

This is the shapely buttress easily seen from the road, that terminates the short south-east ridge of Spidean a' Choire Lèith.

Approach: From the car park at NG 935 566, follow the path on the right of the Allt an Doire Ghairbh to an easing at 370m. Cross the Allt climb a slight gully trending left and deepening to reach a plateau right of the crag. Make a leftward traverse to the buttress. This is largely reversing the descent from Coire Dubh Mòr.

Descent: The summit is optional but nearby. Return to the plateau and reverse the approach.

There are two main icefalls split by a tapering rocky rib. These are well seen from the road, the left icefall being wide while the right one is narrow. Although the ice forms readily, the buttress faces due south and is seriously affected by the sun. Even early in the season it may not be a good choice on a sunny day and is rarely in condition in March.

1 Pyramid Left Icefall 180m V,5 ** *(1986/1987)*
The wide left-hand icefall has a steep second pitch. There can be a choice of vertical icicles here; the choice and difficulty will depend on the precise formation, which will always be spectacular. Easier ice leads to an interesting final mixed section.

2 Pyramid Right Icefall 180m V,4 * *(1977)*
The right-hand icefall is sustained and serious with little protection, but is never too steep. For an easier route (IV,4), or if the direct line is not complete, avoid the steep initial section by moving out on to the central rib for a pitch (as on the first ascent).

LIATHACH
South Side

Pyramid Buttress

1. Pyramid Left Icefall	V,5 **	
2. Pyramid Right Icefall	V,4 *	
3. Busman's Holiday	V,5 *	
4. Pyramid Right Edge	III *	
5. Pottering About	II	
6. The Tight One	IV,5	
7. Spidean's Sting	III,4	
8. The Potter's Apprentices	IV,4 *	
9. Toll Gate West	II *	
10. Salvation	VI,7	
11. Soul-Searcher	IV,5	
12. The Sneak	V,6 **	
13. Toll Gate East	II **	
d. descent		

Rab Anderson

304 LIATHACH

Pyramid Left Icefall, V,5, Pyramid Buttress, Liathach. Climber Graeme Ettle   John Lyall

3 Busman's Holiday   120m   V,5 *   (1995)
The icefall in the depression between Pyramid Right Icefall and Pyramid Right Edge. Steep thick ice left of the depression corner (45m), the continuation in the corner on thinner ice (35m), then a thinly iced corner and right traverse into the finishing gully of Pyramid Right Edge, entering it lower than the latter (50m).

4 Pyramid Right Edge   180m   III *   (Early 1980s)
Follow the right ridge of the buttress, starting up a groove with a steep finish. Further turfy grooves lead logically up the crest to a final barrier which forces a traverse left into an easy finishing gully.

COIRE LIATH MHÒR - TOLL A' MEITHEACH

(NG 936 579)   Alt 700m   South-East facing   Map p273

The backwall of this hanging corrie east of Pyramid Buttress comprises steep tiers sporting cascades of ice in numerous short steep drops. The approach and descent are by the path, as for Pyramid Buttress. On either side of the backwall are prominent gullies, Toll Gates West and East. At the top left of the backwall, between Toll Gate West and a snow gully to its left (the common descent gully, the opposite side of Way Up) is a buttress with four routes.

5 Pottering About   60m   II   (1996)
Climbs the icefall on the left of the buttress, finishing up corners. Start just right of the descent gully.

6 The Tight One   60m   IV,5   (1997)
Climbs the recessed cleft 20m left of Spidean's Sting, the most obvious line towards the left of the crag. Start with an off-width crack, then up to the cleft. Climb its left side, then traverse right and finish up a clean-cut narrow chimney topped with a chockstone.

7 Spidean's Sting   70m   III,4   (1995)
There is a prominent chimney in the centre. The chimney was climbed to a capstone. The traverse out right below it to a shelf and subsequent short steep wall was the crux.

8 The Potter's Apprentices   80m   IV,4   (1996)
This route goes up grooves right of centre of the buttress. It starts 5m right of a roof low on the buttress and about 30m right of Spidean's Sting. Climb the shallow gully direct, steeper than it looks, make delicate moves through a steep chimney to a terrace (45m). Trend right through steep mixed ground, finishing up a chimney (35m).

9 Toll Gate West   200m   II *
The left-hand of the deep gullies splitting the backwall.

10 Salvation   55m   VI,7   (1987)
An impressive icefall can form down the centre of the lower tier, rarely if ever reaching ground level. Levitate past the gap onto the steep ice screen above, which leads right to a stepped corner-line (25m). Climb the corner and the icefall left of a cave above, leftwards onto the big terrace above the first tier. Abseil descent.

11 Soul-Searcher   210m   IV,5   (1987)
Climb the central scoop line in the bottom tier, which is right of Salvation, trending slightly right, then go diagonally right on easy angled ice for 25m to an icy groove-chimney in the next tier. A good steep pitch up the chimney leads to easier climbing in the same chimney-line and onto snowfields below the main ridge.

12 The Sneak   90m   V,6 **   (1994)
The retiring icefall which forms up the left wall of Toll Gate East and which can look incomplete from below. There are three steep ice pitches, particularly the third, with big belay ledges and good rock belays between.

13 Toll Gate East   200m   II **
The right-hand of the prominent gullies bordering the steepest part of the backwall, and the deeper of the two. A fine route with spectacular scenery which forms a lot of ice and can be Grade III unless built up with snow.

STÙC A' CHOIRE DHUIBH BHIG - SOUTH

Map p273

On the south-east flank of the small top just west of Stùc a' Choire Dhuibh Bhig, are two obvious gullies. These, and routes further east, are approached direct from the road or the Coire Dubh path.

14 Gully 1A   180m   IV,4   (1979)
The westerly of the two obvious gullies, with a dog-leg to the right at mid-height. Innocuous looking, but concentrated difficulties in the first 60m when not banked out!

306 | BEINN EIGHE

15 Hidden Buttress   160m   II/III   *(1985)*
Climb the buttress left of Gully 1A, following a shallow depression over numerous icy steps.

16 Gully 2A   180m   III   *(Early 1980s)*
The right-hand of the two prominent gullies usually has one long steep ice pitch low down.

The terraced buttress right of Gully 2A maintains its height circling Stùc a' Choire Dhuibh Bhig, until it reaches a wide easy gully broadening at the top. Right of this again, the crag shortens towards Stringless Gully and Triceratops.

17 Snow White   200m   IV,4   *(1987)*
The major icefall between Gully 2A and the easy gully to the right. Starting from the lowest tier, the icefall widens and steepens at mid-height. It is clearly visible from the Coire Dubh car park.

The next routes are visible from the path high up on a short band of rock ringing the east buttress of Stùc a' Choire Dhuibh Bhig. Descend by walking right above the band of cliffs and down the ridge.

18 Stringless Gully   150m   I/II   *(1976)*
This is the first obvious steep sided deep gully approximately 200m left of the right-bounding ridge.

19 Triceratops   90m   Very Difficult   *(1970)*
This route follows the right ridge of Stringless Gully. Start at the lowest point of the ridge, turn the first of three pinnacles on the right and climb the other two direct to the top.

20 Fairy Queen   80m   IV,5   *(1987)*
An obvious icefall forms in a bay some 30m right of Stringless Gully. It is climbed in two fine steep pitches; the first an ice cased corner and the second with devious climbing up an icicle clinging to the headwall. Move right to finish.

BEINN EIGHE

Maps p194, 307

An extensive ridge of mostly quartzite with many peaks, two Munros and three big corries on its north side. All the climbing is in these corries, but the approach is easiest from Glen Torridon to the south. The highest peak is Ruadh-stac Mòr (NG 951 611, 1010m), which along with Coinnich Mhòr (NG 944 600, 976m) at the head and Sàil Mhòr (NG 938 605, 980m) at the west end, form the magnificent cirque of Coire Mhic Fhearchair. The next corrie, Coire Ruadh-staca, is formed between Ruadh-stac Mòr and Ruadh-stac Beag, with the second Munro, Spidean Coire nan Clach (NG 966 597, 993m) at its head. The third corrie is formed between Spidean Coire nan Clach and the east end of the ridge, with Sgùrr Bàn (NG 974 600, 970m) and Sgùrr nan Fhir Duibhe (NG 981 600, 963m) round its head.

COIRE MHIC FHEARCHAIR

(NG 945 605)   Maps p194, 307

Coire Mhic Fhearchair is one of the finest corries in Scotland and is justly famous for its magnificent Triple Buttresses. Secluded from the road by a relatively long approach, they dominate the lonely corrie and offer routes of great length and character. Some of the climbs here, both summer and winter, compare with the best available anywhere in Britain.

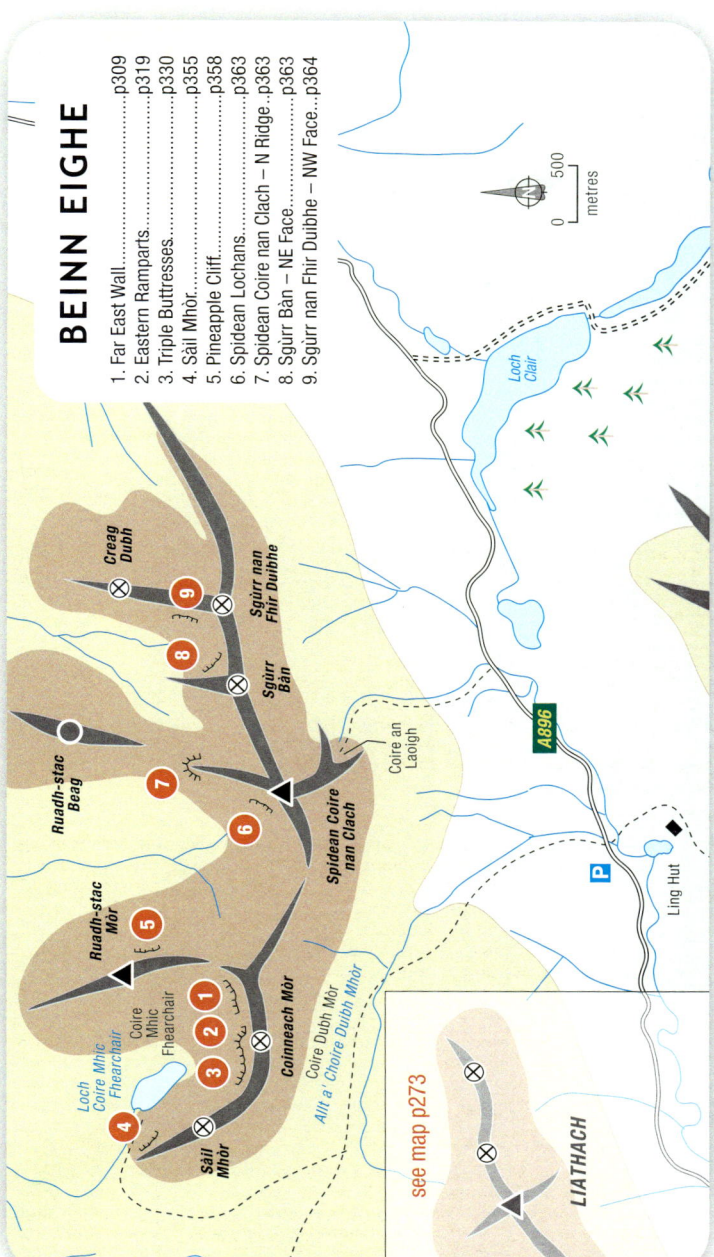

In winter the corrie is a paradise for modern style mixed climbing, and comes into condition very quickly. The steep blocky quartzite provides good axe placements, reliable protection and sensational lines. There is less reliance on frozen turf than, for example, in the Cairngorms, and the corrie usually holds more snow than one might imagine from the view from the car park. Good ice conditions are rarer, but the easier gullies of Sàil Mhòr fill readily. When in condition, two of the most spectacular ice routes in Scotland are to be found in the corrie.

Approach: The best approach is to follow the well made Coire Dubh path between Liathach and Beinn Eighe starting from the Coire Dubh car park in Glen Torridon (NG 959 569). Fork right at a cairn about 2km beyond some stepping stones and follow a path contouring below Sàil Mhòr and rising gradually to the lip of the corrie. This takes about 2hrs and a further 40mins to the foot of the Triple Buttresses.

For the more technical routes on the upper walls (Far East Wall, Eastern Ramparts, Central, West Central and Fuselage Walls), an approach over the top is quicker and rucksacs can be left at the top. This is not recommended for first time visitors as the panorama of the cliff from the loch is not to be missed. Follow the Coire Dubh path for about 2km until it flattens out and the hillside on the right becomes scree covered. The scree is a fine descent either in summer or in winter when snow covered. For ascent it is best to follow a stream which bounds the scree on the left; initially on the stream's right as far as the first rock band, then crossing to its left and finally trending further left to reach grassy fields below Coinneach Mhòr.

For most of the climbing, go to the east cairn of Coinneach Mhòr, then descend to the col leading to Ruadh-stac Mòr (or cut the corner on the east and go more direct to the col). From here, descend the gully into the corrie (scree or easy snow). After a climb on the Eastern Ramparts or the Far East Wall, it is possible to descend in two abseils if a second climb is contemplated and the top is known (two 50m abseils for the Ramparts, slightly shorter for the Far East). For climbs on the West Buttress quartzite, go to the west cairn of Coinneach Mhòr; this is virtually at the top of West Buttress. Routes on the West Central Wall can be approached by two abseils after spying the line from a viewpoint near the top of Central Buttress. Fuselage Gully Right Fork can also be descended, particularly in winter.

Descent: Reversing one of the high level routes above. The line near the stream is the simplest; the scree is slightly quicker for those who like it. The scree can be reached either from its start on the ridge or at two different points during the stream descent.

Seen from Loch Coire Mhic Fhearchair, the wall in the top left of the corrie is the Far East Wall. To its right is Far East Gully and then the steep left flank of the East Buttress, known as the Eastern Ramparts. Because the crests of the triple buttresses incline to the west, each buttress has an extensive left wall of steep quartzite facing north-east and a much narrower right wall tucked into the flanking gully. The left wall of Central Buttress is known as Central Wall, and the gullies have the obvious nomenclature East Central Gully, West Central Gully and Far West Gully (usually called Fuselage Gully).

The buttresses are composed of three tiers, the upper tiers of quartzite standing on a plinth of sandstone. The terrace above the sandstone tier, Broad Terrace, rises from left to right, so that the sandstone of the West Buttress offers much longer and better climbs than that of the East. Two further fault lines cross the buttresses. The middle fault starts on the left at the base of the Eastern Ramparts proper, continues across the top of the lower quartzite tier of East Buttress and marks the level where more continuous climbing on the left walls of Central and West Buttresses begins. The highest fault is the line of the Upper Girdle, a sensational 700m climb across all three buttresses. It crosses the Eastern Ramparts about one third of the way up and on the crests of the Central and West Buttresses it marks the level where the steep climbing on the final towers begins.

Although the Far East Wall and the steep left walls of the triple buttresses offer good lines, the nature of the climbing on the crests of the buttresses is such that numerous variations are possible, different climbs on successive tiers being easily combined. In summer the sandstone is treacherous when wet and the cliffs do not dry quickly. The quartzite holds are not too slippery (although the cracks are) so the quartzite sections of the classic Triple Buttress routes can be climbed in the wet. Vegetation on the sandstone and big loose blocks on the quartzite are further problems that will be encountered. Lest this should sound discouraging, it should be added that the climbing is very satisfying and the situations are outstanding. On the quartzite very steep walls may sometimes be climbed with surprising ease using big, flat holds; certainly the climbing is easier than it looks. Some of these climbs must be amongst the best and most sensational in Scotland, summer and winter. The sandstone climbing is more technical and can be deceptively hard at times.

Far East Wall

(NG 949 602) Alt 800m North-West facing Map p307 Diagram p310

Although somewhat slow to dry this wall has some excellent routes on sensationally steep quartzite. Descent at either side is feasible though the left-hand scree gully from the col below Ruadh-stac Mòr is more convenient. The main wall catches the sun in the afternoon and evening, consequently drying out faster from light rain than much of the Eastern Ramparts which gets the sun only in the morning. But the rock is more compact, so the main drainage points are more stubborn.

1 Nightcap Groove 45m HVS 5b *(1980)*
Climb the short prominent groove on the extreme left of the wall.
Winter: **VI,7** *(1992)*
Technical and well enough protected, but short.

2 Morning Wall 60m VS *(1983)*
This climbs the little grey wall between Nightcap Groove and Sidewinder. Start in an easy broken groove up and left of Sidewinder.
1. 40m 4c Scramble up the groove, then continue straight up to reach the right end of a grass ledge. Step round right, go up a crack and back up left to a ledge above a square-cut overhang.
2. 20m 4c Climb above the ledge, traverse left into a short corner, then go up and slightly right to a bulge. Mantelshelf over this and continue to the next terrace and easy ground above.

3 Sidewinder 90m Severe 4a *(1966)*
This route takes the obvious line of weakness slanting slightly right in the left end of the cliff. Start 6m left of the left end of the grass terrace that runs along under the steep grey wall. Climb a fault into a niche, then up to a grass platform. Continue straight up by steep walls and grooves to the foot of a right-slanting crack and follow this to its end. Step left and follow a fault over some dubious rock to the top.
Winter: **V,6** *(2002)*
By the summer route. The pitches are interchangeable with Glow Worm, and with the same first pitch, but the second pitch gives a good technical crux in gaining the base of the main right-slanting ramp.

4 Glow Worm 80m V,6 * *(1990)*
A winter ascent of a line based on Sidewinder, but taking a parallel line below the right-slanting crack to belay near Sting, then crossing Sidewinder to finish on its left.

On the left side of the Far East Wall is an impressively compact, steep grey wall with a white streaked bulging nose towards its left side. Just left of the nose is a shallow overhanging groove, the line of Moonshine. Left again the wall is bounded by a much more prominent groove, with the first belay of Sting at its foot. Three routes climb the main wall between the nose and the right-bounding big corner of Sundance. The three have a common start, reaching the horizontal fault by a fine left-slanting corner. Thereafter, The Reaper takes a crack-line on the right, Seeds of Destruction goes directly up, and Angel Face goes diagonally left above the bulging nose.

BEINN EIGHE
Coire Mhic Fhearchair
Far East Wall

1. Nightcap Groove	HVS 5b	9. Seeds of Destruction	E3 ***
2. Morning Wall	VS	10. The Reaper	E2 **
3. Sidewinder	Severe 4a	11. Sundance	E2 *
4. Glow Worm	V,6 *	12. The Root of all Evil	E2 **
5. Sting	HVS *	13. Hydroponicum	HVS
7. Moonshine	E4 ***	14. Meccano	E3 **
8. Angel Face	E2 ****		

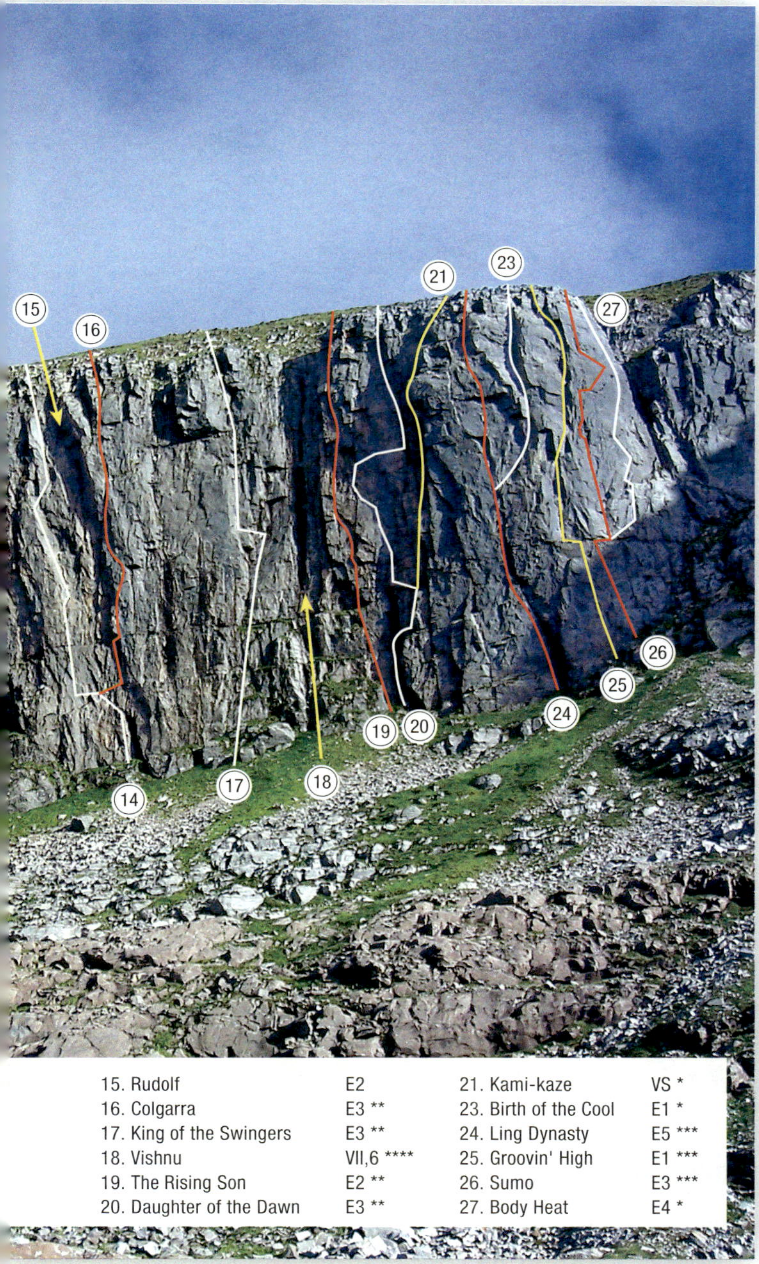

311

15. Rudolf	E2	21. Kami-kaze	VS *
16. Colgarra	E3 **	23. Birth of the Cool	E1 *
17. King of the Swingers	E3 **	24. Ling Dynasty	E5 ***
18. Vishnu	VII,6 ****	25. Groovin' High	E1 ***
19. The Rising Son	E2 **	26. Sumo	E3 ***
20. Daughter of the Dawn	E3 **	27. Body Heat	E4 *

Andy Nisbet

312 BEINN EIGHE

5 Sting   90m   HVS * *(1974)*
This takes a prominent crack on the left side of the steep grey wall that lies to the right of Sidewinder. Start a few metres right of the end of the grass terrace running under the grey wall.
1. 40m 4b Climb an obvious left-trending groove to a grass ledge, traverse right and gain a niche at the base of the prominent groove.
2. 15m 5a Step off a large flake on the left and follow a steep crack to a peg runner. Move left to ledges.
3. 35m 4c Climb a short wall and a bulge then up the prominent hanging chimney to easy ground.
Winter: **VII,7 **** *(1997)*
A sustained route by the summer line. Requires snowy conditions for the first pitch (which was split by a belay on the grass ledge before the traverse) to be wintry.
Variation: **Sting Direct   90m   E1** *(2000)*
1. 45m 5c Take an obvious crack-line starting a little way up the lower groove and follow it all the way to the top of the huge flake on pitch 2.
2. 45m 5b Follow the normal route initially (pitch 2), then grooves directly to the top (i.e. – left of the final chimney).

6 Sunscream   110m   E5 * *(2000)*
This fine varied route takes a direct line based on the wall and slight hanging groove left of Moonshine. Not as well protected as other routes hereabouts. Start at the base of the groove of The Sting.
1. 35m 6a Climb directly up through a bulging nose to a depression in the centre of the wall. Follow the obvious line trending slightly right on dwindling holds until a scary step up gains better holds leading directly to the horizontal fault. Pull left through the overhang to small ledges.
2. 25m 6b Climb up left across twin grooves to gain the arete forming the right edge of a deep groove (just right of Sting). Move delicately up, then make a desperate move back right to better holds at the base of a slim hanging groove. Climb the strenuous groove until a standing position can be gained on a jug on the right arete. Continue straight up for 10m (common with Moonshine), then pull left into a niche under the huge roof and belay on the left.
3. 50m 5b Step left round the edge into a corner, then up this to a swing back right on to the face. Climb straight up past a small niche and continue up the fine wall to easy ground and the top.

7 Moonshine   95m   E4 *** *(1988)*
The main pitch takes the shallow overhanging groove left of the bulging nose of the buttress. Sustained technical climbing but arguably only E3. Start on the long grassy ledge under the buttress, about 10m from the left end, by a small rock scar.
1. 25m 5b Go straight up the wall, then move right into a flake-line and follow this to belay by the horizontal break.
2. 35m 6a Go diagonally left to gain the base of the groove. Climb the groove with increasing difficulty to a foothold on the left arete. Climb straight up until level with a huge overhang on the left, then move right and up to a ledge.
3. 35m 5b Climb the short awkward corner above, then move left and up a long easy wall to finish.

8 Angel Face   95m   E2 **** *(1988)*
A highly recommended route taking a sensational and improbable line above the bulging nose of the wall. Protection is good apart from bold moves to gain the tiny ramp on pitch 2. Take plenty of RPs. Start at the left end of a long flake which is embedded against the right side of the lower wall on the long grass terrace.
1. 15m 5a Climb a narrow ramp leftwards, move right into a shallow groove, and climb it to a grass ledge at the base of a bigger groove on the right. This is below a main horizontal ledge which has no belay.
2. 35m 5c Take the left-leaning groove to the horizontal ledge. Traverse left about 5m along the fault to a small pedestal. Climb the wall above, then move left to

FAR EAST WALL 313

Moonshine, E4, Far East Wall, Coire Mhic Fhearchair, Beinn Eighe. Climber Gary Latter

gain a tiny ramp. Go up this to a crack, then make a long step left into the base of a thinner crack. Climb the crack to a small roof. Traverse delicately left under the roof to the edge of nowhere, then return unexpectedly right to a belay above the right end of the ledge.
3. 45m 5b Climb the crack, and when it becomes unfriendly move slightly right and up to a large flake-ledge. Go on up the wall above to a smaller flake-ledge. Traverse left to a large block. Now trend rightwards across slabbier ground to a steep blocky finish.

9 Seeds of Destruction   95m   E3 ***   *(1988)*
A superb route with very sustained climbing up the wall left of The Reaper. A double set of medium sized RPs is useful for pitch 2. Start as for The Reaper and Angel Face, at a large detached flake.
1. 15m 5a As for Angel Face.
2. 20m 5c Climb the left-leaning groove to the horizontal fault and traverse left to the pedestal of Angel Face. Move right past a poor peg runner and pull over a

bulge into a shallow corner. Belay on the right under a smooth groove.
3. 30m 5c Climb the groove to a big ledge on the right. Step down and traverse left until a left-facing corner can be gained. Climb the corner to the right end of the large flake-ledge of Angel Face. Climb the wall above to the next ledge.
4. 30m 5c Go up to a small rock scar, then steeply up and left to a rest at a horizontal break. Traverse right, then go up into a curving groove on the right. Above this go straight up steep blocky ground to finish.

10 The Reaper   95m   E2 **   *(1980)*
The original route on this wall takes a bold line up the vertical crack towards the right side. Its first two pitches up to the horizontal fault were subsequently used by Angel Face and Seeds of Destruction.
1. 15m 5a As for Angel Face.
2. 25m 5c Climb the left-leaning groove to reach the prominent horizontal fault (as for Angel Face). Traverse right until below the left side of the large recess above. Climb steeply to reach a crack (which is not visible from the fault) in the left side of the recess. Climb the crack and belay in a niche.
3. 25m 5b Continue up the crack to a ledge on the left.
4. 30m 5a Go up right into a shallow corner, move further right then zigzag to finish up an obvious chimney.

11 Sundance   95m   E2 *   *(1974)*
To the right of the grey wall is an obvious steep corner-crack cutting through several overhangs in the upper part of the crag. A fine line with a strenuous crux but a little mossy. Start directly beneath.
1. 25m Climb up steep but grassy rocks to the horizontal fault.
2. 25m 5b Climb a crack in a wall over a bulge and up to a bigger bulge. Enter a hanging chimney which leads to a good ledge.
3. 20m 5a Climb the wall on the left to the next overhang which is climbed on good holds.
4. 25m 5a The final overhang is turned via a grass ledge on the impending right wall. Continue up mossy walls to the top.

12 The Root of all Evil   100m   E2 **   *(1995)*
Climbs the big left-facing corner on the wall just right of Sundance to join and finish up Hydroponicum. Typical Coire Mhic Fhearchair; sustained, overhanging, excellent holds and protection, but slow to dry. Start as for Sundance.
1. 30m Climb the right-slanting crack but break off right and belay under a smaller corner right of the big corner.
2. 20m 5b Climb the smaller corner until obvious holds lead out to its left arete. Pull round the arete into the big corner just above its second roof. Climb the big corner until 3m below a big roof.
3. 15m 5c Traverse left to a hidden crack and climb it (sustained) until a step out right gives a rest below the main roof system. Pull out right to belay as for Hydroponicum.
4. 35m 5a Finish as for Hydroponicum.

13 Hydroponicum   100m   HVS   *(1995)*
Takes an improbable left-slanting line through overhanging ground. Unfortunately mucky in places. Well enough protected but very exposed and perhaps worthy of an extra grade for this. Start about 20m right of Sundance.
1. 40m Climb thickly turfed ledges up left to an apex below a short steep corner.
2. 25m 5a Climb the corner and continue diagonally left on a ramp to belay below the last roof.
3. 35m 5a Pass the roof on the left, close to the big right arete of Sundance and climb a shallow cracked groove line to the top.
Winter: **VIII, 8 ****   *(2005)*
The line is the same as the summer route but with a different belay after pitch 2. Start at the vegetated triangle running up into the centre of the Far East Wall.

1. 43m Climb turfy steps on its right side, then move left to belay in an alcove at the apex of the triangle.
2. 12m Make strenuous moves into a chimney on the left and continue to a semi-hanging stance beneath a massive flake.
3. 30m Climb delicately up leftwards to a glacis under a large roof; move left and up round the left edge of the overhangs in a sensational position (crux) and gain the bottom of a short chimney-groove (crux, sustained with protection difficult to place); hanging belay (optional).
4. 15m Climb the chimney, then move left into a steep but helpful finishing groove.

14 Meccano 95m E3 ** (1992)
A fine sustained route which climbs a slabby ramp on the wall left of the big corner of Colgarra. Pitch 3 was led with a peg for aid, but seconded free.
1. 20m 4c Colgarra, pitch 1.
2. 25m 5b Step up and traverse 6m left to a left-slanting left-facing shallow corner, then climb this to the horizontal fault. Hand traverse right then pull up to a short corner. Climb the corner, and another above, then use an in situ sling to gain a slab (seconded free at 6a). Belay just on the left, at the base of the ramp.
3. 50m 5c Climb the ramp to its top, then move right and follow a series of shallow grooves (left of the corner of Rudolf) to the top.

15 Rudolf 95m E2 (1992)
This takes the big left-facing corner up which Colgarra starts; it is slow to dry and vegetated at the top. Start immediately left of the slit cave of Colgarra.
1. 25m 5a Climb a shallow crack-line, then take a direct line up the wall (touching Colgarra), then a steep left-leaning corner to the horizontal fault. Belay at the base of a groove which leads up to the big groove.
2. 25m 5c Climb the groove to a roof, then move left to a small ledge.
3. 45m 5b Climb up on the right, then move into the main corner. Follow this to the top.

16 Colgarra 100m E3 ** (1976/1988)
This unusually steep route goes up the centre of the cliff, starting at a deep slit cave. In its upper reaches it takes a hanging chimney visible from below immediately right of the big left-curving corner of Rudolf. Another route of great character.
1. 20m 5a Climb the left side of the cave and up diagonally left to a grass ledge.
2. 20m 5b Traverse right beyond the line of the groove of Rudolf, then go up past the horizontal fault and pull into the main corner. Follow this to a step right and belay at a large jammed flake.
3. 10m 5a From just above the belay swing right onto the steep wall and go up a flake-crack to a smaller flake.
4. 20m 6a Climb the thin groove above to reach good holds leading up and left into the hanging chimney, which is climbed to a grass ledge.
5. 30m 5b Climb up and slightly left to a small overhang, over this and follow a crack (not the ramp on the left) to easy ground.

17 King of the Swingers 100m E3 ** (1992)
A route up the big corners left of Vishnu. It was led free, but a short pendulum move reduces the grade to a consistent E1.
1. 25m 4b Climb unpleasantly to the base of the big corner left of Vishnu, which starts at the level of the horizontal fault.
2. 25m 6b Climb the corner to a roof. Place high runners and one out left in a crack through the roof, then traverse just below a small overlap 3m below (or pendulum, which reduces the grade to 5b) to gain a crack which leads to a ledge below another big corner.
3. 50m 5a Climb the corner then move left below an overhang to a ledge. Climb a vegetated groove until it is possible to finish up the rib on the right.

316 BEINN EIGHE

18 Vishnu   110m   VII,6 ****   (1988)
A fierce winter route up the major fault-line left of The Rising Son. Although some of the climbing was on ice, much was mixed. Protection is poor on the icy sections but better on the mixed.
1. 15m Starting on the right an introductory pitch leads up left to a belay below the initial groove.
2. 20m Climb the groove on deceptively steep ice to a belay in a deep recess below big icicles.
3. 20m An overhanging chimney leads out right to a small ledge from where a mixed line up an overhanging groove leads to another small ledge and good belay.
4. 50m Climb the vertical corner above until the ice can be regained above its steepest section. Now a deep gully leads over two steep sections to easier ground and the final snow slopes.

19 The Rising Son   100m   E2 **   (1986)
Start at the recess of Kami-kaze.
1. 25m 4c Climb up and left to belay on a grass ledge.
2. 30m 5b From the right end of the ledge go right and up over a bulge (loose block) to a position immediately under a line of overhangs (seen from below). Traverse left under the overhangs for about 5m, then go up steeply for about 10m until able to make a delicate move left to a small stance below an overhung niche.
3. 15m 5b Climb through the niche and past a ledge to belay.
4. 30m 4c Continue trending slightly left to gain a major fault which leads to the top.

20 Daughter of the Dawn   100m   E3 **   (1993)
A sensational line up the vertical wall left of Kami-kaze. A direct finish would be better but harder.
1. 25m 4c As for the first pitch of Kami-kaze.
2. 20m 5c Traverse 5m left and go up left to a smaller ledge. Step right into a crack in a pale wall and climb it leading into a corner and tiny ledge at its top.
3. 10m 5c Pull out left into another corner and up this to a roof. Pull out left again and go up to a ledge on the left.
4. 45m 5b From the right end of the ledge, climb up flakes, pull out right, place high runners and traverse right into a big left-facing corner, followed slightly left to a wide notch at the top.

21 Kami-kaze   100m   VS *   (1966)
This follows the big fault-line on the left of the large protruding buttress which forms the right-hand section of the cliff. Start at a damp, overhung recess about 30m left of a deep slit cave.
1. 25m Climb up the recess until it is possible to traverse right to a shallow groove. Go up this then right to belay below a chimney-crack in the obvious fault-line.
2. 25m Climb the chimney to belay in the base of a deeper wider chimney.
3. 25m Climb this overhanging chimney until it becomes a cave under the huge beak. Traverse sensationally out left and up a groove to easier ground.
4. 25m Finish up the groove above.
Winter: **VI,7 *****   (1988)
Outrageous situations, but highly amenable rock, make this one of the best mixed climbs in the area. Chimneying features prominently, so sacks should not be carried. The summer line is followed and is sustained but generally well protected unless icy; (the first pitch is the boldest).

22 Fascist Groove Thang   100m   E7 **   (1995)
Climbs the wall left of Ling Dynasty. Start at the obvious groove 20m left of Birth of the Cool.
1. 45m 5b Climb the groove, loose at first, past two ledges to belay on a slab or the inset ledge above.
2. 25m 6c With a runner in the corner above, traverse right under a small overlap

*Kami-kaze, VI,7, Far East Wall, Coire Mhic Fhearchair, Beinn Eighe.
Climber Andy Cunningham*

to a good hold. Move up left on to a ramp, then follow a hairline crack to a spike. Gain the right end of the overlap above and make difficult moves through a bulge into the base of a holdless groove (Fascist Groove). Continue with difficulty up and across the right wall of the Fascist Groove, moving up to belay below a large crack.
3. 30m 5c Climb the steep crack until the angle eases, follow the left arete, then a crack to broken ground.

23 Birth of the Cool   100m   E1 *   (1976)
To the right of Kami-kaze the steep grey pillar is cleft by an obvious chimney-line in the lower part. The climb follows this line then breaks right through a belt of overhangs and finishes up a prominent corner. Harder and with poorer rock than Groovin' High. Start at the wet slit cave at the base of the chimney.
1. 25m 4c Climb loose rock on the left side of the cave.
2. 15m 5a Continue up the steep chimney-crack to a ledge.
3. 15m 5b Climb a steep crack and the wall on the right to a good ledge.
4. 20m 5b Go right along the ledge, climb a narrowing groove and exit to the right with difficulty.
5. 25m 4b Climb the corner to the top.

24 Ling Dynasty   110m   E5 ***   (1987)
This route starts up Birth of the Cool and continues straight up a magnificent crack and through the big roof above. Follow Birth of the Cool for three pitches to the ledge where it goes right.
4. 25m 6b Step left into the crack and climb it to a roof. Pull out rightwards into

the continuation of the crack and climb it to the big roof (very sustained). Traverse right to a belay (which is more comfortable than it looks) at the right end of the roof.
5. 15m 6a Return left and climb the wide crack in the roof. Go leftwards up the thin ramp above to belay.
6. 15m 4c Move right and up a corner to the top.

25 Groovin' High 90m E1 *** (1973)
A superb route following a big corner on the right side of the clean grey pillar. Start 6m right of the slit cave of Birth of the Cool.
1. 30m 4c Climb short walls and corners to a large ledge below the big corner.
2. 20m 5a Climb the steep corner.
3. 40m 5b Continue by the fine corner system above to reach a small ledge at 20m (possible belay). Continue in the same line to the top.

26 Sumo 85m E3 *** (1987)
This takes the vertical crack-line and wall just right of Groovin' High, with an excellent crux pitch, technical, clean and very sustained. Start 2m right of Groovin' High.
1. 30m 4c Climb corners and short walls to a large ledge 3m right of Groovin' High. Crawl right to belay. Or start further right and go direct to the belay.
2. 30m 5c Climb a steep corner, then the crack-line to enter a groove below a roof. Move left to good holds and re-enter the groove beside the roof. A strenuous bulge leads to a belay.
3. 25m 5b Take the shallow groove above to horizontal cracks. Traverse right into a corner, climb it and return diagonally left until above the belay at a small roof. Finish rightwards up a slight ramp and back left on big holds to the top.

27 Body Heat 90m E4 * (1996)
Climbs the wall right of Sumo, starting as for that route.
1. 35m 4c Climb Sumo to a ledge. Traverse right, then go straight up to belay at a pointed block.
2. 20m 6b Climb above the block and follow a ramp up right until a move left gains a stopping place at large flat holds. Move slightly left on to a steep wall (RPs in a thin horizontal crack), then straight up to a flake hold (good nut). A hard move leads to better holds and a hanging belay on the slabbier rock above.
3. 35m 5b Follow a flake-line above to an overlap. Move right and follow a shallow groove and wall to the top.

28 Body Swerve 90m E4 * (2006)
1. 35m 4c As for Body Heat.
2. 30m 6a Follow the ramp of Body Heat to the flat holds on the left, then traverse right for a few moves on small positive edges. Go up, then move rightwards to a good break and welcome protection. Continue straight up before a bold move left gains a short flake and easier climbing, which then leads to ledges on the right.
3. 25m 5b Turn the roof above on the right, then follow cracks and walls to easier ground (possibly the same finish as Body Heat).

29 Far East Gully 70m III,5 (1998)
The gully bounding the right end of Far East Wall, cutting in behind the grey pillar. Includes a chimney section with an awkward move over a chockstone.

30 Karaoke Wall 45m HVS (1992)
Right of the grey pillar (containing Groovin' High) is Far East Gully, then a shorter wall which tapers off rightwards. This route takes the obvious line just right of the gully.
1. 20m 5a Climb the crack, which gradually increases in width, to a ledge at its top.
2. 25m 4b Continue in the same line up the groove above.

31 Epilogue 50m VS 5a (1993)

Start 5m right of Karaoke Wall at a parallel crack-line. Climb this for 20m to a ledge. Traverse right along the ledge until above a large corner. Climb the wall above moving leftwards near the top.
Variation: **Divine Ambition   50m   E1** *(2003)*
A direct version of Epilogue.
1. 30m 6a Climb the parallel crack-line as for Epilogue for 20m to a ledge. Make a difficult move to continue up to a bay.
2. 25m 5a Continue up a corner above to easy ground.

Eastern Ramparts

(NG 947 602)   Alt 800m   North-East facing   Map p307   Diagram p320

This is the left flanking wall of the East Buttress. It is long and complex and the climbs are not easy to find on first acquaintance. The ledge of the Upper Girdle runs across it at about one third height, except at the left where the lower section is much shorter; eventually the ledge runs into the hillside. This point, and the big corner of Claustrophobic Corner above are good location features. Also useful is the initial right-facing corner of Eastern Promise, about 35m right of the Upper Girdle start. The Pale Diedre, a left-facing corner at the right boundary of pale rock above the Upper Girdle, is a prominent feature in the centre of the face. At the base of the diedre a grassy shelf, Bottom Shelf, runs rightwards above a small lower tier of quartzite. This is the start of the middle fault of the Triple Buttresses. The best descent is down the easy gully beyond Far East Wall but the steep broken ground at the left end of the cliff is also an option (about Difficult, one abseil in winter).

1 The Trundler   45m   HVS 5a *(1992)*
Start beside Cornice Groove, on the left. Climb an easy corner, then move left into a second corner and follow this to roofs. Pull out right then climb fine cracks in the wall left of Cornice Groove to finish.

2 Cornice Groove   50m   VS *(1969)*
At the left end of the cliff, just before it falls back towards Far East Gully, there is a slim V-groove with an overhang at 30m.
1. 35m 5a Climb the groove turning the overhang on the left.
2. 15m Continue more easily to the top.
Winter: **VI,7 *** *(2000)*
A combination of ice and mixed climbing up the groove, which collects snow.

3 Corniced Arete   55m   VS *(1980)*
1. 25m 4c Start beside Cornice Groove and climb the arete on the right for 10m. Make a short traverse right and continue up and right to a good stance below and just right of a small roof.
2. 30m 4c Climb the crack on the left side of the roof and go straight up to a larger roof composed of huge blocks. Climb this on large jugs to finish.

4 The Modern Idiot   55m   E1 *(1992)*
Between Cornice Arete and Olympus is an arch of roofs low down. Start below its left end.
1. 25m 5b Go diagonally right and pull through the roof at the second small corner from the right end. Go straight up cracks, then traverse 2m left and belay as for Cornice Arete.
2. 30m 5b Climb the right-slanting corner above until forced to traverse right below an overhang. Pass it on the right then finish straight up.

5 Olympus   70m   HVS ** *(1980)*
A sustained route, but easier than it looks, taking a line up the middle of the imposing wall right of Corniced Arete making for a vague depression about three-quarters of the way up the cliff. Start near the beginning of the Upper Girdle just left of a large right-facing corner (Claustrophobic Corner).

1. The Trundler	HVS 5a		9. The Great Wall of China	E3
2. Cornice Groove	VS		10. Turkish Delight	E3 **
3. Corniced Arete	VS		11. Feast of the East	E1 *
4. The Modern Idiot	E1		12. Eastern Promise	VS *
5. Olympus	HVS **		14. Rampart Wall	HVS **
6. Claustrophobic Corner	E1 *		15. Pale Rider	E1 **
7. The Ho Chi Min Trail	E2 *		16. Paleface Wall	E3 *
8. Heavy Flak	E1 *		17. The Pale Diedre	E2 ***

BEINN EIGHE
Coire Mhic Fhearchair
Eastern Ramparts

19. Tainted Galahad	E2 **	26. Shang-High	HVS
20. Rampage	E2	27. Fear of the Dark	E1
21. The Unknown Soldier	E1 *	28. The Tower of Darkness	E4 *
23. Forgotten Warrior	HVS *	29. Fairytale Groove	HVS *
24. Samurai	HVS	31. Gnome Wall	Hard Severe
25. Simpleton	HVS *	33. Gashtrognome	VI,7 **

1. 35m 4c Move right and back left above the initial roofs to reach ledges. Go left on to pale rock, then climb up and right to reach a small flaky ledge below a steepening in the wall.

2. 35m 4b Climb the wall and a shallow corner on the right before swinging up left on to a ledge beneath an obvious 6m flake-crack. Climb the crack, move 3m right and finish up the wall.

6 Claustrophobic Corner   70m   E1 * (1988)

Scramble up to start below the large right-facing corner which lies above the start of The Upper Girdle.

1. 35m 5a Climb up on to a pedestal in the corner proper. Climb the corner for about 5m to an overhang. Make bold moves out across the left wall and pull into a subsidiary corner. Climb this to regain the main corner. Traverse left and climb the left rib of the corner to a ledge.

2. 35m 5b Go diagonally right and break through the band of overhangs at a jutting block on the right. Climb the wall above slightly leftwards.

7 The Ho Chi Min Trail   70m   E2 * (1988)

A good route with a sensational first pitch. Scramble up to start in the centre of a usually wet recess right of Claustrophobic Corner.

1. 35m 5c Climb the bulging wall on good holds, then move right into the right corner of the recess. Climb this to the roof and pull over using an unusual wedged block (crux). Traverse left by a flake-crack which bends upwards into a shallow groove. Go up the groove until a short left traverse leads to a tiny square ledge.

2. 35m 5b Return to the groove and climb it steeply until it peters out under the roofs. Go diagonally right under the roofs and pass them at their end. Climb the wall above to an easier groove leading to a short corner and roof, passed on the right.

8 Heavy Flak   80m   E1 * (1978)

Scramble up easy ground for 10m to belay at the right side of the wet recess (or climb more direct at about 4b).

1. 20m 5a Step right and up then traverse left to a vertical crack which is climbed to a belay in a recess.

2. 10m Climb up the fault to belay behind the huge flake.

3. 20m 5b Step left and climb the groove to belay under a roof on the left.

4. 30m 5a Traverse right for 5m and climb large flakes leftwards until a groove leads to the top.

9 The Great Wall of China   90m   E3 (1993)

Climbs the wall between Heavy Flak and Turkish Delight. Start 5m right of the scrambly start of Heavy Flak below a flake-corner.

1. 30m 5a Climb this to a low ledge. Step right, climb an open corner leading to the Upper Girdle and continue to a ledge below a roof.

2. 20m 6a Climb the wall just right of the roof (crux), then traverse left delicately above its lip. Go up the right side of a huge flaky pinnacle and belay on top.

3. 40m 5c Gain a ledge with perched block on the right, then follow a crack-line to a small roof. Go left round the roof and up steps above.

10 Turkish Delight   95m   E3 ** (1987)

This takes a crack-line up the vague buttress between Heavy Flak and a big left-facing roofed corner system on the right. Sustained and well protected. Start below the right end of a short ledge below the Upper Girdle.

1. 35m 4c Climb a shallow corner to the ledge. Continue slightly rightwards to the Upper Girdle. Climb onto big blocks under the roofed fault, then traverse left to a block under a shallow crack-line just left of the more obvious right-facing double roofed corner of Feast of the East.

2. 25m 5b Climb the crack, which bends right over a bulge, then immediately move left up the wall away from the fault and up to a block below a thin crack.

3. 10m 5c Climb the crack to an awkward belay in a red corner.
4. 25m 5b Climb the overhanging crack above, then go straight up to finish at the left end of the fault.

11 Feast of the East   90m   E1 * *(1992)*
This takes the diagonal crack-line which cuts through the prominent left-facing roofed corner system. Start about 8m left of the obvious corner of Eastern Promise.
1. 30m 5a Climb a shallow corner, go right and left to pass a roof, then continue to the Upper Girdle. Belay at a huge block below the roof at the base of the corner system.
2. 15m 5c Climb onto the block, then go up the clean-cut corner with two overhangs (strenuous but well protected) to a small ledge.
3. 25m 5b Continue in the same line, now a wide crack in places, passing through the corner system.
4. 20m 4c Go up left to a big ledge, pull out left up an overhanging wall, then finish easily above.

12 Eastern Promise   95m   VS * *(1969)*
About 35m right of the wet recess there is a clean, pale right-facing corner in the lower tier. Start below this.
1. 30m 4b Climb the corner to mid-height, traverse left and continue up the wall to belay on the Upper Girdle.
2. 25m 4c There is a huge roof some 15m above. Climb up to its right, then step left to gain and climb a narrow chimney to a ledge with a block.
3. 40m 4c Climb the steep wall and grooves above to the top.
Winter: **VI,7 *** *(1991)*
Follow the summer line. Top end of the grade; intimidatingly steep but co-operative and well protected. Pitch 3 was entirely on ice on the first ascent; there was little ice on the second ascent.

13 Siege Tactics   110m   E1 *(1995)*
Takes a line parallel to Pale Rider and forming an X with Rampart Wall. The lower and left of the two square roofs above the Upper Girdle and mentioned in the description of Rampart Wall is a key locating feature. Start mid-way between Eastern Promise and Rampart Wall/Pale Rider; 10m left of a point below the square roof.
1. 40m 5c Climb fairly directly to the Upper Girdle via a vague depression which is the right hand of several pale lines of smooth rock. One hard move stepping out right on to a small square orange slab; there may well be an alternative easier line.
2. 25m 5b Climb directly up past the right end of the square roof to a good recessed ledge.
3. 35m 5a Pull out above the ledge and take a slightly right trending line to belay below the chimney at the left end of the capping wall (close to Pale Rider).
4. 10m 4b Climb the small tower just left of the chimney on huge holds.

14 Rampart Wall   115m   HVS * *(1969)*
Below and a little to the left of the pale diedre which features prominently in the middle of the upper cliff there is a left-facing corner in the lower tier (taken by Pale Rider). This is some 50m right of Eastern Promise. Start below this corner, about 5m left of the start of Bottom Shelf. The climb takes a slanting leftwards line from this point, passing some prominent square-cut overhangs at half-height.
1. 25m 4c Start up a small rectangular grey rib and climb trending left for 20m to a bulge. Move right and back up left over a flake to a ledge level with the base of the left-facing corner of Pale Rider.
2. 20m 4c Climb a flake-crack for 6m then traverse left into the next crack. Go up to a block on the Upper Girdle just left of a large shallow cave.
3. 40m 5a Climb a bulging crack to a pointed pinnacle. Move round the pinnacle and make a delicate traverse left to another crack-line which is climbed to a large flake. Climb the corner forming the right side of this flake, then traverse left across

its top into a large bay and go up easy ground for 15m.

4. 30m 4c Climb a narrow slab on the right to a ledge and continue up short walls to the top.

Winter: **VII,8** ***   (2002)

A sensational line through some unlikely ground. Four pitches with belays as for summer. Start 10m left of the summer route and go up to the second of two ledge systems; this is about 10m up. Traverse right to near the summer route, ignoring tempting direct crack-lines. Follow a grassy crack in a right-facing corner which is about 10m left of Pale Rider corner to reach the belay ledge. The traverse on pitch 2 is very thin and the technical crux. Tension was used for the delicate traverse on pitch 3 but it is short and there are possibilities for freeing it. On pitch 4, the narrow slab is smooth and a steeper groove on the left was climbed (Eastern Promise winter may have shared some of this pitch, which ices up.)

15 Pale Rider   110m   E1 **   (1986)

This takes the most prominent crack-line on the wall left of The Pale Diedre. The crack-line is characterised by two projecting blocks just at the point where its angle eases. Start below a left-facing corner, as for Rampart Wall.

1. 45m 4c Climb directly up to the base of the corner. Immediate entry is barred by a detached block, so go up left and enter above the block by delicate moves across pale rock. Follow the corner to the Upper Girdle and belay 10m further left just below and left of the crack-line, about 20m left of The Pale Diedre.

2. 35m 5b Climb the crack to a small ledge beside the projecting blocks. Go easily up right to belay on a large ledge.

3. 20m 4c Return left to the original line, which has a blank section below a bulge. Instead go left round an edge and straight up the wall above to belay below a short chimney on the left.

4. 10m 5a Climb the wall on the right to finish.

16 Paleface Wall   100m   E3 *   (1988)

A direct line up the pale wall left of Pale Diedre. A series of fine technical pitches on the best rock. Pitches 2/3 and 4/5 can be combined. Start at a 6m pinnacle below a rib, in whose left side is set the initial corner of Pale Rider.

1. 45m 5b Climb the front face of the pinnacle. Go up the wall above, then right and back left into a shallow corner on the crest of the rib. Go up this to the Upper Girdle.

2. 20m 5b Some 10m left of The Pale Diedre is a clean right-facing corner. Gain this from the left and climb it to a ledge.

3. 10m 5c Climb the shallow corner above the right end of the ledges to jugs. Move left and go up to a ledge.

4. 15m 5c Climb the crack above the right end of the ledge. Move left round a roof and make a thin move left before going straight up to a big ledge.

5. 10m 5b Climb the horizontally faulted wall directly above (strenuous). A rattling flake is a crucial hold. Sometimes wet but avoidable.

17 The Pale Diedre   105m   E2 ***   (1980)

This is the obvious line in the middle of the upper part of the cliff. Start below and slightly left of this at the foot of a right-facing diedre. A most enjoyable climb.

1. 40m 5b Climb the diedre directly to overhangs at 24m. Move left then go up right to below the pale diedre.

2. 40m 5c Climb the diedre; excellent!

3. 25m Finish up the easy groove on the right.

18 Boggle   110m   E1   (1961)

This devious line has an original description worthy of Robin Smith, its creator. Start as for The Pale Diedre. "Zigzag to reach the left end of the ledge about 12m up. Climb a corner for 6m to a ledge on the left then pull up into the pale smooth corner on the right. Climb this to below roofs crawl left over loose blocks and go up and right to reach the Upper Girdle below the pale shallow diedre. Move right

EASTERN RAMPARTS 325

*The Pale Diedre, E2, Eastern Ramparts, Coire Mhic Fhearchair, Beinn Eighe.
Climber Robert Durran*

and climb by cracks, grooves, flakes, corners, hand traverses and mantleshelves away up and right onto the crest of the pillar bounding the diedre. Step left and climb a corridor between roofs to top."

19 Tainted Galahad   110m   E2 **   (1988)
A line between Boggle and Rampage, passing left of the square-cut roof.
1. 40m Start as for Rampage and belay on top of the large pinnacle.
2. 15m 5a Step right as for Rampage, then climb the obvious corner to belay 3m below the square roof.
3. 15m 5c Step down and left on to a foothold on the arete. Swing down under a bulge on the left, then surmount it (crux). Move left and climb a crack to a flake near Boggle. Return right and belay in a corner.
4. 40m 5a Climb the corner to just below its top. Traverse right on to easier

ground. Go diagonally right, climb an awkward bulge by a large flake and finish by short corners and walls on the left.
Variation: **Direct Finish   30m   E3 6a** *(2004)*
For pitch 4, climb the corner, exit right, then move back left and go directly up to a long narrow ledge with a flake-corner at the right end. Climb a bulging crack in the wall above to the top.

20 Rampage   110m   E2 *(1977)*
This climb lies to the right of Boggle and features a pale coloured wall in its upper half, just right of a prominent square-cut roof at mid-height. Stars are unknown. Start 6m right of The Pale Diedre.
1. 45m 5a Climb a right-slanting fault past a strenuous bulge to a ledge below a large pinnacle. Climb the groove on the right of the pinnacle and belay on the top, on the Upper Girdle.
2. 20m 4c Climb up and right to the top of a second pinnacle.
3. 25m 5c Climb up for 6m to a small recess, step right, move up the wall and into the groove on the right. Continue up this and over a bulge to a good ledge on the right.
4. 20m 4b Climb the chimney to the top.

21 The Unknown Soldier   110m   E1 * *(1993)*
1. 45m 5a Climb a parallel fault 10m right of Rampage, passing a ledge at 25m, to the Upper Girdle.
2. 20m 4c Climb a right-facing yellow corner, move right and up to another big ledge.
3. 15m 5b From the right end of the ledge go up a steep wall. Step right and go up a second steep wall (a nut for aid was used due to the onset of rain, but it would go free perhaps at 5c) to a ledge out right. A short corner led to a block on the left.
4. 30m 5a Go up the fault above, then move right to climb the very steep blocky rib between Rampage and Forgotten Warrior.

22 The Unknown Warrior   130m   VII,7 * *(1999)*
A winter line starting up The Unknown Soldier, continuing up Forgotten Warrior and finishing up Samurai. An independent finish up Forgotten Warrior looks worth a try for a party with daylight to spare. The summer lines were not followed precisely, so a full description is given. Start at a break 15m left of the cave which is about 15m up on the first pitch of Samurai (and 10m left of Samurai winter).
1. 45m Climb about 10m to a ledge below a large triangular shape of rougher rock. Go right and back left to a V shape formed by a right to left ramp between the triangle and a smaller triangle to its right. Go slightly rightwards up a crack-line in smooth rock to a good ledge level with a pinnacle on the right. The pinnacle seems to be a dead end so pull out left on an undercut flake-crack (well seen from the cliff base) and climb a thin crack in a small smooth ramp (crux) to the Upper Girdle. Alternatively, find the start and follow your nose.
2. 10m Traverse right along the Girdle past a section where the ledge disappears and belay in a niche immediately after the ledge reappears (Forgotten Warrior belay).
3. 40m Climb Forgotten Warrior pitches 2 and 3, but apart from the start, keep to the fault-line. At the top, move out right under the perched block (a chockstone) to belay as for Samurai.
4. 35m Finish up Samurai (the final gully on ice on this occasion).

The section of cliff around Samurai contains two parallel crack-lines. Samurai takes the right-hand line, with a shallow cave on pitch one. The following route takes the left-hand line, leading directly to a square-cut notch in the cliff top.

23 Forgotten Warrior   115m   HVS * *(1992)*
This climbs a right-slanting crack and chimney-line, clearly seen from 30m below the start. From the start itself, only the final square-cut notch is obvious. The grade is uncertain, as the climb was done in the wet, and perhaps has not been repeated,

but provided sustained climbing on good rock. Begin 5m left of Samurai.
1. 45m 4c Climb the crack-line to reach and follow a right-facing corner. At the Upper Girdle, traverse right back to the original line.
2. 20m 5a Climb the crack-line, then the rib on its right and swing back left into the top of the crack-line to gain the ledge above.
3. 20m 4c Continue up the crack-line until forced out left to ledges.
4. 30m 4c Return to the crack-line above its steep section, then gain the base of the square-cut notch either directly or by a spectacular loop out right on good rock. Climb the notch to the top.

24 Samurai   110m   HVS   (1966)
Although each pitch has some hardish moves the climbing on this route is not sustained. Start 30m right of The Pale Diedre at the foot of the right-hand fault which slants slightly to the right past a cave at 20m.
1. 45m 5a Climb the fault turning the cave on the left, and belay on the Upper Girdle.
2. 30m 5a Avoid the overhanging chimney ahead; instead traverse right from the foot of the chimney into a vertical crack. Climb this for 12m, then move left round a nose and go up a steep wall to a ledge. Continue up the fault to a stance at perched blocks.
3. 35m 4c Traverse right underneath a perched block for 6m and climb the right-hand of three faults, a narrow chimney; traverse left along a horizontal crack to finish up an easy chimney (the central fault).
Winter: **VII,7 ****   (1997)
Sensational and helpful as ever. Start about 6m left of the summer route at a shallow right-facing corner with the first move gaining the top of an awkward block (same as Forgotten Warrior).
1. 20m Climb the corner and traverse right to the cave of Samurai (the direct start up to the cave looks better but has not been climbed).
2. 30m Climb directly out of the cave and up the fault to a steep wall below the Upper Girdle. Go up and traverse a flake on the left to gain the Girdle. Walk along the Girdle to regain the summer line.
3. 35m The 'overhanging chimney' was climbed direct followed by the move under the 'perched block'.
4. 35m As for summer, finishing up the shallow chimney of the central fault.

About 15m right of Samurai there is a steep crack running up the left side of a partly detached flake, starting about 6m up the cliff. Some 3m to the left of this is a line of twin cracks which gives the start of the next two climbs. There are a number of other possible ways up the lower tier around here but this appears to be the easiest.

25 Simpleton   120m   HVS *   (1980)
A vague crack-line just right of Samurai offers some good climbing on clean rock but feels a bit close to other routes. Notable features are a huge protruding block below the Upper Girdle which is just to the right of the route; two overhangs just above the Upper Girdle – a square overhang on the lower left and a more triangular one on the upper right; and a steep corner with a small roof just above the triangular overhang. Start below twin cracks 15m right of Samurai.
1. 45m 4b Climb the crack-line to a grassy ledge 10m below the Upper Girdle, then go diagonally right onto the huge flat-topped block and up to the Upper Girdle.
2. 25m 4c Traverse left into a crack-line which leads between the two roofs. Follow this into a short chimney immediately left of the triangular roof and belay below the steep corner.
3. 20m 5b Continue up the deceptively leaning corner (nut for aid; it would go free at 5c) to reach the right end of a big ledge on Samurai and below its right-hand chimney-fault.
4. 30m 4c Climb a wide right-slanting crack, then move back left on to the rib right of Samurai. Go up this to finish up a steep, crack seamed tower.

328 BEINN EIGHE

Fairytale Groove, VII,8, Eastern Ramparts, Coire Mhic Fhearchair, Beinn Eighe. Climber Es Tressider

26 Shang-High   120m   HVS   (1976)
A feature of this route is the prominent chimney in the upper tier, some 25m right of Samurai. A line does in fact start from Bottom Shelf but on the first ascent the lower chimney was avoided by climbing the wall on the left, approximately the same route subsequently taken by Simpleton.
1. 45m As for Simpleton.
2 and 3. 75m Climb the crack above for 6m then move right and up a steep wall until it is possible to move right to belay in the prominent chimney. Climb the chimney to a large slotted roof and turn this by a crack on the left. Continue up steep rock to the top.
Winter: **VII,7 *****   (1992)
Steep and strenuous, but a good winter line. Follow approximately the summer line to the Upper Girdle (finishing by the left side of the flat topped block, the best locating feature). From the Upper Girdle, follow the chimney-line direct, climbing through the slotted roof before moving left into another chimney.

At the right end of The Ramparts is a large white wall above The Upper Girdle. Between the white wall and the chimney-line of Shang-High on the left is formed a grey tower, The Tower of Darkness. The white wall is bounded on either side by a corner system and above its right side is a huge detached flake, very obvious from the base of the cliff.

27 Fear of the Dark   100m   E1   (1988)
Climbs the discontinuous corner system which bounds the white wall on its left. Start at the lower chimney of Shang-High.
1. 40m 5a Climb the right side of the chimney and the wide crack at the right side of the roof to belay on The Upper Girdle.
2. 10m Walk right and belay under the white wall.
3. 20m 4c A crack in the white rock above is the natural line but looks hard.

Instead climb a reddish corner left of the two white areas and move left to belay as for The Tower of Darkness.
4. 40m 5b Traverse right round an arete. Climb the arete a metre or so, then move right into the main corner. Climb the corner to a roof. Traverse right, then go up the wall and over a bulge into a finishing groove (which is 10m left of the large detached flake and just right of a big roof).

28 The Tower of Darkness   100m   E4 *   (1988)
Climbs the impressive grey tower, with a fingery crux. Start just right of the lower chimney of Shang-High, which is a wide roofed fault, at a long thin crack-line.
1. 45m 5b Climb the crack to a belay under the broad rib left of the pale wall.
2. 25m 5a Climb the rib to a block ledge under the tower. There is a reddish roofed groove above the left edge of the ledge.
3. 30m 6a Climb the thin crack above the right end of the ledge and go up to a roof. Step right under the roof and go up to another roof on the right edge of the tower. Finger traverse left, then go up the wall (crux) to an overhanging crack which leads to the top.

29 Fairytale Groove   100m   HVS *   (1988)
The route takes the big corner which bounds the right side of the white wall. Start below a narrow chimney right of the lower chimney of Shang-High (old cairn).
1. 45m 4b Climb straight up, passing the chimney on its right, to reach the Upper Girdle at the same place as Gnome Wall (which comes in from the right). Belay on the right, under the pale wall (as for Fear of the Dark).
2. 45m 5a Traverse right, then go up into a roofed recess. Pull out left from the recess into the main corner and follow it to easier ground.
3. 10m Climb a short wall to the easy crest of East Buttress.
Winter: **VII,8**   (2001)
Follow the summer line into and up the wide crack above the roofed recess for about 6m. The main corner moves left here but go right up cracks for 15m to a big ledge. Move right to a rib and finish up this easier blocky rib to reach East Buttress.

30 Happy Ever After   100m   E1   (1994)
Climbs a prominent groove in the rib right of Fairytale Groove. Start right of Gnome Wall and below the groove.
1. 40m 5a A crack in a pillar was chosen as a start, but there are other options.
2. 25m 5b Traverse right along the Upper Girdle underneath the undercut rib. Climb a groove just before the Gnome Wall recess and traverse left on to the rib as soon as possible. Climb the rib to the base of the groove.
3. 35m 5b Climb the groove using a wide crack on the left wall, then moving on to the right arete before finishing up blocky ground.

31 Gnome Wall   150m   Hard Severe 4a   (1959)
This route takes a line of weakness near the right-hand end of the Ramparts, and escapes onto the crest of East Buttress near a projecting gargoyle which is visible on the right skyline from the start of the route. Tom Patey's original description may indicate to connoisseurs of his routes what to expect. Start just up and right from the right-hand end of Bottom Shelf, where scrambling is required to continue rightwards. 'Work up leftwards to gain the Upper Girdle (45m). Traverse right along the Upper Girdle to where the ground above becomes more broken and belay in a recess (25m). Lunge onto a grassy ledge on the left. Climb a wet lichenous crack and a slab to reach a deep rock crevice on the right. An airy ledge to the right leads to an exposed 20m of climbing on excellent rock. Finish on easy rock just right of the gargoyle.'
Winter: **V,7** *   (1988)
The summer line gave interesting and unusual climbing to the belay below the gargoyle. A ferocious last pitch follows. Go up left to a pinnacle. Step off this and go up the wide crack immediately left of the gargoyle (30m). Continue to easy ground.

32 The Gash 50m Very Difficult *(1962)*
On a lower quartzite tier between Broad Terrace and the right end of the Eastern Ramparts. This is the bizarre, deeply cleft chimney which runs up left from Broad Terrace to end about 30m right of the start of Gnome Wall, to which it makes a good introduction. Start on Broad Terrace just right of a 'bad step'. Climb into a chimney leading to a large dry cave, go through behind chockstones (a tight squeeze), and finish up the clean rib on the left.
Winter: **III,4**
A possible start to East Buttress. Climbed as part of the following route.

**33 Gashtrognome 210m VI,7 ** *(1998)
Takes the line of least resistance up the concave scoop formed just left of East Buttress to a spectacular escape on to the buttress. The Icefall Start to East Buttress leads directly to this route.
1. 25m Climb The Gash to beyond its through route.
2. 35m Go up a shallow gully to a terrace and walk 10m right until below a pale corner (probably icy).
3. 20m Climb the corner and its left arete to a ledge up left.
4. 35m Step back down and traverse right above the corner along a ledge. Where the ledge ends, climb a left-facing corner, then take a left-curving line to below a big roof.
5. 20m Continue left across a pale slab and up a groove to a ledge.
6. 30m Go left again until just right of the Gargoyle. Pull right on to a sensational jutting ledge 'the diving board'. Continue right, still sensational, to easier ground.
7. 45m Go up the easing angle and a final short wall (on East Buttress).
Scramble to the top.

Triple Buttresses

(NG 945 603) Alt 700m North facing Map p307, Diagrams p332, p336

Coire Mhic Fhearchair is home to the famous Triple Buttresses which dominate the corrie and provide classic mountaineering routes up their crests. Because the buttresses angle to the north-west, their left sides provide long north-east faces with many routes. The left side of East Buttress is the Eastern Ramparts, already described. The left side of Central Buttress s Central Wall, home of many winter routes, while the left wall of West Buttress, West Central Wall, is much steeper and holds both sensational summer and hard winter routes.

East Buttress - Sandstone Tier

The original route up the buttress avoided most of the difficulties of the sandstone tier on the left and this may well be the preferred option in summer or winter because the more direct sandstone starts are considerably harder. Two summer routes and two winter routes are described on this tier, but other alternatives are possible, both summer and winter, particularly on the left.

1 Icefall Start 50m V,5 *(1983)*
A substantial icefall forms in a wet depress on left of the highest section of the sandstone tier and forming from a spring at the 'bad step' on Broad Terrace. It provides two pitches of steep ice, with steeper options available.

2 Mango 70m VS *(1977)*
Start 12m left of The Chimney at a small overhang.
1. 45m Climb up to a groove passing a loose block. Move right to a groove on the right, swing left and up to a ledge.
2. 25m Continue up rightwards to easier ground.

**3 The Chimney 65m VI,7 ** *(1986)
This is the conspicuous chimney near the right end of the sandstone tier. It has been

climbed in summer (Very Difficult) but is wet and loose. In winter it gives an excellent start to the buttress.
1. 25m Climb the steep chimney to a belay where the angle appears to ease and the chimney opens out to form a corner above.
2. 35m Continue directly up the corner till a short ramp can be followed to a flake. Move over this and up to a short corner below the terrace, a few metres left of the chimney-line.
3. 5m Climb the short corner to Broad Terrace.

4 Bloodstone Start   70m   Severe *(1972)*
Start mid-way between The Chimney and East Central Gully. Gain a ledge underneath a short, wet overhanging chimney. Go right round a rib and back left up towards a fault, and then a steep crack, to enter a recess with twin rock spikes above. Pass the spikes and go up right towards East Central Gully, then back left more easily to Broad Terrace.

East Buttress - Quartzite Tiers

5 East Buttress   210m   Difficult *** *(1907)*
An enjoyable, classic climb up the crest of the buttress, often climbed in boots. It has an imposing appearance but the holds are very positive and it is only slightly harder in the wet. Start on Broad Terrace about 10m from its right end. This point may be reached by traversing all the way along Broad Terrace from the left, easy but with one wet and exposed section, or by climbing the sandstone tier by one of the routes described above. Climb the steep face on good holds to a large ledge (30m). Continue up an interesting and varied series of pitches, often slightly right of the crest, to the top. A short vertical corner right of the crest is the crux and also the last difficulty before scrambling. Keeping further left is Very Difficult and also good.
Winter: **IV,5** ***
Follow the summer route, often by traversing along Broad Terrace which has one exposed icy section, about Grade II. It is climbable in any conditions and can often be used to salvage a day for those originally intent on harder things. The crux is as for summer.

6 East Central Gully   250m   III *
The normal start is to traverse all the way along Broad Terrace from the left and enter the gully easily from the base of East Buttress quartzite. The gully provides several ice pitches, none too long or steep.
Variation: **Direct Start   V,4**
The sandstone section of the gully is the logical direct start but is deceptively hard and serious. The ice is often hollow, covering a deep crack, and there is minimal protection. It makes a good start to the climbs on Central Wall. In summer the gully is Severe and usually wet.

Central Wall

Central Wall is the name given to the north-east facing left flank of the upper part of Central Buttress. It is bounded on the left by East Central Gully and on the right by the crest of Central Buttress. The lower part of the wall is formed by what appears from below to be a tower about 45m high rising from East Central Gully at the level of Broad Terrace. The top of the 'Tower' is in fact a gently sloping terrace from which most of the summer climbs start. It can be reached most pleasantly in summer by climbing up the first 35m of East Buttress Ordinary Route and then traversing across East Central Gully.

In winter the easiest access is to traverse above the sandstone tier of East Buttress into East Central Gully and follow this until one can break out right onto the Tower (Grade II). A more satisfying approach is to climb the first pitch of East Central Gully (Grade V,4), then take the right fork between the Tower and Central Buttress, finally breaking out left onto the Tower (Grade IV,4). The right fork can

1. Icefall Start	V,5		10. East Wall	VI,7 *
3. The Chimney	VI,7 **		12. East Central Wall	V,4 ***
5. East Buttress	IV,5 ***		13. Patey's Direct Route	V,6
6. East Central Gully	III		14. Pelican	VI,6 ***
8. The Cool Cleft	V,5 **		18. Piggott's Route	VI,7 ****
9. Assegai	V,6		21. Hamilton's Route	VI,6 **

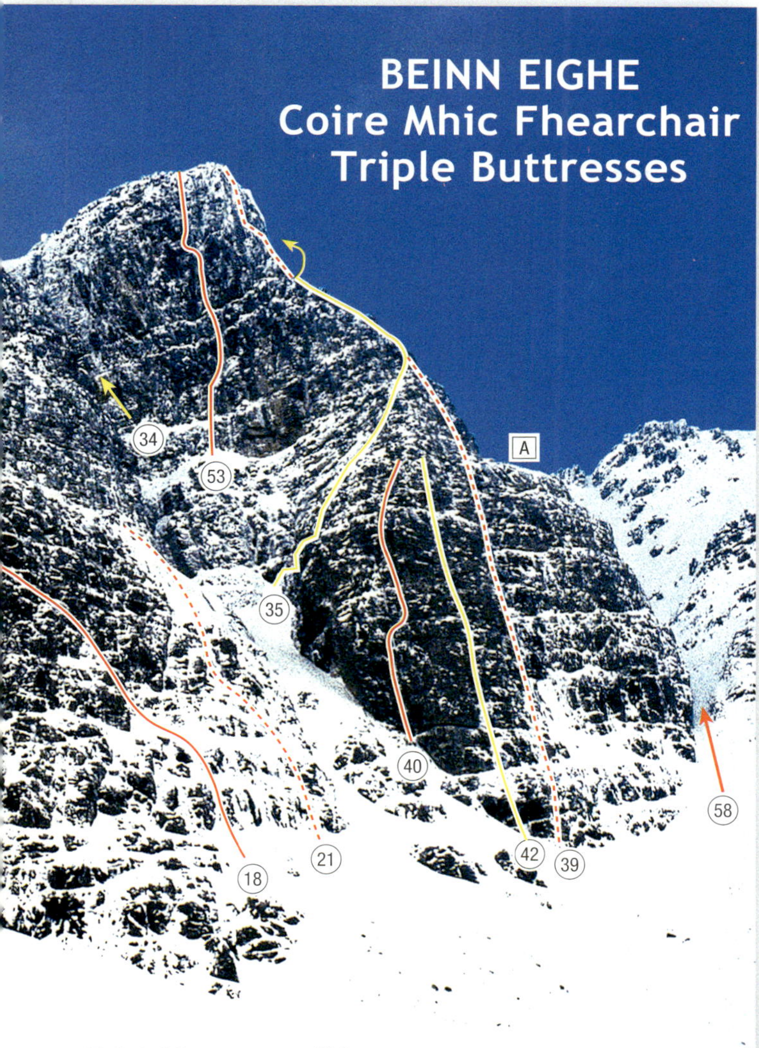

BEINN EIGHE
Coire Mhic Fhearchair
Triple Buttresses
34
53
35
A
40
42
39
58
18
21

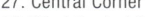

27. Central Corner	VII,8	42. Junior	E1
34. West Central Gully	VII,8 ***	53. Mistral	VII,7 ***
35. W.Buttress, W-C Start	IV,4 ***	58. Fuselage Gully	I **
39. W.Buttress Direttissima	VII,8 ***		
40. Sideshow	HVS	A. Broad Terrace	

Rab Anderson

also be reached by the traverse across East Buttress (Grade II) if the initial chimney of East Central Gully is insufficiently iced. The winter climbs Pelican and Flight of the Condor naturally start up the right fork, and this is included in the length given.

7 East Central Ribs   100m   Severe 4a   *(1954)*
The climb follows the crest of three successive quartzite ribs, just right of East Central Gully. The ribs are steep and exposed and bordered on the right by a narrow cleft. Start just above the Tower in the cleft right of the first rib. Follow the cleft for a few metres then traverse left by a short, difficult overhang to the crest. Follow the crest for 25m and get to the right edge. Traverse onto the right flank and into a groove which leads up for 3m to a large ledge on the crest; continue up this for 15m to a narrow arete leading to the second rib. Start the second rib on the left and traverse with difficulty to the crest, which is followed to the top of the second rib (40m). The final rib is straight ahead. Start up an overhanging chimney on the left (5m), then a vertical wall to a ledge (10m) followed by easier rock to the top.
Winter: **V,6**   *(1997)*
Following the summer route except that the second tower was climbed direct but the third less direct; after the overhanging chimney, a ledge was traversed right into the top of another chimney which led up and left back to the crest.

8 The Cool Cleft   120m   V,5 **   *(1983)*
This takes the shallow curving narrow cleft immediately right of East Central Ribs. It readily forms ice, particularly late in the season. Climb an icy chimney for 30m. Continue up to a very steep icy section 12m high (crux). Follow the right-curving continuation fault more easily to the top (70m). On the first ascent, the crux section lacked ice and instead the rib on the left was climbed, as for East Central Ribs.

9 Assegai   90m   VS 5a *   *(1976)*
Immediately right of East Central Ribs is a parallel rib, about 30m high, and right again is a line of slanting and steep narrow slabs ending on the right at a prominent corner. There is a rockfall scar on the wall on the right; start just left of it. Climb slabs to the horizontal fault of the Upper Girdle, then a groove on the left to a good stance. Traverse left then up, and cross to another stance. Climb straight up strenuously (crux) then climb a loose block into an overhanging chimney and up to a stance. Follow the chimney, then go right to a wall and a stance on the edge. Finish up a wall of loose blocks.
Winter: **120m   V,6**   *(1993)*
This winter ascent was based on the summer line. Start 5m right of The Cool Cleft.
1. 35m Climb a wide steep chimney, then go right to belay below the chimney of the summer route.
2. 40m Move left into a corner, then into cracks just to the right, before moving back right to the summer line above its chimney.
3. and 4. 45m Follow the summer line.

10 East Wall   140m   VI,7 *   *(1989)*
The route takes a big stepped corner system in the steep buttress between Assegai and Fulmar Chimneys. The rockfall scar is in the left wall of the corner system which trends up right. Start below and right of the rockfall scar.
1. 30m Climb leftwards and follow a chimney just right of the back of the corner system. At its top move right to a huge block belay below vertical twin cracks.
2. 15m Climb the left-hand crack, but finish by the last moves of the right crack.
3. 35m Take a short corner on the left with a jutting block. Move left, then up to a squeeze chimney. Avoid this by a traverse left and descend 10m into the main corner system. Follow this to a big ledge on the left.
4. 25m Go more easily right and back left by a chimney to the crest.
5. 35m Easy ground to the top.
Summer: **Severe**   *(1954)*
This route was 'unidentifiable' in the last guide, but is thought to have followed more or less the line of the winter route described above.

CENTRAL WALL 335

*The Cool Cleft, V.5. Central Wall, Coire Mhic Fhearchair, Beinn Eighe.
Climber Robin Clothier*

11 Fulmar Chimneys 90m Very Difficult *(1970)*
From the top of the Tower, easy ground slopes up left. Go up this for 15m, then traverse 5m right to a small grass corner at the foot of a deep-cut chimney. There is a flake embedded in the grass on the left. Climb the chimney finishing to the right. Continue up a second chimney and easy rock trending right to a nook below the final steep wall. Traverse right past a curious triangular truncated block to the foot of a steep, clean chimney and go up this to the top.

12 East Central Wall 370m V,4 *** *(1981)*
This is a winter version of Fulmar Chimneys, a good first excursion away from the buttresses with a fine mountaineering atmosphere. Climb East Central Gully through the sandstone (crux, grade reduced to IV,4 by the normal start to East Gully, along Broad Terrace), then take the right fork between the Tower and Central Buttress. From the top of the gully between the Tower and Central Buttress go up leftwards on broken ground until about 10m below and right of a very prominent crack. Now the route is based on Fulmar Chimneys. Traverse 5m right along an overhung ledge to the base of the chimney. Climb this and a further right-slanting chimney to reach a triangular bay with ice in the overhanging corner at its top. The ice is very steep and may be avoided by climbing a shallow chimney to the right of the bay which leads to easy ground.

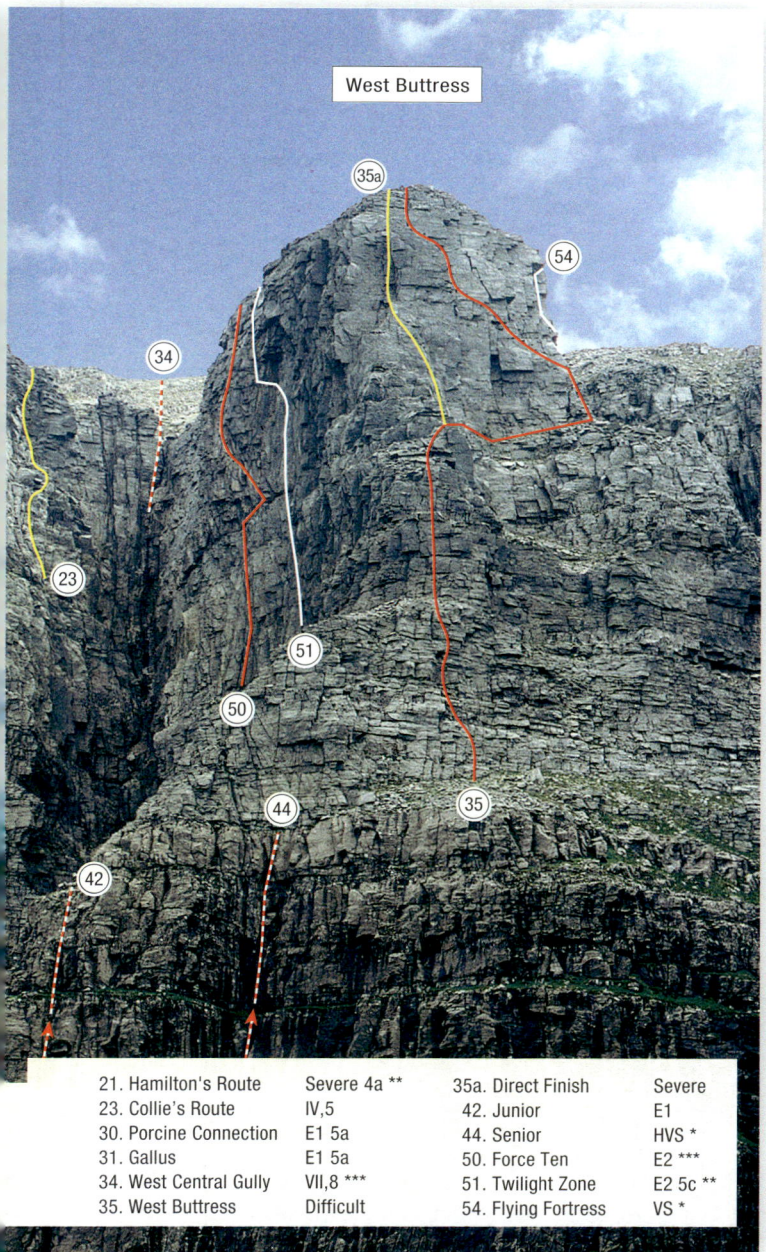

West Buttress

21. Hamilton's Route	Severe 4a **	35a. Direct Finish	Severe
23. Collie's Route	IV,5	42. Junior	E1
30. Porcine Connection	E1 5a	44. Senior	HVS *
31. Gallus	E1 5a	50. Force Ten	E2 ***
34. West Central Gully	VII,8 ***	51. Twilight Zone	E2 5c **
35. West Buttress	Difficult	54. Flying Fortress	VS *

Andy Nisbet

13 Patey's Direct Route   105m   Hard Severe 4b   *(1957)*
This is a steep and direct route up the right side of Central Wall, in the line of the gully between the Tower and Central Buttress. Start where this gully peters out, at a level a little below the top of the Tower and under a shallow depression in the steep wall above. The route follows a line of thin cracks on the left of the depression which continue after mid-height as a V-groove with an overhang at the top. Climb the cracks for 35m. A steep 10m wall then leads to an easier angled wide chimney with a flat 'card-table' on the right at mid-height. Avoid the start of the V-groove by taking the crack on the left for 12m and then traversing back right. Continue up the groove and turn the top overhang on the left.
Winter: **V,6**   *(1988)*
Follow the summer line throughout.

14 Pelican   105m   Severe *   *(1977)*
To the right of Patey's Direct Route is a prominent, steep chimney-crack line. This is climbed direct all the way.
Winter: **180m   VI,6 *****   *(1987)*
1. 45m Climb the gully to the right of the Tower (access to the Tower is now on the left).
2. 25m Continue up the gully by a steep ice pitch to belay under a prominent chimney with two sections.
3. 20m The first section of the chimney is very narrow and may be climbed by a shallow corner on the right. The second section tapers and forces an awkward, strenuous exit.
3. 35m Above is a large roof. Avoid this by a ramp on the left, pulling through the left end of the roof into an icy groove which leads to the Upper Girdle. Pull through the bulge above and go up a groove to a stance.
4. 35m Continue up the groove (more like a shallow chimney) to a ledge. Move left into another groove system and up this to belay.
5. 20m Follow the groove to the top.

15 Condor Crack   75m   Severe   *(1986)*
This lies on the wall between Pelican and upper crest of Central Buttress. Start either by descending left from the terrace below the final tier of Central Buttress or approach most easily via Parker's Route (Route 24).
1. 20m Scramble up easy rock until it steepens. Step up and go easily left along the line of the Upper Girdle to an awkward step down, then up. Climb over some blocks easily seen from the start.
2. 25m 4b Muscle up a left-slanting off-width flake-crack and step left then right into a crack-line. Follow this to more blocks.
3. 30m Climb over the blocks and step right to a little slab which leads to a band of steeper rock. Pass this by a shallow chimney, then easier rock to the top.

16 Flight of the Condor   250m   VII,8   *(1989)*
The route takes a line up the right side of Central Wall, passing left of a big left-facing corner on the final tier. Start by traversing above the sandstone of East Buttress into East Central Gully and on to the base of the gully right of the Tower. Two short pitches in the gully lead to an easy ramp which goes out right towards the crest of Central Buttress. Climb straight up to the Upper Girdle. An obvious off-width flake crack can now be seen up on the left (Condor Crack pitch 2). Traverse left a short distance, then up a groove until a long step left gains the base of the crack. Climb the crack (short but desperate when verglassed, 30m). Climb the wall above, trending slightly right to a ledge. Traverse right, then descend to the right to gain the top of a big left-facing corner (here joining Central Buttress, Flying Finish). Climb an easy chimney to blocky ground (35m). Now the normal finish to Central Buttress, winter; go diagonally left to a big pinnacle, then back right round an edge to a bay. The short chimney at the back leads to snow slopes.

17 Flying Finish (to Central Buttress)   75m   Hard Severe   *(1997)*
Start 10m along the Upper Girdle, traversing from the base of Central Buttress final

CENTRAL WALL — 339

Hamilton's Route, Severe, Central Buttress, Coire Mhic Fhearchair, Beinn Eighe. Climber John Ellison

tier, just before a dangerous looking column of rock.
1. 35m 4b Climb a chimney to a ledge, then trend left up flake-cracks past an awkward block to the arete right of a big left-facing corner, an obvious feature on the face when seen from the left. Climb the chimney just right of the arete to an airy ledge.
2. 40m Climb an easy chimney on the left, then finish left and right by a big pinnacle (as for Flight of the Condor, also the easiest finish to Pigott's Route).

Central Buttress

As always, there are three tiers, sandstone, lower quartzite and upper quartzite. Any combination of routes on each tier can be made but some old and new combinations of consistent grade are described initially followed by other routes which are on one tier only.

340　BEINN EIGHE

*Central Buttress – Pigott's Route, VI,7, Coire Mhic Fhearchair, Beinn Eighe.
Climber Grahame Nicoll*

18 Central Buttress – Pigott's Route　270m　Severe 4b ＊＊　　　　　*(1922)*
This line nearest the crest is most commonly followed in summer and winter and generally referred to as 'Central Buttress'. A classic route in all senses, taking a magnificent line up the crest of the buttress but quite vegetated in the sandstone and many ledges with loose blocks on the quartzite. When damp (or wet, when it is still possible), it is recommended to start as described for Hamilton's Route (called Slab Route) or to miss out the sandstone by starting up West Central Gully. This is about Moderate but not exposed and soloing assumed for the recommendation.

The route starts up the sandstone via the obvious diagonal line running up from right to left (not so obvious from directly underneath). Start on the grass terrace just above the lowest rocks, about one-third of the way from the right-hand end, where a pinnacle block leans against the face. Climb from the block to a terrace, move right and reach a black cave clearly visible from below (30m). From the top of the cave follow the grassy rake up left to Broad Terrace and the quartzite.
Continue quite close to the arrival point, from the highest point of the grass on Broad Terrace, in a bay just right of the crest. Climb up trending left to a stance in a corner (20m). Traverse left to the crest, round it, and up an exposed chimney on good holds. Go up easy ground to the foot of the final tier.

The route up the final tower takes a big groove which starts just left of the crest and bends up right to follow the crest. Climb a big open groove over several short steps to a platform. On the right is a short overhanging chimney-crack with a crack to its right. Climb the chimney with difficulty, the only Severe move on the route but definitely so, (sack hauling and combined tactics may help; or avoid it by a loop on the right on to the frontal face, particularly useful in the wet – see Direct Route) and move up to an obvious crack. An esoteric finish is now to traverse horizontally left on a narrow ledge across a vertical wall to reach easier ground but more normally, go up right on big blocks towards the frontal face, then pull up left to a flake on the wall and overlooking the crack. Step left under a bulge to the top

of the crack and then a bay. Climb a short overhanging wall on the right or, easier, go left to a big pinnacle and right to the top (the winter choice).
Winter: **VI,7** **** *(1971/1978)*
A magnificent winter route, long and hard with the crux near the top. The awkward overhanging chimney-crack in this final tier is the crux by far. The shallow groove immediately to its left has also been climbed and is technically easier, although with several thin moves.

19 Central Buttress – VS Route   280m   VS **** *(1976/1998)*
Constructed as a VS line on all tiers and offering arguably the best climbing (particularly for a VS leader!). The big corner (Central Corner) in the sandstone is high in the grade (especially with rucksacks) but the quartzite tiers are low in the grade. Start via the very prominent diedre on the left flank of the sandstone tier.
1. 50m 4a Climb to the terrace below the corner, then a right-slanting line to the base of the corner itself.
2. 50m 4c The corner provides a superb long pitch; the pitch can also be split.
Walk right along Broad Terrace until about 40m right of the crest (and Pigott's) where the highest sandstone forms a platform 10m above Broad Terrace. This is below the right-hand of two right-facing corners which each start about 20m up.
3. 20m 4a Climb on to the platform and straight up to the left end of a ledge (same as Hamilton's Route).
4. 20m 4b A fairly direct line up the wall above, slightly right, then left to finish up a corner.
5. 40m 4a Climb steep blocky ground.
6. 40m Scramble to the Upper Tier.
7. 30m 4b Start just right of the crest and a block resting against the face at a small right-facing corner with jammed flakes (i.e. between Pigott's and Hamilton's). Climb this and a wider corner-crack above. An easy way leads left to Pigott's. Instead, move out right on to the crest.
8. 30m 4a Follow the crest steeply on good holds to the top.

20 The Generation Game   220m   E2 5c * *(1994)*
A direct and hard version of Central Buttress, picking good pitches. Climbed when damp; possibly E1. Start to the left of the grassy start to Pigott's Route. Go left to a vague shallow groove, then trend right to a small ledge (4c). Go up an obvious pod, then straight up a vertical wall to belay just left of Pigott's lower ramp-line (5c, thin). Cross Pigott's and climb easily up and right to the terrace. On the quartzite, start below 'a corner halfway between Pigott's and Hamilton's' (presumably the corner of The Porcine Connection). Climb the wall to the right of the corner and over a couple of overlaps (50m, 5b/c). Now a direct line to the final tower. This was climbed by a chimney and flake-line starting as for Hamilton's but cutting back left on to the tower itself on gigantic flakes to the top, perhaps coinciding with the 'VS Route' near the top (4c).

21 Hamilton's Route   270m   Severe 4a ** *(1936)*
The other traditional line, up the right side of the buttress, more sustained but no harder. Not as good a line but better climbing, particularly on the Upper Tier. An easy but pleasant route up the right-hand side of the sandstone has been chosen as a start (Slab Route, Difficult), although Hamilton did not start this way.

Start at the right end of the grass terrace below the face, about 10m left of West Central Gully. Climb slabby rock parallel to the gully, choosing the easiest line on good rock, for 70m to meet a barrier slab beneath Broad Terrace. Trend left up this, spaced protection, to the Terrace close to where the route continues.

Start about 40m right of the crest (and Pigott's) where the top of the sandstone rises above Broad Terrace and forms a platform 10m up. This is right of an obvious right-facing corner in the centre of the wall which starts about 20m up. Climb to reach the quartzite and straight up to the left end of a ledge (20m, 4a). Or reach the same point by going right and back left, easier but some loose rock. Traverse right along the ledge (about 15m), then trend up right to the edge of the buttress, overlooking West-Central Gully (20m). Go up a big groove slanting back left and continue to below a short bulging corner. Traverse back right round an edge to climb a short corner (or climb the bulging corner – 4b). Continue on easier ground to the base of the final tower. Start this about 10m right of the crest below a huge flange of rock curving up right. Go diagonally right on flakes to gain the right end of a ledge on top of a large detached flake below the flange. Climb slabs diagonally rightwards (4a) to reach and follow big open chimneys to the top, keeping always on the right side of the buttress.

Winter: **VI,6** ** *(1998)*

A similar standard to Pigott's, perhaps a little more sustained but without the very awkward crux. Slab Route makes a fine start if an icefall which forms on the smooth slabs just below Broad Terrace is formed. Or the icefall can be climbed on its own, reached easily from West Central Gully. Otherwise, gain the quartzite start easily via West Central Gully. Start up a vegetated groove right of the summer start and only about 20m from West Central Gully. Follow this into a corner on the right which leads to the end of the traverse on the summer route. Follow the summer route thereafter, including the final tower.

22 Central Buttress – Grade IV Line   300m   IV,5 ***   *(2001)*

A constructed winter line up Central Buttress at an easier grade to provide a magnificent (but devious) mountaineering route. Start up Slab Route to the barrier slab (see Hamilton's Route). Either climb this or if not iced, traverse right to a grassy groove near West Central Gully and climb this to Broad Terrace. Follow Hamilton's Route (winter) until the top of the big groove (which often ices). Traverse left along a terrace to join easy ground on the crest (Pigott's) and return right to below the final tier. Now finish up Collie's Route:

23 Collie's Route   110m   IV,5   *(1990)*

This is an easier finish to the right of Hamilton's Route, approximately following Collie's original summer line, which reached here by West Central Gully. Also a good option for those running out of steam on Pigott's or Hamilton's. Difficult in summer.
1. 35m From the crest of the buttress below the final tier (Pigott's), make a descending traverse rightwards along the Terrace for 25m to just past a rib which forces the terrace to narrow. Climb up turfy ledges in a stepped corner system to below a short steep corner.
2. 25m Either go up left and traverse back right on to the top of the short corner or climb the corner direct (well protected but 6) to a ledge. Move right up flakes to a steep wall, then round its right end to reach an easier line leading up left.
3. 50m Follow this line up left to a short awkward corner and a short chimney which lead to the final crest.

24 Parker's Route   300m   Very Difficult

The easiest line up the buttress, much of which is scrambling, is mostly of historical interest. The route started up West Central Gully and left along Broad Terrace to the crest, not far from the top of Central Corner. Climb by a series of blocks and cracks, trending slightly right, to the middle horizontal fault. Continue on easy rock to the Upper Girdle below the final tower. The original line here is uncertain and may have coincided partly with Pigott's, but it seems both probable and appropriate to traverse right along its base beyond Hamilton's Route and finish by Collie's Route (Difficult).

Alternative routes on first the sandstone and then the quartzite are now described.

Central Buttress - Sandstone Tier

25 Central Reservation   70m   HVS   *(1992)*

This climbs a set of slabs leading out left to the left edge of the tier. Start at the same point as Central Corner.
1. 25m 4b Move out left then up to the base of the first slab, which is climbed on its left side. The only belay is below the right-hand corner of the next steep slab.

2. 45m 4c Climb the corner, then the following slab by its left edge. Continue (unprotected) to the top.

26 Swinging in the Rain   70m   HVS * (1992)
A good wee route up the face left of Central Corner.
1. 40m 5a Climb straight up into a left-facing corner about 5m left of Central Corner. Follow it to its end, then move left into a small corner (which is the continuation of a crack-line from below).
2. 30m 4c Finish up the corner and the slabs above.

27 Central Corner – Winter   VII,8 (1999)
Central Corner is the very prominent diedre on the left flank of the tier and described as part of the Central Buttress – VS Route. The winter route follows the summer line. The corner can fill with snow and some ice and was climbed in these conditions.

28 Puddock   70m   HVS * (1985)
This climbs the steep grooves just right of Central Corner. Start from a grass terrace and go up to belay below the grooves. Follow the left-hand groove to reach a good ledge below a short overhanging corner. Climb the corner and exit left to ledges. Continue more easily to Broad Terrace.

29 Readymix   90m   Severe (1968)
This is the best way of starting up Central Buttress – Pigott's Route at a consistent grade. Pigott's itself starts up an obvious fault running diagonally up left. Below the grass ledge at the foot of this fault there is another grass terrace which runs almost all the way round the buttress just above the lowest rocks, and is reached most easily by scrambling up to the right. The route starts from this terrace, at the point where it is scree covered for a short distance, about 15m left of the pinnacle block of Pigott's Route.
1. 25m Climb 5m to the top of a small projecting rib, then up left onto a small slab to gain the foot of a groove. Climb to a small ledge at 12m, then more steeply to a large ledge.
2. 25m Regain the groove above by traversing right to avoid a bulge, then trend left to reach a good ledge and belay.
3. 40m The leftward trend continues up a short wall and then, by an exposed move, around a pillar of rocks, which is climbed. Finish up a steep wall.

Slab Route is next to the right and used as the start to Hamilton's Route (Route 21).

Central Buttress - Lower Quartzite Tier

In addition to the routes described above, there are other options both on the lower and upper quartzite tiers. From the crest (Central Buttress – Pigott's Route) rightwards is a long wall leading to Hamilton's Route at the far (West Central Gully) end. The upper half of this wall holds several right-facing corners which are the key to finding the routes. The first main corner is a direct version of Pigott's Route. The second, about one-third along the wall, is Porcine Connection, with The Generation Game to its right. The third, about two-thirds along the wall is the basis of Gallus while the fourth, smaller and towards the right end, is taken by Central Buttress – VS Route.

30 Porcine Connection   100m   E1 5a (1995)
A line up the lower quartzite tier, i.e. immediately above Broad Terrace, climbing the left-hand of the two central right-facing corners starting about 20m up. Start about 15m right of Central Buttress – Pigott's Route and 25m from the right edge of the buttress below the corner. Trend up right to below a very prominent right-facing corner (25m). Climb delicately up into the corner and follow it (35m). Trend right via a crack to join easier ground.

West Buttress, IV,4, Coire Mhic Fhearchair, Beinn Eighe. Climber Rab Anderson

31 Gallus 75m E1 5a (2000)
Start just right of Porcine Connection at a ragged vertical crack.
1. 35m 5a Climb the crack for 20m to the bottom of the corner (touching Porcine Connection). Traverse a wide foot ledge right to a blunt rib below and right of the right-hand corner. Climb this for 5m then traverse left to a hanging stance at the foot of the right-hand corner.
2. 40m 4c Move back right to the rib, then climb diagonally up and right to a horizontal break which is followed right to a detached pillar overlooking the corner of Central Buttress – VS Route. Carefully climb the left-hand side of the pillar to a large grass ledge.

Central Buttress - Upper Quartzite Tier

Condor Crack (Route 15) and the Flying Finish (Route 17) are strictly on Central Wall but are usually accessed by traversing left from the crest. Next is Central Buttress – Pigott's Route, then the VS Route, then The Generation Game, Hamilton's and Collie's. Below are a couple of additional routes.

WEST BUTTRESS 345

32 Dusk 65m E1 *(1996)*
A harder finale up the final tower, and must be close to easier routes, but this author couldn't find it! Start round right of the large detached flake of Hamilton's Route, beneath a smaller such feature a short way up the wall.
1. 25m 5b Climb up to just right of the flake, then cross Hamilton's and head up slightly rightwards on good edges into a slim left-facing groove. Ascend this by a fine finger-crack to the ledge just above.
2. 40m 5b Continue up the open chimney come corner above, with difficult moves above a large ledge near the top.

33 Nunn's Route 100m Scottish IV, aid *(1969)*
Start in West Central Gully and climb easily up left as for the start of the Terrace below the final tier. On the right side of Central Buttress is an overhanging wall with a cave at its base and leading into a chimney system. Climb out the top of the cave on aid and up the much easier chimney system to join Collie's Route where it turns left. It has been freed (very strenuous) but the party abseiled off in darkness.

34 West Central Gully 350m VII,8 *** *(1987)*
The gully is easy except for a very steep 70m step sporting an ice smeared overhanging chimney leading to steep, pure ice climbing. A very hard and fine climb. From the base of the step ascend the chimney forming the back of the gully and belay beneath a prominent overhang (25m). Climb into the chimney-groove on the left of the overhang, move up to another overhang and follow an ice-choked crack to small ledges on the left (20m). Take the mixed groove on the left to the overhang; step right on to icy smears and follow these to good, thick ice and easy ground 50m from the top (25m).

West Buttress

The lowest tier of the West Buttress is easily the most formidable of the sandstone tiers on the triple buttresses, and contains some excellent climbs. The middle quartzite section is fairly broken on the crest and can be climbed almost anywhere, but the final tier rears up imposingly to provide situations as fine as any in the corrie. The steep left wall of the quartzite, rising from broken ground somewhat above the level of Broad Terrace also provides good climbs, of a similar but sterner character than Central Wall.

As with Central Buttress, climbs on different tiers may be connected together at will, allowing numerous permutations. For convenience, the normal route up the buttress is described first in its entirety. The other climbs on the initial (Sandstone) and final (Quartzite) tiers are then described separately.

35 West Buttress 300m Severe 4a (sandstone), Difficult (quartzite) * *(1919)*
Missing out the sandstone by starting up Fuselage Gully reduces the grade to Difficult. Start near the extreme right of the buttress, close to Fuselage Gully. Climb an open scoop followed by an overhang to the right on to a grass terrace. Go up to the right of a slight crack, traverse left across a corner to a slab and climb it to another grass ledge. Go slightly right and up a poorly defined groove to a sloping moss ledge. Climb the slab above working slightly left to reach Broad Terrace. The buttress is now quite easy angled. Climb on the right of the buttress crest, with short walls and occasional interest, to the base of the final tower, whose steep frontal face has been likened to a massive upstanding domino. A direct finish at Severe provides a better alternative. For the normal route, traverse/walk right on scree ledges for about 20m to the edge where the buttress turns towards Fuselage Gully. Climb a line of weakness and traverse back left along ledges. Climb a shallow chimney in a big corner to a ledge just below the top of the steep frontal face of the final tower. A short narrow chimney leads to a walk along the final crest.
Variation: **Direct Finish 60m Severe 4a *** *(1960)*
This takes the left side of the steep frontal face. From below the final tower climb

a clean 9m wall strenuously on good holds. This leads to a recess on the left of the tower, whence an easy move left gives access to a flake-crack slanting up right. Climb this, with a fine exposed finish behind an enormous projecting block. Climb the wall above to the top.
Winter: **400m IV,4 ***** *(1979)*
Another superb mountaineering route. The two options skirt the sandstone tier either on the left via West Central Gully or on the right via Fuselage Gully, the options joining to share a finish up steep frontal face of the final tower.

West Central Start
This provides wonderful scenery. Start up West Central Gully, easy slabby ground or banked out. Once into the wide part of the gully proper, keep to the right and climb a narrow right branch into a cave. Crawl out right on to the buttress, then go up into a bay exited by a chimney on the right. Go up to a steep band, the crux when climbed direct, but there may be an easier option. Now on easier ground, continue to the final tier and finish by the summer route going right, then back left.

Fuselage Gully Start
Climb some way up Fuselage Gully (Far West Gully) and go left at the first break in its steep left wall (this is high up but still sandstone). Follow the easiest practicable line to Broad Terrace. Alternatively, continue up the gully until above the sandstone and traverse easily left along Broad Terrace (should be soloable). Go along the Terrace to its apparent end where it goes round a bend. Climb shallow corners just right or on the crest to reach the final tier after about four pitches, joining the West Central Gully Start after about 60m. A line up a large shallow scoop in the face right of the crest has also been climbed (as on the first ascent).

36 Corner Finish to West Buttress 60m VS * *(1971)*
On the right-hand side of the steep frontal wall is a clean-cut corner topped by an overhang with a hole in it. This forms the right side of steep frontal face of the final tower.
1. 35m Climb the corner to the overhang, passing a ledge on the right at 25m. Climb the overhang through the hole to a big ledge on the normal route.
2. 25m Climb the shallow chimney of the normal route for 9m, then step right below an overhang and traverse round to the foot of a crack in a hanging corner. Climb this to another overhang and move left to finish.
Winter: **VI,7 *** *(2000)*
By the summer route, sustained and well protected.

37 Still Game 60m VI,7 * *(2007)*
A crack-line up the smooth wall between the Corner Finish and the Right-Hand Finish. Some wide cracks provide a variety of torquing techniques; large hexes and Friends up to 4 are useful. Start at the right end of a lower wall, just left of the edge where the buttress turns towards Fuselage Gully. The aim is to gain a corner formed past the right end of a prominent roof.
1. 25m After a step up, climb diagonally left to gain the shallow vertical corner. Climb it to the right end of the roof, then the easier continuation corner before heading up left on the normal West Buttress route to a point about 5m from the right end of the upper wall; this is below the crack-line.
2. 20m Climb up left to a roof, then squirm right past it to a ledge below the crack-line. Climb the crack-line to a ledge below a right-facing corner.
3. 15m Climb the corner to the top of the buttress.

38 Right-Hand Finish to West Buttress 35m Very Difficult *
This tackles a large right-facing corner system in the top tier, above the point where the normal route traverses back left. Above is a steep flake-chimney. Climb this until moves can be made left onto a ledge. Climb the exhilarating wall above the right side of the ledge on excellent holds.
Winter: **V,6 **** *(1986)*
Climb the chimney and corner direct without the detour left on to the ledge.

WEST BUTTRESS

39 West Buttress Direttissima   310m   VII,8 ***   (1986/2005)
This very fine and direct winter line follows the large open corner of the summer route, Senior, on the lower tier. On the top tier it takes the Direct Finish. Gain the base of the obvious corner-line in the sandstone tier, either by an icefall, or by an easy traverse along a shelf.
1. 30m Climb the corner, or ice to its right and step left to belay.
2. 20m Step back right and climb the corner direct via a steep crack with a difficult exit to a good belay.
3. 30m Move up the corner a little, then go right and up to gain a girdling ledge. Continue on ice above with increasing difficulty to an awkward belay at a huge flake.
4. 25m Step back left into the corner, then climb this strenuously to reach the crest of the buttress.
5. 6. and 7. 110m Continue up the crest of the buttress to the quartzite, then take the normal route to below the final tower.
8. 20m The line is now that of the Direct Finish. Climb a short wall, then another short wall with a thin crack; step left and continue to a recess formed by a huge flake at the foot of the impressive final flake-line.
9. 30m Move up then left to gain the flake-line which leads to a fine finish over an obvious projecting block.
10. 35m Climb a short chimney and easy ground to the top.
Variation: **Original Line**
3a. 40m Reach the girdling ledge, then traverse left along it to gain the frontal face. Belay below an obvious groove barred by a bulge, just past a narrowing of the ledge where a step has to be made over a loose block.
4a. 40m Once the initial bulge is overcome the difficulties ease and a shallow groove leads to the crest of the buttress.

West Buttress - Sandstone Tier

40 Sideshow   80m   HVS †   (1976)
On the left side of the sandstone tier, overlooking West Central Gully, an obvious groove runs almost to the top of the tier. Start below and left of an obvious spike. Climb up and right past the spike into the groove, go up this to an overhang which is turned on the right and continue in the same groove to a ledge. Move up and right to a large rock ledge below a flared chimney. Climb the chimney to a grass ledge then take the rocks above to easy ground.

41 Cyclonic Westerly   90m   E3 **   (1992)
A fine route on perfect rock but serious, with a sustained balancy and unprotected section. A total contrast in styles when combined with Force Ten or Shoot the Breeze on the quartzite tier. Start as for Junior.
1. 10m 4c Climb to the base of the Junior corner.
2. 25m 5c Move out left on juggy rock to the base of a shallow corner in Junior's left arete. Step left and climb the wall direct (crux) to a steep line of flakes, which lead to a good ledge.
3. 40m 5b Move out left under a roof onto the slabbier face. Trend right, then follow a left-slanting groove to a roof. Pull through this, then follow two more grooves (not far left of Junior) to a huge ledge.
4. 15m 4c Climb easily through the final tier.
Variation: **E1**   (1992)
Instead of climbing the wall direct on pitch 2, go diagonally left across the face to belay near Sideshow (5a). Climb a short corner, then make a long rightwards deviation to regain the direct route a few metres below the roof of pitch 3 (5b).

42 Junior   90m   E1   (1976)
The straight steep corner mid-way between the big central corner and the left edge of the buttress. The lower section is usually wet and the corner can collect rubble.

Blood, Sweat and Frozen Tears, VIII,8, West Buttress, Coire Mhic Fhearchair, Beinn Eighe. Climber Martin Moran

1. 45m 5b From the lower grass ledge climb up to the corner and follow it directly to belay on a large ledge on the left.
2. 20m 5a Continue in the corner to a ledge on the left below an overhang. Step left and climb the steep wall into a groove. Follow the groove to a grass ledge terrace.
3. 25m Climb easily to the top of the sandstone tier.
Variation: **Direct Start   10m   E3 5c**   *(1996)*
A desperate and badly protected start, but it does avoid the green slime! Start left of the corner and climb steep rock to gain a prominent jutting horn of rock. Hard and unprotected moves lead right into the Junior corner.

43 Relayer   90m   Scottish VS   *(1976)*
Start 15m right of Junior. Climb an easy groove to a ledge and belay. Follow the groove over a small bulge to a ledge, move up and right into a small niche and traverse right to another small niche. Climb up to a small overhang, traverse right, then go back up left to the foot of a small prominent corner. Climb a little way up the groove and go left along a ledge. Move up over a small bulge and right into a short corner; climb this and the rocks above to a grass ledge and finish up an obvious easy groove.

44 Senior 90m HVS * (1976)
This is the big central corner in the sandstone tier, often wet. It is climbed directly throughout, taking the right-hand of two cracks at mid-height.

The slabs and walls right of Senior give good climbing. Two routes have been made here (90m VS), one of which takes a line about 30m right of the corner. Descriptions have not been recorded.

West Buttress - Quartzite Tier - West Central Wall

Above the sandstone the quartzite of the West Buttress is fairly broken on the crest, and not too steep, for some way until it rears up in a final imposing tier above the level of the Upper Girdle, which traverses its left face as a twin (upper and lower) ledge system. On this face, Twilight Zone starts from the lowest steep rocks, but all the other summer routes start from the Second Terrace. This can be reached by two 50m abseils down the line of Twilight Zone (or any of the other routes but with a first anchor near the cliff top); the descent can be planned from the good view from the top of Central Buttress. To approach from below, traverse onto West Buttress from Fuselage Gully (above the sandstone) and climb the buttress easily until a steeper tier suggests a traverse left onto the face. Climb a short loose pitch (Very Difficult) to gain the Second Terrace.

45 Maelstrom 90m HVS (1996)
This takes a left-facing corner system in the left side of the upper part of West Central Wall, moving left to pass left of a big isolated roof near the top (the roof is perhaps the best locating feature). The corner defines the left side of the big inset slab on pitch 2 of Earth, Wind and Fire. The climbing is mucky and loose at times and winter is the best season. Start about 15m left of the mossy groove of Blood, Sweat and Frozen Tears (which is at its mossiest between the two Girdle ledges) at the next but shallower groove left.
1. 25m 4c Climb the groove which splits into two. Take the right-hand which leads to the lower of the Girdle ledges.
2. 25m 4c To the left is the very mossy groove which is the start of the winter difficulties. Much more pleasant is an arete which is 5m right of the belay and beyond another groove. Climb this to the upper ledge and move left to a chimney. Pull up left and enter the slightly overhanging chimney. Climb it and the subsequent corner for about 15m.
3. 40m 4b Traverse left, move up then left again into a parallel corner which passes left of the big roof. Follow this to the top.
Winter: **VII,7 **** (1992)
The winter line bypasses the first tier but offers a very sustained route, protected with a large rack of rocks and thin pegs. Although often very icy, it requires good conditions for there to be sufficient ice to be helpful, but is climbable whatever. Start in West Central Gully where it steepens, at the height of the Girdle Traverse (Grade II to here). Follow the lower Girdle ledge right for about 15m to an icy groove, very mossy in summer. Climb this to the upper ledge, then move right along this ledge past a break to the chimney of summer. Continue as for summer to the top.

46 Earth, Wind and Fire 90m HVS (1991)
Start towards the left end of the Second Terrace, left of a rockfall scar and left of a very mossy groove (taken by the winter route, Blood, Sweat and Frozen Tears).
1. 30m 4b Pull through an initial overhang and go right until close to the vegetated groove. Return left under a smooth wall until a corner leads to the lower of the Upper Girdle ledges.
2. 25m 4c Go up to the upper ledge and break through the overhangs at their smallest point. Climb a big inset slab near its left arete.
3. 35m 4c Break out right to a ledge. Climb a shallow chimney, then go right to a blocky fault which leads to easy ground.

47 Blood, Sweat and Frozen Tears   100m   VIII,8 ********   (1993)
This is an outstanding and very sustained route up the big vegetated groove right of Earth, Wind and Fire (the left-hand of two big grooves, the right being Chop Suey). Above the Upper Girdle, the groove continues between the inset slab of Earth, Wind and Fire and the arete of Shoot the Breeze. The route can be approached via West Central Gully (II), or via two 50m abseils. The line can be seen from the top of Central Buttress (although the groove is less obvious from here than from below) and the first abseil is from a point 6m right of a big perched block. The second is from the belay at the end of pitch 2. Low in the grade; the first ascent thought VII,8.

1. 30m Climb the groove, at times on the right wall, to belay on the lower ledge of the Upper Girdle.

2. 20m Continue up the groove, then move left onto a steep slab to reach the upper ledge of the Upper Girdle. Pull through the overhangs above the ledge (at the same point as Earth, Wind and Fire), then immediately swing right into the continuation corner. Climb this and move left to a block belay.

3. 50m Go left and climb a big left-facing corner past a difficult overhang.

48 Shoot the Breeze   90m   E2 *******   (1992)
A stunning route, one of the wildest at its grade in Scotland, with a well protected crux and a Troll Wall ambiance. Start just right of the rockfall scar.

1. 30m 5b Climb up to and follow a corner-crack which forms the right edge of the scar, then continue to the lower of the Upper Girdle ledges.

2. 30m 5a Continue up the corner to the upper ledge. Move leftwards through the capping overhangs at an obvious break. Go up about 5m, then traverse left and climb a big arete which leads into the corner on the left. Belay where the corner slants right.

3. 30m 5c Regain the arete by a foot ledge and climb it into the top of the corner. Return to the arete, follow this to overhangs, then pull left into a short corner. Climb this with difficulty to easier, steep blocky ground which leads to the top.

49 Chop Suey   100m   E1   (1992)
This follow a line of big grooves; it is dangerously loose in places. Start about 10m left of the pinnacle of Twilight Zone at the huge groove, the most prominent feature in this section of cliff (but partially hidden until one is below it).

1. 30m 5b Climb the groove to the lower of the Upper Girdle ledges.

2. 30m 5a Climb the right wall of the groove to the upper ledge, then follow the ledge leftwards across the groove. Weave a line leftwards through overhangs to join the long upper groove.

3. 25m 5b Follow the groove to easier ground.

4. 15m 5a Climb a blocky step to the top.

50 Force Ten   95m   E2 *******   (1992)
This gives sustained climbing in spectacular positions with only the occasional hollow block. Above the Upper Girdle it takes an undercut white streaked and left-slanting ramp, which is well seen from the loch. Start as for Chop Suey.

1. 30m 5b Climb the sharp right arete of the huge groove to the lower of the Upper Girdle ledges.

2. 20m 5c Continue just right of the arete to the upper ledge. Pull through the capping overhang and climb the ramp out leftwards to belay near its top.

3. 30m 5b Make a short traverse left round the arete, then climb steep cracks (just right of the long groove of Chop Suey) to blocky ground.

4. 15m 5a As for Chop Suey, climb a blocky step to the top.

51 Twilight Zone   160m   E2 5c ******   (1977)
There have been disagreements about the grade. The route climbs the very steep smooth looking section of the wall, passing left of large roofs near the top. Start in West Central Gully at the centre of a small buttress where the quartzite begins.

Climb cracks and grooves to a terrace (45m). Go up an open corner to a large pinnacle (15m). Climb the pinnacle and the groove behind until forced into a second groove which is followed to a belay on the Upper Girdle. Go right for 3m and climb grooves and steep slabs to a spike belay (20m). Move left and gain a groove leading to the large roof; climb this for 10m, then step left and climb a steep wall to belay at the left end of the roof. Climb the left arete to a corner and finish up this.

52 Wall of the Winds   115m   E1 * *(1990)*
This route is based on a continuous line of grooves 10m left of Mistral. Start midway between the initial corner of Mistral and the pinnacle of Twilight Zone.
1. 10m Climb an easy blocky groove.
2. 35m 5a Go up a continuation groove onto a pinnacle that looks like a flake from below, then up to the Upper Girdle.
3. 45m 5b The continuation is unattractive, so take a flake on the left which leads into a shallow groove. Climb this for about 8m. Traverse left to another groove which is followed to good runners. A short descent allows a return traverse to the shallow groove. A right-trending line through the left of a roof system leads to a chimney not far left of the V-corner of Mistral.
4. 25m 4c Finish up the chimney.

53 Mistral   120m   E1 * *(1976)*
At the top right of the east wall of West Buttress is an obvious deep V-corner. The route leads fairly directly to the corner. Start at an obvious groove at the foot of the wall.
1. 20m 4b Climb the groove to a good ledge below a chimney.
2. 35m 5a Climb the chimney past a wedged flake and overhang. Continue up a steep crack moving right at the top to a stance on a ledge 10m below the Upper Girdle. (If wet the chimney may be avoided by the wall on the right.)
3. 10m Continue up the crack to the Upper Girdle.
4. 30m 5b Climb a bulge and the steep wall above to a small block overhang (well seen from the foot of the climb). Step left onto the nose and climb steeply to enter the deep V-corner.
5. 25m 4c Climb the corner to the top.
Winter: **135m   VII,7 *** *(1991)*
The winter line is based on the summer line of Mistral. Start up West Central Gully and, where it widens above the sandstone, break out right by a short ice pitch onto the base of the wall. Go out right and easily up the left side of West Buttress until a ledge leads back left to the start of Mistral (the second icy groove from the right). This is the start of the serious climbing.
1. 40m Climb the icy V-groove and the three tiered overhanging chimney directly above. Traverse right and belay below another chimney.
2. 25m Climb the chimney (it has a wide crack in its right wall) to the Upper Girdle. Return left to belay directly above the previous pitch.
3. 30m Climb the crux (pitch 4) of Mistral, very sustained.
4. 40m Traverse left and finish up the final chimney of Wall of the Winds.

West Buttress - Fuselage Wall

Diagram p353

This is the west side of West Buttress's top tier, a wall which faces towards Far West Buttress and is separated from it by Fuselage Gully. At its base is a ledge which provides a walk from Fuselage Gully round on to the crest under the top tier of West Buttress. Being high and exposed to north-westerly winds, this is a good early winter season venue.

Approach: The direct approach is either up or down Fuselage Gully. In winter the descent of Fuselage Gully, using a 15m abseil from the aircraft wreckage, gives a quick access to these short steep routes.

BEINN EIGHE

54 Pension Plan 60m V,7 *(2007)*
Where the top tier of West Buttress turns round towards Fuselage Wall, right of the Right-Hand Finish to West Buttress and left of a big roofed corner (Flying Fortress), is a shallower corner system. Start just round the edge of the buttress, on the left end of Fuselage Wall.
1. 25m Make a step up right on blocks, then return left on jutting blocks in a steep cracked wall. Climb a crack near the left edge of the wall into a narrow chimney and continue to a ledge below the shallower corner.
2. 25m Climb blocks to the base of the corner, then steeply up it to a narrow chimney and ledge above.
3. 10m Avoid the roof at the top of the corner by climbing the wall on the left via a big flake.

55 Flying Fortress 60m VS * *(1989)*
The prominent square-cut corner capped by a large roof. Start just round the edge of the buttress, on the left end of Fuselage Wall.
1. 30m 4b Climb stepped blocks up rightwards, then up to the foot of the corner.
2. 30m 4c Climb the corner and turn the roof on the right to finish.
Winter: **V,7 *** *(2000)*
By the summer route. Spectacular, but short and well protected.

56 Fuselage Wall 60m Severe 4a *(1962)*
In the centre of the wall about 20m up there is a 3m high pinnacle, more easily seen from the side than below. Climb steep cracks to reach the neck behind the pinnacle from the left. Cross the neck to the right and climb straight up for 10m, then traverse left round an exposed corner into a scoop. Alternatively climb directly to this point from the top of the pinnacle, passing a small overhang. Trend right to a large platform and over the final eaves to easier ground.
Winter: **70m V,7 *** *(1987)*
A direct version of the summer route.
1. 30m Follow the summer route to the neck behind the pinnacle.
2. 15m Climb straight up a shallow corner and crack to a good ledge on the left.
3. 25m Climb the flake beside the belay and continue up the fault over a small roof to follow a corner leading to the top.

57 Fight or Flight 70m V,6 ** *(2006)*
Sustained climbing up the centre of the wall, but well protected and with no desperate moves. The capping roof yields unexpectedly. Start 10m left of Fuselage Gully, where a groove leads up left to roofs below the pinnacle.
1. 25m Climb the groove to blocks, return right up a huge flake and go up a short overhanging chimney capped by a chockstone to a diagonal ledge.
2. 20m Go left up the ledge and return right over a big flake to the base of a left-facing corner directly above the belay. Climb the corner to a ledge below roofs.
3. 25m Go up left to a niche and pull out left on to a hanging slab between roofs. Return right above the roof and climb blocky ground to the top.

58 Bombs Away 70m V,7 * *(2005)*
Climbs the right side of Fuselage Wall. Very steep and improbable, but extremely helpful and well protected. Start 5m up Fuselage Gully.
1. 30m Climb steeply up ledges leading left on to the wall. Don't head towards the pinnacle, but move back right on to steeper ground and climb up to below a steep wall.
2. 15m Go diagonally right on a gangway of blocks under the wall. From its top, gain a short roofed groove. Pull out left round the roof (crux) and go up another groove to pull out left again.
3. 15m Pull right on to a small hanging slab and climb a short crack to roofs. Make a slightly descending traverse into a hidden chimney and climb this to a big ledge on the right.
4. 10m Climb a bulging chimney to finish.

BEINN EIGHE
West Buttress & Fuselage Wall

Andy Nisbet

35.	West Buttress	Difficult *, IV,4 ***
36.	Corner Finish	VS *, VI,7 *
38.	Right-Hand Finish (S)	Very Difficult *
38a.	Right-Hand Finish (W)	V,6 *
54.	Pension Plan	V,7
55.	Flying Fortress	VS *, V,7 **
56.	Fuselage Wall	Severe 4a, V,7 *
57.	Fight or Flight	V,6 **
58.	Bombs Away	V,7 *
59.	Fuselage Gully	I **

TORRIDON

Fight or Flight, V,6, Fuselage Wall, Coire Mhic Fhearchair, Beinn Eighe.
Climber Jonathan Preston

59 Fuselage (Far West) Gully 400m I **

This is the obvious gully between the West and Far West Buttresses. It gives probably the best easy gully climb in the corrie, assuming the left branch is taken. It contains the wreckage of a Lancaster bomber which crashed in 1952. The engines and wheels can be found in the scree below. Grade II in lean conditions. In summer it provides an amusing 'scramble', mostly up a rubble chute, though not particularly loose or dangerous, but culminating in a short tricky pitch (about Difficult) leading to a clamber through the aircraft wreckage.

60 The Upper Girdle 750m Severe *** (1960)

The line is obvious all the way. A remarkable expedition, with at least half a dozen Severe pitches and tremendous situations. Start a short way right of the left end of the Eastern Ramparts. This section is the most entertaining, the traverse being continuously difficult and exposed for about 180m. From East Buttress things go easily all the way across to West Central Gully, apart from a single awkward pitch on Central Wall. West Central Wall is by far the most impressive section, and has three serious pitches. The most appropriate finish is by the Direct Finish to West Buttress.

Winter: **VI,7 ** ** (1987)

The girdle was accomplished in two parts. The girdle of the Eastern Ramparts was done in about ten pitches and a finish made up East Central Gully. In the second part the Central and West Buttresses were crossed. The lower of the two possible traverse lines on West Central Wall was taken, giving spectacular positions.

Far West Buttress

The pillar to the right of Fuselage Gully has been climbed by a corner starting about 5m right of the step below the wreckage **Fuselage Pillar** (45m VI,7 2000).

Far West Buttress   60m   Severe 4a *(1954)*
Start at an obvious corner left of the centre of the buttress. Climb steep rock for 12m, then traverse left for 5m on large but poor holds to a belay below a right-angled corner. Go up to the corner, climb it and finish up the left-hand edge.
Winter: **V,6 ****   *(1991)*
An excellent route with two technical but well protected pitches, following the summer line.

SÀIL MHÒR

(NG 938 606)   Alt 981m   Map p307
When entering Coire Mhic Fhearchair from the north-west the beetling crags and terraces of Sàil Mhòr on the right cannot fail to impress. They are generally too broken and vegetated, or wet and smooth to give good rock climbs but come into their own in winter. The gullies are numbered right (outside the corrie) to left.

Approach: By the path into Coire Mhic Fhearchair.

Descent: Go to the summit of Sàil Mhòr and follow the ridge towards Coinneach Mhòr. At the far end of the col between these two, turn right and descend a shallow gully, glissading as far as possible, until easier slopes lead down to the path.

The routes are described from right to left as this is the way one would normally approach them.

1 Morrison's Gully (No.1 Gully)   300m   I *
The big gully on the north face of Sàil Mhòr, obvious before reaching the corrie. No difficulty.

2 Expanding Universe   100m   VI,5 *   *(2004)*
Although short, this route provides two excellent and contrasting pitches, the first on thin ice, the second up steep turfy chimneys. Start at the base of a big obvious groove, some 200m up and on the left wall of Morrison's Gully.
1. 30m Climb the thinly iced groove, poorly protected, to a good belay below steep chimneys.
2. 50m Continue directly up the chimneys to easier ground.
3. 20m A short step leads up on to the shoulder and the end of the difficulties.
Easy ground on Sailing Buttress (about 200m of Grade II) leads to the top, but it should be possible to climb down and right to gain a ledge leading back into the gully.

3 Sailing Buttress   400m   III,4   *(1996)*
Climbs the buttress left of Morrison's Gully to join Lawson, Ling and Glover's Route when finishing up its upper crest. Pass the vertical wall at the base of the buttress by starting up Morrison's Gully and traversing left at the first opportunity. A left-trending line was then taken to a pinnacle on a big terrace below a barrier wall. The terrace was then traversed right to near its end to find (with difficulty) the easiest line through the wall. Above the wall, the difficulty eased quickly.

4 Lawson, Ling and Glover's Route   400m   II ***   *(1899)*
A fine mountaineering route through excellent scenery with only a couple of awkward sections. The next obvious gully, starting above the north-west end of the lochan, is Jenga (No.2 Gully). Climb the gully till it turns sharply left then break out up easy slopes on the right to gain the crest. This is followed to the top over rocky steps and pinnacles to the summit of Sàil Mhòr.

SÀIL MHÒR

4. Lawson, Ling and Glover's Route II ***
5. Jenga VI,7 ***
6. The Darkness Beckons VII,7 ***
7. Overkill V,7 **
8. Achilles V,5 **
9. White's Gully II *
10. Smears for Fears V,4

Rab Anderson

5 Jenga (No.2 Gully)   300m   VI,7 ***   (2000)
An impressive deep gully with a fierce headwall. The gully is easy until it turns left. Soon there is a chockstone pitch which can bank out and leads to the headwall. Continue up the back of the gully until forced to traverse left. Either climb ice in the left corner or a pile of blocks just to the right until steep ground forces a return traverse to near the gully bed (45m). Climb the gully into a small cave (25m). Chimney out the top of the cave to the final groove which finishes on a flat platform on the crest of the buttress, here joining Lawson, Ling and Glover's Route (25m). Follow this to the top.

6 The Darkness Beckons   215m   VII,7 ***   (2001)
Imposing tiered sandstone cliffs form a continuous wall down and left of Jenga (No.2 Gully). The following route is based on a big left-facing corner-line starting near the top of the lower couloir. Start where Jenga turns left, 30m below its first main pitch.
1. 17m   Make a delicate traverse left to gain the corner (a direct start might be recommended).
2. 18m   Sustained climbing up the corner; swing left at the top to below the continuing cleft.
3. 20m   Go up the V-wedge corner, then escape right 5m along an exposed ledge to a block.
4. 30m   Go 5m right and climb a fine chimney in a detached pillar to a terrace; traverse 10m left to a cracked block back in the corner-line.
5. 25m   Enter the innocuous groove on the left and struggle up it to a larger terrace; traverse 10m left to below a break in the next tier.
6. 55m   Climb the break to easier snows below the next tier.
7. 50m   Go up the left side of the tier to gain easier ground; 200m of easy climbing to the summit of Sàil Mhòr.

7 Overkill   225m   Scottish VS   (1968)
This climb lies on the steep left wall of Jenga. The first pitch is the crux by far and looks hard but can be avoided by a traverse in along a grass ledge from Jenga thereby 'reducing' the grade to modern VS, but very dry conditions are required for any pleasure. A prominent groove cuts into the bulging area at the base of the cliff, where the gully wall turns east to form the main face. Start near the foot of the gully, below the groove which rises towards a line of rounded ribs.
1. 40m   Climb the groove on its left wall to a steep, black section and go up this moving right to finish.
2. 25m   Climb short walls and ledges trending slightly left to a corner system below a prominent triangular overhang.
3. 30m   Climb the corner system passing the overhang on the right to a ledge below a sharp right-angled corner.
4. 40m   Climb the corner and its left wall to a good ledge. A groove left of an overhang then leads to a terrace.
5. 90m   Climb four short walls and intermediate terraces to easier ground.
Winter: **V,7 ***   (2000)
A much better route in winter, up a fine exposed face with a couple of short hard sections, well protected. Traverse in from Jenga gully along an easy but narrow grass ledge. From here, climb as for the summer line until after the sharp corner. The natural winter line then goes slightly right and back left.

8 Achilles   250m   V,5 **   (1986)
About halfway along the lochan a steep narrow cleft on the right sometimes gives rise to a splendid icefall. After an easy snow introduction climb four pitches mainly on ice, including a free standing ice pillar, to the first substantial terrace (120m). The next band is taken by a groove on the left. Above this a deep chimney on the right may offer a good finish; however on the first ascent darkness forced a traverse left into White's Gully from where the easiest line was taken to the top.

BEINN EIGHE

9 White's Gully (No.3 Gully)   120m   II *   (1910)
A broad gully running up from the head of the lochan is joined a third of the way up by a narrow gully whose foot is a quarter of the way down the lochan. The route follows this narrow gully and is easy up to the final 30m, which is a chimney with three chockstones.

10 Smears for Fears   100m   V,4   (1986)
This route may be used as a finish for Achilles or White's Gully. Take the first break left above the narrowing in White's Gully. Climb an ice cased corner to a difficult cornice finish.

COIRE RUADH-STACA

The central of the three great northern corries of Beinn Eighe.

Pineapple Cliff - Creag Mhòr

(NG 954 608)   Alt 800m   South-East to North-East facing   Map p307   Diagram p359

This cliff lies in on the east flank of Ruadh-stac Mòr, highest top of the Beinn Eighe range. It is composed of good quartzite but with a few wedged and loose blocks typical of lower grade climbs on this rock. The climbs are varied and full of character but with shorter difficulties than in Coire Mhic Fhearchair.

Approach: From the bealach at the south end of the Ruadh-stac Mòr ridge (above the south-east corner of Coire Mhic Fhearchair) descend 60m to the east and find a goat track just above the lowest tier. Follow it descending slightly northwards for 600m to the base of the cliff, 3hrs.

Descent: Probably climb with rucksacks in summer although descent can be made at the north end. In winter, it is possible to leave rucksacks at the bealach.

Parallel ridges slant rightwards up the hillside separated by well-defined gullies. On the approach two flat fronted ridges separated by a gully are seen bounded on their right by a narrow gully and a thinner ridge. The thinner ridge has a large wall, the biggest feature of the cliff, forming its right side (hidden on the approach) and a huge stepped pinnacle leaning against it (The Independent Pineapple), which is not obvious from below. Right of this wall is a gully with a very prominent chockstone, then a smaller ridge and a long smaller wall.

1 Sidestep   75m   Severe
This is the left-hand and higher of the two flat fronted ridges. Climb the ridge direct for 45m to a ledge. From the right-hand end of the ledge climb the right flank and back to the crest (loose rock) to another ledge (15m). From the right-hand end of this ledge again climb the right flank to the crest and reach easy ground.
Winter: **110m   IV,6**   (1995)
By the summer route.

2 Milk Shake   120m   II   (2002)
The straight gully between the two flat fronted ridges has two steps which can bank out or be quite tricky when lean.

3 Spog aig Giomach   100m   VS 4b   (1971)
This is the right-hand and lower of the two flat fronted ridges. Large comfortable stances are separated by short steep pitches. Start 6m left of the lowest point of the ridge by climbing a steep, reddish wall for 12m to a grassy stance. Climb the 15m corner above with an overhang to be avoided at 10m, then a short chimney. Move 5m left and follow a steep crack and chimneys to the halfway terrace. Walk a few metres right, climb back up left, and follow an easy crest to the top of the cliff (45m).

360 BEINN EIGHE

Winter: **IV,6** *(1991)*
Follow the summer line, except at the top of pitch 1 where a deviation left into a chimney followed by a traverse right across the initial corner leads to the stance.

4 Three Tier Chimney   130m   III,4 *(1991)*
The narrow gully parallel to and left of Thin Man's Ridge. This is mostly easy but has one strenuous pitch of three piled chockstones and a final short chimney pitch.

5 Thin Man's Ridge   130m   Hard Severe 4b ** *(1971)*
The thinner ridge on the right, forming the left edge of the large wall. Large people will encounter peculiar difficulties on this climb. Start at the base of the crest of the right-hand of the two main ridges (or round to the right up a series of corners, followed by a traverse left to the crest). Climb 30m to a large terrace on the crest in front of an impressive tower. Traverse right into a very narrow chimney and climb this for 5m. It is now possible to pass right through the tower inside the chimney, to emerge on its far side. A 10m groove leads to the crest from where rucksacks can be hauled up the front of the tower. A few metres of horizontal ridge lead to the halfway terrace. The face above has been climbed by accident, hard and vegetated, but the route continues up the pillar of rock over to the right. Climb it slightly round to the right by a steep diedre for 15m, then trending right for another 15m to a detached block and belay. Traverse delicately left for 6m across the front of the pillar. Scramble for 30m to a final 5m wall which leads to the top.
Winter: **V,7 ** *(2000)*
By the summer route with the lower right-hand start, except that the final 5m wall was passed by a chimney on its immediate left (top of Three Tier Chimney).

6 The Independent Pineapple   120m   Severe 4a * *(1972)*
A huge stepped pinnacle leans against the right wall of Thin Man's Ridge. This route takes a fine natural line up this wall via the pinnacle. Start at a right-angled corner about 20m left of Chockstone Gully. Climb the double cracks in the back of the corner and continue left to reach a shelf running up the face (40m). Climb the shelf past two mossy chimneys to the top of the Independent Pineapple. To escape from the pinnacle return down the shelf for 12m, make a delicate traverse left for 6m and climb two chimneys to the top of the cliff.
Winter: **IV,6 ** *(1991)*
Follow the summer route, a well protected natural line.

7 Pineapple Sunday   100m   E2 5b ** *(2000)*
Climbs the outside face of the pinnacle to provide spectacular situations. Start at the foot of Chockstone Gully about 5m out from the chockstone. The protection is good but strenuous to place.
1. 45m 5b Climb a steep crack leading over a bulge (crux) into a groove. Move left to a ledge and immediately back into the groove. Trend right up the wall until above the chockstone, then climb straight up walls left of a big crack to a ledge below the right-hand of two cracks in the face of the pinnacle.
2. 35m 5a Move into the left-hand crack and climb it until it ends. Return to the right-hand crack and climb its continuation to near the pinnacle top until a step on to the right arete leads to a juggy finish up the pinnacle.
3. 20m 5b Climb the steep wall behind the pinnacle to finish up a groove (left of the clearly easier finish to Pineapple Chimney and also left of a corner).

8 Pineapple Chimney   100m   VS * *(1977)*
A fine chimney separates the right-hand side of the Independent Pineapple from the wall.
1. 25m Start by climbing Chockstone Gully until a narrow ledge leads left into a groove which leads to the chimney.
2. 25m 4b Traverse the ledge left and climb the groove to an easing below the chimney.
3. 25m 4a Climb up into the chimney, then make a subterranean traverse behind the Pineapple to the opposite side. Climb easily to its top.

Lip Service, V,5, Pineapple Cliff, Coire Ruadh-staca, Beinn Eighe. Climber Dave McGimpsey

4. 25m 4c Climb the wall above trending right for 6m, then an awkward move right leads round a corner to ledges. Finish up corners above.
Winter: **VI,7 ***** *(2000)*
By the summer route except that the outside of the chimney was climbed direct to the top of the Pineapple.

9 Chockstone Gully   100m   III * *(1984)*
This is the straight gully to the right of Thin Man's Ridge, unmistakable by the huge chockstone near its foot. Requires a good build-up to be Grade III.

10 Midge Ridge   100m   Very Difficult *(1971)*
A rightmost ridge, right of Chockstone Gully, provides a rather broken climb, better in winter. Start 15m right of the gully. Ascend to the ledge above then climb an obvious narrow wall and corner. Continue up the line of least resistance. The ridge narrows at the top.
Winter: **IV,5** *(1987)*
Start just right of Chockstone Gully near the toe of the buttress. Climb a groove then another groove beside the chockstone, turn the next steep wall by a chimney on the right and follow a groove to the crest of the ridge. Climb easily up and right to the finishing chimneys.

362 BEINN EIGHE

11 Jambo   120m   V,7 * *(2004)*
Right of Midge Ridge is a bay enclosed by overhanging walls. This route takes a right-slanting corner through the walls and leading to a right diagonal line of chimneys. Start on the right side of the bay and climb cracks leading to the corner. Climb the corner and traverse right to a ledge (20m). Climb two successive chimneys leading right (30m). Climb a flake-chimney and a short wall leading to easier ground. Go up this to a final wall (45m). Traverse right and finish up steep turf.

12 Jinx   140m   IV,5 * *(2001)*
The line of least resistance up the face right of Midge Ridge and Jambo. Start at the initial chimney of Autumn Rib (narrow and right-slanting).
1. 25m Climb the chimney, then squeeze through a slot on the left to gain a higher ledge.
2. 20m Traverse this ledge left, slightly descending and with a final crawl, to its very end.
3. 20m Step left into the base of a chimney-crack and climb it.
4. 40m Trend left up steep broken ground.
5. 35m Finish rightwards up a long groove.

13 Autumn Rib   90m   Hard Severe 4b *(1977)*
At the northern end of the cliff are three right-slanting chimney systems, the left and central being close together with the central one particularly cavernous. This route starts up the narrow left-hand chimney (loose) leading to a platform at 15m. Climb the rib between the left and central chimneys, short but sustained and on good rock, exact line unsure.

14 Lip Service   110m   V,5 * * *(2006)*
Climbs the left chimney. Start at the initial narrow chimney of Autumn Rib.
1. 20m Climb the chimney.
2. 30m Traverse the platform right and go up under a chockstone into the deep upper chimney come cave.
3. 25m Move outwards on the left wall to reach ice which flows down from the lip of the cave. Climb this to the lip, the difficulty depending on its thickness but graded for good placements. Continue to a bay.
4. 35m Climb an upper gully to below a final chimney. Here a line of ice led out on to the left wall.

15 Smilodon   100m   Severe 4a *(2001)*
Based on a deep groove in the centre and right of the crest of the buttress between the central and right chimneys. Start 10m left of the right chimney. This is below the groove, which starts about 20m up. Climb a short cracked wall and chimney leftwards to a ledge. Go left to the crest and back right to the base of the groove. Climb the groove to where two blocks protrude from a ledge on the left. Climb the wall on the left to step back into the groove for its last move. Go up a section of easy gully and finish by a short bulge.
Winter: **IV,5 *** *(2003)*
By the summer route except that the groove was climbed direct throughout.

16 Chocked   100m   IV,6 * *(2005)*
A crack-line just right of Smilodon. Rather close, but the middle pitch is superb.
1. 30m Climb the initial section of the right chimney, then take a slab leading left to below the crack-line.
2. 35m Climb the crack-line, which leads into the easy gully of Smilodon.
3. 35m Finish up this.

17 Quickstep   120m   IV,5 *(2004)*
The rightmost buttress, right of the right chimney system. Five short pitches. Start up a prominent narrow chimney on the left side, facing the rest of the cliff. Staying

on the left side, climbs short walls to a corner below a thin pinnacle. From the top of the pinnacle, step left into a steep groove which leads to easier ground. Go down behind a bigger pinnacle and climb a wall on the left before returning right to thread a way amongst finishing short walls.

SPIDEAN COIRE NAN CLACH

The second highest peak of Beinn Eighe.

Spidean Lochans

(NG 964 599)   Alt 650m   North-West facing   Map p307

Two lochans are located on a shoulder on the north-west side of Spidean Coire nan Clach. The outlet from the northern one flows over a rock band and offers two icefalls, **Christmas Day Special** (80m III 1996) climbs the left-hand of the pair and has a large ledge and block after about 30m. The right-hand one **Whiteout** (80m IV,4 1996) is slightly steeper with poor rock belay potential.

Above these is a rock band leading to open slopes and to two craggy areas leading to the summit. The right-hand crag is split by a narrow gully which trends left near its top (Grade II). Start up a chimney (optional) at the right end of the lower rock band. The best gully on the left-hand section cuts up its centre and has a few rock steps (Grade III).

High on the right (south-west) of the face, starting at a height of about 780m and finishing on the ridge about 500m west of the top of Spidean Coire nan Clach, is the following route on a dome shaped buttress at NG 961 596.

Bartlett's Dilemma   90m   IV,4   (2003)
1. 40m Start just right of the toe of the buttress and go up an icy or turfy gully trending slightly right.
2. 30m At this point the gully continues easily up and right, but step left and continue up mixed ground until a smooth wall forces a step right around a flake, continue up until below an open chimney.
3. 20m Continue up towards the chimney and climb it to the top.

North Ridge of Spidean Coire nan Clach   100m   III,4   (2004)
The base of the ridge forms an overhanging wall (NG 968 602, alt 750m). Heading up right (west) the right side of the ridge becomes progressively easier. The route takes an obvious line of weakness leading diagonally left with one steep section (potentially very loose) to reach a pinnacle on the crest. The crest soon becomes easy scrambling and walking.

SGÙRR BÀN

North-East Face

(NG 976 601)   Alt 850m   North facing   Map p307

A very steep cliff, more accessible than Coire Mhic Fhearchair, but with much less scope and shorter routes.

Approach: Park near NG 977 578 and follow the Coire an Laoigh footpath almost until it levels off, then break off right and follow the lip of its upper corrie rightwards. Climb broken rocks left of a gully which leads to the col between Sgùrr Bàn and Sgùrr an Fhir Duibhe (the gully is loose scree but good when snow filled). Make an unpleasant descent of loose scrambling leftwards to the base of the cliff, 2hrs. Subsequent descents will be by abseil.

Descent: Down the gully from the col offering fine scree or glissading to regain the footpath. About an hour to the road.

The most prominent feature of the cliff is a right-slanting ramp which becomes a gully and splits the cliff into two halves. The right half is bigger but with less good rock (and a big rockfall scar). Where the ramp first becomes a gully, the right wall is formed by a rock island. The wall opposite this island is the left half of the cliff, and has a steep prow with three crack-lines which provide the best rock climbs. This steep wall is bounded on its left by a gully.

The Grotto 80m III * *(1999)*
The gully is unfortunately short, but with a remarkable 15m subterranean pitch. It starts from near the base of the ramp, easy at first. A big chockstone blocks the gully and a pitch was climbed on the wall to its left followed by a short traverse back in. The gully is now blocked by an apparent overhanging wall. Enter a cave at the base of the wall, then back and foot outwards, go under a chockstone, then back and foot inwards to exit through a hole. The gully is easy to finish.

Ban the Bomb 50m E1 5a *(1999)*
From the base of the gully section, scramble up left for 10m on to a ledge (about Very Difficult). Start here. The rock is poorer than on the prow. Go diagonally left along a flake-line passing under clean white rock to reach a pinnacle-block. Go up from here on grey rock trending first right then left to the top.

Faith 50m E2 5b * *(1999)*
The left-hand crack-line. Start from the same ledge. Pass a roof by moving out left and back right (low in the grade but requires faith).

Hope 50m E2 5c ** *(1999)*
The middle crack-line, which leads directly up from the start of the scramble to the ledge. It has two hard bulges separated by steep rock. The hope is that the crack is dry; otherwise add a grade for bridging.

Charity 50m E1 5b * *(1999)*
Start level with the top of the rock island. The right crack-line is on the right side of the prow and passes right of its band of overhangs.

The Ramp 200m I *(1999)*
Best included on the ascent of Sgùrr Bàn from the east (Sgùrr nan Fhir Duibhe) by dropping down from the col and climbing the ramp and gully to finish nearly on the summit.

Scarface 75m E1 5b *(1999)*
Climbs the impressive crest of the right section but a big rockfall scar drops some hints. Start round on the front face about 10m up a ramp which forms the base of the cliff.
1. 30m 5b Climb a left-facing corner, much harder than it looks, in several steps to a big flake-line (visible from the top of the left section of cliff).
2. 30m 4c Traverse right to the last flake. Stand on it to pull on to the wall above and climb this trending slightly right to reach the left edge of the huge rockfall scar.
3. 15m 5a Climb leftwards through the steep final wall.

SGÙRR NAN FHIR DUIBHE

North-west Face

(NG 982 601) Alt 850m North-West facing Map p307

A high, somewhat broken cliff, too loose for summer but offering easier winter routes which come into condition readily (although dangerously loose if not frozen).

Approach: By the Coire an Laoigh footpath, but break off right to climb the shallow gully leading to the col between Sgùrr Bàn and Sgùrr an Fhir Duibhe. If the gully is not snow filled, start on the right. A slight descent and easy traverse leads to the base of the cliffs, 2hrs.

Descent: Return to the col and reverse the approach.

Clearly seen from the col is a smooth steep wall at the base of a ridge. The left branch of Double Gully is well seen just to its right. Left of this ridge but largely hidden from the col is an easier angled but very pinnacled ridge, Ragged Muffin Ridge. At the left side of the face are two parallel gullies which lead to the two main gaps forming the Black Carls section of the crest, which lies north-east of Sgùrr nan Fhir Duibhe summit. Routes described right (near the col) to left.

Double Gully Right 100m I (1997)
The gully at the right end of the cliff, right of the smooth wall. The right gully appears to head into a big cul-de-sac but sneaks out right.

Double Gully Left 120m III (1999)
The well-defined left gully has two ice pitches.

The Dark Ridge 130m IV,6 (1999)
The steep fronted ridge near the right end of the cliff. Start easily up its left-hand side until a chimney leads back right to the crest below a steep wall (50m). Climb the short wall (crux), then traverse left to a corner and round its bounding wall to a groove (20m). Climb the groove, then the right-hand of two faults to gain the crest. Follow the crest to the top (60m).

Black Gully 130m II (1999)
The gully left of The Dark Ridge has several small steps and one larger one, passed on the right. The main gully trends left, close to Ragged Muffin Ridge.

Ragged Muffin Ridge 110m IV,4 (1997)
Follows the crest of the ridge over several pinnacles including chimneying behind an alarmingly slender tower on pitch 3. Difficult in summer (1957) but very loose.

Rockhoppers Ridge 130m III,4 (1997)
The less defined ridge left of Ragged Muffin Ridge, starting with a steep wall (crux), then a chimney, huge square topped block and easier to the top, close to the summit of Sgùrr nan Fhir Duibhe.

Carla's Gully 80m II (1999)
The gully leading to the most obvious gap in the Black Carls section of ridge. At the top is a short pitch (Grade I if banked out) and a through route emerging on the col.

Rubble without a Cause 90m IV,4 (1999)
The buttress between the two gullies. Start near the base of Carla's Gully and climb a tricky groove (might be Grade III with loose blocks well frozen) leading to an easy finish passing right of an upper tower.

Bodach Gully 80m II (1999)
The left but less defined gully has a harder pitch.

Knoydart

W	1897 Apr 17	Raeburn's Gully	H.Raeburn, J.H.Bell,H.C.Boyd, W.Brown
W	1897 Apr 18	North-East Ridge	J.H.Bell, W.Garden, T.Gibson, H.Raeburn, H.Barrow, W.Barrow, W.Brunskill, W.Brown

followed immediately in their wake...

S	1939 Jul	Moss Gully	K.McLaren, J.Bennet
W	1962 Apr 14	Gaberlunzie	A.G.Nicol, R.W.P.Barclay, T.W.Patey

There was an unsuccessful attempt on this gully as early as May 1928.

W	1962 Apr 15	Viking Gully	A.G.Nicol, T.W.Patey
S	1967 Jun 22	Round House	G.A.White, J.A.Gillcrest
S	1967 Jun 22	Battlement Slab	D.S.Nicol, P.Gunn
S	1967 Jun 22	Portcullis	I.S.Clough, B.Rex

Deteriorating weather conditions forced the FA party to follow easier ground on the left for the final 60m.

W	1971 Apr	Para Handy Gully	A.Ewing, W.Sproul
S	1971 Jul 13	Culverin, Cannonade, Sentinel, Parapet, Bastion	M.Horsburgh, K.Schwartz
W	1978 Feb 8	Face Route	A.Nisbet, P.Tipton
W	1978 Feb 8	West Pillar	D.Dinwoodie, A.McIvor
W	1978 Feb 9	Landlubbers Buttress	A.Nisbet, P.Tipton
W	1978 Feb 17	Tir na Og	A.Foster, C.Higgins
W	1978 Feb 19	Summit Route	A.Foster, C.Higgins
W	1978 Mar	Transatlantic Bong, Thunderchicken	C.Higgins, K.Sims
W	1979 Feb 9	East Rib	C.Higgins, R.Speiss
W	1979 Mar 24	Eastern Chimney	D.Broadhead, S.Gallacher, D.Rubens
S	1980 Aug	Direct Route	B.McMillan, G.Strange
W	1984 Feb 19	Celtic Sea	R.J.Allen, W.Jeffrey, D.N.Williams
W	1984 Feb 19	Western Approaches	R.J.Allen
W	1986 Feb 2	Marguerite	R.Everett, S.Richardson

Named after a summit (Pointe Marguerite) in the Grandes Jorasses.

W	1986 Feb 28	Penny Wheep Gully	S.Kennedy, G.Rowbotham, S.Thirgood
W	1986 Mar 1	Bottleneck Gully	W.Jeffrey, D.N.Williams

Several lines are believed to have been climbed in Co're Dhorrcail by Heriot-Watt students in the early 1980s, but details have not been reported.

W	1991 Feb	Strider's Gully	P.Duggan

Possibly climbed previously.

W	1991 Feb	White Settler	W.Jeffrey, D.N.Williams

Possibly climbed previously.

W	1994 Jan 8	North Spur	S.Kennedy, S.Ritchie
S	1996 Jun 26	A Good Day Spoilt	M.Harris, M.Ballance
W	2003 Feb 16	Peekaboo Gully, Skinny Gully	D.Morris

Glen Shiel & Kyle of Lochalsh
Meall na Teanga

W	1986 Feb 15	Central Gully	D.A.Hetherington

Cluanie Dam Area

S	1988	Persistent Arete	R.Lupton, B.Taylor
S	1996 May 14	Persistent Reward	R.Simpson, D.Morrison

Druim Shionnach - West Face

S	1938 Aug 1	Silver Slab	J.W.Haggas, S.Thompson, P.B.White
W	1994 Feb 16	Cave Gully	S.Kekus, A.Nisbet
W	1994 Feb 20	Capped Gully	A.Nisbet, G.Vaughn, M.Webb
W	1995 Jan 11	Bow Peep	J.Lyall, A.Nisbet
W	1995 Jan 24	Silver Corner	B.Davison, A.Nisbet
W	1995 Feb 8	Cross-Bow	S.Dring, K.Grindrod, J.Lyall, Z.Webster
W	1995 Mar 25	Boxers Buttress	A.Nisbet
W	1995 Mar 26	Deceptive Chimney	S.McKenna, A.Nisbet, I.Stewart
W	1995 Dec 24	Silver Edge	A.Nisbet, G.Nisbet
W	1996 Mar 14	Silver Slab	B.Davison, A.Nisbet
W	2005 Nov 28	Hurting II	S.Allan, A.Nisbet
W	2006 Jan 1	Bowling Alley	D.McGimpsey, A.Nisbet

FIRST ASCENTS

W 2006 Mar 17   Eurhythmics, Poems   A.Nisbet, J.Preston

Mid-way Buttress
W 1996 Mar 24   Mid-way Gully   P.Grant, M.Lee
W 2005 Nov 28   Mid-way Buttress   S.Allan, A.Nisbet

Creag Coire an t-Slugain
W 1993 Apr 6   Pioneer Gully   A.Nisbet, G.Wallace
Andy Nisbet was looking for Aonach air Chrith and went up the wrong valley by mistake in the mist.
W 1994 Mar 31   Ridge and Furrow   P.Foulkes, A.Nisbet
Now superseded by the direct lines.
W 1995 Feb 1   Tipperary   J.Ashby, M.Dennis, R.Jarvis, A.Nisbet
W 1995 Feb 8   The Triangle   P.Clayton, A.Nisbet, A.Partington
W 1995 Feb 16   Left Ridge   J.Hart, A.Nisbet
W 1995 Mar 25   Speckles, Flaky Ridge   A.Nisbet
W 1996 Apr 2   Far Left Gully   D.Morrison
W 1996 Dec 31   Right End Buttress   A.Nisbet
W 1997 Jan 3   Rowaling   A.Clapperton, A.Nisbet
W 1997 Feb 2   The Ridge Direct   J.Ashby, J.Hubbard, A.Nisbet
W 1997 Feb 15   Ploughshare Groove, Hidden Gully A.Nisbet, G.Nisbet
W 1997 Feb 20   Rose Garden   J.Gillman, A.Nisbet, D.Roberts
W 1997 Dec 3   The Furrow (Direct)   A.Mullin, A.Nisbet, J.Preston
W 2003 Feb 16   Hourglass Groove   J.Colverd, E.Gillespie, A.Nisbet
W 2004 Jan 3   Trumpet   D.McGimpsey, A.Nisbet
W 2004 Mar 5   Hypotenuse   A.Nisbet
W 2005 Feb 22   Hong Kong   H.Chan, A.Nisbet
The start by A.Nisbet on 5 Mar 2004

Aonach air Chrith - North-West Face
W 1994 Mar 20   Mica Schist Special   P.Coleman, M.Moran, S.Richmond
W 1994 Mar 24   My Mother Says No   G.Craig, K.Lindsay, A.Nisbet, R.Patey, M.Valentine
W 1995 Feb 8   Mummy Knows Best   I.Foskett, G.Moore, M.Moran, I.Reid
Direct Finish by J.Burton, S.Collins, J.Preston on 20 Feb 1997
S 1995 May 6   Boa Constrictor   A.Nisbet, G.Nisbet
W 1996 Jan 23   Get into the Groove   K.Burch, E.Herring, A.Nisbet
Rib Start by R.Murray, A.Nisbet, G.Stockbridge on 22 Mar 1996
W 1996 Jan 25   The Deerstalker   E.Herring, A.Nisbet
W 1996 Jan 29   Thin Groove Alley   S.Ainsworth, A.Inglis, M.E.Moran, N.Veitch
W 1996 Mar 13   (Dreaming of the) Deep Freeze   B.Davison, A.Nisbet
W 1996 Mar 17   Airy Icefall, Airy Corner   C.Kirk, M.Knowles, A.Jones, A.Nisbet
W 1996 Nov 30   Boa Constrictor   A.Nisbet, G.Nisbet

Sgùrr an Lochain - North-East Face
W 1990   Flying Gully, also Left Branch   M.Moran and parties
W 1994 Feb 1   Lochain Buttress   N.Kekus, T.Masters, R.Reynolds
W 1996 Apr 4   Direct Evasion   M.Welch, A.Britton, M.Grange, A.Lowry
Direct Variation by N.Edwards, C.Gardiner, M.Moran on 27 Feb 2000
W 1996 Dec 22   Enchanted Falls   N.Taylor
W 2007 Jan 18   Once Bitten, Twice Shy   M.Moran, A.Nisbet
W 2007 Feb 10   The Beast and The Beast   M.Moran, I.Parnell

Sgùrr a' Bhac Chaolais
S 1985 May 29   Mayfly   J.R.Sutcliffe, N.Fletcher
W 1994 Mar 1   Snowdrop   D.Houfe, A.Nisbet, N.Sinclair, D.Wolfe
W 1995 Dec 27   Mayfly   S.Allan, A.Nisbet

The Saddle
W 1926 Easter   Big Gully   A.J.Rusk and party
The ascent was made in 'mixed' conditions. Part ice part vegetation.

368 FIRST ASCENTS

S	1961 Easter	Easter Buttress	D.Piggot, G.S.Johnstone
W	1994 Feb 7	Big Gully	J.Ashby, J.Colverd, D.Gunevan, A.Nisbet
W	1994 Feb 13	Little Gully	B.Davison
W	1994 Mar 13	Cioch Buttress	R.Groth, M.Mauger, A.Nisbet, K.Rogers
W	1994 Dec 30	Biped Buttress	A.Nisbet, G.Nisbet
W	1995 Feb 22	My Learned Friend	J.Gillman, A.McGuffie, A.Nisbet, K.Wigley
W	1996 Feb 6	Easter Buttress	P.Franzen, A.Nisbet, M.Wight
W	2001 Jan 1	Millenium Chimney	D.Joy, S.Naylor, A.Nisbet

Beinn Sgritheall

W	1964 Sep 14	North Buttress	H.M.Brown, A.Smith
S	1965 Oct 20	North Buttress	H.M.Brown, A.Dunsire
W	1995 Jan	Sgritheall Gully	B.Lowe

May have been climbed before.

Creag Lundie Slabs

Locals have soloed here for many years.

S	1996 Jun 2	The Lost Knuckle	D.Morrison, R.Simpson
S	1998 May 22	Other routes	M.Hudson, A.Holden

Sgùrr nan Conbhairean

W	1992 Feb 23	Ceannacroc Couloir	D.Broadhead, G.Drinkwater
W	1995 Jan 21	Fog Monster	A.Powell, M.Dickenson, N.Williams
W	1995 Jan 21	Misty Byway	S.Elworthy, R.Cross
W	1995 Dec 29	Sunny Side Up	A.Powell, S.Elworthy
W	1996 Jan 14	Icestasy, Liquid Gully	I.Appuhamy, A.Nisbet
W	1996 Jan 26	Anne Frank's Chimney, Crystal Couoir	J.Lyall, A.Nisbet
W	1996 Feb 18	East Ridge	P.Benaiges, C.Constable, R.Hinde, A.Nisbet
W	1998 Jan 29	The Green Man	R.Hester, G.Jones, A.Nisbet
W	2002 Oct 31	Category Five (West Crag)	A.Nisbet

Sàil Chaorainn - West Face

W	2000 Mar 27	Distant Groove, left edge	A.Nisbet

A' Chràlaig - Lochan na Cràlaig

W	2001 Jan 16	Curly Gully, Curled Buttress	D.McGimpsey, A.Nisbet
W	2002 Mar 14	Kraken, Spiked	A. and P.Lunn, A.Nisbet

Mullach Fraoch-Choire - South-East Face

W	1996 Feb 17	Frayed at the Edges	A.Nisbet

Ciste Dubh - South-East Face

W	1995 Dec 23	Kissed Ye Quick, The Undertaker	A.Nisbet, G.Nisbet
W	1996 Feb 22	The Mantleshelf	C.Constable, R.Hinde, A.Nisbet
W	1996 Nov 20	Rest in Peace	J.Lyall, A.Nisbet, G.Nisbet

Sgùrr an Fhuarail

W	1996 Jan 28	One for the Road	J.Ashby, P.Thorogood, M.Welch

Sgùrr a' Bhealaich Dheirg

W	1986 Dec 30	Resolution Gully	H.Irvine, A.Keith

Direct Finish by A.Nisbet, C.Platten on 17 Mar 1999

W	1997 Feb 25	Beinn Gunn's Buttress	R.Cooke, C.Darwin, A.Nisbet
W	1997 Mar 20	Solution Gully	A.Nisbet, N.Smith, R.Storm
W	2004 Mar 8	Resolve	J.Preston, M.Kinsey

Five Sisters of Kintail

S	1956 May	California	H.Barber, C.A.Simpson

FIRST ASCENTS

W	1957 Jan 2	Forked Gully	J.H.Barber, C.A.Simpson
W	1957 Jan 2	Trident Gully	J.G.Burns, H.Kindness
W	1957 Jan 3	Solo Gully	J.G.Burns
W	1957 Jan 3	Dog's Leg Gully	J.H.Barber, G.Burns
W	1984 Dec 30	Saighead Slot	U.Jessop, P.A.Brownsort
W	1984 Dec 30	Hidden Gully	U.Jessop, P.A.Brownsort, T.Lee, F.Alexander
W	1985 Jan 1	Window Gully	J.McKeever, G.Jones
W	1985 Mar 20	Brenda's Cleavage	P.A.Brownsort, A.Keith, F.D.Munro, D.Tytler
S	1985 Sep 21	Babylon Buttress	P.A.Brownsort, R.Blackburn, F.D.Munro
W	1986 Jan 2	Edge of Reason	H.Irvine, U.Jessop
W	1986 Jan 2	Grovel Gully	A.Matthewson
W	1986 Mar 27	Twisting Gully	P.A.Brownsort
W	1986 Mar 30	A' Charraig Gully	P.A.Brownsort
W	1987 Jan 3	Little Gully	E.Barnfield, D.Johnson
W	1987 Jan	Left-Hand Gully	M.Potter
S	1987 Aug	Flying Ridge	A.Matthewson
W	1995 Nov 18	Babylon Buttress	T.Archer, E.Ewing, P.Toniolo, S.Walter
W	2004 Jan 27	Canine Buttress	V.Chelton, D.McGimpsey, A.Nisbet
W	2004 Feb 8	Hanging Garden, Flying Ridge	D.McGimpsey, A.Nisbet

Short routes above Shiel Bridge by A.Cain, C.Rowland and others during 1980s.

Beinn Fhada

S	1949 Jun 9	Needle's Eye Buttress	R.Grieve, R.Brown
W	1951 Apr 14	Right-Hand Gully	C.L.Donaldson, J.Russell, G.Dutton
S	1952 Jul 20	The Needle	W.J.Cole, J.R.Marshall, I.Oliver
S	1955 Jul 12	Guide's Rib	G.H.Kitchen, R.J.Porter
S	1955 Jul	Porter's Climb	G.H.Kitchen, R.J.Porter
S	1955 Jul	Continuation Climb	G.H.Kitchen, R.J.Porter
S	1961 Easter	Summit Buttress	D.Piggot, G.S.Johnstone
W	1983 Feb 19	Left-Hand Gully, Tropical Buttress	S.Kennedy, N.Morrison
W	1984 Mar 3	Summit Buttress	A.B.Lawson, R.Richard
S	1989 Jun 24	The Kintail Blanket	A.Matthewson, A.Tibbs
W	1991	Instructors Gully	P.Grant, D.Morrison
W	1992 Nov 17	Fisherman's Blues	S.Kennedy, M.Macleod, D.Ritchie
W	1994 Jan 26	The Funnel	D.Joynes, A.Nisbet, N.J.Worsey
W	1994 Feb 6	Needle's Eye Buttress	J.Ashby, J.Colverd, D.Gunevan, A.Nisbet
W	1994 Feb 27	The Wind Machine	D.Houfe, A.Nisbet, N.Sinclair, D.Wolfe
S	1996 May	Tramlines	A.Nisbet, D.Thomson
W	1996 Dec 27	Guide's Rib	G.Ettle, J.Lyall, R.Milne
W	2000 Dec 30	Needle's Eye Buttress Direct	M.Shaw, I.Humberstone
W	2000 Mar 1	Tramlines	D.McGimpsey, A.Nisbet
W	2001 Jan 29	Summit Central Buttress	D.McGimpsey
W	2006 Mar 21	Fatties Gully, Lightning Gully, Atta Buttress	A.Nisbet

Biod an Fhithich

S	1971 Apr	Hump	R.Burnett, R.Sharp
S	1971 Jul 30	Wrong Turn	M.Horsburgh, D.Regan, K.Schwartz
S	1971 Sep 5	Ankle Ridge	M.Horsburgh, K.Schwartz
S	1974 Feb	Intro One, Intro Two	A.C.Cain, N.Cain

Precise line uncertain; routes as described by A.Mullin, A.Nisbet, 27 Jul 1999

S	1974 May 5	Biodirect	C.Rowland, A.C.Cain
S	1974	Ginger's Gully	A.C.Cain, D.Lewis
S	1998 Sep	Biodiversity	A.Mullin, A.Nisbet
S	2000 Sep 25	Bionic	A.Nisbet, D.McGimpsey

Cragaig

Routes on The Tongues unknown, as described by C.Moody

S	1998 Apr 15	Pine Processionary	C.Moody, L.Gordon Canning
S	1998 Apr 17	Fritillary	C.Moody, L.Gordon Canning

FIRST ASCENTS

S	1998 Apr 17	Drinking with the Priest	W.Gordon Canning, L.Gordon Canning
S	1998 Apr 18	Elchaig Arete	C.Moody, R.Lupton, L.Gordon Canning, W.Gordon Canning

White Dyke
Written up in a mini-guide by Alan Taylor in 1983, giving only the following FAs

S	1983 Jun	Terminal Groove, Maurice's Slab	M.McCleod
S	1983	Clare, Heart of Darkness, Defying Destiny	A.Taylor

Duncraig - Creag an Duisilg

S	1971 May 29	Shenavall	R.Schipper, B.Chambers
S	1971 May 29	Cypress Avenue	S.Docherty, N.Muir
		Direct start by M.E.Moran, A.Nisbet on 11 May 1996	
S	1971 Jun 4	Lonesome Traveller	N.Muir
S	1971 Jun 4	Easy Rider	R.Schipper, S.Crymble
S	1971 Jun 5	The Three Legged Race	S.Docherty, N.Muir, D.Regan
S	1971 Jun 7	Chanter	N.Muir, R.Schipper
S	1971 Jun 12	Can of Worms	N.Muir, S.Docherty, R.Schipper
S	1971 Jul 24	Trundle	D.Regan, A.Kimber

Two easier routes by N.Muir not found. Routes were climbed by A.C.Cain & others but lost in the Moritorium (not all were new). Included a steep pitch on the Western Cliff by A.C.Cain and D.Scott and two very vegetated lines with J.Davies.

S	1989	Hang Over, Long Reach, Levitation	N.Smith, R.Lupton
S	1989	Gordon's Route	G.Bisset
S	1989	Pine Martin, Wild at Heart	N.Smith
S	1996 May 11	Jim Kerr Knew my Father	M.E.Moran, A.Nisbet
		Probably the route climbed by J.Kerr around 1982 but not recorded.	
S	1996 May 25	Hamish Quick-Death	I.Dring, M.E.Moran
S	1996 May 26	James Bond is Alive and Well and Living in Plockton, Seals Guaranteed or your Money Back---	I.Dring, M.E.Moran
S	1996 May 27	Brigadier Braggart's Little Secret, The Queen's Garden Party	I.Dring, M.E.Moran
S	1996 May 28	It Ne'er Rains but it Pours	I.Dring, M.E.Moran
S	1996 Jun 24	The Hanging Traverse of Babylon	M.E.Moran, M.Welch
S	1996 Jun 26	Crocodile Shoes	M.E.Moran, A.Nisbet
S	1996 Jun 26	My Sex Romp with Llama Sid	M.E.Moran (unsec)
S	1996 Jun 27	Bungle in the Jungle	M.E.Moran, A.Nisbet
S	1997 May 1	King Prawn Deathwish	I.Dring, M.E.Moran
S	1997 May 29	Roseroot Ramp, Plockton Plonkers	R.Chapman, A.Jago, M.E.Moran
S	1997 May 29	Miracle of the May Midge	M.E.Moran (unsec)
S	1998 May 23	No Stars No Moon No Nothing	I.Dring, J.Codling

Glen Carron
Glen Carron South

S	1954 May 15	Mica Ridge	A.Watson, A.Watson (senior)
W	1978 Dec 31	Short and Silly	J.R.Mackenzie
W	1987 Jan 3	North Gully	R.Archbold, D.Nichols
S	1988 Jul 23	Munroist's Reward	R.Everett, D.Gaffney
S	1988 Jul 24	Monar Magic	R.Everett, D.Gaffney
S	1993 May 26	Left Edge Route	A.Nisbet
S	1993 Jun 13	The Far Side	R.Blackburn, A.Keith
W	1994 Mar 16	The Gully that Time Forgot	I.Lee-Bapty, E.Todd, P.Westall
S	1995 May 27	The Dreaded Lurgi	A.Nisbet, G.Nisbet
W	1995 Dec 29	Moruisg Icefall	I.A.Sumner, P.Lester

Right-hand version by A.Nisbet and party in Mar 1996 Iced corner to right by M.Moran and party, 1996

W	1996 Jan 30	In the Pink	J.Ashby, P.Thorogood, M.Welch
W	1996 Feb 2	The Fast Lane	M.E.Moran, A.Nisbet, G.Nisbet
W	1996 Feb 2	High Flier, The Big Dipper, Running on Empty	M.E.Moran, A.Nisbet
W	1996 Feb 2	The Ice Channel	A.Bull, M.Kinsey, M.Welch
W	1996 Feb 3	The Stonker, The Wee Nipper	J.Lyall, A.Nisbet, M.Welch

FIRST ASCENTS

W	1996 Feb 8	Willy Wonka	L.Atchison, R.Avis, S.Challoner, S.Potter, M.Welch
W	1996 Feb 8	Aerial Runway	A.Nisbet
W	1996 Mar 18	Whites of their Ice	C.Kirk, M.Knowles, A.Jones, A.Nisbet
S	1996 Jun 27	Disposable Slab, Close to the Edge (Variation)	J.R.Mackenzie

An ancient peg near Disposable Slab suggested a previous ascent.
Route as described by W.McKerrow, J.R.Mackenzie on 31 Aug 1996.

S	1996 Aug 31	The President's Men	W.McKerrow, J.R.Mackenzie
W	1997 Jan 4	The Topper	A.Gorman, D.Williamson, H.Wyllie
W	1997 Jan 6	Wee Dribble	A.Cunningham, F.Fotheringham
S	1999 Aug 23	Rock Surfer, Brittle Times	R.Biggar, J.R.Mackenzie
W	2000 Dec 16	Mica Ridge, Spiral Search	D.McGimpsey, A.Nisbet
W	2001 Feb 8	White Heather Club	J.Ashby, L.Sell-Blackaby, M.Moran
S	2002 Sep 1	Slapstick	E.Christison, B.Fyffe, D.McGimpsey, A.Nisbet
W	2003 Jan 4	Hellfire and Brimstone	G.Robertson, M.Halls, P.Ebert
W	2003 Jan 20	Occluded Ridge	V.Chelton, N.Harrison, D.McGimpsey
W	2003 Feb 25	Chemical Alley	D.Allan, D.Moy
W	2003 Feb	The Shiner, FB Gully	P. and G.Robertson
W	2003 Mar 17	The Bow	D.Allan, D.Bell, E.Christison, D.McGimpsey
W	2003 Mar 19	Stirling Moss	D.Allan, J.R.Mackenzie
W	2003 Mar 19	Downhill Racer	J.R.Mackenzie (in descent)
W	2003 Feb 18	Unnamed buttress	B.Davison, D.McGimpsey

Fuar Tholl

S	1933 Oct 14	Original Route	C.Ludwig, J.D.MacLennan
S	1952 Jul 25	Enigma	W.J.Cole, J.R.Marshall, I.Oliver
S	1961 Oct 7	The Nose Direct	T.W.Patey

A 'more direct' line was climbed in 1973 by D.Dinwoodie, B.Lawrie, but the original seems fairly direct.

S	1968 Aug 3	Nimrod	G.Anderson, J.R.Brumfitt, P.Macdonald
S	1969	Investigator	M.Boysen, D.Alcock
S	1969	Snoopy	D.Alcock, M.Boysen
S	1969	Sherlock	M.Boysen, D.Alcock
S	1969	Sleuth	I.Clough, H.MacInnes
S	1969	Blue Finger	I.Clough, H.MacInnes
S	1969	Cold Sweat	H.MacInnes, C.MacInnes
S	1969	Boat Tundra	I.Clough, H.MacInnes
S	1969	The Fuar	I.Clough, H.MacInnes, M.C.MacInnes
S	1969	Right End Buttress	M.Boysen
W	1970	Sleuth, Original Winter Route	A.Fyffe, H.MacInnes, K.Spence

Sleuth Start by D.McGimpsey, A.Nisbet on 29 Feb 2000

W	1971 Jan 24	The Pile	P.Christie, P.Macdonald
S	1971 Jun 17	Nebula	D.Barr, P.Macdonald
S	1972 Jun	Benn Gunn, Direct Route, All the Way	G.Shields, R.Sharp
S	1974 Apr	Private Eye	M.Boysen, P.Braithwaite, P.Nunn
W	1976 Feb 22	Right End Buttress	W.S.McKerrow, D.M.Nichols
W	1978 Feb 19	Fuar Folly	R.J.Archbold, D.M.Nichols
W	1984 Mar 31	Tholl Gate	P.Butler, M.Fowler
W	1986 Feb 15	Fuhrer	M.Fowler, C.Watts
W	1986 Feb 3-4	Cold Sweat	M.E.Moran (backroped)
W	1986 Feb 22	Olfactory	B.Owen, D.Rubens, G.Macnair, G.Cohen
W	1987 Jan 10	Cold Hole, Pipped at the Post	M.Fowler, C.Watts
W	1988 Mar 4	Evasion Grooves	S.Jenkins, M.E.Moran
W	1989 Feb 23	The Ayatollah	I.Dring, M.E.Moran
W	1989 Mar 3	Reach for the Sky	S.Jenkins, M.E.Moran
W	1989 Mar 11	Mainline Connection	R.Anderson, R.Milne
W	1990 Feb	Chock-a-Block Gully	P.Potter, M.Garret, M.Sales.
W	1991 Feb 16	Tubular Bells	D.Wills, M.Fowler
W	1991 Feb 16	Investigator	M.Fowler, D.Wills
W	1992 Mar 11	Newton's Law	M.Moran, J.Newton, J.Yates
W	1992 Mar 13	Lair Wall	M.Moran, K.O'Neale, W.O'Neale
W	1992 Mar 15	Luck of the Irish	M.Moran, C.O'Callaghan, C.Swift

372 FIRST ASCENTS

W	1993 Mar 23	Sandstorm (1PA)	M.Moran, A.Nisbet

Variation and FFA: B.Wilkinson, R.Thomas, Mar 2005

S	1993 Jun 24	Fuar Feast	A.Nisbet, G.Nisbet
W	1993 Dec 12	Blue Finger	A.Nisbet, G.Nisbet
W	1993 Dec 17	Mixed Post	D.Jarvis, A.Nisbet
W	1994 Feb 15	Nebula	S.Richardson, R.Webb
W	1994 Feb 20	Il Duce	S.Richardson, D.Heselden
W	1994 Feb 20	Right Gully	M.Reid, M.Sizer, P.Sizer, M.Welch

Left Gully by M.Moran and party, around 1990

W	1994 Feb 22	Central Gully Direct	A.Nisbet, G.Vaughn, M.Webb
W	1994 Mar 26	Butcher's Dog	B.Cowie, I.Gray
S	1994 Jul 18	Via Wellington	A.Nisbet, G.Nisbet
W	1995 Jan 12	Fuar Folly Direct	J.Lyall, A.Nisbet

The original intention of Fuar Folly was this line.

W	1995 Feb 19	Solicitor's Rib	J.Gillman, A.McGuffie, M.Moran, K.Wigley
W	1997 Jan 4	Enigma	S.M.Richardson, C.Cartwright
W	1998 Mar 1	The Ramp	J.Gibbs, A.Nisbet, A.Petts
W	1998 Mar 7	Snoopy	C.Dale, A.Nisbet
W	1998 Mar 8	Irish Grooves	I.Lee-Bapty, A.Nisbet, A.Wildsmith
S	1999 May 20	A Right Cheek	A.Nisbet
S	1999 Jul 31	Moriarty	B.Davison, A.Nisbet
W	2000 Dec 31	Spare Rib	D.Joy, S.Naylor, A.Nisbet
W	2001 Jan 16	Hanging Imminent	H.Burrows-Smith, J.Lyall
W	2002 Feb 24	Supersleuth	G.Robertson, P.Benson, J.Currie
S	2003 May	Spare Rib	I.Thow
W	2005 Feb 13	Welsh Grooves	H.Chan, A.Nisbet, V.Parfitt
S	2005 Aug 8	Placa	A.Nisbet
W	2005 Nov 26	Summit Rib, Western Pinnacle	A.Nisbet

Sonny Wall & Whispering Buttress

Routes by C.Las Heras, R.I.Jones, 23 Apr 2005
A Dog named Corrie by the owners of Corrie, names unknown, same date

Sgòrr Ruadh

S	1898 May 26	Robertson's Buttress	A.E.Robertson

Probably starting up Robertson's Gully, then transferring on to the buttress.

S	1904 Apr 4	Raeburn's Buttress	H.Raeburn, E.B.Robertson

Climbed in winter conditions after starting up Narrow Gully and traversing on to the buttress after its first two pitches. The first summer ascent is unknown (but A.Nisbet climbed the described route and variation in June 1998).

S	1948 Jun	Academy Ridge	Inverness Royal Academy C.C.
S	1955 Jul	Upper Buttress, Original Route	I.H.Ogilvie, P.M.Francis
S	1961 Oct 8	Splintery Edge	T.W.Patey
W	1967 Dec 20	Brooker's Route	W.D.Brooker, S.H.Wilkinson

Originally named as Raeburn's Buttress Direct.

W	1969 March	Post Box Gully, Brown Gully	A.Fyffe
W	1969	Steppin	A.Fyffe and party
W	1969	The Slant	H.MacInnes and party
W	1969(?)	Croydon Chimney (1PA)	H.MacInnes and party

FFA: M.Moran and party around 1990

W	1969 Mar	Easy Gully	J.Cleare, P.Gillman
W	1972 Feb	Upper Buttress, Original Route	P.Nunn, A.Riley

Details unknown for the Grade III nearby.

W	1976 Jan 31	Robertson's Gully	A.Nisbet, N.Spinks
W	1976 Feb 1	High Gully	M.Hillman, A.Nisbet

Variation by P.Potter, A.Macdonald on 30 Jan 1988

W	1978 Feb	Narrow Gully	G.Cohen, D.Rubens
W	1983 Apr 4	Wildcat Gully	P.J.Biggar, I.Haig
W	1987 Dec 6	Fox's Face	S.Jenkins, M.E.Moran
W	1988 Apr 2	Ruadh Awakening	R.Anderson, R.Milne
W	1988 Nov 21	First Blood	S.Jenkins, M.E.Moran
W	1989 Feb 17	Raeburn's Superdirect	M.E.Moran, P.Potter
W	1989	Tango in the Night	S.Aisthorpe, N.Forwood, P.Yardley
W	1994 Jan 2	Academy Ridge, Direct Finish	A.Keith, D.Bearhop

FIRST ASCENTS

W	1994 Jan 7	Parallel Lines	F.Bennet, J.Irvine
W	1994 Jan 16	Robertson's Buttress	B.Findlay, G.Strange
W	1995 Mar 1	Riotous Ridge	D.Bradshaw, J.Colverd, A.Nisbet
W	1995 Mar 18	The Key, Highland Scottische	A.Nisbet
W	1995 Mar 20	Tophet Gully	S.Duncan, A.Nisbet
W	1996 Mar 24	Battersea Buttress	R.Brayshay, C.Milne, A.Nisbet
W	1996 Nov 26	The Sandstone Virgin	J.Lyall, A.Nisbet, J.Preston
W	1996 Nov 28	Gopher's Gully	M.E.Moran, A.Nisbet
W	1996 Dec 21	Spanner in the Works, The Last Waltz	A.Nisbet, J.Preston
W	1997 Dec 4	Tritium Chimney	M.E.Moran, A.Nisbet

Start as described by S.Allan, K.Grindrod, A.Nisbet, 23 Mar 2006

W	1998 Jan 6	The Jigsaw	H.Davies, G.Bardsley, A.Nisbet
W	1998 Mar 11	Gravesend	I.Lee-Bapty, A.Nisbet, A.Wildsmith
W	1998 Apr 16	Raeburn's Buttress (Variation)	R.McAllister, A.Nisbet
W	1999 Jan 14	Raeburn's Buttress (Direct)	D.McGimpsey, A.Nisbet
W	2001 Jan 6	Splintery Edge, Pit Bull Polka	D.McGimpsey, A.Nisbet
W	2001 Dec 22	Ruayahua	E.Brunskill, D.Morris
W	2006 Feb 22	Sticky Fingers	M.Edwards, D.McGimpsey, A.Nisbet
W	2006 Apr 9	Frivolity	A.Nisbet

Meall nan Ceapairean

W	1996 Feb 7	Restful Buttress	P.Franzen, A.Nisbet, M.Wight
W	1998 Nov 6	Stressful Buttress	A.Nisbet (backroped)

Maol Chean-dearg

W	1968 Dec 22	Hidden Gully	H.M.Brown, R.J.Rankin, R.Aitken
S	1969 Dec 29	Ketchil Buttress, Ketchup Buttress	H.M.Brown, D.Macnab
S	1971 Aug 1	No Birds	K.Schwartz
S	1971 Aug 1	But Midges	K.Schwartz, M.Horsburgh
W	2001 Dec 22	Ketchil Buttress, Ketchup Buttress	D.McGimpsey, A.Nisbet

An Ruadh-stac

S	1960 Aug	North Face	C.J.S.Bonington, T.W.Patey
S	1967 Aug 21	Foxtrot	D.Stone, B.T.Hill
W	1983 Dec	Right Icefall	I.Thow
W	1993 Dec 30	North Face Route	A.Matthewson, A.Tibbs
W	1994 Mar 20	Quartzice	R.Everett, S.Richardson
W	1996 Feb 21	Left Icefall	C.Constable, R.Hinde, A.Nisbet

Glas Bheinn

W	1972 Apr	Black House	T.Briggs, P.Nunn, C.Rowland
W	1974 Apr	Adul Suh	P.Braithwaite, P.Nunn
S	1984 May 26	Slab and Groove, Clean Compromise	G.Cohen, D.Rubens
S	1984 May	Left-hand Route	P.Nunn, M.Richardson
W	1995 Jan 4	Frozen Pipes	A.Matthewson, A.Tibbs, H.Tibbs
W	1995 Jan 4	New Kelso Couloir	R.Blackburn, E.Blackburn
W	1996 Jan 29	Greenhorn Gully	J.Ashby, P.Thorogood, M.Welch
W	1999 Mar	Right-Hand Gully	R.Webb, N.Wilson
W	1999 Dec 14	The Beast's Lair	J.Lyall, R.Webb
W	2000 Feb	Slab Boys	M.Eurolander, R.Webb

Bad a' Chreamha

S	1983 Nov 11	Floating Rib, Spare Rib	J.Davies, A.C.Cain

Reraig Coastal Cliff

Explored by M. & A.Moran in Sep 2001

Applecross
Meall Gorm

FAists not known for several of the easier routes

S	1953 May 2	Blue Pillar	A.G.Nicol, T.W.Patey
S	1953 May 2	Cobalt Buttress	J.M.Taylor, C.D.Thomson, R.P.U.Tait
S	1955 Aug 18	Blaeberry Corner	W.D.Brooker, A.J.R.A.Norton

374 FIRST ASCENTS

W	1958 Feb	Blue Pillar	J.Brown, T.W.Patey
S	1965 May 15	Rattlesnake	P.Macdonald, A.R.M.Park
W	1970 Feb 10	Cobalt Buttress	I.Clough, G.Drayton, C.Young
W	1970	Gorm Gully	A.Fyffe and party
W	1971 Feb	Blaeberry Corner	K.Spence, J.Horsfield, B.Jones, P.Thomas
S	1971 Sep 4	The Smooth Creep	S.J.Carroll, P.Macdonald

Steve Carroll was chatting up the barmaid in the Garve Hotel on the way home and she called him a 'smooth creep', hence the silly name!

W	1978 Mar 25	The Six-track Mono Blues	M.G.Geddes, B.P.Hall, A.McIntyre, J.Porter
W	1980 Feb	Way Out	R.Robb, S.Young
W	1980 Feb 5	Stonner Falls	P.Anderson, K.Murphy
W	1982	Trident Gully, Right Branch	A.C.Cain, G.Wallace

Precise line unknown as the description was lost in the Moratorium. Also claimed by P.Langhorne, N.Eagers, 21 Feb 1986 who climbed the described line.
Direct Finish by M.Moran and party on 10 Feb 1999

W	1986 Feb 15	Trident Gully, Left Branch	N.Eagers, P.Langhorne
W	1986 Feb 16	Spiral Terrace	P.Langhorne, N.Eagers

Direct Finish by G.Lewis-Evans, A.Nisbet, D.Winterbone on Jan 18 1998.

W	1986 Mar 2	Wee Beastie	J.Douglas, P.Langhorne
W	1987 Mar 15	Lobster Gully	M.Fowler, A.Saunders
W	1991 Jan 8	Blue Moon	S.Aisthorpe, J.Lyall
W	1993 Dec 13	Rattlesnake	G.Ettle, J.Lyall
W	1993 Dec 17	Blue in the Face	G.Ettle, J.Lyall
W	1994 Jan 9	Scampi Fries	F.Bennet, J.Irving
W	1995 Jan	Gormless Grooves	P.Bass, A.Lockley, M.Welch
W	1995 Feb 25	The Vegetable Sheep	A.Nisbet, G.Nisbet
W	1995 Mar 7	Global Warming	D.Bunker, K.Law, A.Nisbet, A.Nolan
S	1996 Sep 6	The Blue Lamppost	A.Nisbet, G.Nisbet
W	1996 Dec 27	Blue Velvet	R. and C.Anderson
W	1997 Feb 27	Boulder Problem Buttress	R.Cooke, A.Nisbet
W	1998 Jan 20	Bypass Buttress	G.Lewis-Evans, A.Nisbet, D.Winterbone
W	1999 Feb 9	Trident Gully, Central Branch	S.McMurrow, M.Moran
W	1999 Feb 10	Shamrock Gully	U.Mulcahy, S.McMurrow, A.Nisbet
W	2000 Feb 21	Wedge Buttress	C.Dale and party

Upper part climbed several times before.

Sgùrr a' Chaorachain - A' Chìoch & North Buttresses

S	1908 Jun 6	Glover's Route	G.T.Glover, W.N.Ling

First winter ascent unknown.

S	1952 Mar 28	Jupiter	J.M.Taylor, W.D.Brooker, T.W.Patey
S	1952 Mar 30	Totem	T.W.Patey, J.M.Taylor
S	1952 May 31	North Wall	T.W.Patey, G.B.Leslie, J.M.Taylor, J.Morgan
S	1952 Jun 1	Turret Buttress	G.B.Leslie, T.W.Patey, J.M.Taylor
S	1953 May 2	Dexter	T.W.Patey, C.D.Thomson, R.P.U.Tait
S	1953 May 2	Sinister	J.M.Taylor, A.G.Nicol
S	1960 Aug 12	Cioch Nose	T.W.Patey, C.J.S.Bonington
S	1968 Jun 3	Cleavage, The Maxilla	R.Hobbs, C.W.Dracup
S	1968 Jun 9	Cioch Nose Direct	T.W.Patey, H.MacInnes
S	1968	Sideburn	G.Anderson, A.Ewing
S	1969 May	Snothard	C.W.Dracup, R.Hobbs
S	1969 May 25	Cioch Corner	C.W.Dracup, R.Hobbs
S	1969 May 25	Lap of the Gods	R.How, J.R.Sutcliffe
S	1969 May 25	Gritstone Grooves	R.F.Allen, M.Allen
S	1970 May	Cioch Corner Superdirect	J.E.Howard, C.Rowland
S	1970 Jul	Parting	A.Ewing, F.Harper
S	1971	African Waltz	A.S.Macdonald, R.Popham
S	1975 May	Forgotten Corner	R.J.Archbold, G.Cohen
S	1975 Oct	Mantissa	R.J.Archbold, D.Dinwoodie
W	1977 Feb	No.4 Gully	C.Rowland, A.C.Cain
W	1979 Jan 14	South East Spur	A.Nisbet
W	1980 Jan	Anonymous Gully	N.D.Keir, G.Muhlemann
W	1984 Jan 15	Sinister	S.Allan, A.Nisbet
W	1984 Jan 16	White Dwarf	S.Allan, A.Nisbet
S	1984 Jun 2	Lost Wall	D.Rubens, G.Cohen

W	1986 Feb 2	Turret Buttress	M.Hamilton, G.Cohen
W	1986 Feb 16	Voyager	A.Nisbet, J.Mothersele
W	1991 Jan 12	Dexter	G.Ettle, A.Nisbet
W	1991 Feb 11	Jupiter	B.Davison, A.Nisbet
W	1993 Mar 3	Totem	D.Coburn, R.McFadden, A.Nisbet, R.Peak
S	1993 Oct	Chopper Chimney	M.Welch, M.Arkley
W	1993 Dec 27	North Wall	B.Davison, A.Nisbet
W	1995 Jan 23	North Gully	B.Davison, A.Nisbet
W	1995 Feb 26	The Gully in 3D	A.Nisbet, D.Parr, D.Walsh, D.Williams
W	1996 Feb 25	Chocks Away, Very Y-Gully	G.Bardsley, H.Davies, A.Nisbet
W	1996 Dec 31	Tomahawk	J.Lyall, M.Sclater, D.Williamson
W	1997 Jan 3	High Domain	S.Allan, J.Lyall
S	1996 Sep 14	Independence Day	M.Arkley, D.Counsell
S	1997 Jun 1	Impulse	G.Reilly, F.Templeton
S	2002 Sep 12	Rapid Pulse	G.Ettle, J.Lyall
W	2003 Feb 5	Cioch Nose Superdirect	C.Dale, M.Moran

An ascent was made by J.Sylvester, D.Toombs in 1986 but not recorded and it is uncertain what conditions were like.

W	2006 Mar 9	Far North Gully	A.Nisbet

Sgùrr a' Chaorachain - Summit Buttress

S	1972 Jun	Big Daddy (1PA)	G.Shields, R.Sharp

FFA: B.Davison, A.Nisbet, 1 Aug 1999

W	1986 Feb 2	Excitable Boy	P.Long, B.Owen

Triple Echo Finish by M.Fowler, S.Sustad, 24 Feb 1995

W	1986 Feb 2	Blade Runner	P.Long, B.Owen
S	1989 Jun 19	Synergy	P.Potter, M.Welch
W	1995 Jan 3	Yodel	M.Welch, R.Shillaker
W	1997 Jan 3	Wanda Lust	S.Allan, J.Lyall
S	1997 May 31	Airwaves	M.E.Moran, A.Nisbet

Sgùrr a' Chaorachain - South Face & Upper Cliff

S	1961 Oct 11	Sword of Gideon	T.W.Patey
S	1968 Apr 11	Swordstick	T.W.Patey, J.Cleare
S	1969 May 25	Recess Rib	J.A.Austin, K.Wood
S	1970 Jun 18	Trundler	B.Beattie, T.McKenny, C.Brooker
S	1970 Jun 27	Bumblyone	T.Cardwell, B.Beattie, C.Brooker
S	1970 Jun	Bumblytwo	B.Beattie, K.Hiles, E.Gautier
S	1970 Jun	Broken Buttress	C.R.Brooker, P.Barroud, A.Bartholomew
S	1970 Jul 7	Anduril	B.Beattie, J.Napoleoni
S	1970 Aug 23	The Smoke	T.Cardwell, B.Beckett, D.Smith
S	1970 Aug 25	Striker	T.Cardwell, D.Knight, J.Pollard
S	1971 Apr 25	Dougie's Climb	G.Anderson, P.F.Macdonald, D.B.Scott
S	1971 May	Swordthrust	W.March
S	1971 Jun 12	Park Lane	T.Cardwell & party
S	1971 Aug 20	Ganglion	K.V.Crocket, C.Stead
S	1971 Aug 21	Gideon's Wrath	K.V.Crocket, C.Stead

Direct Finish by T.Doe, A.Brooks on 19 Jun 1973

S	1971 Jul 6	Vine Street	T.Doe and party
S	1972 Jun	Big Daddy	G.Shields, R.Sharp
S	1973 May 25	Lost Supper (finished up Sword Swallower)	T.Doe, J.Duncan

As described by T.Doe, A.Brooks on 19 Jun 1973 (Gideon's Wrath Direct Finish)

S	1973 Jun 20	North Circular	T.Doe, J.Duncan
S	1973 Sep 2	Yer Dirt Box	T.Doe, R.Carr
S	1974 Apr 8	Sausage Machine	T.Doe, N.Pattinson, P.Thomson, L.Ray
S	1974 May 14	Rastus	T.Doe, J.McDougal, L.McInnes
S	1975 Jun 10	Jemima	T.Doe, R.Wood, D.Allen
S	1975 Jun 10	Lulu Belle	T.Doe, D.Allen
S	1984 Jun 10	Rig Veda	G.Cohen, S.Brener
S	1984 Jul	Pommel	D.Rubens, D.Broadhead
W	1987 Mar 22	Bee Gully	M.Fowler, A.Saunders
S	1988	Sanctuary	P.Potter, M.Welch
S	1991 Jul 5	Hotline	J.Lyall, A.Nisbet
S	1993 Jun 15	Sword Swallower	J.Lyall, A.Nisbet

376 FIRST ASCENTS

S	1993 Jun 15	The Kings of Midian	J.Lyall, A.Nisbet

Patey used Midian's start for Sword of Gideon.

S	1996 Jun 14	Roadhog's Wall	M.E.Moran (unsec)
S	1997 May 31	Crossed Swords	A.Nisbet

As described but much climbed previously

S	1997 Jun 16	Astrocyte	A.Nisbet, G.Nisbet
W	1999 Feb	Skullsplitter	R.G.Webb, N.Wilson
S	2005 Aug 14	Orcrist	R.I.Jones, A.Nisbet

Beinn Bhàn

S	1891 Jul	Traverse of A' Chioch	L.W.Hinxman
S	1950 Jul	North Buttress of A' Chioch S.Paterson	D.J.Bennet
S	1961 Oct 13	Upper Connecting Ridge of A' Phoit	T.W.Patey
W	1968	Upper Connecting Ridge of A' Chioch	J.Brown, T.W.Patey
W	1969 Mar 1	March Hare's Gully	C.J.S.Bonington, T.W.Patey
W	1969 Mar 2	North Gully, A' Chioch	A.Fyffe, C.MacInnes, M.Alburger
W	1971 Feb	Upper Connecting Ridge of A' Phoit	B.Goodwin, J.Grieve, D.Tierney
W	1971 Feb	Wall of the Early Morning Light	K.Spence, J.Horsfield, B.Jones, P.Thomas

The first route to breach the great back wall of Coire na Poite.

W	1974 Apr	Gingerbread	A.C.Cain, C.Rowland
W	1976 Feb 1	Mad Hatter's Gully	M.Freeman, G.Stephen
W	1977 Feb 12	Silver Tear	N.Muir, A.Paul
W	1978 Feb 11	Alice's Buttress	R.J.Archbold, J.C.Higham
W	1978 Feb 19	Moonshine	D.M.Jenkins, C.Stead

The route as described by D.McGimpsey, A.Nisbet in Jan 2003.

W	1978 Feb	Deep Gully	D.M.Jenkins, P.F.Macdonald
W	1979 17 Feb	The Chimney	A.Nisbet, B.Sprunt

Gully of the Gods was the intention, but the subterranean line was not spotted.

W	1979	Meandertha	A.Taylor, C.Robertson
W	1980 Jan 26-27	Der Riesenwand	A.Nisbet, B.Sprunt

The first ascent involved a bivouac!
Direct Start by I.Parnell, G.Robertson on 10 Feb 2007

W	1980 Feb 4	Dormouse Chimney	M.Freeman, J.Moreland
W	1980 Feb 5	Hors d'Oeuvres	P.Anderson, K.Murphy
W	1980 Feb 7	Donkey's Doobrie	P.Anderson, K.Murphy
W	1980 Feb 7	Skidmark Buttress	R.Robb, S.Young
W	1980	Crab Nebula	D.Dinwoodie, A.Williams
S	1981 Aug 4	Rory-Pory	D.Dinwoodie, R.A.Smith
W	1981 Dec 30	Sheet Whitening	M.Fowler, S.Fenwick, M.Lynden

This is the same route as Guttersnipe (SMCJ 1983). On 9 Jan 1982, M.Geddes, N.Rayner and T.Walne climbed 'a gully (800ft, Grade IV) in the coire north of the Giant's Coire, Beinn Bhàn' – presumably Coire Toll a' Bheinn. Never recorded.

W	1983 Feb 24	The Cooler	D.Dinwoodie, A.Paul

The 'even steeper' finish by G.Ettle, M.Garthwaite on 9 Jan 1997

W	1983 Feb 26	Adventures of Toad	D.Dinwoodie, A.Paul
W	1983 Apr 3	Gully of the Gods	M.Fowler, S.Fenwick
W	1983 Apr 3	Der Rise and Shine	A.Saunders, B.Simmonds
W	1984 Feb 8	The Acid Queen	D.Dinwoodie, C.Maclean
W	1984 Mar 17	Great Overhanging Gully (3PA)	M.Fowler, P.Butler

FFA: C.Cartwright, D.Heselden, Feb 1994

W	1984 Mar	Threatening Behaviour	S.Fenwick, P.Thornhill
W	1984 Mar	Breach of the Peace	F.Thornhill
W	1984 Mar	Indecent Exposure	S.Fenwick, N.Bankhead
W	1986 Feb 2	Harlequin Rib	H.M.A.Towler, G.S.Strange, J.C.Higham, B.S.Findlay, R.J.Archbold

Right-Hand version by C.Dale and party on 12 Feb 2003

W	1986 Feb 17	Sniper's Gully	J.Mothersele, A.Nisbet
W	1986 Feb 23	Mock Turtle Icefall	D.Gardiner, D.Hawthorn
W	1986 Mar 1	In X.S.	C.Downer, D.Scott
W	1986 Mar 1	Couldoran Gully	J.Lyall
W	1986	The Dwarf Icefall	B.Jardine and partner
W	1988 Mar 18	Flying Penguin Gully	P.Potter, M.Welch
W	1986 Mar 1	Grey Hair Gully	J.Lyall
W	1989 Feb 21	Flesheater	I.Dring, M.E.Moran

FIRST ASCENTS 377

W	1989 Mar 17	Das Rheingold	M.E.Moran
W	1990	Right Face	S.Jenkins and party
W	1991 Feb	Divine Retribution	C.Cartwright, R.Clothier
W	1993 Jan 14	Indigenous	P.Mynch, M.Moran
W	1994 Jan 5	Man's Best Friend	G.Ettle, J.Lyall
W	1994 Feb 14	Teapot	S.J.H.Reid, J.Rowlands
W	1995 Mar 4	The Magician's Boy	R.G.Webb, N.Wilson
W	1995 Feb 8	Criminal Trespass	P.Clayton, A.Nisbet, A.Partington
W	1995 Feb 10	Toll a' Bhein Gully, Missing Persons	A.Nisbet, G.Nisbet
W	1995 Feb 10	Solitary Confinement	A.Nisbet
W	1996 Nov 24	Consolation Buttress	G.Ettle, P.Munford, A.Nisbet
W	1996 Dec 28	North Buttress	A.Nisbet, G.Nisbet
W	1997 Jan 9	Bhantasia	G.Ettle, M.Garthwaite
W	1998 Jan 19	Illegal Grass	G.Lewis-Evans, A.Nisbet, D.Winterbone
W	1998 Jan 20	Beinn Bhan Grooves	G.Ettle, J.Preston
W	1998 Mar 5	White Bhan Man	G.Ettle, K.Grindrod, J.Lyall
W	1999 Feb 27	The Bill	A.Nisbet
W	1999 Mar 4	Breach of Contract	A.Nisbet, C.Preece, O.Preece

The gully leading to the central col on the A' Chioch ridge was climbed by D.Morrison, R.Simpson and A.Fisher in winter 1999

W	1999 Dec 19	The Weed	D.McGimpsey, A.Nisbet
W	2000 Feb 20	Genesis	A.Cave, D.Heselden
W	2000 Dec 28	Gingerbread	G.Ettle, I.Taylor
W	2000 Dec 30	Insufficient Evidence	D.McGimpsey, A.Nisbet
W	2001 Feb 5	Suspense Buttress Direct	J.Ashby, L.Sell-Blackaby, M.Moran
W	2001 Feb 9	Countdown to Disaster	B.Fyffe, O.Samuels
W	2001 Feb 28	Winklepicker, Musselman, Bounty Hunter	D.McGimpsey, A.Nisbet
W	2001 Mar 2	Cliffhanger	D.McGimpsey, A.Nisbet
W	2002 Jan 4	Silent Witness	A.Nisbet
W	2002 Mar 14	The Godfather	M.Moran, P.Tattersall
W	2003 Dec 30	Revelations	J.Edwards, S.Barron
W	2004 Jan 17	Biblical Knowledge	J.Edwards, G.Hughes
W	2004 Jan 31	Realisation	S.Yearsley, M.Bass
W	2004 Dec 21	Weakest Link	D.McGimpsey, A.Nisbet
W	2005 Feb 22	Gryphon	I.Small, D.McGimpsey
W	2005 Feb 24	Skinflint	A.Nisbet, J.Preston; D.McGimpsey, I.Small
W	2006 Mar 3	Speeding Ticket	A.Nisbet

Applecross Crags
Ardheslaig
Routes by combinations of T.Doe, J.Brinsley, B.Depper on 18 Sep 1974 except The Mother-in-Law, Very Gneiss by T. Doe and party on 24 Oct 1974. Other routes unknown.

Ardheslaig Sea-Cliff
Routes by M.Moran and party in 2002.

Loch na Creige Crag
The four routes were climbed by P.Potter, M.Welch in the spring of 1988.

A' Bhainlir
S	2005 May 7	Vantage Slab	A.Nisbet

Arch Crag
S	2003 Sep 28	Cas Chrom	S. Kennedy, R. Hamilton

Sand
S	1988 Jun 16	If	P.Potter, M.Welch
S	1988 June	Mandela's Birthday	M.Welch, J.Holmes

Camusteel Sea-Cliffs
The routes are taken from a guide written by Terry Doe, generally without first ascentionists. Rush Pigeon by A.Macdonald, P.Potter, 2 Oct 1988.

Torridon
Kinlochdamph Crag

S	1999 Apr 26	Cat's Claw	M.Moran
S	1999 Apr 28	Needle's Edge	M.Moran (unsec)
S	1999 May 1	Sleeping Dog Climb	A.Moran, M.Moran

Poshpaws Start by M.E. & A.J.Moran, 4 May 2004

S	1999 May 1	Crusade Corner	M.Moran
S	1999 Jun 11	Ivy League	M.Moran, A.Nisbet, W.Skidmore
S	1999 Jun 16	Hasta la Bista	J.Allott, M.Moran

Direct Finish by M.E.Moran, J.Preston, 13 May 2004

S	1999 Jun 23	Here be Dragons, Beauty and the Beast	M.Moran, A.Nisbet
S	1999 Jun 23	Den of Iniquity	M.Moran (unsec)
S	1999 Jun 24	Beasts' Lair, Raven Seek thy Brother	M.Moran, A.Nisbet
S	2000 May 10	Command and Conquer	M.Moran, D.Ross, M.Welch
S	2004 May 13	Tiberian Sun	M.E.Moran, J.Preston
S	2005 Mar 30	War of Attrition	M.E.Moran, A.J.Moran

Ben Shieldaig

S	2004 May 23	Gateway	S.Kennedy, R.Hamilton
S	2004 May 23	Prawn Man	R.Hamilton, S.Kennedy

Shieldaig Crags

The following routes may have been climbed previously. The Shieldaig area has also been used for bouldering in the past.

S	2005 Mar 20	Sheep Shed Shuffle	J.Sutherland, G.McPartlin, A.Hendriks
S	2005 Sep 10	Archie Gemmell	J.Sutherland, A.Hendriks
S	2006 Apr 23	Unpaid Bills	J.Sutherland, A.Hendriks
S	2006 May 28	Threesome	C.Wilson
S	2006	Routes on West Crag	C.Wilson, R.Johnson

Creag Dhubh an t-Sall

S	2001 Sep 27	Apis	M.Moran
S	2001 Sep 27	Vespa, Bombus	M.Moran, A.Nisbet.
S	2002 Jul 14	Hoverfly	D.McGimpsey, E.Christison
S	2002 Jul 14	Bumble	D.McGimpsey

Creag na Speireag

S	1996 Apr 6	Rock Agus Roll, Nematode, Che Guevara, Gondola	C.Moody, M.McLeod
S	1996 May 12	Cuir Tigear Na Do Thanc	C.Moody, M.McLeod, R.Lupton

Variation by D.McGimpsey, A.Nisbet, 20 Jun 2002

S	1996 May 12	Telegraph Pole	C.Moody, M.McLeod, R.Lupton
S	2001 May 12	Someone's Crack, Pea Soup, Lysfoss, South Wall	C.Moody, C.Grindley
S	2001 Sep 27	Big Ears, One Cog Missing	M.Moran, A.Nisbet
S	2002 Jun 20	Waggonner	D.McGimpsey, A.Nisbet

One fall taken without lowering off.

Beinn Damh

S	1967 Aug	Aquila	L.Cardy, G.Halleyard
W	1979 Feb 12	Boundary Gully	R.Butler, D.Howard, D.McCallum, C.Roylance

Originally called Aquila Gully, repeated and named as Boundary Gully by P.Moffat, P.J.Biggar on 3 Feb 1991.

W	1979 Feb 12	Stag Gully	R.Butler, D.Howard, D.McCallum, C.Roylance

Left Fork by P.J.Biggar, R.A.Biggar, 13 Feb 1994

W	1984 Mar 3	Aetos	I.Crofton, G.Caplan
W	1987 Jan 1	Neerday Gully	P.J.Biggar

The first of five gullies in Little Coire by P.J.Biggar, R.A.Biggar, 1987-1994. Many buttresses climbed by B.Wilkinson, J.Baillie in 2000.

W	1991 Jan 3	The Professor's Lum	P.J Biggar, R.A.Biggar
W	1991 Jan 13	Stirrup Gully	J.Elliot, P.J.Biggar

FIRST ASCENTS

Retreat from below the easy upper section. Complete ascent by A.Nisbet on 20 Mar 1996.
W	1995 Jan	Traveller's Trail	J.Ashby, R.Jarvis, M.Moran
W	1995 Feb 28	Stalker's Gully	D.Bradshaw, J.Colverd, M.Moran
W	1995 Dec 30	Moonloop	J.Graham, N.Bullock
W	1997 Jan 8	Mystic Gully	A.Nisbet, J.Preston
W	1997 Feb 11	The Thin White Line	M.C.Jacob, P.J.Biggar
W	1997 Feb 15	The Slanter	P.J.Biggar
W	1998 Mar 4	Erica's Ridge	J.Gibbs, A.Nisbet, A.Petts, C.Platten
W	2001 Feb 8	Calluna (Right Finish)	A.Foster, J.Gibb, A.Nisbet

Left Finish by D.McGimpsey, A.Nisbet on 4 Mar 2001
W	2004 Feb 26	Ermine	A.Nisbet, J.Preston
W	2005 Feb 25	Lingo	A.Nisbet, J.Preston
W	2005 Mar 14	Fraoch Groove	A.Nisbet (backroped)
W	2006 Mar 1	Foxy Grooves	M.Edwards, D.McGimpsey, A.Nisbet

Creag an Fhithich

S	1994 Aug 6	Crystal Horizon, Tombstone, Fiery Cross, Procession	S.Kennedy, C.Grindley
S	1994 Aug 6	Maculate Slab	S.Kennedy
S	1995 May 25	Congregation, Gem Find	T.Leggat, A.Nisbet
S	1999 Apr 25	Four Trees, routes on Chimney Climb wall	D.Allan

Annat Bouldering

Routes on upper walls by D.MacLeod, M.Tweedley in 2004
Boulders and Slipstanes Wall by T.Pinnons in 2006

Creag na Botaigean

S	1995 May 6	Two Bolts and Some Bailer Twine	C.Moody, R.Watson
S	1996 May 9	Dhanakosa	I.Taylor (unsec)
S	2000 Jul 29	Lammergeier	D.McGimpsey, A.Nisbet
S	2000 Jul 30	Phantom Fencer, Tjasa	D.McGimpsey, A.Nisbet

Seana Mheallan

All routes by R.and C.Anderson in May and June 1990 except:
S	1993 May 11	No Brats	I.Taylor, C.Moody
S	1993 May 12	Reject	C.Moody, I.Taylor
S	1994 May	Sandwich	I.Taylor, C.Moody
S	1999 May 18	Forgotten Corner, Skirting the Issue, Rejection	A.Fyffe, A.Salisbury
S	1999 May 31	Dirty Dancing	A.Cunningham, A.Fyffe
S	2000 June 25	Thunderbird	D.Cuthbertson, J.George
S	2006 May 14	Neville the Hedgehog	P.Mather, R.Mather

Seana Mheallan West

S	1994 Jul 3	Nasal Abuse, Mechanical Sheep, Skate, Polythene Bag, Clingfilm	C.Moody, R.Watson
S	1994 Jul 16	Fleeced, Unmasked, Flaky, Archangel, Bedrock, Moaning Minnie	S.Kennedy, C.Grindley
S	1994 Sep	Mr Bean	S.Kennedy, D.Ritchie, S.Thirgood
S	1995 Jul 11	Hadrian's Wall	M.McLeod, C.Moody
S	1998 May 12	Off With Her Head, Wriggle, Porpoise Scandal, Bleached Whale, Dolphin Friendly	L.Gordon Canning, C.Moody
S	1998 Jun 17	The Age of Confusion	C.Moody, L.Gordon Canning
S	1998 Jun 22	The Black Queen	A.Nisbet, G.Nisbet
S	1998 Jul 2	Incognito, Turned Turtle, The Knob, Wilma, Pebble	J.Lyall, A.Nisbet
S	1999 Jun 9	Fish and Chips, Sleeping Sickness	L.Gordon Canning, C.Moody
S	1999 Jun 13	Cairnaholics Anonymous	A.Nisbet, G.Nisbet, C.Watkins
S	1999 Jun 13	Cairn Terrier, Clockwork Rat	A.Nisbet, C.Watkins
S	2000 Jul 15	Outswinger	D.McGimpsey, A.Nisbet
S	2000 Jul 16	Skye and Kyle against Trugs, Quartz Warts	C.Moody, C.Grindley

FIRST ASCENTS

S	2002 Aug 10	Lap Land, Heather Said Sunshine, Better than a Slap in the Face	C.Moody, C.Grindley
S	2002 Aug 10	Luing Rib	C.Moody
S	2003 Apr 19	Mind the Trench, Trench at Top	C.Moody
S	2005 Apr 23	Right Edge, The Black Steaked	C.Moody, A.Nisbet
S	2006 Apr 29	Tarsam, Yak	C.Moody, C.Grindley, B.Taylor

Path Crag

S	2005 Aug 7	Path Corner, Foxglove Crack, Lower Leftist, Swirl	C.Moody, C.Grindley.
S	2005 Apr 23	White Fingers, Path Flake, Space Face, Spaceman, Pitching	C.Moody, A.Nisbet

Celtic Boulders

These have been climbed on for many years but the following were perhaps first ascents. Many of the routes as described were climbed by N.Hinchcliff and friends.

S	2002	6b arete on The Ship	W.Moir, N.Morrison
S	2003 Apr 5	Trend Setter	T.Rankin (unsec)
S	2004	Frantic	D.MacLeod
S	2004	Wall to its right	M.Tweedley
S	2005	right arete on The Ship	M.Smith
S	2007 Feb	The Mission	R.Betts

Creag nan Leumnach

S	1994 Feb 13	Global Warming	C.Moody
S	1994 Mar 26	The White Streak	N.Smith, C.Moody
S	1994 May 14	Blind as a Frog, Block and Beak, A Million Years BC, Don't Just Sit There, Sky a Jy	S.Kennedy, C.Moody
S	1994 May 14	Big Tree	C.Moody
S	1994 May 23	Squeezin' yer Heid, Warmer Cleaner Drier	C.Moody, I.Taylor
S	1994 May 25	The Great Brush Robbery	I.Taylor, C.Moody,
S	1994 May 25	Torridown Man	C.Moody, I.Taylor
S	1996 May 26	Cross Dressing	I.Taylor, T.Fryer
S	1996 Aug 8	The Vanishing Frog	I.Taylor (unsec)
S	1999 Aug	Kermit's Crack	P.Thorburn, I.Taylor
S	1999 Aug	Completely out to Lunge	I.Taylor, P.Thorburn

Creag nan Uaimh

S	1994 May 23	Reach the Road, Caterpillar Ridge, Kanko the Bone	C.Moody, I.Taylor
S	1994 May 23	En Route, Holly Tree Rib	C.Moody

Hairpin Crag

S	1990	Walsh's Groove	M.Moran
S	1992 Jul 4	The Black Struggle	C.Moody, B.Taylor
S	1992 Aug 8	Grey Matter, Nut the Rock	C.Moody, R.Lupton
S	1993 May 8	The Text Book, Black and Blue	C.Moody, B.Taylor
S	1993 May 9	Indian Winter, Wind Break	I.Taylor, C.Moody
S	1993 May 10	Becalmed, Bundle of Apathy	I.Taylor, C.Moody
S	1997 Jun 8	Windy Wall, Nut the Rock Direct Finish	G.Latter, P.Thorburn
S	2005 May 15	Speckled Frog, Man-Eating Troll	R.I.Jones, A.Nisbet
S	2006 May 21	A Range Apart	M.Dent, R.I.Jones

Possibly climbed before as a rusty peg was found.

S	2006 May 21	Bluebell Crack	R.I.Jones, M.Dent

Sgorr a' Chadail

S	1952 Aug 4	Reflection Wall	W.J.Cole, J.R.Marshall
S	1993 Apr 28	The Pale Wall, Mirror Image	A.Nisbet, G.Nisbet
S	1993 Apr 29	Trench Foot, Reflections of my Mind	A.Nisbet, G.Nisbet
S	2005 Jul 5	False Identity, Chadailac	I.Small, C.Cartwright

FIRST ASCENTS

Inveralligin Sea-Cliffs
Early explorations were carried out by school groups from Cathkin High School and Stonelaw High School, who jointly owned the old schoolhouse from the late 1960s until 1986. No formal routes were noted or recorded until August 1985, when Ian Hunter and Lindsay McGibbon, both former pupils of Cathkin High School, did The Evil One on Boathouse Crag and Sammy's Belt and Six of the Best on Sammy's Buttress. The crags were visited several times from March 1999 to August 2001 by I.B.B.Hunter with some of M.Hale, G.White, T.Davidson, S.Spencer, P.Fidler, R.Brown, J.Cassidy and M.B.Duffy. A.Nisbet climbed three routes on Boathouse Crag in June 2005.

Creag Alligin
Routes first climbed by M.Welch and M.Arkley in October 1993, with later visits by M.Moran, A.Nisbet and parties.

Discovery Rock
Routes climbed by M.E.Moran, J.Allott, B.Moore and party, 26 May 2003 and M.Moran and J.Preston, 2 Nov 2004.

Big Bill's Crag
S	2004 Nov 2	Who Needs Kalymnos?	M.E.Moran, J.Preston

Beginners Slabs
Pink Slab by R.Brown, J.R.Mackenzie on 18 Sep 1993. Others by A.Nisbet on 10 Sep 1999.

Diabaig
S	1975 Aug 3	Route One	J.A.Austin, E.Grindley
S	1975 Aug 4	Route Two, Route Three	J.A.Austin, E.Grindley
S	1976 Aug 9	The Black Streak	J.A.Austin, R.Valentine
S	1976 Aug 10	Gamhnachain's Crack, Charlie's Tower	J.A.Austin, C.Rose, R.Valentine
S	1976 Aug	Upper Corner	J.A.Austin, R.Valentine, J.Ratcliffe
S	1982 Apr 24	Foil, Boab's Corner	C.Moody, R.Sharples
S	1982 May 23	Plunge	D.Hayter, C.Moody
S	1983	The Pillar	M.Hamilton
S	1984 May	Dire Wall	A.Nisbet, R.F.Allen
S	1984 May	Northumberland Wall	A.Nisbet, R.McHardy
S	1985 Jun 8	Dead Mouse Crack	J.Brown and partner
S	1987 Apr 16	An Eyeful	G.Latter, I.Griffiths, D.Griffiths

The Gritty Finish by S.Crowe, 1993

S	1987 May 27	Rubblesplitskin	K.Howett
S	1987 May 27	Edgewood Whymper	K.Howett, D.Cuthbertson
S	1987 May 28	Local Hero	K.Howett, D.Cuthbertson
S	1987 May 29	Condome	K.Howett, D.Cuthbertson

Instant Muscle (1988) would seem to be the same route.

S	1987 May 29	The Con-Con	D.Cuthbertson, K.Howett

Direct variation (named Rough Justice) by D.Griffiths, C.Bell, 15 Jul 1988

S	1987 Jun 10	Wall of Flame	K.Howett, C.Thomson
S	1988	Final Demand	D.Griffiths
S	1988 Apr 30	Bromide	W.Hood, C.Moody, B.Williamson
S	1988 Aug	Going Home	G.Latter, K.Howett
S	1988 Aug	Afterglow	K.Howett, G.Latter
S	1990 May	An Offensive Man, Animal Magic, Porpoise Pun	K.Howett, A.Taylor, T.Prentice
S	1990	Batwing	B.Kerr, T.Prentice, A.Todd
S	1990 Jul 29	Evasion	S.Allan, D.Etherington

Pitch 2 by G.Latter, A.Clapperton on 15 Jul 1996

S	1990 Jul 29	Bogie	S.Allan, D.Etherington, A.Nisbet
S	1990 Oct 24	The Mynch	G.Fry, M.Moran, P.Mynch
S	1991 Mar 26	The Grunter	W.Hood, L.Skuodas
S	1991 Apr 15	Diabaig Corner	R.Lupton, C.Moody
S	1991 May 31	Dire Straights	S.Jenkins, M.Moran

A line starting up Dire Straights but perhaps finishing up Upper Corner was climbed by J.Brown, A.C.Cain around 1980.

S	1991 Sep 1	Brimstone	J.Lyall, A.Nisbet

Perhaps climbed before.

FIRST ASCENTS

S	1993 Sep 18	Pink Slab	R.Brown, J.R.Mackenzie
S	1993 May 8	The Frieze	M.Moran, A.Nisbet
S	1993 May 23	Shunned	A.Cunningham, J.Pickering
S	1993 Jun 1	Diabaig, the Hard Way	N.Foster (unsec)
S	1993 Jun 19	Terrier Trauma	K.Milne, J.Ashdown
S	1994 May 10	Grandad's Wall, Copping's Crack	M.Moran, J.Copping, T.Rankin, B.Riley
S	1994 May 10	Dental Trauma	M.Moran, J.Copping, T.Rankin
S	1994 May	Big Glossy Book Route	C.Moody
S	1994 May	The Gooseberry	A.Tibbs, H.Tibbs, A.Matthewson
S	1994	(Once upon a time in) The Wild West	S.Crowe (unsec)
S	1995 May 21	Continuation Route	A.Andrew and party
S	1996 Apr	Oor Wullie pitch 2	T.Fryer, I.Taylor
	As described by J.Lyall, A.Nisbet, 1 Apr 1998		
S	1996 Jul 15	The Dominie	G.Latter, A.Clapperton
	Pitch 1 by G.Latter, P.Thorburn, 1997		
S	1997 Jul 26	Apprentices Route	N.Kenworthy, D.W.M.Whalley, K.Holland
S	1998 Jun 29	Feelin' Groovy	G.Latter
S	1998 Oct 12	Calcite Corner, Pointless Eliminates	G.Latter, A.Siddons
S	2003 Aug 31	Apprentice Bhoys	S.Kennedy, A.MacDonald
S	2005 May 1	Emerald	S.Kennedy, A.MacDonald
S	2005 May 15	Deputy Dawg, Musky, Like Pine Bark	C.Grindley, C.Moody
S	2005 Jun 25	Top Cat	A.Nisbet

Diabaig Peninsula

S	1998 Sep 5	Epsilon, Delta, Gamma	A.Brockington, J.Fisher
S	1998 Sep 5	Beside the Point, The Ice Bulge, Brave New World, The Sea The Sea	J.Fisher, A.Brockington
S	1998 Sep 5	The Feelies	A.Brockington, J.Fisher
S	1998 Sep 5	Beached Boat Buttress	J.Fisher, A.Brockington
S	1998 Sep 5	Ewar Woowar, Alice's Overhang	J.Fisher
S	1998 Oct 3	The Low Girdle	F.Bennet, J.Fisher
S	1998 Oct 3	Rolling Home	J.Fisher, F.Bennet
S	1998 Oct 3	Submission, Boatman's Call	S.Grey, A.Reid, J.Reid
S	1998 Oct 3	The Applecross Jam	A.Coull, A.Sharpe, J.Fisher, F.Bennet
S	1998 Oct 3	8-Ace, Red Crescent	S.Grey, A.Reid, J.Reid
S	1998 Oct 4	Ugly Mug, Ugly Wall	F.Bennet, J.Fisher
S	1998 Oct 4	Pretty Scoop, Pretty Crack	J.Fisher
S	1999 Jul 11	Jammy Dodger	R.McAllister and others
S	2000 Apr 30	Mustn't Grumble	R.Simpson, B.Watson
S	2000 May 14	Aquamarine	R.Durran (unsec)
S	2000 Jul 22	Pretty Midgie	J.Currie, T.Rankin
S	2000 Jul 22	Diabaig Tiger	T.Rankin, J.Currie, G.Robertson
S	2000 Jul 22	Right of Tenure, The Act	G.Robertson
S	2000 Jul 28	A Mugs Game, Handsome Hog	D.McGimpsey, A.Nisbet
S	2000 Aug 3	Diabug	A.Nisbet
S	2000 Sep 1	Parasol (Loch a' Bhealaich Crag)	D.McGimpsey, A.Nisbet
S	2001 Jun 17	Hot Head	J.Preston, J.Lyall
S	2004 Jun 12	Rolling Baba	M.E. and A.J.Moran
S	2005 Jun 2 to 5	Rubha na h-Airde routes	D.Gilyeat, A.Morley, B.Woodley
S	2006 Jun 2	Shipwrecked	B.B. and J.Woodley, S.Tight
	Only one member of the party was aged over 11.		

White House Crag

S	1993 Oct	Rendezvous	M.Welch, M.Arkley
	Approached by canoe from Applecross.		
S	1998 May 8	Rock Stripper, The Full Monty, Walking on Crystals, Quartz Inspector's Slab	R.Brown, J.R.Mackenzie
S	1998 May 16	Indecent Exposure, Promiscuous Groove	R.Brown, J.R.Mackenzie, G.Cullen, A.Nisbet
S	1998 May 16	Bare Faced Cheek	R.Brown, J.R.Mackenzie, G.Cullen

Beinn Alligin

W	1973 Feb	West Coast Boomer	D.Gardner, N.Crawford, C.Ferguson

W	1981 Feb	Backfire Ridge	S.Chadwick, G.Powell
W	1984 Apr 15	Backyard Gully	S.Chadwick
W	1985 Feb 10	Diamond Fire	S.Chadwick, G.Livingston, G.Strange
W	1986 Feb 1	Backyard Buttress	R.Archbold, J.C.Higham, H.M.A.Towler
W	1986 Feb 15	Koh-i-Noor	M.E.Moran, M.Hardwick
W	1986 Feb 18	Ice Gem	M.E.Moran, S.Chadwick
W	1986 Mar 2	Crown Jewel	M.E.Moran, N.Adey, M.Guest
W	1986 Mar 2	Moonstone	M.E.Moran
W	1987 Jan 18	Bilas	D.Rubens, D.Broadhead
W	1987 Feb	Errors Cleft	S.Chadwick, I.Davidson
W	1988 Mar 15	Diamond Cleft	C.Munro, S.Chadwick
W	1989 Feb 26	Light of Bengal	I.Barron, S.Kennedy
W	1989 Feb 26	Shezan	M.Macdonald, A.Scrase
W	1993 Jan 27	Hatchet Man	S.Chiles, H.Davis, A.Nisbet, P.Worthington
W	1993 Feb 27	Under the Hammer	A.Nisbet, G.Ollerhead
W	1994 Apr 8	Gardeners' Choice	B.Davison, C.Ottley
W	1995 Jan 25	Black Opal	A.Gorman, S.Chadwick
W	1996 Feb 20	Depth Charge	S.Chadwick, M.E.Moran
W	1996 Mar	Curve Stone	S.Chadwick, S.Gorman
W	1996 Dec 5	Wall of the Outcry	M.E.Moran, A.Nisbet
W	1999 Jan 9	For the Chop	B.Davison, A.Nisbet
W	1999 Jan 21	Wailing Wall	D.McGimpsey, A.Nisbet
W	2001 Feb 11	Coire nan Laogh icefalls	J.Preston, B.Clarke, M.Weldon

Beinn Dearg

W	1994 Apr 6	North Ridge	D.Broadhead
S	1994 Jun	North Ridge	A.Nisbet, G.Nisbet
W	2000 Dec	Red Rag	R.Webb, N.Wilson
W	2001 Jan 27	Red Dwarf	D.McGimpsey, A.Nisbet
W	2001 Jan	Red Chimneys	R.Webb, M.Hind

Liathach

S	1894 Jun 11	Northern Pinnacles	W.Douglas, L.Hinxman, W.Rennie, W.MacDonald, J.Gall Inglis
S	1899 Easter	East Buttress	Lawson, W.N.Ling, G.T.Glover
W	1900 Easter	Northern Pinnacles	S.M.C. Party
W	1928	Gully 1K	F.S.Goggs
W	1928	Left-Hand Trinity Gully	G.Sang, W.N.Ling, G.T.Glover
S	1939 Jun	P.C. Buttress	R.S.Horseman, H.K.Hartley
S	1947 Jun 30	Bell's Buttress	Dr. and Mrs. J.H.B.Bell
S	1952 Aug 4	Reflection Wall	W.J.Cole, J.R.Marshall
W	1955 Mar 29	Central Trinity Gully, Right-Hand Trinity Gully	D.Stevens, R.Urquhart
W	1955 Mar 31	3rd Pinnacle Gully, Twisting Gully	R.Urquhart, D.Stevens
W	1955 Mar 31	Left-Hand Trinity Gully	M.Robson, A.Delafield
S	1959 Easter	Dru	D.J.Temple, P.J.Crabb
W	1966	Hillwalk	unknown
W	1967 Feb	George	I.G.Rowe, M.Kelsey
W	1968	Chi Squared	C.Rowland, R.Toogood

First recorded by D.Rubens and party in 1984.

S	1970 Aug	Triceratops	R.W.L. and D.G.Turnbull
W	1976 Dec	Stringless Gully	A.Barney, P.Nunn, C.Rowland, R.Toogood
W	1977	Hidden Gully	C.Rowland (solo)
W	1977	Spidean Way	C.Rowland, B.Griffiths
W	1977 Feb	Footless Gully	C. and A.S.Rowland

Originally recorded as Gloveless Gully after a glove was dropped en route!

W	1977 Feb	Pyramid Buttress	D.Jenkins, C.Rowland, M.Webster
W	1978	West Gully	C.Rowland, R.McHardy
W	1978 Feb 11	Poachers Fall	R.McHardy, A.Nisbet

Eventually climbed after three attempts by C.Rowland over 1977/78 including one with McHardy in 1978 (Nisbet felt like the poacher).

W	1978 Feb 12	Sinister Prong	J.Grant, J.R.Mackenzie
W	1979	Gully 1A	C.Rowland and party
W	1979 Feb 24	Vanadium Couloir	A.Paul, D.Sanderson
W	1980s	Pyramid Right Edge	B.Ledingham, C.Rowland

384 FIRST ASCENTS

W	1980s	Gully 2A	C.Rowland and party
W	1984 Feb	Headless Gully	S.Kennedy, A.Nisbet
W	1984 Feb 21	Titanium Gully	D.Rubens, G.Macnair, G.Cohen
W	1984 Apr 1	Umbrella Fall	M.Fowler, P.Butler

The described start on the lower tier may have been the original start but was certainly climbed by B.Davison, C.Ottley, 7 Apr 1994.

W	1985	Hidden Buttress	C.Rowland, K.Hopper
W	1985 Mar 10	Jerbil	M.Fowler, B.Craig
W	1986 Jan 3	Terminal Buttress	G.Nicoll, J.Hotchkis

A similar line hereabouts was climbed in winter 1983 by C.Rowland, K.Hopper and B.Ledingham.

W	1986 Feb 15	The Executioner	A.Nisbet, J.Mothersele
W	1986 Feb 22	The Andes Couloir	A.Cunningham, A.Nisbet
W	1986 Feb 22	Bell's Gully	R.Anderson, M.Hamilton
W	1986 Feb 23	Salmon Leap	A.Cunningham, A.Nisbet

Variation by R.Page, Y.Astier, 29 Mar 1995

W	1986 Feb 23	Dru Couloir	R.Anderson, M.Hamilton
W	1986 Feb 23	Pyramid Left Icefall	K.Hopper, C.Rowland

The direct line (as described) by C.Rowland, M.Antoine in 1987

W	1986 Feb 24	The Deerhunter	A.Cunningham, A.Nisbet
W	1986 Feb 25	Snow Goose	A.Cunningham, A.Nisbet
W	1986 Feb 25	The Snotter	A.Cunningham, A.Nisbet
W	1987 Jan 2	Bannockburn	C.Forrest, W.Moir
W	1987 Jan 11	Test Department (2PA)	M.Fowler, C.Watts

Free ascent of the complete icicle on 6 Mar 1999 by B.Davison, A.Nisbet; S.Anderson, M.Moran. At least 10 more ascents in the following week, including the variation finish by C.Piccolruaz, J.Oberhauser on 12 Mar 1999

W	1987 Jan 11	Bell's Buttress, Left Chimney	G.Cohen, D.Broadhead
W	1987 Jan 13	Soul-Searcher	M.E.Moran
W	1987 Jan 13	Hooded Claw	A.Nisbet, A.Cunningham
W	1987 Jan 13	Brain Drain	A.Nisbet, A.Cunningham
W	1987 Jan 14	White Tiger	A.Cunningham, A.Nisbet
W	1987 Jan 15	Snow White	A.Nisbet, A.Cunningham
W	1987 Jan 15	Fairy Queen	A.Cunningham, A.Nisbet
W	1987 Jan 17	Salvation	M.E.Moran (unsec)
W	1987 Jan 17	Toll Dubh Chimney	D.Rubens, D.Broadhead
W	1987 Feb 14	Valentine Buttress	D.Broadhead, W.Tring
W	1987 Feb 15	Rambler's Rib	D.Broadhead, S.Sillars
W	1988 Feb 16	The Temptress	A.Cunningham, A.Nisbet
W	1989 Feb 25	Thumbscrew	I.Barron, S.Kennedy
W	1989 Feb 25	Thumbscrew Direct	G.Nicoll, S.Pearson
W	1990 Jan 4	Holy Trinity	R. and C.Anderson
W	1991 Feb 17	Brain Strain	D.Wills, M.Fowler
W	1992 Dec	North East Buttress	S.Archer, E.Brunskill
W	1993 Jan 23	Last Orders	S.Pearson, G.Cohen
W	1993 Jan 30	Fat Man's Folly	D.Broadhead, D.Rubens
W	1993 Mar 1	Echo Couloir	S.Birch, C.Collin, M.Moran

Left start (as described) by A.Nisbet, G.Nisbet on 19 Mar 1994

W	1993 Mar 3	The Shining Path	S.Birch, M.Moran
S	1993 Apr 28	The Pale Wall, Mirror Image	A.Nisbet, G.Nisbet
S	1993 Apr 29	Trench Foot, Reflections of my Mind	A.Nisbet, G.Nisbet
W	1994 Feb 7	Head Hunter	N.Kekus, S.Anderson

Probably climbed before in mistake for Headless Gully

W	1994 Feb 21	First Face	A.Nisbet, G.Vaughn, M.Webb
W	1994 Feb 22	Fubarbundy	C.Cartwright, D.Heselden
W	1994 Feb 23	The Stem	C.Cartwright, D.Heselden
W	1994 Mar 3	The Sneak	D.Houfe, A.Nisbet, N.Sinclair, D.Wolfe
W	1994 Mar 7	Over Sixties Icefall	M.Johnston, A.Nisbet, D.Thompson
W	1994 Mar 17	Under Thirties Icefall	R.Groth, M.Mauger, A.Nisbet
W	1994 Apr 13	Cube's Chimney, The Faultfinders	S.Blagbrough, J.Lyall
W	1995 Jan 10	Campanology, The Final Gong	J.Lyall, A.Nisbet
W	1995 Jan 19	Red Herring	E.Herring, A.Nisbet, R.Perriss
W	1995 Feb 9	Eagle Gully	K.Grindrod, J.Lyall
W	1995 Feb 24	Busman's Holiday	A.Nisbet, G.Nisbet
W	1995 Mar 15	Bell's Right Buttress, Bannock Gully	I.Dillon, A.Nisbet
W	1995 Mar 21	Spidean's Sting	M.Welch, D.Green, I.Grimshaw

W	1995 Mar 25	Forking Gully	A.Fyffe, J.Hepburn
W	1995 Mar 29	The Doctor's Ear	K.Duncan, A.Nisbet, I.Stewart
W	1996 Feb 1	West Face of the Dru	S.Ainsworth, A.Inglis, A.Nisbet, N.Veitch
W	1996 Feb 20	Holy Ghost	C.Constable, R.Hinde, A.Nisbet
W	1996 Feb 24	The Potter's Apprentices, Pottering About	M.Welch, M.Arkley
W	1996 Feb 26	Icicle Gully	G.Bardsley, H.Davies, A.Nisbet
W	1996 Mar 3	Trinity Arete	A.Nisbet, A.Partington
W	1996 Mar 25	Bell's Left Buttress	R.Brayshay, C.Milne, A.Nisbet
W	1996 Apr 7	Spring Gully	A.Jago, A.Nisbet, S.Watts
W	1997 Jan 2	The Tight One	I.Grimshaw, T.Hawkins
W	1997 Feb 11	WPC Gully	A.Lockley, J.Moore, A.Nisbet
W	1998 Jan 4	Georgina	H.Davies, G.Bardsley
W	1999 Mar 6	The Bender	B.Davison, A.Nisbet
W	1999 Mar 10	Gully Obscura	A.Bull, M.Kinsey, A.Nisbet
W	1999 Mar 12	Brainless Fall	V.Chelton, D.McGimpsey, A.Nisbet
W	1999 Mar 13	Brainstorm	B.Davison, D.McGimpsey, A.Nisbet, S.Ohly, D.Wilkinson
W	1999 Mar 14	The Torture Chamber	B.Davison, D.Wilkinson
W	1999 Mar 27	Titanium Buttress	B.R.Shackleton, W.Jeffrey, N.Tilston
W	1999 Dec 27	Round the Bend (1PA)	S.Allan, A.Nisbet
W	2000 Jan 22	Nil Can't	J.Abery, R.Bennie, E.Gillespie, J.Leedale, A.Nisbet, J.Preston
W	2000 Feb 19	Sinister Prawn, Wacky Races	D.McGimpsey, A.Nisbet
W	2000 Feb 21	Coriolis	P.Astle, N.Cooper, A.Nisbet
W	2000 Mar 4	Chinook	S.Anderson, M.Moran, M.Welch
W	2000 Dec 19	North Ridge	D.McGimpsey, A.Nisbet
W	2001 Jan 29	Nanda Gully	P.Faulkner, B.Mason, A.Nisbet
W	2001 Feb 11	Penelope Pitstop	D.Amos, E.Gillespie, A.Nisbet
W	2001 Mar 30	Didi Buttress	A.Nisbet
W	2002 Feb 27	Drumnadrookit	E.Brunskill, A.Nisbet
W	2004 Dec 26	Pearl Ridge, Boxing Day Romp	J.Higham, R.Higham
S	2005 Jul 5	False Identity, Chadailac	I.Small, C.Cartwright

Beinn Eighe - Far East Wall

S	1966 May 30	Kami-kaze	J.Brumfitt, W.Sproul
S	1966 Oct 16	Sidewinder	A.Fyffe, P.Williams
S	1973 Jul 7	Groovin' High	R.Archbold, J.Ingram, G.Strange
S	1974 May 5	Sting	J.Ingram, G.Strange
	FFA: S.Blagbrough, A.Nisbet, Jun 1988		
S	1974 May 5	Sundance R.Archbold, G.Cohen	
	FFA: G.Cohen, G.Nicoll, June 1988		
S	1974 Jun 30	Birth of the Cool	R.Archbold, G.Cohen
	FFA: M.Hamilton, G.Cohen, Jul 1978		
S	1976 Aug 21	Colgarra	R.Archbold, G.Cohen
	FFA: S.Blagbrough, A.Nisbet, 14 Jun 1988		
S	1980 May 17	Nightcap Groove, The Reaper	B.Sprunt, G.Strange
S	1983 Jun 19	Morning Wall	R.Archbold, G.Strange
S	1986 Jun 22	The Rising Son	S.Pearson, D.Rubens
S	1987 Jun 20	Sumo	A.Cunningham, A.Nisbet
S	1987 Jul	Ling Dynasty	G.Livingston, A.Nisbet
W	1988 Feb 6	Kami-kaze	A.Cunningham, A.Nisbet
W	1988 Feb 14	Vishnu	A.Cunningham, A.Nisbet
S	1988 Jun 1	Angel Face	C.Forrest, A.Nisbet
S	1988 Jun 9	Seeds of Destruction	A.Nisbet, W.Todd
S	1988 Jun 10	Moonshine	C.Forrest, A.Nisbet
W	1990 Feb 12	Glow Worm	A.Nisbet, S.Dring
S	1991 Jun	Karaoke Crack	A.Fyffe, N.Ritchie
S	1992 Jun 11	Rudolf	B.Davison, J.Lyall, A.Nisbet
S	1992 Jun 12	King of the Swingers	B.Davison, J.Lyall, A.Nisbet
S	1992 Jun 13	Meccano	B.Davison, J.Lyall, A.Nisbet
W	1992 Oct 24	Nightcap Groove	G.Ettle, A.Nisbet
S	1993 May 28	Daughter of the Dawn	A.Nisbet, G.Nisbet
S	1993 Jun 14	Epilogue	J.Lyall

Divine Ambition by S.Ritchie, J.A.Edwards on 19 Apr 2003

S	1996 Jun 16	Hydroponicum	J.Allott, A.Nisbet
S	1996 Jun 25	Body Heat	R.Campbell, P.Thorburn
S	1996 Jun 26	Fascist Groove Thang	P.Thorburn, G.Latter
S	1996 Jun 28	The Root of all Evil	J.Allott, A.Nisbet
W	1997 Jan	Sting	M.E.Moran, A.Nisbet
W	1998 Apr	Far East Gully	R.McAllister, A.Nisbet
S	2000 Jun 23	The Sting Direct	T.Rankin, G.Robertson, J.Currie
S	2000 Jun 23	Sunscream	T.Rankin, G.Robertson
W	2002 Jan 31	Sidewinder	M.Moran, P.Bass
W	2005 Nov 28	Hydroponicum	J.Bracey, R.Cross, M.Moran
S	2006 Jul 15	Body Swerve	I.Taylor, T.Fryer

Beinn Eighe - Eastern Ramparts

S	1959 Aug 16	Gnome Wall	T.W.Patey
S	1961 Oct	Boggle	R.Smith, A.Wightman
S	1966 May 30	Samurai	J.Brumfitt, W.Sproul
S	1969 May 27	Rampart Wall, Cornice Groove	J.A.Austin, D.G.Roberts
S	1969 May	Eastern Promise	D.Millar, K.Wood

Unwittingly renamed Forge by N.Muir, A.Paul in '977

S	1976 Aug 20	Shang-High	R.Archbold, G.Cohen
S	1977 Aug 18	Rampage	N.Muir, A.Paul
S	1978 July 12	Heavy Flak	M.Hamilton, G.Cohen
S	1980 May 17	Simpleton	A.Nisbet, N.Spinks
S	1980 May 18	Corniced Arete, Olympus	A.Nisbet, N.Spinks
S	1981 May 18	The Pale Diedre	B.Sprunt, G.Strange
S	1986 Aug 10	Pale Rider	A.Nisbet, B.Lawrie
S	1987 Jun 21	Turkish Delight	A.Cunningham, A.Nisbet
W	1988 Feb 17	Gnome Wall	A.Cunningham, A.Nisbet
S	1988 Jun 1	Fairytale Groove	C.Forrest, A.Nisbet
S	1988 Jun 8	Tainted Galahad	J.Mothersele, A.Nisbet

Direct Finish by I.Small, A.Hume, J.Walker, 7 Aug 2004

S	1988 Jun 10	The Tower of Darkness	C.Forrest, A.Nisbet
S	1988 Jun 13	Claustrophobic Corner, Fear of the Dark	S.Blagbrough, A.Nisbet
S	1988 Jun 14	Paleface Wall	I S.Blagbrough, A.Nisbet
S	1988 Jun 15	The Ho Chi Minh Trail	S.Blagbrough, A.Nisbet
W	1991 Feb 12	Eastern Promise	B.Davison, A.Nisbet
W	1992 Feb 18	Shang-High	B.Davison, A.Nisbet
S	1992 May 30	Feast of the East	A.Nisbet, G.Ollerhead
S	1992 Jun 12	The Trundler, The Modern Idiot	B.Davison, J.Lyall, A.Nisbet
S	1992 Oct 1	Forgotten Warrior	A.Nisbet, M.Sclater
S	1993 Jun 4	The Unknown Soldier	J.Lyall, A.Nisbet
S	1993 Jun 14	The Great Wall of China	J.Lyall, A.Nisbet
S	1994 Jul 17	Happy Ever After	A.Nisbet, G.Nisbet
S	1995 Jun 24	Siege Tactics	J.Allott, A.Nisbet
W	1997 Jan 9	Samurai	A.Nisbet, J.Preston
W	1998 Apr 12	Gashtrognome	R.McAllister, A.Nisbet
W	1999 Jan 10	The Unknown Warrior	B.Davison, A.Nisbet
W	2000 Nov 21	Cornice Groove	A.Nisbet, J.Preston
W	2001 Mar 25	Fairytale Groove	B.Fyffe, E.Tresidder
W	2002 Mar 1	Rampart Wall	B.Davison, D.McGimpsey, A.Nisbet

Beinn Eighe - Triple Buttresses & Sàil Mhòr

S	1899 Apr 2	Lawson, Ling and Glover's Route	
S	1907 Jun	East Buttress Ordinary Route	G.B.Gibbs, E.Backhouse, W.A.Mounsey

A winter ascent was only claimed on 17 Dec 1978 by D.Donoghue, M.Orr but previous ascents were then said to have been under snow.

W	1910 Apr 26	White's Gully	S.White and party
S	1919 Jul	West Buttress Ordinary Route	G.S.Bower, J.B.Meldrum
S	1922	Pigott's Route	A.S.Pigott, M.Wood
S	1936 Jun 4	Hamilton's Route	J.F.Hamilton, W.Kerr
S	1954 Jun 9	East Central Ribs	L.S.Lovat, T.Weir
S	1954 Jun 12	Far West Buttress, East Wall	L.S.Lovat, T.Weir
S	1957 Aug 2	Direct Route, Central Wall	T.W.Patey
S	1960 Aug 9	West Buttress, Left-Hand finish	C.J.S.Bonington, T.W.Patey
S	1960 Aug 11	The Upper Girdle	T.W.Patey, C.J.S.Bonington

FIRST ASCENTS 387

S	1962 Jun	The Gash	T.W.Patey, A.G.Nicol, K.A.Grassick, J.M.Taylor
S	1962 Jun	Fuselage Wall	T.W.Patey, J.M.Taylor
S	1963 Jun	East Central Gully	W.Proudfoot, D.MacKenzie, D.Williamson, P.Acock
S	1968 Jun	Overkill	R.McHardy, P.Nunn, C.Rowland
S	1968 Jun 3	Readymix	M.Green, J.R.Sutcliffe
W	1969 Dec 28	Nunn's Route (1PA)	P.Nunn, A.Riley, D.Goodwin, C. and S.Rowland

Freed by P.Thornhill, A.Nisbet on 25 Jan 1984 but the route was not completed

S	1970 Oct	Fulmar Chimneys	J.Hogan, D.Bell
W	1971 Feb	Central Buttress – Pigott's Route	K.Spence, J.Rowayne, K.Urquhart

Climbed by Spence over two days with course students, access for the second day via West-Central Gully. Complete ascent by A.McIntyre, A.Rouse in Feb 1978.

S	1971 May	West Buttress, Direct Finish	W.March
S	1972	Bloodstone Start	W.S.McKerrow, D.M.Nichols
S	1976 Apr 24	Assegai	P.Baines, D.M.Nichols
S	1976 Aug	Senior	D.M.Jenkins, P.F.Macdonald
S	1976 Aug	Junior	R.McHardy, J.McLean

Direct start by C.French, T.Prentice on 25 Jul 1996

S	1976 Aug	Sideshow	R.McHardy, B.J.Chislett
S	1976 Aug	Relayer	R.McHardy, B.J.Chislett
S	1976 Aug	Mistral	R.McHardy, B.J.Chislett
S	1976 Sep	Central Corner	A.Nisbet, N.Spinks

Used as the start of Central Buttress – VS Route. First quartzite tier by J.Colverd, E.Gillespie, A.Nisbet on 23 Mar 1998. Top tier unknown

S	1977 Aug 17	Pelican, Mango	N.Muir, A.Paul
S	1977 Aug 18	Twilight Zone	N.Muir, A.Paul
W	1979 Jan 13	West Buttress	R.MacGregor, A.Nisbet
W	1981 Dec 22	East Central Wall	P.Barrass, A.Nisbet
W	1983 Feb 12	The Cool Cleft	R.Arnott, E.Clark, A.Nisbet, S.Thirgood

The direct version was climbed by P.Thornhill, C.Watts, A.Saunders, M.Fowler on 9 Apr 1983. They called it Eighe and Spoon Race

S	1985 Jun 15	Puddock	B.S.Findlay, G.Strange
W	1986 Feb 1	Achilles	B.S.Findlay, G.Strange
W	1986 Feb 1	West Buttress, Right-Hand finish	M.Hamilton, G.Cohen
W	1986 Feb 14	Smears for Fears	A.Cunningham, W.Todd
W	1986 Mar 30	East Buttress, The Chimney	R.Anderson, G.Nicoll
W	1986 Apr 5	West Buttress Direttissima	R.Anderson, R.Milne

This was the name given to the winter combination of Senior on the lowest tier with the Bonington/Patey variation finish at the top. Senior was climbed direct by G.Robertson, E.Tressider, 27 Jul 2005

S	1986 Jun 27	Condor Crack	D.Roberts, J.Scarborough
W	1987 Jan 3	Fuselage Wall Direct	R.Anderson, G.Nicoll
W	1987 Jan 9	Pelican	A.Cunningham, A.Nisbet
W	1987 Feb 21	The Upper Girdle, Part 1	M.Fowler, C.Watts
W	1987 Mar 14	The Upper Girdle, Part 2	M.Fowler, A.Saunders
W	1987 Apr 5	West Central Gully	M.Fowler, M.Morrison

1 rest on axes attached to rucksack straps used! FFA: G.Robertson, E.Tressider, Feb 2002

W	1988 Nov 21	Direct Route (Central Wall)	A.Nisbet, P.Yardley
W	1989 Feb 16	East Wall	B.Davison, A.Nisbet
W	1989 Feb 17	Flight of the Condor	B.Davison, A.Nisbet
S	1989 Jul 20	Flying Fortress	A.Tibbs, S.Steer
W	1990 Jan 3	Central Buttress, Collie's Route finish	S.Allan, A.Nisbet
S	1990 Sep 15	Wall of the Winds	J.Lyall, A.Nisbet
W	1991 Jan 9	Far West Buttress	S.Aisthorpe, J.Lyall
W	1991 Feb 14	Mistral	B.Davison, A.Nisbet
S	1991 Aug 31	Earth, Wind and Fire	J.Lyall, A.Nisbet
W	1992 Mar 29	Maelstrom	A.Nisbet, S.Roberts
S	1992 May 26	Shoot the Breeze	A.Nisbet, G.Ollerhead
S	1992 May 28	Force Ten	A.Nisbet, G.Ollerhead
S	1992 Jun 29	Cyclonic Westerly	A.Nisbet, G.Ollerhead

Variation avoiding the crux climbed by the same party the same day.

S	1992 Jun 29	Chop Suey	A.Nisbet, G.Ollerhead
S	1992 Jun 2	Central Reservation, Swinging in the Rain	J.Lyall, A.Nisbet

388 FIRST ASCENTS

W	1993 Jan 29	Assegai	M.Moran, A.Nisbet
W	1993 Mar 26	Blood, Sweat and Frozen Tears	M.Moran, A.Nisbet
S	1994 Sep 15	The Generation Game	A.Cave, J.Brown
S	1995 Jul 26	Porcine Connection	D.Rubens, C.Rubens
W	1996 Mar 30	Sailing Buttress	A.Nisbet
S	1996 Jul 17	Dusk	G.Latter, A.Clapperton
S	1996 Sep 5	Maelstrom	A.Nisbet, G.Nisbet
W	1997 Feb 4	East-Central Ribs	J.Hubbard, A.Nisbet
S	1997 Jun 10	Flying Finish (to Central Buttress)	A.Nisbet, A.Goring, P.Patterson, I.Sneddon
W	1998 Nov 17	Hamilton's Route	D.McGimpsey, A.Nisbet

First winter ascent of Slab Route (Central Buttress Icefall Start) unknown.

W	1999 Jan 21	Central Corner	A.Mullin, S.Paget
W	2000 Mar 4	Jenga	B.Davison, D.McGimpsey, A.Nisbet, D.Wilkinson

Named after an earlier attempt when removal of a crucial block caused a pile to collapse, Davison flying with them. On the helicopter flight out, Nisbet spotted Spring Gully (Liathach) which he climbed 3 days later!

S	2000 Jun 3	Gallus	S.R Scott, D Carr
W	2000 Nov 15	Flying Fortress	A.Nisbet, J.Preston
W	2000 Dec 18	Direct Finish to West Buttress	A.Mullin (roped solo)
W	2000 Dec	Fuselage Pillar	A.Mullin (roped solo)
W	2000 Dec 27	Overkill	D.McGimpsey, A.Nisbet
W	2001 Feb 15	Central Buttress – Grade IV Line	D.Amos, E.Gillespie, A.Nisbet

The first complete ascent; the sections climbed before.

W	2001 Jan 29	The Darkness Beckons	C.Dale, M.Moran
W	2004 Feb 9	Expanding Universe	E.Tresidder, G.Robertson
W	2005 Dec 17	Bombs Away	A.Nisbet, J.Preston
W	2006 Dec 17	Fight or Flight	D.McGimpsey, A.Nisbet, J.Preston
W	2007 Jan 2	Still Game	D.McGimpsey, A.Nisbet
W	2007 Mar 2	Pension Plan	D.McGimpsey, A.Nisbet

Beinn Eighe - Coire Rudha-staca

S	1971 Jul 12	Thin Man's Ridge	D.Howard, C.S.Rose, R.W.L.Turnbull
S	1971 Sep	Spog aig Giomach	C.S.Rose, R.W.L.Turnbull
S	1972 Jul	The Independent Pineapple	C.S.Rose, D.Howard
S	1972 Sep	Midge Ridge	C.S.Rose, S.Peterson
S	1976 Oct 17	Autumn Rib	S.Ackerley, A.Nisbet
S	1977 Oct 15	The Pineapple Chimney	B.Clough, A.Nisbet, M.Thorp
W	1984 Apr 7	Chockstone Gully	R.Archbold, G.Strange
W	1987 Jan 10	Midge Ridge	G.Nicoll, R.Anderson
W	1991 Jan 13	The Independent Pineapple	G.Ettle, A.Nisbet
W	1991 Feb 15	Three Tier Chimney	B.Davison, A.Nisbet
W	1991 Dec 21	Spog aig Giomach	J.Lyall, A.Nisbet
W	1995 Jan 26	Sidestep	B.Davison, A.Nisbet
S	2000 Jul 23	Pineapple Sunday	D.McGimpsey, A.Nisbet
W	2000 Dec 17	Pineapple Chimney	A.Nisbet, J.Preston
W	2000 Dec 17	Thin Man's Ridge	N.Johnson, D.McGimpsey
S	2001 Jul 18	Smilodon	A.Nisbet
W	2001 Nov 28	Jinx	D.McGimpsey, A.Nisbet
W	2002 Jan 26	Milk Shake	D.McGimpsey, A.Nisbet
W	2003 Jan 5	Smilodon	D.McGimpsey, A.Nisbet
W	2004 Nov 28	Quickstep	A.Nisbet, D.Preston
W	2004 Dec 19	Jambo	D.McGimpsey, A.Nisbet
W	2005 Feb 8	Chocked	D.McGimpsey, A.Nisbet
W	2006 Feb 21	Lip Service	M.Edwards, D.McGimpsey, A.Nisbet

Beinn Eighe - Other Crags

S	1957 Aug	Ragged Muffin Ridge	T.W.Patey
W	1996 Dec 25	Spidean Lochans, Christmas Day Special and right gully finish	B.Davison
W	1996 Dec 27	Spidean Lochans, Whiteout and left gully finish	B.Davison
W	1997 Mar 3	Rockhoppers Ridge, Double Gully Right	C.Kempster, J.Preston, J.Preston

W	1997 Mar 3	Ragged Muffin Ridge	R.Callard, S.Hinshelwood, A.Nisbet
W	1999 Jan 5	Rubble without a Cause	R.McAllister, A.Nisbet
W	1999 Jan 5	Double Gully Left, Carla's Gully, Bodach Gully	A.Nisbet
W	1999 Mar 27	The Dark Ridge, Black Gully, The Ramp	B.Davison, A.Nisbet
S	1999 Jul 29	Scarface, Ban the Bomb, Faith, Hope, Charity	B.Davison, A.Nisbet
W	1999 Dec 2	The Grotto	A.Nisbet
W	2003 Dec 30	Bartlett's Dilemma	J.Sutherland, A.Gorman
W	2004 Nov 19	North Ridge of Spidean Coire nan Clach	V.Chelton, D.McGimpsey, A.Nisbet, J.Preston

INDEX

3rd Pinnacle Gully	287
4th Pinnacle Gully	289
8-Ace	261

A
A' Charraig Gully	67
A' Chioch, Traverse	171
Academy Ridge	120
Access Gully	275
Achilles	357
Acid Queen, The	167
Act, The	261
Adul Suh	132
Adventures of Toad, The	173
Aerial Runway	94
Aetos	203
African Waltz	146
After the Horse has Bolted	242
Afterglow	254
Age of Confusion, The	220
Airwaves	156
Airy Corner	54
Airy Icefall	53
Alice's Overhang	263
Alice's Buttress	173
All the Way	116
Andes Couloir, The	290
Anduril	159
Angel Face	312
Animal Magic	245
Ankle Ridge	75
Anne Frank's Chimney	61
Anonymous Gully	145
Anthrax	77
Apis	200
Applecross Jam, The	261
Apprentice Bhoys	253
Apprentices Route	258
Aquamarine	262
Aquila	203
Archangel	224
Archie Gemmell	199
Assegai	334
Astrocyte	157
Atta Buttress	72
Autumn Rib	362
Ayatollah, The	108

B
Babylon Buttress	67
Backfire Ridge	270
Backyard Buttress	270
Backyard Gully	270
Bald Slab	60
Ban the Bomb	364
Bannock Gully	291
Bannockburn	291
Bare Faced Cheek	265
Bartlett's Dilemma	363
Bastion	32
Battersea Buttress	122
Battlement Slab	32
Batwing	245
Beached Boat Buttress	263
Beag Pardon	275
Beast and The Beast, The	54
Beast's Lair, The	133
Beasts' Lair	196
Beauty and the Beast	195
Becalmed	234
Bedrock	224
Bee Gully	160
Beinn Alligin, Ridge Traverse	266
Beinn Bhan Grooves	179
Beinn Gunn's Buttress	64
Bell's Buttress	294
Bell's Buttress, Left Chimney	293
Bell's Gully	294
Bell's Left Buttress	293
Bell's Right Buttress	294
Bender, The	281
Beside the Point	261
Better than a Slap in the Face	223
Bhantasia	177
Biblical Knowledge	179
Big Daddy	154
Big Dipper, The	94
Big Ears	200
Big Glossy Book Route	255
Big Gully	58
Big Gutter	60
Big Tree	233
Bilas	268
Bill, The	187
Biodirect	73
Biodiversity	73
Bionic	73
Biped Buttress	58
Birth of the Cool	317
Bitch Witch	263
Black and Blue	236
Black Gully	365
Black House	132
Black Opal	271
Black Queen, The	224
Black Streak, The	254
Black Streaked, The	223
Black Struggle, The	236
Blade Runner	154
Blaeberry Corner	139
Blanco	76
Bleached Whale	224
Blind as a Frog	231
Block and Beak	233
Blood, Sweat and Frozen Tears	350
Bloodstone Start	331
Bluebell Crack	234
Blue Finger	102
Blue in the Face	140
Blue Lamppost, The	140
Blue Moon	138
Blue Pillar	139
Blue Velvet	141
Boa Constrictor	51
Boab's Corner	258
Boat Tundra	102
Boatman's Call	262
Bodach Gully	365
Body Heat	318
Body Swerve	318
Boggle	324
Bogie	256
Bombs Away	352
Bombus	200
Boomerang	76
Bottleneck Gully	33
Boulder Problem Buttress	142
Boundary Gully	206
Bounty Hunter	168
Bowling Alley	42
Bow Peep	44
Bow, The	90
Boxer's Buttress	44
Boxing Day Romp	300
Brain Drain	284
Brain Strain	284
Brainless Fall	277
Brave New World	262
Breach Gully	186
Breach of Contract	184
Breach of the Peace	184
Brenda's Cleavage	67
Brigadier Braggart's Little Secret	83
Brimstone	253
Brittle Times	91
Broken Buttress	162
Broken Cracks	60
Broken Flip Flop	199
Bromide	258
Brooker's Route	124
Brown Gully	122
Bumble	200
Bumblyone	160
Bumblytwo	160
Bundle of Apathy	236
Bungle in the Jungle	80
Busman's Holiday	204
But Midges	130
Butcher's Dog	102
Bypass Buttress	136

C
Cairn Terrier	219
Cairnaholics Anonymous	219
Calcite Corner	249
California	65
Calluna	206
Campanology	295
Can of Worms	83
Canine Buttress	66
Cannonade	30
Capitalist Pig	79
Capped Gully	44
Captain Haddock	242
Carla's Gully	365
Carn na Feola North Ridge	271
Cas Chrom	191
Cat's Claw	196
Category Five	62
Caterpillar Ridge	234
Cave Gully	44
Ceannacroc Couloir	60
Celtic Sea	39
Central Buttress – Pigott's Route	340

INDEX

Central Buttress,
  Grade IV Line 342
Central Buttress,
  VS Route 341
Central Corner 343
Central Couloir 122
Central Gully 41
Central Parallel Gully 101
Central Reservation 342
Central Trinity Gully 296
Chadailac 302
Chanter 82
Charity 364
Charlie's Tower 257
Che Guevara 201
Chemical Alley 90
Chi Squared 274
Chimney, The
  (Beinn Bhàn) 182
Chimney, The (Coire
  Mhic Fhearchair) 330
Chinook 282
Chock a Block Gully 100
Chocked 362
Chocks Away 154
Chockstone Gully
  (Meall Gorm) 138
Chockstone Gully
  (Pineapple Cliff) 361
Chop Suey 350
Chopper Chimney 154
Christmas Day Special 363
Cioch Buttress 58
Cioch Corner 148
Cioch Corner
  Superdirect 149
Cioch Nose 147
Clare 77
Claustrophobic Corner 322
Clean Compromise 132
Cleavage 149
Cliffhanger 167
Clingfilm 223
Clockwork Rat 222
Close to the Edge 91
Cobalt Buttress 142
Coffin Gully 63
Cold Hole 109
Cold Sweat 102
Colgarra 315
Collie's Route 342
Command and
  Conquer 198
Completely out to
  Lunge 233
Con-Con, The 256
Condome 256
Condor Crack 336
Congregation 208
Consolation Buttress 171
Continuation Route 245
Cool Cleft, The 334
Cooler, The 176
Copping's Crack 243
Coriolis 299
Corn in Egypt 61
Corner Climb 78
Corner Finish to
  West Buttress 346
Corner Route 190
Cornered 213
Cornice Groove 319
Corniced Arete 319
Couldoran Gully 167
Countdown to Disaster 182
Crab Nebula 170
Crack Climb 77
Crack of Ages 215
Crackpot 60
Crescent Gully 139
Criminal Trespass 187
Crocodile Shoes 80
Cross Dressing 231
Cross-Bow 44
Crossed Swords 161
Crown Jewel 268
Croydon Chimney 122
Crusade Corner 196
Crystal Couloir 61
Crystal Horizon 208
Cube's Chimney 295
Cuir Tigear Na Do
  Thanc 201
Culverin 30
Curled Buttress 63
Curly Gully 63
Curve Stone 270
Custodian, The 118
Cyclonic Westerly 347
Cypress Avenue Direct 81

D

Dark One, The 212
Dark Ridge, The 365
Darkness Beckons, The 357
Das Rheingold 182
Daughter of the Dawn 316
Dead Mouse Crack 252
Deceptive Chimney 46
Deep Freeze 53
Deep Gully 166
Deep North Gully 270
Deep South Gully 269
Deer Hunter, The 282
Deerstalker, The
  (Aonach air Chrith) 53
Deerstalker, The
  (Seana Mheallan) 215
Defying Destiny 77
Delta 261
Den of Iniquity 195
Dental Trauma 245
Depth Charge 269
Deputy Dawg 258
Der Rise and Shine 182
Der Riesenwand 180
Dexter 152
Dhanakosa 209
Diabaig Corner 245
Diabaig Diamond 263
Diabaig Tiger 261
Diabaig, the Hard Way 246
Diabug 263
Diagonal 190
Diamond Cleft 270
Diamond Fire 270
Didi Buttress 298
Dire Straights 247
Dire Wall 247
Direct Evasion 54
Direct Route 32
Dirty Dancing 216
Disposable Slab 91
Distant Groove 61
Divine Retribution 180
Doctor's Ear, The 293
Dog named Corrie, A 118
Dog-leg Crack 213
Dog-Leg Gully 66
Dog's Leg Gully 67
Dolphin Friendly 224
Dominie, The 255
Donkey's Doobrie 166
Don't Just Sit There 233
Dormouse Chimney 171
Double Gully 49
Double Gully Left 365
Double Gully Right 365
Dougie's Climb 163
Downhill Racer 89
Dreaded Lurgi, The 87
Drinking with the
  Priest 76
Dru 289
Dru Couloir 289
Drumnadrookit 285
Dundee Cake 242
Dusk 345
Dwarf Icefall, The 182

E

Eag Dubh 268
Eagle Gully 291
Earth, Wind and Fire 349
East Buttress (Liathach) 274
East Buttress (Coire
  Mhic Fhearcair) 331
East Central Gully 331
East Central Ribs 334
East Central Wall 335
East Rib 37
East Ridge 60
East Wall 334
Easter Buttress 58
Eastern Chimney 37
Eastern Promise 323
Easy Gully (Five Sisters) 66
Easy Gully
  (Sgòrr Ruadh) 122
Easy Rider 82
Easy Slab 78
Echo Couloir 290
Edge of Enlightenment 212
Edge of Reason 66
Edgewood Whymper 250
Elbow Room 213
Elchaig Arete 75
Eliminator 215
Emerald 252
En Route 234
Enchanted Falls 55
Encore 189
Endless Dribble 199
Enigma 112

INDEX

Epilogue	318
Epsilon	261
Erica's Ridge	204
Ermine	206
Errors Cleft	270
Eurhythmics	46
Evasion	256
Evasion Grooves	109
Ewar Woowar	262
Exception, The	190
Excitable Boy	154
Executioner, The	279
Expanding Universe	355
Exterminator	215
Eyeful, An	247

F
Face Route	37
Fairy Queen	306
Fairytale Groove	329
Faith	364
False Identity	302
Far East Gully	318
Far Left Gully	46
Far North Gully	154
Far Side, The	87
Far West Buttress	355
Fascist Groove Thang	316
Fast Lane, The	94
Fat Man's Folly	292
Fatties Gully	72
Faultfinders, The	292
FB Gully	88
Fear of the Dark	328
Feast of the East	323
Feelies, The	262
Feelin' Groovy	250
Fiery Cross	208
Fight or Flight	352
Final Demand	249
Final Gong, The	295
First Blood	127
First Face	287
Fish and Chips	220
Fish Eagle	264
Fisherman's Blues	70
Fistfighter	213
Flake Climb	78
Flaky	220
Flaky Ridge	49
Fleeced	220
Flesheater	170
Flight of the Condor	336
Floating Rib	133
Flying Finish	336
Flying Fortress	352
Flying Gully	54
Flying Penguin Gully	187
Flying Ridge	66
Fog Monster	61
Foil	254
Footless Gully	276
For the Chop	268
Forcan Ridge	57
Force Ten	350
Forgotten Corner (Seana Mheallan)	216
Forgotten Corner (Sgurr a' Chaorachain)	146
Forgotten Warrior	326
Forked Gully	65
Forking Gully	290
Four Trees	207
Foxglove Crack	226
Fox's Face	125
Foxtrot	130
Foxy Grooves	207
Fraoch Groove	204
Frayed at the Edges	63
Frieze, The	247
Fritillary	75
Frivolity	129
Frozen Pipes	132
Fuar Feast	105
Fuar Folly Direct	105
Fuar, The	108
Fubarbundy	282
Fuhrer	104
Full Monty, The	266
Fulmar Chimneys	335
Funnel, The	72
Furrow, The	47
Fuselage (Far West) Gully	354
Fuselage Wall	352

G
Gaberlunzie	35
Gallus	344
Gamhnachain's Crack	253
Gamma	261
Ganglion	157
Gardener's Choice	267
Gash, The	330
Gashtrognome	330
Gateway	198
Gem Find	208
Generation Game, The	341
Genesis	179
George	285
Georgina	286
Get into the Groove	53
Gideon's Wrath	158
Gin Crack	240
Ginger's Gully	73
Gingerbread	177
Global Warming (Creag nan Leumnach)	231
Global Warming (Meall Gorm)	136
Glover's Route	145
Glow Worm	309
Gnome Wall	329
Godfather, The	180
Going Home	254
Gondola	202
Good Day Spoilt, A	39
Gooseberry, The	259
Gopher's Gully	127
Gordon's Route	85
Gorm Gully	139
Gormless Grooves	139
Grandad's Wall	243
Gravesend	120
Great Brush Robbery, The	233
Great Overhanging Gully	182
Great Wall of China, The	322
Green Man, The	62
Greenhorn Gully	132
Grey Hair Gully	167
Grey Matter	236
Gritstone Grooves	145
Groove and Prow	78
Groovin' High	318
Grotto, The	364
Grovel Gully	67
Grunter, The	253
Gryphon	173
Guide's Rib	70
Gully 1A	305
Gully 1K	296
Gully 2A	306
Gully 5	289
Gully 7	291
Gully 8	291
Gully in 3D, The	153
Gully Obscura	298
Gully of the Gods	180
Gully that Time Forgot, The	96

H
Hadrian's Wall	223
Hamilton's Route	341
Hamish Quick-Death	80
Handsome Hog	264
Hang Over	85
Hanging Garden	67
Hanging Imminent	111
Hanging Traverse of Babylon, The	82
Happy Ever After	329
Harlequin Rib	174
Hasta la Bista	198
Hatchet Man	269
Headhunter	276
Headless Gully	277
Heart of Darkness	78
Heather Said Sunshine	223
Heavy Flak	322
Hellfire and Brimstone	88
Here be Dragons	196
Hidden Buttress	306
Hidden Gully (Creag Coire an t-Slugain)	49
Hidden Gully (Five Sisters)	66
Hidden Gully (Liathach)	275
Hidden Gully (Maol Chean-dearg)	130
High Domain	153
High Flier	94
High Gully	122
High Tide, Green Grass	190
Higher Gully	275
Highland Scottische	127
Hillwalk	279
Ho Chi Min Trail, The	322
Holly Tree Rib	234
Holy Ghost	297
Holy Trinity	297

INDEX

Hong Kong	47	Kanko the Bone	234	**M**	
Hooded Claw	281	Karaoke Wall	318	Mackintosh Slab	219
Hope	364	Kermit's Crack	231	Maculate Slab	207
Hors d'Oeuvres	166	Ketchil Buttress	129	Mad Hatter's Gully	174
Hot Head	259	Ketchup Buttress	129	Maelstrom	349
Hotline	163	Key, The	127	Magician's Boy, The	182
Hourglass Groove	49	King of the Swingers	315	Mainline Connection	112
Hoverfly	200	King Prawn Deathwish	84	Mandela's Birthday	192
Hump	73	Kings of Midian, The	159	Man-Eating Troll	234
Hunter Killer	214	Kintail Blanket, The	71	Mango	330
Hurting II	42	Kissed Ye Quick	63	Man's Best Friend	170
Hydroponicum	314	Knob, The	224	Mantissa	148
Hypotenuse	49	Koh-i-Noor	268	Mantelshelf, The	63
		Kraken	63	March Hare's Gully	173
				Marguerite	35
I				Mark of a Skyver	215
Ice Bulge, The	262	**L**		Mary Greaser Crack	78
Ice Channel, The	96	Lair Wall	99	Maurice's Slab	78
Ice Gem	268	Lammergeier	209	Maxilla, The	148
Icefall Start		Landlubbers Buttress	38	Mayfly	56
(East Buttress)	330	Lap Land	224	Meanderthal	176
Icicle Gully	299	Lap of the Gods	149	Meccano	315
If	192	Last Orders	295	Mechanical Sheep	222
Il Duce	108	Last Waltz, The	128	Mica Ridge	88
Illegal Grass	184	Lawson, Ling and		Mica Schist Special	52
Impulse	145	Glover's Route	355	Middle of the Road	216
In the Groove	213	Left Edge Route	87	Midge Direct	199
In the Pink	96	Left Gully	275	Midge Ridge	361
In X.S.	170	Left Icefall	130	Mid-way Buttress	46
Incognito	219	Left in the Lurch	216	Mid-way Gully	46
Indecent Exposure		Left Parallel Gully	100	Milk Shake	358
(Beinn Bhàn)	186	Left Ridge	46	Millenium Chimney	58
Indecent Exposure		Left-Hand Gully		Million Years B.C., A	233
(White House Crag)	265	(Beinn Fhada)	69	Mind the Trench	223
Independence Day	153	Left-Hand Gully		Miracle of the	
Independent		(Five Sisters)	66	May Midge	84
Pineapple, The	360	Left-hand Route		Mirror Image	302
Indian Winter	236	(Glas Bheinn)	132	Missing Persons	187
Indigenous	171	Left-Hand Trinity Gully	296	Mistral	351
Instructors Gully	69	Levitation	85	Misty Byway	61
Insufficient Evidence	187	Liathach Main Ridge		Mixed Post	109
Intro One	75	Traverse	274	Moaning Minnie	220
Intro Two	75	Light of Bengal	268	Mock Turtle, The	174
Investigator	116	Lightning Gully	72	Modern Idiot, The	319
Irish Grooves	99	Like Pine Bark	259	Monar Magic	88
It Ne'er Rains but it		Ling Dynasty	317	Moonloop	206
Pours	83	Lingo	206	Moonshine	
Ivy League	196	Lip Service	362	(Beinn Bhàn)	176
		Liquid Gully	61	Moonshine (Coire	
J		Little Gully (Five Sisters)	67	Mhic Fhearchair)	312
J.S.	199	Little Gully (The Saddle)	59	Moonstone, The	268
Jambo	362	Little Plum	190	Moore's Last Sigh, The	242
James Bond is Alive		Lobster Gully	140	Moriarty	114
and Well and		Local Hero	250	Morning Wall	309
Living in Plockton	81	Lochain Buttress	55	Morrison's Gully	355
Jammy Dodger	261	Lonesome Traveller	80	Moruisg Icefall	92
Jemima	165	Long Reach	85	Moss Gully	39
Jenga	357	Long Tall Jonny	242	Mother-in-Law, The	189
Jerbil	290	Looks Different	213	Mottled Wall	264
Jigsaw, The	124	Lost Knuckle, The	59	Mr Bean	223
Jim Kerr Knew my		Lost Supper	158	Mugs Game, A	264
Father	81	Lost Wall	148	Mummy Knows Best	52
Jinx	362	Low Diagonal	60	Munroist's Reward	87
John Muir Trail	39	Low Girdle, The	262	Musky	258
Junior	347	Lower Leftist	226	Musselman	167
Jupiter	150	Luck of the Irish	99	Mustn't Grumble	262
		Luing Rib	223	My Learned Friend	58
K		Lulu Belle	165	My Mother Says No	52
Kami-kaze	316	Lysfoss	202		

INDEX

My Sex Romp with
 Llama Sid 80
Mynch, The 243
Mystic Gully 206

N

Nanda Gully 299
Narrow Buttress 78
Nasal Abuse 220
Nebula 111
Needle, The 70
Needle's Edge 196
Needle's Eye Buttress 70
Needle's Eye Buttress
 Direct 70
Neerday Gully 203
Nematode 201
Neville's Post 242
Neville the Hedgehog 219
New Kelso Couloir 132
Newton's Law 99
Nightcap Groove 309
Nil Can't 279
No Birds 130
No Brats 219
No Stars No Moon
 No Nothing 84
No.1 Gully (Liathach) 287
No.1 Gully (Sgùrr
 a' Chaorachain) 152
No.2 Gully (Liathach) 287
No.2 Gully (Sgùrr
 a' Chaorachain) 152
No.3 Gully 152
No.4 Gully 152
No.5 Gully 153
North Buttress
 (Liathach) 298
North Buttress
 (A' Chioch) 171
North Circular 159
North Face 130
North Gully (A' Chioch) 171
North Gully
 (Sgòrr Ruadh) 129
North Gully (Sgùrr
 a' Chaorachain) 150
North Gully (Sgùrr
 nan Ceannaichean) 92
North Ridge 299
North Ridge of
 Spidean 286
North Ridge of Spidean
 Coire nan Clach 363
North Spur 33
North Wall 148
North-East Buttress 298
North-East Ridge 33
Northern Pinnacles, The 299
Northumberland Wall 253
Nose Direct 99
Nunn's Route 345
Nut the Rock 236

O

Occluded Ridge 89
Off With Her Head 224
Offensive Man, An 245
Olfactory 100
Olympus 319
One Cog Missing 200
One for the Road 64
Once Bitten, Twice Shy 54
Oor Wullie 258
Orcrist 159
Original Route 108
Othello 242
Outswinger 220
Over Sixties Icefall 281
Overhanging Crack 78
Overhanging Groove 79
Overkill 357

P

P.C. Buttress 291
Pale Diedre, The 324
Pale Rider 324
Pale Wall, The 301
Paleface Wall 324
Pandora's Box 189
Para Handy Gully 33
Parallel Lines 122
Parapet 32
Parasol 265
Park Lane 160
Parker's Route 342
Parting 145
Patey's Direct Route 336
Path Corner 226
Path Flake 228
Path of Righteousness 213
Pea Soup 202
Pearl Ridge 300
Pebble 226
Peekaboo Gully 29
Pelican 336
Penelope Pitstop 280
Penny Wheep Gully 37
Pension Plan 352
Perfect Day 199
Persistent Arete 41
Persistent Reward 41
Phantom Fencer 210
Pile, The 100
Pillar, The 247
Pine Martin 85
Pine Processionary 76
Pineapple Chimney 360
Pineapple Sunday 360
Pioneer Gully 49
Pipped at the Post 109
Pit Bull Polka 129
Pitching 226
Placa 102
Plockton Plonkers 84
Ploughshare Groove 47
Plunge 258
Poachers Fall 282
Poems 42
Pointless Eliminates 250
Policeman's Gully 187
Polythene Bag 223
Pommel 163
Porcine Connection 343
Porpoise Pun 245
Porpoise Scandal 224
Portcullis 32
Porter's Climb 70
Post Box Gully 120
Pottering About 305
Potter's Apprentices,
 The 305
Prawn Man 198
President's Men, The 91
Pretty Crack 265
Pretty Midgie 265
Pretty Scoop 265
Private Eye 116
Problem Arete 60
Procession 208
Professor's Lum, The 203
Promiscuous Groove 266
Puddock 343
Pyramid Left Icefall 302
Pyramid Right Edge 304
Pyramid Right Icefall 302

Q

Quartz Inspector's Slab 266
Quartz Warts 224
Quartzice 130
Queen's Garden Party,
 The 83
Quickstep 362
Quite Gneiss 190

R

Rack Rental 242
Raeburn's Buttress
 via Narrow Gully 123
Raeburn's Gully 38
Raeburn's Buttress
 (Direct) 123
Raeburn's Superdirect 125
Ragged Muffin Ridge 365
Rambler's Rib 279
Ramp, The (Sgùrr Ban,
 Beinn Eighe) 364
Ramp, The (Fuar Tholl) 99
Rampage 326
Rampart Wall 323
Range Apart, A 234
Rapid Pulse 143
Rastus 165
Rattlesnake 140
Raven Seek thy Brother 195
Reach for the Sky 114
Reach the Road 233
Readymix 343
Realisation 173
Reaper, The 314
Recess Rib 161
Red Chimneys 272
Red Crescent 259
Red Dwarf 272
Red Herring 289
Red Rag 272
Reflection Wall 301
Reflections of my Mind 300
Reject 218
Rejection 218
Relayer 348
Rendezvous 265
Resolution Gully 65

INDEX

Resolve	65	
Rest in Peace	64	
Restful Buttress	131	
Revelations	179	
Ridge Direct, The	47	
Right Cheek, A	99	
Right Edge	223	
Right End Buttress (Creag Coire an t-Slugain)	49	
Right End Buttress (Fuar Tholl)	110	
Right Face	177	
Right Gully	54	
Right Icefall	130	
Right of Tenure	261	
Right Parallel Gully	101	
Right-Hand Finish to West Buttress	346	
Right-Hand Gully (Beinn Fhada)	69	
Right-Hand Gully (Fuar Tholl)	110	
Right-Hand Gully (Glas Bheinn)	131	
Right-Hand Trinity Gully	297	
Rig-Veda	163	
Riotous Ridge	129	
Rising Son, The	316	
Roadhog's Wall	162	
Roaming the Gloaming	133	
Robertson's Buttress	120	
Robertson's Gully	120	
Rock Agus Roll	201	
Rock Around the Block	214	
Rock Stripper	265	
Rock Surfer	91	
Rockhoppers Ridge	365	
Rolling Baba	261	
Rolling Home	262	
Root of all Evil, The	314	
Rory-Pory	167	
Rose Garden	47	
Roseroot Ramp	84	
Round House	32	
Round the Bend	281	
Route One	254	
Route Three	253	
Route Two	253	
Route with a View	215	
Rowaling	47	
Rowantree Crack	218	
Ruadh Awakening	127	
Ruayahua	122	
Rubble without a Cause	365	
Rubblesplitskin	250	
Rudolf	315	
Running on Empty	96	

S

Saighead Slot	65	
Sailing Buttress	355	
Salmon Leap, The	282	
Salmon Slit	189	
Salvation	305	
Samurai	327	
Sanctuary	163	
Sandpiper	216	
Sandstone Virgin, The	127	
Sandstorm (Fuar Tholl)	105	
Sandstorm (Seana Mheallan)	216	
Sandwich	216	
Scampi Fries	139	
Scarface	364	
Schtroumpf, The	133	
Scooby Did	190	
Scooby Doo	190	
Scoop, The	190	
Sea Otter	264	
Sea, The Sea, The	262	
Seals Guaranteed or your Money Back	80	
Seams Obvious	213	
Seeds of Destruction	313	
Seems the Same	213	
Senior	349	
Sentinel	30	
Separate Reality	78	
Sgritheall Gully	59	
Shaggy Crack	190	
Shamrock Gully	136	
Shang-High	328	
Sheep Shed Shuffle	199	
Sheet Whitening	170	
Sheneval	82	
Sherlock	114	
Shezan	268	
Shilling Corner	78	
Shiner, The	88	
Shining	76	
Shining Path, The	290	
Shipwrecked	263	
Shoot the Breeze	350	
Shoot the Cuckoo	214	
Short and Silly	92	
Shunned	256	
Sideburn	145	
Sideshow	347	
Sidestep	358	
Sidewinder	309	
Siege Tactics	323	
Silent Witness	186	
Silver Corner	44	
Silver Edge	44	
Silver Slab	44	
Silver Tear	174	
Simpleton	327	
Sinister	152	
Sinister Prawn	285	
Six-track Mono Blues, The	142	
Skate	223	
Skidmark Buttress	166	
Skinflint	168	
Skinny Gully	29	
Skirting the Issue	216	
Skullsplitter	159	
Sky a Jy	233	
Skye and Kyle against Trugs	220	
Slab and Groove	131	
Slab Boys	131	
Slab Climb	77	
Slab Route	190	
Slant, The	120	
Slanter, The	203	
Slapstick	91	
Sleeping Dog Climb	196	
Sleeping Sickness	223	
Sleuth	113	
Sleuth, Original Winter Route	113	
Small Gutter	60	
Smears for Fears	358	
Smilodon	362	
Smoke, The	160	
Smooth Creep, The	140	
Sneak, The	305	
Sniper's Gully	170	
Snoopy	115	
Snothard	147	
Snotter, The	275	
Snow Goose	282	
Snow White	306	
Snowdrop	56	
Society of Whispers	118	
Solicitor's Rib	101	
Solitary Confinement	187	
Solo Gully	67	
Solution Gully	64	
Someone's Crack	202	
Sonny Jack	118	
Sorrow	78	
Soul-Searcher	305	
South Gully	92	
South Wall	202	
Space Face	226	
Spaceman	226	
Spanner in the Works	125	
Spare Rib (Bad a' Chreamha)	133	
Spare Rib (Fuar Tholl)	100	
Speckled Frog	234	
Speckles	49	
Speeding Ticket	184	
Spidean Way	280	
Spidean's Sting	305	
Spiked	62	
Spiral Search	88	
Spiral Terrace	136	
Splintery Edge	128	
Spog aig Giomach	358	
Spring Gully	299	
Squeeze 'Em In	213	
Squeezin' yer Heid	231	
St. Andrew's Slab	76	
Stag Gully	204	
Stalker's Gully	204	
Steppin	120	
Sticky Fingers	125	
Still Game	346	
Sting	312	
Stirling Moss	89	
Stirrup Gully	207	
Stonker, The	94	
Stonner Falls	139	
Stressful Buttress	131	
Sticky Fingers	125	
Strider's Gully	38	
Striker	160	
Stringless Gully	306	
Submission	262	
Summit Buttress	69	

Summit Central Buttress	69	Tramlines	72	**W**	
Summit Rib	110	Transatlantic Bong	39	Wacky Races	280
Summit Route	39	Transoceanic Chicken	117	Waggonner	201
Sumo	318	Traveller's Trail	204	Wailing Wall	269
Sundance	314	Trench at Top	224	Walkers Climb	77
Sunny Side Up	61	Trench Foot	300	Walkin on Crystals	266
Sunscream	312	Trend Setter	228	Wall of Flame	254
Sunset Slab	77	Triangle, The	49	Wall of the Early	
Supersleuth	113	Triceratops	306	Morning Light	176
Susie's First	242	Trident Gully	67	Wall of the Outcry	269
Suspense Buttress	167	Trident Gully,		Wall of the Winds	351
Suspense Buttress Direct	167	Central Branch	138	Walsh's Groove	236
Suspense Gully	170	Trident Gully,		Wanda Lust	154
Swinging in the Rain	343	Left Branch	138	Wanderer, The	242
Swirl	228	Trident Gully,		War of Attrition	196
Sword of Gideon	159	Right Branch	138	Warmer Cleaner Drier	233
Sword Swallower	159	Trinity Arete	296	Way Out	138
Swordstick	161	Tritium Chimney	124	Way Up	281
Swordthrust	160	Tropical Buttress	70	Weakest Link	167
Synergy	154	Trumpet	49	Wedge Buttress	142
		Trundle	83	Wee Baldy	60
T		Trundler, The	319	Wee Beastie	138
Tainted Galahad	325	Tubular Bells	110	Wee Dribble	94
Tango in the Night	128	Turkish Delight	322	Wee Nipper, The	94
Tarsam	220	Turned Turtle	224	Weed, The	184
Teacher's Pet	241	Turquoise Gully	142	Welsh Grooves	100
Teapot	173	Turret Buttress	153	West Buttress	345
Telegraph Pole	201	Twilight Zone	350	West Buttress	
Temptress, The	285	Twinkle Toes	133	Direttissima	347
Terminal Buttress	298	Twisting Gully		West Central Gully	345
Terminal Groove	77	(Five Sisters)	65	West Coast Boomer	267
Terrier Trauma	257	Twisting Gully (Liathach)	290	West Face of the Dru	289
Test Department	284	Two Bolts and Some		West Gully	280
Text Book, The	236	Bailer Twine	210	West Pillar	37
Thin Groove Alley	53			Western Approaches	38
Thin Man's Ridge	360	**U**		Western Pinnacle	117
Thin White Line, The	203	Ugly Mug	264	Whaleback	189
Tholl Gate	108	Ugly Wall	264	White Bhan Man	177
Threatening Behaviour	186	Umbrella Fall	281	White Dwarf	150
Three Legged Race,		Under the Hammer	268	White Fingers	226
The	81	Under Thirties Icefall	281	White Heather Club	92
Three Tier Chimney	360	Undertaker, The	64	White Settler	39
Threesome	199	Unknown Soldier, The	326	White Streak, The	231
Thumbscrew	276	Unknown Warrior, The	326	White Tiger	282
Thunderbird	216	Unmasked	220	Whiteout	363
Thunderchicken	39	Unpaid Bills	199	White's Gully	358
Tiberian Sun	196	Upper Buttress,		Whites of Their Ice	96
Tight One, The	305	Original Route	129	Who Needs Kalymnos?	242
Tipperary	47	Upper Connecting		Wide Deceiver	213
Tir na Og	37	Ridge of A' Phoit	177	Wild at Heart	85
Titanium Buttress	292	Upper Corner	247	Wild West, The	247
Titanium Gully	292	Upper Girdle, The	354	Willy Wonka	96
Tjasa	209			Wilma	226
Toll a' Bhein Gully	187	**V**		Wind Break	236
Toll Dubh Chimney	290	Valentine Buttress	293	Wind Machine, The	70
Toll Gate East	305	Vanadium Couloir	293	Window Gully	67
Toll Gate West	305	Vanishing Frog, The	231	Winklepicker	167
Tomahawk	152	Vantage Slab	191	WPC Gully	291
Tombstone	208	Vegetable Sheep, The	138	Wriggle	224
Top Cat	259	Very Gneiss	189	Wrong Turn	75
Tophet Gully	125	Very Y-Gully	154		
Topper, The	94	Vespa	200	**Y**	
Torridonian, The	216	Via Wellington	109	Y Gully	170
Torridown Man	231	View to a Hill	215	Yak	220
Torture Chamber, The	276	Viking Gully	37	Yankee Groove	77
Totem	152	Vine Street	161	Yer Dirt Box	162
Touch Too Much, A	213	Vishnu	316	Yodel	156
Tower of Darkness, The	329	Voyager	150		